THE STATE OF EDUCATION
POLICY RESEARCH

THE STATE OF EDUCATION POLICY RESEARCH

Edited by

David K. Cohen
Consortium for Policy Research in Education, University of Michigan

Susan H. Fuhrman
Consortium for Policy Research in Education,
Teachers College, Columbia University

Fritz Mosher
Consortium for Policy Research in Education

LEA LAWRENCE ERLBAUM ASSOCIATES, PUBLISHERS
2007 Mahwah, New Jersey   London

Director of Editorial: Lane Akers
Editorial Assistant: Anthony Messina
Cover Design: Tomai Maridou
Full-Service Compositor: MidAtlantic Books and Journals, Inc.

This book was typeset in 10/12 pt. Times Roman, Italic, Bold, and Bold Italic, with Helvetica.

Lawrence Erlbaum Associates, Inc., Publishers
10 Industrial Avenue
Mahwah, New Jersey 07430
www.erlbaum.com

CIP information for this volume can be obtained by contacting the Library of Congress.

ISBN 978-0-8058-5833-4 — 0-8058-5833-4 (case)
ISBN 978-0-8058-5834-1 — 0-8058-5834-2 (paper)
ISBN 978-1-4106-1684-5 — 1-4106-1684-3 (ebook)

Books published by Lawrence Erlbaum Associates are printed on
acid-free paper, and their bindings are chosen for strength and durability.

Printed in the United States of America

10 9 8 7 6 5 4 3 2 1

The editors dedicate this book to our late colleague, Thomas K. Glennan, Jr. (1935–2004). Tom played an active role in planning for the December, 2003, meeting in Philadelphia that led to this volume, and we are grateful that he was able to join us on that occasion.

As the first Director of the National Institute of Education and a long-time policy analyst and researcher at the RAND Corporation, Tom helped to launch many of the most constructive lines of research described here. He was both a mentor and a model for so many of us who try to inform policy and practice through the systematic application of disciplined inquiry and, as he would have insisted, through principled design and development.

We, along with at least three generations of policy researchers and policy-makers, and the students and teachers of America, have lost a guiding influence and a good friend. We hope he would have approved what we offer here. However, we can imagine hearing from him in response a very warm and amused, "Yes, but then. . . ."

Contents

I. INTRODUCTION TO EDUCATION POLICY RESEARCH

II. THE MAKING AND EFFECTS OF EDUCATION POLICY

VI. POLICY AND PROFESSIONALS

VII. IN CONCLUSION

Tables and Figures

TABLES

FIGURES

Preface

David K. Cohen, Susan H. Fuhrman, and Fritz Mosher

EDUCATION POLICY RESEARCH: TAKING STOCK

Government has played an increasingly large role in public education in recent years. For example, states have set more rigorous academic standards and held schools accountable for student achievement by requiring a variety of performance assessments. The federal government has also passed measures linking school and student achievement levels to federal funding. The growth of such policies has been accompanied by the growth of research on education policy, and that has drawn greater attention to the research, in part because the research often investigates the success or failure of policies. It has also come under greater scrutiny, particularly by those seeking scientific evidence that policies are having an effect on schooling. The purpose of this volume is to take stock of education policy research today, analyzing strengths and weaknesses across the field through examination of key issues facing education policymakers and researchers.

Education policy research is both a relatively new and an expanding field. It is new partly because the federal government made few significant education policy decisions until the mid- to late 1960s, and partly because state policymaking during the 19th and early 20th centuries was quite restrained. However, the passage of the Elementary and Secondary Education Act in 1965 made the federal government an important partner in educational policy. Federal agencies also began to follow the example of Robert McNamara's Defense Department, and sponsor research on the implementation and effects of government programs. In response to the expanded federal role, in the 1970s state governments started to expand their policy interests. As social research grew in both higher education and think tanks, analysts began to examine how federal and state policies actually reached recipients and how local schools and districts responded. Further, concomitant growth in higher education and domestic policy research helped to encourage vast changes in knowledge production and use, one of which was the burgeoning of policy research in education.

Policy research in education continued to expand rapidly through the ensuing decades, as the volume of education policymaking at all levels of government grew and education became a major electoral and legislative issue. In the 1990s, many states adopted wide-ranging accountability and assessment policies, and the 2001 No Child Left Behind Act greatly increased the federal role in public education. Studying the impact of such policies has become a significant academic and applied industry, attracting more and more scholars from key social science disciplines.

As policymaking has expanded, government has assumed greater responsibility, not only for resource allocation and the regulation of quality, but also for the heart of the enterprise: teaching, learning, and school outcomes. The expanded scope of governmental responsibility for school operations and effects has spurred a parallel expansion of the scope of policy research in education. As policy increasingly aimed to influence instruction and student outcomes, policy researchers turned their attention more closely to the core issues of instruction. The emphasis of new policies on instructional improvement has reconfigured the boundaries of, and relations within, policy research.

At the same time, education research in general has come under attack as being insufficiently rigorous. Critics charge that its generalizations are made on small samples and that it reveals little about cause and effects. The U.S. Department of Education has pressed researchers to conduct studies more scientifically, and policy research is now responding to this press. It is argued frequently in this volume that more rigorous education research must be grounded in practice—that much more knowledge is needed on how policy and practice interact—and deeper examination of the policy–practice links seems to many researchers a promising response to critics' challenges. There is much agreement that more evidence of the effects of policy on public schooling is needed, but the acquisition of that evidence faces many challenges.

The expansion of policy research, criticism of its methods, and the challenges it faces in increasingly complex environments of policy and practice suggest that a volume assessing the state of the field and making recommendations for future directions would be useful. This book discusses the connections of policy, research, and practice as well as assessing what we know about the design and implementation of policies, about whether they work in schools, and about the extent to which research knowledge informs policies themselves. A clear, if complex, view of the state of education policy research emerges from the chapters in this volume, which have been written by researchers and policy experts in education, economics, and related disciplines. The book is intended to articulate the state of the field in a way that will be useful to policymakers seeking research to inform their decisions and to researchers seeking to improve the quality of their efforts.

OVERVIEW OF THE VOLUME

The volume is arranged thematically, with chapters in each section exploring a key thematic area of education policy research. We begin with a section considering the making and effects of education policy. Chapters in this section cover political aspects of education policy, governance in U.S. education, the relations between policy and practice, privatization trends in education, and the role of race in education policy. In the next section on resource allocation, chapters cover methods for estimating the effects of resources as well as the relations of resources to equity. A section on the boundaries of K–12 education with the preschool and postsecondary education sectors contains two chapters surveying connections at each boundary. The next section is devoted to education research itself, with chapters on what we know and need to know about the effects of education policy and on two different and representative efforts in practice-based research. A final section takes up the theme of policy and the teaching profession, with chapters on teacher quality and state policy around teaching. Each section is followed by an expert commentary that discusses common themes among the section's chapters and poses key questions for policy, research, and practice suggested by the authors' analyses. As the following chapter summaries indicate, this volume demonstrates that the state of education policy today is characterized by a complex variety of viewpoints and problems.

The volume begins with Robert Floden's introductory chapter, "Philosophical Issues in Education Policy Research." He describes three major and contrasting approaches to education policy research and examines key philosophical issues related to each approach. He focuses on issues of epistemology and political theory. This chapter serves to define the field and explain what sorts of argument and evidence are typical within it.

The section on The Making and Effects of Education Policy begins with Lorraine McDonnell's account of the political dimensions of education policy, "The Politics of Education: Influencing Policy and Beyond." She identifies key limitations of education policy research, such as a lack of attention to local policy and to politics itself as an object of study. To address these limitations, McDonnell uses a framework that encompasses the three categories of political variables she finds most relevant to understanding education policy: institutions, interests, and ideas. Institutional fragmentation in education policy means that policymaking in the United States shifts easily across institutional arenas, often with the result of increasing the advantages of particular interest groups. The author suggests that interests and their interactions with new ideas are important to education reform and that for reform to succeed, it must become institutionalized. The chapter offers directions for research, such as better understanding of local politics, focusing on the incentives of key political actors, and gathering more information on political attitudes and behavior.

The next chapter examines what we know about the shifting influence of government involvement in education. In "Educational Governance in the United States: Where Are We? How Did We Get Here? Why Should We Care?" Susan H. Fuhrman, Margaret E. Goertz, and Elliot Weinbaum survey the federal, state, and local levels of governance and the interactions among them. They show that local governance is still powerful but more influenced by state and federal policy than in the past. According to the authors, education governance is decentralized; there is little uniformity in policies across the nation. They examine the impact of decentralized governance structure on four policy domains—education funding, teacher quality, instructional guidance, and accountability—and conclude that decentralized governance entails wide variation in the schooling available to the nation's children. Suggestions are offered for future study to meet the challenges of this complicated policy environment. For example, the educational systems of other countries can provide useful lessons for U.S. public education.

In "Policy and Practice," David K. Cohen, Susan L. Moffitt, and Simona Goldin summarize what we know about the relations between policies and what actually happens in classrooms and schools. They review the history of the influence of education policy on practice; then they examine the implications of that history for education research. The authors argue that successful policy implementation depends on effective interactions among four key factors—policy aims, policy instruments, the capabilities (such as practitioner knowledge and values) attached to individuals and institutions, and the environments of practice in which policies are carried out. In examining the interactions among the factors, the authors emphasize a key dilemma: that the effectiveness of education policies depends on the very individuals and institutions whose problems the policies are meant to correct. Policies should be designed so that they can be well used by those responsible for putting them into practice.

The chapter by Paul Hill, "New Political Economy of Public Education: Policy and Research," examines the current trend towards privatization in schooling, particularly charter schools and the voucher movement. The author examines both the political context that has driven the trend and the main consequences of the trend. He foresees emerging coalitions of interest groups that combine groups favoring development of new options for disadvantaged children, groups favoring strong learning standards, and groups favoring limiting public oversight of schools to a concern with equity and performance. Hill demonstrates that so far, charter school and voucher options have only had modest effects, so we should not be deceived by the claims of private education advocates that a free market in education is necessarily best. We should continue to scrutinize how private schools function in relation to public education and examine empirically the variations in quality and outcomes among private options.

A final chapter in this section, "As Moths to a Flame: Education Policy Research and the Controversial Issues of Race," by Jeffrey Henig, examines the ways in which race has been addressed in education policy since *Brown v. Board of Education*. Henig maps the research literature, then focuses on specific areas of research that shed light on how race affects and is affected by education policy. These areas of inquiry include desegregation, tracking, and school choice; arguments for and against race-based policies; civic capacity; and the declining significance of race. He concludes with reflections on ways that public debates and academic disciplines have shaped the research agenda around race.

In his commentary, James P. Spillane finds several cross-cutting themes in this section: the segmented nature of the U.S. education system, the shifting policy terrain over the past decades, and the need for more relevant research. Spillane also recommends diversifying policy research methodologies (to include, for example, narrative approaches), treating instruction as an explanatory variable in order to develop a more nuanced understanding of the relations between policy and practice, and focusing more research on the work practices involved in policy implementation.

The next section on Policy as Resource Allocation begins with Lisa Barrow and Cecilia Elena Rouse's "Causality, Causality, Causality: The View of Education Inputs and Outputs From Economics." This chapter discusses methodologies for estimating the causal effects of resources on education outcomes. It examines the notion of the education production function and various ways of estimating it, including multilevel statistical models. The problems involved in drawing causal inferences from these models are reviewed. The chapter also examines what the authors believe to be the best evidence from economics on the effects on student outcomes of a few important inputs: spending, class size, teacher quality, the length of the school year, and technology. The authors conclude that while the number of studies using credible strategies is low, there is certainly evidence that what schools do matters. One important policy implication is that because it is difficult to evaluate attempts to improve outcomes after the fact, research and evaluation should be part of policy change from the beginning.

The section's second chapter is by W. Norton Grubb: "The Elusiveness of Educational Equity: From Revenues to Resources to Results." Grubb examines the relationship of educational resources to inequality in students' opportunities to learn. The chapter reviews different understandings of equality of educational opportunity. There is a great deal of uncertainty about how educational equity is to be defined and about whether equity should be applied to revenues and expenditures, the resources they can buy, or to outcomes. The author shows that progress in equity over the past few decades has been more in equalizing funding across districts within states than in addressing other types of inequality that affect students. He maintains that a better understanding is needed of the translation of revenues into the complex range of resources within schools that might matter to the results of schooling. A new approach to education finance is advocated, one that recognizes a broader variety of school resources as well as nonschool resources such as parent effects and student behavior. This approach can help identify and explain the most important inequalities in schooling. A key policy implication of this new approach is that policy related to equity should shift from a focus on funding to a focus on equity of effective resources for schooling.

Commenting on this section, Helen F. Ladd identifies four related sets of questions about resources: questions about the effects of resources, the quantity of resources needed for adequacy, how resources can be made more productive, and how the distribution of resources affects equity. Deeming that the section's chapters might have addressed resource adequacy and productivity more fully, Ladd briefly reviews policy and research approaches to adequacy—contrasting what she calls a professional judgment approach with an economic approach—and to productivity, focusing here on whole-school reform models and governance changes intended to improve educational outcomes.

In the first chapter of the section, Across the Sectors, "Boundaries With Early Childhood Education: The Significance of the Early Childhood Frontier for Elementary and Secondary Education," W. Steven Barnett and Debra J. Ackerman describe the current state of the early childhood sector and of its articulation with K–12 education. Most preschool programs are privately operated and much more diverse than public education programs. The growing policy interest in making preschool universal suggests that a collision between the two very different sectors is on the horizon. The chapter examines the potential impact of the preschool sector on school choice, curriculum and assessment policies, and teacher certification. The sectors are currently not well articulated; cross-sector difficulties regarding standards, teacher certification, class size, scheduling, and funding remain to be solved. Nevertheless, the integration of preschool with K–12 education could offer benefits, such as the implementation at higher grade levels of preschool standards emphasizing the whole child. The authors call for future research to discover which policies and types of articulation make for effective alignment between sectors.

In "Separation of K–12 and Postsecondary Education Policymaking: Evolution, Impact, and Research Needs," Michael W. Kirst argues that the separation of K–12 and higher education policies and research has been an impediment to educational improvement in both sectors. This chapter examines key aspects of the separation, such as the disconnection between high school assessments and college placement tests, and then explores the evolution of the separation and the problems of governance arising from it. Kirst concludes with a discussion of policy levers that might bring the sectors closer together, including more state-level coordination in standards and assessments, finance, data systems, and accountability.

The commentary on this section, by J. Lawrence Aber, construes the three major sectors of the U.S. education system as lacking a comprehensive set of societal values or goals to guide successful "border crossings" across the sectors. To that end, he recommends establishing a conceptual framework that explains the disjunctures across sectors and ways to resolve them, as well as conducting rigorous policy experiments to test intentional change strategies across *both* the early childhood and postsecondary borders.

The section on The Role of Education Research begins with Fritz Mosher's "Knowledge and Policy." In this chapter, he contends that we now know too little to attain the stated goals of education policy, particularly the achievement of proficiency in core subjects by all students. Policies premised on the assumption that we do know are likely to lead to frustration and could easily call the enterprise of public education into question. Reviewing recent reform policies and related research, the author concludes that the education policy research leaves policymakers without knowledge of what works to improve schooling. The field lacks much of the infrastructure and incentives—including learning assessments that could inform better instruction—that will be required if it is to produce the knowledge and tools needed adequately to inform education policy and practice. The author suggests that much more strategic management and funding of research is needed in order to encourage schools to learn over time what is required for improvement and the ultimate attainment of the nation's ambitious policy goals.

In "Learning, Teaching, and Keeping the Conversation Going: The Links Between Research, Policy, and Practice," Barbara Neufeld describes the applied research of the organization she founded, Education Matters, Inc. The organization has supported reform efforts in a number of cities, particularly Boston, by providing formative evaluations of reforms in instructional practice. Neufeld provides rich illustrations of the nature and use of the organization's work, and then describes key challenges that are likely to face those evaluating reforms in progress. These challenges include the reluctance of district personnel to respond to evidence as well as the difficulty of maintaining helpful relationships with school personnel while providing rigorous feedback meant to spur instructional improvement.

The section ends with a review of a well-known comprehensive school reform program: "Research In, Research Out: The Role of Research in the Development and Scale-Up of Success for All," by Robert E. Slavin, Nancy A. Madden, and Amanda Datnow. The authors argue that successful reform requires that the means of improving the core technology of instruction be discovered through an ongoing, evidence- and practice-based process of implementation, evaluation, and adjustment. The chapter describes how the Success for All program has put evidence-based practices in place and established an internal system that shows whether the practices are succeeding. The components of Success for All, including a culture of data-driven decision making, are reviewed. The authors recommend that increased funding and rigorous evaluation of evidence-based programs is needed in order to generate knowledge of what works to improve classroom learning.

Carol Hirschon Weiss's commentary on this section cautions against expecting too much of education research. She reminds us that scientific research is always marked by controversy and debate. Education research, no matter how conclusive, will continue to have to pass muster with policymakers who may or may not be interested in being guided by evidence. She suggests that researchers may have to become more engaged in the "rough-and-tumble of political argument" if their work is to have greater impact.

The final section on Policy and Professionals begins with Richard M. Ingersoll's "Misdiagnosing the Teacher Quality Problem." This chapter investigates three common assumptions about the teacher shortage that is often thought to be lowering the quality of instruction in the nation's classrooms. The first assumption is that teaching is plagued by overly restrictive entry barriers that discourage high-quality teaching candidates. The second is that our traditional teacher preparation sources are not producing enough teachers to meet demand. Third, teacher education is inadequate, resulting in high levels of underqualified teachers. The author argues that all three assumptions are flawed. Entry barriers are not particularly restrictive, the supply of teachers may be higher than is thought, and teacher quality problems are not necessarily linked to preparation programs. Using data from the Schools and Staffing Survey, Ingersoll argues that the shortage stems chiefly stems from other causes, particularly teacher attrition related to working conditions and high rates of teacher misassignment. Also discussed are policy implications, such as improving school management of human resources, and research implications, such as the need for comparative studies to better understand misassignment.

Complementing Ingersoll's consideration of a crucial professional problem is Thomas B. Corcoran's survey of the teacher policy landscape, "The Changing and Chaotic World of Teacher Policy." Focusing on state policy as the salient force in shaping teacher quality, this chapter surveys areas of state influence, including teacher licensing standards, teacher education policies, compensation and evaluation, induction, professional development, and data policy and systems. The author assesses what is known in each area and concludes by considering what critical questions the policy research community should address to support policymakers in efforts to improve the quality of teaching.

In commenting on this section, Allan Odden, Anthony Milanowski, and Herbert G. Heneman III stress that ineffective human resources management practices and labor market problems are the chief hindrances to ensuring that there are highly qualified teachers in all the nation's classrooms. They recommend a number of directions for research and policy to improve the quality of the teaching force, including investigation of knowledge- and skill-based pay systems and redesign of teacher licensure and work structures.

The volume closes with the editors' "Conclusion: A Review of Policy and Research in Education." They survey the trajectory of education policy over the past 50 years and identify enduring problems in education policy—particularly resource allocation, race, the quality of teaching, and access to schooling. This concluding chapter also reviews the role of education research in relation to the issues explored in the volume and discusses major implications and recommendations for policy and research. Throughout the volume, it is suggested, the authors call for closer connections between policy, practice, and research. Major efforts to gain knowledge of how policies influence teachers and students are urged.

ACKNOWLEDGMENTS

The State of Education Policy Research has been made possible in part by the generous support of the Spencer Foundation (Grant No. 200500061). The volume has also been made possible in part through key funding to the Consortium for Policy Research in Education from the Department of Education's Institute of Education Sciences (Grant No. R308A960003). The data presented, the statements made, and the views expressed are solely the responsibility of the editors and authors.

CPRE unites some of the nation's leading research institutions to improve elementary and secondary education through research on policy, finance, school reform, and school governance. CPRE studies alternative approaches to education reform to determine how state and local policies can promote student learning. The consortium's member institutions at the time of the production of the volume were the University of Pennsylvania, Harvard University, Stanford University, the University of Michigan, and the University of Wisconsin–Madison. In December 2003 and January 2005, CPRE and the Spencer Foundation cosponsored meetings on the state of education policy research and commissioned a series of papers in connection with the meetings. This volume is the result of those efforts.

The editors would like to thank Lane Akers, Vice President, Editorial, at Lawrence Erlbaum Associates, for support of the project. The support of Rebecca Larsen, Editorial Assistant, and Anthony Messina, Editorial Assistant, at Erlbaum has also been very helpful. Among the many friends and associates of CPRE from whose general and specific guidance we benefited we would particularly like to thank the chapter authors as well as Christopher Cross, Denis Doyle, Richard Elmore, the late Tom Glennan, Carl Kaestle, James Kelly, Elliott Krause, Brian Rowan, William Schmidt, James Spillane, and Jon Supovitz, all of whom participated in the meetings to plan the volume. We are also grateful for the communications assistance of Kelly Stanton Fair at CPRE. The consortium's Mark Rohland did yeoman's service in editing the chapters and preparing the volume for publication. Finally, the editors gratefully acknowledge the invaluable advice of Paul D. Goren, Vice President of the Spencer Foundation, throughout the creation of this volume.

Contributors

Lawrence Aber, New York University. Lawrence Aber is a Professor of Applied Psychology and Public Policy at the Steinhardt School of Education, New York University. Dr. Aber earned his Ph.D. from Yale University and an A.B. from Harvard University. He previously taught at Barnard College and at the Mailman School of Public Health at Columbia University, where he also directed the National Center for Children in Poverty. He is an internationally recognized expert in child development and social policy. His basic research examines the influence of poverty and violence, at the family and community levels, on the social, emotional, behavioral, cognitive, and academic development of children and youth. Dr. Aber also designs and conducts rigorous evaluations of innovative programs and policies for children, youth and families, such as violence prevention, literacy development, welfare reform, and comprehensive services initiatives. He has received a William T. Grant Faculty Scholar Award as well as a Visiting Scholar Award from the Russell Sage Foundation. Dr. Aber testifies frequently before Congress, state legislators, and other deliberative policy forums. The media, public officials, private foundations and leading non-profit organizations also frequently seek his opinion or advice about pressing matters concerning child and family well-being.

Debra J. Ackerman, Rutgers University. Debra J. Ackerman is an Assistant Research Professor at the National Institute for Early Education Research (NIEER) at Rutgers University, where she received her Ph.D. in education. Her work at NIEER focuses on policies related to early childhood education and the professional development of the early care and education workforce. Dr. Ackerman's recent publications include NIEER policy reports on kindergarten readiness, full-day kindergarten, and increasing the effectiveness of preschool, as well as journal articles examining child care wages and issues related to upgrading the qualifications of early care and education teachers.

W. Steven Barnett, Rutgers University. W. Stephen Barnett is a Professor of Education Economics and Public Policy and Director of the National Institute for Early Education Research (NIEER) at Rutgers University. His research includes studies of the economics of early care and education, including costs and benefits, the long-term effects of preschool programs on children's learning and development, and the distribution of early educational opportunities. Dr. Barnett earned his Ph.D. in economics at the University of Michigan. Recent publications include *The State of Preschool: 2005 State Preschool Yearbook,* the third in a series of annual reports profiling state-funded prekindergarten programs, and, with Leonard Masse, a benefit-cost analysis of the Abecedarian program in *Economics of Education Review.*

Lisa Barrow, Federal Reserve Bank of Chicago. A senior economist in the research department at the Federal Reserve Bank of Chicago, Dr. Barrow received a B.A. in economics from Carleton College and A.M. and Ph.D. degrees in economics from Princeton University. Her research interests are in labor and public finance economics with a focus on education issues. She has studied school choice, how the "market" values public school spending, and how the economic value of education varies by race and ethnicity in addition to work on how demographic changes affect aggregate labor market statistics. In current work she is examining high school math teacher quality in Chicago and using randomized trials to evaluate the effectiveness of computerized algebra instruction. Before joining the Chicago Fed in 1998, Dr. Barrow was a visiting assistant professor at the School of Industrial and Labor Relations at Cornell University. She has served as a lecturer at the University of Chicago's Irving B. Harris Graduate School of Public Policy Studies.

David K. Cohen (Coeditor), University of Michigan. David K. Cohen is John Dewey Collegiate Professor in the School of Education, and Walter Annenberg Professor of Public Policy, in the Ford School of Public Policy, at the University of Michigan. His research interests include education policy, the relations between policy and practice, and school improvement. With Brian Rowan and Deborah L. Ball, he has directed the Study of Instructional Improvement, a large, mixed-methods study of efforts to improve learning in high-poverty elementary schools at the University of Michigan.

Thomas B. Corcoran, Teachers College, Columbia University. Mr. Corcoran is a co-director of the Consortium for Policy Research in Education (CPRE). Prior to joining CPRE, he served as Policy Advisor for Education for New Jersey Governor Jim Florio, Director of School Improvement for Research for Better Schools, and Director of Evaluation and Chief of Staff of the New Jersey Department of Education. He has served as a consultant to urban school districts and national foundations on issues of improving quality and equity. Mr. Corcoran's research interests focus on ways of improving the use of research findings and clinical expertise to inform policy and practice, the effectiveness of different approaches to professional development, the impact of changes in work environments on the productivity of teachers and students, the efficacy of state teacher policies, and the evaluation of high school reforms. He is a member of the National Research Council's Science Learning Study, the International Baccalaureate Organization's Research Committee, the New Jersey Quality Teaching and Learning Commission, the advisory committee for the Mathematics and Science Partnerships Knowledge Management Project supported by NSF, and the Merck Institute for Science Education Critical Friends Group.

Amanda Datnow, University of Southern California. Dr. Datnow is an Associate Professor in the Rossier School of Education at the University of Southern California. She was formerly a faculty member at the Ontario Institute for Studies in Education of the University of Toronto and at Johns Hopkins University. She received her Ph.D. in education at UCLA. Her research focuses on the politics and policies of school reform, particularly with regard to the professional lives of educators and issues of equity. She has conducted numerous prior studies of comprehensive school reform and studies of other related school change issues. She is currently conducting a study of data-driven decision making in four school systems. Dr. Datnow is the author or editor of six books and the author of over 40 articles and book chapters. In 2005, she won the American Educational Research Association's Early Career Award.

Robert E. Floden, Michigan State University. Robert E. Floden is a Professor of Teacher Education, Measurement and Quantitative Methods, Educational Psychology, and Educational Policy at the Michigan State University College of Education. Floden has an A.B. in philosophy from Princeton University as well as an M.S. in mathematical statistics and a Ph.D. in philosophy of education, both from Stanford University. Floden's work has been published in the *Handbook of*

Research on Teaching, the *Handbook of Research on Teacher Education*, and many journals. His academic honors include serving as Editor of *Review of Research in Education* and Features Editor of *Educational Researcher*, being elected president of the Philosophy of Education Society, and receiving an Alexander von Humboldt Fellowship and the Margaret B. Lindsey Award for Distinguished Research in Teacher Education. He has been studying teacher education and other influences on teaching and learning for almost three decades. He is currently coprincipal investigator of Michigan State University's Teachers for a New Era initiative and coprincipal investigator on a project developing measures of teachers' mathematical knowledge for teaching algebra.

Susan Fuhrman (Coeditor), Teachers College, Columbia University. Dr. Fuhrman was recently appointed President of Teachers College, Columbia University. From 1995 to 2006 she was the Dean, and the George and Diane Weiss Professor of Education, at the University of Pennsylvania's Graduate School of Education. She is also the Chair of the Management Committee of CPRE, which she founded in 1985. Dr. Fuhrman is currently the principal investigator of the Center on Continuous Instructional Improvement (CCII), a research and development center funded by the Hewlett Foundation that focuses on creating tools and policy supports for instructional improvement processes. She has conducted research on state policy design, accountability, and standards-based reform, and she has written widely on education policy and finance.

Margaret E. Goertz, University of Pennsylvania. Dr. Goertz is a Professor of Education Policy in the Graduate School of Education at the University of Pennsylvania and a codirector of the Consortium for Policy Research in Education (CPRE) at Penn, where she specializes in the study of state and federal education finance and governance policy. Dr. Goertz has conducted extensive research on state education finance and school reform policies, teacher and state accountability policies, and state and federal programs for special needs students. She is currently studying the impact of state accountability policies on high schools and the implementation of the No Child Left Behind Act. She is a past president of the American Education Finance Association. Dr. Goertz has spoken and published extensively in the areas of state education reform and education finance. In 2005 she published a chapter on state education policy in Congressional Quarterly Press's *The State of the States*.

Simona Goldin, University of Michigan. Simona Goldin holds a master's degree in management and urban policy analysis from the New School University. She is currently a doctoral student at the University of Michigan in the Educational Foundations and Policy program. Her research interests include the relationships between policy and practice and the role of students in policy implementation.

W. Norton Grubb, University of California, Berkeley. Dr. Grubb is a Professor and the David Gardner Chair in Higher Education at the School of Education, the University of California, Berkeley, where he is also the Faculty Coordinator for the Principal Leadership Institute. He received his doctorate in economics from Harvard University in 1975. He has published extensively on the economics of education, public finance, education policy, community colleges, and social policy for children and youth. He also consults extensively with high schools, community colleges, and public policy groups about both institutional and policy reforms. He has worked for the Organisation for Economic and Co-operation and Development, for which he wrote reports on adult education in Canada and Austria and on tertiary education. Among his many works are *Learning to Work: The Case for Reintegrating Education and Job Training*, *Working in the Middle: Strengthening the Education and Training of the Middle-Skilled Labor Force*, and *Education* *for Occupations in American High Schools*, an edited volume on the integration of academic and occupational education. In 2004 he coauthored a book with Marvin Lazerson about the vocational transformations of American schooling, *The Education Gospel: The Economic Power of Schooling.*

Herbert G. Heneman III, University of Wisconsin-Madison. Dr. Heneman is the Dickson-Bascom Professor (Emeritus) in Business, Management, and Human Resources at the University of Wisconsin-Madison. He also serves as a participating faculty member in the Industrial Relations Research Institute and as a Senior Research Associate in the Wisconsin Center for Education Research. His research is in the areas of staffing, performance management, union membership growth, work motivation, and compensation systems. He is currently investigating the design and effectiveness of group bonuses and knowledge- and skill-based pay systems for teachers. Dr. Heneman is the senior author of four textbooks on human resource management. He is a member and former chair of the Human Resources Division of the Academy of Management.

Jeffrey R. Henig, Columbia University. A Professor of Political Science and Education at Teachers College and a Professor of Political Science at Columbia University, Dr. Henig earned his B.A. at Cornell University and his Ph.D. in political science at Northwestern University. Past research has focused on the boundary between private action and public action in addressing social problems. Most recently, he has been focusing on the politics of school choice, charter schools, and coalition building for urban school reform. He is the author or coauthor of seven books, including *Rethinking School Choice: Limits of the Market Metaphor* and *Mayors in the Middle: Politics, Race, and Mayoral Control of Urban* Schools. *The Color of School Reform: Race, Politics and the Challenge of Urban Education* and *Building Civic Capacity: The Politics of Reforming Urban Schools* were named the best books written on urban politics in 1999 and 2001, respectively, by the Urban Politics Section of the American Political Science Association.

Paul T. Hill, University of Washington. Dr. Hill is a Research Professor at the University of Washington's Daniel J. Evans School of Public Affairs. He is also Director of the Center on Reinventing Public Education, which studies alternative governance and finance systems for public K–12 education. Dr. Hill's recent work on education reform has focused on school choice plans, school accountability, and charter schools. He chaired the National Working Commission on Choice in K–12 Education, which issued its report, *School Choice: Doing it the Right Way Makes a Difference,* in 2003. Dr. Hill holds a B.A. from Seattle University and an M.A. and a Ph.D. from Ohio State University, all in political science. He is a non-resident Senior Fellow of the Brookings and Hoover Institutions.

Richard M. Ingersoll, University of Pennsylvania. Dr. Ingersoll, a former high school teacher, is currently a Professor of Education and Sociology at the University of Pennsylvania. Dr. Ingersoll's research is concerned with the management and organization of elementary and secondary schools and the character and problems of the teaching occupation. Over the past decade he has done extensive research on the problems of teacher shortages and underqualified teachers. His research on these issues has been widely reported in the media and featured in numerous major education reports, such as those published by the National Commission on Teaching and America's Future and the Education Trust. In 2004 he received the Outstanding Writing Award from the American Association of Colleges for Teacher Education for his book, *Who Controls Teachers' Work? Power and Accountability in America's Schools.* This book looks at how much control and accountability are exerted over teachers and their work in schools and what impact this has on school performance.

Michael W. Kirst, Stanford University. Since 1969, Dr. Kirst has been a Professor of Education and Business Administration (by courtesy) at Stanford University. As a policy generalist, Kirst has published articles on school finance politics, curriculum politics, intergovernmental relations, and education reform policies. He is the author of 10 books, including *From High School to College* in 2004 and *The Political Dynamics of American Education* in 2005. Kirst was a member of the California State Board of Education from 1975 to 1982 and its president from 1977 to 1981. He was a cofounder of Policy Analysis for California Education (PACE) in 1983, and is a member of the management and research staff of the Consortium for Policy Research in Education (CPRE). Before joining the Stanford faculty, Kirst held several positions with the federal government, including staff director of the U.S. Senate Subcommittee on Manpower and Poverty.

Helen F. Ladd, Duke University. Dr. Ladd is the Edgar Thompson Professor of Public Policy Studies and Economics at Duke University. Most of her current research focuses on education policy. She is the editor of *Holding Schools Accountable: Performance-Based Reform in Education.* She is also the coauthor (with Edward Fiske) of *When Schools Compete: A Cautionary Tale,* about school reform in New Zealand, and of *Elusive Equity: Education Reform in Post Apartheid South Africa.* From 1996 to 1999 she cochaired a National Academy of Sciences Committee on Education Finance and has published background papers and a final report on the committee's work. During the past few years she has written articles on teacher quality, charter schools, school-based accountability, market-based reforms in education, parental choice and competition, intergenerational conflict and the willingness to support education, and the effects of HUD's Moving to Opportunity Program on educational opportunities and outcomes.

Nancy A. Madden, Success for All Foundation. Dr. Madden is currently president of the Success for All Foundation. She received her B.A. in psychology from Reed College in 1973 and her Ph.D. in clinical psychology from American University in 1980. From 1980 to 1998, she was a research scientist at the Center for Research on the Education of Students Placed at Risk at Johns Hopkins University, where she directed the development of the reading, writing, language arts, and mathematics elements of Success for All. Dr. Madden is the author or coauthor of many articles and books on cooperative learning, mainstreaming, Chapter 1, and students at risk, including *Effective Programs for Students at Risk* and *Every Child, Every School: Success for All.*

Lorraine M. McDonnell, University of California, Santa Barbara. Dr. McDonnell is a Professor of Political Science at the University of California, Santa Barbara. Her research focuses on the politics of education policy, especially the role of competing societal values and how they shape education reforms. She is also interested in the relationship between the differing norms of the institutions that share authority over education governance and their ability to be responsive and effective political decision makers. Her recent book, *Politics, Persuasion, and Educational Testing,* examines the politics of student assessment.

Anthony Milanowski, University of Wisconsin-Madison. An Assistant Scientist with CPRE at the University of Wisconsin-Madison, since 1999 Dr. Milanowski has coordinated the CPRE Teacher Compensation Project's research on standards-based teacher evaluation and teacher performance pay. He is also a coprincipal investigator of a study of principal performance evaluation and is participating in a study of class size reduction. He received a Ph.D. in industrial relations from the Industrial Relations Research Institute at the University of Wisconsin-Madison, an M.A. in public policy from the La Follette Institute there, and a B.A. in philosophy from the University of Wisconsin-Milwaukee. He has taught courses in compensation, staffing, and human resource management for the Schools of Business and Education at Wisconsin-Madison. Before coming to CPRE, Dr. Milanowski worked for many years as a human resource management professional. His research interests include performance evaluation, pay system innovations, teacher selection, and the teacher labor market.

Susan L. Moffitt, University of Michigan. Dr. Moffitt is a Research Area Specialist at the University of Michigan's Ford School of Public Policy. She received her Ph.D. in political science from the University of Michigan in 2005. Her research considers how knowledge creation and distribution advance public policy implementation and regulation in the context of Title I of the Elementary and Secondary Education Act. She also investigates education statistics, public advisory committees, and the federal drug approval process. In the fall of 2006, Moffitt began a two-year term as a Robert Wood Johnson Scholar in Health Policy Research at Harvard University.

Fritz Mosher (Coeditor), Consortium for Policy Research in Education. Frederic A. (Fritz) Mosher is an independent consultant on education policy and research planning, management, and funding. He is Senior Consultant to the Consortium on Policy Research in Education (CPRE) for dissemination and outreach. He has also been a Senior Advisor to the Spencer Foundation and a RAND Corporation Adjunct Staff member. He has been an advisor to the Assistant Secretary for Research and Improvement in the United States Department of Education and to Achieve, Inc. In 1998, he retired from Carnegie Corporation of New York after 36 years as a program specialist and policy analyst. Over that time he worked in the full range of the corporation's programs, including international affairs, U.S. governmental reform, education at all levels, and the role of universities in the planning and development of national education systems in Anglophone Africa. In recent years he focused on the policy issues involved in transforming the U.S. public education system into one that would enable substantially all students to reach high standards of achievement. He is a cognitive/social psychologist by training, with a Ph.D. from Harvard University.

Barbara Neufeld, Education Matters, Inc. Dr. Neufeld is president and founder of Education Matters, Inc., a nonprofit educational research and evaluation firm that, since its inception in 1984, has focused on issues associated with improving teaching, learning, and leadership in urban areas. Dr. Neufeld has served as principal investigator for numerous evaluations, including the Effective Schools Programs in Connecticut elementary schools; Dr. James Comer's School Development Program in New Haven and Hartford, CT; early development of the Coalition of Essential Schools; professional development designed to improve instruction in mathematics; middle school reform in San Diego, Corpus Christi, TX, Louisville, KY, and Minneapolis, MN; the Boston Annenberg Challenge; Boston's literacy coaching models; and high school renewal in the Boston Public Schools. Dr. Neufeld has taught elementary school in the South Bronx and in New Haven. She was a Lecturer in Education at the Harvard Graduate School of Education from 1985 to 1997.

Allan R. Odden, University of Wisconsin-Madison. Dr. Odden is a Professor of Educational Leadership and Policy Analysis at the University of Wisconsin-Madison. He is also a codirector of the Consortium for Policy Research in Education (CPRE). He was a Professor of Education Policy and Administration at the University of Southern California from 1984 to 1993 and Director of Policy Analysis for California Education (PACE). From 1975 to 1984 he held various positions at the Education Commission of the States. He was president of the American Educa-tion Finance Association (AEFA) in 1979–1980 and received AEFA's Distinguished Service Award in 1998. His research and policy emphases include school finance redesign and adequacy, effective resource allocation in schools, the costs of instructional improvement, and teacher compensation. Odden has written widely, publishing over 200 journal articles, book chapters, and research reports as well as 30 books and monographs. A 2006 book, coauthored with Marc Wal-lace, is entitled *New Directions in Teacher Pay*.

Cecilia Elena Rouse, Princeton University. Dr. Rouse is a Professor of Economics and Public Affairs at Princeton University. She received her Ph.D. from Harvard University. Her primary research and teaching interests are in labor economics, with a particular focus on the economics of education. She has studied the economic benefit of community college attendance, evaluated the Milwaukee Parental Choice Program, examined the effects of education inputs on student achievement, tested for the existence of discrimination in symphony orchestras, studied unions in South Africa, and examined the effect of financial aid on college matriculation. Her current re-search evaluates Florida's school accountability and voucher programs. In addition, she is cur-rently conducting randomized evaluations of technology-based programs in schools in three large urban school districts as well as a randomized evaluation of strategies for increasing educational attainment among community college students. Dr. Rouse is currently a senior editor of *The Fu-ture of Children*, a Princeton-Brooking publication, and an editor of the *Journal of Labor Eco-nomics*. She is the founding director of the Princeton Education Research Section and currently director of the Industrial Relations Section as well. She is also a member of the MacArthur Foun-dation's Research Network on the Transition to Adulthood. In 1998–1999 she served a year in the White House at the National Economic Council.

Robert E. Slavin, Johns Hopkins University. Dr. Slavin is currently director of the Center for Data-Driven Reform in Education at Johns Hopkins University and chairman of the Success for All Foundation. He received his B.A. in psychology from Reed College in 1972 and his Ph.D. in social relations in 1975 from Johns Hopkins. Dr. Slavin has authored or coauthored more than 200 articles and 20 books, including *Educational Psychology: Theory into Practice*; *Coopera-tive Learning: Theory, Research, and Practice*; *Show Me the Evidence: Proven and Promising Programs for America's Schools*; *Effective Programs for Latino Students*; and *One Million Chil-dren: Success for All*. He received the American Educational Research Association's Raymond B. Cattell Early Career Award for Programmatic Research in 1986, the Palmer O. Johnson Award for the best article in an AERA journal in 1988, the Charles A. Dana Award in 1994, the James Bryant Conant Award from the Education Commission of the States in 1998, the Outstanding Leadership in Education Award from the Horace Mann League in 1999, and the Distinguished Service Award from the Council of Chief State School Officers in 2000.

James P. Spillane, Northwestern University. The Spencer T. and Ann W. Olin Professor in Learn-ing and Organizational Change at Northwestern University, Dr. Spillane teaches in the School of Education and Social Policy at Northwestern and is a Faculty Fellow at the Institute for Policy Re-search. A graduate of the National University of Ireland, Dr. Spillane taught elementary school before earning a Ph.D. from Michigan State University in 1993. Spillane's work explores the pol-icy implementation process at the state, district, school, and classroom levels, focusing on inter-governmental relations and relations between policy and school leaders' and teachers' practice. He is principal investigator of the Distributed Leadership Study, a program of research investi-gating the practice of school leadership. Dr. Spillane serves on the editorial board of numerous national and international journals. He is the author of *Standards Deviation: How Schools Misunderstand Education Policy*, *Distributed Leadership*, and many journal articles.

Elliot H. Weinbaum, University of Pennsylvania. Dr. Weinbaum is a researcher at the Consortium for Policy Research in Education (CPRE) at the University of Pennsylvania. His research interests include intergovernmental relationships and policymaking, performance-based accountability, and the impacts of policy on school improvement. He is currently an investigator in a national study of high schools and the roles that outside organizations play in high schools' strategies to improve instruction. Other recent research has examined the effects of statewide accountability systems on district improvement efforts aimed at high schools. Dr. Weinbaum spent his elementary and secondary school years in the Philadelphia public schools; he holds a B.A. from Yale University and a Ph.D. from the University of Pennsylvania.

Carol Hirschon Weiss, Harvard University. Dr. Weiss is the Beatrice B. Whiting Research Professor in the Harvard University Graduate School of Education. She holds a Ph. D. in sociology from Columbia University. She has published 11 books, including *Evaluation: Methods for Studying Programs and Policies*, which has been translated into five languages including Hungarian, Ukrainian, and Thai, and *Organizations for Policy Analysis: Helping Government Think*. She has published over 145 articles in the periodical literature and has been on the editorial boards of a score of journals. She has been a Fellow at the Center for Advanced Study in the Behavioral Sciences, a Guest Fellow at the Brookings Institution, a Senior Fellow at the U.S. Department of Education, and a Congressional Fellow. She has done pioneering research on the politics of evaluation and has spent 25 years studying the influence of research and evaluation on public decisions.

THE STATE OF EDUCATION
POLICY RESEARCH

I

INTRODUCTION TO EDUCATION POLICY RESEARCH

1

Philosophical Issues in Education Policy Research

Robert E. Floden

Policy research in education takes many forms. Individual journals can be dominated by some particular model of policy research, but the field as a whole is much more varied. One issue of *Educational Evaluation and Policy Analysis*, for example, may focus on studies that use complex linear models to estimate relationships between characteristics of schooling and pupil achievement, but the range of the field is suggested by a scan of the editorial board of *Educational Policy*, which includes critical theorists, philosophers, school reformers, economists, psychologists, and political scientists. Some policy research publications describe the effects of particular government policies, such as the introduction of a new accountability system in a state. But other publications paint a broad-brush picture of the ways in which districtwide adoption of textbooks "deskills" the teaching force.

The range of philosophical issues entangled with education policy research is also broad. Epistemological questions can be raised about descriptive and explanatory claims about policies, their contexts, and their effects. Issues in ethics and political theory have application both to judgments about the value of policies and to decisions about how policy researchers should fit within the political process. Metaphysical questions could be raised about what counts as a policy: Is it a written document? The intention of the legislator who sponsored the bill? A pattern of governmental action?

Given that variety of policy research approaches and applicable branches of philosophy, this chapter can only introduce some of the philosophical issues in education policy research. To simplify the discussion, the chapter will roughly divide the research into three categories, using a study in each to illustrate the work done there. For each of the categories of research the chapter will then discuss philosophical issues within two branches of philosophy—epistemology and political theory. This discussion, though just an introduction to the possible philosophical discussions, will call attention to issues that may not be apparent to those who conduct and use policy research.

THREE APPROACHES TO EDUCATION POLICY RESEARCH

We can pick out three contrasting approaches within education policy. Each approach has its associated broader field of inquiry, typical research questions, and research methods.

One approach draws on *economics* to address questions about the "production" of education outcomes and about the operation of markets for education personnel and services. Typical questions include the following: How are expenditures on schooling related to pupil learning? How would changes in structure of the education market (e.g., changing restrictions on how teachers are hired) affect prices (e.g., teacher salaries) and productivity (e.g., the pupil learning gains associated with teachers earning a given salary)? Research to address these questions often uses large sets of data collected as part of the regular operation of the education system, with analysis methods based on econometric models. An example is Goldhaber and Brewer's study (1997) of the relationship between teacher certification status and student achievement. The study analyzed data collected by the National Center for Education Statistics as part of the National Education Longitudinal Study of 1988 (NELS:88), which included information on the certification status of teachers and information on pupil achievement, linked to individual teachers.

A second approach involves *organizational studies* that draw on political science, sociology, and organizational theory to address questions about ways in which formal policies play out as they are implemented. Typical questions include these: What was the intent of the policy? What happened as educators and others tried to implement it? What factors influenced implementation? How was the policy as implemented different from the policy as intended? What were the effects of the policy? How well did the intended effects compare with the actual effects? Research to answer these questions often uses a mixture of document analysis, survey, interview, and observation. Typical methods of analysis include coding of themes in interview responses, statistical analysis of survey data, and analyses of documents. An example is Supovitz and Weathers's study (2004) of a school superintendent's implementation of a "snapshot" system of indicators to monitor progress toward key district goals. The research team used systematic interviews and a survey carried out for the study, together with information they had gained through long-term work with the district.

A third approach to education policy research draws on *critical theory* to address questions about how policies and discourses work to legitimate and reproduce inequalities in social status and income. Typical questions include: How do recent government actions and social trends operate to maintain current, unequal social structures? How are educators, even well-meaning educators, co-opted into ways of teaching that keep the poor and rich in their current relative positions? The scholarship that is used to answer these questions often builds on theories about society and political discourse, often referring to what is written by policymakers, news reporters, and other scholars. The analysis is aimed at reinterpreting stated policies to bring out assumptions about social class and reveal likely ways in which policies maintain current social positions. Apple's discussion (2001) of market-based approaches to teacher education draws on policy changes around the world in arguing that changes proposed for teacher education, both from politically conservative and politically liberal education leaders, are motivated by admirable aspirations but will likely lead to the reproduction of class hierarchies.

ECONOMIC APPROACHES TO EDUCATION POLICY RESEARCH

The rubric "economic approaches" is defined broadly here to include the range of work that has studied education using models that treat education as a process by which characteristics of people and organizations are used to predict the costs and outcomes of education. School finance studies examine relationships among funding formulas, regulations, economic conditions, and funds available for education. So-called "production function" studies examine the associations between inputs such as characteristics of schools, teachers, and students and outputs such as dropout rates, student achievement levels, and student learning. Much of the research is done by scholars with expertise in economics, but those with backgrounds in statistics, sociology, political science, and other disciplines are also involved.

Such research becomes *policy* research when connections are made between the models and education policies, either current or contemplated. For example, Goldhaber and Brewer's study (1997) is linked to policy discussions about the effects of teacher certification policy. The intent of current policies is taken to be the exclusion of people from teaching if they do not meet some specified minimum level of education, knowledge, and skill. For example, for teacher certification, most states require completion of a state-approved teacher preparation program, receiving a passing score on one or more teacher tests, and passing a criminal background check. Certification is intended to be a requirement for employment as a regular classroom teacher. Because schools employ many people who have not met those requirements (contrary to the intent of the policy), comparisons can be made between those who have completed certification and those who have not. A comparison of particular interest is in the effect teachers have on student learning.

Epistemological Issues in Economic Education Policy Research

Epistemology considers arguments about claims to knowledge. What is required to justify a claim? What are ways in which a skeptic might attack a claim? How can skeptical attacks be countered?

Several types of knowledge claims in economic education policy research are of particular interest: claims about causation, claims about human motivation (cast by economists as claims about incentives), and predictions about consequences of policies. These knowledge claims involve going beyond description of current circumstances to make assertions about what will happen, or is likely to happen, in the future.

The justification for claims about the future has been a central theme in epistemology. In the 18th century, David Hume (1740; 1748) made powerful skeptical arguments against the possibility of justifying any claims about the future or about the causal connections among events. Claims about the future always invoke evidence about the past as the basis for predictions about the future. Hume points out, however, that such claims about the future rely on the assumption that the future will resemble the past. The justification for that assumption depends, in turn, on the fact that the future has, so far, resembled the past. Such circular reasoning gives no firm foundation for argument. Similarly, the justifications given for claims that one event causes another start from the observation that the events have always or typically been seen to follow another, moving to the conclusion that such constant conjunction is due to one event causing the other. But nothing in that argument implies that the conjunction will continue to occur in the future. Hence arguments in support of causal claims depend on assumptions—that the future will resemble the past and more generally that there are regularities across time and context—that go beyond empirical evidence.

Hume's skepticism has not deterred scientists from making and defending causal claims, but it has underscored the uncertainty that is an inevitable part of scientific arguments. In social science, including economic education policy analysis, concerns about causal inference are a continuing theme both in philosophy and in statistical methodology. Rubin (1974) and Holland (1986) have written seminal analyses of modern statistical procedures for making causal inferences. They trace the discussion of causal inference back to philosophers like Hume, agreeing that arguments for cause require unconfirmable assumptions as well as empirical data. To make inferences about causal effects, assumptions must be made about what would have happened under other circumstances. Thus causal inferences depend on counterfactual claims, which, being contrary to fact, cannot be directly validated.

Because many economic education policy studies rely on observed, rather than experimentally manipulated, variations in key variables, they are particularly subject to skeptical concerns about the basis for causal claims. Studies of the effects of resources on education outcomes, for example, use data about existing variations in resources across organizational units such as districts or schools. Because units vary along many dimensions besides the amount of resources, inferences about whether variation in resources *causes* variation in outcomes must use analyses that try to determine what the association between resources and outcomes would have been if, counterfactually, the units had varied only along that dimension. Economists and other quantitative analysts have developed sophisticated statistical procedures—analysis of covariance, multiple regression, instrumental variables analysis—to make the counterfactual inferences. In the end, the validity of an inference will depend on claims that the models used in these analyses accurately represent the causal connections operating on the events studied.

The point here is not that such sophisticated analyses are improper, but that grounds for skeptical challenge will always be present. Statistical sophistication does not eliminate the need for assumptions, which may prove to be wrong. Some skepticism is always defensible. The stronger, or less plausible, the assumptions, the more reason for skepticism.

In Goldhaber and Brewer (1997), data from three waves of the National Longitudinal Study of 1988 (NELS) were used as the empirical basis for causal inferences about the impact of resources, particularly the teachers' years of experience and degree level, on 10th-grade pupils' mathematics achievement. The study's elaborate model, including measures of reported teacher behavior, other teacher characteristics, school characteristics, student background, and prior student achievement, is used to support claims about what the association between teacher qualifications and mathematics would have been, had all other things been equal (i.e., the impact of teacher qualifications on achievement). The authors conclude that,

> traditional (OLS) educational production function models do show some educational resources to be significant in influencing tenth-grade mathematics test scores. Although school-level variables do not, in general, seem to have much effect on student achievement, some teacher characteristics do. Teachers who are certified in mathematics, and those with bachelor's or master's degrees in math, are identified with higher test scores. (p. 520)

The authors are aware that the particular model used as the basis for inference affects the conclusions that will be draw about causal connections: "subtle differences in model specification can result in very different interpretations of whether teachers, for example, affect student outcomes" (p. 520). The causal inference to be drawn depends both on the empirical data and on the assumptions made about other causal linkages.

Which assumptions to make are connected to the policies that might be used to alter some variables. Two options might be considered, for example, for moving from this study's conclusion about the effects of teacher degrees on mathematics achievement. One option a state might consider would be requiring districts to staff all 10th-grade mathematics classes with teachers who have master's degrees in mathematics. An alternative option would be to require all current teachers of 10th-grade mathematics classes to complete such a master's degree. Both policies would change the qualifications of 10th-grade teachers, but one would do so by changes in the particular people teaching, the other would do so by changing the education completed by those already in the classroom. That difference, compounded by the wide variability in what it means to have a master's degree, might lead to these two policies having quite different effects.

A different line of epistemological work would give other reasons for skepticism about economic education policy studies. Many studies based on economic theory make assumptions about human action and motivation that have been critiqued by philosophers of social science. One assumption often made in economics is that people's decisions are affected by rational assessments of the costs and benefits of available courses of action. A person's choice of a career, for example, is assumed to be based, in large part, on assessments about the costs of preparation for the career, the expectations for securing employment in a desired location, the monetary and non-monetary rewards of employment across the length of a career, and so on. Economic policy discussions of merit pay, for example, describe the incentives and costs that people may perceive in differing institutional and organization arrangements—pay scales, licensing requirements, and so on.

About such models, philosophers raise general questions about whether human action is directed by such rational processes and about whether universal models (e.g., that people's choices are governed by perceived costs and benefits) are valid, as well as specific concerns about the special emphasis on economic concepts like incentives and costs. Some philosophers, such as Charles Taylor (1971), have argued that human action cannot be *predicted*, but can only be *understood* by interpretive methods that examine the meanings that individuals make of their particular situations. Social scientists who place a similar emphasis on the importance of meaning and particularity (e.g., Erickson 1986) might likewise object to the ways in which economic education policy analyses assume that written responses on large-scale surveys are valid indicators of the variables analysts take them to measure.

Political Theory and Economic Education Policy Analysis

Economic education policy studies can be read as efforts to describe the way education processes work, without taking a position on the value of those processes. That is, they may seem to assume a separation between fact and value, in which the analyst selects a topic because it is linked to current policy debates, but the analysis done is designed to illuminate the consequences of different policies, not to advocate one position over another. If that were so, the study would inform policy choices by describing likely consequences. But the choice would be made on the basis of value choices, of policymakers or their constituents, informed by the policy analysis.

In the Goldhaber and Brewer paper, for example, the authors conclude that "teachers with mathematics degrees are clearly associated with higher student scores on the NELS mathematics test" (p. 520). They stop short of making any claims about whether teachers should pursue mathematics degrees or whether schools should hire teachers with such degrees. Their conclusion has evident relevance to policy decisions about teacher certification and employment, but they (implicitly) leave the choices about policy directions to others. In other words, reports of economic education policy studies are often cast in language that suggests that they are value neutral.

Philosophers (and philosophically minded social scientists) have repeatedly debated whether or in what ways social science could be value neutral. Weber (1949), for example, argued that the concepts social scientists choose to use to describe and explain are selected because of their associations to valued aspects of society, so values always play some part in social science. Taylor (1967) makes a similar point for political science. He says that although some descriptions seem to be value neutral, for attempts to explain anything of significant interest, some choice about a theoretical framework must me made. That choice will not be based entirely on what "facts" are most obvious or evident. Instead, it will be based in part on decisions about what aspects of social life are most important, in other words, on values. He contrasts Marxist explanations, for which social class is the central feature, with explanations that see political parties or constitutional structures as the main explanatory characteristics.

Economic education policy analyses, then, are not value free. Production function studies feature particular outcomes, often student achievement test scores or changes in test scores. They conceptualize the amount of associated resources—dollars, teacher qualifications, amount of instructional time—as a prime determinant of the outcome. They therefore are tilted toward policy discussions about levels of resource provided and about one set of education outcomes, suggesting the range of policy options that will be considered. In that way, the policy analyses carry particular values that are implicit in the ways problems are framed.

The way in which values enter into education policy analysis are sometimes more overt. In debates about the connections between resources and student outcomes, the discussion has sometimes been cast as whether "money matters" (e.g., Hanushek, 1994; Hedges, Greenwald, & Lane, 1994), a shift in language that makes the judgments of value explicit. Hanushek, for example, reasons from his literature review of production function studies, which found at best inconsistent associations between measures of school resources and pupil achievement. In his paper, he moves that conclusion to say that:

> Improvement of our schools is, I believe, a very important national policy goal to pursue. It would be very unfortunate if policymakers were confused into believing that throwing money at schools is effective. More serious reform is required if we are to realize the full benefits of our schools. (p. 8)

His use of "throwing money at schools" can be seen as exaggeration for rhetorical effect, but even discounting for that exaggeration, his paper lines up with a value position in favor of restraining education spending and of limiting the attention paid to differences in funding levels across schools. Other education policy issues, including use of market mechanisms, school choice, and teacher credentialing policies, are ones where education policy analyses are written to align with one or another policy position.

If education policy analysis is inevitably value laden, what might be said about the proper role of the policy analyst in policy development? Should the analyst try, as much a possible, to leave the value choices up to others, emphasizing the technical function of providing information about education processes? Should the analyst try to make value positions explicit, so that readers can consider value commitments as they decide what use to make of an analysis? Should the policy analyst be pressing to be an ongoing part of the policy debate, drawing on social science expertise but also working to shape policy, drawing on other beliefs and understandings?

Discussions about the proper role of the policy analyst go beyond the strictly philosophical literature, as analysts themselves have tried to understand and evaluate how analysis has figured into the development of policy. Cohen, Moffitt, and Goldin (this volume) and Cohen and other colleagues (e.g., Cohen & Garet, 1974; Lindblom & Cohen, 1979; Cohen & Barnes, 1993) have argued that the connections among research, policy, and practice are complex and reciprocal. They dethrone top government officials as the makers of policy at the same time as they cast the influence of policy research (and other research) as an indirect stream of ideas, acting diffusely over time to alter the "climate of opinion." While there is much to be said for this view, it may give too little credit to roles played by policy analysis and by policymakers.

Many have written that the U.S. education system is "loosely coupled," implying that the connections between research, policy, and practice will not match the optimistic (or megalomaniacal) researcher's or policymaker's vision of empirical study being the defining determinant of a policy that dramatically and uniformly transforms instruction. But research does get picked up by policymakers and used (or at least cited) as the basis for policies, some of which have far-reaching consequences, some intended, others not. The Tennessee class size study, for example, offered strong evidence that elementary school pupils made larger learning gains in smaller classes. That conclusion was picked up by California policymakers, who established policies that did dramatically reduce class sizes (though they also had other, unanticipated) effects. Granted, policymakers may have had other reasons for reducing class size, and the effects on pupil achievement were not, at least initially, parallel to those found in the research study. But the example shows that some links among policy analysis, policy, and practice are substantial.

Cynical commentary on the ways in which policy analyses figure into policy decisions may also underestimate contributions made. Given that policy analyses often point to the complexities operating, it would be reasonable for policymakers to give these analyses only a small amount of weight. Analyses may have more weight when they substantially reduce uncertainty about likely outcomes and when political positions are not closely associated with policy options (Cronbach, et al., 1980). Gathering policy analyses may also have beneficial social effects, beyond whatever role they actually play in decision making. Having a system that regularly gathers data on policies may inspire public confidence in government, which in turn contributes to the efficiency of government operations (Floden & Weiner, 1978).

ORGANIZATIONAL APPROACHES TO EDUCATION POLICY ANALYSIS

"Organizational" approaches is shorthand for work that examines the ways that education policies are carried out. These studies often prepare descriptions of stated or intended policies by interviews and examinations of documents. They then describe ways in which the policies are enacted, giving explanations for discrepancies between the formal policy and its real-life instantiations. Supovitz and Weathers (2004), for example, studied a school district's system of data indicators designed to keep track of the district's progress in education reform and communicate the reform vision to district staff. Through formal and informal interviews with the district superintendent, the investigators gathered information about the intended purpose and operation of the system of indicators, which was oriented to give a district-level perspective on implementation of reforms aligned with district goals. The system deliberately does not present data on individual schools or teachers. With the intended purpose and operation in mind, the investigators conducted interviews of principals who participated in the system, together with a survey administered to all principals in the district's schools. Using these data, the investigators described the actual operation of the system, the degree to which it served its intended purposes, and the unanticipated effects of the system, such as the spread of ideas about better educational practices across schools.

Epistemological Issues in Organizational Policy Research

Organizational studies highlight claims about reasons for action, such as assertions about what those formulating a policy hoped it would accomplish and how others believe they were affected by the policy. Conclusions of the studies have causal import, describing the extent to which intended consequences were produced and sketching other effects. The arguments supporting all these claims take a different form from that of the arguments economic policy analysts make for their claims. Where economic analyses highlight statistical procedures to control for differences across cases, organizational analyses highlight methods thought likely to elicit candid responses in interviews and surveys, or use a variety of evidence to construct an interpretation that fits with the varying accounts across actors in a situation. This approach to policy research treats people's reports of their intentions and perceptions as trustworthy, absent some reason for skepticism. It treats self-reports about determinants of action as similarly trustworthy.

Philosophers have found the concept of "intention" problematic. The term connotes a desire to bring something about, which comes before taking action, but in many cases the intention accompanies the action, rather than preceding it. For complex actions, such as drafting an education policy, the intention may only become clear to the author as the policy is drafted and revised. A single action may have several intended consequences. Or an intended action may have several foreseen consequences, some intended, some not.

For evaluating claims about intention in the context of organizational education policy analysis, the philosophical work suggests that a range of evidence be considered in attributing intention. That evidence would include stated intentions, but would also include other information, including circumstances that might lead the person to mislead, or to misunderstand his or her own motives. The evidence would also include other actions the person has taken that could be seen as either consistent or inconsistent with the stated intention.

Two distinguishable kinds of evidence bear on claims about the connection between a policy and what educators do. Observations of action are one source of evidence. As for the case of economic policy research, the evidence should go beyond reporting that something occurred after the policy was established. The analyst should consider the possibility that something other than the policy was the cause of observed action or change in action. The organizational analyst typically has fewer cases than the economic policy analyst to use for comparison. Often, as in the work reported in Supovitz and Weathers (2004), only a single organizational unit is studied, so the opportunities for checking on other possible explanations must rely on data within the case, rather than across cases (King, Keohane, & Verba, 1994).

The second source of evidence is the reports from the educators themselves, who talk about policies and their effects. Philosophers would probably say that the conclusions based on such self-reports are part of an explanation for action on the basis of reasons, rather than a causal explanation. Explanation on the basis of reasons starts with premises about intentions and beliefs attributed to the actor, describes circumstances, and shows that the action taken was rational, given that state of affairs. Historians often provide such explanations, giving an explanation that rests on the rationality of the action taken, given what those involved believed.

The explanation on the basis of reasons may be inconsistent with a causal explanation for a variety of reasons, including deception and self-deception. People in public positions often appear to give reasons for their actions that are going to play well in the press, though the reasons may not be what they actually had in mind. Psychological studies by Nisbett and Ross (1980) have shown that people sometimes give descriptions of their reasons for a judgment that are at odds with the observed circumstances. These discrepancies do not mean that explanations should ignore reasons, restricting attention to causal explanations. Attention to human rationality is an important moral stance, honoring individuals as autonomous persons. Psychology has also shown that people actively interpret their surroundings; this rules out overly simple causal effects on human action. In fact, using the term "action" indicates that reasons play an important part. As one philosopher has put it,

> We should not easily set aside an agent's reason explanation in favor of a causal explanation. To give reasons for belief and reasons for action is to be concerned with justification and truth, autonomy, and responsibility. To set such reasons aside may be oppressive. It may also make us miss the point of what is going on. (Føllesdal, 1982, p. 314)

To support conclusions about the consequences of policies, then, investigators should consider both reasons and causes. The reasons actors report are an important source of information, but investigators should also look more broadly, using all available information to put together an explanation of the reasons that might be behind action. Causal explanations should also be considered, with reasoning based on the same logic used in economic analyses.

The conclusions and supporting evidence in the Supovitz and Weathers report (2004) illustrate the use of the mix of evidence to draw conclusions that include causal effects and explanations in terms of reasons. For example, the investigators looked at the consequences for principals who were themselves engaged in visiting other schools to collect the "snapshot" data on implementation of reform. They found that "Both the influence of the snapshot experience and its perceived utility was [sic] amplified for those principals who were involved in conducting snapshots in comparison to those who just were recipients of the snapshots" (p. 14). This is in part a causal claim, supported by the survey evidence: "Comparisons of the survey responses indicated that the principals who participated in collecting the snapshot data were more influenced by the snapshot experience" (p. 14). The report also shows how the principals themselves gave reasons for this strong influence. One principal said about the experience of going to collect snapshot data:

> You can come back to your building after you've done a visitation like that and you learn from that experience, and so okay, I know I need to do this or don't need to do that, or I've not done that very well. . . . But certainly you come back and you do realignments—that's what the process is about. I was glad to I was able to do that, because it helps me make a better assessment in terms of what I need to do with my staff. (p. 14)

With obvious reason to question this self-report (and similar reports from other principals), the investigators have good reasons for explaining the effects of involvement in collecting snapshot data.

Political Theory and Organizational Education Policy Research

Organizational studies of the implementation and effects of policies are typically case studies with a strong evaluative component. They take the intentions of the policy as a starting point, then document and explain the policy's consequences. Some reports may be written for the scholarly community, but the policy community itself is often an important audience. For that audience, the big questions are these: To what extent did the policy achieve its goal? If the consequences were far from what was intended, can adjustments be made, or should the policy be abandoned? If the consequences were roughly in line with the goal, what can be done to make the policy even more effective? For effective policies, how can they be adapted for other contexts?

When the policy community is a major audience, the work of these policy analysts may be more like program evaluation, with its strong applied orientation, than like academic research, with its emphasis on abstract theory. That practical orientation has advantages and disadvantages. On the positive side, work shaped to fit the immediate questions of policymakers is more likely to be used by them. It will attend to the issues of current interest, may highlight adjustments that are easily achievable, and may be written in language close to the language policymakers use.

Some may criticize the analysts, however, for staying *too* close to the interests of the policy audience. One criticism is that studies that focus on immediate, practical concerns do not contribute to theory, and thus have only local, limited application. The familiar debates about the merits of basic and applied research play out in the context of policy research. A different line of criticism is that taking the goals of a policy as a given provides an implicit endorsement of those goals, rather than taking a broader view of what goals are of the most value. In the early evaluation literature, Scriven (1975) argued for "goal-free" evaluation, saying that evaluators have a responsibility to assess the positive and negative effects of education programs, whether or not those effects are part of what the program developers intended. Scriven might make the same argument about organizational education policy analysts, exhorting them not to give any particular weight to the intentions of the current policymakers. Arguments can be made on both sides about the proper stance for policy analysts. Analysts are more likely to influence policymakers if they orient their reports toward ways to accomplish current policy goals. Analyses that take a critical perspective (as do those in the next section) may have long-term impact on policy goals, but are less likely to be drawn on by those currently in control.

CRITICAL THEORY

Critical theorists, unlike the two previous groups, deliberately take positions in opposition to the current policy structure. Their starting point is the belief that the current modes of social and political organization operate to maintain existing differences of power and privilege. They do not typically carry out primary empirical research, relying instead on what others have written. The writings they draw on include empirical research, like that carried out by the other groups, but also include statements made by a wide range of those in the policy community.

Apple's (2001) analysis of the policies being considered for teacher education starts from a broad characterization of possible policies. He characterizes the policies under discussion as "proposals to totally deregulate teacher education so that competition among institutions of higher education, private for-profit training agencies, and school districts themselves will supposedly reinvigorate teacher education and make these programs more cost-effective and efficient" (p. 182). His analysis works from an equally broad depiction of the ideas that he thinks motivate consideration of the policies, namely what he calls "conservative modernization," which is a combination of a press for market-based approaches and strong standards.

His argument is that, while the ideas that make up conservative modernization sound appealing, they have hidden dimensions that make them anything but. He repeatedly uses words like "seemingly" and "overtly" to signal that what appears benign on the surface is actually a set of ideas that will lead to undesirable outcomes, in particular, to the reinforcement of social stratification, unequal opportunities, and inequitable treatment along class and race lines. He says, for example, about standards that "such regulatory reforms are supposedly based on shared values and common sentiment," (p. 189) then goes on to say that they are actually determined by those in power.

Epistemological Issues in Critical Theory

The conclusions drawn in the critical theory are based largely on theoretical analyses of power relations in society. Following the thinking of theorists like Habermas and Marx, the critical theorists see the operation of the social world as determined by differences in power and privilege, differences that are associated with race, class, and gender. Those in power, largely White, upper class, and male, have an interest in holding on their power. They do so, whether intentionally or unconsciously, by controlling policies and by shaping the terms of communication.

Policy analysts like Apple work to show that policies, even when described by those in and out of power as reasonable or perhaps even admirable, usually operate to preserve the status quo. The epistemological question about critical theory is what is required to support such claims.

Those writing within the tradition of critical theory support their analyses by pointing to general conditions that they believe are evident to anyone who looks carefully—who makes what Apple calls an "unromantic appraisal" (p. 183). They take the ways a policy's proponents talk and note that the same policy can be seen, perhaps should be seen, in the light of how it actually serves the powerful. For example, proposing high standards for teachers argue that the higher standards will raise teachers' professional status. Apple suggests that these policies can also be seen as "attempts to centralize control over what teachers are to do even though their rhetoric is couched in the language of increasing professional competence" (p. 183).

If one accepts the premise that those in power control the terms of discussion, to their own benefit, then the task for analysts is to show how seemingly progressive policies are not. The skeptical epistemological question is whether that initial premise also needs support, or could be challenged by the evidence.

Political Theory and Critical Theory

Critical theorists could never be faulted for pandered to policymakers. They are intentionally oppositional. As a result, they are unlikely to shape policy by direct work with policymakers. Their goal, however, is to improve policy by revealing what remains hidden in policy analyses that take the stated intentions of policymakers at face value and accept current public agreement on education goals as a given. Other policy analysts can supply empirical information on the effects and operations of policies, which may lead to changes when stated goals are not being met. The critical theorists persistently raise questions both about the stated goals and about the interpretations other analysts make about observed events. The economic and organizational analysts may fault critical theorists for not caring enough about the "data"; critical theorists fault the other analysts for failing to take an "unromantic" look at the data, failing to see that the terms of the discussion have be set by the powerful, so that troubling persistence of inequities remain hidden.

> Thus, rather than taking neoliberal claims at face value, we should want to ask about their effects that are too often invisible in the rhetoric and metaphors of their proponents. (Apple, 2001, p. 184)

CONCLUSION

I have illustrated some of the philosophical questions that can be asked about education policy research. The illustrations are located in epistemology and in applied political theory. In the first instance, the question is what counts as an adequate warrant for knowledge, with the answer dependent on the type of claim and the context in which the claim is evaluated. For political theory, the question chosen as an illustration is what the connection should be between the policy analyst and the policymaker.

I have suggested that these questions would be answered differently across three approaches to education policy analysis, approaches associated with economics, organizational theory, and critical theory. For epistemology, the types of claims vary, with causal claims more prominent in the first approach, explanations based on reasons more prominent in the second, and reinterpretations that reveal hidden structures in the third. (The division is by no means clear however; organizational analysts make some causal claims, critical theorists explain some actions in terms of reasons, and so on.) The consequence is that a deeper exploration of the epistemological issues would move differently in each area. Such exploration could sharpen the arguments analysts make to defend their claims, or suggest ways in which analysis or reporting should be changed to counter plausible skeptical critiques.

I have also suggested that analysts across approaches attempt to play varying roles in the process of shaping policy. A simplified description is that the economic analysts provide technical expertise for predicting effects of policies, acting instrumentally to allow policymakers to factor likely effects of policies into their decision making. The organizational analysts are similarly instrumental, but focus more on describing how intended policies are implemented, with explanations of the course of implementation that highlight the reasoning of those working in the system. The critical theorists shift attention to revealing differences between the stated, progressive intentions of policies and the ways in which policies can be seen to serve interests of the powerful. Analysts in each approach can argue that they are working to improve education. Each takes a position, often implicit, about what "improve" means and what his or her role is in identifying or establishing that meaning.

Education policy analysts often take up philosophical issues like the ones discussed here, though they may not label what they do as philosophy (Floden, 2005). Chapters in this volume, for example, discuss the evidence needed to support causal inferences and consider what role policy analysts could or should have in shaping policy. Perhaps seeing the philosophical dimension of these issues will permit analysts to learn from extant work in philosophy and give philosophers substantive examples on which to try out their abstract arguments.

REFERENCES

Apple, M. W. (2001). Markets, standards, teaching, and teacher education. *Journal of Teacher Education 52*(3), 182–196.

Cohen, D. K., and Barnes, C. A. (1993). Pedagogy and policy. In *Teaching for understanding: Challenges for policy and practice*, ed. D. Cohen, M. W. McLaughlin, and J. Talbert, 207–239. San Francisco: Jossey-Bass.

Cohen, D. K., and Garet, M. S. (1975). Reforming educational policy with applied social research. *Harvard Educational Review 45*(1), 17–43.

Cronbach, L. J., Arnbron, S., Dornbusch, S., et al. (1980). *Toward reform of program evaluation.* San Francisco: Jossey-Bass.

Erickson, F. (1986). Qualitative methods in research on teaching. In M. C. Wittrock (Ed.), *Handbook of research on teaching* (3rd ed., pp. 119–161). New York: Macmillan.

Floden, R. E. (2005). When is philosophy of education? In K. R. Howe (Ed.), *Philosophy of education 2005: Proceedings of the sixtieth annual meeting of the Philosophy of Education Society* (pp. 1–13). Champaign-Urbana, IL: Philosophy of Education Society.

Floden, R. E., and Weiner, S. S. (1978). Rationality to ritual: The multiple roles of evaluations in governmental processes. *Policy Sciences 9,* 9–18.

Føllesdal, D. (1982). The status of rationality assumptions in interpretation and in the explanation of action. *Dialectica 36,* 301–316.

Goldhaber, D. D., and Brewer, D. J. (1997). Why don't schools and teachers seem to matter? Assessing the impact of unobservables on educational productivity. *Journal of Human Resources 32*(3), 505–523.

Hanushek, E. A. (1994). Money might matter somewhere: A response to Hedges, Laine, and Greenwald. *Educational Researcher 23*(4), 5–8.

Hedges, L., Laine, R., and Greenwald, R. (1994). A meta-analysis of the effects of differential school inputs on student outcomes. *Educational Researcher 23*(3), 5–14.

Holland, P. W. (1986). Statistics and causal inference. *Journal of the American Statistical Association 81,* 945–970.

Hume, D. (1740). *A treatise of human nature.* Repr., New York: Oxford University Press, 2000.

Hume, D. (1748). *An enquiry concerning human understanding.* Repr., New York: Oxford University Press, 1999.

King, G., Keohane, R. O., and Verba, S. (1994). *Designing social inquiry: Scientific inference in qualitative research.* Princeton, NJ: Princeton University Press.

Lindblom, C. E., and Cohen, D. K. (1979). *Usable knowledge: Social science and social problem solving.* New Haven, CT: Yale University Press.

Nisbett, R., and Ross, L. (1980). *Human inference: Strategies and shortcomings of social judgment.* Englewood Cliffs, NJ: Prentice-Hall.

Rubin, D. B. (1974). Estimating causal effects of treatments in randomized and nonrandomized studies. *Journal of Educational Psychology 66*(5), 688–701.

Scriven, M. (1975). *Evaluation bias and its control* (Occasional Paper Series No. 4). Kalamazoo, MI: Western Michigan University, Evaluation Center. http://www.wmich.edu/evalctr/pubs/ops/ops04.html

Supovitz, J. A., and Weathers, J. (2004). *Dashboard lights: Monitoring implementation of district instructional reform strategies.* Philadelphia: University of Pennsylvania, Consortium for Policy Research in Education.

Taylor, C. (1967). Neutrality in political science. In P. Laslett and W. G. Runciman (Eds.), *Philosophy, politics, and society* (3rd ser., pp. 25–57). Oxford: Blackwell.

Taylor, C. (1971). Interpretation and the sciences of man. *Review of Metaphysics 25*, 3–51.

Weber. M. (1949). *The methodology of the social sciences.* E. A. Shils and H. A. Finch (Trans. and Ed.). Glencoe, IL: Free Press.

II

THE MAKING AND EFFECTS
OF EDUCATION POLICY

2

The Politics of Education: Influencing Policy and Beyond

Lorraine M. McDonnell

Because it constitutes the processes and institutions through which valued societal benefits are distributed, politics gives public schooling its rationale, defines its mission, and allocates resources to accomplish that mission. Consequently, education policy analysts have always examined political factors in their research. Nevertheless, as they sought to understand better the school-level effects of education policies, research on the politics of education narrowed. For several decades, the study of politics focused primarily on how political factors influence the design, enactment, and implementation of specific policies.

This intellectual narrowing limited the knowledge base in three ways. First, because the policies of greatest interest to researchers (and funders) originated at the federal and state levels, little research was conducted on the politics of local school districts. From the late 1970s to the late 1990s, few analyses focused, for example, on how local school boards conceive of their roles and make policy decisions, which topics dominate district agendas, or how education issues fit into the broader politics of local communities.[1]

Second, by viewing politics as essentially an independent variable that helps explain specific policy outcomes, researchers paid less attention to aspects of education policy where politics and political functions are, in effect, the dependent variable. One prominent example is student testing policy. For many years, testing was seen as the sole province of psychometricians and educators, with research focused on the technical properties of standardized tests. Political factors were seen as motivating conditions that explained the emergence of policies such as minimum competency testing. But testing was not explicitly conceptualized as advancing identifiable political purposes. It is only recently, as testing policies have become more controversial, that researchers have focused on their political functions in promoting particular curricular values and in imposing greater political accountability on the educational enterprise.

Third, the tight connection between the study of politics and education policy analysis has meant that little research has been conducted on the broader role of politics in education, independent of particular policies. Other functions of politics, such as mobilizing citizen participation,

---

[1]For example, in the 1997 edition of a major politics of education textbook (Wirt & Kirst, 1997), more than 50% of the studies of local education politics cited were conducted prior to 1980, and almost none of the cited research had been conducted on education politics in any communities other than large cities.

serving as a focal point for deliberation, and exposing participants to the values and interests of others, have largely been ignored. Although these other aspects of education politics may not be directly relevant to understanding specific policies, they do provide an important context for understanding such issues as the differential impact of federal and state policies in local communities and changes in how political elites, the media, and the public frame policy problems and solutions over time (Baumgartner & Jones, 1993).

These gaps in our understanding of education politics have been remedied in several critical areas over the past five or six years. Of particular importance to education policy research is new work on the politics of urban education (Henig, et al., 1999; McDermott, 1999; Orr, 1999; Portz, Stein, & Jones, 1999; Rich, 1996; C. N. Stone, 1998; C. N. Stone, et al., 2001). Somewhat ironically, given past neglect of this topic in policy research, these recent studies were motivated by the failure of top-down policies, such as desegregation and various school reform initiatives, to have a significant impact in urban areas. Another area where new research can contribute to a better understanding of policy is the cultural politics of education, particularly debates over which values should be taught in the schools (Binder, 2002; Deckman, 2004; DelFattore, 2004; McDonnell, 2004).[2]

Now is an especially good time to take stock of what is known about the relationship between education politics and policy and to identify areas where additional research is needed. Not only has new research broadened empirical knowledge about education politics and policy, but some recent studies have also provided alternatives to the now-outmoded theories that have defined politics of education research for several decades. In this chapter I review the extant research on education politics and policy, using a framework that encompasses the broad categories of political variables most relevant to understanding policy: institutions, interests, and ideas. In a final section, I discuss several areas where future research could be most productively concentrated.

POLITICAL INSTITUTIONS AND PUBLIC EDUCATION

In explaining why particular policies are adopted, what policymakers expect them to accomplish, and the extent to which they are implemented and actually change teaching and learning, researchers have assumed that institutional characteristics are critical factors. In making this assumption, they are drawing on a body of theoretical literature arguing that institutions matter because they define the framework in which policymaking occurs and thus shape its outcomes, and because different institutional arrangements advantage some societal interests and policy alternatives at the expense of others (Kelman, 1987; March & Olsen, 1989, 1995).[3] These effects occur through the structure of rules and norms that determines who may participate in the policymaking process, who is granted formal authority to choose among proposals, and what procedures must be followed before those with formal authority can make a decision. In education policy, institutional arrangements are particularly critical to explaining policy outcomes because political power is exercised and policy decisions made in multiple venues or arenas. As Mazzoni

---

[2]Although it is less relevant to understanding particular education policies, research is also now being produced on the political socialization of students after a 30-year hiatus (e.g., Conover & Searing, 2000; Niemi & Junn, 1998).

[3]Even researchers who start with very different models of politics and assumptions about the role of institutions agree that they are important to explaining outcomes. For example, Moe (2000) presents a model in which political institutions largely reflect the interests of dominant groups, while March and Olsen (2000) assume that those same institutions embody rules and norms encouraging the development of shared identities that extend beyond self-interest. Nevertheless, both sets of authors see institutions as critical for understanding education policy and for changing its outcomes.

(1991) notes, these arenas are never neutral in their allocation of access and power: "They legitimate a set of participants, establish the institutional and social context—including the governing 'rules of the game'—mediate the potency of resources and strategies, and encourage some means (and discourage other means) of reaching agreements" (p. 116).

If we look across research on education politics and policy, three basic conclusions emerge about institutions. The first is the much discussed (and often lamented) one that U.S. public education is fragmented institutionally. Not only do multiple levels of government share authority over public education and responsibility for its funding, but power is also fragmented among institutions within each of those levels. The source of this fragmentation is deeply rooted in the nation's history and culture as well as in its Constitution (James, 1991; Madison, Hamilton, & Jay, 1788/1961; Morone, 1990),[4] with institutional fragmentation often having resulted from demands to make schools more responsive and to address emerging problems within a bureaucratic structure (Tyack, 1993).

Contemporary policy and institutions reflect and reinforce these historical trends. Consider, for instance, the institutional fragmentation associated with the pattern of categorical funding that has characterized the federal role over the past 30 years. In responding to the needs and interests of various student populations, from the disabled to those enrolled in vocational education, Congress has fostered the establishment of federal, state, and local bureaucracies to administer these programs and deliver services to students. In addition, the enabling legislation has often created formal roles for groups representing these students, their parents, and the professionals who serve them. Once such a multiplicity of governance structures is in place, the institutions themselves hamper coherent policy, as each agency's autonomy hinges to some extent on resisting coordination (Wong, 1994).

Ambivalent attitudes reflecting the public's desire to have the federal government provide specific benefits such as funding for early childhood education while also wanting it to exert less influence over local programs further complicate the picture (Elam & Rose, 1995; Elam, Rose, & Gallup, 1994; Johnson & Immerwahr, 1994). The interplay of contradictory public demands and fragmented institutions has produced an educational policy system that appears to some critics to be nothing more than an overly bureaucratized monolith (Moe, 1990), but the real problem is more complex and may be just the opposite. Cohen and Spillane (1992) argue that reformers' ambitious attempts at strong policy have inevitably been implemented through a large and loosely jointed governance system: "While the design of American government incarnates a deep mistrust of state power, the design of most education policy expressed an abiding hope for the power of government and a wish to harness it to social problem solving. . . . The collisions between rapidly pp. 7, 11).

Multitiered influence is not confined to formal governmental bodies. Education politics and policies at all levels have been heavily influenced by a variety of voluntary networks comprising groups representing elected officials (e.g., National Governors' Association, National Conference of State Legislatures), corporations (Business Roundtable, National Alliance of Business), teacher unions (American Federation of Teachers, National Education Association), professional organizations (National Council of Teachers of Mathematics), education reformers (Carnegie Forum on Education and the Economy, National Board for Professional Teaching Standards), foundations (Carnegie Corporation, Ford, Pew, Fordham), public policy institutions (Brookings, Heritage), and groups advocating broad ideological positions (Eagle Forum, People for the American Way). The agendas and strategies of these organizations vary considerably, but all have influenced the array of education policy alternatives and have made the political environment much

---

[4]This discussion of institutional fragmentation is excerpted from McDonnell & Weatherford, 2000.

denser. The overall effect has been to make the range of policy choices richer, but also to make it more difficult for any one institution or level to act authoritatively.

Rather than an unresponsive and centralized system, American education politics is better described as a multiplicity of loosely connected institutions that are highly responsive to narrowly defined functional and geographic constituencies. Not only the design and implementation of policy, but also the complex and shifting politics of education are shaped by this context of competing demands and ideals. The result is a continuing and vigorous debate: first over the roles and responsibilities of different branches and levels of government, and second over how to develop the nexus of negotiated rules and expectations that would allow separate institutions to share authority.

The second conclusion flows from the first: the fragmentation of authority and responsibility means that policymaking can be shifted quite easily from one institutional arena to another, and it is often done to increase the strategic advantage of particular interests. The most prominent example is the role of courts. Judicial decisions, particularly in school finance, desegregation, and the education of disabled students and those with limited English proficiency, have forged major new policy directions. The courts have strongly influenced education both directly and by constraining other political actors. For example, elective bodies are often in the position of reacting to an agenda set by the courts, and of having to legislate the specifics of a general policy direction established by judicial fiat (see, e.g., Melnick, 1995; Reed, 2001).

A group with a rights-based claim pursues it through the judiciary, often after determining that legislative majorities are unlikely to be responsive. A decision in the group's favor commands the legislature's attention, at the same time that it circumscribes how elected officials balance this claim against those of other interests. Although the courts' influence has been concentrated in only a few critical areas, some analysts have suggested that the growing judicial role is part of a larger "antipolitical" trend, where reform advocates "seek to spare themselves the rigors and uncertainties of interest mobilization and coalition-building by shifting consideration of key issues from legislatures and school boards to institutions that are less 'political' and more authoritative, such as courts and markets" (Plank & Boyd, 1994, p. 264).

Although research has focused on the role of courts and the strategic advantage to be gained or lost by moving from one arena to another, less attention has been paid to how institutional norms with regard to participation and decision making vary across arenas. Yet these differences can be significant in understanding why participation patterns vary and why different arenas produce different types of policies. For example, in his analysis of choice legislation in Minnesota, Mazzoni (1991) suggests that major policy changes are more likely to occur if policy entrepreneurs can move the process out of the stable legislative subsystem where established groups and their legislative and bureaucratic supporters dominate institutional agendas to the broader and publicly visible "macro arena" where a more diverse set of policy elites and the public can be mobilized.

One mechanism for moving policy ideas into the macro arena that a number of states, including Minnesota, have used is the appointed commission where a broad array of interests are represented, and decision making is more consensual than in the legislative subsystem characterized by bargaining. Although such commissions have been effective in moving new ideas into the policy arena and in dealing with ideological differences among participants, they typically lack the authority to enact policy. Consequently, commission recommendations must be sent to the legislature or another authoritative arena for ratification. For example, in examining why state standards setting in mathematics and science in California was so divisive, McDonnell and Weatherford (1999) found that because the state board of education and its political principal, the governor, had to ratify the standards commission's work, those who opposed the standards developed by the commission had no incentive to seek compromise in that venue since they knew they could press their case in another arena.

Although studies such as the Minnesota case in the 1980s and the California case in the 1990s are suggestive, more systematic knowledge is needed about the incentives and norms shaping the different arenas that consider education policy. This information is particularly important now that the scope of centralized authority, with its emphasis on decision making through bargaining, has grown simultaneously with expanded school-site governance where deliberative norms and consensual decision making are more likely.

Another arena growing in importance is the initiative and referendum in states and localities. As of 2003, 24 states and about half of all cities permit voters to propose policies and enact them into law through the ballot process (Matsusaka, 2004). Like the shift from legislatures to courts or commissions, use of the initiative process is typically based on a strategic calculation that a policy proposal will fare better in this arena than in the legislature. Traditionally, initiatives and referenda most relevant to education were those dealing with school tax levies, construction bonds, and tax limitation measures, beginning with California's Proposition 13 in 1978 and subsequently approved in 38 other states (Wong, 1999). More recently, initiatives have also dealt with the substance of education. Among the most prominent are those that voucher proponents have sponsored to authorize either state-funded voucher programs or tuition tax credits for parents who send their children to private schools. Unlike tax limitation measures, over half of which have been approved, the voucher and tax credit initiatives appearing on state ballots over the past 15 years have been defeated (Moe, 2001).[5]

Much of the research literature tends to be normative, either criticizing the initiative process for providing wealthy interests with a mechanism easily manipulated to their advantage or applauding it for giving voters a way to regain control from legislatures beholden to special interests (Matsusaka, 2004). Although there is some empirical research on the determinants of public support for ballot propositions and the extent to which they are consistent with minority preferences (e.g., Donovan & Bowler, 1998; Gamble, 1997; Hajnal, Gerber, & Louch, 2002), few studies focus specifically on initiatives related to education.[6] Especially useful would be ones that advance our understanding of the conditions under which arena shifts occur by examining the factors that shape a group's decision to advance its policy proposal by directly appealing to voters.

Finally, an institutional perspective on education politics points to the centrality of local institutions and to the need to develop a better understanding of them. Recent comparative research on urban districts and school reform has highlighted the critical role of local political institutions in facilitating or hindering changes in education policy and practice. We also need similar research, using common theoretical frameworks and data collection strategies, on the politics of education in nonurban communities. Such studies would help in understanding the political dynamics of those communities and how and why they may differ from urban ones. They would also provide information about the broader political context in which U.S. public education is now operating, when the majority of voters live outside urban areas and distinctive patterns are emerging in the voting behavior of those living in rural and exurban areas as compared with voters in cities and suburbs.

---

[5]Moe (2001) argues that for the voucher movement, ballot propositions are probably a no-win strategy because public opinion is more easily manipulated during initiative campaigns in contrast to the legislative process where it cannot be so readily molded by one side or the other and has only an indirect effect on the policy outcome (369).

[6]In one of the few studies focusing on education referenda, Lentz (1999) examined the predictors of passage of school financial referenda in Illinois between 1981 and 1989. She found that although predictors of passage vary by type of community, economic conditions and community homogeneity are significant predictors for all community types.

In addition to a more complete and systematic overview of local political institutions and their effects on schooling, additional in-depth case studies focusing on specific puzzles and enduring dilemmas are needed. Because research on the local politics of education was neglected for so long, knowledge about it often rests on old information and conventional wisdom that has gone unexamined even as it continues to dominate political rhetoric. One example is the popular belief in local control for promoting participation in the educational enterprise and ensuring greater responsiveness to community interests. That core belief has posed a dilemma for policymakers attempting to advance social goals that transcend the parochial interests of local communities and that may involve redistribution from some localities to others.

In studying the tension between conditions promoting equal educational opportunity and ones maintaining strong self-government, McDermott (1999) found local control to be more problematic than typically assumed from conventional wisdom. After examining the response of New Haven and three suburban districts to a state supreme court desegregation decision, she concluded that local control has been a barrier to desegregation and efforts to improve learning opportunities for students attending urban schools. At the same time, it has not met a reasonable standard for democratic control because local school politics is characterized by low levels of participation, with decision-making processes largely closed to ordinary citizens. For those familiar with failed attempts to desegregate across district lines, McDermott's finding that suburbanites viewed regional problems such as poverty as urban issues and that no institutions could pursue redistribution across town lines is unsurprising. Similarly, her finding of low levels of citizen participation is consistent with other studies. What is more revealing is the reason for this lack of public involvement. McDermott looked beyond public apathy to explain low participation, and found that "professional educators, and by extension, boards of education, have generally tended to see community involvement as an issue of public relations, not democratic politics per se" (81). Her research suggests that a partial explanation for tepid public participation in school governance is the lack of opportunity for meaningful citizen involvement.

Just as McDermott's research challenges conventional wisdom by providing further insight into an enduring dilemma, other recent studies have tackled unresolved institutional and political questions by investigating them from perspectives not typically used in education research. One example comes from two studies (Henig, et al., 1999; Rich, 1996) that analyze why Black-majority cities governed by Black leaders have fallen so far short of public expectations for education reform. By taking an explicitly racialized perspective in their comparative study of Black-led cities, the authors document the role of race not just in complicating access to needed private resources typically held by white elites, but also in defining the role of the school system as part of a broader employment regime. Henig and his colleagues note that,

> rather than looking at schools and their jobs in negative terms—as sources of patronage, inefficiency, and intransigence, and waste—we take seriously the positive roles that schools play in the local political economy, as sources of citywide economic development, community identity and stability, and upward mobility for individuals and groups. (p. 118)

Consequently, they investigate the implications of the public school system being the largest employer in Baltimore, Detroit, and Washington, DC.[7] One result is a more nuanced analysis of why teacher unions, Black ministers, and community activists oppose reform efforts if they seem to threaten jobs.

---

[7]Even in Atlanta, in an economically growing region, the Atlanta Public Schools is the sixth largest employer, with more workers than either Coca-Cola or the Georgia Power Company.

These are just two examples of a growing, but still limited, research literature that focuses on local political institutions, attempting to move beyond conventional wisdom in finding reasons for policy shortcomings and political dysfunction. What they share is a realization that even with the growth of top-down policy, local political institutions are still critical players that need to be examined from theoretical perspectives that view them as explicitly political bodies situated in an environment broader than just the school system.

THE POLITICS OF EDUCATION INTERESTS

The dominance of rational choice models in economics, policy analysis, and political science over the past 20 years placed the concept of *interest* front and center in research in those fields. Studies in this genre begin with the assumption that political actors know their self-interest and pursue it in the political arena through bargaining with other actors who are also pursuing their self-interest and whose support is needed to build a coalition representing enough votes to enact a given policy. Consequently, in formulating explanations for policy outcomes and predictions about future results, those with a material stake in the outcome and, therefore, an incentive to mobilize in support or opposition to a particular policy need to be identified. However, a number of scholars have argued that a model of politics and policymaking premised solely on self-interest is incomplete, and that some policy outcomes cannot be adequately explained by self-interest alone (Kelman, 1987; Mansbridge, 1990; Reich, 1988). The concept that captures this alternative set of motivations is *ideas*, and includes the notion of a public interest that transcends self-interest and, in the case of education, theories about how children ought to be educated and who ought to be responsible for that education.

Much of the debate over the validity of interests versus ideas in explaining policy outcomes has been waged deductively and on normative grounds, rather than based on empirical research. However, over the past decade, researchers have realized that neither model provides a full explanation. Much of public policy is motivated by self or group interest, whether it be politicians' desire to be reelected or interest groups' efforts to enhance their members' material advantages. Nevertheless, ideas are often necessary to persuade others to accept even the most self-interested policy options. Furthermore, comprehensive and far-reaching policies are more likely than narrow, specialized ones to be motivated by ideology and by concepts that transcend self-interest (Kelman, 1987). In fact, ideas and interests are so intertwined that it is often difficult to measure their independent effects (Kingdon, 1993). One can acknowledge, for example, that teacher unions seek to improve their members' salaries and working conditions, but they also represent professional values that may lead them to espouse policy options that may benefit the educational enterprise generally, but not necessarily the self-interest of all their members (e.g., peer evaluations leading to the dismissal of unqualified teachers).

Although education is a policy domain where the distinction between interests and ideas is often blurred, this section reviews research focused primarily on the interests that define education policy, while the next one examines idea-based politics. However, the two sections overlap, reflecting the sometimes tight connections between interests and ideas in education politics and policy. One area where the overlap is evident is the proliferation of organized interest groups. In 1980, the *Encyclopedia of Associations* listed 976 groups focused on education; by 1995, that number had increased by a third to 1,312 (Baumgartner & Leech, 1998, p. 103). As the number of groups has increased, so has the diversity of voices represented, and for some of those groups, the pursuit of their interests and the promotion of ideas are inextricably linked.

In examining research on the role of interests in education policy, we can draw three broad conclusions. First, because research on major interest groups, such as teacher unions, has examined their influence on specific policies over time and across jurisdictions, it is possible to assess the long-term impact of these groups. However, there is little systematic research on other groups that have been identified as important, such as textbook and test publishers.

As teacher unions gained collective bargaining rights, but also recognized the limits on what could be obtained at the bargaining table, they pursued a dual strategy of collective bargaining and political action—supporting electoral candidates and lobbying. By the 1980s, the American Federation of Teachers (AFT) and the National Education Association (NEA) had become an influential interest in many states, even in the South, where collective bargaining was not legalized. However, teacher unions have never represented a monolith in their political positions, and their differences became especially significant as a variety of reforms dominated education policy agendas beginning in the 1980s. For example, when a series of reforms to promote teacher professionalism were proposed, the AFT and NEA affiliates in Florida and Pennsylvania took divergent positions. Some state affiliates within the same national organization even differed in their policy positions, as when the NEA affiliate in Arizona accepted the principle of peer evaluation in the 1980s, while the California affiliate rejected it (McDonnell & Pascal, 1988). More recently, in their 11-city study, Stone and his colleagues (2001) found that,

> in only three cities was the teachers' union a member of the reform coalition, and thereby in a position to put professional development on the table as an element of the improvement agenda. In another three, the teachers were active (if not always highly visible) opponents of reform. And in the remaining five they were largely nonplayers in broad school improvement efforts. (p. 83)

The reasons for these differences depend to a large degree on local circumstances, particularly the historical relationship between the teacher union and the school district and their leaders. However, teacher organizations, regardless of the level of the system at which they operate, must all make a similar calculation in deciding whether to defend the status quo, accommodate reform proposals, or shape new approaches. Because they are voluntary membership organizations whose survival depends on accommodating member preferences and also interest groups seeking benefits from the political system, teacher organization leaders must assess the cost of pursuing a reform strategy that might alienate members as compared with acceding to membership preferences and perhaps risking a negative public image. The cost of pursuing reform may be particularly high if members believe that union leaders are doing so at the expense of pressing for higher salaries and better working conditions (McDonnell & Pascal, 1988).

Balancing the union's traditional role with one of reform advocacy has become more difficult as new players have entered the education arena and proposed policies, such as expanded school choice and stricter accountability, that are perceived to be at odds with the interests of organized teachers. For example, in their analysis of the status of teacher unions in Michigan and Pennsylvania after the election of Republican governors in the 1990s, Boyd, Plank, and Sykes (2000) found that,

> the unions in both states have failed to advance a politically viable alternative to the reform strategies favored by their adversaries. Their energies are largely devoted to protecting their members against erosion in their economic position and to defending the public school system against the threat of vouchers. As the unions' power has diminished, however, their capacity to accomplish either of these ends has fallen into some doubt. (p. 175)

In assessing the long-term political impact of teacher unions, we can conclude that their influence has varied considerably across states and localities, and that the major gains the unions secured through political action and collective bargaining in the 1970s and 1980s have not been matched recently. Teacher unions also have a mixed track record in blocking reforms they oppose. What is more significant than their opposition is the extent to which, beginning with the state-level reforms of the late 1980s and continuing today, teacher unions have been sidelined in the enactment of major new education policies.

The business community has been prominent among the new players shaping the education policy arena over the past 20 years. Business leaders were active in the progressive coalition at the beginning of the 20th century that pressed for greater professionalism, centralization, and accountability in public education at the state and local levels (Tyack, 1974). Their involvement at the federal level had largely been limited to the support of vocational education. However, by the 1960s, business leaders were at first indifferent and then opposed to an increased federal presence in the nation's schools. Their opposition stemmed from a fear that an expanded role would result in higher taxes; an aversion to getting involved in a politically charged policy arena that was dealing with issues such as desegregation; and with the availability of a capable and plentiful domestic labor force, a lack of concern about educational quality (Manna, 2003).

The situation changed in the 1980s. Concern over the need to maintain a well-trained labor force in the face of global competition and frustration over the slow progress of educational change led to more sustained and policy-oriented business involvement at the state level. By the 1990s, its presence was also felt at the federal level, especially in the Business Roundtable's support of Goals 2000, other standards-based initiatives, and more recently, the No Child Left Behind Act (NCLB). As Manna (2003) concludes, "the political leverage that business leaders provided to federal reformers from both major parties is hard to understate" (p. 11).

As with the teacher unions, business involvement in reform efforts in the 11 cities Stone and his colleagues (2001) studied has varied. In Pittsburgh, Boston, and Los Angeles, it was broad-based and institutionalized, while it was less broad-based but institutionalized in Baltimore and Houston. In Washington, DC, it was institutionalized but guarded, and in Detroit, business involvement was contested. In the other four cities, Atlanta, Denver, St. Louis, and San Francisco, business played only a small role in reform efforts (78). Henig and his co-authors (1999) explain why business involvement at the local level has not always fit the "celebratory" tone that characterizes the existing literature on education partnerships. They note that even businesses physically located within central cities may not depend on graduates of urban high schools for their entry-level workers. Consequently, the economic incentive is less compelling if they can recruit, for example, from surrounding suburbs. Business leaders are also reluctant to get involved in local education politics if controversial issues are likely to arise that might pose risks for their corporate image. Finally, Henig et al. conclude from their study of Black-led cities that business elites there and in other cities with large minority populations fear either becoming enmeshed in racial conflicts or being cast as White nationalists.[8] In contrast, African American political leaders are concerned about whether alliances with business will be sustained over the long haul and whether they will be portrayed as elitists by grassroots opponents if they work too closely with business leaders.

---

[8]One example was the case of Houston, where the business role was highly visible, but its image was tarnished in the Latino community because of business involvement in the selection of an African American superintendent at a time when members of the Latino community felt they had a strong claim to be considered for the office (Longoria 1998; Stone et al., 2001, p. 83).

Although the increasingly prominent role of business groups at all three governmental levels has prompted greater research attention to their motivations and strategies, we lack recent and systematic research about their overall impact on education politics and policy. Most of the studies from which we can learn about the role of business have as their unit of analysis particular policies such as NCLB or state and local reforms where business groups are one set of players.[9] Consequently, it would be useful to conduct studies where the unit of analysis is a major business organization or organizations (e.g., the Business Roundtable and its state affiliates) in the expectation that it would yield more systematic information about overall impact.

While we know less about business groups than teacher unions, research knowledge about both is greater than for a number of other interests that have become increasingly significant in education policy. These include textbook and test publishers (particularly after the passage of NCLB), ancillary service providers such as those offering tutoring, foundations, community-based organizations, and various nonprofits. Contemporary media accounts suggest that these groups can be quite influential, and that some, such as test publishers, have much to gain from current policies that greatly expand requirements for standardized testing. Lack of systematic and up-to-date knowledge about these organizations suggests that research is needed that focuses on specific interest groups or categories of groups as the unit of analysis and that examines them in the context of specific policies such as NCLB and also comparatively over time, place, and issues.

A second conclusion from the extant research on education interests is that those with the greatest stake in the system, namely students and their parents, have had an organized and sustained presence in only a few areas of education policy, most notably special education. Special education is an interesting case of political action. Its advocates' early success came largely because professionals working in special education recognized that a focus on securing educational rights for students with disabilities constituted not only a powerful lever for advancing their case, but also a way to unite a diverse coalition with professionals in control of the programs that resulted. Melnick (1995) concludes that although the emphasis on rights was at first perceived by special education professionals as an attack on their expertise and discretion, they soon realized that such an approach would actually increase their control over special education policy.

However, the consensus among advocacy groups—including those representing parents of students with disabilities—that marked the policy's initial passage has not been reflected in its subsequent implementation. The reasons stem from the funding shortfall between the 40 percent of excess costs authorized in the legislation and actual appropriations, and the rights accorded parents to bring actions against schools (Posner, 1998). The funding shortfall often put state and local governments and those groups representing general education at odds with the interests of special educators and parents, as special education was increasingly seen as an underfunded mandate, consuming a disproportionate amount of state and local revenues and compromising other educational priorities.

The interests of parental groups have also at times differed from those of special educators, particularly with regard to expanding parents' procedural rights to challenge decisions about service provision made by professionals. As the coalition around the original legislation has frayed, the way in which the policy problem is defined has varied among groups. In her analysis of groups testifying before Congress in all federal special education legislation since 1975 as well as those that filing amicus briefs in special education cases before the Supreme Court, Itkonen (2004) found that family disability groups typically premise their political action on the argument

---

[9]Another example of a study examining business involvement as part of the analysis of a particular policy issue is Witte's (2000) analysis of the Milwaukee and Cleveland voucher programs.

that special education is a civil rights entitlement protected by the federal government, and they tell a hopeful story of the positive outcomes that will result if students with disabilities are served. In contrast, professional groups, particularly school administrator organizations, view special education as a set of procedural rules governing a grant-in-aid program. They advocate for greater state or local control, for equitable funds distribution, and against expansions to the statutes (e.g., through new eligibility categories), and they typically tell stories of decline, focusing on the negative consequences of federal legislation (e.g., that special education mandates undermine the ability of state and local governments to provide high-quality education for all students). Itkonen found, after controlling for organizational characteristics such as staff size and age of group, that groups framing the policy problem as a civil rights issue and portraying the results of federal policy in a hopeful manner tend to be more effective in advancing their interests than those pressing for less federal control and relying on stories of decline.

In other areas of education, parents have also organized in informal, grassroots networks. The most recent examples are those formed in opposition to state-mandated tests. To date, the organized testing backlash has been concentrated in suburban communities in a few states such as Massachusetts and New York. Somewhat ironically, the parents of those students who are least likely to feel the adverse effects of high-stakes testing (suburban, upper-middle-class, White students) are the ones who have organized thus far. Whether they will be successful in organizing a broad spectrum of parents and the public will largely depend on how urban, minority, and working-class parents react if and when sanctions are imposed on large numbers of their children.

Although the interests of poor, working-class, and minority parents have been represented by various interest groups and public interest law firms in desegregation, school funding, and related cases, grassroots organizing by these parents is typically limited and sporadic. The reasons are the same as those that bias political participation more generally in the United.States: limits on parental time, a dearth of strategic and financial resources, and despite rhetoric to the contrary, little effort on the part of school officials to involve parents as full participants in the policy process. Stone and his colleagues (2001) note, "research indicates that the actions of school systems are an especially important factor in the degree to which parents become actively engaged. Yet among our eleven cities, only Pittsburgh made any systemwide effort to involve parents" (p. 83). In other cities, there were limited efforts in a few schools, but it was not a consistent, district-wide priority. As a result, the co-authors conclude that "despite vocal support for parental involvement from the U.S. Department of Education and many state departments of education as well, urban parents are scarcely visible as *active* stakeholders in the current school improvement movement" (p. 83).

Even for more affluent parents who have the resources to press the system, school officials have been more willing to address concerns about individual children than to respond to collective demands for change. Part of the explanation lies in how educators conceive of their roles. As teaching has become more professionalized, educators have been reluctant to accept parental and public participation in education governance on an equal basis and instead have encouraged parental involvement on limited terms that they define (viz., parental assistance with homework, participation in the PTA, classroom volunteering; Farkas, 1993; Hess, 1995; McDermott, 1999). Whether one interprets the current situation as due to a lack of parental incentives to do more than press for their own children's welfare or as caused by a system stacked against their collective action, parents' limited voice as an educational interest is often used as a major rationale for transforming their status and that of their children from one of clients to consumers through various school choice strategies (Chubb & Moe, 1990; Schneider, Teske, & Marschall, 2000).

A third conclusion emerging from research on education interests relates to an earlier point. With the notable exception of teacher unions, much of what we know about education interest groups comes not from studying the groups as the unit of analysis, but rather from research on specific policy issues and local communities. As a result, our knowledge of education interests is spotty, and unconnected to the research base on interest groups outside of education. So, for example, the broader interest group literature is quite informative about what scholars call "demand aggregation"—how groups mobilize, how group leaders relate to their membership, and how they recruit members or otherwise maintain themselves (Cigler, 1994). However, we lack systematic information on these topics for most groups active in the education arena. We even lack another type of more descriptive information available from large-scale surveys of interest groups in other policy domains—namely, a systematic overview of the various tactics that groups use in their attempts to influence policy.

THE POLITICS OF EDUCATIONAL IDEAS

Although it is never an entirely clean distinction, we might think about interests and ideas by considering their respective roles in explaining different types of policies. Material interests are more likely to explain the politics of ongoing policies, particularly within legislative bodies where interests are well defined and relationships among interest groups, legislators, and the bureaucrats implementing policy are well established. Most of the political action is focused on refining the rules governing an established policy and bargaining over the distribution of an already-defined set of resources. This type of policymaking characterizes Mazzoni's (1991) "stable legislative subsystem" and Baumgartner and Jones's (1993) "structure-induced equilibrium" where institutions are created to sustain a given policy and where for a long period only incremental changes are made at the margin of the policy, leaving its core idea intact. Baumgartner and Jones describe such an equilibrium as a "policy monopoly" that includes a definable institutional structure limiting access to the policy process and a powerful supporting idea. "These buttressing policy ideas are generally connected to core political values which can be communicated directly and simply through image and rhetoric" (p. 7).

However, policy monopolies and the interests they serve can be disrupted with major policy changes resulting. These occur because ideas challenging an established policy monopoly capture the imagination of the media, policymakers, and the public. They provide new understandings of policy problems and new ways of conceptualizing solutions. These ideas can fuel powerful changes as they are communicated through a variety of rhetorical mechanisms, including stories about decline or negative consequences resulting from the current policy monopoly and stories of hope about what can be accomplished with a new framing of the policy problem and solution (D. Stone, 2002, p. 138). Yet new ideas "are not controlled or created by any single group or individual, but are the result of multiple interactions among groups seeking to propose new understandings of issues, political leaders seeking new issues on which to make their name, agencies seeking to expand their jurisdictions, and voters reacting to the whole spectacle" (Baumgartner & Jones, 1993, p. 237). Even when new ideas lead to policy changes, the old policy monopoly often continues until the institutional structures and norms through which new policies are implemented are also transformed. For example, charter schools and vouchers represent new ideas about how schools should be organized to enhance student learning. They are part of the policy discourse, and new policies reflect their underlying ideas, but it is not yet clear the extent to which they will significantly alter the institutional structure of public education and create a new policy monopoly.

Central to the success of idea-based policy change are policy entrepreneurs—political actors who promote policy innovations—and the policy issue networks they use to communicate their ideas to those with shared interests and with whom they are linked by formal and informal contacts (Kingdon, 1995; Wirt & Kirst, 2001). A good example of this process is the role of policy entrepreneurs and issue networks in the diffusion of ideas about school choice. Drawing on a survey of state education policy experts, Mintrom (1997) found that policy entrepreneurs were identified as advocates of school choice in 26 states. Then using event history analysis models of the diffusion of school choice ideas across the U.S., Mintrom and Vergari (1998) found that greater involvement in policy networks significantly increased the likelihood that policy entrepreneurs achieved their legislative goals. However, the explanatory variables for getting the school choice issue on a state's legislative agenda differed from those explaining whether or not a choice policy was subsequently enacted. The researchers found that in getting the choice issue on the agenda, policy entrepreneurs used both interstate or external policy networks and internal, in-state networks comprising individuals with ties to members of the local policymaking community. The external networks served as sources for generating new ideas, while the internal networks provided relevant contacts and a source of information about how best to present proposals for innovation to garner serious attention. However, once the issue was on the agenda, the factors that predicted legislative approval were different. At the approval stage, not only was the presence of an internal network significant, but approval was more likely if the teacher union did not strongly oppose the policy and if student test scores had declined, signaling a need for policy change.

This example illustrates the critical role of policy entrepreneurs and issue networks in spreading new ideas and in altering established policy monopolies. But it also shows how ideas and interests intersect. In this case, the strength of union opposition had no effect on the likelihood of legislative consideration of school choice, but such opposition did reduce chances for legislative approval. In essence, the influence of a critical group whose interests could be threatened by school choice was not a significant factor in determining whether this new idea was seriously considered, but the group's position did make a difference to whether it was transformed into policy.

Keeping in mind the caveat that distinctions between interests and ideas are rarely unambiguous, we can draw two conclusions from research on the role of ideas in education politics. The first is the obvious one that ideas have always been central to defining American public education, and they continue to shape its politics. Ideas about the training needed to prepare citizens for responsible self-government provided the original rationale for public schools. However, the basis for public schooling was never completely political. From the very beginning of the republic, political and economic motivations were intertwined, and the links grew even stronger as the nation industrialized. For example, in describing the common school movement, James (1991) notes that "it brought together Protestant-style civic religion and a republican fervor carried forward from the American Revolution, along with socially and politically conservative values stressing nativism, work discipline, time control, sobriety, and other traits associated with the maintenance of moral order and civic cohesion in a nascent capitalist economy" (p. 178).

The values and ideas motivating education policy have changed over time, but there is no question that ideas continue to undergird major policy shifts. One need only think of the notion of *fiscal neutrality* behind school finance reform, the rejection of the "separate but equal" doctrine in school desegregation, the concept of *opportunity to learn* justifying standards-based curricular reforms, and countless other ideas that have inspired policy changes. Cremin (1989) reminds us of Aristotle's dictum: "It is impossible to talk about education apart from a conception of the good life; people will inevitably differ in their conceptions of the good life, and hence they will inevitably differ on matters of education; therefore the discussion of education falls squarely within the domain of politics" (pp. 103–104). All these policy ideas embody "conceptions of the good life" that spell out a set of goals and a course of action to attain it. But in doing so, they also challenge other conceptions of what schooling should accomplish.

A number of analysts have examined the competing goals of education as a basis for understanding major policy disputes. In a recent example, Hochschild and Scovronick (2003) provide a useful conceptual framework for understanding the bases of contention in policies ranging from school finance reform to bilingual and special education. They argue that from its inception, American public education has been defined by two broad goals with a third added more recently. The first is to promote individual attainment, articulated in the ideology of the American dream promising that all U.S. residents will have a reasonable chance to achieve success as they define it. The second is the collective purpose of promoting democracy through the teaching of democratic values and practices, and the provision of equal opportunity for all children. A third goal that has become prominent over the past two decades is the expectation that schools should meet the distinctive needs of particular racial, ethnic, religious, and gender groups.

By examining a variety of policy debates through the lens of each of these goals, we can begin to understand why the politics surrounding some education policies have been so virulent and difficult to resolve. Although Hochschild and Scovronick assume that all three goals are valid, the legitimacy of the third one continues to be questioned in debates over policies ranging from affirmative action to special education. Even when a goal's legitimacy is not in question, its advocates must compete for scarce resources and for time in the school curriculum, with one goal typically preeminent at a given time. The result, as Baumgartner and Jones's model would predict, is continual jockeying among proponents of those goals not currently in ascendancy to upset the status quo and to gain a higher place on the public agenda for the values they espouse. Consequently, "the combination of multiple goals, competing interests, and a fragmented governance structure has often made policies incoherent and decisions unstable" (Hochschild & Scovronick, 2003, p. 18).

Although the primacy of an idea can be measured by the level of resources devoted to policies promoting it, perhaps a more powerful indicator is the extent to which it is reflected in what students are taught. For that reason, researchers have turned their attention to studying political activism aimed at influencing what values are taught in the schools. From this growing body of research comes a second conclusion: studies focused on the cultural politics of education have enhanced our understanding of the motivations and strategies of groups often considered to be outside mainstream politics, and in several instances, these studies suggest augmentations or revisions to existing social science frameworks.

Cultural activists are not important to an understanding of politics in the same way as, for example, teacher unions, whose influence is more widespread and sustained. Rather, groups promoting particular cultural identities and moral values are significant because their concerns raise abiding philosophical issues such as which educational decisions should be the prerogative of the state and which should remain within the purview of the family. Foundational questions of this type have influenced the contours of American public education since its inception, requiring those governing the schools to decide not only the boundaries between family and state, but also what constitutes sectarian and religious values and what constitutes civic and secular ones. To hark back to Hochschild and Scovronick's framework, these groups' demands have also forced schools to consider how much of their curriculum should be common to all students and how much should reflect the beliefs and identities of specific groups. In periods of increased activism, groups pushing a values agenda have shaped policy debates through key judicial decisions, and in some cases, through policies affecting large numbers of students such as the termination of the California Learning Assessment System (CLAS) in the mid-1990s (McDonnell, 2004).

Although most recent studies have focused on specific policies that have been the flashpoints for values-based controversies (e.g., school prayer and curricular content), a few have examined the actors who precipitated these disputes and the institutions that have been the target of their campaigns. One example is Deckman's (2004) study comparing Christian Right candidates for local school boards with candidates not affiliated with the Christian Right or subscribing to their issue positions. On the basis of a nationally representative survey of candidates running in the late 1990s, she found that 19 percent of candidates either belonged to a Christian Right group or supported one and also supported the issue agenda endorsed by those groups. Although the media have paid considerable attention in recent years to the Christian Right's efforts to train and recruit candidates to run for local political offices, few of Deckman's study respondents, regardless of whether they were part of the Christian Right, received direct assistance from interest groups or political parties. In addition, there was no statistically significant difference between the proportion of Christian Right candidates who won in contested races (46 percent) and non-Christian Right candidates who won (52 percent). However, Christian Right candidates were significantly more likely than non-Christian Right candidates to say that applying their "religious or moral beliefs" to school policy was an important factor in their decision to run for office.[10]

Binder's (2002) study compares two very different curricular values—Afrocentrism and creationism—through seven cases grounded in a well-specified theoretical framework. Consequently, the study contributes to our understanding of the politics of ideas, and also provides a revision to social movement theory that can be tested in studies outside education. Binder found that despite having very different constituencies, there were notable similarities between Afrocentrists and creationists. Both made comparable arguments about oppression by the majority culture and about their children's welfare; educators were skeptical about the factual claims of both groups; and both had to mount their challenges through the bureaucratic channels of school districts. Binder concludes that Afrocentrists were more successful in getting their values embodied in curriculum because they appeared to be offering a solution to problems of urban school failure, and school administrators were sympathetic to their arguments that African history and culture had been excluded from the curriculum. In contrast, the creationists were attempting to change the curriculum in suburban schools that appeared to be effective in educating their students; they were trying to change the higher status science curriculum as opposed to history; and their opponents had the added lever of the courts because creationism raised issues of separation of church and state.

Binder also found that Afrocentrists and creationists often directed their arguments for change at insiders within the school establishment, and not just at outsiders such as mobilizable members of the public. She concludes, "once we have taken note of the fact that insiders are sometimes the targets of challenger frames and even occasionally, they, themselves, become challenge advocates, then we have to recognize that the old line separating 'insiders' from 'outsiders' in challenge events is suspect" (p. 217). The finding that challengers' frames or arguments sometimes connected with insiders' frames helps explain why Afrocentrists were more successful, even if only at a symbolic level, and it suggests an important enhancement of classical social movement theory. The status of creationists, some of whom were elected to a school boards, also allowed Binder to make an important distinction between political and institutional power. As school

---

[10]To understand how Christian Right candidates govern once they are in office, Deckerman augmented her survey research with two case studies: one of a district where Christian Right members constituted the governing majority and one where they were a minority coalition. She reported that where the Christian Right was in the majority, the board members found little success in imposing their moral and religious agenda because of community opposition. In contrast, where the Christian Right coalition was in a minority position, it could maintain its role as an "outsider" critic of the system and shape both the board's agenda and the terms of its debate. Deckerman concludes that "in terms of the intersection of religion and politics, the cases demonstrate that conservative Christians are perhaps more effective as critics of the system in a minority setting than as policymakers with the authority to govern" (2004, p. 164).

board members, creationists had formal political authority over educators. However, because they did not share their professional socialization and were not involved in routine education decision making, they lacked the legitimacy that would have converted their political authority into institutional power over district policy and practice.

Binder's analysis brings us full circle back to the topic with which this chapter began—the role of institutions in education policy. Her conclusions that "political power in school systems often does not translate into bureaucratic power in that same organization," and that "political 'insider' status, or 'polity membership,' is one of those concepts begging to be revamped" (pp. 228–229) remind us that challengers to the educational status quo must disrupt existing patterns of interest among policymakers and organized groups. However, even when they are successful at the enactment stage, they must also permeate well-established bureaucratic interests during implementation. Whether the ideas used to promote change are ones such as standards and accountability that ultimately become widespread and create a new policy monopoly, or are ones that remain at the fringes such as Afrocentrism, their advocates must find a way to convert whatever political influence they can garner into sustained institutional influence. Otherwise those ideas will not endure or shape classroom teaching and learning.

CONCLUSIONS AND IMPLICATIONS FOR FUTURE RESEARCH

Education policy research, by its almost sole focus on the political determinants of federal and state policies, has narrowed how politics is conceptualized. As a result, serious gaps in our understanding of local education politics are just beginning to be remedied. Additionally, research is still limited on how education policies are used to accomplish political purposes such as ensuring that schools are democratically accountable, functioning as venues for public participation, and socializing students into their roles as citizens.

Even if our attention is confined just to a narrow conception of politics and its effect on policy, there are still gaps in the knowledge base. Researchers need to augment studies of a specific policy or group of policies with ones that take as their primary focus the institutional actors shaping those policies. This approach would increase our understanding of political actors' incentives and the conditions under which they pursue particular strategies. Such studies might, for example, examine a range of interest groups, or differences in participant access and decision-making norms across policymaking venues, whether they are school-site councils, local boards of education, legislatures, or courts. Research with institutional actors as the primary units of analysis should be comparative across time, place, and policy issues. It also needs to be grounded in the substantial research literature that already exists in political science, economics, and sociology on political institutions.

This review has presented an institutional view of politics almost exclusively, and has not considered the political attitudes and behavior of individuals with regard to public education. The reason is simple: there are few rigorous studies of this topic that use sophisticated analytical techniques. We know little about how parents and the public form their attitudes; what role expert information plays in attitude formation as compared with other influences such as friends, neighbors, and elites; how the media may work as an agenda setter; how attitudes are related to each other; and how they change or remain stable over time. Survey data have been collected for decades, yet they have not been subjected to the same analyses as citizens' preferences in other issue domains.

For more than three decades, the major source of public opinion data on education has been the Phi Delta Kappa/Gallup Poll on the Public's Attitudes Toward the Public Schools. More recently, other sources such as Public Agenda (e.g., Farkas et al., 1999; Johnson & Immerwahr, 1994; Johnson et al., 1995; Public Agenda, 2002) have surveyed public and parental attitudes, while the news media and other organizations have focused their polling on education issues at irregular intervals, often around the time of national elections (e.g., Hart & Teeter, 2004). The Gallup Poll is a useful source of information on national trends in public opinion on issues such as vouchers and standardized testing. Because of their more in-depth treatment of issues, over-samples of specific groups such as minority and traditional Christian parents, and the use of focus groups to augment nationally representative surveys, the Public Agenda reports have provided useful insights into what parents and the public expect from schools and how they view their roles in the educational enterprise. The media and other intermittent polls are useful for obtaining snapshots of where the public stands on issues currently on the political agenda.

However, all these polls report only marginals and a few cross-tabulations (most often on parental status, political affiliation, and race/ethnicity). Consequently, we lack any comprehensive information about the independent effect of various demographic variables on opinions, and also about how respondents' positions on moral value questions and policy issues outside education affect their stance on education policy issues. Another notable lack is systematic information about the public's level of factual knowledge about education issues on which they express opinions.

A variety of studies are necessary to remedy these gaps. We need sophisticated secondary analyses of the data that have been collected through Gallup and other polls. This research should be grounded in the literature on public opinion and attitude formation, and it should rely on the most advanced analytical techniques. Researchers should also play a more active role in designing new surveys that examine one or two issues in considerable depth,[11] or that measure the relationship between attitudes about education and positions on other policy issues. To understand attitude formation better, experimental and focus group studies also need to be conducted.

Although knowledge about public attitudes toward education is sketchy, information abut public participation is even more limited. Over 10 years ago, the Gallup poll asked about public participation in the schools and reported on differences between parents and nonparents.[12] But we lack comprehensive, up-to-date information about general levels of participation, and we know little about the reasons why people become active in school politics. This information is particularly important as the proportion of voters with school-age children continues to decline, and

---

[11]An example of one of the few such studies is Moe's (2001) study of public opinion on vouchers. It is based on a nationally representative survey and presents a multivariate analysis of the determinants of support for vouchers. However, it begins by examining levels of satisfaction with the public schools and the basis for that assessment. As a result, the study presents a comprehensive picture of public opinion about issues such as social equality, diversity, and school prayer, and how it varies by demographic group and relates to attitudes toward the public schools.

Sikkink's (1999) analysis of the social sources of alienation from public schools is also based on nationally representative survey data, but it does not focus on a policy issue. Rather it examines why some religiously conservative individuals feel alienated from the public schools while others do not. This study is an example of how research on individual attitudes can complement the institutionally focused research in studies such as Binder's (2002) and Deckman's (2004).

[12]Close to half the respondents with no children in the public schools reported attending a school play, concert, or athletic event in a local public school within the past year. Only 10%, however, had attended a school board meeting, and an even lower proportion had served as a member of a public-school-related committee. In most cases, reported rates of participation in school activities by respondents without school-age children were about half that reported by parents of school-age children (Elam, Rose, & Gallup 1994).

fewer people have first-hand knowledge of the schools and are only loosely connected to the ones in their communities. We know, for example, that turnout for school board elections is typically smaller than for general elections, and that part of the problem may be structural because in many communities school board elections are scheduled in off years from the general election, resulting in less visibility for candidates and fewer incentives for voters to turn out (Berry & Howell, 2005; Townley, Sweeney, & Schmieder, 1994).[13] However, we lack even systematic aggregate data on turnout for school board election across the country, as well as individual-level data on voters' motivations and what distinguishes participants from nonparticipants.

Three decades of focused research on federal and state education policies have produced the useful byproduct of increased knowledge about the politics driving those policies. We understand better how the structures and norms of different institutional venues provide different strategic opportunities for participants, and how they vary in the policy outcomes they produce. The strong link between material interests and idea-based conceptions of what constitutes an appropriate education is recognized now. But strangely missing from this analytical portrait of education politics is a depiction of the politics closest to schools and classrooms. Most notable for its absence is systematic knowledge about the preferences and expectations of the public, both parents and nonparents. Ten years ago, David Matthews (1996) asked, "Is there a public for the public schools?" Unfortunately, education policy analysis has not yet provided a research-based answer to that question.

REFERENCES

Baumgartner, F. R., & Jones, B. D. (1993). *Agendas and instability in American politics.* Chicago: University of Chicago Press.

Baumgartner, F. R., & Leech, B. L. (1998). *Basic interests.* Princeton, NJ: Princeton University Press.

Berry, C. R., & Howell, W. G. (2005). Democratic accountability in public education. In W. G. Howell (Ed.), *Besieged: School boards and the future of education politics* (pp. 150–172). Washington, DC: Brookings Institution Press.

Binder, A. J. (2002). *Contentious curricula.* Princeton, NJ: Princeton University Press.

Boyd, W. L., Plank, D. N., & Sykes, G. (2000). Teachers unions in hard times. In T. Loveless (Ed.), *Conflicting missions? Teachers unions and education reform* (pp. 174–210). Washington, DC: Brookings Institution Press.

Chubb, J. E., & Moe, T. M. (1990). *Politics, markets, and America's schools.* Washington, DC: Brookings Institution Press.

Cigler, A. J. (1994). Research gaps in the study of interest group representation. In W. Crotty, M. A. Schwartz, & J. C. Green (Eds.) *Representing interests and interest groups.* Lanham, MD: University Press of America

Cohen, D. K., & Spillane, J. P. (1992). Policy and practice: The relations between governance and instruction. *Review of Research in Education* 18:3–49.

Conover, P. J., & Searing, D. D. (2000). A political socialization perspective. In L. M. McDonnell, P. M. Timpane, & R. Benjamin (Eds.), *Rediscovering the democratic purposes of education* (pp. 91–124). Lawrence: University Press of Kansas.

---

[13]Although the research is limited, we also know that rules governing whether school board elections are at-large or by district have affected the number of Blacks elected to school boards, with the number increasing in district elections (Marschall, 2005). The situation for Latinos is different: the effect of ward structures on their representation on local boards depends on whether Latinos are a majority or a minority of the population in a district (Meier & Juenke, 2005).

Cremin, L. A. (1989). *Popular education and its discontents.* New York: Harper and Row.

Deckman, M. M. (2004). *School board battles: The Christian right in local politics.* Washington, DC: Georgetown University Press.

DelFattore, J. (2004). *The fourth R: Conflicts over religion in America's public schools.* New Haven, CT: Yale University Press.

Donovan, T., & Bowler, S. (1998). Direct democracy and minority rights: An extension. *American Journal of Political Science 42*(3), 1020–1024.

Elam, S. M., & Rose, L. C. (1995). The 27th annual Phi Delta Kappa/Gallup poll of the public's attitudes toward the public schools. *Phi Delta Kappan 77*(1), 41–56.

Elam, S. M., Rose, L. C., & Gallup, A. N. (1994). The 26th annual Phi Delta Kappa/Gallup poll of the public's attitudes toward the public schools. *Phi Delta Kappan 76*(1), 41–64.

Farkas, S. (1993). *Divided within, besieged without: The politics of education in four American school districts.* New York: Public Agenda Foundation.

Farkas, S., Johnson, J., & Duffett, A., with Aulicino, C., & McHugh, J. (1999). *Playing their parts: Parents and teachers talk about parental involvement in public schools.* New York: Public Agenda Foundation.

Gamble, B. (1997). Putting civil rights to a popular vote. *American Journal of Political Science 41*, 245–269.

Hajnal, Z. L., Gerber, E. R., & Louch, H. (2002). Minorities and direct legislation: Evidence from California ballot proposition elections. *The Journal of Politics 54*(1), 154–177.

Hart, P. D., & Teeter, R. N. (2004). *Equity and adequacy: Americans speak on public school funding: A national opinion survey conducted for the Educational Testing Service.* http://www.tc.columbia.edu/centers/hechinger/Resources/proceedings/politics/re7286color.pdf

Henig, J., Hula, R., Orr, M., & Pedescleaux, D. (1999). *The color of school reform: Race, politics, and the challenge of urban education.* Princeton, NJ: Princeton University Press.

Hess, G. A., Jr. (1995). *Restructuring urban schools: A Chicago perspective.* New York: Teachers College Press.

Hochschild, J., & Scovronick, N. (2003). *The American dream and the public schools.* New York: Oxford University Press.

Itkonen, T. (2004). *Stories of hope and decline: Interest groups and the making of national special education policy.* Ph.D. dissertation, University of California, Santa Barbara.

James, T. (1991). State authority and the politics of educational change. *Review of Research in Education 17*, 169–224.

Johnson, J., with Farkas, S., Friedman, W., Immerwahr, J., & Bers, A. (1995). *Assignment incomplete: The unfinished business of education reform.* New York: Public Agenda Foundation.

Johnson, J., & Immerwahr, J. (1994). *First things first: What Americans expect from the public schools.* New York: Public Agenda Foundation.

Kelman, S. (1987). *Making public policy.* New York: Basic Books.

Kingdon, J. W. (1993). Politicians, self-interest, and ideas. In G. E. Marcus & R. L. Hanson (Eds.), *Reconsidering the democratic public* (pp. 73–89). University Park, PA: Penn State University Press.

Kingdon, J. W. (1995). *Agendas, alternatives, and public policies.* 2nd ed. New York: HarperCollins.

Lentz, C. (1999). Predicting school referenda outcomes: Answers from Illinois. *Journal of Education Finance 24*(4), 459–482.

Longoria, T., Jr. (1998). School politics in Houston: The impact of business involvement. In C. Stone (Ed.), *Changing urban education* (pp. 184–198). Lawrence: University Press of Kansas.

Madison, J, Hamilton, A., & Jay, J. (1788/1961). *The federalist papers.* C. Rossiter (Ed.). Reprint. New York: New American Library.

Manna, P. (2003). *The politics of education policy in the American federal system.* Paper presented at the annual meeting of the Midwest Political Science Association, Chicago.

Mansbridge, J., ed. (1990). *Beyond self-interest.* Chicago: University of Chicago Press.

March, J. G., & Olsen, J. P. (1989). *Rediscovering institutions.* New York: Free Press.

March, J. G., & Olsen, J. P. (1995). *Democratic governance.* New York: Free Press.

March, J. G., & Olsen, J. P. (2000). Democracy and schooling: An institutional perspective. In L. M. McDonnell, P. M. Timpane, & R. Benjamin (Eds.), *Rediscovering the democratic purposes of education* (pp. 148–173). Lawrence: University Press of Kansas.

Marschall, M. J. (2005). Minority incorporation and local school boards. In W. G. Howell (Ed.), *Besieged: School boards and the future of education politics* (pp. 173–198). Washington, DC: Brookings Institution Press.

Matsusaka, J. G. (2004). *For the many or the few.* Chicago: University of Chicago Press.

Matthews, D. (1996). *Is there a public for the public schools?* Dayton, OH: Kettering Foundation Press.

Mazzoni, T. L. (1991). Analyzing state school policymaking: An arena model. *Educational Evaluation and Policy Analysis 13*(2), 115–138.

McDermott, K. (1999). *Controlling public education.* Lawrence: University Press of Kansas.

McDonnell, L. M. (2004). *Politics, persuasion, and educational testing.* Cambridge, MA: Harvard University Press.

McDonnell, L. M., & Pascal, A. (1988). *Teacher unions and educational reform.* Santa Monica, CA: RAND.

McDonnell, L. M., & Weatherford, M. S. (1999). *Standards setting and public deliberation: The case of California.* Los Angeles: University of California, Los Angeles, National Center for Research on Evaluation, Standards, and Student Testing.

McDonnell, L. M., & Weatherford, M. S. (2000). Seeking a new politics of education. In L. M. McDonnell, P. M. Timpane, & R. Benjamin (Eds.), *Rediscovering the democratic purposes of education* (pp. 174–206). Lawrence: University Press of Kansas.

Meier, K. J., & Juenke, E. G. (2005). Electoral structure and the quality of representation on school boards. In W. G. Howell (Ed.), *Besieged: School boards and the future of education politics* (pp. 199–227). Washington, DC: Brookings Institution Press.

Melnick, R. S. (1995). Separation of powers and the strategy of rights: The expansion of special education. In M. K. Landy & M. A. Levin (Eds.), *The new politics of public policy* (pp. 23–46). Baltimore: Johns Hopkins University Press.

Mintrom, M. (1997). Policy entrepreneurs and the diffusion of innovation. *American Journal of Political Science 41*(3), 738–770.

Mintrom, M., & Vergari, S. (1998). Policy networks and innovation diffusion: The case of state education reforms. *The Journal of Politics 60*(1), 126–148.

Moe, T. M. (1990). Political institutions: The neglected side of the story. *Journal of Law, Economics, and Organization 6*, 213–254.

Moe, T. M. (2000). The two democratic purposes of public education. In L. M. McDonnell, P. M. Timpane, & R. Benjamin (Eds.), *Rediscovering the democratic purposes of education* (pp. 127–147). Lawrence: University Press of Kansas.

Moe, T. M. (2001). *Schools, vouchers, and the American public.* Washington, DC: Brookings Institution Press.

Morone, J. A. (1990). *The democratic wish: Popular participation and the limits of American government.* New York: Basic Books.

Niemi, R. G., & Junn, J. (1998). *Civic education: What makes students learn?* New Haven, CT: Yale University Press.

Orr, M. (1999). *Black social capital: The politics of school reform in Baltimore, 1986–1998.* Lawrence: University Press of Kansas.

Plank, D. N., & Boyd, W. L. (1994). Antipolitics, education, and institutional choice: The flight from democracy. *American Educational Research Journal 31*(2), 263–281.

Portz, J., Stein, L., & Jones, R. R. (1999). *City schools and city politics: Institutions and leadership in Pittsburgh, Boston, and St. Louis.* Lawrence: University Press of Kansas.

Posner, P. L. (1998). *The politics of unfunded mandates: Whither federalism?* Washington, DC: Georgetown University Press.

Public Agenda. (2002). Reality check 2002. http://www.publicagenda.org/specials/rcheck2002/reality.htm

Reed, D. S. (2001). *On equal terms.* Princeton, NJ: Princeton University Press.

Reich, R. B., ed. (1988). *The power of public ideas.* Cambridge, MA: Ballinger.

Rich, W.C. (1996). *Black mayors and school politics.* New York: Garland.

Schneider, M., Teske, P., & Marschall, M. (2000). *Choosing schools: Consumer choice and the quality of American schools.* Princeton, NJ: Princeton University Press.

Sikkink, D. (1999). The social sources of alienation from public schools. *Social Forces 78*(1), 51–86.

Stone, C. N., ed. (1998). *Changing urban education.* Lawrence: University Press of Kansas.

Stone, C. N., Henig, J. R., Jones, B. D., & Pierannunzi, C. (2001). *Building civic capacity: The politics of reforming urban schools.* Lawrence: University Press of Kansas.

Stone, D. (2002). *Policy paradox.* Rev. ed. New York: Norton.

Townley, A. J., Sweeney, D. P., & Schmieder, J. H. (1994). School board elections: A study of citizen voting patterns. *Urban Education 29*(1), 50–62.

Tyack, D. B. (1974). *The one best system.* Cambridge, MA: Harvard University Press.

Tyack, D. B. (1993). School governance in the United States: Historical puzzles and anomalies. In J. Hannaway & M. Carnoy (Eds.), *Decentralization and school improvement: Can we fulfill the promise?* (pp. 1–32). San Francisco: Jossey-Bass.

Wirt, F.M. & Kirst, M.W. (1997), *The political dynamics of American education.* Berkeley, CA: McCutchan.

Wirt, F. M., & Kirst, M. W. (2001). *The political dynamics of American education.* 2nd ed. Richmond, CA: McCutchan.

Witte, J. F. (2000). *The market approach to education.* Princeton, NJ: Princeton University Press.

Wong, K. K. (1994). Governance structure, resource allocation, and equity policy. *Review of Research in Education 20*, 257–289.

Wong, K. K. (1999). *Funding public schools: Politics and policies.* Lawrence: University Press of Kansas.

3

Educational Governance in the United States: Where Are We? How Did We Get Here? Why Should We Care?

Susan H. Fuhrman, Margaret E. Goertz, and Elliot H. Weinbaum

Unlike systems in most industrialized nations, the governance of public education in the United States is a largely decentralized system with authority spread among governmental entities. Key decisions related both directly and tangentially to instruction are debated and decided by the leaders of 50 states, just over 14,000 school districts, and almost 96,000 schools, and are influenced by the interests, preferences, and abilities of more than three million schoolteachers (National Center for Education Statistics, 2006). Constitutional authority for the provision of education resides in the states. Forty-nine states further disperse power and authority to local education agencies and, to a lesser extent, to schools and parents. This fragmented governance system poses challenges for policymakers, bureaucrats, researchers, advocates, and teachers who want to improve our educational system.

GOVERNANCE STRUCTURE

From the founding of the nation until the 1950s, both responsibility for and control of education rested firmly in the hands of local communities through over 80,000 elected school boards. Though the role of individual states in the provision and governance of public education varied widely, states generally had little capacity to oversee education in any comprehensive way. Similarly, the role of the federal government was limited to data collection and financial support for a small number of targeted education programs. Since the historic U.S. Supreme Court decision in *Brown v. Board of Education of Topeka, Kansas* in 1954, educational governance has undergone a series of shifts, redistributing authority and responsibility across the federal, state, and local levels of government. In general, power and authority have grown at the state and (to a lesser degree) federal levels. However, alongside the growth in state and federal power, local districts have increased capacity while simultaneously devolving power to communities and parents.

The trajectory over the past 50 years has left each level of government with a particular purview. The federal government has been concerned with ensuring equal educational opportunity to all students, but particularly those from traditionally disadvantaged groups and students with special needs (Hill, 2000). States have most actively engaged in defining curriculum standards, creating systems to assess student attainment of these standards, setting performance targets for various system actors, and financing schools (McDonnell & McLaughlin, 1982). And while local school districts have been subject to an increased level of policymaking from above, they have simultaneously created their own standards and policies, frequently in the areas of curriculum, instruction, and recruitment of, and professional development for, staff (Massell & Goertz, 2002). While significant authority has been consolidated at the federal, state, and district levels, power has also been shifted to communities and parents through site-based councils, charter schools, and increased use of parental choice to spur innovation and competition at the local level.

The growing centralization and standardization of certain areas of education policymaking coexists uneasily with the public's desire for local control of its schools. It results in a system that is very tightly controlled around some issues—e.g., civil rights, state standards, and assessments—and very loosely controlled around other functions, most notably teaching and learning.

In order to better understand this system and its implications, we ask: What does the United States' current system of educational governance look like? What is the impact of this intergovernmental arrangement on the functioning of the educational enterprise in this country? We begin with a review of the research on the educational governance system in this country, focusing on the distribution of authority at the federal, state, and local levels and on the implications of this distribution of power for the exercise of educational policymaking. We then examine the different ways that historians, political scientists, economists, and sociologists view the development and functioning of this system. We then discuss the implications of the education governance system for policies that directly shape public education in this country: those on education finance, teacher quality, instructional guidance and support, and the design of accountability systems. We conclude with suggestions for future research on education governance in the United States.

The Federal Role

Prior to 1954, the federal government played a minimal role in the governance of public education. The federal Office of Education, established in 1867, was charged with gathering data about educational enrollment and attainment. It had a limited coordination function and no authority over other governmental entities. Any other federal involvement generally involved the disbursement of federal funds for a particular purpose (e.g., vocational programs, compensation for the presence of federal land in a district, and Depression-era funding for teacher salaries and school construction; Tyack, 1974).

Since 1954, however, federal involvement in education has expanded substantially. In considering the federal role both before and after this time, Jack Jennings (2001) identified "four major reasons why the federal government became involved in education: to promote democracy; to ensure equality of educational opportunity; to enhance national productivity; to strengthen national defense" (p. 5).

Public schools are used to promote democracy by developing an educated population that can fulfill the responsibilities of citizenship. Though the intent to create an educated citizenry through the development of public schools is not specified in the U.S. Constitution (but is evident in many of the state constitutions drafted shortly after), the federal government demonstrated its commitment to establishing common schools by setting aside land to fund public schools, requiring new states entering the union to provide public schools, and creating tax codes that encourage public school funding. More recently, the federal government has been concerned with improving the quality of public education by requiring states to establish challenging educational standards. In 1989, the Education Summit convened by President George H. W. Bush and the nation's governors called for all schools to strive toward lofty goals. Goal number three (of six goals articulated following the summit) stated that "By the year 2000, American students will leave grades four, eight, and twelve having demonstrated competency in challenging subject matter including English, mathematics, science, history, and geography; and every school in America will ensure that all students learn to use their minds well, so they may be prepared for responsible citizenship, further learning, and productive employment in our modern economy" (Executive Office of the President, 1990). President Bush unsuccessfully proposed a system of voluntary national standards and test in support of these goals in his America 2000 initiative. President Clinton subsequently took a "carrot and a stick" approach to promote and support nascent state standards through the Improving America's Schools Act (IASA) of 1994, which required states to establish challenging content standards, and through the Goals 2000 Act, which provided funds to states and localities to design and implement these standards. While these policies, and subsequent legislation, such as the No Child Left Behind (NCLB) Act of 2001, were directed at improving education for all students, most of the federal government's effort and resources have been concerned with creating greater educational opportunity for targeted groups of students.

The federal government's focus on equality of educational opportunity dates to the *Brown v. Board of Education* decision and has emphasized giving certain groups of students—racial/ethnic minorities, poor students, students with disabilities, English language learners and children of illegal aliens—more equal access to schooling and appropriate programs of education. Concerns about the preservation of states' rights, fear of federal control and regulation of education, and the politics of race and religion led federal policymakers to design policies that targeted students with particular needs rather than the educational system as a whole.

The Elementary and Secondary Education Act (ESEA) of 1965 began a long tradition of enacting discrete federal programs on behalf of particular populations with special needs. Other federal initiatives that followed included protections and programs for English language learners in 1967, protection from gender-based discrimination in 1972, and, with the passage of the Education of All Handicapped Children Act in 1975, mandatory service provisions for students with disabilities. Until the late 1980s, however, the quality of these programs was of limited interest to the federal government.

Particular federal programs were also developed to meet the other two goals identified by Jennings (2001). Federal efforts to build particular skill sets and raise the overall level of education among Americans was one way that the government has sought to enhance national productivity. Vocational training has played the largest role in this effort. Starting with the Smith-Hughes Act in 1917 and continuing with the Perkins Vocational and Technical Education Act of 1984 and the School-to-Work Opportunities Act of 1994, the federal government has maintained a commitment to providing opportunities for students to learn skills that can be immediately put to use by the modern economy.

Spurred on by the Cold War and the "space race" with the Soviet Union, the federal government has also attempted to use public education to strengthen national defense. The National Defense Education Act of 1958 funded efforts to improve math and science standards and instruction in an attempt to develop a cadre of citizens who would be more fully equipped to compete on an international battleground. Subsequent national efforts, most prominently those supported by the National Science Foundation, have continued this tradition.

The efforts of the federal government have generally taken three approaches to policymaking, loosely defined. First, through the courts, the federal government has become involved in guaranteeing individuals' absolute or constitutional rights as they relate to education. In guaranteeing educational access based on race, gender, or disability, the federal courts have stimulated Congress into action. As a result, the federal government has issued mandatory guidelines about how public education must be made available, and to whom.

Second, the federal government offers funding as an incentive to create and offer certain programs. Title I of ESEA provides major incentives for states and districts to offer supplemental services to students in poverty, and more recently, to establish more challenging educational standards and accountability systems. State can decline Title I funding (although it constitutes a major portion of a state's federal funding for elementary and secondary education). While a few states have threatened to opt out of NCLB, none has decided to do so. Instead, the states offer public education programs that comply with federal guidelines. The same holds true of the vocational or other discretionary programs of which the federal government funds a portion.

A third tool available to federal policymakers is the use of the so-called "bully pulpit" to influence public opinion and leadership about educational issues. The publication of the *A Nation at Risk* in 1983 (National Commission on Excellence in Education) may be the best example of this. While that report did not contain new information or describe tested remedies, it fomented a flurry of action and reaction in the education arena. A year later, the publication of *The Nation Responds: Recent Efforts to Improve Education* (U.S. Department of Education, 1984) continued this pressure, as did a variety of speeches and materials released by federal offices and, to a lesser extent, by states. While there has been very little research on the effectiveness of the bully pulpit, it seems clear that the federal government has frequently been able to catalyze activity (if not necessarily improvement) not through policymaking, but through rhetorical and publicity efforts.

Regardless of the policy instrument, the federal government's focus on target problems and student populations resulted in a system of fragmented and isolated categorical programs. Concerned that state and local policymakers did not embrace its equity agenda, federal education programs of the 1960s and 1970s were designed to bypass state education policies. The federal government used targeting provisions, service mandates, and compliance audits to ensure that educationally disadvantaged students and other underserved populations received access to federally funded programs and other services (McDonnell & McLaughlin, 1982; Moore, Goertz, & Hartle, 1983). Federal program fidelity was also fostered through the development of a "vertical" system of policy implementation—one of close relationships and communication among federal, state, and local program staff committed to the goals of their specific program (McLaughlin, 1982; Orland, 1994). Often characterized as program "silos" or "picket fences," this governance structure increased student access to educational services (although often through "pull-out" programs), but did little to address the quality of these programs. For example, early evaluations of Title I programs showed a great deal of variation in the content and quality of remedial programs (Borman, 2000).

Starting in the late 1980s, the federal focus began to shift from student access and procedural accountability to program quality and educational accountability. With the call for national goals in 1989, the Bush America 2000 proposal, and the passage of Goals 2000 and IASA (which was a reauthorization of ESEA), the federal government turned to standards-based reform (Smith & O'Day, 1991) as a lever of school reform, rather than programmatic inputs and processes. The premise of "high standards for all students" and the initiation of schoolwide programs in Title I moved the focus of federal policy away from "picket fences" to core instructional improvement in schools (McDonnell, 2004). Although enforcement of its provisions was weak (Cohen, 2002), and states varied considerably in how they responded to the law's requirements (Goertz & Duffy, 2001), IASA sent a strong message to states that a focus on standards and performance should take precedence over the process requirements that once garnered federal attention.

In response to uneven implementation of IASA across the 50 states, Congress enacted NCLB, which requires states to test more and set more ambitious and uniform improvement goals for their schools, and prescribes sanctions for schools that fail to meet these goals. Although NCLB is regularly cited as the largest incursion of federal action into the elementary and secondary educational arena in the history of the United States, states retain the authority to set content and performance standards, design assessments, and apply sanctions (Fuhrman, 2004). In continuing to assuage fears of centralized control of education, the federal government still leaves the decisions about educational content and instruction to states and localities. Thus, the success of NCLB, as with IASA, depends on the willingness and capacity of states and localities to enact policies and practices that reflect both the spirit and the letter of the law.

With the continued existence of categorical programs and the unwillingness of national policymakers to mandate course content or qualities, federal policy allows a great deal of variation at the state level. We will now turn to a discussion of the role of the states in elementary and secondary educational governance and policy.

The State Role

States, which have constitutional authority for public education, delegated that responsibility to local school districts or local education agencies (LEAs) for most of American history. State departments of education were small and interfered little in the operation of local school systems. In the second half of the 20th century, however, states exponentially increased the level of regulation and oversight that they demanded of local districts. Wirt and Kirst (2001) point to three values that drive state involvement in education: equity, efficiency, and local choice. First, states have sought to assure some degree of equal educational opportunity by mandating minimal levels of service, in part through finance equalization, which dates back to the 19th century. States have pursued equity goals by giving monetary grants to districts and by mandating particular school "inputs" like the presence of school libraries or science labs and rosters of course offerings. Frequently spurred by federal action, states pursued equity measures such as racial desegregation in schools in the 1950s, programs for poor students in schools in the 1960s, finance equalization in the 1970s, and higher minimum programmatic standards in the 1980s and 1990s.

Second, states have sought efficiency, most frequently through consolidation and standardization. For example, states consolidated the number of LEAs in order to more efficiently oversee their activities. As a result, the number of local school districts in the United States dropped from 127,531 in 1932, to 89,000 in 1948, to under 15,000 today (Tyack & Cuban, 1995). States have standardized financial accounting, teacher certification requirements, and other processes to ensure minimum quality. The more recent focus on student testing at the state level can also be interpreted as a move toward both measuring and motivating greater levels of efficiency. Following efforts to increase and equalize state funding for education, states wanted accountability for their new investment. Testing is seen as one way to both measure and motivate greater levels of efficiency. Testing and standardization also allow for more comparisons among LEAs.

Third, states are guided by a value of preserving local choice. Even now, in contrast with most other industrialized nations, the local educators in the United States have an unusual level of discretion, although state involvement in local education has grown.

In part, state authority has expanded in response to changes at the federal level. Beginning with the passage of ESEA in 1965, federal funds supported staff positions at the state level to assist with the implementation of, and compliance with, federal programs. State departments of education began to grow exponentially with the federal government funding between one-third and two-thirds of state education agency staff. In 1972, three-fourths of the staff members in state departments of education had been in their jobs for less than three years (Wirt & Kirst, 1975). However, in a clear case of ontogeny replicating phylogeny, throughout the 1960s and into the 1970s the growth of state departments of education mirrored federal programs and took place in program "silos," with many states developing their own categorical programs in response to local needs and pressures without giving significant thought to program integration or impact.

Despite the federally driven growth of state departments of education and increased state funding, research in the early 1980s found that state legislators, governors, and boards of education were not playing a significant role in federal education programs, and did not know much about them (Moore, Goertz, & Hartle, 1983). The loose connections between states and the federal government meant that "central agencies [could] make serious demands on others with relative ease; they need only mobilize the political resources to enunciate a policy or begin a new program. But the costs of enforcing demands are much greater" (Cohen & Spillane, 1993, p. 42). This research shows that even with funds devoted to enforcement of federal programs, states' own priorities and proclivities often eclipsed the federal agenda.

Despite their autonomy, states often act in similar ways. Research by Marshall, Mitchell, and Wirt (1989) showed that, despite some variation, states in their study emphasized seven areas for their education reform efforts: finance, personnel, student testing, program definition, governance, curriculum materials, and building and facilities, and in a similar descending level of priority. Additionally, in most of the states, relatively similar programs were pursued within each domain. For example, within finance, states focused on funding equalization strategies; within personnel, states set teacher certification and training requirements. The researchers attributed this broad general agreement to "national reform currents" ideas that were shared commonly across the country due to court action or national efforts. In areas where there was less agreement across states—governance was the most apparent example of divergent approaches across states—local preferences and traditions of governance played a larger role in influencing state action. In this way, the state is "caught" between the policy mandates and messages sent by the federal government and the demands and preferences of local politics and districts.

As states became increasingly involved in the educational enterprise, their share of educational expenditures grew from 30 percent in the 1940s to about 50 percent in the mid–1980s, though variation among the states continued to be significant (Wirt & Kirst, 2001). For the first time, state funding began to comprise a larger share of school funding than did locally raised funds. Some have argued that the state school finance movement was the most important factor in raising the profile of states in school governance (Kirst, 2004). The growth of the state departments of education and simultaneous increase in state expenditures caused states to exert an authority that they had possessed but rarely used. Occasionally, this authority was thrust upon them by courts demanding remedies to inequities in school finance. Since the Supreme Court decision in *San Antonio* v. *Rodriguez* in 1973, state courts and legislatures have been the final arbiter of school finance issues. These efforts have sought to redress inequities and sufficiently meet the needs of all students, regardless or residence, wealth, color, or ability.

In addition to finance remedies, states exerted authority in ensuring that academic standards were high enough to educate a productive and competitive workforce. This interest in standards paralleled, and frequently preceded, the federal efforts in this area. Increased international competition, the much publicized publication of *A Nation at Risk*, and the low relative performance of

American students in international academic exams caused governors and legislatures, newly emboldened by their substantial financial contributions, to create new standards and assessments to encourage and measure higher performance.

Like federal policymakers, states addressed education reform on a relatively piecemeal basis. In reviewing education policymaking in the 1980s, researchers from the Consortium for Policy Research in Education found that "most state reform packages lacked coherence." As at the federal level, the impetus for state education reform came from either the courts or coalitions of interest groups and legislators. There was not great interest at the state level in overhauling public education in major ways. "States tended to reject complicated reform recommendations in favor of more limited ones" (Consortium for Policy Research in Education, 1989, p. 2). Just as states were loosely connected to federal policy, many of the reforms were implemented at the local level in quite different form than their state-level progenitors had imagined. With relatively little coordination of state policies, significant gains in achievement through much of the 1980s were hard to find (Firestone, Fuhrman, & Kirst, 1989).

As a result of the apparent inefficiency, states began to look at their education policies more holistically. In an effort to embark on more successful reform, governors and chief state school officers were early supporters of the systemic reform movement. Systemic reform, based on the work of Smith and O'Day (1991), was designed to address the disconnected state policies of the past by asking states to create high-level statewide academic standards, to align policies in assessment, accountability, and teacher preparation and certification, and to demand progress toward performance standards. Nearly every state and many national organizations, including the National Council of Teachers of Mathematics, the National Governors Association, the Business Roundtable, and the American Federation of Teachers, created and supported state standards documents. Some of these organizations, and others like the Council for Basic Education and Achieve, also began to evaluate state standards documents. Though there was not always a consensus about the clarity and quality of state standards, the presence of outside organizations evaluating standards encouraged many states to go through revision and improvement processes.

However, as standards documents and ideas were translated into policies at the state and local levels, there was debate and resistance to the changes (Massell, Kirst, & Hoppe, 1997). State standards and accountability systems varied in specificity, directiveness, and effectiveness, and state compliance with the new requirements of IASA also ranged widely, with many states resisting the increased centralization of authority and incursion into what had traditionally been a local role (Anderson & Turnbull, 1998). In many cases, the early standards documents were the source of controversy at the local level. As the public has become more comfortable with the idea of statewide education standards and states have improved the quality of those standards, the idea of standards-based reform has gained greater acceptance. Controversy continues in some states, however, over the content of those standards, particularly in science.

While states are being pushed further to attach consequences to performance standards, the question remains as to what real effects this will have in terms of classroom instruction and student achievement. Studies of state standards-based reform policies have found that schools and school districts are paying attention to state standards and aligning curriculum, school improvement plans, local assessments, and professional development with state curricular frameworks and assessments (Goertz, 2001; Fuhrman, 2001; Gross & Goertz, 2005). And states with strong accountability policies prior to NCLB (those with significant consequences for students and schools) showed larger gain on the National Assessment of Educational Progress (Carnoy & Loeb, 2004; Hanushek & Raymond, 2004; NAEP). However, research also shows that districts and schools do not necessarily possess the capacity to effectively change practice in response to more guidelines, assessments, and sanctions (Corcoran & Christman, 2002; Gross, et al., 2005;

Hatch, 2002; Spillane, 2004). Many have suggested that long-lasting change at the classroom level will have to be driven not by the state or federal government policymakers but by local education agency leaders who are in regular contact with schools and teachers (Elmore, 1993; Massell, 2000; McLaughlin & Talbert, 2003). Though local districts may not always possess the knowledge and skills needed to guide instructional improvement, their role in the governance system continues to be pivotal, as they can encourage or discourage effective practice at the local level.

The Local Role

The history of local control of education in the United States has generally been a case of slow and steady erosion. Local school districts are creations of their states; states define their boundaries, governance structures, and responsibilities. Until the 1960s, both responsibility and control of education rested firmly in the hands of local communities through their elected school boards and school administrators. Since that time, the authority of local school boards and superintendents has been assaulted on two fronts. Expanded control by states and the federal government over central decisions about education—standards, curriculum, resource allocation, qualifications of staff and oversight of schools—has narrowed the locus of decision making from above. Within the local system, teacher unionization and political demands for greater community and parental control through site-based management, charters, vouchers, and contracting have further reduced the authority and reach of local boards of education.

In spite of increased state and federal activism, local school districts retain primary responsibility for curriculum and instruction, the hiring and assignment of teachers and principals, the funding of schools, and the operation and maintenance of school buildings. School districts mediate between school and state authorities, interpret state standards as they develop their own, and manage instructional reform. Districts are oftentimes the only or the major source of assistance to schools as they develop more effective curriculum and instruction. And their policies structure and channel schools' interactions with external agents and ideas.

The public prefers that major decisions concerning the education of their children remain in the hands of their local school officials (Rose & Gallup, 2002, 2003). In most communities, where school districts are small and board members are known to the public, elected school boards are viewed as effective mechanisms of democratic control. Some commentators question whether school boards are truly representative bodies, as most school board elections are apolitical, with few contested seats and low voter turnout (Hess, 2002). Others argue that low turnout is a sign of a community's satisfaction with its schools at a given point in time, and that when citizens become dissatisfied with the status quo, they will seek new school board members (Wirt & Kirst, 2001). And citizens report participating in other forms of involvement in their schools—attending local school events, following the activities of their local school board, signing a petition, and fund raising (Public Education Network/Education Week, 2004).

In many large school districts, however, local school bureaucracies have grown larger and increasingly complex and have been criticized for being unresponsive to community needs and for being incapable of educating children (see, e.g., Bryk, Kerbow, & Rollow, 1997). Parents and local residents feel disenfranchised and powerless and have sought other avenues for expressing their interests in their children's education. Concern over this lack of responsiveness, as well as concerns about accountability and poor performance, have led some states and school districts to enact three kinds of governance change: (1) devolution of authority to schools and their communities, (2) expansion of parental authority over where their children attend schools, and

(3) movement of centralized control from the school board to the mayor's office or other entities (Corcoran & Goertz, 2005).

Most schools report they have some type of advisory body, but their influence is generally limited to matters of school planning, parent involvement, and fund raising. In its various forms, site-based management provides greater school-site autonomy over some combination of budget, personnel, and program decisions. Most site-based management plans also include a school-based governance structure that involves parents and teachers (and sometimes community members) in the decision-making process. The results of this experiment in democratic localism have been mixed. Structures that have expanded local participation have enabled some schools to create more democratic decision-making processes, while in other schools power has been consolidated in the hands of the principals. Where councils have real power, the members are typically elected by parents and staff in the school, but it has been difficult to get parents involved in school governance. Researchers have not found a direct relationship between more democratic decision making and instructional change. Rather, schools with strong democratic practice were more likely to engage in restructuring practices which, in turn, often stimulated instructional innovation, but the extent of these changes has varied widely (Bryk, et al., 1998; David, 2000; Malen, Ogawa, & Kranz, 1990).

Choice is a popular concept in the United States, and advocates of school choice argue that a market system is more responsive to parents, creates conditions for more effective schools, and is a more efficient mechanism for governing education than local school boards or large district bureaucracies (Chubb & Moe, 1990; Hill, this volume). Nearly all of the states provide some form of public choice through charter schools or interdistrict or intradistrict enrollment options, and the NCLB Act gives parents of students attending low-performing schools the option to transfer to higher-performing schools within their districts. The law also lists conversion to a charter school as a restructuring option for schools that fail to improve over time. In 2005, 3,000 charter schools served nearly 740,000 students, although half of these schools were concentrated in five of the 40 states with charter school laws (U.S. Charter Schools, 2005). In 1999, prior to the enactment of NCLB, one-quarter of all districts already provided intradistrict choice, and 14 percent of all public school students (and nearly one-quarter of African American students) exercised that choice option (Gruber, et al., 2002; Bielick & Chapman, 2003). Only four states have state-financed tuition or voucher programs, and these apply only to a small number of students or districts. The findings from research on vouchers and charter schools are inconsistent, and so far the reported effects on student achievement, whether positive or negative, are small (Gill, et al., 2001; Miron & Nelson, 2004).

A third kind of governance change alters the nature of democratic control by moving authority from the school board to the mayor's office. The type and level of mayoral involvement in local school systems ranges from appointing a subset of school board members to appointing both the full board and the superintendent of schools. The specifics reflect each city's educational and political context and history. Proponents of this approach argue that mayoral control provides a single point of electoral accountability for education, improves the management of the school system, facilitates the integration of education with other children's services, and, ultimately, will improve educational quality and student performance (Kirst, 2002). While mayoral takeover generally produces more efficient financial and administrative management, its impact on instruction remains tenuous and unclear, reflecting in part the extent to which the mayor and his appointees, particularly the superintendent of schools, focus their efforts on school improvement strategies (Cibulka & Boyd, 2003; Cuban & Usdan, 2002; Kirst, 2002; Rich, 1996).

The education governance system in the United States has undergone considerable change in the past 50 years. The federal government has set strong goals for the equity and excellence of the country's educational system. Its reliance on states to meet these goals has made states stronger and more fundamental actors in the system. Yet at the same time that states are limiting the authority of local school districts, they must depend on these governmental units to refocus teaching and learning toward more rigorous academic standards. Parental demand for charter schools, home schooling, or private schools paid for with publicly funded vouchers adds still another element to a "complex and fragmented structure, in which it appears that everybody—and therefore nobody—is in charge" (Kirst, 2004, p. 16).

In the next section, we look at how scholars from various disciplines view the development and operation of this intergovernmental system.

RESEARCH PERSPECTIVES ON INTERGOVERNMENTAL RELATIONS

Scholars have viewed the development and functioning of our intergovernmental system, with its historic deference to local districts and growing state and federal power, through the lenses of their disciplines.

Historians tend to see our education system's evolution as part of our nation's overall resistance to potentially tyrannical centralized power. Powers granted to Congress were few and controlled; most functions were reserved for the states, and this was the case with education. Early schools were either private or funded with a mix of public and private dollars; many were affiliated with churches. Keeping education partially private was a way of limiting the role of government in people's lives (Reuben, 2005). In the 1840s and 1850s when state legislatures established free, tax-supported schools, they were responding to calls for "common" schools as a means to develop an educated citizenry (Kaestle & Smith, 1982; Reuben, 2005). States also consolidated some districts and created state offices intended to provide improvement and curricular support and gather statistics. (Reuben, 2005; Walsh, 1998). However, the South resisted; the large slaveholders who dominated politics were uninterested in educating white laborers and were fearful of educating slaves (Reuben, 2005). Although, of course, the South eventually created public schools after the Civil War, Northern fear of any national funds going to support segregated schools kept the federal government's role minimal. Another depressor on the growth of the federal role had to do with religion. Catholics saw public schools as promoting Protestantism, while non-Catholics resisted giving any aid to Catholic schools. The ESEA of 1965, a landmark in terms of increasing the federal role in education, was made possible politically only because the Civil Rights Act of 1964 erased the concerns about fostering segregated schools and because aid was directed at disadvantaged children, including those in Catholic schools, so aid was going to the students, not the religious schools per se.

Contrasting slightly with historians' analyses, political scientists tend to view our federal system of education through the perspective of pluralistic politics. As Madison argued in *The Federalist Papers*, No. 10, interests that lack majorities in individual states can aggregate to have power at the federal level that they lack at the state level. Underrepresented groups have continually looked to the federal level to direct funding and programs to poor and minority districts and schools. As discussed previously, federal education policy is frequently justified on equity grounds, and the federal dollar goes disproportionately to poorer areas. The argument that federal action is necessary to assure equity has supported the expansion of the federal government into areas like standards, accountability and teacher policy that abut states' traditional areas of authority, as in NCLB.

At the state level, the regrouping of political interests after World War II led to an increased state role in many policy areas, including education. The *Baker v. Carr* decision in 1962, requiring "one man, one vote," shifted the balance of power in state legislatures to urban areas. Their representatives wanted to see states embark on more redistributive policies, such as new school finance formulas, that acknowledged urban tax and education burdens. The greater policy role at the state level, and the growing proportion of state budgets going to education through more equalizing finance formulas, attracted more general interests, such as business elites, to education policy. No longer would school interests—teachers and administrators—have the arena of education policy to themselves. It was the activity of business elites that propelled states into the excellence agenda of the 1980s, leading them to engage in curriculum and teaching policy issues they had previously delegated to locals. (McDonnell & Fuhrman, 1985).

Political scientists also use institutional explanations for shifts in power among levels of the federal system. Hence the rise of state power vis-à-vis locals in the 1970s and 1980s can also be traced in part to the growth and modernization of state governments. Redistricted state legislatures became more professionalized. Citizen legislatures that met a few months every other year gave way to full-time legislatures with large, specialized staffs. Governors developed policy offices too. These bulked-up institutions were anxious to flex their muscles; it is not surprising that they expanded their policy interests (Rosenthal & Fuhrman, 1980a, 1980b). The astounding volume of education policy in the 1980s, and the expansion of state interest into questions of what should be taught and who should teach, reflect this newfound power.

Rather than examining historical or political shifts, economists are likely to examine the comparative advantages of various levels of government, concentrating on resources such as fiscal base and information. Higher levels of government have broader tax bases and therefore greater and more varied fiscal resources. Thus, states and the federal government have comparative advantages over local entities when it comes to funding. However, the specific mix of the tax base also matters. Local districts are typically almost entirely dependent on property tax revenue for the local share of funding. Further, the property tax is almost a dedicated tax for education since the largest proportion of local funding, by far, goes to education as opposed to other services. While the property tax as a revenue source can be less than progressive, depending on how it is structured, it is also relatively resistant to business cycles and therefore more stable than the sales, income, and business taxes used by higher levels of government. The importance of the property tax as a steady and significant stream for education funding helps explain in part the persistence of local districts, despite incursions on their power (Peterson, 1995; Peterson, Rabe, & Wong, 1986).

Economists also focus on how information is distributed across the system. Those closest to the ground, local educators, have much more information about the actual business of education. Higher-level policymakers must depend on them for the provision of education. According to principal-agent theory, the principal, the policymaker, "hires" agents, educators, to further a goal, since the principal is at some distance from the classroom and cannot achieve the educational goals himself. The principal and the agent are in different contexts, have different information, and face different constraints; the agent will not necessarily do the principal's bidding simply upon a request to do so. So the principal's challenge is to design incentives strong enough to induce agents to further the principal's goal. Principals also try to direct agents' behaviors through mandates, and the more that incentives have strings or conditions attached, the more they come to look like mandates or regulations (McDonnell & Elmore, 1987). However powerful the incentives or tight the strings, the agent may not entirely control the factors that affect outcomes or have the necessary knowledge and skill to achieve the goal. To some extent, the principal must compromise, accepting the best outcome possible, given that he must hire an agent rather than accomplishing the goal himself. This theory helps explain why higher-level policy is never mechanically translated into practice; rather it is most often modified by locals who adapt it to fit their situation (Moe, 1989).

Sociologists have also studied the intergovernmental system. Organizational theorists are concerned with the interdependencies and relationships among institutions. Because instruction is so buffered, so difficult to reach through policies or administrative actions, or so "loosely coupled" (Meyer & Rowan, 1977; Weick, 1978), higher levels of government have faced severe challenges in trying to guide instruction (Cohen & Spillane, 1993). Districts, states, and the federal government have tried numerous approaches, from direct regulation to ratcheting up incentives through strong accountability systems. The constant struggle to govern the classroom affects relationships among governments as well as the interactions among policy and practice. Therefore, not only are classrooms affected by the federal government's NCLB requirement to engage in more testing and to tighten the connection between curriculum and testing, but so too are schools, districts, and states. They not only mediate the relationships between the classroom and the federal policy but they also adjust their own policies, and their spheres of influence are modified. Does the balance of, and shift in, power examined and explained by these various disciplinary perspectives affect the substance of education policy in the United States? We turn to this question in the next section.

IMPLICATIONS OF DECENTRALIZED GOVERNANCE STRUCTURE FOR POLICY

This section of the chapter examines the impact of the decentralized governance structure on four policy domains: education funding, teacher quality, instructional guidance, and accountability.

Education Finance

The decentralized structure of education in the United States and its heavy reliance on states and local communities to fund schools has led to inequities in educational resources both within and across the states. State policymakers determine the financial structure of public K–12 education; that is, how revenues are raised and allocated across the school districts in their states. This has resulted in 50 separate state systems of funding education with considerable variation in the sources of education revenue and in the average revenue behind each student. In 2001–2002, school districts received, on average, 49 percent of their revenues from state aid, 43 percent from local sources, and 8 percent from federal sources. State support ranged, however, from a low of 32 percent to a high of 72 percent across the United States, while reliance on local revenues ranged from a low of 13 percent to a high of 63 percent (National Center for Education Statistics, 2004). There were large differences in spending across the states as well. In that same year, the average per-pupil expenditure was $7,734, but the lowest-spending state, Utah, spent only half as much ($5,132) as the highest-spending state, New Jersey ($10,235), after adjustment for regional cost differences (Education Week, 2005). Evans, Murray, and Schwab (1999) found that in 1992 variation across the states accounted for two-thirds of the total variance in per-pupil spending nationally.

Spending can vary considerably within states, particularly those in which the majority of funds are raised locally, because the level of local education revenues available to schools is driven by the interaction of the wealth and tax effort of a community. Since the late 1960s, poor and underresourced school districts in 45 states have challenged the constitutionality of funding disparities in state courts (Hunter, 2006). Litigation activity in the 1970s and 1980s led states to increase their share of education funding to its current level. In states with court-ordered reform, inequities in education expenditures decreased, usually because states targeted additional state aid to the lowest-spending and/or lowest-wealth districts (Evans, Murray, & Schwab, 1999; Goertz & Natriello, 1999). But funding disparities persist. In 18 states, the 25 percent of districts serving the greatest number of students in poverty received at least a $100 per pupil less in 2001–2002 than the 25 percent of districts with the lowest poverty concentrations, in spite of the greater level of student need. In 10 states, the difference exceeded $500 per student. Similar funding inequities were observed when comparing districts with the highest and lowest minority enrollments in each state (Carey, 2004). Even after adjustment for student poverty and special needs, the coefficient of variation in education revenues exceeded 10 percent in 40 of the 50 states, and few state school finance systems had neutralized the relationship between district wealth and education resources (Education Week, 2005).

These inter- and intrastate expenditure disparities raise the question of whether school districts across the country have the level of resources needed to bring all students to a proficient level of performance, as required under NCLB. Although they continue to debate whether "money makes a difference," researchers have concluded that effective teachers can raise student achievement (see, e.g., Barrow & Rouse, this volume; Hanushek & Rivkin, 2004).

Teacher Quality

Although there is consensus that teachers matter, there is less agreement about the characteristics of a good teacher (e.g., level and type of preparation, test scores, years of experience, or certification) or about ways to increase the supply of quality teachers (such as raising salaries, expanding pathways into the teaching profession, or changing the salary structure). However one measures teacher quality, states and school districts are under pressure to place better trained teachers in every classroom, particularly in the classrooms of poor, minority, and low-achieving children.

States have had minimum requirements for entrance into the teaching profession in place for decades, but states differ considerably in the substance of these policies. States require that prospective teachers complete an approved teacher education program and/or a prescribed course of study, but these requirements generally focus on the type rather than the content or quality of the courses taken or on the success of the program graduates in the classroom. Until the enactment of NCLB, only half of the states required teachers to major in the subject they plan to teach; another 11 states allowed perspective teachers to have either a major or minor in their teaching field. Although all new teachers must now have a subject major in their teaching area, decentralized higher education governance systems make it difficult for most states to influence the content of either subject matter or education courses. Therefore, the content and quality of teacher preparation programs can, and do, vary widely within as well as across states.

To ensure that prospective teachers have a minimum level of knowledge and skills, a majority of states assess the basic skills (41 states), subject matter knowledge (30 states) and/or the professional knowledge (35 states) of their teaching candidates prior to issuing a license (Council of Chief State School Officers, 2002). The performance of new teachers is not comparable across the states, however, as states select their own assessments and establish different passing scores. In 2002, 44 states allowed individuals with a college degree to seek licensure through an "alternative route," but programs in only 24 states included both preservice and mentoring components, and only 18 states required program entrants to pass a basic skills or subject matter test (Education Week, 2003). Other state teacher policies, such as induction programs and recertification, are implemented at the school and school district level, increasing variability in design, practice, and impact.

The lack of uniform teacher preparation programs within a state can be a problem because teacher labor markets are regional and in some large urban areas are relatively closed systems. Boyd et al. (2003) found, for example, that 60 percent of new teachers in New York State took a job within 15 miles of their hometown or where they attended college; nearly 85 percent stayed within a 40-mile radius. It is possible that this localization depresses teacher salaries in comparison to other professions that operate in a national market. Within these regions, teachers generally choose schools that mirror the urbanicity of their home communities, with graduates of urban high schools choosing to teach in urban schools and graduates of suburban high schools going to suburban districts. This means that the graduates of poor-quality high schools, who often go to college with weak skills, may bring these weak skills back into the urban classroom (Haycock, 2004; Strauss, 1999). Disparities in education spending, teacher salaries, and working conditions between central cities and suburban communities also affect where teachers choose to work. As a result, poor, minority, and low-achieving students are taught by substantially less qualified teachers, particularly in urban areas (Ingersoll, 2004; Lankford, Loeb, & Wyckoff, 2002; see Haycock, 2004, for citations to additional research).

Instructional Guidance and Support

Although the federal government requires states to adopt standards in at least reading and mathematics, they do not review or approve the content of these standards. Federal law forbids its agencies from mandating, directing, or controlling the specific instructional content, curriculum, programs of instruction, or academic achievement standards and assessments of states, districts, or schools (Fuhrman, 2004), although the government can and does use grants to support the adoption of instructional programs with a particular focus. Thus, states determine the substance of academic standards.

In 2004, all but one state had developed content standards in reading and mathematics, and all but two in science and social studies as well (Education Week, 2005). States have not adopted common standards, however. Although many states have aligned their mathematics and science standards, and to a lesser extent their reading standards, to those developed by the professional organizations in these fields, states differ in the coverage, rigor, specificity, and clarity of their curricular frameworks. One evaluation reported that content standards in only five of the 30 states reviewed were clear, specific, and covered what the reviewers considered essential reading and math skills in each grade (Cross, Rebarber, & Torres, 2004). Other analyses also showed variation in the quality of standards both across and within states (Education Week, 2005; Rothman, 2004). Some states have developed both professional and community consensus around the content of the standards. Other states have faced philosophical battles over what should be taught (e.g., evolution or social science content) and how (e.g., different approaches to teaching mathematics and reading). (See, e.g., Pearson, 2004, and Schoenfeld, 2004, respectively, on the reading and math wars.)

How does this decentralized process of setting standards affect what students are taught? In contrast to other countries, standards in the United States are unfocused and lack coherence, reflecting a "splintered vision" of what students should know (Schmidt, McKnight, & Raizen,

1997). A lack of agreement on what constitutes eighth-grade mathematics, for example, has resulted in considerable diversity in students' opportunities to learn mathematics—opportunities that are apportioned differentially by school size, location, and racial/ethnic composition (Cogan, Schmidt, & Wiley, 2001). In addition, standards in most states are not as challenging as those in high-performing nations, and the multiplicity of standards has led to a curriculum in the United States that is "a mile wide and an inch deep" (Rothman, 2004). Finally, while states have increased coursework requirements for high school graduation over the last 20 years, too few students are gaining the knowledge and skills they need to success in college and the workplace (Achieve, 2004; Education Trust-West, 2004). No state currently requires every high school student to take a college- and work-preparatory curriculum to earn a diploma. Only five states, for example, require all students to complete four math courses for graduation, and nearly half of the states do not specify which mathematics or science courses students need to take (Achieve, 2004).

Further variation is injected into the system as schools and school districts interpret and implement state standards. Education policymaking is not a zero-sum game in the United States; increased state policymaking is accompanied by more district policymaking (Fuhrman & Elmore, 1990). This is particularly true with regard to state standards, where districts have developed their own curricular frameworks, curricular materials, student assessments, instructional monitoring, and professional development to support the state reform. The level and type of district instructional guidance and support vary considerably, however, reflecting differences in district size, student performance, capacity, philosophy, and leadership (see, e.g., Hannaway & Kimball, 2001; Massell & Goertz, 2002; Shields, et al., 2004; Spillane, 2004; Weinbaum, 2005).

Accountability

When Congress enacted the NCLB Act, states were at different stages of meeting the accountability requirements of the new law. Only 22 states had single accountability systems in place by 2000–2001. Only 13 states tested consecutive grades between grades 2 or 3 and at least grade 8 in the same subject areas using the same assessment. No state had a system in place that met all of the provisions of NCLB (Goertz & Duffy, 2001).

There has been considerable discussion in the policy, political, and research communities about the type and extent of flexibility states have in responding to the requirements of the NCLB Act. With regard to accountability, some provisions allow no flexibility. For example, some state accountability systems used a performance index that combined performance on reading and mathematics (a compensatory model). States now have to hold schools and districts accountable separately for reading and mathematics (a conjunctive model). States must calculate Adequate Yearly Progress (AYP) separately for all students and all subgroups of students in a school and school district. Also, states must follow the NCLB provisions for establishing "starting points" for the AYP targets, as well as timelines for implementing specified sanctions on Title I schools. States still establish their own standards in reading, mathematics, and science; design their own assessments, which must be aligned with state standards; and set their own proficiency standards. Other areas of flexibility include setting the growth trajectory for improvement and the minimum number of students required for inclusion in accountability calculations, using confidence intervals[1] to calculate AYP, and determining whether NCLB sanctions should be applied to non-Title I schools (Forte Fast & Espenbach, 2004). States may choose how to incorporate NCLB

---

1. A confidence interval is a statistical technique that accounts for measurement error. Because test results from smaller groups may be less reliable than those from larger groups, confidence intervals can be applied to effectively reduce the percentage of students required to be at proficiency for subgroups with smaller numbers of test takers.

accountability requirements into their state accountability systems, leaving many states with two sometimes conflicting accountability policies (Goertz, 2005).

All states have developed accountability policies that meet the requirements of NCLB. But the discretion granted states in the design of their content standards, accountability plans, and assessment policies means that the concept of "proficient" means different things in different states. For example, the percentage of fourth-grade students achieving proficiency on their 2005 state reading assessments ranged from 36 percent in South Carolina to 88 percent in Tennessee, although the range in performance on the NAEP fourth-grade reading assessment was almost identical—26 percent in South Carolina and 27 percent in Tennessee (Dillon, 2005). The percentage of schools not making AYP in 2005 ranged from a low of 2 percent in Wisconsin to a high of 66 percent in Hawaii and 64 percent in Florida (Olson, 2005).

States also differ in how they hold students accountable for performance. Currently, 20 states, educating about one-half of all public school students, require students to pass an examination as a condition of graduation. The content, coverage, and rigor of these tests range, however, from basic skills in reading and mathematics to end-of-course assessments in core courses. Twelve states also require students in lower grades to pass tests as a condition of promotion to higher grades (Zinth, 2005).

Clearly, the decentralized nature of educational governance has allowed for considerable variability at the state and local levels in terms of education financing, teacher quality, standards setting, and accountability. While the federal government has increasingly (particularly with the passage of NCLB) set minimum requirements in some of these areas, a great deal of discretion is left to the states and localities. Given the implications of teacher preparation for the educational experience of students, the lack of federal oversight of teacher preparation programs allows for great variation from the outset. Those teachers then go to work in schools that have been provided with widely differing resources as a result of the varying sources and levels of funding in each district around the country. They are guided in their teaching by state- and district-level standards that vary widely in terms of quality and content because of the input and authority of numerous policymakers and education leaders at the state and local levels and the absence of consensus about the quality of standards in many areas. The type and quality of ongoing guidance and support that the teachers receive in their efforts to teach these standards is largely determined at the district and sometimes the school level. And finally, teachers and students are then held to quite different, often fluctuating, and occasionally contradictory systems of accountability. In sum, the multitiered system of educational governance allows for very disparate teaching experiences and educational experiences for students, depending largely on the particular school, district, and state in which one finds oneself.

CONCLUSIONS

The dynamic nature of the intergovernmental system suggests continued research as future shifts occur. We also need more research that comes at these questions from a multidisciplinary perspective and that focuses on the consequences of alternative power arrangements. Potentially fruitful future research would include projects that track shifts in power as a result of NCLB, study the comparative advantages of different governmental levels, and take comparative approaches to various governmental arrangements.

As noted previously, several aspects of NCLB affect relationships among levels of government. Policies on testing and accountability constrain state and local activity while policies on parental choice and supplemental education services will likely yield a growth in charters and privatization. These shifts in power will both influence and be influenced by the intergovernmental structure that we have described here. Additionally, the success of these initiatives will be circumscribed by the effect of the intergovernmental structure on education finance, instruction, accountability, and teacher quality. Studies of NCLB should focus, of course, on whether students are learning more and why, but they should also focus on how relationships among federal, state, and local governments and new educational providers are changing and on the implications of those changes for the future of education.

Future studies might look at the comparative advantages of different governmental levels with somewhat broader frames than past studies. For example, economists who study adequacy or productivity might collaborate with political scientists examining institutional and interest alignments to determine how the latter affect the definitions of adequacy and productivity and how these aspects of resource deployment then alter political arrangements. Given the shifts in educational governance and authority, it would be helpful to analyze how interest alignments create additional (or create a dearth of) resources for particular educational efforts.

Even though the state standards movement and NCLB have led to some homogenization of intergovernmental arrangements in the United States, it will be important for researchers to examine the consequences of differently constructed governance systems (e.g., loose or tight organizational arrangements, vertical and horizontal structures) around key functions. Such studies could use comparative research, focusing on countries like New Zealand, which couples standards reforms with substantial devolution of authority to schools, to look at contrasting arrangements and their differential effects. It might even be possible within particular states to deliberately alter balances of power among schools, districts, and states in design experiments that would study a range of outcomes under different governance structures.

Clearly, the delicate and shifting balance of America's intergovernmental structure around education provides a variety of challenges when we strive for widespread educational improvement. However, when thoughtfully examined, the system also provides an opportunity for identifying particularly successful arrangements that will yield more efficient and effective practice.

REFERENCES

Achieve, Inc. (2004). *The expectations gap: A 50-state review of high school graduation requirements.* Washington, DC: Author.

Anderson, L. M., & Turnbull, B. J. (1998). *Living in interesting times: Early state implementation of new federal education.* Washington, DC: Policy Studies Associates, Inc.

Bielick, S., & Chapman, C. (2003). *Trends in the use of school choice: 1993 to 1999. Statistical analysis report.* (NCES 2003-031). Washington, DC: National Center for Education Statistics.

Borman, G. (2000). Title I: The evolving research base. *Journal of Education for Students Placed at Risk 5,* 1–2, 27–45.

Boyd, D., Lankford, H., Loeb, S., & Wyckoff, J. (2003). Understanding teacher labor markets: Implications for educational equity. In M. L. Plecki & D. Monk (Eds.), *School finance and teacher quality: Exploring the connections* (pp. 55–83). Larchmont, NY: Eye on Education.

Bryk, A. S., Kerbow, D., & Rollow, S. (1997). Chicago school reform. In D. Ravitch & J. P. Viteritti (Eds.), *New schools for a new century* (pp. 164–200). New Haven, CT: Yale University Press.

Bryk, A. S., Sebring, P. B., Kerbow, D., Rollow, S., & Easton, J. Q. (1998). *Charting Chicago school reform: Democratic localism as a lever for change.* Boulder, CO: Westview Press.

Carey, K. (2004). *The funding gap 2004: Many states still shortchange low-income and minority students.* Washington, DC: The Education Trust. Retrieved January 22, 2007 from http://www2 .edtrust.org/NR/rdonlyres/30B3C1B3-3DA6- 4809-AFB9-2DAACF11CF88/0/funding2004.pdf

Carnoy, M., & Loeb, S. (2004). Does external accountability affect student outcomes? A cross-state analysis. In S. H. Fuhrman & R. F. Elmore (Eds.), *Redesigning accountability systems for education* (pp. 189–219). New York: Teachers College Press.

Chubb, J. E., & Moe, T. M. (1990). *Politics, markets, and America's schools.* Washington, DC: The Brookings Institution.

Cibulka, J. G., & Boyd, W. L. eds. (2003). *A race against time: The crisis in urban schooling.* Westport, CT: Praeger.

Cogan, L. S., Schmidt, W. H., & Wiley, D. E. (2001). Who takes what math and in which track? Using TIMSS to characterize U.S. students' eighth-grade mathematics learning opportunities. *Educational Evaluation and Policy Analysis 23*(4), 323–341.

Cohen, D. K., & Spillane, J. P. (1993). Policy and practice: The relations between governance and instruction. In S. Fuhrman (Ed.), *Designing coherent education policy* (pp. 35–95). San Francisco: Jossey-Bass.

Cohen, M. (2002). Unruly crew: Accountability lessons from the Clinton administration. *Education Next 2*(3), 42–47.

Consortium for Policy Research in Education. (1989). *State education reform in the 1980s* (CPRE Policy Brief No. RB-03). New Brunswick, NJ: Author.

Corcoran, T. B., & Christman, J. B. (2002). *The limits and contradictions of systemic reform: The Philadelphia story.* Philadelphia: University of Pennsylvania, Consortium for Policy Research in Education.

Corcoran, T. B., & Goertz, M. (2005). The governance of public education. In S. Fuhrman & M. Lazerson (Eds.), *The public schools* (pp. 25–56). New York: Oxford University Press.

Council of Chief State School Officers. (2002). *Key state education policies on PK–12 education.* Washington, DC: Author.

Cross, R., Rebarber, T., & Torres, J. (2004). *Grading the systems: The guide to state standards, tests, and accountability policies.* Washington, DC: Thomas B. Fordham Foundation and AccountabilityWorks.

Cuban, L., & Usdan, M., eds. (2002). *Powerful reforms with shallow roots: Improving America's urban schools.* New York: Teachers College Press.

David, J. L. (2000). Educators and parents as partners in school governance. In R. Pankratz & J. M Petrosko (Eds.), *All children can learn: Lessons from the Kentucky reform experience* (pp. 207–224). San Francisco: Jossey-Bass.

Dillon, S. (2005). Students ace state tests, but earn D's from U.S. *New York Times*, Retrieved November 26, from www.nytimes.com/2005/11/26/education/26tests.html

Education Trust-West. (2004). *The A–G curriculum: College-prep? Work-prep? Life-prep? Understanding and implementing a rigorous core curriculum for all.* Oakland, CA: Author.

Education Week. (2003). Quality counts 2003. If I can't learn from you: Ensuring a highly qualified teacher for every classroom. Special issue, *Education Week 22*, no. 17, January 9.

Education Week. (2005). Quality counts 2005. No small change: Targeting money toward student performance. Special issue, *Education Week 24*, no. 17, January 6.

Elmore, R. (1993). The role of local school districts in instructional improvement. In S. Fuhrman (Ed.), *Designing coherent policy: Improving the system* (pp. 96–124). San Francisco: Jossey-Bass.

Evans, W. N., Murray, S. E., & Schwab, R. M. (1999). The impact of court-mandated school finance reform. In H. F. Ladd, R. Chalk, & J. Hansen (Eds.), *Equity and adequacy in education finance: Issues and perspectives* (pp. 72–98). Washington, DC: National Academy Press.

Executive Office of the President. (1990). *National goals for education.* Washington, DC: U.S. Government Printing Office.

Firestone, W.A., Fuhrman, S. H., & Kirst, M. W. (1989). *The progress of reform: An appraisal of state education initiatives* (CPRE Research Report No. RR-014). New Brunswick, NJ: Consortium for Policy Research in Education.

Forte Fast, E., & Espenbach, W. (2004). *Revisiting statewide educational accountability under NCLB.* Washington, DC: Council of Chief State School Officers.

Fuhrman, S. H., ed. (2001). *From the capitol to the classroom: Standards-based reform in the states. One hundredth yearbook of the National Society for the Study of Education, part 2.* Chicago: University of Chicago Press.

Fuhrman, S. H. (2004). Less than meets the eye: Standards, testing, and fear of federal control. In N. Epstein (Ed.), *Who's in charge here? The tangled web of school governance and policy* (pp. 131–163). Denver, CO: Education Commission of the States; Washington, DC: Brookings Institution Press.

Fuhrman, S., & Elmore, R. (1990). Understanding local control in the wake of state education reform. *Educational Evaluation and Policy Analysis 12*(1), 82–96.

Gill, B., Timpane, M., Ross, K., & Brewer, D. (2001). *Rhetoric versus reality: What we know and what we need to know about vouchers and charter schools.* Santa Monica, CA: RAND.

Goertz, M. E. (2001). Redefining government roles in an era of standards-based reform. *Phi Delta Kappan 83*(1), 62–66.

Goertz, M. E. (2005). Implementing the No Child Left Behind Act: Challenges for the states. *Peabody Journal of Education 80*(2), 73–79.

Goertz, M. E., & Duffy, M. C. (2001). *Assessment and accountability across the 50 states* (CPRE Policy Brief No. RB-33). Philadelphia, PA: University of Pennsylvania, Consortium for Policy Research in Education.

Goertz, M. E., & Natriello, G. 1999. Court-mandated school finance reform: What do the new dollars buy? In H. F. Ladd, R. Chalk, & J. Hansen (Eds.), *Equity and adequacy in education finance: Issues and perspective* (pp. 99–135). Washington, DC: National Academy Press.

Gross, B., & Goertz, M. E., eds. (2005). *Holding high hopes: How high schools respond to state accountability policies* (CPRE Research Report No. RR-056). Philadelphia: University of Pennsylvania, Consortium for Policy Research in Education.

Gross, B., Kirst, M., Holland, D., & Luschei, T. (2005). Got you under my spell? How accountability policy is changing and not changing decision making in high schools. In B. Gross & M. Goertz (Eds.), *Holding high hopes: How high schools respond to state accountability policies* (CPRE Research Report No. RR-056), (pp. 43–80). Philadelphia: University of Pennsylvania, Consortium for Policy Research in Education.

Gruber, K. J., Wiley, S. D., Broughman, S. P., Strizek, G. A., & Burian-Fitzgerald, M. (2002). *Schools and staffing survey, 1999–2000: Overview of the data for public, private, public charter, and Bureau of Indian Affairs elementary and secondary schools.* Washington, DC: U.S. Department of Education, U.S. Government Printing Office.

Hannaway, J., & Kimball, K. (2001). Big isn't always bad: School district size, poverty and standards-based reform. In S. H. Fuhrman (Ed.), *From the capitol to the classroom: Standards-based reform in the states. One hundredth yearbook of the National Society for the Study of Education, part 2* (pp. 99–123). Chicago: University of Chicago Press.

Hanushek, E. A., & Raymond, M. E. (2004). Does school accountability lead to improved student Performance? NBER Working Paper No. 10591.

Hanushek, E. A., & Rivkin, S. G. (2004). How to improve the supply of high-quality teachers. In D. Ravitch (Ed.), *Brookings papers on education policy: 2004* (pp. 7–44). Washington, DC: Brookings Institution Press.

Hatch, T. (2002). When improvement programs collide. *Phi Delta Kappan 83*(8), 626–634, 639.

Haycock, K. (2004). The elephant in the living room. In D. Ravitch (Ed.), *Brookings papers on education policy: 2004* (pp. 229–263). Washington, DC: Brookings Institution Press.

Hess, F. M. (2002). *School boards at the dawn of the 21st century: Conditions and challenges of district governance.* Washington, DC: National School Boards Association.

Hill, P. T. (2000). The federal role in education. In D. Ravitch (Ed.), *Brookings papers on education policy: 2000* (pp. 11–57). Washington DC: Brookings Institution Press.

Hunter, M. A. (2006). *Litigations challenging constitutionality of K–12 funding in the 50 states.* New York: Campaign for Fiscal Equity. Retrieved January 22, 2007 from http://www.schoolfunding.info/litigation/In-Process%20Litigations-09-2004.pdf.

Ingersoll, R. M. (2004). Why some schools have more underqualified teachers than others. In D. Ravitch (Ed.), *Brookings papers on education policy: 2004* (pp. 45–88). Washington, DC: Brookings Institution Press.

Jennings, J. (2001). *A brief history of the federal role in education: Why it began and why it's still needed.* Washington, DC: Center on Education Policy.

Kaestle, C. F., & Smith, M. S. (1982). The federal role in elementary and secondary education, 1940–1980. *Harvard Educational Review 52*(4), 384–408.

Kirst, M. (2002). *Mayoral influence, new regimes, and public school governance* (CPRE Research Report No. RR-049). Philadelphia: University of Pennsylvania, Consortium for Policy Research in Education.

Kirst, M. (2004). Turning points: A history of American school governance. In N. Epstein (Ed.), *Who's in charge here? The tangled web of school governance and policy* (pp. 14–41). Washington, DC: Brookings Institution Press.

Lankford, H., Loeb, S., & Wyckoff, J. (2002). Teacher sorting and the plight of urban schools: A descriptive analysis. *Educational Evaluation and Policy Analysis 24*(1), 37–62.

Malen, B., Ogawa, R. T., & Kranz, J. (1990). What do we know about school-based management? A case study of the literature—A call for research. In W. H. Clune & J. F. Witte (Eds.), *The practice of choice, decentralization, and school restructuring.* Vol. 2 of *Choice and control in American education* (pp. 289–342). London: Falmer.

Marshall, C., Mitchell, D., & Wirt, F. (1989). *Culture and education policy in the American states.* New York: Falmer.

Massell, D. (2000). *The district role in building capacity: four strategies* (CPRE Policy Brief No. RB-32). Philadelphia: University of Pennsylvania, Consortium for Policy Research in Education.

Massell, D., & Goertz, M. E. (2002). District strategies for building capacity. In A. M. Hightower, M. S. Knapp, J. A. Marsh, & M. W. McLaughlin (Eds.), *School districts and instructional renewal* (pp. 43–60). New York: Teachers College Press.

Massell, D., Kirst, M., & Hoppe, M. (1997). *Persistence and change: Standards-based reform in nine states* (CPRE Research Report No. RR-037). Philadelphia: University of Pennsylvania, Consortium for Policy Research in Education.

McDonnell, L. (2004). *Politics, persuasion, and educational testing.* Cambridge, MA: Harvard University Press.

McDonnell, L., & Elmore, R. (1987). Learning from experience: Lessons from policy implementation. *Educational Evaluation and Policy Analysis 9*(2), 171–178.

McDonnell, L., & Fuhrman, S. (1985). The political context of school reform. In V. D. Mueller & M. P. McKeown (Eds.), *The fiscal, legal and political aspects of state reform of elementary and secondary education* (pp. 43–65). Cambridge, MA: Ballinger.

McDonnell, L., & McLaughlin, M. (1982). *Education policy and the role of the states.* Santa Monica, CA: Rand Corporation.

McLaughlin, M. (1982). The role of the states in federal education programs. *Harvard Educational Review 52*(4), 562–583.

McLaughlin, M., & Talbert, J. (2003). *Reforming districts: How districts support school reform.* Seattle, WA: Center for the Study of Teaching and Policy.

Meyer, J. W., & Rowan, B. (1977). Institutionalized organizations: Formal structure as myth and ceremony. *American Journal of Sociology 83*(2), 440–463.

Miron, G., & Nelson, C. (2004). Student achievement in charter schools: What we know and why we know so little. In K. Bulkley & P. Wohlstetter (Eds.), *Taking account of charter schools: What's happened and what's next?* (pp. 161–175). New York: Teachers College Press.

Moe, T. (1989). The politics of bureaucratic structure. In J. Chubb & P. Peterson (Eds.), *Can the government govern?* (pp. 267–330). Washington, DC: Brookings Institution.

Moore, M., Goertz, M., & Hartle, T. (1983). Interaction of federal and state programs. *Education and Urban Society 15*(4), 453–478.

National Center for Education Statistics. (2005). *Digest of education statistics, 2006* (NCES 2006-030). Washington: Author. Retrieved January 22, 2007 from http://nces.ed.gov/pubsearch/pubsinfo.sp?pubid = 2005025.

National Commission on Excellence in Education. (1983). *A Nation at risk: The imperative for educational reform.* Washington, DC: Author.

Olson, L. (2005). Defying predictions, state trends proved mixed on schools making NCLB targets. *Education Week*, September 7, 1, 26–27.

Orland, M. (1994). From the picket fence to the chain link fence: National goals and federal aid to the disadvantaged. In K. Wong & M. Wang (Eds.), *Rethinking policy for at-risk students* (pp. 179–196). Berkeley, CA: McCutchan.

Pearson, P. D. (2004). The reading wars. *Educational Policy 18*, 216–252.

Peterson, P. E. (1995). *The price of federalism.* Washington, DC: Brookings Institution Press.

Peterson, P. E., Rabe, B. G., & Wong, K. K. (1986). *When federalism works.* Washington, DC: Brookings Institution.

Public Education Network/Education Week. (2004). Learn. Vote. Act. The public's responsibility for public education. Retrieved January 22, 2007 from www.PublicEducation.org/portals/Learn_Vote_Act/default.asp.

Reuben, J. (2005). Patriotic purposes: Public schools and the education of citizens. In S. H. Fuhrman & M. Lazerson (Eds.), *The public schools* (pp. 1–24). New York: Oxford University Press.

Rich, W. (1996). *Black mayors and school politics.* New York: Garland Press.

Rose, L. C., & Gallup, A. M. (2002). The 34th annual Phi Delta Kappa/Gallup poll of the public's attitudes toward the public schools. *Phi Delta Kappan 84*(1), 41–46.

———. The 35th annual Phi Delta Kappa/Gallup poll of the public's attitudes toward the public schools. *Phi Delta Kappan* 85 (1): 41–52.

Rosenthal, A., & Fuhrman, S. (1980a). Education policy: Money is the name of the game. *State Legislatures 6*(8), 4–10.

Rosenthal, A., & Fuhrman, S. (1980b). Shaping state education policy. *Compact 14*(3), 22–23, 27.

Rothman, R. (2004). Benchmarking and alignment of state standards and assessments. In S. H. Fuhrman & R. F. Elmore (Eds.), *Redesigning accountability systems for education* (pp. 96–137). New York: Teachers College Press.

Schmidt, W. H., McKnight, C., & Raizen, S. (1997). *A splintered vision: An investigation of U.S. science and mathematics education.* Dordrecht, Netherlands: Kluwer.

Schoenfeld, A. H. (2004). The math wars. *Educational Policy 18*, 253–286.

Shields, P. M., Lash, A., Padilla, C., Woodworth, K., & Laguarda, K. G. (2004). *Evaluation of Title I accountability systems and school improvement efforts (TASSIE): Second-year findings.* Washington, DC: U.S. Department of Education.

Smith, M.S., and O'Day, J. (1991). Systemic school reform. In S. H. Fuhrman & B. Malen (Eds.), *The politics of curriculum and testing. Politics of Education Association Yearbook, 1990* (pp. 233–267). London: Taylor & Francis.

Spillane, J. P. (2004). *Standards deviation: How schools misunderstand education policy.* Cambridge, MA: Harvard University Press.

Strauss, R. P. (1999). Who gets hired to teach? The case of Pennsylvania. In M. Kanstroom & C. E. Finn, Jr. (Eds.), *Better teachers, better schools* (pp. 103–130). Washington, DC: Fordham Foundation Press.

Tyack, D. B. (1974). *The one best system: A history of American urban education.* Cambridge, MA: Harvard University Press.

Tyack, D., & Cuban, L. (1995). *Tinkering toward Utopia: A century of public school reform.* Cambridge, MA; Harvard University Press.

U.S. Charter Schools. (2005). State by state. www.uscharterschools.org.

U.S. Department of Education. (1984). *The nation responds: Recent efforts to improve education.* U.S. Government Printing Office, Washington, DC.

Walsh, J. M. (1998). *The intellectual origins of mass parties and mass schools in the Jacksonian period: Creating a conformed citizenry.* New York: Garland.

Weick, K. (1978). Educational organizations as loosely coupled systems. *Administrative Science Quarterly 23*, 541–552.

Weinbaum, E. (2005). Stuck in the middle with you: District response to state accountability. In B. Gross & M. E. Goertz (Eds.), *Holding high hopes: How high schools respond to state accountability policies* (CPRE Research Report No. RR-056) (pp. 95–121). Philadelphia: University of Pennsylvania, Consortium for Policy Research in Education.

Wirt, F. M., & Kirst, M. (1975). *Political and social foundations of education.* Berkeley, CA: McCutchan.

Wirt, F. M., & Kirst, M. (2001). *The political dynamics of American education.* 2nd ed. Richmond, CA: McCutchan.

Zinth, K. Student promotion/retention policies. Retrieved January 22, 2007 from http://www.ecs.org/clearinghouse/65/51/6551.htm.

4

Policy and Practice

David K. Cohen, Susan L. Moffitt, and
Simona Goldin

In 1950, the relations between policy and practice in education were not a puzzle of much interest to anyone.[1] There was no federal education policy to puzzle about, and, though states made
education policy, it seemed not to puzzle anyone, at least not in print. States contributed to local
school funds, but the main issues concerned amounts, not effects on practice. It was widely
assumed that more money would buy more educational resources, which would create better education, which would enable more learning. So pervasive were these ideas that, though policy
typically was thought to have substantial effects on practice, warrants for the claim were rarely
investigated. Discussion centered on how much should be spent on what, for whom.

Money was not the only instrument of policy. States set standards for teacher certification and
licensing, and regulated school safety and curricula.[2] Here too, the effects on practice were
assumed to be plain: setting certification standards would translate into better-educated teachers,
which would enable more learning. Generous assumptions about the potency of policy fit the condition of government: the federal Office of Education did little besides collect data, and most state
education agencies were quite weak. If states needed only to appropriate funds and broadly regulate schools in order to influence practice, weak government would do.

Since then, education policy has had five boom decades, but the more policy there was, the
more doubts grew about its potency. There are more state and federal monies, more mandates and
incentives, dozens of policies and programs, and recent policies embody much more ambitious
efforts to change practice. Yet the relations between policy and practice are now much more
controversial than they were in the 1950s, and there are more doubts about the efficacy of
policy.

The doubts and controversy were fueled by research. In the two decades following *Brown v.
Board of Education*, researchers showed that funding differences among U.S. schools had modest and inconsistent effects on teaching and learning, and that the educational resources that
money bought also had modest and uneven effects. Despite large differences in average

---

1. This chapter was originally drafted for a meeting of the Consortium for Policy Research in Education in January
2005, which was supported in part by a grant from the Spencer Foundation.

2. Kenneth Meier (1993) defines regulation as "government restriction of individual choice to keep conduct from tran-
scending acceptable bounds" (p. 82).

achievement among schools, and especially troubling differences between schools that enrolled the children of affluent and poor parents, the educational resources that most people thought significant were weakly related to school-average student performance.

These studies provoked others, for schools plainly made a difference: when children learn algebra, they do so in classrooms, not on the street, and many learn to read only in school. To explain such effects, some scholars moved from studying the impact of familiar resources like money, teachers' degrees, and facilities, to studying the impact of instructional practices, organizational arrangements, and educators' knowledge and skill. They showed that practice-embedded knowledge and action affected learning. They also showed that teachers' and students' knowledge and academic practices, and the organizations in which they work, mediate between the conventional resources that schools deploy, on the one hand, and learning on the other.

Those inquiries began to clarify how schools made a difference, and they implied a novel idea: the effects of resources depend on their use. Schools and teachers did different things with the same resources, with different effects on learning. That seemed to imply that the classical instruments of education policy—funding and regulation—were not as potent as had been thought.[3] The headline news in the early 1970s was that resources had relatively weak and inconsistent effects on practice. That shook inherited ideas about the power and effects of policy, and helped to generate new ideas about what it might take for policy to influence practice. The more fundamental point, which never made any headlines, was that if the effects of resource allocation or regulation depend on practitioners' use, then policy depends on practice. Resource provision is crucial, for students and teachers cannot use books or laboratories they don't have, but books do not unfold automatically in students' minds (Hanushek, 1996). Resource provision creates opportunities for use, but resources are only effective if used well. It would be reasonable to infer that policies would be more likely to influence practice if they cultivated practitioners' use of policy, and less likely to influence practice if they only allocated and regulated resources.

Studies of implementation, which began in response to President Lyndon Johnson's Great Society, took a similar path. The early studies seemed to assume that efficacy resided in policy: well-designed policies would contain the resources, incentives, and oversight that were needed to shape practice, so most early studies focused on compliance. The authors recognized that some discretion or adaptation was unavoidable, but that was not thought to add value to the policy. Implementers' discretion was in fact thought to weaken policy. If policies could drive practice, study of implementation would be unnecessary: evidence of resource allocation and regulation would do.[4]

These ideas were upset by evidence that education policy did not have the expected effects. One case arose when, a few years after the 1965 Elementary and Secondary Education Act (ESEA) passed, the NAACP Legal Defense and Education Fund reported on state and local misuse of funds under Title I. Instead of spending the money on poor children, as the act required, some localities spent it on fire engines, band uniforms, and other things that were plainly prohibited (Martin & McClure, 1969). Another case was the General Electric Tempo study of Title I, for it reported that Title I had no average effect on learning (Mosbaek, et al., 1968). As the researchers searched for explanations they found that though some schools spent Title I money on

---

3. For example, Eric Hanushek (1996) argues that the effects of resources depend on their use, hence that resources should be tied to incentives in order to maximize effects on student outcomes.

4. The literature on implementation is extensive. Several useful accounts are McLaughlin (1991a, 1991b), Elmore (1978), Elmore (1979–1980), Van Meter and Van Horn (1975), Pressman and Wildavsky (1979), Lindblom (1959), Mazmanian and Sabatier (1989), and Lipsky (1980).

reading, others spent it on music instruction or field trips. They concluded that since practitioners put the program to such varied noninstructional uses, it could hardly improve achievement.

Both cases showed that practice shaped how policy turned out. Drawing on such research, Richard Elmore titled early ideas about the potency of policy a "noble lie," and argued that policy should be made by "mapping backward" from practice, to rest policy design with the needs of practitioners (1979–1980, p. 603).[5] Milbrey McLaughlin and Paul Berman took a similar view in the RAND Change Agent Study, in which they portrayed teachers' motivation as a key to implementation: "projects begun with broad-based support were not only more likely to have been implemented in a mutually adaptive way, but they also stood a better chance of attaining a stable continuation" (1978, p. 21). The growing sense that implementers' discretion was unavoidable was taken to mean that policy could not design practice; McLaughlin wrote, "policy cannot mandate what matters" (1991, p. 187). Practice was too complex, and policymaking too remote, for policymakers to prescribe for practitioners (McLaughlin, 1991a).

That nicely represented what came to be known as the "bottom up" perspective: practitioners' will was their own, unreachable by policy yet crucial to its success. Practice shaped policy. Practitioners knew things that policymakers could not, and used the knowledge to modify policy. McLaughlin and other researchers saw teachers' adaptation of policy as the result of professional judgment about policies' utility: "one ironic consequence of this street-level policymaking and professionals' priority for client service is that reformers often may not get what they want, but get what they need as policy is put into practice" (1991a, p. 189).[6] Many studies in the 1970s and 1980s agreed with these ideas, most influentially in Michael Lipsky's *Street-Level Bureaucracy*, which argued that policy was effectively made in practice (1980). In less than a decade, inherited assumptions about the potency of policy had been reversed by ideas about the potency of practice, all of them arising in research on implementation.

The difference was not academic, for at the same time researchers argued that policy should be understood from the bottom up, state and federal governments made increasing efforts to direct practice with policy, from the top down. In the 1970s states mandated basic skills instruction and minimum competency testing. The latter sought, for the first time in U.S. history, to regulate learning and teaching by requiring outcomes and attaching incentives to their attainment. Government began to turn away from efforts to shape practice by allocating or regulating resources, toward efforts to shape practice by requiring outcomes. The state policies drew mixed reviews: researchers frequently portrayed them as efforts to "de-skill" teachers, but the evidence suggests that practice responded. NAEP scores improved sharply for African American and Hispanic students between the mid-1970s and mid-1980s. One cannot draw tight causal connections, and other factors probably were partly responsible, but better NAEP scores were roughly what the state policies sought (Smith & O'Day, 1990).

Policymakers took a bolder step in the same direction in the mid-1980s, as they launched standards-based reform. They complained that academic standards were generally weak, that students were not educated for the complexities of life and work in an "information age," that more

---

5. "The notion that policymakers exercise—or ought to exercise—some kind of direct and determinant control over policy implementation might be called the 'noble lie' of conventional public administration and policy analysis" (Elmore (1979–1980, p. 603).

6. Ten years after the RAND Change Agent Study, though, McLaughlin began to revise her account, and allowed for the potential for policy to impact practice: "belief or commitment can follow mandated or 'coerced' involvement at both the individual and the system level . . . we did not see or did not recognize instances in which belief follows practice. Individuals required [by policy] to change routines or take up new practices can [thereby] become 'believers'" (McLaughlin 1991b, p. 149).

academically demanding instruction was in order, and that educators should be called to account for what schools produced. These policies sought to drive practice by building a new framework around schools. The key instruments were content standards, tests that were aligned to standards, and accountability that offered incentives for schools to boost test scores. California and Kentucky pioneered the new approach in the mid-to-late 1980s, and it spread quickly. By 1993 more states had adopted a version of the policy, and most others fell into line following President Clinton's Goals 2000 and President Bush's No Child Left Behind (NCLB).

Yet as state and federal policies moved more aggressively to shape practice, research painted a darker picture. Many researchers doubted the efficacy of policy, and criticized policies that pressed for results. Some argued that such policies would not influence practice, but others discerned damage. Yet when researchers investigated results-oriented policies, some reported constructive effects. Martin Carnoy and Susanna Loeb's first study of state accountability systems found that states with more stringent accountability systems had stronger student NAEP performance (2002). David Grissmer and his colleagues reported similar effects in comparing student performance in Texas, which had a relatively strong accountability system, with that in California, which had a relatively weak system (2000). At the same time, other researchers report contrary effects: Audrey Amrein and David Berliner (2002) made such claims in a multistate study, and Walt Haney (2000) persistently doubted the Texas policies.

RECONSIDERING THE RELATIONSHIP

Given this contentious history, how might one understand the relations between policy and practice? In 1941, Carl Friedrich wrote, in a book that few subsequent students of implementation seem to have read, "Public policy, to put it flatly, is a continuous process, the formation of which is inseparable from its execution. Public policy is being formed as it is being executed, and it is likewise being executed as it is being formed" (p. 356). Roughly three decades later, Giandomenico Majone and Aaron Wildavsky offered a less concise but similar view: policy

> shapes implementation by defining the arena in which the process takes place, the identity and role of the principal actors, the range of permissible tools for action, and of course by supplying resources. The underlying theory provides not only the data, information, and hypotheses on which subsequent debate and action will rely, but also, and most importantly, a conceptualization of the policy problem. (Majone & Wildavsky, 1979, p. 174)

These views imply that policy and practice depend on each other. Policies and programs[7] cannot specify practice, but depend on practitioners to realize them in varied situations, while practice depends on policy to frame action and offer resources. Our discussion of the relations between policy and practice begins from these ideas, and from the puzzles about the primacy of policy versus practice that have absorbed researchers since the late 1960s. We discuss the primacy puzzle and, in that analysis, begin to sketch a theory. With the sketch in place, we develop the theory further.

As a theoretical matter, we see the relationship between policy and practice as a dilemma, not a matter of primacy. Governments and private agencies identify problems and propose solutions, whether for welfare, drug use, or weak schools, yet the key problem solvers are the offending, needy, or damaged organizations and people. Governments can devise instruments—incentives,

---

7. The terms are equivalent for our purposes, so we use them interchangeably.

ideas, money, leadership, rules, and more—to encourage implementation. Governments also often have more power than the objects of policy. These things can help, but only if attended to and used well by those who are said to be the problem, and others who may assist. Only welfare recipients and caseworkers can move from welfare to work. Only teachers and students can improve weak schools. Only drug users and counselors can enable addicts to become productive workers.

This dilemma can be difficult to manage even in seemingly simple situations, as when teachers try to help students improve weak compositions. Teachers often see students as the problem, but students are the key problem solvers. Teachers can offer examples, assign exercises, coax, and make suggestions, but they depend on students to use the advice and examples to write better compositions. Teachers have more knowledge, power, and authority, but students' will and ability are their own. Like other higher-ups, teachers depend on the people with problems to solve them, despite the frequent imbalance in power and authority. If students will not do as teachers propose, teachers must settle for what students can or will do.[8]

The policymakers who define problems and devise remedies are rarely the chief problem solvers. They depend on the very people and organizations that have or are the problem to solve it. Yet those that have or are the problem depend on policymakers or others for many of the resources—ideas, incentives, money, and more—that may enable a solution. The dilemma helps to call attention to the tensions between authoritative direction and human agency, and highlights mutual dependence in the relations between policymaking and practice.

Though several researchers refer in one way or another to features of the dilemma, they generally have viewed things in terms of primacy—i.e., from the angle either of those who make and manage direction setting, or of those who put directions into practice. In the example just above, they consider implementation from either the teachers' or the students' angle. From the first vantage point, that of those with governmental power, the main issues appear to concern how control, compliance, and management influence policy outcomes (Bardach, 1977; Mazmanian & Sabatier, 1989; Bardach 1977),[9] while from the second point of view, that of the objects of policy, they appear to concern how the work that implementers do, and the situations in which they do it, influence their response to policy (Berman & McLaughlin, 1978; Elmore, 1979–1980; Lin, 2000; Lipsky, 1980; Berman & McLaughlin 1978; Elmore 1979–1980; Lin 2000). In the example above, the teachers' view might have them facing students who act out, malinger, or fail to use their help, and thus require control, incentives, and other measures. The students' view might have them coping with teachers who control them too closely, take no account of their wishes, or don't grasp what it takes to learn. This example could be replicated, substituting managers and policymakers for teachers, and teachers, social workers, or prison staff for students.

In these discussions of primacy, the issue typically appears as one of political hierarchy, and categories of analysis are attached to political positions. From what many call the "top," the main issues concern how control, compliance, and management influence policy outcomes (Mazmanian & Sabatier 1989; Bardach, 1977; Mazmanian & Sabatier, 1989), while from what

---

8. Though this point has not been central to most analyses of implementation, several scholars have called attention to it. Richard Elmore wrote that "Unless the initiators of a policy can galvanize the energy, attention, and skills of those affected by it . . . the effects of policy are unlikely to be anything but weak and diffuse" (1979–1980, p. 611). Milbrey McLaughlin wrote that policy implementation is a "problem of the smallest unit," and that policies cannot "mandate what matters" (1991a, p. 189; p. 187 respectively). Elmore and McLaughlin (1988) wrote that the fate of reforms ultimately depends on those who are the object of distrust. Ann Chih Lin writes that "Every grand idea and good wish that policymakers have lies in the hands of others who implement them" (2000, p. 14).

9. Top-down theorists often consider policymakers to be those at higher levels of government—i.e., federal and state officials.

is termed the "bottom," they concern the work that implementers do, where they do it, and how these shape policy. Policy and practice are portrayed in conflict, as policymakers attempt to secure compliance from implementers who respond by ignoring, evading, or attempting to buffer themselves from policy.[10]

Though conflict is familiar in the relations between policy and practice, positional differences do not capture the most salient features of the relationship. Policymakers seek to exercise power as they try to lead society and solve problems by changing service delivery in government and private sectors. Typically they also craft such actions to help secure or maintain political office, and to reinforce the legitimacy of policy and the relevant agencies. As policymakers try to affect service delivery, they also try to advance their political interests and legitimate their actions. The exercise of power touches all three domains. Yet the changes in service delivery for which policy often calls imply change in the practices that deliver services, or in the services that clients use, or in how they use them, or some combination of these. The sharper the departures from conventional practice that policy urges, the more radical are the entailed changes for practitioners and service recipients, and the more the changes place practice at risk of failure. For more ambitious policies require practitioners to acquire new capabilities, and to unlearn present capabilities which sharpens the dilemma. More ambitious policies create even more incompetence among the practitioners whose incompetence already is implied in the policies' aims; if new competencies cannot be acquired, practice will fail.

Practice failure can become a problem for policy, for if policy success depends on practice, policies that disturb practice without improving it can be a threat. The more uncertain practitioners are about what to do, the more the risk of implementation failure, or service delivery disruption, or resistance by practitioners or clients, or some combination of these. That can erode trust in practice, and because the problem can be traced to policy, contagion can threaten the legitimacy of policies or programs, and even the authors' political interests. Such things play out in different ways, often in anticipated actions, reactions, and adjustments before matters spill into public view. But however they happen, the more policy puts practice at risk of failure, the more likely it is to damage the legitimacy and political interests of practitioners, policymakers, or both.

Policy and practice thus contain opportunities for cooperation and conflict. Practitioners depend on policymakers and others in the environment for resources to assist their work, including policy implementation, and policymakers depend on practice for success. Practitioners have incentives to implement policy, for policymakers exercise authority and control resources. Yet policymakers have incentives to adjust to practitioners' capabilities, because failure in practice can affect the interests and legitimacy of policymakers. This web of mutual dependence can encourage the trust, collegiality, cooperation, and communication which can enable effective implementation, but the more that policies depart from conventional practice, the greater the chance of conflict between policymakers and practitioners, for such policies enlarge the gap between the practices that implementers have mastered and those that policy implies they should learn, and increase the chances of practice failure.

In the next section we discuss the resources—skill, knowledge, incentives, and money, among others—that can widen or narrow that gap, and thus influence the chances for cooperation or conflict. We note here only that as practitioners' resource needs grow, so do the fiscal and political demands on policymakers and others in the environment, and that helps to increase the chance of conflict.

---

10. Commentators often portray this as conflict over goals.

These theoretical points have an empirical aspect, for "top" and "bottom" in hierarchies turn out to be rubbery categories. Arguing about which has primacy obscures key features in the relations between policy and practice. Title I of the 1965 ESEA was a federal program, so one might assume that viewing its implementation from the top would begin and end in Washington. But this program devolves extensive authority for program decisions to states: they allocate funds, screen local applications, and assist and evaluate local programs. The federal government is the top agency for states, and they are the federal agency's bottom of first resort. But those agencies in Albany and Sacramento also are the top agencies for local education agencies (LEAs), even as the school principals' top in those LEAs is the central office, and the teachers' top is the principal. In modern societies, in which political organization grows ever more dense and elaborate, one agency's top is more and more likely to be another's bottom.

The problems of control and compliance that researchers identify with the policymaking top also are problems for organizations and individuals that researchers identify with the bottom, and for those in between. The problems of control and compliance that state Title I offices have, vis-à-vis LEA central offices, very closely resemble the problems of control and compliance that LEA central offices have with schools. Similarly, LEA central office workers who deal with problems of control and compliance vis-à-vis principals, teachers, and students also must manage their work as "street-level" bureaucrats, working at the bottom, vis-à-vis central and state agencies. The roles that have been identified with opposition between top and bottom actually are mixed together in offices at many levels. Nearly all of those embroiled at all levels of policy and practice are both central controllers and street-level bureaucrats, trying to influence those for whom they make policy while trying to negotiate for themselves with those who make policy for them. They often occupy these different roles at the same time, with respect to the same policy or program, working as street-level bureaucrats and policymakers at the same time.[11] The dilemma that we sketched earlier is presented in many locations, and many individuals and agencies experience it from both sides.

There are some limiting cases: the central government is subordinate to no higher domestic agency, though it depends on many, and students exercise no positional authority over others on whom they depend for services. But nearly all others who relate policy and practice are at neither extreme: they try to influence those who depend on them for resources and guidance while at the same time attempting to respond to those who seek to influence them by offering guidance and resources.

In these cases, the key to the relations between policy and practice is not positions in hierarchies, but mutual dependence, and the cooperation or conflict that it engenders.[12] Which it is depends less on positional authority than on the distance between policy and practice, and on the resources that might help to bridge that distance. The central problem of implementation, for policymakers and practitioners, is whether and how to bridge that gap. The central questions for analysts are what contributes to the distance, and what resources might help to bridge it.

Our answer to both questions turns on four factors. One is the aims that policies set: some set very modest and uncomplicated aims, while others set ambitious and complex aims. The further

---

11. Some political scientists use principal-agent theory and its hierarchy to explain intraorganizational issues (see, for example, Brehm & Gates 1997). The theory recognizes control and compliance problems at several points along an implementation path, which might imply that a "bottom" can also be a "top." But it treats these relations as layered and in isolation from each other. In our formulation, individuals or groups of individuals can be simultaneously a top and a bottom.

12. For a helpful and somewhat parallel discussion, see Elmore (2005).

aims depart from conventional practice, the greater the resources—social, human, and fiscal—that will be needed to realize them in practice.

Those resources are of three sorts. One comprises the instruments that policymakers and managers deploy to support change in practice—our second factor. They include money, mandates for action, incentives to comply with requirements, flexibility to adapt policy to local conditions, ideas (including everything from visions of a new state of affairs to systematic study of implementation and effects), to inform implementers' understanding and actions, and combinations of these and others. These are socially created tools, intended to encourage assent to policy and to help realize aims in practice.[13] They intend to mobilize the capability to implement, and thus to sustain policymakers' political interests and their legitimacy.

Another set of resources is commonly referred to as "capacity," though we prefer capability.[14] This is the third factor, which refers to the resources that practitioners and others bring to policy; capability includes interests, values, will, skill, and knowledge, among other things. These categories mirror several of those used to characterize instruments, which is no accident, for when instruments are effective, it is partly because they help to mobilize the capabilities that would enable the practitioners or organizations that are or have been the problem to turn themselves into the solution.

A last set of resources arises in the environments of practice, which is our fourth factor. Environments play at least two roles. Policy instruments and capabilities are formed in and operate through environments, hence are shaped by them. In the United States, for example, most elementary school teachers learn little about the subjects that they will teach, because of the professional environments of higher education and the political environments of government. These environments limit the capabilities that teachers bring to the implementation of academically ambitious curricula or demanding academic standards. In addition, environments are congeries of agencies and individuals, which can enable or constrain relations between policy and practice. For instance, familiarity with each other's work is a significant influence on policymakers' and practitioners' ability to communicate and understand what is at stake between them. That familiarity is influenced by such features of the environment as the size and organization of political systems. Educational policy in the United States is made by a great variety of agencies in a very large society: roughly 15,000 local school boards, 50 state governments (which include legislatures, governors, and state school agencies), the federal legislature and executive, and an extraordinary array of local, state, and federal judiciaries. Each state sets its own finance and curriculum policies, as well as standards for teacher education and certification. Nearly all of these agencies also interpret and implement policy made by other government agencies. Policymakers in these agencies also are influenced by and influence many other non-government organizations, including parent advocacy groups, research and analysis organizations, churches, disciplinary groups, professional associations, institutions of higher education, and many others. In contrast, France is a much smaller nation-state with a highly centralized school system, in which most important decisions are made in Paris. Though France is larger than many nation-states, centralization

---

13. We use instruments in a similar sense to McDonnell and Elmore (1987). They refer to policy instruments as "the mechanisms that translate substantive policy goals (e.g., improved student achievement, higher quality entering teachers) into actions" (p. 134). They do not address either adaptability or instruments' salience for practice. For a discussion of the former, see McLaughlin (1991a). For a discussion of the latter, see Cohen and Hill (2001, pp. 2–8, pp. 148–151, pp. 166–167, p. 180, p. 184).

14. Warehouses have capacity, while people and organizations have capabilities.

reduces the chance of fragmentation that is endemic in the United States, and increases the chance for understanding between policymakers and practitioners. Those chances increase even more in Singapore, a small and centralized nation-state that is roughly the size of Rhode Island and has one centrally managed school system. Size and fragmentation increase the costs of communication, while coherence and compactness reduce them. Less understanding between policymakers and practitioners reduces the chances to see common interests and interdependence, and increases the chances of conflict.

The four factors interact. One key influence on any policy's success in practice is the extent of consistency among its aims, the capabilities that practitioners require to implement them, the instruments deployed to encourage revised practice, and the resources available in the environment. There is, however, no One Best Form of consistency, for aims, instruments, capability, and environments combine variously.

We discuss these four factors, and their interactions, below.

AIMS

Other things being equal, the greater the change in practice that policies seek, the more difficult it is to manage the dilemma of implementation. Some policies seek only modest extension of current practices: they add five minutes a day to the 10 already spent on composition, or include a new wetland in existing shoreline preservation, or spread extant Medicare benefits to new patients. Others call for change that has little technical content; they shift school schedules, or require patients to communicate with nurses rather than doctors. Their difficulty varies with the extent to which the changes depart from current practice, or encounter resistance. Other policies have technically more ambitious aims, like replacing computation with conceptual mathematics, or adding new environmental regulation; they depart more from current practice, and make the revision of practice more difficult (Spillane, 2000).

The revision of practice often is complicated by ambiguous policy aims. In some cases that is because aims are general: policies often set objectives for organizations that are so varied that very specific aims would be unworkable. In these cases, mutual dependence leads policymakers to take certain features of practice into account. In some other cases, policies are ambiguous because they envision states of affairs so novel that they can be imagined but not specified in much detail. In still other cases, ambiguity results when coalitions use vague phrases to paper over differences. Majone and Wildavsky wrote that "In most policies of interest, objectives are characteristically . . . vague (because that is how we can agree to proceed without having agreed also on exactly what to do)" (1979, pp. 168–169). Federal education policy typically has been general and thus ambiguous, to manage both state and local variability and differences within coalitions. Yet such useful ambiguity affects relations with practice, for "the more general an idea and the more adaptable it is to a range of circumstances, the more likely it is to be realized in some form, but the less likely it is to emerge as intended in practice" (Majone & Wildavsky, 1979, p. 176). The generality and ambiguity that attract policymakers make it difficult for practitioners to know what is expected of them (Brodkin, 1990).

That is likely not to be a problem if pressure for results is modest. That was true for most federal education policies for decades, in part because of the environment. Schooling is central to social policy in the United States, yet it has been limited in scope and strength. Though several European nations directly address social inequality with health care, education, incomes, and tax policies, the United States restrained social policy to modest welfare, health, unemployment insurance, and old-age pensions (Katznelson & Weir, 1985). One reason was that public schools were thought to guarantee equal opportunity and reduce the need for other intervention (Katznelson & Weir, 1985; Weir, Orloff, & Skocpol, 1988). Yet economic liberalism and skepticism about government kept schools and governments weak: states delegated central functions like test and text writing to private firms, and local control created enormous economic and social inequality among school systems. Education was central to social policy, but it was offered modestly and unequally by weak state and federal governments.

Schooling thus has had a paradoxical role in U.S. social policy: strong in principle, popular belief, and policy, but relatively weak in practice. Access to schools was seen as the key to opportunity, and the United States opened access earlier and more broadly than most other developed nations; yet schools were modestly and quite unequally supported. There was less to access than met the eye, since schools' capabilities to equalize opportunity were very uneven, and far from commensurate with either the rhetoric of policy or popular belief.

Policy reflected that dualism. Title I of the 1965 ESEA was both a radical departure and a modest initiative. On the radical side, it aimed to improve schools for poor children, and led to more federal influence on states and schools. School improvement might not seem radical compared to income transfers or tuition vouchers, yet in the mid-1960s ESEA involved Washington in schools, leading federal officials to try to help schools improve, to advise states and localities, and to evaluate their progress.[15] These relatively strong aspects of Title I led local educators to try to improve schools despite pervasive inequality and weak knowledge, and that was far from current practice: school improvement was unknown, and state and federal intervention was rare. That sharpened the dilemma, for practitioners at all levels of the federal system faced large new tasks with small capabilities.

Yet Title I was also weak. Its formula grant came close to being general aid, designed in part to restrain central influence. The federal government had to decide how much to spend, apportion it, and mail checks, while localities had only to spend the money on a broad category of school resources for a particular purpose, and fill out applications to that effect. These things were familiar: Congress knew how to appropriate funds, and educators knew how to spend on schools. Distributing funds was a bit novel for the Office of Education and required learning, yet it was familiar federal work. This aspect of Title I pressed implementers beyond extant skill and knowledge, but not so far as to make it very difficult to manage the dilemma.

Title I's ambiguous aims reflected that tension, and implementation was an exercise in managing the ambiguity.[16] For three decades there were cautious federal efforts to improve schools with something close to general aid, but Presidents Clinton and Bush made Title I the core of their effort to drive state and local practice with standards-based reform. The aims of Title I changed from vague pronouncements about improved schools for poor children to more specific requirements for students' academic progress. When the Improving America's Schools Act of 1994 (IASA) and NCLB focused policy on educational achievement, they seemed to sweep ambiguity out of federal and state education policy.

Yet great ambiguity remains. Most important decisions about the actual content of the new aims were delegated to the states, and, in some cases, to localities. Thus a key provision of NCLB—the criterion by which schools are judged to have achieved "proficiency"—varies among states, which choose their own tests and set their own proficiency standards. What appears to be

---

15. Michael Kirst, interview, September 1995.

16. These paradoxical features of Title I closely resembled much state school policy, in which weak school finance equalization policies were seen as powerful means to equalize educational opportunity.

unprecedented clarity in Title I's aims dissolves into a blur as states decide (Olson, 2002; Saulny, 2005; Olson 2002). Ambiguity also increased with arguments about whether tests can measure learning with sufficient validity to decide about students' proficiency.

These political and technical sources of ambiguity are little different today than in 1965. States have most of the political authority in U.S. public education: in 1965 that was displayed in the vague aims in Title I's legislative language, while in 1994 and 2001 it was displayed in the delegation of aim setting to states. These were two different ways to cede crucial decisions to the states, thus creating openings for different solutions to the same problem. The uncertain validity of tests to measure students' achievement was known in 1965, but it was not salient to policy because Title I did not aim explicitly at tests or use them for accountability. Doubts about tests only surfaced intermittently in succeeding decades, when every-five-year evaluations sought to estimate the effects of Title I, and Congress debated the program's fate. By 2003, however, tests were in the foreground because they had been made the central aim of Title I. All the ambiguities that researchers had known about for decades became highly salient to policy, and burst into public debate.

One source of ambiguity is new, though, for as standards-based reform pressed policy further into practice, the ambiguity of policy aims increased. Learning is much more complex than federal funds transfer, and Americans are deeply divided about what is important to teach and learn, and how best to do so. Teaching and learning also are not well understood, certainly not well enough to scientifically specify the most effective ways to teach and learn multiplication or composition to a great range of students in a great range of circumstances. Standards-based reform opened up large domains of ambiguity when it moved aggressively into the weakly understood and contested domain of instruction. Though ambiguity is likely not to be a problem as long as pressure for results is modest, standards-based reforms coupled ambiguous aims to rising pressure for results. That increased the potential for conflict between federal officials and those in states and localities, but the sweeping delegation of key decisions enabled states and localities to tailor policy aims to their circumstances and helped to manage the conflict. The arguments about NCLB accountability suggest intense conflict, yet the actions suggest mutual adjustment. Conflict and cooperation coexist.

The further policy aims depart from conventional practice, the more acute the dilemma becomes, because such aims reduce practitioners' capabilities and increase the risk of practice failure. Ambiguous aims also can influence the dilemma by making it difficult for practitioners to know how to do what policy proposes. But this effect depends on the extent to which policy presses for results.

Whatever the aims of policy, the resources to achieve them lie elsewhere: in practitioners' capabilities, in the strength and salience of the instruments that policy deploys, and in the environments of policy and practice. As Ann Lin writes, the incentives to reconcile policy and practice mean that policy is "a joint project" (Lin, 2000, p. 164).

POLICY INSTRUMENTS

Most policies create a gap with practice by moving at least a bit beyond it, but policies cannot succeed unless that gap is bridged. Doing so depends in part on the instruments that policies deploy. They offer funds, mandate or forbid actions, create incentives to comply, offer flexibility to adapt to local conditions, and deploy ideas to inform practice. These and other instruments are socially created tools; their aim is to encourage assent to policy and offer resources to change practice. They are best thought of as the capabilities that policy brings to its relations with practice. Since success tends to sustain policymakers' interests and legitimacy, while failure tends to erode them, such instruments are political as well as technical, and their invention and operation is shaped in part by political considerations.

Instruments vary in strength, or their influence in practice, and in salience, or how closely they connect with what must happen in practice to achieve policy aims. Strong but not salient instruments will be less effective, for they tell practitioners to do something but leave them to figure out what and how. Strong incentives to achieve aims that are far beyond most implementers' capabilities are a case in point. Instruments that are salient for practice but weak also are unlikely to be effective, for while they offer help that bears on practice, they exert little influence. Technical assistance to produce performances that implementers had no reason to produce is a case in point (Fuhrman & Elmore, 1992; 1995). Instruments that are strong and salient are more likely to help, but they are difficult to craft, and become more so as policy departs further from conventional practice.

Strength and salience are not inherent in instruments; they are instead partly a function of the distance between aims and capabilities: instruments which are strong and salient for policies that depart only a bit from conventional practice are unlikely to be equally strong and salient for policies that depart much more dramatically. To illustrate these points, consider the instruments that four federal programs deploy. Impact Aid helps schools that serve families at federal installations, and three instruments suffice: money, flexibility to spend it, and occasional oversight with audits. The government compensates for a burden imposed but, since it seeks no change in behavior, it creates no incompetence. Flexibility was essential and noncontroversial, and was feasible since no significant change in practice was required.

Flexibility delegates responsibilities to practitioners, either because policymakers want to avoid conflict or because circumstances require adjustments to differences in local capability or other circumstances. This instrument addresses the dilemma of implementation, for it promises to increase the chance of success by delegating agency for policy to practice. Allowing such adaptation could mobilize support for policy as well, inviting practitioners to engage policy on terms that suit their values and interests. Like other instruments, however, the effects of flexibility depend on how practitioners use it. That, in turn, depends on other policy instruments and on practitioners' capability. The 1994 reauthorization of Title I (IASA) set very ambitious new aims, including greatly improved academic work for disadvantaged students. It required states to devise and use strong academic standards and tests that were keyed to the standards, and to make schools accountable for students' performance. At the same time, the legislation gave states great flexibility to devise standards and tests, and to set the student performance criteria for which they would be accountable. That flexibility did not produce deep engagement with the policy in the last half of the 1990s: a few states continued with reforms they already had under way, but most superficially implemented Title I. State and local capabilities to devise standards and improve instruction were far from commensurate with IASA's ambitious aims, and flexibility was not coupled to other instruments. IASA offered little assistance to improve practitioners' capability, and no potent incentives for states and localities to devise demanding standards and tests, or to set stiff requirements for student performance. The Clinton administration faced a hostile House of Representatives and opposition in many states, and federal officials did not think they had the influence to push states to take a more aggressive approach to changing practice. They expected political and legislative losses elsewhere if they pressed harder.[17] Weak policy instruments, modest

---

17. Those estimates were mistaken. At the end of the second Clinton administration, Michael Cohen was appointed Assistant Secretary of Education for Elementary and Secondary Education; he vigorously enforced IASA's requirements, and more states complied.

capability in practice, and political dependence combined with flexibility to promote weak responses in practice.[18]

The salience and strength of policy instruments vary not only with other instruments and capability, but also with policies and environments. Title VI of the 1964 Civil Rights Act (CRA) sought to change behavior on America's most painful social problem by withholding federal funds from agencies that discriminated on the basis of race. This instrument was salient because money is essential to schools' operation; it was relatively strong, for once Title I began, federal funds became a part of school budgets: jobs and operations depended on them. But federal officials hesitated to use it, for they

> soon learned that the withholding of funds is a two-edged sword. The recalcitrant state agency is punished, but the Federal program is also wounded through loss of vital local support, political attacks, and general disruption of cooperative relationships needed for the successful operation of other programs. (Orfield, 1969, p. 7)

The threat of fund loss was salient, but it was only intermittently strong because of federal dependence on success in practice and on political support. That limited how far federal officials would push practice, which resistant Southern officials quickly sensed.

The salience and strength of policy instruments also vary with the actions at which policy aims. Title VI was relatively effective for such acts as denying African American children access to "White" schools, but less so for segregated classes or teachers' treatment of students. For the latter had something to do with teachers' beliefs and attitudes, and with common, sometimes nonracial, ability grouping. Fund loss was not as salient to teachers' beliefs and attitudes as to system budgets. In addition, withholding funds was relatively blunt: it was relatively strong in dealing with problems that infected entire jurisdictions, but less so in dealing with complex problems like racially imbalanced classrooms. A tool that was salient and strong for one situation was not for another that seemed quite similar.

The more complex the change that policies seek, the more difficult it is to devise salient and strong instruments. The curriculum reforms of the late 1950s and early 1960s urged ambitious change, yet offered little assistance to practice, apart from limited summer workshops. Some teachers could apply and take the time, but there was room for only a few of those who needed help. Most teachers had no opportunities to learn about how students might respond, how teachers might learn the new material, and how they might teach in light of students' responses. If one reason was the lack of many workshops, another was the lack of suitable instruments to enable teachers' learning. For example, there was no curriculum for teachers that built on the student curriculum, to help teachers learn how to use the student curriculum well. If it had existed it might have included examples of students' work, analyses of the thinking involved, and how

---

18. Some readers may see our analysis as a version of principal-agent theory, but we do not. The two chief components of principal-agent models, as applied to government agencies, are goal conflict and information asymmetry (Waterman and Meier, 1998). The rest of principal-agent theory and application builds on those components; it often is said that without goal conflict or information asymmetry, there isn't an interesting principal-agent story. Goal conflict is pervasive in the United States, but fundamental implementation problems would persist even if goals or preferences were perfectly aligned throughout the school system, and even if all principals were privy to all agents' information. The problems of aligning implementers' capabilities, policy goals, and instruments can be exacerbated by goal conflict and/or information asymmetry, but they are independent of goal conflict and/or information asymmetry. Thus a central problem for Title I and many other policies and programs is that they have goals that few if any have the capabilities to implement, and for which policy or program instruments typically offer tepid and partly salient support, at best. In such situations, principals are unlikely to behave differently if they know everything that agents know; for neither group knows nearly enough to implement policies broadly and effectively.

accomplished teachers used the materials and students' work to improve practice. It would have been difficult to create such an instrument, for considerable expertise in teaching and learning would have been needed, along with professional and political influence to gain support and encourage use. No government or private agencies tried to do such work, and it seems that few of those who built student curricula could even imagine what to do; they wrote the student materials and let teachers cope.[19] That sharpened the dilemma for practitioners, inviting them to produce performances which were far from current practice, yet provided little help and few incentives.

The strength and salience of policy instruments do not inhere in the instruments, but depend on how the instruments relate to practitioners' capabilities, to the actions at which policies aim, and to the environments of policy and practice. It can be difficult to align these relations. The instruments that IASA and NCLB have deployed seem strong, historically considered: clear academic standards, tests aligned with the standards, and schools' accountability for students' performance go far beyond Title I's initial instruments. In 1965, the key instrument was the formula grant, which targeted money to education for poor children in particular schools. In its time that was a sharp departure, but it was a virtual entitlement: once the formula was written and a federal appropriation made, state and local grants were set. States and LEAs had to write proposals and offer assurances, but their grants depended less on the proposals' merits than on the incidence of poverty and a legislative intent that nearly all districts should receive funds. There were few incentives to change practice, and little help. The formula grant was well aligned with a legislative intent to offer something like general aid, but not with the intent to improve schools. Funds alone would not be strong or salient for that purpose.

That was because resources' effects depend on practitioners' use, which also holds for IASA and NCLB. Standards, tests, and accountability appear much stronger than the 1965 originals, but their effects depend no less on practitioners' use. That is a key problem for NCLB, because its instruments are not very salient to the practices at which they aim. Teaching and learning must change if Title I is to succeed, yet NCLB's instruments do not reach these practices very well. Academic standards can be a useful frame for practice, but few teachers can turn them into lessons that advance learning. They can exemplify policy goals, but not in the detail, or with the salience to instruction, that would enable most teachers and students to use them. That makes the dilemma of implementation more acute, and increases the likelihood that practitioners will respond in ways that have limited educational value. Many states responded by adopting tests of basic skills, to create relatively easy outcome measures. In these cases the tests are used as a sort of curriculum, but are likely to leave many students with narrow and superficial knowledge.

Incentives also are essential to learning, but are more likely to be effective if they are salient to instruction. The incentives attached to accountability in standards-based reform, however, do not operate on instruction; they operate on states, and through them, on districts, and through them, on schools, and through them, on teachers. Moreover, there are no incentives for students to perform, even though they are as important to outcomes as teachers. The target of accountability incentives is not instruction, but students' test scores, and the incentives operate outside instruction. They affect teachers through many layers of government; if they operate on students at all, they do so through teachers and schools. These features reduce the incentives' salience for instruction, and that reduces the probability that they will greatly improve instruction. In such schemes of multilevel government accountability it would be impossible to attach incentives for performance to a particular instructional design, unless the design was a part of the accountabil-

---

19. Peter Dow, in *Schoolhouse Politics: Lessons from the Sputnik Era* (1993), offers an account of these problems in connection with his analysis of one such curriculum—Man: A Course of Study.

ity scheme itself. That would have been a political and technical near-impossibility in the United States in 2000.

Though some of NCLB's instruments are strong, they are not salient to the practices that could realize the policy. That sharpens the dilemma of implementation, and is likely to encourage responses that do not help to improve instruction. Teachers may try to reduce the risk of failure by boosting outcomes without improving learning: they prep students for tests, help them to cheat, alter scores, or inflate average scores by keeping low-performing students away. Such responses are to be expected if policies set implausible aims, or if they set plausible aims but fail to deploy instruments that are strong and salient enough to support their achievement, or if instruments are strong but not salient, or strong and salient but operate on incapable practitioners. In such cases, attaching consequences to performance increases the chances that practitioners will try to reduce risk by complying without improving practice.[20] It is reasonable to expect practitioners to act roughly rationally, given any set of aims and instruments, and they are likely to try to reduce risk if they are required to do things that they cannot.

What practitioners can and cannot do, however, depends in part on their capabilities.

CAPABILITY

The resources that individual practitioners bring to policy arise from four sources: values, interests, dispositions, and skill and knowledge. These resources constitute capability. But capability is not a fixed trait. Capabilities that are sufficient for policies which depart only a bit from conventional practice, with some support from policy instruments, are unlikely to be sufficient for policies that depart much more dramatically, especially if there is not strong support from policy instruments. Capability is a function of the distance between policy aims and instruments, given some level of conventional practice.

Values are one source of capability; policy aims may offend the values of practitioners or organizations. Teaching evolution deeply offends some educators, who believe that it introduces incorrect or evil ideas, while not teaching evolution deeply offends others. Such values influence capability by enhancing or weakening the will to implement policy, or by impeding or enhancing acquisition of the skills and knowledge required to implement. Values vary with environments. Aversion to evolution is more likely in the U.S. South, while support is more likely in affluent urban areas. Policies that reduce speed limits are more likely to be accepted in densely populated and urbanized states, and less likely to be accepted in states in the wide-open spaces of the American West, where such limits are thought to infringe on basic liberties. Even when programs have no prominent value content, they come into play. Adding 10 minutes of daily writing may reduce recess or music, requiring practitioners to adjust their priorities, not in principle but in the daily conduct of valued work. Such conflict can reduce practitioners' will to do as policies propose, just as consistency can increase it (Lin, 2000).

Practitioners' interests are a second source of capability. A policy that requires firms to cease dumping PCBs in rivers may cost them money or market share. Requiring educators to test students and track their progress is costly. Even if manufacturers or educators agree with the policies, implementation can damage their interests by reducing profits, cutting products, or changing work. That can diminish the will to implement, just as policies that enhance practitioners' interests can reinforce it. Rewarding corporations for protecting the environment, by trading

---

20. Traditional notions of information asymmetry do not seem to help here. Though gaming is one reaction to incentives *sans* capability, this does not hinge on agents' private information and how it enables them to shirk, drift, sabotage, and otherwise pervert democratic processes.

pollution-reducing practices, is intended to enhance their will to advance policy by enhancing their interest, just as paying teachers to learn more about their subjects could increase their will to improve instruction, by showing them how more knowledge could advance their professional interest in student learning. Such interests vary with environments. Towns that are situated on polluted rivers far downstream from the pollution source are likely to have a greater interest in the creation and implementation of remedial policies than those that are situated at the source, where families depend on polluters for jobs and towns depends on them for taxes and economic development.

Knowledge and skill are a third source of capability. Motorists use their skill in driving and knowledge of speeding fines to deal with speed limits, and judges use their knowledge of federal and state sentencing guidelines, and their skill at weighing evidence, to decide criminal cases. When policies urge change in practice, they often create incompetence by requiring practitioners to do things that they do not know how to do (Bardach, 1977). To deal with this problem, policies sometimes require or support education for practitioners.

Dispositions are a fourth source of capability. Teachers with very similar values, interests, and knowledge nonetheless approach their work quite differently: some are warmly engaged and eager to work, while others are diffident and less eager. Similarly, some managers are aggressive in pursuit of their objectives, while others are more timid. Such differences contribute to capability by influencing the will to work, the motivation to learn, and engagement with practice.

Organizations and environments influence capability as well. One example is that affluent school districts typically employ better educated teachers, who use resources more effectively than their colleagues in less advantaged districts. Another is that schools with better leadership, which also are more often found in affluent communities, appear to make better use of teachers' knowledge and skill. Schools in less affluent communities, by contrast, have more staff turnover, which reduces capability by impeding the development of stable knowledge among practitioners. Since policies operate in environments, such differences count. Title I, for instance, is a modest federal supplement to state and local operations: the entire federal contribution is now between 8 and 10 percent of total local revenues. The program's influence in practice thus depends at least as much on what local school organizations bring to bear in implementing the program as on the resources that the program brings. Yet states and local school systems have very unequal capabilities, owing to very large differences in finance, in family education, and in income; many of the states and localities that need Title I the most have the least capability to bring to implementation. The program's effect is shaped by the very inequalities that it aims to ameliorate.

Organizations and environments also influence capability by enabling or impeding the exchange of knowledge about practice, and about the interests, values, and knowledge that inform practice. One case in point concerns cooperative practice, for schools appear to be more effective when educators work together, share aims and professional norms, and build knowledge; learning also can be more effective when students work together (McLaughlin & Talbert, 2001; Rosenholtz, 1991; Spillane, 1999). Another case in point concerns the size and complexity of service delivery organizations, for the larger and more complex they are, the more difficult it is to exchange knowledge about practice. Other things being equal, for example, implementing a school improvement policy is likely to be less difficult in a medium sized subdistrict of New York City than in the entire city, for the communication, learning, and oversight would be more difficult for the entire city (Elmore & Burney, 1997). In these cases and many others, the behavior or attributes of organizations affect capability by way of their influence on individuals in the organizations. For as organizations grow larger and more complex, maintaining or improving performance requires more coordination and communication.[21] As societies grow more complex, the population of public and private agencies grows. They send more and more messages, each originating in or filtering through a distinctive situation. They reduce the chances for understanding, for as more messages flow through such fragmented fields, the costs of working together rises (Cohen and & Spillane, 1992).

Capability is also an attribute of organizations and environments. Some school systems use inspectors to monitor and improve instruction. Teachers' promotion to tenure and school headships depends on proven excellence in practice, and the resulting capability can help to sustain or improve individuals' performance. In addition, the inspectorates become repositories of capability: they institutionalize knowledge, skill, and the disposition to maintain or improve practice. Organizations can also degrade capability. In the United States, excellence in teaching is not required to maintain teaching or administrative posts, and there are no inspectorates. To the extent that it exists, instructional expertise is concentrated among classroom teachers. The lack of such capability outside classrooms makes it more difficult to sustain or improve performance inside them.

Several points flow from this discussion. One is that capability is specific to tasks, or sorts of tasks; there appears to be little or no generic capability. When policies propose to change practice they create incompetence, but the "incompetence is not, of course, a trait like having brown eyes. It is a description of a relationship between a task or function in the situation up to a given, though ultimately arbitrary, standard of some sort" (Bardach, 1977, p. 126). If policy moves only a modest distance from conventional practice, it often is feasible for practitioners to overcome their newly acquired incompetence and acquire new capabilities on their own, or with a little help. But the further from conventional work policies move, the more incompetence they create. More capabilities would have to be unlearned and learned, with more help, if practitioners were to become competent.

A second point is that practitioners' capability arises not from a single attribute—skill and knowledge are most often mistaken for the whole—but from combinations of knowledge, values, interests, and dispositions. Practitioners are likely to find it more difficult to acquire or use knowledge when policies negatively affect their interests or values, or when they are not disposed to engage with practice. Values can also help to create interests, as when lobbying for charter schools yields enabling legislation that creates networks of charter sponsors, educators, and parents, which become a significant interest group in state politics. Capability subsists in such interactions, and is maintained, enhanced, or degraded by them.

Third, organizations contain and enhance capability by enabling and institutionalizing the exchange of knowledge about practice and about the interests, values, and knowledge that inform practice. Or they inhibit capability by impeding such exchange. Such capability is perhaps a form of social capital that grows when organizations enable and institutionalize work together on practice (Bryk & Schneider, 2002).

Finally, because the elements of capability interact, policymakers may have more than one point of leverage. Policies often try to mobilize knowledge and skill indirectly, by offering incentives for certain results and leaving it to implementers to exert or acquire the required capability. That can work if practitioners have or can easily acquire it, but the elements of capability are not

---

21. There is a reciprocal relationship: organizations that have many highly capable managers and practitioners find it much easier to mobilize collective capability, and those that can mobilize capability make it easier for individual practitioners to maintain or improve performance, and vice versa.

interchangeable. Policies that offer incentives alone are less likely to work if practitioners cannot easily learn what they need to know. Recent standards-based policies make schools accountable for student performance, and reward or penalize them accordingly. A few states set relatively demanding targets, but most set more modest goals. Teachers in both sorts of states acquire an enhanced interest in students' performance, but those in states with less demanding targets require only a modest increase in skill and knowledge. They need only to work harder, or in more focused ways, and learn on their own or from each other (Skrla, Scheurich, & Johnson, 2000). But states with tougher requirements create more incompetence, and imply a need for more professional learning, which teachers are less able to do on their own. As policies depart further from current practice, interest alone is less likely to provoke improved knowledge, skill, or practice. Policies that press practitioners to produce performances for which they lack capability sharpen the dilemma of implementation and increase the chances that practitioners will attempt to comply without actually improving students' learning.

Capability is relational: it waxes and wanes in interactions among the aims that are set by policy, the instruments that are deployed, and practitioners' interests, values, skills, knowledge, and dispositions. These interactions are situated in schools, governments, and other organizations, which also affect capability. One can speak accurately of capability only if one speaks in relational terms, and one can shape capability only by shaping those relations.

CONCLUSION

A dilemma lies at the heart of relations between policy and practice: policies seek to correct problems in the definition or delivery of social and educational services, yet the key problem solvers are the failing schools, welfare clients, or drug addicts that policy identifies as the problem. The success of policy depends on the flawed clients, practitioners, and organizations that policy would correct. The central puzzle for policy and practice is how to enable these people and organizations to change and improve. Policies may offer incentives, ideas, money, and more, yet they will help only if they are used well by those said to be the problem, and others assisting them.

This view is useful in several ways. For one thing, dilemmas can be managed more or less well, but rarely resolved. For another, it helps to highlight key elements in the relationship between policy and practice—aims, instruments, capability, and environments—and to show that the influence of each depends on the others. It also reveals the role of consistency in these relations: for instance, the strength of incentives to cooperate depends on how far policy aims depart from practice, on how strong and salient the instruments are, on practitioners' capabilities, and on support in the environment. The less consistency there is among these things, the less likely it is that policy and practice can get what they need from each other.

The dilemma also reveals the importance of mutual dependence: policymakers rely on practitioners for their success, and practitioners rely on policymakers for resources and guidance. Both have incentives to cooperate. Policymakers' legitimacy and political interests depend on policies' fate in practice, so policymakers have reasons to accommodate practitioners' concerns and capabilities. Practitioners have incentives to execute policy, for it arises in legitimate authority, it can offer valuable resources, and failure could weaken the interests and legitimacy of practice. But the further policy departs from extant practice, the more likely is conflict. In either case, one cannot understand policy without reference to practice.

The dilemma also highlights an enduring tension between policy and practice. For example, standards-based policies assume that state and local school systems have served poor children badly, and try to take forceful measures to get them to correct the problem. From this perspective, NCLB is on the mark in its use of tough instruments to mobilize educators' will to improve, to identify weak professionals, and to spur schools to perform. Yet if educators are to improve weak schools, it makes sense for policy to offer the assistance, encouragement, and trust that they need to do the job. Advocates of the first view tend to see advocates of the second as apologists for those who have long failed poor children, and who would defeat policies like NCLB by allowing weak performance. Advocates of the second view tend to see partisans of the first as inflexible enforcers who are likely to defeat school improvement by driving practitioners into mechanistic compliance. It is easier to agree that policy depends on practice than to decide which view is correct.

The dilemma implies that each view has a portion of truth. The people and organizations that have been the problem often are complicit in social damage, and cannot simply be trusted to do the right thing; it makes sense to treat them with some skepticism and call them to account. Yet because they are the chief available agents of improvement, it also makes sense to give them the help and trust that could enable them to improve. In a reasonable world, policymakers and practitioners would choose both, for short of creating entirely new systems of service provision, policies would be more likely to improve practice if they blended the two approaches. One example is policy that combines instruments that require performance with instruments that are calibrated to practitioners' capabilities to improve.[22]

There is a sense in which recent education policy did choose both. IASA and NCLB have left localities and states to devise their own tests and standards; IASA even let them shape the schedule of compliance. Both statutes have deployed instruments that trust those who had or were the problem to solve it, as they see fit. NCLB insists on strict compliance on a breathtaking schedule, but it delegates key decisions about compliance to states and localities. In these respects, IASA and NCLB embody the mutual dependence that we discussed earlier. That dependence creates incentives for policy to adjust to practice, and as states have lowered proficiency criteria to enable at least a semblance of success, the federal government has accepted the adjustments. Since the success of policy depends on practice, it behooves policymakers to accept such adjustments. The adjustments have been a way for policymakers and practitioners to manage the combination of aims that imply dramatic departures from conventional practice, with instruments and capabilities that cannot produce the desired changes in practice. Tacitly easing aims by reducing the criteria of success has been the chief way to manage this lack of consistency.

Improved knowledge is another way to manage the great distance between the aims that standards-based policies set on the one hand, and the instruments that they deploy and schools' capabilities on the other. If evidence were systematically collected on the operation and effects of policies in order to illuminate the causes of success and failure, and if there were systematic inquiry into educational processes and school improvement, the ensuing knowledge could help to improve practices, instruments, and capabilities.

Knowledge is a key instrument of policy in any event, but it assumes crucial importance with standards-based reform, for these policies can succeed only if schools improve learning.[23] The policies propose to do that by requiring academic standards, tests, and accountability; the aim is to create a frame that will insure that schools teach, and students learn, the things that are speci-

---

22. Milbrey McLaughlin (1991a) wrote that "Experience shows that some balance of pressure and support is essential. Pressure is required in most settings to focus attention on a reform objective; support is needed to enable implementation" (p. 188).

23. On ideas as policy instruments, see Weiss and Gruber (1984) and Cohen and Hill (2001).

fied in standards and tests. That greatly expands what educators need to know, for these policies hold schools accountable for students' learning. If schools lack knowledge of effective practice, they will not greatly improve learning. Those practice failures would make standards-based policies a political liability, for either state-maintained schools or the policies would lose legitimacy if failure became epidemic. As a result, issues that once were chiefly of academic interest, like valid ways to measure learning, or alignment among curriculum, instruction, and outcomes, now have real political import. By requiring schools and school systems to be more effective, these policies set a new priority on the production and use of valid knowledge about teaching, learning, and school management.

Though better schools are badly needed, neither IASA nor NCLB nor any state policies have been written or executed in ways that enable such learning. There is, for example, little provision for continuing formative studies. In addition, though NCLB did provide for more focused research on schooling and school improvement in the new Institute of Education Sciences (IES), that agency has a huge agenda and a modest budget. In addition, NCLB's tight compliance schedules mean that even if the funds had been much more ample, and more research had been done, much of it would have been concluded after the key decisions were made. Inquiry could not have proceeded at the rapid pace of NCLB's compliance schedule. This situation has encouraged practitioners to adjust their interpretations of policy down to something closer to conventional practice, and it has encouraged policymakers to accept many adjustments. Though NCLB rhetorically recognizes the importance of new knowledge, it has neither placed a very high priority on producing it, nor made a serious effort to frame implementation as a means to generate and use knowledge.

Several decades ago, Mazmanian and Sabatier (1989) addressed this matter:

> [if a] valid causal theory linking target group behavior to policy objectives is not available or is clearly problematic . . . then the proponents of the statute must make a conscious effort to incorporate in it a learning process through experimental projects, extensive research and development, evaluation studies, and an open decision process involving as many different inputs as possible. (p. 273)

It is a wise observation, even more apposite today than it was then, but few policymakers appear to have noticed. Why have they so seldom used systematic knowledge to learn and inform action?

Part of the answer lies in the environment. Those who make policy in our fragmented governments typically are poorly informed about practice, and practitioners often are equally in the dark about policy. Given the loose sprawl of American government, it can be difficult even to arrange regular consultation between practitioners and policymakers, and it is more difficult to inform policymakers and practitioners about each other's concerns and capabilities. The structure of government might not be such a problem if social and professional organization in education made room for regular exchanges among professionals between these sectors, so that there were more communication and common knowledge. But such exchange is rare.

Another part of the answer lies in the weakness of practice. The organizations that represent education professionals have traditionally restricted themselves to work on bread-and-butter issues, and have not invested in efforts either to improve practice or to build professional knowledge and coherent standards of professional practice. When such initiatives were undertaken, quite recently, they came from other organizations than those that represent education professionals. Had professional organizations initiated such efforts, they would have been led to invest in systematic inquiry, for they could not have made much progress without it. Their capability to engage with and inform policymakers would have been appreciably greater. Lacking such initiatives, practicing professionals have not been in a strong position either to represent the conditions of practice to policymakers and others, or to argue convincingly for solutions.

Still another part of the answer lies in the weakness of the organizations that sponsor research and conduct professional education. The state governments that have constitutional authority for schooling have never invested in systematic inquiry, nor have local educational authorities. The federal government did very modestly invest in research, but most of those investments were not targeted on efforts either to improve practice or to build professional knowledge and coherent standards of practice. The colleges and universities in which most educational research and professional education take place have done little to improve this situation. Little academic research has focused on educational practice, improving practice, or improving professional knowledge and skill. University teacher education has been painfully superficial, equipping practitioners neither with strong skills and knowledge nor with much capability to acquire knowledge for practice elsewhere. Hence neither researchers nor professional educators have been able to speak convincingly to policymakers or practitioners concerning the conditions of practice and their implications for policy.

Standards-based reform has created a new frame for education policy in which both practitioners and policymakers share an unprecedented need for much better knowledge about schooling and school improvement. Without such knowledge it will be impossible to deliver on the policies' promise of greatly improved teaching and learning, yet these policies have neither significantly enhanced the capability to produce such knowledge, nor devised ways in which practitioners and policymakers might use it. One question that researchers might address in the coming decades is how this paradoxical situation affects policy and practice.

REFERENCES

Amrein, A. L., and Berliner, D. C. (2002). *The impact of high-stakes tests on student academic performance: An analysis of NAEP results in states with high-stakes tests and ACT, SAT, and AP test results in states with high school graduation exams.* Tempe, AZ: Education Policy Studies Laboratory.

Bardach, E. (1977). *The implementation game: What happens after a bill becomes a law.* Cambridge, MA: MIT Press.

Berman, P., and McLaughlin, M. W. (1978). *Implementing and sustaining innovations* (R-1589/8-HEW).Vol. 8 of *Federal programs supporting educational change.* Santa Monica, CA: RAND.

Brehm, J., and Gates, S. (1997). *Working, shirking, and sabotage: Bureaucratic response to a democratic public.* Ann Arbor, MI: University of Michigan Press.

Brodkin, E. Z. (1990). Implementation as policy politics. In D. J. Palumbo and D. J. Calista (Eds.), *Implementation and the policy process: Opening up the black box* (pp. 107–118). New York: Greenwood.

Bryk, A. S., and Schneider, B. (2002). *Trust in schools: A core resource for improvement.* New York: Russell Sage Foundation.

Carnoy, M., and Loeb, S. (2002). Does external accountability affect student outcomes? A cross-state analysis. *Educational Evaluation and Policy Analysis 24*(4), 305–331.

Cohen, D. K., and Hill, H. C. (2001). *Learning policy: When state education reform works.* New Haven, CT: Yale University Press.

Cohen, D. K., and Spillane, J. P. (1992). Policy and practice: The relations between governance and instruction. In G. Grant (Ed.), *Review of research in education 18*, 3–49. Washington, DC: American Educational Research Association.

Dow, P. B. (1993). *Schoolhouse politics: Lessons from the Sputnik era.* Cambridge, MA: Harvard University Press.

Elmore, R. F. (1978). Organizational models of social program implementation. *Public Policy 26*(2), 185–228.

Elmore, R. F. (1979/1980). Backward mapping: Implementation research and policy decisions. *Political Science Quarterly 94*(4), 601–616.

Elmore, R. F. (2005). Agency, reciprocity, and accountability in democratic education. In S. Fuhrman and M. Lazerson (Eds.), *The public schools* (pp. 277–301). New York: Oxford University Press.

Elmore, R. F., and Burney, D. (1997). School variation and systemic instructional improvement in Community District #2, New York City. Pittsburgh, PA: University of Pittsburgh, Learning Research and Development, High Performance Learning Communities Project.

Elmore, R. F., and McLaughlin, M. W. (1988). *Steady work: Policy, practice, and the reform of American education.* Santa Monica, CA: RAND.

Friedrich, C. J. (1941). *Constitutional government and democracy: Theory and practice in Europe and America.* Boston: Little, Brown.

Fuhrman, S. H., and Elmore, R. F. (1992). *Takeover and deregulation: Working models of new state and local regulatory relationships* (CPRE Research Report No. RR–24). New Brunswick, NJ: Consortium for Policy Research in Education.

Fuhrman, S. H., and Elmore, R. F. (1995). Ruling out rules: The evolution of deregulation in state education policy. *Teachers College Record 97*(2), 279–309.

Grissmer, D. W., Flanagan, A., Kawata, J. H., and Williamson, S. (2000). *Improving student achievement: What state NAEP test scores tell us.* Santa Monica, CA: RAND.

Haney, W. (2000). The myth of the Texas miracle in education. *Education Policy Analysis Archives 8*(41).

Hanushek, E. (1996). School resources and student performance. In G. Burtless (Eds.), *Does money matter? The effect of school resources on student achievement and adult success* (pp. 43–73). Washington, DC: Brookings Institution Press.

Katznelson, I., and Weir, M. (1985). *Schooling for all: Class, race, and the decline of the democratic ideal.* New York: Basic Books.

Lin, A. C. (2000). *Reform in the making: The implementation of social policy in prison.* Princeton, NJ: Princeton University Press.

Lindblom, C. (1959). The science of muddling through. *Public Administration Review 19*(2), 79–88.

Lipsky, M. (1980). *Street-level bureaucracy: Dilemmas of the individual in public services.* New York: Russell Sage.

Majone, G., and Wildavsky, A. (1979). Implementation as evolution. In J. L. Pressman and A. B. Wildavsky (Eds.), *Implementation: How great expectations in Washington are dashed in Oakland. Or, why it's amazing that federal programs work at all, this being a saga of the Economic Development Administration as told by two sympathetic observers who seek to build morals on a foundation of ruined hopes* (pp. 163–180). Berkeley, CA: University of California Press.

Martin, R., and McClure, P. P. (1969. *Title I of ESEA: Is it helping poor children?* Washington, D.C.: Washington Research Project of the Southern Center for Studies in Public Policy and the NAACP Legal Defense of Education Fund.

Mazmanian, D. A., and Sabatier, P. A. (1989). *Implementation and public policy.* Lanham, MD: University Press of America.

McDonnell, L. M., and Elmore, R. F. (1987). Getting the job done: Alternative policy instruments. *Educational Evaluation and Policy Analysis 9*(2), 133–152.

McLaughlin, M. W. (1991a). Learning from experience: Lessons from policy implementation. In A. R. Odden (Ed.), *Education policy implementation*, 185–196. Albany, NY: State University of New York Press.

McLaughlin, M. W. (1991b). The RAND change agent study: Ten years later. In A. R. Odden (Ed.), *Education policy implementation* (pp. 143–156). Albany: State University of New York Press.

McLaughlin, M. W., and Talbert, J. E. (2001). *Professional communities and the work of high school teaching.* Chicago: University of Chicago Press.

Meier, K. J. (1993). *Politics and the bureaucracy: Policymaking in the fourth branch of government.* Belmont, CA: Wadsworth.

Mosbaek, E. J., et al. (1968). *Analysis of compensatory education in five school districts.* Washington, DC: General Electric, TEMPO.

NAACP Legal Defense and Education Fund. (1969). *Title I: Is it helping poor children?* Washington, DC: Washington Research Project of the Southern Center for Studies in Public Policy and Author.

Olson, L. (2002). A "proficient" score depends on geography. *Education Week*, February 20, 1.

Orfield, G. (1969). *The reconstruction of Southern education: The schools and the 1964 Civil Rights Act.* New York: Wiley-Interscience.

Pressman, J. L., and Wildavsky, A. B. (1979). *Implementation: How great expectations in Washington are dashed in Oakland. Or, why it's amazing that federal programs work at all, this being a saga of the Economic Development Administration as told by two sympathetic observers who seek to build morals on a foundation of ruined hopes.* Berkeley, CA: University of California Press.

Rosenholtz, S. J. (1991). *Teacher's workplace: The social organization of schools.* New York: Teachers College Press.

Sarason, S. B. (1971). *The culture of the school and the problem of change.* Boston, MA: Allyn and Bacon.

Saulny, S. (2005). State to state: Varied ideas of proficient. *New York Times*, January 19, late edition, B8.

Sexton, P. C. (1961). *Education and income: Inequalities of opportunity in our public schools.* New York: Viking.

Skrla, L., Scheurich, J. J., and Johnson, Jr., J. F. (2000). *Equity-driven, achievement-focused school districts: A report on systemic school success in four Texas school districts serving diverse student populations.* Austin, TX: Charles A. Dana Center.

Smith, M. S., and O'Day, J. (1990). Systemic school reform. In *Politics of Education Association yearbook*, 233–267. London: Taylor & Francis.

Spillane, J. P. (1999). External reform initiatives and teachers' efforts to reconstruct their practice: The mediating role of teachers' zones of enactment. *Journal of Curriculum Studies 31*(2), 143–175.

Spillane, J. P. (2000). Cognition and policy implementation: District policy-makers and the reform of mathematics education. *Cognition and Instruction 18*(2), 141–179.

Waterman, R. W., and Meier, K. J. (1988). Principal-agent models: An expansion? *Journal of Public Administration Research and Theory 8*(2), 173–202.

Weir, M., Orloff, A. S., and Skocpol, T. (1988). *The politics of social policy in the United States.* Princeton, NJ: Princeton University Press.

Weiss, J., and Gruber, J. (1984). Using knowledge for control in fragmented policy areas. *Journal of Policy Analysis and Management 3*, 225–247.

Van Meter, D. S., and Van Horn, C. E. (1975). The policy implementation process: A conceptual framework. *Administration and Society 6*(4), 445-488.

5

New Political Economy of Public Education: Policy and Research

Paul T. Hill

Engineer Richard Pei gleefully tells newcomers to RAND about the wonders of Chinese baseball, a hybrid of standard baseball and politics. All the normal rules of baseball apply, except one: anybody can move the bases anywhere at any time. That's where it resembles politics.

Many people have been moving the bases in education. In the mid-1970s, the politics of education was predominantly about government action; how much would be appropriated for government-funded programs, how it was to be spent, and under what rules public employees would act.

Today, the politics of education are about that and much more. In the mere eight years since Wirt and Kirst published the latest edition of their classic *The Political Dynamics of American Education* (1997) many new actors have entered the competition to influence the ways public money is spent and children are educated. Jeffrey Henig (2005, pp. 191–196) identifies several constituencies that might be attracted to dramatically different ways of funding and overseeing public education, including African Americans and Latinos dissatisfied with the education provided their children, conservative Jewish voters interested in saving Jewish private schools, and homeowners who fear losses in their property values. These groups might join others who have long sought changes, including Catholics who want public support for parochial schools, companies that hope to operate publicly funded schools, parents and educators associated with charter schools, and financial services organizations hoping to do business with independent charter or voucher-funded schools. Henig further notes that some of these interests might find at least a temporary home in the Republican Party, which would like to weaken entities that now buttress the Democratic Party, particularly teachers' unions.

Henig might also have mentioned homeschoolers on the left and right who want their children to avoid educational institutions altogether. Homeschoolers are united in wanting public schools and colleges to give children credit for what they have learned at home, and many want access to government funding to pay for testing, materials, and online instruction. He might also have mentioned some big-city mayors who believe troubled public school systems undermine their cities' futures, and have given up efforts to improve conventional public school system.

These groups are moving in similar directions, but they haven't yet coalesced around a simple set of ideas. In general, they favor letting families choose schools other than those run by traditional school districts, transferring of public funds to entities running schools no matter whether they are governmental or private, and giving schools freedom over choice of instructional methods and staff pay and hiring. The groups are still somewhat divided about the desirability of some versus no public oversight (charter schools versus vouchers or tuition tax credits) and public funding for religious education and "virtual schools" that essentially serve children who stay at home with their parents.

All these groups have some agendas consistent with the theme of privatization. In its most general definition, privatization is the reliance on nongovernmental actors to perform functions once performed by government. Some of the new actors (vendors to school districts, for- and non-profit educational management organizations) are in business to do things that public school districts now do, so privatization is their main agenda. Others (mayors, philanthropies, pro-choice minority groups like the Black Alliance for Educational Options [BAEO], the federal government) have mixtures of agendas, some focused simply on changing public school districts internally and some on creating alternatives to district activities.

Though Wirt and Kirst acknowledged some of these developments in 1997, some actors are much more prominent now than before, and some of their agendas are new. No one could have predicted the Gates, Broad, and Walton foundations' determination to dramatically increase the numbers of charter schools, nor the movement of some traditionally centrist foundations like Heinz, Annie E. Casey and Kauffman into the pro-charters camp. Nor was Congress certain to enact the No Child Left Behind requirement that children in consistently low-performing schools be offered options including charter schools.

In the politics of education, the bases have been moved outside what was once considered the ballpark boundaries, as groups discontented with the current state of affairs search for ways to change things to their advantage. Though these changes were unanticipated only a few years ago, from today's perspective their development looks unsurprising. A combination of private and within-government groups (e.g., teachers' unions and the district-level administrators of federal and state programs) had dominated conventional education policy thoroughly. After fulfilling the obligations imposed by teacher union contracts and categorical program requirements, schools and districts had few remaining discretionary funds. Funds that might have been combined to support needed investments (e.g., in teacher training) were fragmented because separate central office units controlled small amounts. Moreover, the share of public education funds spent on students other than the handicapped had fallen steadily for years.

Districts were unable to create satisfactory options as new immigrant groups emerged and the educational needs of center-city African American children became increasingly severe. Many parents who wanted alternatives to the schools provided by their districts were forced to pay private school tuition. People with new ideas on how to reach students doing poorly in public schools could not get needed permission or funding. Universities controlled certification, and district human resource offices made sure only people from conventional backgrounds could get teaching jobs.

A Chinese baseball master could predict what happened: frustrated groups sought ways to deflect the flow of government funds and set up competing structures—schools, training systems, and ways of giving parents choices—that the existing structure had blocked. The same expert could predict the response of the "haves"—blocking and thwarting efforts to expand the game.

THEORIES EXPLAINING TRANSFORMATION OF
THE POLITICAL ECONOMY

There are counterparts to the Chinese baseball master in the political science and business literatures. Frank Baumgartner and Bryan Jones wrote in *Agendas and Instability in American*

Politics (1993) about how the politics of a policy area like public education can pass through a series of "punctuated equilibriums." Policy and politics can be stable for long periods as an idea structures the operations of government and supporters and beneficiaries form a "policy monopoly" to protect the idea by keeping opponents out of the decision-making process. As they argue, the equilibrium can be upset, especially if previously indifferent or excluded groups are mobilized on behalf of a new idea—an alternative mode of government operation incompatible with the previously dominant one. If the newly mobilized groups are strong enough they can undermine the institutional arrangements that protected the previous policy. Supporters of the new idea then try to construct a new policy equilibrium, which, because it necessarily excludes some interests, can last only so long before it also is challenged.

If the baseball expert had been familiar with Baumgartner and Jones, he might have predicted that this group competition would also have set off a competition in moralizing. As we have seen in education, some groups trying to expand the game have adopted a free-market ideology, and others have labeled school choice "the new civil right." Groups defending their stakes in the system have justified them as results of democratic processes and painted their opponents as undemocratic proponents of market Darwinism. The baseball expert might also have speculated that if the same groups were to trade positions (i.e., the ins outside and the outs inside) they might also trade ideologies.

The counterpart to Chinese baseball in the business literature is Clayton Christensen's *Innovator's Dilemma* (1997). Based on studies of several industries, Christensen's book shows that the inevitable process of product improvement—in which a company makes a highly successful product increasingly expensive and feature-laden in order to satisfy its most demanding users—can ultimately lead to the company's demise. As he argues, companies enhance their products in order to satisfy their most demanding customers and to increase the prices that can be charged for them. A new company with a much simpler product can attract the low-end users of the dominant product—those who do not need or want to pay for all the features that have been added—and attract new customers for whom the dominant product is far too complex and expensive. As the new product gains market share, demand for the previously dominant product falls and its unit cost rises dramatically, until the company that produced the dominant product is unable to continue selling it for a profit. The new product gains market share and ultimately becomes the dominant one. Ultimately, however, improvement of the new product—which is needed to satisfy the most demanding and lucrative customers—ultimately makes it susceptible to disruption as well.

To understand why there is so much energy behind privatization, one needs only to review the many ways in which the education policy process was, until recently, locked up tight. Virtually all the money in public education is already spoken for,[1] and is barely enough to cover the salaries of administrators, teachers, and support personnel.[2] As Stephen Carroll has shown (2005), even as

1. Forthcoming research by Marguerite Roza and colleagues will illustrate that control of public school districts' funds is fragmented among so many within-system groups that actual spending has little connection with official district priorities. They will show that teacher salaries cause significant spending disparities from school to school, and that actual spending on individual disadvantaged children varies tremendously within a given district. After they weight school budgets for individual student attributes, they find that school budgets vary by $14,960 in one typical district. In addition, central office expenditures for services delivered to schools, which are not reflected in school budgets, add significantly to the horizontal inequities in funding.

2. On this point see the Appendix, a school board member's analysis of the source of structural deficits in one urban district, Seattle. Years of school improvement efforts that involved hiring extra teachers have put the district in a position where its main cost drivers, teacher salaries, are increasing automatically at over 5 percent each year while the district budget is flat or falling slightly. The result; no money for anything new, many things other than teachers' salaries being cut dramatically.

new money comes into the system, it is hard for districts to resist demands to spend it on teachers—more teachers to reduce class size and higher salaries and benefits for incumbents.

Parents or educators wanting to experiment with new schools rarely get the chance to do so; many districts consider the schools they offer as a fixed set. Though higher-income families can create alternatives for themselves by moving or paying private school tuition, poorer families are completely dependent on what the districts offer. Their schools generally get the newest and least qualified teachers, as scarce experienced teachers use their seniority advantages to work elsewhere (see Guin, 2004; Haycock, 2000). According to Roza and Hill (2004), teacher salary averaging means that schools with low-cost teachers pay more for their teachers than those teachers cost in salary and benefits, and that the difference is transferred to schools that can attract more senior staffs. Low-income families know that teachers leave their schools as soon as they can, leading to constant turbulence in teaching and home–school relations (Guin, 2004).

These arrangements are solidified in laws, contracts, regulations, and district practices. They are not inevitable concomitants of government-provided education, though insiders defend their advantages as fairly won in the democratic process. Thus parents and others who want to try new things and redistribute opportunity are understandably skeptical about the value of government and want some funds controlled, teachers allocated, and schools provided by someone other than government. Thus the preference for privatization.

Are such profound changes necessary? Wouldn't poor and minority children benefit more if they just got access to better teachers and if schools were fully desegregated to provide more challenging peer support? Many of the new supporters of privatization long sought such changes and have concluded the system isn't capable of making them—especially since the very groups that now control public education would have to give up something to make such things happen. This view gains support, for example, from a forthcoming book edited by Jane Hannaway and Andrew Rotherham. It reports several studies showing how teacher collective bargaining agreements channel teaching talent and money away from schools serving the most disadvantaged children.

Pressure for privatization comes from groups that think they cannot get what they need from within the conventional structure. The solution, they think, is to tap into public funds in new ways and create new actors—new kinds of school providers, new vendors of online instruction, new sources of teachers—to claim government support and compete for students. Few people who want the things that privatization will bring are driven by the desire to create utterly unfettered markets. They just want something else tried, and if that fails something else again. No matter what reforms are tried, if government adopts them and they work poorly, the demand for privatization could rise again.

This paper takes a decidedly Bentleyan approach to the political economy of education, and thus a neutral stance on privatization. It treats group action as an inevitable result of need, and ideology as a rationalization for interest. (Bentley rejected these rationalizations as mind-stuff.) Groups on the outside are bound to reject as invalid the processes by which those on the inside made their gains, and vice versa.

> Politics is always a group phenomenon. It indicates the push and resistance between groups. The balance of the group pressures is the existing state of society. Pressure is broad enough to include all forms of the group influence upon group, from battle and riot to abstract reasoning and sensitive morality. It allows for humanitarian movements as easily as for political corruption. Groups exert their pressure, whether they find expression through representative opinion groups or whether they are silent, not indeed with the same technique, not with the same palpable results, but in just as real a way. (Bentley, 1908, pp. 258–259)

Despite the great diversification of groups and agendas, the standard conception of policy-making is still relevant. It moves from demands and support through legislative decision making to the administration of government programs and thence to events in classrooms leading to changes in student learning. However, the numbers of actors involved in the policy system and the diversity of agendas they pursue have increased dramatically in the past five years.

In addition to the newly aroused interest groups identified by Henig (2005), there are new within-government actors, including legislative committees that write tax laws and can authorize credits and deductions that channel public funds outside the school district structure, and new bureaucracies supporting charter schools. Thus parts of government are now actively providing government support for family choice and creation of new school options, via tuition tax credits[3] and philanthropic spending on alternatives to district-run schools. Funds previously controlled by school districts can be deflected to schools other than those provided by school districts, via the mechanisms of family choice and government funds following children to schools chosen by parents.

Though legislatures still appropriate funds to run schools and school districts, groups unhappy with the system have found ways to develop their own options. Private parties can also determine how public funds are divided up between schools, as funds follow children to the schools their parents choose. School boards and state education agencies can determine curriculum and instruction in schools they control in some localities, but in others these choices have been delegated out to schools and heavily influenced by parent preferences.

Charter schools, privately run schools operating with public funds, blur the once-bright line between public and private schooling. Jews and Protestants have joined Catholics in trying to get government vouchers to pay for the choices they have made. Foundation investments are driving school districts' choices of reform strategies, and the federal government has joined with foundations to develop new private sources of teacher and administrator training.

New entrants and methods of bypassing existing institutions are signs that the old equilibrium is under pressure. Though, in Baumgartner and Jones' terms, a new policy monopoly hasn't yet emerged, the preexisting one is being broken. The forces now breaking the policy monopoly have been evident for some time. However, the existing system has heretofore been able to contain them within its boundaries. Philanthropies have been supported by tax expenditures for years, and have tried to influence educational policy and practice. Parents of handicapped children have been able to demand alternatives to district-provided schools. Unions have been able to deflect public resources by negotiating district support for their own operations and increasing the share of public funding that goes for teacher salaries. All of these activities could have been labeled privatization, but they were not, because the groups whose agendas jointly controlled public education were accustomed to them and accepted them as normal accommodations in the course of business.

The entry of new groups with broader agendas has upset the equilibrium among the groups that established their place within the system at earlier times. Everyone in the system has less control of events than they once had. State legislative education committees find their turf invaded by

---

3. Tuition tax credits are a popular idea that nonetheless has been enacted only in a few places. According to the Center for Education Reform Web site (2005), "Limited school tax credits/deductions (that include private school tuition) exist in Minnesota and Iowa. Arizona offers a tax credit for donations to privately funded voucher programs. Illinois, Indiana, Michigan, and Wisconsin are giving tax credits serious consideration. South Dakota, Utah, Virginia, Idaho, Maryland, Missouri, and Oregon have reviewed the idea."

committees that write tax laws; state departments of education find themselves pushed around much more aggressively by a privatization-friendly federal government. School districts find themselves in competition for students and money that once automatically came to them. Moreover, in times of scarce funding, many districts find that they have committed all their funds to salaries and operations and must seek business and foundation support for teacher training and school improvement efforts. (On the gradual erosion of districts' capacity to adapt, see Hill, 2000.) This further weakens district autonomy and increases philanthropies' substantive leverage. Parents' credible threat to leave schools can force districts to create new options of their own and reallocate funds to strengthen schools facing competition.

Groups whose claims were established at an earlier time inevitably try to block the claims of groups mobilized at a later time. New groups on the outside therefore have little choice but to attack what others hold. Privatization is the natural refuge of a group that has been unable to move government. This fact has nothing to do with the moral merits of one group's claims versus another's. But that has not stopped groups from moralizing their claims, with outsider groups arguing for social justice and a new deal true to the values of public education, and insider groups defending the status quo as the essence of public educating.

A CONTEST OVER THE MEANING OF PUBLIC EDUCATION

The very definition of public education is now contested. Is public education indeed the exact system we have, such that challenges to current arrangements are intrinsically hostile to public education? Or is the meaning of public education elastic enough to cover both the current arrangements and alternatives that outsiders press for? Can the proposed arrangements that today look like privatization become a means of delivering public education in the future?

I am one of those who have argued that public education is not a particular institution but an objective, to which particular institutional arrangements might or might not contribute (2001). From this perspective, public education is both a goal—to educate every child so that he or she can be a full and effective participant in our country's economic, community, and political life—and a problem to be solved. Until the goal is fully met, institutional arrangements must be in flux, and none can be privileged against criticism or competition. The argument that public education is a specific institution implies that the institution is sacred even if it does not provide the benefits sought by those who constructed it.

Others will argue that particular values and processes define public education—communitarian values that rule out competitive or private provision of services, and deliberative processes that lead to uniform actions approved by a majority. Ideas like "public schools are our last public space" (Barber, 2004) suggest that public education is incompatible with differentiation of services and providers.

These differences can be debated, and they will. In the debate, crude Bentleyans will ask smooth philosophers whether the arrangements we now call public education approximate their definition of public education closely enough to merit the name.

CONSEQUENCES TO DATE

It is one thing to say that pressures for privatization are inevitable and morally equal to demands made earlier by groups that gained control of the public schools apparatus, and quite another thing to say that actual privatization efforts have accomplished what their supporters hoped they would.

What's the evidence? I will try to review the results of the new politics of public education from two perspectives: (1) the overall health of public education broadly defined, including all publicly funded K–12 education, and (2) benefits and harms to the groups pressing for new allocations of money and authority and to those resisting. This overview is severely handicapped by a shortage of good research. Education policy research and evaluation have fallen far behind developments in the real world. Though many studies attempt to score points for or against the desirability of privatization, few studies try to understand developments in detail. In the conclusion I will identify the kinds of research that must be done if we are to understand, predict, and help community leaders calibrate policies about these new developments.

General Effects on Publicly Funded Education

Are children in district-run public schools any worse off as a result of the wins experienced by those who would create charter schools or allow parents to use vouchers? What about the children whose parents have taken advantage of new choices? Is teaching any less attractive an occupation, or are school districts any less able to operate good schools?

Groups opposing privatization have raised all these possibilities, and none of them stretches credulity. Money transferred to charter and voucher schools comes out of district budgets, and children who leave existing schools take money with them. These processes could harm the schools that children leave. Loss of funds could also force district-wide cutbacks that interfere with needed services to schools and investments in teachers, which could make teaching less attractive. Finally, the overall quality of publicly supported education in a community could decline if the charter schools and voucher-redeeming private schools to which they transfer are of low quality.

Despite the surface plausibility of these predictions, none of them has yet been borne out. There are isolated examples of small districts (e.g., Inkster, Michigan) that have lost funding because of the location of charter schools nearby, but no general pattern. Opponents of privatization could still be right: negative consequences could still be on the way, but taking longer than expected to appear. To date, however, the evidence on all the negative predictions is mixed at best.

It is hard to see widespread negative effects of choice programs on existing public schools. This is true in part because many localities with choice programs also have growing student populations, so losses to charters and other schools are unnoticed. Moreover, in urban neighborhoods like Chicago's Near South Side, significant numbers of students attending charter schools are drawn away from parochial schools. Even in cities with stable student populations, it is not clear how much the existence of charter schools increases the numbers of students who leave the district schools every year. A recent study of Seattle (Anderson, 2004) showed that 7 percent of the student population left every year for reasons other than graduation—usually to attend school in other jurisdictions or private schools. If only one-fourth of those students chose to attend charter schools, they could fill four average-sized charter schools every year, without affecting the district's overall student population.

The funding arrangements for choice programs further help explain this "null effect" on district finances. Charter and voucher schools generally receive less than 100 percent of the local per-pupil expenditure. Districts retain part of the funds, paradoxically increasing their average per-pupil expenditure even as their student population declines. If in the future choice advocates succeed in increasing charter and voucher schools' share of per-pupil expenditures, districts could lose the financial buffer they have enjoyed.

Results are also murky about the consequences of choice plans for district-run school quality. The expectation that schools of choice would draw off the most advantaged students have not been borne out; in fact the debate has now shifted to the question of whether charter schools draw a disproportionately difficult-to-educate population (Buckley, Schneider, & Shang, 2004). Evidence from Florida suggests that competition from schools of choice can force districts to change their spending patterns and invest in improving schools threatened with population loss (Camilli & Bulkley, 2001). This could lead to some hurtful cutbacks in other schools. Student achievement results are hard to find. Bettinger (1999) presents a typically mixed picture: average student achievement has risen in Michigan district-run schools subject to competition from charters. He attributes the results to two factors: (1) the loss of the lowest-achieving students to charter schools and (2) a decline in remaining public school students' achievement that is too small to offset the gains realized when the lowest-achieving students departed.

It is difficult to trace any connection between privatization initiatives and changes in the overall size and quality of the teaching force working in a geographic area. These almost certainly respond to major economic factors—the demand for college-educated workers, trends in teacher pay relative to other occupations, and the quality of benefits offered by school districts—far more than to the political factors discussed here.

Are schools of choice drawing away the best teachers? No one thinks so. Murphy and DeArmond (2003) provide evidence that charter schools (and parochial schools, the most common destination of students receiving vouchers) draw from a similar but not identical labor pool as do district schools. Given their lower per-pupil funding, schools of choice pay lower salaries and therefore attract younger staff. Most schools of choice either require teachers to be certified but allow teachers to gain certification while on the job. They attract some young teachers who would not work in district-run schools. According to Caroline Hoxby (2000), charter schools pay premiums for teacher attributes that are not rewarded by public school systems—high SAT scores, degrees from competitive colleges, and quantitative college majors—and do not reward teachers for some attributes that school districts value, e.g., MA degrees from schools of education.

What about children whose parents choose charter schools or use vouchers? Here debate rages. Results vary from slight advantages for children whose parents exercise choice, to slight disadvantages, to no difference in measurable outcomes. (See for example Howell et al., 2001, 2003; Krueger & Zhu, 2003; Rouse, 1998; Witte, 1998.) The results of voucher trials in New York City, Milwaukee, and Washington, DC, are hotly debated. Available studies of charter schools are very hard to interpret because none draws from a true nationally representative sample of charter schools. Drawing a nationally representative sample would be extremely difficult. Charter schools are a state-level phenomenon: each state has its own goals for charter schools, standards for granting charters, and funding and regulatory arrangements. Even within states, most studies are small and opportunistic; they represent some charter schools but not the state's charter schools in general (Zimmer & Gill, 2004). There are, moreover, no statewide studies whatever for 28 of the states with charter schools (Hill, 2005a). Though studies are rapidly becoming more sophisticated, the best-designed ones (Bifulco & Ladd, 2004; Hanushek et al., 2005; Sass, 2006) draw different conclusions in part because they focus on different states (Hill). The first issue of the new MIT journal *Education Finance and Policy,* set to be published in 2006, includes peer-reviewed versions of the articles by Tim Sass and by Robert Bifulco and Helen Ladd, plus review essays written from several different policy perspectives. It is likely to sustain rather than to resolve uncertainties about the student achievement effects of charter schools.

Results on outcomes other than test scores are starting to trickle in. Students who use vouchers to attend Catholic schools (but not other schools supported by vouchers) gain on civic knowledge and tolerance, as do students in District of Columbia charter schools (Buckley & Schneider, 2004). There are no clear results on long-term outcome measures like persistence in school, graduation rates, or college attendance and completion.

On one measure, however, charters and other schools of choice are a big success. Parents are generally much happier with their children's education than parents whose children remain in district-run schools (Schneider, Buckley, & Kucsova, 2003). These results could be precursors to good things like student persistence in school and graduation rates, and they could be evidence of the importance of letting parents match subtle attributes of schools—climate, emotional support, studiousness—to what they know about their children (Office of Educational Research and Improvement, 2000).[4] However, there are strong competing hypotheses, including cognitive dissonance reduction—I chose this school, therefore it must be better. The available research supports only speculation on these issues.

Whatever its causes, parent satisfaction can be an important factor in the new politics of education. The newest groups to take an interest in privatization, including Henig's trio of African Americans, Latinos, and Jews, want more than anything else to gain some control over the kind of education their children receive. With privatization they can gain the experience of choosing schools and the satisfaction of knowing that educators must work to gain their loyalty. These gains have immediate symbolic value, long before it is clear whether privatization has led to increases in student learning. Some current supporters of privatization could lose their enthusiasm if charter and voucher schools do not improve student learning. However, supporters unhappy with district-run schools might take a long time to draw negative conclusions about schools of choice, especially if foundations and charter school providers withdraw external support from the least effective schools and continue investing in new ideas and reproducing the most effective schools.

Nothing in the privatization movement, or in the political science and business theories that predicted it, requires that new schools work immediately or every time. As Christensen (1997) notes, the fact that a particular company is ripe for disruption doesn't mean that just any alternative product will take away its market. In his terms, a disruptive innovation must offer something attractive, both to people who have been buying the dominant product but are not happy with it and to potential customers who have been on the sidelines. A given charter school, or even a generation of charter schools, might not fulfill parents' and supporters' hopes. But dissatisfaction with the current dominant product creates opportunities for successive waves of potentially disruptive innovations.

Similarly, in terms introduced by Baumgartner and Jones (1993), the new ideas that undermine an established policy monopoly might not all be worked out perfectly in advance and immediately fulfill all their proponents' hopes. In the beginning it is probably enough for the previously disaffected to see that things are being done differently. Disappointed groups might eventually look elsewhere, but in the case of education privatization, no one knows how long it will take to get to the long run.

---

4. Nationally, White students make up 48 percent of the charter school population and 58 percent of the population served by conventional public schools. Charter school student populations are disproportionately White in Arizona, California, Colorado, and Georgia and disproportionately minority in Florida, Massachusetts, Michigan, Minnesota, New Jersey, North Carolina, Pennsylvania, Texas, and Wisconsin, See also Cobb and Glass (1999).

In the next section we will explore whether the groups that have pressed for privatization are happy with what they have accomplished and are likely to press for more of the same in the future.

The Spread of Privatization

Critics of groups like the BAEO and the National Council of La Raza claim that their working with such strange bedfellows as the Children's Scholarship Fund and the Walton Foundation will ultimately harm the very children they hope to benefit. The claim (made most recently in a national philanthropic meeting by Professor Jeannie Oakes of UCLA)[5] is that minorities for privatization have been fooled into thinking they can make common cause with their historic enemies: business interests, libertarians, economic conservatives, and Republicans. Critics claim that such groups will eventually lose out badly in pro-privatization coalitions and will be forced back into coalition with traditional constituents of the civil rights community, such as the unions and groups opposing separation of church and state.

This allegation is decidedly non-Bentleyan—it assumes that group interests are secondary to ideology, and that moral stances are the appropriate guide to coalition building. Groups like African American educators that have benefited in the past from coalitions with groups ideologically committed to work through government should stay on the left.

The furious response from leaders like Howard Fuller of the BAEO is decidedly Bentleyan. They acknowledge the past value of the civil rights coalition but argue that the real basis for it has eroded. In particular they cite the consequences of teacher collective bargaining agreements, which sustain patterns of within-district teacher allocation ensuring minority children get the least qualified teachers, and union defense of low-performing teachers. They also argue that groups associated with civil liberties and separation of church and state have worked against voucher programs that would give disadvantaged children access to available seats in stable parochial schools.

Critics like Oakes predict that poor people's groups making common cause with business and conservative groups will lose badly when their strange bedfellows' whole agenda is realized. Without the bulwarks of school district central offices, teachers' unions, and rights-based entitlements for handicapped children, they argue, minority groups will have no defense against the greed and selfishness of the advantaged. Minority groups themselves are split on this, with the NAACP and Mexican American Legal Defense and Education Fund generally staying close to the old civil rights coalition, and the Urban League and the National Council of La Raza more open to alternatives. Leaders of urban pro-privatization groups retort that they will take their chances, having lived with the greed and selfishness of their erstwhile partners on the left.

All parties in this debate are arguing about possible future events. The privatization strategy is only starting to take effect, and treacherous bedfellows would still be hiding their harmful intentions, if such they had. Some within the public education establishment fear that right-wing groups favoring privatization hope to derail the pro-women's and gay rights agendas of the teachers' unions; others fear business interests will abandon education issues as soon as they have succeeded in reducing tax support for public education.[6] No one can say for sure what another

---

5. Luncheon Session, Philanthropy Roundtable Conference, moderated by Juan Williams with Jeannie Oakes and Howard Fuller, Atlanta, October 19, 2004. Attended by the author. Oakes's statement at this event appears to have been drawn from her book, *Becoming Good American Schools: The Struggle for Civic Virtue in Education Reform* (2000).

6. Henig (2005) argues that there is a basis for the latter fear. However, pro-choice groups are increasingly forced to argue that public funding for charter schools is too low and needs to be increased (see Finn, Hassel, & Speakman, 2005).

person has in his or her heart. But to date insinuations against the motives of people like Bill Gates, Eli Broad, and the Walton family have no basis other than the *argumentum ad hominem*.

In any case, pro-choice African American and Hispanic leaders will be the first to know whether their pro-privatization alliances have gone sour. They are not likely to be convinced by protagonists on the left side of the culture wars or defenders of the current system.

For the present, it is possible to assess only the short-term consequences of these changes in the political economy of education. Table 5.1 provides the author's own overview.

As the table shows, the practical significance of measures promoted by privatization advocates is relatively small. To date the results neither fulfill the hopes of privatization supporters nor justify the ferocious opposition to them by within-system actors like teachers' unions, school boards, and schools of education. As Henig (2005) notes, the choice debate has "high reverberation," with pro- and anti-choice camps exaggerating the significance of current proposals, motivated less by the character of particular measures than by fears about where those measures could ultimately lead.

How the family options provisions of No Child Left Behind are implemented could determine whether privatization initiatives in education grow or peter out. No Child Left Behind requires school districts to offer the parents of children in consistently low-performing schools the option to transfer to better-performing schools in the same district. Cities like Chicago, Cleveland, New York, St. Louis, and Los Angeles are forced to ask whether they can, by changing the ways they fund and oversee schools and changing the rules governing who may teach in and lead schools, increase the number of good schools they offer.

TABLE 5.1
Privatization Initiatives and Their Consequences to Date

	Significance	*Prospects for Expansion*
Charter schools	3,500 schools serving 700,000 children in 41 states, mostly concentrated in metropolitan areas.	No Child Left Behind could greatly accelerate expansion in big cities.
Contracting-out for schools	Use concentrated in a few big cities.	Could replace chartering as the principal way of creating new schools.
Pressures on districts to find new school providers	Roughly a score of new providers nationwide.	Depends on how many districts turn to new providers.
New sources of teachers	Alternative certification programs in 47 states. New teacher training institutions.	Could grow substantially in urban areas with perceived weak teaching forces and need for new schools.
Publicly funded vouchers	Limited to children in a few large central cities.	May depend on future federal legislation, based on new pilot voucher program in DC.
Privately funded vouchers	Available to about 500,000 children nationwide.	Unlikely to grow substantially without changes in tax laws.
Tuition tax credits	Available in one-third of the states.	Future significance depends on whether they are allowed on federal income taxes.

The numbers of children and schools potentially involved are tremendous. Testing done in the 2002–2003 school year showed that 27,000 Baltimore students, one-third of the district's total enrollment, were eligible to transfer to higher-performing schools, yet only 301 seats in such schools were available. (Fields, 2003). Even if all empty places in parochial schools were added into the mix, Baltimore would still have 20,000 students with no place to go. In Chicago, 270,757 students were eligible to transfer, but only 1,097 seats were available at 38 schools (Cholo & Dell'Angela, 2004). There were 20 applicants for every available seat, and nearly a quarter million eligible families made no effort to choose, probably in recognition that there was no place to go. Dozens of other urban districts required by No Child Left Behind to offer choices to children in low-performing schools have been unable to do so; higher-performing schools are full, and the only available alternatives are low-performing.

Major urban districts are attempting to increase the number of good schools in a variety of ways. Chicago, for example, has committed to closing its 60 lowest-performing schools and creating 100 new ones. Like Philadelphia (Bulkley, Mundell, & Riffer, 2004), Chicago will ask its district central office to create some new schools but also offer charters and contracts to independent groups willing to develop new schools in low-income neighborhoods. The charter and contract schools will also be free to hire teachers not now employed by the school district, and to offer different compensation packages.

Chicago and Philadelphia have both used chartering but developed an additional instrument, contracting. By using their inherent power to enter into contracts for provision of educational services, these districts have bypassed their state charter laws' caps on the allowable numbers of charter schools. They are also working to create funding and accountability arrangements that are more attractive to both school providers and public oversight agencies. These districts are also learning how to establish and oversee such contracts, and apply what they learn more broadly and help other districts to do so.

The future of vouchers is far less certain. Private vouchers provide a charitable opportunity for wealthy individuals, but statewide enactment of voucher programs has proven extremely difficult. To date, private voucher programs have helped preserve threatened Catholic schools in a few cities and provided vehicles for research and policy advocacy, but they show little sign of spreading. Tuition tax credits could lead to great expansion of privately administered but publicly funded vouchers. Their legal status and political prospects are uncertain. However, continued failure of big-city school improvement efforts, combined with more conservative courts and a large Republican majority in some future Congress, could increase tuition tax credits' significance.

IMPLICATIONS

For Policy

A Bentleyan from another planet, looking on developments in the political economy of American K–12 education, would expect slow but steady erosion of the advantages enjoyed by groups that captured government in the 1960s and 1970s. She would expect groups pressing for privatization to continue pressing for policy change, electing allies to office, finding ways to divert money from the control of elected officials allied with school boards and unions, creating new suppliers of teachers, schools, and support services, and drawing families away from low-performing, district-run schools. She might expect rural and wealthy suburban areas to be unaffected, but the big cities to develop a much more diverse set of education providers and different ways of using technology and student and teacher time. She might marvel at the turbulence and inventiveness of a free society. It would not even occur to her that cities had lost a unifying force. She would assume that there was less conflict, both because people would be able to act in their own interests and because the diversity of educational experience could feed a dynamic economy.

Since all earthlings would look alike to her, the alien Bentleyan would not notice whether some groups were getting inferior educations, or whether as a result of diverse schooling, groups were more isolated from one another. But we earthlings would notice. Privatization critics could be proven right—privatization could lead to less sophisticated and aggressive groups' getting even worse schools than they have now. Moreover, schools could find market niches by pandering to religious and social philosophies, separating Americans even more than they are now.

Even if the alien were able to understand these issues, she might be skeptical that such adverse outcomes could occur. Success would put pressure on the pro-privatization coalition, exposing differences between those who expect to benefit from totally free markets and those who believe in common standards for all children's learning and favor prudent regulation against predictable failures of the market (Moe, 2002; National Working Commission on Choice in K–12 Education, 2003). The leaders of minority and disadvantaged groups that pressed for privatization would not ignore early signs of tension with free-market fundamentalists, and they would seek to form new coalitions with groups that favored standards and parsimonious community oversight. The new school entrepreneurs probably would not abandon serving disadvantaged children in order to try attracting suburban White families away from schools that were working perfectly well for them. Pro-privatization lawyers, fresh from winning lawsuits that required accounting for public funds on a per-pupil basis, with equal spending on rich and poor, probably would not accept anyone's violating these principles.

No one can say for sure where the emerging new political economy of K–12 education will ultimately lead. The identities and agendas of contending groups are sure to change over time. Unions, school boards, state legislative committees, advocates for disabled children, and colleges of education are unlikely to leave the scene, but neither are groups like the BAEO, alternative school and teacher providers, foundations in favor of experimentation with new models of public education, legislative tax committees, free-market advocacy groups, and pro-choice litigators. Given the balance of forces at work today it seems likely that more public and private funds will bypass the traditional administrative structure of public education, union and education school monopolies will come under continuing challenge, and communities will increasingly rely on multiple providers for public education.

Given the widespread concerns about the risks of totally free markets, it seems increasingly likely that strong new tripartite coalitions will emerge. These will combine groups favoring development of new options for poor and minority children, groups favoring strong universal student learning standards, and groups favoring limited public oversight of schools, focusing only on equity and performance. Their slogan might be "standards, transparency, and contestable provision," a mixture of agendas whose appeal cuts across traditional divisions between moderates on the left and right. The "contestable provision" element of the slogan closely resembles the Blair government's "Third Way" education reforms in England. The Blair reforms do not automatically favor private school providers, but they foster competition and seek to put governmental and private providers on an equal footing (Hill, 2005).

Settlement on such a solution might be stable for a long time. Its stability would be based on preventing formation of lasting within-government monopolies and allowing continuous entry of groups demanding novel kinds of schooling and new school and teacher providers. However, such a solution would make it impossible for anyone to put the game back into the old, cramped ballpark where it was played from 1954 to roughly 1985.

For Research

To date much of what we know about the privatization movement—its members, their motives, the ways they attract parents, the kinds of schools the movement leads to, and its effects on school districts and district-run schools—either isn't so or is correct only by chance. Both privatizers and their opponents have projected consequences of actions from the assumed motives of their sponsors.

Our national debate about school choice might be different if we knew for sure who is actually running charter schools and what their politics and social values are. We don't have good data on this question, though most people who spend time in charter schools observe that teachers and administrators are often "cause" people about education, not privatization. The charter school movement might be somewhat right of center at the top, where the policy entrepreneurs and foundation heads reside, but be somewhat left of center in the schools themselves. Similarly, the families sending their children to charter schools might prove to be mostly social liberals and Democratic voters.

We also know relatively little about what happens in charter schools and other schools of choice. No one has ventured to explain the odd patterns of favorable and unfavorable test scores reported from the New York and DC voucher experiments. Researchers are just starting to understand charter schools as instructional organizations and to figure out why it can take years for a new charter school to become effective. Politically charged debates about whether charter schools are innovative have drowned out simpler questions about what kinds of new choices they present families, and whether families are learning to tell the difference between charter schools that can and can't benefit their children. Scholars like Anthony Bryk and Paul Teske are starting to ask such questions, but there are very few relevant studies.

We know a little about who teaches in charter schools but very little about how the charter school option is likely affect the K–12 teaching force in the future. Charter schools hire some highly educated young people who might not otherwise enter teaching, and some young people who start in charter schools eventually move into district-run schools. Nobody knows, however, whether nontraditional charter school teachers displace teachers from more traditional sources or how the former affect the overall size and composition of K–12 teaching force.

Despite all the publicity it has received, research on charter school student outcomes is still scarce and relatively primitive. It is not possible to judge a national movement from an unrepresentative sample of schools, or to make sense of mean outcomes when variations among schools are enormous. The best studies available today are noble efforts for the beginning stages of a new inquiry, but they cannot carry the freight of policy implications that activists—and sometimes their authors—claim.

In general, research on vouchers and charter schools has stretched too far for policy relevance. Dueling researchers—e.g., as documented in *The Charter School Dust-Up* (Carnoy et al., 2005)—have acted as if any positive or negative statement about the privatization movement could sink or save it. As this paper shows, the school privatization movement is the result of a vast change in the political economy of public education. The forces at work for and against privatization will be little affected by research findings, unless these all point in the same direction and accumulate over a long time.

Researchers need to regard charter schools as objects of serious study. They are not just like district-run public schools, and they are likely to be around for some time. K–12 public education will be better served by research focused on understanding schools of choice than by studies designed to support or castigate them.

REFERENCES

Anderson, A. B. (2004). *Charter schools in Washington state: A financial gain or drain?* Working Paper, Center on Reinventing Public Education, Seattle. http://www.crpe.org/workingpapers.shtml

Barber, B. R. (2004). Taking the public out of education. *School Administrator,* May. Retrieved January 22, 2007 from http://www.aasa.org/ publications/saarticledetail.cfm?ItemNumber = 1375&snItemNumber = 950&tnItemNumber = 1995

Baumgartner, F. R., and Jones, B. D. (1993). *Agendas and instability in American politics.* Chicago: University of Chicago Press.

Bentley, A. (1908). *The process of government.* Chicago: University of Chicago Press.

Bettinger, E. (1999). *The effect of charter schools on charter students and public schools.* Occasional Paper No. 4, National Center for the Study of Privatization in Education, New York.

Bifulco, R., and Ladd, H. (2004). *The impacts of charter schools on student achievement: Evidence from North Carolina.* Working Paper, Sanford Institute, Durham, NC.

Buckley, J., and Schneider, M. (2004). *Do charter schools promote student citizenship?* New York: National Center on Privatization in Education.

Buckley, J., Schneider, M., and Shang, Y. (2004). *Are charter school students harder to educate? Evidence from Washington D.C.* New York: National Center on Privatization in Education.

Bulkley, K., Mundell, L., and Riffer, M. (2004). *Contracting out schools: The first year of the Philadelphia diverse provider model.* Philadelphia: Research for Action.

Camilli, G., and Bulkley, K. (2001). Critique of "An evaluation of the Florida A-Plus Accountability and School Choice Program." *Education Policy Analysis Archives 9*(7). http://epaa.asu.edu/epaa/v9n7/

Carnoy, M., Jacobsen, R., Mishel, L., and Rothstein, R. (2005). *The charter school dust-up: Examining the evidence on enrollment and achievement.* Washington, DC: Economic Policy Institute.

Carroll, S. G. (2005). *California's K–12 schools: How are they doing?* Santa Monica, CA: RAND.

Center for Education Reform. (2005). *Just the FAQs—Tuition tax credits and tax deductions.* http://www.edreform.com/index.cfm?fuseAction = document&documentID = 59&sectionID = 67&NEWSYEAR = 2006

Cholo, A. B., and Dell'Angela, T. (2004). 100 new schools to be created. *Chicago Tribune,* June 23, 1 Metro.

Christensen, C. M. (1997). *The innovator's dilemma: When new technologies cause great firms to fail.* Cambridge, MA: Harvard Business School Press.

Cobb, C. D., and Glass, G. V. (1999). Ethnic segregation in Arizona charter schools. *Education Policy Analysis Archives 7*(1). http://epaa.asu.edu/epaa/v7n1/

Fields, R. (2003). City transportation problems stall transfers to better schools. *Baltimore Sun*, October 23, 1A.

Finn, C. E., Hassel, B., and Speakman, S. (2005). *Charter school funding: Inequity's next frontier.* Washington, DC: Thomas B. Fordham Institute.

Guin, K. (2004). Chronic teacher turnover in urban elementary schools. *Education Policy Analysis Archives 12*(42). http://epaa.asu.edu/epaa/v12n42/

Hannaway, J., and Rotherham, A. J., eds. (Forthcoming). *Collective action: The cost and consequences of collective bargaining in education.* Cambridge, MA: Harvard Education Press.

Hanushek, E. A., Kain, J. F., Rivkin, S. G., and Branch, G. F. (2005). *Charter school quality and parental decision making with school choice.* NBER Working Paper No. 111252, National Bureau of Economic Research, Cambridge, MA. http://papers.nber.org/papers/w11252.pdf

Haycock, K. (2000). Honor in the boxcar: Equalizing teacher quality. *Thinking K–16 4*(1), 1–5, 7–8, 10–12.

Henig, J. (2005). Understanding the political conflict over school choice. In J. Betts and T. Loveless (Eds.), *Getting choice right: Ensuring equity and efficiency in education policy,.* Washington, DC: Brookings Institution Press.

Hill, P. T. (2000). The federal role in education. In D. Ravitch (Ed.), *Brookings papers on education policy: 2000* (pp. 11–39). Washington, DC: Brookings Institution Press.

Hill, P. T. (2001). What is public about public education? In T. E. Moe (Ed.), *A primer on American public education* (pp. 285–316). Stanford, CA: Hoover Press.

Hill, P. T. (2005a). Assessing achievement in charter schools. In R. J. Lake and P. T. Hill (Eds.), *Hopes, fears, and reality: A balanced look at American charter schools in 2005* (pp. 21–32). Seattle: Center on Reinventing Public Education, National Charter School Research Project.

Hill, P. T. (2005b). Lessons from Blair's school reforms: The "specialist school" formula pays off. *Policy Review 131*. http://www.policyreview.org/jun05/hill.html

Howell, W. G., Wolf, P. J., Campbell, D. E., and Peterson, P. E. (2003). School vouchers: Results from randomized field trials. In C. M. Hoxby (Ed.), *The economics of school choice* (pp. 107–144). Chicago: University of Chicago Press.

Howell, W. G., Wolf, P. J., Peterson, P. E., and Campbell, D. E. (2001). Effects of school vouchers on student test scores. In P. E. Peterson and D. E. Campbell (Eds.), *Charters, vouchers, and public education* (pp. 136–159). Washington, DC: Brookings Institution Press.

Hoxby, C. M. (2000). *Would school choice change the teaching profession?* NBER Working Paper No. 7866, National Bureau of Economic Research, Cambridge, MA. http://post.economics.harvard.edu/faculty/hoxby/papers.html

Krueger, A. B., and Zhu, P. (2003). *Another look at the New York City school voucher experiment.* NBER Working Paper No. 9418, National Bureau of Economic Research, Cambridge, MA.

Moe, T. M. (2002). The structure of school choice. In P. T. Hill (Ed.), *Choice with equity* (pp. 179–212). Stanford, CA: Hoover Institution Press.

Murphy, P. J., and DeArmond, M. M. (2003). *From the headlines to the front lines: The teacher shortage and its implications for recruitment policy.* Seattle: Center on Reinventing Public Education.

National Working Commission on Choice in K–12 Education. (2003). *School choice: Doing it the right way makes a difference.* Washington, DC: Brookings Institution Press.

Oakes, J. (2000). *Becoming good American schools: The struggle for civic virtue in education reform.* San Francisco: Jossey-Bass.

Office of Educational Research and Improvement. (2000). *The state of charter schools 2000.* Washington, DC: U.S. Department of Education, Office of Educational Research and Improvement.

Rouse, C. E. (1998). Private school vouchers and student achievement: An evaluation of the Milwaukee Parental Choice Program. *Quarterly Journal of Economics 113*(2), 553–602.

Roza, M., and Hill, P. T. (2004). How within-district spending inequities help some schools to fail. In D. Ravitch (Ed.), *Brookings papers on education policy: 2004* (pp. 201–228). Washington, DC: Brookings Institution Press.

Sass, T. (Forthcoming). Charter schools and student achievement in Florida. *Education Finance and Policy 1*(1).

Schneider, M., Buckley, J., and Kucsova, S. (2003). *Making the grade: Comparing DC charter schools to DC public schools.* Occasional Paper No. 71, National Center for the Study of Privatization in Education, New York.

Wirt, F. M., and Kirst, M. W. (1997). *The political dynamics of American education.* Berkeley, CA: McCutchan.

Witte, J. F. (1998). The Milwaukee voucher experiment. *Educational Evaluation and Policy Analysis 20*(4), 229–252.

Zimmer, R., and Gill, B. (2004). *Assessing the performance of charter schools.* Education Commission of the States Guest Column No. 5588. Denver, CO: Education Commission of the States.

APPENDIX

Payroll Cause of Schools' Budget Wars
Seattle Post-Intelligencer, January 25, 2005, B7
by Dick Lilly

It's time for a hiring freeze.

It's the cost of payroll and not, as some would claim, the overhead cost of running school buildings, that's really the cause of Seattle Public Schools' budget woes. A hiring freeze leading to a smaller, stable workforce is the only sure, enduring way off the treadmill.

Consider this example: Using money from I-728, the class size reduction initiative, the district allocated $170 to schools for every student enrolled. In 2001–02, the year the program started, the average cost for an elementary school teacher was a little less than $55,000, including benefits, so for every 325 students, principals got enough money to hire another teacher. Across the district, probably 100 teachers were hired. Thanks largely to I-728, class sizes in grades K–4 have fallen to an average of 22.

Next year (2005–06), we will be budgeting average elementary teacher cost at more than $65,000, including benefits. Most, if not all, of the I-728 teachers or their replacements are still in our classrooms, so these 100 teachers will cost us an additional $10,000 each, a total of $1 million more per year.

About 2,300 Seattle teachers are paid through an allocation formula set out in the state's Basic Education Act. Problem is, Seattle employs more than 800 additional teachers not included in the basic education formula. They help us lower class sizes and deliver essential bilingual and special education services mandated but not paid for by the state and federal governments. Those 800 teachers include the 100 or so paid through I-728, other grants and the local levy.

No matter which fund pays their salaries, all teachers qualify for annual pay increases—"step increases"—based on experience and additional education. These increases average approximately 3 percent per year. Fortunately, the state pays step increases for the 2,300 Basic Education Act teachers. Grants and the local levy cover the increases for the other 800 teachers working in Seattle, a total of roughly $1.5 million per year. That's more than the savings from closing four elementary schools annually from now on. There could hardly be a clearer demonstration that the school district budget problem is payroll, not the number of school buildings.

And the payroll problem is really worse. Teachers' aides and administrators also at times qualify for pay and benefit increases not covered by the state. Plus, there's our recent wage settlement with the Seattle Education Association (SEA), the teachers' union. Including benefits, step increases, one-time pension costs shifted to local districts by the state and our contracted pay increases, the cost of an elementary school teacher will rise from $60,953 this year to $65,853 next year, about 8 percent. Seattle Public Schools, not the state, will pay the contracted—and much deserved—wage increases for all teachers.

For the 800 teachers paid locally from levy and grants, the 8 percent jump will add almost $4 million next year, including the estimated $1.5 million for step increases. For the 2,300 teachers covered by the state, as much as half the 8 percent planned increase remains a local responsibility (the pension costs passed back by the state and the new-contract wage increases), totaling about $5.6 million. Together, added cost is pushing $10 million.

Clearly, the problem is payroll growth and the solution is to freeze hiring of teachers, teachers aides and administrators. That will let retirements and other attrition reduce the workforce to the level that can be sustained.

Yes, under this plan class sizes will rise. But closing schools ALSO means class sizes will rise, something that proponents of school closing have not confronted. There aren't enough empty classrooms for the teachers from closed schools, so the students from closed schools will push up class sizes by a couple kids in the surrounding schools, about what would happen with a hiring freeze.

I oppose closing schools just to balance the budget because, as I have shown, payroll cuts through a hiring freeze can do the same job, actually tackling Seattle Public Schools' real problem, which is unmanaged payroll growth. This along with several other strategies for which there isn't space here, are a real, workable alternative to the administration's ill-conceived plan to close schools. Which would you choose, the loss of your neighborhood school and larger class sizes—or just larger class sizes? Sure, neither is exactly what we'd like, but closing schools is a lot worse.

Dick Lilly is a member of the Seattle School Board. The views expressed here are his own.

6

As Moths to a Flame: Education Policy Research and the Controversial Issues of Race

Jeffrey R. Henig

Race, for researchers in education policy, is like a flame to a moth. It can loom large, almost obscuring other issues, but the heat it generates can warn some away. Because education policy researchers typically want to address matters that make a difference in the real world, they cannot easily ignore a factor so potent that it played a major role in reshaping America's cities and suburbs and plays so central a role in statistical models to account for student test scores, even as those models incorporate more and more independent variables expected to expose the apparent racial patterns as spurious. Because education researchers are in and of the societies they study, the awkwardness, uncertainty, and contentiousness that mark the way Americans stumble around the race issue also affect the research they do and choose not to do.

This chapter offers a broad overview of the treatment of race as an issue and nonissue in the education policy research field. The cumulative literature on race and education is massive and internally complex. Perhaps there is someone smart and well-read enough to fully digest and make sense of it; I am not that person. Much of what is written about race and education does not deal directly with public policy. Much that is written about race and education policy involves accounts of classroom practices, policy commentary, or legal analysis but not original and systematic research. Even filtering out those important areas and zeroing in on race and education policy research leaves an intimidating mixture of such different problem definitions, disciplinary approaches, and methodological approaches that coherence and comparison are unlikely. I open with some descriptive information on the kinds of scholarly research currently being published in which race and education policy are central themes. After mapping out the broad terrain of the literature, I narrow the focus to a more manageable set of issues that have received prominent and extensive attention. As a political scientist, I fall back on what I know the most about: those aspects of education policy research that shed light on how race affects and is affected by the way our institutions of democracy and governance go about their business of setting priorities, selecting programs, and implementing policies to better educate America's youth.

The specific areas of inquiry that I focus on include desegregation and white flight; teacher expectations, tracking, and second-generation discrimination; school choice and resegregation; arguments for race-targeted versus race-neutral policies; civic capacity; and the declining significance of race. I conclude with some broad reflections about ways that public debates and controversies have shaped the research agenda, for better and worse, and the ways that academic disciplines and the array of incentives they create for researchers may affect research and public discourse in turn.

MAPPING THE INTELLECTUAL TERRAIN

In order to gain some perspective on the overall shape and context of scholarly writing on race and education I conducted a series of searches using ProQuest Direct and restricting the search to scholarly publications. Table 6.1 summarizes the results. Applying just the search terms "school(s)" OR "education" identified 211,025 articles; the term "race" alone generated 28,940. The intersection of these terms identified a smaller collection of articles; 4,875 articles were published in scholarly outlets focusing on race AND either education or school(s). A little over a quarter (1,377) of this last group of articles also mentioned "policy" or "politics" in the title or abstract. This group was then subjected to more precise coding. A graduate research assistant read every abstract and coded the articles on the basis of their general type (e.g., original research, law review, essay and opinion, or news), the journal type (e.g., race-specific, general education, disciplinary; policy, or law), and their focus (e.g., United States only, other countries, K–12, higher education). This is not meant to be a comprehensive or precise analysis. Undoubtedly different combinations of search terms would identify other articles, and the coding distinctions in some cases may lack reliability. But the basic findings are helpful in orienting the review to follow and suggest some interesting patterns on their own.

Only about one of every six of the scholarly articles published on race and education policy and politics was identified as providing accounts of original research. References in the abstract to words like "this study," "data," "findings," "examine," "analysis," "survey," and "sample" were indicators that tended to identify these articles, although in each case it was a holistic reading of the abstract that led to the classification. Articles coded as "news" included articles that recounted a current event, biographies, interviews with individuals, accounts of speeches, conference announcements, and academic news. The large number of articles in this category reflected in part the heavy representation of one section from one particular journal: the News & Views section of the *Journal of Blacks in Higher Education*, which by itself accounted for 163 articles.[1] Another large category comprised essays; these were analytical pieces and were typically identified by phrases in the abstracts such as "the author argues," "I," "we," "discuss," "theory," and "critique" as well as personal experience narratives. This category picked up such things as editorials, introductions to special issues, and some commentary. It was interesting that so many of the articles captured in the general search were book reviews. In reviewing the landscape one could easily conclude that books have been a disproportionately prominent venue for dealing with race and education policy; conceivably the complexity and political "touchiness" of this subject requires a fuller and more expansive treatment than can be easily accommodated in article form.

---

1. These unsigned articles included such articles as "Reed College's Commitment to Racial Diversity: Affirmative Action 'Lite' " and "For College Freshmen, Race Is Becoming Less of an Issue." Thanks to Jonah Liebert, my research assistant on this project, for his good and perceptive coding.

TABLE 6.1
Scholarly Articles on Race and Education Policy and Politics

Education or school	211,025	
Race	28,940	
Race and (education or school)	4,875	
Race and (education or school) and (policy or politics)	1,377	
Article type	All	
	(1,377)	
Original research	231	
Law	58	
Essay	230	
News	582	
Idiosyncratic	56	
Book review	167	
Historical	27	
Literature review	6	
Historical review	19	
Other	1	

	All (1,377)	*Original research* (231)
Journal type		
Education with race focus	41.5%	2.6%
Race focus	9.3%	6.5%
General education	10.5%	24.7%
Discipline	7.5%	22.9%
Policy	3.3%	10.0%
Law review	3.3%	0.9%
Other	24.6%	31.6%
U.S. vs. non-U.S.		
U.S.	92.1%	80.7%
Non-U.S.	7.9%	19.3%
Level		
K-12	21.5%	40.6%
Higher	37.0%	15.3%
Not school-focused	41.0%	43.6%
Other	0.5%	0.5%
Race focus		
Black	37.1%	19.2%
Latino	1.2%	2.2%
Multi-	61.7%	78.6%
Method		
Quantitative	6.8%	52.4%
Qualitative	48.6%	47.6%
Non-Research	44.4%	0.0%
Other	0.1%	0.0%

Note: Counts derived from searches using ProQuest Direct restricted to scholarly publications.

Perhaps most worth comment in Table 6.1 are the nature and placement of the original research pieces and the distinctions between them and the bulk of the published work. Over half of all the race- and education-related articles appeared in journals that are dedicated to race issues,[2] yet fewer than one in 10 of the original research articles appeared in these venues. In contrast, over half of the original research articles appeared in general education, disciplinary-focused, or general public-policy journals compared with just over one in five of the overall total.[3] This raises a question—to which I return briefly later—about whether scholarship with a primary focus on race is either being marginalized or is marginalizing itself in venues outside the mainstream of research and public policy debate.

SCHOOL DESEGREGATION AND WHITE FLIGHT

The desegregation of America's public schools has been one of the most wrenching exercises the nation has experienced. More than 50 years after *Brown* v. *Board of Education*, battles over the court orders and busing have left deep imprints on partisan realignment in the South: perceptions of the proper role of the judiciary, the distribution of populations between cities and suburbs, and anxieties about the possible resegregation that might accompany the expansion of school choice options like vouchers and charter schools. The 50-year anniversary provided the occasion for numerous symposia and reviews (e.g., in the *Nation*, 2004; the *New York Law School Review*, 2004–2005; the *Review of Research in Education*, 2005; and the *Teachers College Record*, 2005), many with fresh insights and some raising new questions. After half a century, we are still digesting.

It is unsurprising, then, that issues surrounding the desegregation issue dominate the early education policy literature dealing with race and continue to play a central role. Two broad streams of analysis stand out. The first involves empirical analysis of the consequences of desegregation, with special attention to the question of whether court-ordered initiatives improved, worsened, or had no discernable effect on the racial composition of schools and districts. Although much of the work in this area is quantitative, largely descriptive, and focused on technical issues of measurement, the implications that some have drawn played an important role in buttressing conservative arguments about the limitations of government and the unanticipated risks of well-intentioned policies. The second stream has focused less on demographic shifts and more on processes and institutions of governance; rather than seeking a universal answer to the question of whether desegregation has been effective or ineffective, good or bad, it has sought to identify the conditions under which local political leadership and culture led to more or less volatile responses, and it has begun to highlight differences in the way judicial and electoral venues differ in how they process volatile issues involving culture wars and minority rights.

An important touchstone for research on the impacts of desegregation was James Coleman's mid-1970s writing focusing on the issue of "white flight." Looking at racial trends during the 1960s and early 1970s, Coleman concluded that school desegregation prompted a substantial short-term acceleration of "white flight" (Coleman, 1976; Coleman, Kelly, & Moore, 1975).

---

2. "Race-focused" journals were those that had, in their title, terms such as "race," "Hispanic" "Black" (e.g., *Race, Gender, and Class*). "Race and education" journals were those that combined these with a specific reference in the journal title to schools or education (e.g., *Black Issues in Higher Education*).

3. General education journals were those with words in the title like "teacher," "college," "education," or specific education fields like "social studies," "art," or "multiculturalism." "Disciplinary" journals had titles including major scholarly disciplines such as "political science," economics," or "sociology." "General public policy" journals had words in their titles like "policy," "public opinion," "urban," or "administration."

Coleman's work spurred a wave of counter-arguments and alternative analyses. The reverberations were greater than typical for education policy work because of Coleman's considerable visibility and stature as the lead author of the earlier and famously influential report, *Equality of Educational Opportunity*, known generally as the Coleman Report (Coleman et al., 1966). Further adding impact was the sense on the part of many that Coleman's white flight conclusion represented a significant turnabout. The *Equality of Educational Opportunity* study had concluded that Black students do better in classrooms with more advantaged White students, which some had taken as important supportive evidence in favor of more aggressive efforts to integrate schools. Now Coleman was arguing that well-intentioned efforts to desegregate were having the unanticipated effect of decreasing Black central-city students' exposure to Whites.

But what possibly gave Coleman's white flight thesis its biggest impact was the way it nestled comfortably within a theory of politics and government being burnished within the neoconservative movement of the time. During the mid-1970s, traditional conservatives were back on their heels. Their most starkly conservative presidential candidate—Barry Goldwater—had gone down to sharp defeat in 1964. Richard Nixon had recaptured the White House for the Republicans, but his popularity was waning, and what is more, rather than shrink the federal government, his administration had overseen steady increases in expenditures for many of the programs at the core of the welfare state. Rather than run against the goals associated with the growth of government—goals relating to managing the economy for growth, providing income and retirement security, aggressively protecting civil rights, expanding health care, and the like—the new conservative position was to align with these aspirations but argue that well-intentioned efforts to pursue them via government and bureaucracy were destined to fail. Good goals are not enough; when government overreaches, the most likely result is unanticipated negative consequences.

Coleman's white flight analysis prompted a strong and almost immediate response within the research community (Armor, 1978; Cataldo, Giles, & Gatlin, 1975; Clotfelter, 1979; Farley, 1975; Pettigrew and Green, 1976; Rossell, 1975–1976). This kind of hair-trigger researcher response has become a more common feature in American education research, but was relatively uncommon until then. Social scientists are often criticized for being slow to redirect their research agendas in response to societal needs and for being slow, after taking on a policy-relevant problem, to move their study expeditiously from design to findings to publication. This makes the flurry of desegregation and white flight analyses during the mid- to late 1970s impressive, especially since most of these studies had to go through a normally sluggish process of peer review. Either scholars responded on a dime or, more likely, the arc of events—from *Brown* to the national civil rights legislation in the 1960s, to the migration of the Supreme Court's attention from district dual school systems in the South to more subtle forms of de jure segregation in the north—created an incremental buildup of interest, data collection, and analysis within the scholarly community, with researchers accordingly poised to respond rapidly when public interest peaked. Undoubtedly, the fact that the courts were intensely interested played a role. So, almost certainly, did the fact that researchers saw and were engaged by the centrality of the issue in the broad ideological battle over whether wise use of governmental authority or reliance on markets and individual choice was the better path to societal well-being.

Many of those constituting the first stream of desegregation and white flight researchers were sociologists or demographers or relied on the methods associated with those disciplines. For them, school districts were the focus less as policy actors than as convenient units of analysis; districts were the unit at which the relevant data were collected, and because courts defined integration at the district level, this was also the level at which societal interest was most closely pitched. What I am referring to as the "second stream" was characterized by more explicit attention to variation in the ways in which different political venues handled the challenges of framing and implementing policy around the desegregation issue.

A classic example was Robert Crain's *The Politics of School Desegregation* (1969), which examined the ways in which eight northern and seven southern city school systems responded to the pressure to desegregate. Crain avoided the common tendency to pick cases because they were clear examples of either failure or success. The study allowed for—and found—variation in the way that seemingly similar places handled a seemingly similar challenge, and then focused its analysis on the question of explaining why conflict, controversy, and stalemate occurred in some settings while relatively smooth transitions happened elsewhere. Because case selection controlled for broad demographic characteristics of the cities, Crain was able to zero in on the so-called "black box" of local politics. He found that school boards were critical actors, whose members' racial predispositions played an important role in determining whether the board resisted or accommodated demands to integrate, and that cities that generally acquiesced to demands for integration were those with an organized and active civic elite.

Crain attended to formal institutions, particularly the extent to which school board members were appointed or elected, but his primary explanatory variables related to political process, political culture, and political tradition. Another classic of this second stream of desegregation studies, more explicitly zeroed in on an institutional issue. For Hochschild (1984), a critical issue was the distinction between the judicial and electoral arenas as forums for handling tensions between majority interests and minority rights. Her analysis directly challenged the comfortable belief that racial segregation was an aberration in an American landscape marked by values of equality and justice shared by the American public and protected through its democratic processes. She found that popular input had been more likely to derail integration than promote it, that when public involvement was supportive it was more likely to be because key local elites pursued that end, and that the courts—the institution of government least susceptible to popular control—had been the most likely one to take progressive action.

Because they addressed issues that were high on the national policy agenda, these various studies of school desegregation were more widely attended to at the time of their publication than is commonly the case with social science research. But there is an underside to this; two to three decades later some of these works seem to me to be underappreciated precisely because they appear to be anchored in a bygone era. Had the early studies of white flight been framed in the context of a powerful theoretical lens like Hirschman's *Exit, Voice, and Loyalty* (1970), their relevance to contemporary debates about the limits and capacities of government versus markets might be more widely recognized. Crain's and Hochschild's analyses were in general more theoretically grounded—anchored, both, in ideas about democratic theory—but in their presentations, too, explicit theory building was overshadowed by their effort to speak plainly and directly to a critical issue at a critical time. Revisited today, their studies have a lot to say about ongoing debates among public policy scholars about leadership, political institutions, venues, and incrementalism versus change. They speak to these directly and could and should have become part of a more theoretical understanding of how and when political leaders and variable institutions can redirect policies in ways that make them more likely to succeed. Arguably, because they were framed as a response to what were contemporary issues, once those issues passed the analyses seemed passé.

BLACK STUDENTS/WHITE SCHOOLS: TEACHER EXPECTATIONS AND SECOND-GENERATION DISCRIMINATION

As America's schools integrated, through court order or through natural demographic shifts, more attention became focused on what happens when students from different backgrounds, culture, and class come face-to-face with one another and with institutions that have been, and still were, predominantly White-led. Early writings tended to present a picture simultaneously bleak in assessment of the status quo and, paradoxically, optimistic in prospects for positive change. White teachers' low expectations for Black students were self-fulfilling prophecies. Through tracking and various forms of "second-generation discrimination," statistical desegregation between schools was diluted by segregation within schools. Cultural remnants grounded in historical and contemporary segregation and oppression made Black students less able or inclined to do well in school even when opportunities were available. To the extent that these were rooted in out-moded and fading biases and attitudes, such explanations prompted some to assume the problems would fade away as White Americans' racial attitudes matured, as the racial composition of the educational workforce shifted, and as new generations of Black parents—raised in the aftermath of the Civil Rights Movement—exhibited and inculcated in their children a set of expectations less yoked to historical repression. As is often the case, systematic research and policy experience have proven the story to be more complicated than this.

Among the first issues to get sustained attention was the role of teachers' (low) expectations in generating a self-fulfilling prophecy of failure for minority youth. The classic and broadly influential study in this area was *Pygmalion in the Classroom* (Rosenthal & Jacobson, 1968). The study is familiar to many so let me summarize it only briefly here. Researchers administered an intelligence test to elementary school students, but teachers were led to believe the test was specially designed to identify children who may not have been performing well but who could be expected to show a burst of development in the near future. In truth, the researchers randomly selected the students that teachers were informed had been scientifically identified as "late bloomers." When researchers retested the students two years later, there was evidence that the randomly selected students had had greater IQ gains than the control group. The results were taken to mean that teachers' high expectations for these children led them to treat them differently, in ways that stimulated greater intellectual development. The political and policy message that most drew was even more pointed. In the context of racially changing central-city school systems, the study was adduced to explain Black students' poor performance in the classrooms of White teachers who carried racially biased expectations into their classrooms. William Ryan, reflecting on Rosenthal and Jacobson's finding that teachers seemed to exhibit negative attitudes toward children who performed well despite not having been identified as likely late bloomers, gave this interpretation a particularly sharp bite: "Is it possible," he asked, "that we have here a germinal insight into the growing problem of what ghetto teachers call the 'disruptive' child? Could the disruptive child be a modern version of the 'uppity nigger'?" (1976, p. 59).

If raising low expectations were simply a matter of dispelling simple stereotypes, we should by now have seen evidence of a reversal in the performance of minority students in older central-city schools. Even giving just consideration to the potential obstinacy of race-based biases, there is substantial evidence that Whites' racial attitudes in general have liberalized, and massive investment in sensitizing teachers to these matters makes it unlikely that White teachers today would harbor harsher and more rigid views of minority students' potential than their predecessors from earlier decades. In addition, in a substantial number of school districts, Blacks and Latinos now make up a substantial proportion of the teaching corps. A 2001 survey with responses from 70 large school districts found an average of 19.5 percent Black and 8 percent Hispanic, with 16 districts having a combined Black and Hispanic contingent of 40 percent or more.[4] Some central cities like Atlanta, Detroit, and Washington, DC, which became majority-minority cities four or five decades ago, have substantially higher proportions of Black teachers; in these districts

---

4. My thanks to Ken Meier for providing the survey data (Meier 2005).

at least, the portrait of an unsympathetic or culturally tone-deaf White teacher confronting minority students is simply out of date. I know of no evidence that this has led to an improvement in performance of the Black students in those places.[5] This does not mean, of course, that race-based perceptions and racially tilted policies no longer apply. To the extent that they do so, however, the arc of research since then suggests that their effects are more subtle, small, and contingent than the initial reading of the Rosenthal and Jacobson work implied.

Excellent recent reviews make it apparent how much more complicated the story really is (Ferguson, 1998; Jussim & Harber, 2005). Among the complicating issues in the general literature on teacher expectations are the following: evidence that over half of the Black–White test score gap in 12th grade may be accounted for by differences that are evident before children enter their formal schooling years; evidence that, once children do reach school age, subsequent achievement gaps do not increase during the school year but are largely accounted for by differential "fallback" among low-income and minority students during the summer months; evidence that teachers' early impressions of students are generally accurate; evidence that self-fulfilling prophecies, to the extent that they occur, have relatively small size effects; lack of evidence that teacher expectations have effect once children are beyond the very early grades; evidence that self-fulfilling prophecies, to the extent they do occur, are as likely to dissipate as to accumulate over time; and suggestions that teacher expectations may play as least as much of a positive role (drawing some students into performing better than they otherwise might) as a negative one. There is at least some evidence that teachers may hold lower expectations for Black students and that Black students may be more susceptible to the negative effects of teachers' low expectations. But what is striking—especially in light of the powerful strain in conventional wisdom that inflated Rosenthal and Jacobson's "Pygmalion" effect into a prominent explanation for poor performance in inner-city schools—is how little systematic research on the intersection between teacher expectations and race has taken place. Ferguson, for instance, indicates that he could find only three studies testing the accuracy of teacher expectations that provided separate analyses for Black and White students, only four experimental studies examining whether teachers treat Black and White students differently, and only one study that tested to see if teachers' perceptions had a differential effect on test scores depending on the students' race. Interestingly, most of the studies that did explicitly consider race appear to have been done in the 1970s, raising questions about whether researchers, like much of the nation, have concluded that race is either less important than once imagined or simply too hot to handle comfortably, a question to which I'll return later.

Jussim and Harber (2005) conclude that "self-fulfilling prophecies in the classroom do exist, but they are generally small, fragile, and fleeting" (p. 151), while noting that when at-risk groups, including racial minorities, are isolated, such effects "although typically weak" and likely to dissipate "may endure in diluted form for years" (p. 152). Ferguson's conclusions are similar: "My bottom line conclusion is that teachers' perceptions, expectations, and behaviors probably do help to sustain, and perhaps even to expand, the Black—White test gap," but "the full story is quite complicated and parts of it currently hang by thin threads of evidence" (1998, p. 313). None of these reviewers concludes that race is no longer a significant factor affecting students and their performance; to the contrary. Taken together, however, they do raise questions about the extent to which schools are the critical sites at which race-based privileges and disadvantages are created and maintained.

---

5. Indeed, in the recently released NAEP Trial Urban District Assessment (National Assessment of Educational Progress 2005), Washington, DC and Atlanta stood out for combining among the lowest scores for Blacks with the highest scores for Whites, suggesting strongly that the underlying socioeconomic characteristics of their populations mean much more than the demographics of their teacher force.

The evidence about the possibly harmful effects of low teacher expectations is intertwined with controversies over whether and how to channel children into different educational tracks based on differences in background, preparation, ability, or inclination. Some argue that being assigned to a "lower" track is a form of stigmatization that generates a self-fulfilling prophecy that—because it carries the apparent legitimacy and authority of an institutional decision—could be even more powerful than that associated with one teacher's possibly idiosyncratic biases. As much as psychological consequences, however, the tracking controversy has focused on the possibly harmful effects if some children are locked into a less challenging curriculum with less able and qualified teachers.

Controversy over tracking predates the desegregation battle. Over 100 years ago, Progressive reformers instituted various sorting mechanisms as a way to handle the influx of immigrant groups and segregate so-called "unruly" or "difficult" children so they did not disrupt the normal order and educational routines (Tropea, 1987) or to assign students different curriculum on the basis of their natural "merit" (Lemann, 1999). But intersection with race gave those questions new visibility and legal significance. Some analysts have presented tracking as an example of second-generation discrimination in the belief that it is one of the ways some schools and districts tactically maintain predominantly White classrooms even while a school may be becoming more racially mixed because of court order or demographic change. Other forms of second-generation discrimination could include racially disproportionate use of disciplinary action, including suspension and expulsion.

Jeannie Oakes's *Keeping Track* (1985) is almost certainly the best known single work on tracking and among educators, if not necessarily researchers, probably remains the defining work on the subject.[6] Oakes's study is based on detailed data collection in 25 secondary schools. In collecting data, Oakes defined tracking broadly; schools that channeled students into relatively homogenous ability levels in any subject were characterized as engaged in tracking, regardless of whether there was a formal policy. So defined, she found tracking to be nearly ubiquitous, although frequently unacknowledged by the schools. In most of the multiracial schools in her sample, there was a racial pattern in assignment, with non-White students disproportionately in the lower tracks. Low-track classes offered less-challenging content and were taught in ways that put greater emphasis on conformity, order, and discipline. Students in the lower-track classes had lower self-esteem and lower aspirations. Critical questions from a policy standpoint are whether students in Oakes's study were assigned on the basis of true ability and knowledge or teacher perceptions shaded by race, whether different content represented an appropriate and high-quality adaptation of pedagogy to student needs or a partial and poorly delivered curriculum that locked students into a second-tier education, and whether the low-track students' low opinion of themselves was part of the explanation for their poor performance or a result of their internalization of the negative message that schools send by sorting them in the ways that they do. Oakes pulls few punches in her conclusion that on each of these questions tracking appeared to be a reflection of schools' own biases and a powerful legitimation of society's.

As with the literature on teacher expectations, subsequent research has suggested the possible need for a more nuanced understanding that makes distinctions among types of tracking policies and the ways in which tracking may unfold differently in different contexts. Almost no one among the leading researchers is asserting that tracking, as carried out, is a precise and unbiased system for matching individual students with the learning environments that best suit their needs. While there is evidence supporting the view that race can be a factor biasing student

---

6. As a crude indicator, Google Scholar lists *Keeping Track* as having been cited in 440 works. By comparison, Tom Loveless's book, *The Tracking Wars*, which challenges Oakes on many points, is listed in Google scholar as having only 8 citations (accessed September 23, 2005).

assignments to different tracks (Gamoran, 1992), many of the irrational and dysfunctional aspects of tracking as implemented may be attributable to organizational failures that have little to do with race per se (Loveless, 1999; Mickelson, 2003; Riehl, Pallas, & Natriello, 1999).

That schools may simply be bad—rather than racially biased—at doing tracking may not matter if it turns out that students *perceive* race to be at the core of the sorting process. While the research literature is somewhat mixed in its findings about whether placement in low-track classes leads children to internalize feelings of inferiority, at least one systematic meta-analysis suggests that the weight of the evidence supports the somewhat counterintuitive conclusion that it may actually be associated with slightly higher levels of student self-esteem (Kulik & Kulik, 1982). Smith et al. (1998) employed experimental techniques to explore whether the institutional stamp associated with tracking students into different classes had a greater self-fulfilling prophecy effect than does within-class ability grouping and concluded it did not. Ferguson (1998) is supportive of Oakes's assertion that teachers of low-track classes are less enthusiastic, hardworking, and supportive, but notes that the evidence shows small rather than large differences. "Given this similarity of teaching styles and classroom procedures, one should not expect large consequences from alternative grouping and tracking arrangements, except where there are substantial differences in curriculum and courses taken" (pp. 339–340).

To say that research is showing the relationship between tracking and race to be more complicated than initially portrayed is not to say that the relationship is inconsequential. Clotfelter's analysis (2004) of North Carolina data shows that within-school segregation has been growing but primarily at the higher grade levels. Indeed, while between-school segregation is more prevalent than within-school segregation in the elementary levels, in grades 7 and 10, within-school segregation reduces students' exposure to children of other races to a greater extent than does segregation between schools. Conger's analysis (2005) of New York City patterns also finds substantial within-school segregation, even within elementary schools, but there the pattern seemed to be decreasing; moreover, the sharp differences in the extent of within-school segregation across the five boroughs and across different racial groups challenge any simple notions that the process is propelled by racial attitudes of Whites (the fact that segregation is high for Hispanic and foreign-born students, for instance, raises the possibility that the causal mechanism is related to pedagogical issues such as handling of bilingual education). That most within-school segregation seems to occur in later grades, presumably after students' core self-identities have been structured, and that the patterns may reflect pedagogical rather than racial forces, does not mean that minorities do not suffer if they are improperly channeled into lower tracks. Under No Child Left Behind, the nation has begun to grapple with the question of teachers' substantive qualifications, and there is increased attention to the extent to which teachers, particularly at the higher grade levels, really have the expertise they need, and research suggests that teachers in lower tracks are less likely to have majored in the subjects they teach (Ingersoll, 1999).

Most of the research on second-generation discrimination draws on demography, sociology, organizational theory, and psychology; it considers schools, classrooms, teachers, or students as the key unit for analysis, since schools and classroom are where the most sorting takes place, and teachers and students are where the relevant perceptual responses should be found. Some researchers place this into a larger context of politics, power, and control of the institutions of governance. Meier, Stewart, and England (1989), for example, start with the finding that, within large districts, Black students are nearly three times as likely as White students to be placed in a class for the educable mentally retarded and that White students, conversely, are more than three times as likely as Black students to be assigned to a class for gifted students. Such racial patterns are mitigated, however, when a higher percentage of teachers is Black. This, in turn, is more likely when there are more Black administrators; more Black administrators are found in districts with more Blacks on the school board; and, finally, the proportion Black on the school board is associated with Black political resources (higher relative incomes) and reliance on district rather than at-large elections. Rather than focus narrowly on the arguments for or against particular formal policies regarding tracking, this kind of analysis suggests that those interested in reducing racial disparities in assignment to different types of classes might do well to zero in on ways to increase minority groups' political power and to put into place governance institutions that make it more likely they can convert that power into control of office and authority.

SCHOOL CHOICE: MARKETS AS A TOOL FOR EQUITY OR RESEGREGATION

For researchers interested in the way that broad governance institutions affect education policy, it was issues of federalism—in particular states' rights and local control—that until quite recently dominated the field of vision. By the mid-1980s some of those issues were settling into a period of relative quiescence: The fiercest battles over busing were over; the U.S. Supreme Court had issued its major rulings, and there were no near-term prospects that it would reengage in the aggressive campaign to end all vestiges of segregation; and the pattern of predominantly minority central-city districts surrounded by predominantly White suburban jurisdictions had come to be accepted, more or less, as a fact of life. Although research on racial dynamics in schools continued, it was losing some of its prominence and centrality. Surging interest in vouchers, charter schools, and other market-oriented models for stimulating school reform gave the issue of race and resegregation a new second wind.

In recent years, battles over the efficacy of government versus markets have claimed equal time with federalism as a focus of education policy research and debate. Now that school choice options, particularly charter schools, are relatively prevalent and have begun to compile a track record, the debate about market-oriented choice reforms has begun to focus most heavily on the question of whether they lead to better test scores. The issue of impact on achievement is important, and it gets special impetus from the pressure on test scores being exerted by the No Child Left Behind legislation and many states' high-stakes testing regimes. A preoccupation in the early debates, however, was with the potential for market-oriented policies to either exacerbate or alleviate segregation.

Reflecting in part on the historic patterns of white flight and on the specific use of "freedom-of-choice" arguments and policies by some southern districts engaged in the "massive resistance" to integration in the wake of the *Brown* decision, critics of early voucher proposals argued that market-oriented school choice schemes would both allow and encourage White and Black families to re-sort themselves into more homogenous schools settings (Cookson, 1995; Henig, 1994; Wells, 1993). They speculated also that lower-income and minority parents would be disadvantaged in a market-like environment because they would be likely to have less information, less time to research school alternatives, less ability to manage the bureaucratic hurdles of pursuing their choices, and fewer slack resources to devote to handling the complexities of transportation and time management associated with sending one's child somewhere other than the nearest public school. They worried that choice regimes would simply provide advantaged and White families with a new vehicle for ensuring that their children were educated in exclusive settings surrounded by peers who had backgrounds and skin color similar to their own.

In contrast, school choice proponents argued that schools *already* were highly segregated, that highly segregated housing patterns ensured that traditional modes of assignment based on where families lived enshrined this pattern, and that choice systems—by allowing parents to voluntarily sort out on the basis of student interests—would actually do a better job of bringing about racial integration than had command-and-control exercises imposed by the heavy hand of government. (For one early statement of this position see Finn, 1990; for a more recent iteration, see Greene, 2005.) Initially, at least, the competing conjectures were based on theory and analogy. Choice proponents relied both on market theories that predicted minorities unhappy with existing schools would use the exit option to transfer their children to better (and more integrated) schools and on an analogy with magnet schools where choice and integration worked hand in hand (Blank et al., 1983). Since there were no voucher plans in effect and charter schools had not yet been invented, going into the 1990s the prospect for empirical testing was limited.

Over the past 15 years, at least two lines of empirical research have emerged. One, focusing on the professed attitudes and values of White versus minority parents, has tended to produce findings consistent with the claims of choice proponents. The other, which contrasts families' self-professed values with their actual behavior, has been considerably less sanguine about the likelihood that the social goal of racial integration would be furthered in a market-driven system.

Research based on what parents say they consider when selecting schools has tended to suggest that fears of value-based segregation may be overstated. For example, Schneider, Teske, and Marschall (2000) found that low-income and minority parents were actually more likely than White parents to say that academic quality is what is important in choosing schools and that parents "hardly ever cite racial similarity as a relevant criterion in evaluating the quality of schools" (p. 106) and tend to dismiss as peripheral any consideration of the racial composition of schools (see also Kleitz et al., 2000).

Studies looking at choice as actually exercised are less sanguine, with the evidence increasingly suggesting that families rely on the race and socioeconomic status of student populations as shortcuts to finding settings that they believe will be more comfortable or otherwise supportive of their children, even when homogeneity comes at the expense of leaving "better" schools as measured by test score performance. In one early study of transfer patters among public magnet schools, I found that White parents were more likely to select schools that had lower percentages of minority children, while minority families were more likely to select schools in lower-income neighborhoods (Henig, 1996). Saporito and Larreau (1999), also looking at transfer requests within a public school choice program, found that most White families simply eliminated predominantly Black schools from consideration: "Indeed, the role of race is so powerful that it conjures up an image of a 'non-decision' in that 'Black' schools are excluded regardless of their positive attributes on other criteria" (p. 427). In a clever study, Schneider and Buckley (2002) examine how parents used a Web site that had been established to provide parents with various kinds of information about public and charter schools; the site offered information on every public and charter school in Washington, DC, including where they were located, their facilities, faculty, student demographics, and academic performance (see also Elacqua, Schneider, & Buckley, 2005; Weiher and Tedin, 2002).

The suspicions of some that charter schools would exclusively target White middle-class and White parents, in an effort to "skim the cream" of students who would be easier and presumably more profitable to serve, have proven to be largely unfounded. Based on data from 927 charter schools in 27 states, for example, the Department of Education's *The State of Charter Schools 2000* found that "Charter schools were more likely than all public schools to serve Black students (almost 24 percent versus 17 percent) and Hispanic students (21 percent versus 18 percent)" (Nelson et al., 2000, p. 30). But this aggregated finding may mask segregating effects at least within some states and communities. Frankenberg and Lee's analysis of enrollment in 16 states with large charter school populations, for example, found that 70 percent of Blacks in charter schools attended highly minority schools compared with 34 percent in public schools and concluded that charter schools may be producing "pockets of segregation" (Frankenberg and Lee, 2003). Lacireno-Paquet et al. (2002) found that market-oriented charters serve somewhat less disadvantaged students than do traditional public schools or other, more mission-oriented, charter schools. Renzulli and Evans (2005) linked Schools and Staffing Survey (SASS) data on charter schools to Common Core of Data information on student characteristics and to data on the attributes of the districts in which they were located, including student achievement. They found that the percentage of White students in charter schools is often significantly greater than in the districts in which they are located, but that it is also often significantly lower; the fact that the average approximates that for the district is therefore misleading. By examining racial change in the surrounding districts, they found evidence that charter schools under some conditions may be serving as a new option for white flight; controlling for other factors, a 1 percent increase in integration within the surrounding district is associated with a .73 percent increase in the proportion of charter school enrollment that is White. Renzulli and Evans also found no evidence that state policies intended to ensure that charter schools promote, or at least do not harm, racial balance make a difference, which they attribute to the fact that such provisions may simply not be being enforced (see also Cobb & Glass, 1999; Saporito & Lareau, 1999).

Here, as in other areas reviewed in this chapter, as research accumulates and deepens, a common result is that it becomes harder to hold to a view that race is the dominant driving force, eclipsing factors like class, religion, culture, and context. But it also becomes harder to deny the lingering and substantial role that it plays in shaping education politics, policy, and outcomes. The decentralized nature of our federal system complicates matters, as does the fact that for many of the interesting questions researchers are forced to rely on databases that are specific to a particular school, district, or state. The challenge of generalizing from case studies is not unique to education, but arguably the intense localized histories of segregation, desegregation, and racially framed battles for political access and control make it even more hazardous than normal to look for universal patterns abstracted from context, history, and the particularities of place.

In the meantime, while a handful of researchers continue to probe this issue of choice and resegregation, most of the school choice debate has shifted to other issues. In the era of school accountability, high-stakes testing, and No Child Left Behind, the school choice debate, too, has become dominated by the issue of outcomes. It is arguable that the American public—either following or leading the federal courts—has lost some of its focus on race separation and is willing to tolerate or even welcome homogeneous schools as long as they can be convinced that such schools derive from individual families' choices and especially if they prove to facilitate better test scores. Education researchers, reflecting that societal context, are fixing their microscopes on that set of concerns.

RACE-BASED VERSUS RACE-NEUTRAL POLICIES

An important line of research within political science focuses less on the standard questions about "what policies would work" than on "what policies are likely to be passed, implemented, and sustained." There is evidence that Americans' support for or opposition to specific programs is conditioned upon their beliefs about and attitudes toward the putative beneficiaries. There is evidence, too, that the race of the expected beneficiaries is especially critical. Policies believed to be targeted at racial minorities face some higher hurdles, and this has led some analysts to argue that universal policies—even if they appear on their face to spread resources more thinly—are a more effective mechanism for helping minorities and the poor than are policies explicitly targeted on the basis of race or need. Most of the relevant empirical research has focused on social welfare policies generally, but the argument has clear implications for discussions about education reform.

Arguments for framing policies that are race-neutral in the ways they define eligibility and likely program targets can be based on rational efficiency or political strategy. William Julius Wilson (1987) made the case at least partly on the former grounds. Class distinctions among African Americans are important, as he had argued in his earlier work, and policies that ignore that have a potential to waste resources and possibly do some harm as well. Race-based programs—e.g., open housing, anti-redlining regulations, and affirmative action in higher education—may help middle-class Black families, who are quicker to find them and better prepared to exploit them, leaving less wealthy and less educated Blacks even more isolated socially and politically than they had been previously. This led him to conclude that "the problems of the truly disadvantaged may require *nonracial* [emphasis in the original] solutions such as full employment, balanced economic growth, and manpower training and education" (p. 147).

Programs that exclusively provide benefits to any concentrated group also face political hurdles (Wilson & Banfield, 1964), and that is especially the case if the targeted groups is perceived to be weak and undeserving (Schneider, 2001). Gilens (1995) provides compelling evidence that White Americans' attitudes toward Blacks—especially whether they believe that an important explanation for inequality is Blacks' failure to work harder—is a significant factor predicting their support or opposition to welfare programs (see also Lieberman, 1993; Soss et al., 2001). Significantly, these studies suggest that programs believed to primarily benefit Blacks will face resistance whether or not those programs are race-neutral on their face. As Gilens concludes: "Whether race-specific or race-neutral, antipoverty policy in this country has become hostage to White Americans' cynicism toward poor Blacks and specifically to the belief that Blacks' economic problems are of their own making" (Gilens, 1995).

Richard Kahlenberg has taken these lines of evidence and argument and applied them most directly to the issue of education equity and reform (Kahlenberg, 2000). Whether it is the case or not that schools tasked with educating minority students are faced with challenges greater than those with equally low-income White students, Kahlenberg argues that it is simply not worth it to pursue a race-based policy for integrating schools, precisely because the emotional freight and polarizing tendencies make for a losing political hand. In place of race, he proposes a class-based policy for integrating schools. Economic integration would provide many of the positive peer effects that proponents of racial integration desire (although not necessarily those that potentially come from breaking down racial stereotypes) and in many districts would end up increasing racial integration as well. There are at least some indications, too, that the impacts on test scores, and in particular test score gaps, could be substantial; in Raleigh, NC, which initiated economic integration in 2000, the percentage of Black students testing at grade level increased from 40 percent to 80 percent over the past 10 years (Finder, 2005). Economic integration, Kahlenberg reasons, is less likely to trigger political resistance from White and advantaged families, in large part because it is less visible than is integration by race. That does not mean that there would be no resistance, and Kahlenberg proposes to reduce that by building into the policy a promise that no school would become less than 50 percent "nonpoor."[7] Kahlenberg is arguably overly optimistic about the prospects that the American middle class is willing to lose the control it gains from the status quo; if the research cited above is accurate, his proposal to change the formal criterion for integration from race to class may be insufficient to stem resistance if

---

7. Defined as not eligible for free and reduced lunch.

Whites continue to see the effort in racial terms. What is significant about the Kahlenberg argument, however, is the self-conscious effort to shift the grounds on which education researchers typically have addressed the issue of racial conflict. Rather than—or, perhaps more accurately, in addition to—using evidence about schools, students, and classrooms to design idealistic policies that typically fail because of political backlash and the exit option, he proposes that education policy researchers should study the phenomenon of racial politics with an eye toward designing policies that are more likely to get put into effect.

RACE, CIVIC CAPACITY, AND COALITION BUILDING FOR SCHOOL REFORM

Different eras have framed different understandings of where the obstacles to school reform can be found. For much of the 20th century, school reform was seen as a matter of empowering education professionals to find and implement the best means to pursue broadly shared and seemingly unproblematic goals. These professionals, armed as they were with the requisite expertise, could analyze problems and identify solutions; the challenge, where there was one, was to keep politicians and political parties from standing in the way. During the 1960s and early 1970s, spurred in part by racial and ethnic demographic change and political mobilization, a progressive-left critique to this paradigm emerged. Serious conflicts around values and the appropriate ends of education were more evident (explosively manifested, for example, in battles over integration, the racial composition of the teaching workforce, and community control), and professionals' claims to neutral expertise were reinterpreted as rationalizations of the political status quo. By the 1980s, a conservative perspective was ascendant. It returned to the earlier notion that there were some core goals of education that were or should be unproblematic (e.g., a disciplined focus on core literacies), but maintained the more recent portrayal of the professional bureaucracies as part of the problem instead of the solution. School systems were portrayed as uniquely resistant to new ideas—not because educators were serving the interests of a broader political and economic elite, but rather because they were serving interests of their very own.

More recently the dominant framing of the issue has been challenged again. Analysts have now shown that rather than exhibiting outright resistance to change, large central-city school districts frequently suffer from hyperresponsiveness to shifting fads and new notions. While schools districts were once excoriated as bastions of resistance to new ideas, there is a growing recognition that the problem may lie less with the fact that they are closed and impenetrable systems than that they are so open and susceptible to external influence and passing trends. U.S. urban schools do not reject reform so much as they cycle through it spasmodically and without cumulative effect: what has been variously described as "spinning wheels" (Hess, 1998), "reform du jour" (Farkas, 1992), "reforms that go nowhere" (Henig et al., 1999) or "flip flops in school reform" (Hannaway & Stanislawski, 2005). The notion that schools are besotted with reform and the notion that schools resist reforms are not quite so distinct as they may initially appear; as Tyack and Cuban (1995) note reforms are often symbolic and adopted to protect school people "from basic challenges to their core practices" (p. 4).

Against this backdrop, a recent body of research and writing has conceptualized the challenge of school reform less in terms of aspects of the policies themselves than of the political and civic characteristics of communities into which they are introduced. A number of studies have grown out of the Civic Capacity and Urban Education Project, which examined school reform in 11 cities and probed how differences in response were conditioned upon traditions and experiences of collective decision making around schooling but around other issues as well

(Henig et al., 1999). Most of the key obstacles to reform identified in this research are character-istic of large central-city school districts regardless of their particular racial composition, but race emerges as an important intermediary variable, with potential to make reform alliances more frag-ile unless duly taken into account. Most of the literature on the pros and cons of race-conscious policies, discussed in the previous section, puts its emphasis on understanding and accommo-dating the racial sensitivities of Whites, the political majority and dominant power group. Perhaps because it has been more focused at the local level, where racial minorities are often the elec-toral majorities and almost always a force to be reckoned with, the research on civic capacity and urban education has devoted equal attention to understanding racially based political attitudes and behaviors of minority groups.

Political scientists traditionally have seen the political process as a competition among com-peting interest groups. Race, understood within this framework, has tended to be portrayed as one among many attributes that define the boundaries of political interest; just as home ownership confers an interest in keeping property taxes low, or working as a laborer within the construction industry confers an interest in pursuing expansion and growth, so too does membership in a racial minority give individuals an interest in a set of substantive policies and a stake in propelling into power those likely to be most responsive to that agenda. When the Civic Capacity and Urban Edu-cation Project studied school politics in major school districts, however, it found that many of the important cleavages did not reflect race in a direct or obvious way. On the other hand, it found that race still was—and is—a powerful force, less as a delineator of objective interests than as a perceptual filter. Race, from this perspective, is a baseline definer of patterns of trust; it is a reservoir of potent symbols that can be divisive or unifying or both at the same time but that have tended to complicate rather than simplify the challenge of school reform.

Orr (1999) describes how Baltimore's African American community evolved a network of civic associations, fraternal organizations, churches, newspapers, colleges and schools through decades of coping in a White-dominated political and economic environment. These institutions also nurtured a political culture that included a wariness of White business and suburban lead-ers, a tendency to see the public schools as a resource for community development and jobs, and a powerful imperative to "stick together" and hide any intraracial group differences from outsiders lest they be exploited by opponents' strategies to divide and conquer. In many ways and for many purposes, these institutions and culture provided a source of strength. They made it more possible for African Americans to build meaningful lives when they were politically marginalized, and the institutions and culture were a platform for political mobilization when opportunities opened up to capture elected offices. In this sense, Orr argues, these institutions, ideas, and values served as "social capital" in much the way that Robert Putnam conceptualized the term (Putnam, 1993).

Much of what is written about school reform today emphasizes the importance of parent engagement. Schooling is an example of what some have labeled "co-production": favorable out-comes depend not only on what public officials do but on how their actions are complemented or resisted by citizens in their day-to-day lives (Levine, 1984; Sharp, 1980). Strong social capi-tal in minority communities from this standpoint represents a potentially valuable resource. As critics of Putnam's original formulation (1993) have emphasized, however, there are two faces to social capital. Under some conditions, bonds of trust and loyalty within groups come at the cost of exacerbating differences between groups, and this has sometimes been the case on the local playing fields of big-city school politics.

Even where control of the key positions of formal authority within the city and school district had been captured by African Americans, Henig et al. (1999) found little evidence of a dramatic new sense of common purpose among school personnel and the predominantly Black students and parents. To the contrary, there were many indications of a striking class cleavage within the

African American communities. Black teachers exhibited considerable scorn toward the families and parents, while the parents felt that they were looked down upon and not truly welcome in the school communities. On the other hand, they found that race altered the way even these relationships played out—not race simply as skin color and prejudice, but race as a shared political history that resulted in racially framed perceptions and racially grounded loyalties. Ironically, to the extent that it generated a common purpose and capacity to mobilize, race was manifested less in support of broad school reform than in reaction against reform initiatives that were seen as threatening local institutions that had only recently passed into African American hands. Kurt Schmoke was able to become the first African American mayor of Baltimore at least in part because of his ability to tap into the reservoirs of Black social capital that Orr described. But when his efforts to jump-start school reform led him to support an experiment to hire a private firm to run some schools on contract, many in the African American community saw this as an assault on institutions (public schools, public employee unions) and people (teachers) to which they owed a longer-standing commitment of loyalty.

Consideration of how race affects coalitions that can sustain reform also has generated research that questions the easy assumption that African Americans and Latinos comprise a natural alliance. During the 1970s and 1980s, as Latino Americans were beginning to press for influence at the local level, their leaders often found it politically useful to draw the analogy between their claims and those asserted earlier and effectively by the Black community during the civil rights era. The similarities in rhetoric, coupled with the fact that in the minds of White Americans, both groups shared a common status as "minorities," made it easy to assume that the shared interests of Blacks and Hispanics would unite them in a "Rainbow Coalition" that could compete for power with dominant White elites. Meier and Stewart were among the first to put this notion to a test. Their analysis (1991) of school board composition in 118 large schools districts with at least 5 percent Latino enrollment suggested that Whites will often ally with Latinos at the expense of African Americans (Meier & Stewart 1991). Similarly, Shipps (2004) has found evidence in Chicago of a growing fissure between Blacks and Latinos, with the Latinos resenting what they see as the domination of the school system by an African American elite holding tightly to control of the jobs and resources at stake. "Latinos felt they had much to gain by engaging in 'guerilla warfare' against middle-class Blacks who ran the school system and who, they believed, withheld from Latinos the favors and resources of categorical programs and affirmative action" (Shipps, 2004, p. 84). This, in turn, has the potential to make Latinos more responsive to school reform proposals, such as mayoral takeover, contracting out, and school choice that typically are promoted by business interests and resisted by the Black community, which sees them as eroding a public school system that has been an important platform in their community.

DECLINING SIGNIFICANCE OF RACE?

Through the 1960s and into the 1970s, race was a prominent feature in how scholars, politicians, and the public thought and talked about America's schools. By the latter part of the 1970s, however, open attention to race began to slide toward the sidelines of public discourse. Regardless of how much racial matters may have continued to shape ideas and behavior—and my own view is that they have continued to do so to a great extent—race began to be eclipsed to some degree by socioeconomic status as a focal point for debate and an explanatory variable. As public discourse about race became less prominent, education researchers did not universally fall in line. Some fought a rearguard action, insisting that the real issues plaguing America's schools could not be dealt with meaningfully without continuing to grapple with the continuing legacies of racial discrimination. Nonetheless, just as education policy researchers once rode public attention and the policy agenda when they began to delve deeply into such issues as school desegregation, second-generation discrimination, and prospects that school choice might foster resegregation, it appears to me that the community of education policy researchers today has been deflected in some ways from keeping race on center stage. In this and the concluding section that follows it, I step back and—using a very broad brush—draw some general and very preliminary conclusions about how this is occurring and whether it is to good or bad effect.

William Julius Wilson's 1978 book, *The Declining Significance of Race*, marked something of a watershed moment in scholarly and public discourse about race and class in American life. As others have noted (Pettigrew, 1979), the book's provocative title and the fact that it was written by a respected African American scholar gave it extra notoriety and may have invited commentary that simplified and even caricatured what were in fact sophisticated observations that did not dismiss race so much as they recognized that it was a complicated concept that needed to be reconceptualized in light of contemporary circumstances. Focusing his attention on growing class differentiation and the development of a strong and growing highly educated middle class within the African American community, Wilson concluded that "class has become more important than race in determining Black life-chances in the modern industrial period" (p. 150).

The Wilson debate did not immediately or directly penetrate the education policy literature. But it can be argued that the eclipsing of race by class had begun to affect education researchers even earlier. A short "biography" of the famous Coleman Report is illustrative here. The motivation behind this study was solidly anchored in the nation's and Congress's concerns about desegregation, but the findings that cast the longest shadow were those that bore upon family background as the primary drivers of student performance. The point is not so much that people are no longer thinking and writing as much about race and education; that may or may not be the case. But as suggested in the review of published articles presented in Table 6.1 and discussed above, a case can be made that this conversation has itself become somewhat "ghettoized," heavily concentrated in journals that specifically focus on race, much less prominently featured in public policy and disciplinary outlets, and more often presented in theoretical and discursive arguments than in empirical research.

Several factors may have contributed to this apparent tendency to turn to class over race as the independent variable of choice in more empirical research. Battles in the courtroom had played a role in focusing research on desegregation (and funding it). Supreme Court decisions and legal tactics began in the late 1970s to shift the ground on which issues about educational opportunity were adjudicated. *Milliken* v. *Bradley*, by making it much less likely that courts would mandate integration across district lines, in the eyes of many observers marked the end of any hopes that legal approaches based on race would be an effective route to addressing the problems of older central-city school systems (Orfield & Eaton, 1996). Claims of discrimination based on race are treated more favorably by the federal courts than are claims of discrimination based on socioeconomic status, but when the U.S. Supreme Court, in *San Antonio School District* v. *Rodriguez*, essentially delegated adjudication of school financing cases to state courts' readings of state constitutions, it moved the legal battles into an arena in which in which charges of class-based discrimination had more bite. As was the case with racial integration in the 1960s and 1970s, researchers' own desires to be "relevant"—combined in some fashion with lawyers', plaintiffs', defendants', and foundations' willingness to ante up dollars—may have played a role in the tendency to frame research on educational equity in less overtly racial terms.

Another reason race may have become less prominent may have been evidence that the racial gap in educational access and performance was, in point of fact, beginning to shrink. As late as

1975, for example, the dropout rates among non-Hispanic Blacks were twice as high as those for non-Hispanic Whites (22.9 percent of Black 16–24-year-olds versus 11.4 percent for Whites); by 2001 the gap had shrunk appreciably, with 10.9 percent of Black 16–24-year-olds having dropped out versus 7.3 percent for Whites (National Center for Education Statistics, 2003). Although less rapidly than many hoped, the racial gap in test scores also was dropping during the 1960s, 1970s, and 1980s. Hedges and Nowell (1998) reviewed test score data from all six of the major national surveys of high school students' performance and found consistent evidence that the gap in test scores was declining between 1965 and 1992. The sharpest period of decline, in fact, was 1965–1972, the period immediately following the national government's most aggressive actions on behalf of voting rights, equal opportunity, housing integration, school integration, and the war on poverty. To those inclined to believe that specifically racial patterns of inequity were vestigial remnants of historical injustices since corrected, these data may have helped cement the impression that the future of important education policy research lay in the direction of class rather than race (see also Kao and Thompson, 2003).

A more prosaic explanation for why class may have begun to overshadow race has something to do with data and measurement. Systematic research on a national scale typically requires large and expensive databases maintained consistently over time; the willingness of government to fund these depends on elected officials' beliefs about what is and is not important to know. The nation's concern about categorizing and counting people by race goes back to the time of the Founding Fathers; as a result, information on the race of the U.S. population has been collected in every decennial census beginning with the first census in 1790. Following *Brown*, the judiciary generated a new and important "client" for racial data on school enrollment as a means of monitoring compliance with its edicts. School districts are notoriously idiosyncratic about what data they collect and make available, but one of the things researchers normally can count on is the availability of reasonably precise data on racial composition even down to the classroom level. School data on socioeconomic class are more scare and more crude. Most state and local student data systems today rely on school lunch eligibility as an indicator of class. In the wake of the Coleman Report, however, the national government undertook the funding of several large surveys—e.g., High School and Beyond (HSB), the National Education Longitudinal Study (NELS), and the National Longitudinal Survey of Youth (NLSY)—that combined student data with much more detailed information about the characteristics of their families. It is the case for researchers that "if you build a database, they will come"; education policy researchers discovered they could draw on a rich and varied array of indicators relating to class, and not surprisingly they took the bait. At the same time, somewhat ironically, social notions of race were becoming more complicated, and dualist distinctions between White and Black were becoming more problematic. The pressure to attend to distinctions within racial categories—culminating in the option provided in 2000 Census to categorize oneself as racially mixed in a number of different ways—made what had been the more straightforward and convenient approach a trickier challenge for research design.

However important these factors have been, a more straightforward explanation rooted in a combination of psychology and politics may also apply: by 1980 many Americans of different colors and partisan loyalties showed signs of weariness with the emotionally wrenching and polarizing race wars. On many important measures, Americans are strongly supportive of notions of racial justice and exhibit far less blatantly biased attitudes than was once the case. But the failure of the Civil Rights Movement to more permanently erase inequalities and resentments left many with the belief that these problems are immune to public policy. Asked whether they think race relations "will always be a problem for the United States" or "a solution for race relations will eventually be worked out," almost two-thirds (63 percent) of Americans opted for the more pessimistic phrasing in 2003.[8] This translates, especially for some White Americans, into a resistance to policies that explicitly target race. Almost a third (31 percent) of White Americans, in 1999, indicated that they believe that less should be done to integrate the schools, for example, and in 2003 less than half (44 percent) said they generally favored affirmative action programs for racial minorities.

Somewhat ironically, the same frustration that leads some Americans to fatalism about racial equity leads others to an aggressive refusal to allow race and past racial injustices to be used as an explanation for poor education performance. The impetus behind No Child Left Behind includes an insistence that "all children can learn" and consequent rejection of the notion that racially defined test gaps are excusable. When this stance translates into support for substantial public investment in low-income schools, the policy consequences can be directly opposite those that occur when frustration generates fatalism and acceptance of the status quo. Yet these two different reactions can each serve to marginalize public discussion of race and the ways it may still infiltrate behaviors and consequences in classrooms, schools, elections, and governance.

CONCLUSION: IS RESEARCH ON RACE AND EDUCATION BECOMING MORE MATURE OR MORE TIMID?

Academics are frequently caricatured as sequestered denizens of ivory towers, either oblivious or indifferent to social problems that plague the "outside world." Yet as this review makes apparent, public debates and controversies most definitely have shaped the education policy research agenda. For the most part to their credit, education scholars have taken up the challenge to focus their attention on researchable questions that policymakers and the public are genuinely concerned about rather than those that emerge out of the competition among theories within more rarefied debates in the academic disciplines. But there is an underside to this sensitivity to raging concerns and reigning sentiments. Being *au courant* can mean being subject to passing fad and fancy, and engaging in the politically charged debates of the day may make it more difficult to maintain the wary skepticism toward quick and simple answers that is the hallmark of independent search for the truth.

Researchers interested in the world of policy and politics may frame their analyses in the effort to address either of two distinct audiences: the community of scholars to which they belong or the broader policy community within which they hope to find a hearing. Although some have been trained in interdisciplinary programs or hold appointments in multidisciplinary units of public policy or education schools, most education researchers retain an allegiance to an academic discipline, and many draw their intellectual inspiration and favored methodologies from the reigning paradigms therein. Academic disciplines both sharpen focus and narrow range. The models that win favor within scholarly circles are often simplified in ways that the public and policymakers consider naïve. During the 1970s and 1980s, for example, a general trend toward economic and rational choice models within the social science disciplines pushed to the margins elements of race and education that seemed to nonscholars to be most pertinent to the issues at hand: factors relating to emotion, symbolism, loyalties, and suspicions embedded in deep racially defined personal and collective histories and psyches.

8. Polling results in this paragraph come from various sources compiled by Public Agenda (2005).

Some researchers swam against the tide of their disciplines to try to keep abstract theories informed by these more raw considerations and did so to good effect. Much of the research that put race front and center, however, was published in journals or other outlets that self-consciously defined themselves as specializing in race and identity. It is not clear whether this was because the mainstream disciplinary journals were unreceptive or because these scholars self-selected into communities of others who shared their primary concern. Even in the major interdisciplinary education journals, race seems over time to have settled in as "just another independent variable"; the race of students and the racial composition of schools will often appear as a control variable, but its statistical effect is often attenuated by socioeconomic variables, and the racial dimension is not featured in the titles and abstracts that announce the studies' focus.

Just as disciplinary paradigms do, public discourse on controversial issues imposes its own simplifications. There is limited tolerance within the political and policy world for insistence on contingent findings or insistence on the need for further evidence. The pressure is strong to argue that race is either *the* point or *beside the point*. In some of the areas discussed in this chapter, research, in my judgment, has helped sharpen understanding of race and education. Paradoxically perhaps, this may be precisely because it has shown that the consequences of race are dependent upon indirect relationships and interaction with other factors; in other words researchers have made some things more clear because they have shown that things are not so simple as others have claimed.

Is the treatment of race within the education policy literature becoming more mature, then? Is it healthier, more accurate, and ultimately more illuminating if researchers treat race as one among other important dimensions of the education experience; if they force it to compete for our attention with other variables, and attribute to it explanatory power based on empirical results; if they adopt a stance of distance, if not indifference, to the question of whether attention to race is a moral imperative? Or is the dimming of race as a primary concern a mark of timidity, a capitulation on the part of education researchers to prevailing political winds and the national aversion to reopening old wounds? Is the new generation of education policy scholars reshaping the research agenda in productive ways, because it is less encumbered by the emotional and symbolic baggage carried by those who directly experienced the sense of righteousness of the Civil Rights Movement and the blatant resistance and open racism of an earlier age? Or are researchers shying away from race because its political volatility makes it a "hot potato," a risky avenue, especially for junior scholars who worry that they cannot afford to jangle the sensitive nerves of peer reviewers, senior colleagues, and administrators?

My own view is that education policy research can help lead to a more mature debate, and ultimately more effective collective intervention, by showing that the difficulties school districts, cities, states, and the national government experience are due to the fact that the problems we want them to address are multidimensional and obstinate, and that the options for intervention depend, for effectiveness, on context and timing and not simply on good design. Race, I believe, has been and remains an important feature of the problems we confront, and attentiveness to how race affects the prospects for policies to be passed, implemented, and sustained is crucial if are to make headway on the toughest challenges. That means race must be dealt with in a forthright manner, not sidestepped or sublimated, but also not given protected status as a favored explanation that brooks no challenge or complication. Taken as a body, I think education policy research has moved us incrementally toward a more subtle and helpful understanding of the role of race. But the risk that we are prematurely shifting our attention to other concerns strikes me as troubling and real.

REFERENCES

Armor, D. (1978). A response to "The 'White Flight Controversy.' " Comments. *The Public Interest 53*, 113–115.

Blank, R. K., Dentler, R. A., Baltzell, D. C., and Chabotar, K. (1983). *Survey of magnet schools: Analyzing a model for quality integrated education.* Washington, DC: U.S. Department of Education, Office of Planning, Budget, and Evaluation.

Cataldo, E. F., Giles, M., and Gatlin, D. (1975). Metropolitan school desegregation: Practical remedy or impractical idea? *The Annals, 41*, 97–104.

Clotfelter, C. T. (1979). Urban school desegregation and declines in White enrollment: A reexamination. *Journal of Urban Economics, 6*, 352–370.

Clotfelter, C. T. (2004). *After Brown: The rise and retreat of school desegregation.* Princeton, NJ: Princeton University Press.

Cobb, C. D., and Glass, G. V. (1999). Ethnic segregation in Arizona charter schools. *Education Policy Analysis Archives 7*(1), 1–36.

Coleman, J. S. (1976). Liberty and equality in school desegregation. *Social Policy, 6*, 9–13.

Coleman, J. S., Campbell, E., Hobson, C., McPartland, J., Mood, A., Weinfield, F., and York, R. (1966). *Equality of educational opportunity.* Washington, DC: U.S. Government Printing Office.

Coleman, J. S., Kelly, S. D., and Moore, J. A. (1975). *Trends in school desegregation 1968–1973.* Washington, DC: Urban Institute Press.

Conger, D. (2005). Within-school segregation in an urban school district. *Educational Evaluation and Policy Analysis, 27*(3), 225–244.

Cookson, P. (1995). *School choice: The struggle for the soul of American education.* New Haven, CT: Yale University Press.

Crain, R. L. (1969). *The politics of school desegregation.* Garden City, NY: Anchor Books.

Elacqua, G., Schneider, M., and Buckley, J. (2005). *School choice in Chile: Is it class or the classroom?* Paper presented at the annual meetings of the American Political Science Association, Washington, DC.

Farkas, S. (1992). *Educational reform: The players and the politics.* New York: The Public Agenda Foundation.

Farley, R. (1975). Racial integration in public schools, 1967 to 1972: Assessing the effect of governmental policies. *Sociological Forces, 8*, 3–26.

Ferguson, R. F. (1998). Teachers' perceptions and expectations and the Black–White test score gap. In C. Jencks and M. Phillips (Eds.), *The Black–White test score gap* (pp. 273–317). Washington, DC: Brookings Institution Press.

Finder, A. (2005). As test scores jump, Raleigh credits integration by income. *New York Times*, September 25, A1, 24.

Finn, C. E., Jr. (1990). Why we need choice. In W. L. Boyd and H. J. Walberg (Eds.), *Choice in education: Potential and problems* (pp. 3–19). Berkeley, CA: McCutchan Publishing.

Frankenberg, E., and Lee, C. (2003). Charter schools and race: A lost opportunity for integrated education. *Educational Policy Analysis Archives 11*(32). http://epaa.asu.edu/epaa/v11n32/

Gamoran, A. (1992). Access to excellence: Assignment to honors English classes in the transition from middle to high schools. *Educational Evaluation and Policy Analysis, 14*, 185–204.

Gilens, M. (1995). Racial attitudes and opposition to welfare. *Journal of Politics, 57*(4), 994–1014.

Greene, J. P. (2005). Choosing integration. In J. Scott (Ed.), *School choice and diversity: What the evidence says.* New York: Teachers College Press.

Hannaway, J., and Stanislawski, M. (2005). Flip-flops in school reform: An evolutionary theory. In F. Hess (Ed.), *Urban school reform: Lessons from San Diego* (pp. 53–70). Cambridge, MA: Harvard Education Press.

Hedges, L V., and Nowell, A. (1998). Changes in the Black–White gap in achievement test scores. *Sociology of Education, 72*, 111–135.

Henig, J. R. (1994). *Rethinking school choice: Limits of the market metaphor.* Princeton, NJ: Princeton University Press.

Henig, J. R. (1996). The local dynamics of choice: Ethnic preferences and institutional responses. In B. Fuller and R. F. Elmore (Eds.), *Who chooses? Who loses? Culture, institutions, and the unequal effects of school choice* (pp. 95–117). New York: Teachers College Press.

Henig, J. R., Hula, R. C., Orr, M., and Pedescleaux, D. S. (1999). *The color of school reform.* Princeton, NJ: Princeton University Press.

Hess, F. M. (1998). *Spinning wheels: The politics of urban school reform.* Washington, DC: Brookings Institution.

Hirschman, A. O. (1970). *Exit, voice, and loyalty.* Cambridge, MA: Harvard University Press.

Hochschild, J. L. (1984). *The new American dilemma: Liberal democracy and school desegregation.* New Haven, CT: Yale University Press.

Ingersoll, R. M. (1999). The problem of underqualified teachers in American secondary schools. *Educational Researcher, 28,* 26–37.

Jussim, L., and Harber, K. D. (2005). Teacher expectations and self-fulfilling prophecies: Knowns and unknowns, resolved and unresolved controversies. *Personality and Social Psychology Review, 9*(2), 131–155.

Kahlenberg, R. D. (2000). *All together now: Creating middle-class schools through public school choice.* Washington, DC: Brookings Institution.

Kao, G., and Thompson, J. S. (2003). Racial and ethnic stratification in educational achievement and attainment. *Annual Review of Sociology, 29*(1), 417–442.

Kleitz, B., Weiher, G. R., Tedin, K., and Matland, R. (2000). Choice, charter schools, and household preferences. *Social Science Quarterly, 81*(3), 846–854.

Kulik, C. C., and Kulik, V. (1982). Effects of ability grouping on secondary school students: A meta-analysis of evaluation findings. *American Educational Research Journal, 19,* 415–428.

Lacireno-Paquet, N., Holyoke, T. T., Moser, M., and Henig, J. R. (2002). Creaming versus cropping: Charter school enrollment practices in response to market incentives. *Educational Evaluation and Policy Analysis, 24*(2), 145–158.

Lemann, N. (1999). *The big test: The secret history of the American meritocracy.* New York: Farrar, Straus and Giroux.

Levine, C. H. (1984). Citizenship and service delivery: The promise of coproduction. *Public Administration Review, 44,* 178–187.

Lieberman, M. (1993). *Public education: An autopsy.* Cambridge, MA: Harvard University Press.

Loveless, T. (1999). *The tracking wars: State reform meets school policy.* Washington, DC: Brookings Institution.

Meier, K. J. (2005). National minority education study. Electronic files Texas A&M, University, College Station TX.

Meier, K. J., and Stewart, Jr., J. (1991). Cooperation and conflict in multiracial school districts. *Journal of Politics 53*(4), 1123–1133.

Meier, K. J., Stewart, Jr., J., and England, R. E. (1989). *Race, class, and education: The politics of second-generation discrimination.* Madison, WI: University of Wisconsin Press.

Mickelson, R. A. (2003). When are racial disparities in education the result of racial discrimination? A social science perspective. *Teachers College Record, 105*(4), 1052–1086.

National Assessment of Education Progress. (2005). *The nation's report card: Trial urban district assessment.* http://nationsreportcard.gov/tuda_reading_mathematics_2005/

National Center for Education Statistics. (2003). *Digest of education statistics 2003.* Washington, DC: Author.

Nelson, B., Berman, P., Ericson, J., Kamprath, N., Perry, R., Silverman, D., and Solomon, D. (2000). *The state of charter schools 2000: Fourth-year report.* Washington, DC: U.S. Department of Education, Office of Educational Research and Improvement.

Oakes, J. (1985). *Keeping track: How schools structure inequality.* New Haven, CT: Yale University Press.

Orfield, G., and Eaton, S. (1996). *Dismantling desegregation.* New York: The New Press.

Orr, M. (1999). *Black social capital: The politics of school reform in Baltimore.* Lawrence: University Press of Kansas.

Pettigrew, T. F. (1979). The changing, but *not* declining significance of race. *Michigan Law Review, 77*(3), 917–924.

Pettigrew, T. F., and Green, R. L. (1976). School desegregation in large cities: A critique of the Coleman "white flight" thesis. *Harvard Education Review, 46,* 1–53.

Public Agenda. (2005). *Race: Quick takes.* http://www.publicagenda.org/issues/angles.cfm?issue_type = race

Putnam, R. (1993). *Making democracy work: Civic traditions in modern Italy.* Princeton, NJ: Princeton University Press.

Renzulli, L. A., and Evans, L. (2005). School choice, charter schools, and white flight. *Social Problems 52*(3), 398–418.

Riehl, C., Pallas, A., and Natriello, G. (1999). Rites and wrongs: Institutional explanations for the student course-scheduling process in urban high schools. *American Journal of Education, 107,* 116–154.

Rosenthal, R., and Jacobson, L. (1968). *Pygmalion in the classroom: Teacher expectations and student intellectual development.* New York: Holt.

Rossell, C. H. (1975–1976). School desegregation and white flight. *Political Science Quarterly 90,* 675–695.

Ryan, W. (1976). *Blaming the victim.* 2nd ed. New York: Vintage.

Saporito, S., and Lareau, A. (1999). School selection as a process: The multiple dimensions of race in framing educational choice. *Social Problems, 46*(3), 418–439.

Schneider, M., and Buckley, J. (2002). What do parents want from schools? Evidence from the Internet. *Educational Evaluation and Policy Analysis, 24*(2), 133–144.

Schneider, M., Teske, P., and Marschall, M. (2000). *Choosing schools: Consumer choice and the quality of American schools.* Princeton, NJ: Princeton University press.

Schneider, R., Jr. (2001). The culture wars. *Gay & Lesbian Review Worldwide, 8*(3), 4.

Sharp, E. B. (1980). Toward a new understanding of urban services and citizen participation: The coproduction concept. *Midwest Review of Public Administration, 14*(2), 105–118.

Shipps, D. (2004). Chicago: The national "model" reexamined. In J. R. Henig and W. C. Rich (Eds.), *Mayors in the middle: Politics, race, and mayoral control of urban schools* (pp. 59–94). Princeton, NJ: Princeton University Press.

Smith, A., Jussim, L., Van Noy, M., Madon, S. J., and Palumbo, P. (1998). Self-fulfilling prophecies, perceptual biases, and accuracy at the individual and group level. *Journal of Experimental Social Psychology, 34,* 530–561.

Soss, J., Schram, S. F., Vartanian, T.P., and O'Brien, E. (2001). Setting the terms of relief: Explaining state policy choices in the devolution revolution. *American Journal of Political Science, 45*(2), 378–395.

Tyack, D., and Cuban, L. (1995). *Tinkering toward utopia.* Cambridge MA: Harvard University Press.

Tropea, J. L. (1987). Bureaucratic order and special children: Urban schools, 1890s–1940s. *History of Education Quarterly, 27*(1), 29–53.

Weiher, G. R., and Tedin, K. L. (2002). Does choice lead to racially distinctive schools? Charter schools and household preferences. *Journal of Policy Analysis and Management, 21*(1), 79–92.

Wells, A. S. (1993). *Time to choose: America at the crossroads of school choice policy.* New York: Hill and Wang.

Wilson, J. Q., and Banfield, V. (1964). Public-regardingness as a value premise in voting behavior. *American Political Science Review, 58,* 876–887.

Wilson, W. J. (1978). *The declining significance of race: Blacks and changing American institutions.* Chicago: University of Chicago Press.

Wilson, W. J. (1987). *The truly disadvantaged: The inner city, the underclass, and public policy.* Chicago: University of Chicago.

The Making and Effects of Education Policy: Commentary

Policy, Politics, Institutions, and Markets

James P. Spillane

Taking stock of the empirical and theoretical knowledge base, these five chapters together provide an extensive and engaging review of the accumulated wisdom of the past half century on education policy. That is no small achievement considering the vast terrain that falls under the education policy rubric. The chapters highlight the complexities of the education policymaking and implementation processes but do so in a way that leaves the reader not confused or stymied, but with a set of conceptual tools for framing future research work. Most important, the reviews point to important omissions, oversights, and blind spots in the accumulated wisdom and offer pointers for future research.

My commentary attempts to do two things. First, I identify some important themes that cut across two or more of these chapters, themes that savvy readers will already have picked up on. Second, by way of critique I point to some additional issues that the chapters either fail to address or just touch on that I believe are critical as scholars of education policy frame their research agendas over the next several years.

CROSSCUTTING THEMES

Segmented System and Extra System

A persistent theme in education policy scholarship over the past several decades concerns the segmented and unwieldy government system in which policy gets made in the United States and that it must then navigate in the implementation process. Together the five chapters provide a comprehensive treatment of this familiar theme in the education policy literature. Both the Fuhrman, Goertz, and Weinbaum chapter and the McDonnell chapter capture the complexity of making policy in the U.S. system, where authority over education is both vertically and horizontally segmented. Federal, state, and local school districts all make education policy. Further, at the federal and state levels, authority over education is spread among the executive and legislative branches of government, and the courts also have a hand in education policymaking. These arrangements for governing education pose challenges for education policymaking and those who study it.

The segmented institutional arrangements are equally if not even more important when it comes to understanding the implementation process. The terrain from Congress or the statehouse to the schoolhouse provides numerous opportunities for detours. Challenging the rather simplistic top-down and bottom-up perspectives that have framed much of the implementation scholarship, Cohen, Moffitt, and Goldin argue convincingly that the challenges that segmented institutional arrangements pose for policy implementation are best understood in terms of mutual dependence between policy and practice rather than in terms of hierarchical position. Unpacking the mutual dependency argument, these authors highlight how aims, instruments, capability, and environments are the key ingredients in understanding relationships between policy and practice-policy implementation. Whereas Cohen and his coauthors focus chiefly on the mutual dependency between policy and practice, a similar mutual dependency is at play among federal, state, and district policymaking agencies.

But more than segmented institutional arrangements are at play when it comes to understanding the making and implementation of education policy. A vast and sprawling and mostly unregulated extra system is also implicated in education policymaking and policy implementation. As Paul Hill points out, over the past 5 years many new actors with more diverse agendas have engaged in the education policymaking process. Hill goes on to show that shifts in the political economy of schooling over the past decade have resulted in the emergence of new providers of public schooling in the United States. In doing so, Hill surfaces another key consideration in any effort to understand the making and its implementation of education policy: a vast extra system of providers who fall outside the formal government system. Of course, besides these providers, the extragovernmental system of publishers, testing companies, professional associations, universities, and private consultants should be central to any discussion of education policy in the United States over the past half century.

Shifting Terrain

A second and closely related theme picked up in many of these chapters concerns the shifting terrain of the education policy system and the extra system in the United States. The American education system and the extra system have been arrangements in the works for over a century, and indications suggest they will continue to be so. As historians of education have pointed out, this is due in great part to the system's origins in a locally inspired school reform movement. Unlike many of the nation states of Western Europe or former colonies (e.g., Ireland, India), where the education system was designed as an arm of central government or colonial domination, the American system bubbled up from below. The U.S. system did not evolve from any grand Napoleonic plan or attempt by a colonial power to subdue restless colonies. As such, the American education system continues to be in a state of change with respect to which entities have responsibility for which aspects of schooling America's youth.

The Fuhrman, Goertz, and Weinbaum chapter documents considerable shifts in roles and relations among different government agencies and levels of government over the past 50 years. Hill shows how in just 5 years many new actors have entered the policymaking arena with the emergence of new providers of schooling in the United States and efforts to influence the ways public money earmarked for education is spent. This shifting terrain complicates policymaking and policy implementation as well as the work of policy analysts. The No Child Left Behind Act (NCLB) is a critical factor accounting for shifts in the terrain over the past decade, but it has not, as Paul Hill's account makes clear, been the only factor. Moreover, if history is any guide to things to come, the terrain of educational policymaking in the United States is far from settled.

But the shifting terrain is more than an explanatory variable in efforts to account for policymaking and policy implementation. Looking beyond the instrumental view of policies to examine their impact on the education system and the extra system is an area that merits more attention from policy scholars. Policies that are designed to improve mathematics instruction or improve the achievement of poor children through the provision of vouchers or charter schools also, whether intended to do so or not, have the effect of changing the system. As David Cohen pointed out over two decades ago in his seminal Harvard Educational Review essay (1982), education policy leads to growth in the organization of the education system and to an expansion of the extra system-interest groups, agencies, professional associations, and so on. Although few have exploited Cohen's observations, the evidence amassed in these chapters suggests that an important area of study for scholars of education policy might focus on how policymaking and implementation build and reorganize the education system and the extra system.

Relevant Research

A third theme cutting across these five chapters centers on doing research on education policy. Henig concludes that education policy researchers have been responsive, focusing their labors on research questions of interest to the public and policymakers rather than being chiefly driven by the theoretical debates of their disciplines. As Henig points out, this is good for an applied field like education, but researchers' responsiveness to the most recent controversy or debate also has a disadvantage for scholarship on education policy. It is difficult for researchers to maintain that skeptical disposition important for solid scholarship and a safeguard against buying into the latest quick fixes that have become mainstays in education policymaking. In a similar vein, Lorraine McDonnell notes how researchers' responsiveness to policymakers and funders has skewed the accumulated wisdom towards certain aspects of education policy and certain parts of the system rather than others. Few scholars, for example, have studied the politics of local school boards, focusing instead on state and federal education policymaking, usually around particular policies.

Although education policy researchers deserve recognition for their responsiveness to policymakers' and the public's interest, it is important that as a field we stand back from time to time and ask what some of the key omissions and oversights in our knowledge base are. This is especially timely considering the current push in many quarters for research that focuses on policy effects-that tells us what works. Policy effects are undoubtedly important, but as these chapters make clear, better evidence on what works in getting fifth graders to learn mathematics, say, is unlikely to be sufficient in addressing the implementation challenges. Moreover, as Hill underscores in thinking about policy effects, it is not sufficient simply to measure the treated and control groups—one has also to examine the effects of a particular policy for the system as a whole.

Looking at how researchers from various disciplines have examined education policy, Fuhrman, Goertz, and Weinbaum call for more multidisciplinary research. Forging collaborations among economists, political scientists, sociologists, and scholars from other disciplines who work in the area of education policy is likely to lead to some new research agendas that generate new knowledge about policy and its implementation. Moreover, given the vast terrain that the five chapters cover under the rubric of education policy, such multidisciplinary collaborations are essential. However, some of the most difficult work in building collaborations among researchers may come from within education schools. Bringing together researchers who study learning and teaching—often with a particular school subject focus—with those scholars who study school organizations, school administration, and education policy may be as challenging as bringing together scholars from disciplines as diverse as economics and sociology. Yet these sorts of collaborations seem critical to build the capacity in the research community to carry out the next generation of education policy research. Finally, another sort of collaboration that seems essential in advancing the field would involve building bridges to scholarship in other social policy areas that address children, such as human services.

OTHER THEMES

Reading these chapters prompted me to reflect on a few other issues that I believe are important as we review the last 50 years of education policy research with an eye towards forging a research agenda for the next decade or so.

Diversifying Our Research Epistemologies and Methodologies

One issue that merits attention concerns the epistemological and methodological approaches to research in education policy. To begin with, there is a scarcity of theory-testing work, especially on policy implementation. Over the past couple of decades scholars have generate numerous theories about the implementation process. However, few of these theories have been subjected to rigorous empirical testing. Using experimental and quasi-experimental designs to test various hypotheses about the policy implementation process is important.

Strikingly absent in these chapters is any mention of research that takes a narrative approach to analyzing education policy. This is surprising in that narrative or story is a key tool that politicians and policymakers use in making policy and implementing it (Gardner, 1995; McAdams, 2006). Using narrative approaches more to analyze policy, policymaking, and policy implementation might be especially fruitful. For example, analyzing the stories that policymakers use to promote particular policies (e.g., NCLB) or analyzing the policy texts in a particular policy genre such as the education of poor children and children of color (e.g., Title I) over time is likely to surface new knowledge about education policy.

Instructional Practice and Policy

As Cohen and his colleagues suggest, practice is not simply an outcome variable when it comes to education policy. There is much here that needs to be unpacked as scholars construct new research agendas. Few studies treat instruction as an explanatory variable. Factoring in instruction as an explanatory variable in scholarship on education policy involves moving away from views of teaching as a monolithic practice. More sophisticated constructions of teaching are necessary that take into account the subject matter (e.g., mathematics, literacy) and the dimension of teaching (e.g., content, teaching strategies).

Take school subjects by way of example. Instruction is about subject matter. Educational activities in American society are organized quite differently—both in the broader social environment and in local school settings—across different curricular domains. The structure of the education system, including the extra system, looks different depending on the school subject. Federal and state government agencies regulate the different school subjects differently with mathematics and language arts receiving far more attention from policymakers. Differences across subject areas are also reflected in the organization and activities of the extra system, including textbook and test publishers, professional associations, and postsecondary institutions that prepare teachers and school administrators. Further, how schools—a critical level of the system when it comes to the implementation of education policy—manage instruction differs depending on the school subject. Studies of education policymaking and implementation need to be more sensitive to the school subject as a potentially powerful explanatory variable in accounting for both the policymaking and implementation processes.

Getting to Work Practices

Reflecting the state of the knowledge base, these chapters dwell mostly on structures, positions, policy instruments, actors, agencies, and resources—all of which are important. However, there is no discussion of practice per se; that is, the work practices that policymakers, other system and extra-system actors, and stakeholders engage in as they make policy and work on implementing policy. My argument here is not for a description of policymaking processes or implementation processes but rather for a research agenda that attempts to understand the actual work practices involved in implementing or making policy in a particular education agency. For example, much of the current literature dwells on those school or school-district-level conditions that enable or hinder the implementation of state and district policies (e.g., organizational leadership, social trust, human capital). In doing so a somewhat static picture of these organizations and policy implementation emerges that fails to capture the day-to-day life of a school or school district. It is in and through these daily organizational practices that relations between policy and instructional practice get established or not. Ordinary and everyday organizational routines from a grade-level or departmental meeting to the second-grade teachers' informal but weekly morning coffee klatch are critical to understanding relations between policy and practice (Spillane, 2006). These everyday and sometimes mundane routines are critical in any organization from the schoolhouse to the statehouse and beyond.

CONCLUSION

Education policy as a social phenomenon and as a field of study is a vast and changing terrain involving both government and extragovernmental agencies and actors. The vastness of the terrain means that scholars from different disciplines—economics, education, political science, sociology, and so on—are essential for studying education policy. The extent to which scholars from these different traditions can work together to take multidisciplinary approaches to the study of education policy is critical to adding value to the empirical knowledge base over the next decade or two.

REFERENCES

Cohen, D. K. (1982). Policy and organization: The impact of state and federal educational policy in school governance. *Harvard Educational Review, 52*(4), 474–499.

Gardner, H. (1995). *Leading minds: An anatomy of leadership.* In collaboration with E. Laskin. New York: Basic Books.

McAdams, D. P. (2006). *The redemptive self: Stories Americans live by.* New York: Oxford University Press.

Spillane, J. (2006). *Distributed leadership.* San Francisco: Jossey-Bass.

III

POLICY AS RESOURCE ALLOCATION

7

Causality, Causality, Causality: The View of Education Inputs and Outputs From Economics

Lisa Barrow and Cecilia Elena Rouse

Frustrated with decades of research on education that seemingly amounts to little accumulated knowledge on how to improve student academic outcomes, policymakers and researchers are taking stock of what we do and do not know about the effectiveness of educational inputs.[1] As an example, in 2002 the U.S. Department of Education created the What Works Clearinghouse (WWC)—a database meant to provide educators and policymakers with a "trusted source" of information on what "scientifically based" education research has to say about what works and does not work in education. The fact that the federal government was willing to spend $18.5 million (U.S. Department of Education, 2002) to fund such an enterprise reflects the view of many that ultimately we know little about which inputs matter for student success in education.

Why do we seem to know so little? Many economists would argue it is because research has not emphasized isolating causal relationships between education inputs and student outcomes (Angrist, 2004). Rather, education research has focused on other aspects of the issue, such as differences across settings, which usually has not been the major concern for researchers placing a priority on causality.[2] If one believes student outcomes are uniquely tied to the educational setting, then it is fruitless to try to draw general conclusions about the "average effect" of an education input (which, in this view, does not apply to anyone in reality; Cook, 2001).[3] However, the WWC as well as many others in the education research field have started to highlight research that emphasizes isolating the causal relationships between education inputs and student

---

1. We emphasize that "inputs" can be interpreted either narrowly or broadly. District organization (e.g., primary, middle, high school vs. K–8 and high school) can be interpreted as an input, as can the structure of teacher contracts. Similarly inputs may be defined as class size, textbooks, or computers in the classroom. We take the broader interpretation but will only discuss the evidence regarding a few of the thousands of potential inputs to educational outcomes.

2. Of course all researchers attempt to estimate the causal (or unbiased) effect of an input on educational outcomes. However, all research necessarily demands sacrifice, and some researchers will sacrifice causality rather than not estimate differences across settings; others would make the opposite decision. We attempt to draw a distinction between these emphases.

3. See Cook (2001) for a thoughtful discussion of why education research has by and large rejected randomized experiments.

outcomes. Some refer to this emphasis as on "identification" (i.e., "identifying" the impact of a particular input as distinct from other factors) or "internal validity" as termed by Campbell and Stanley (1963).

In this chapter we discuss methodologies for estimating the causal effect of resources on education outcomes; we also review what we believe to be the best evidence from economics on a few important inputs: spending, class size, teacher quality, the length of the school year, and technology. In general we conclude that while the number of papers using credible strategies is thin,[4] there is certainly evidence that what schools do matters. But many unanswered questions remain.

THE THEORETICAL AND EMPIRICAL IDEAL

Economists' View of Education Resources[5]

Economists typically analyze a school's performance and the effectiveness of its inputs using an "education production function." The school produces education using inputs and a production technology. One can then measure the effect of particular inputs on the output (education), usually for each student. Specifically, one can think of a production function as the following equation.

$$E_{ist} = f(NS_{it}, R_{ist}, X_{ist}, e_{ist})$$ (1)

Here E_{ist} represents the output for student i in school s in year t; NS_{it} represents nonschool inputs into student i's educational attainment, such as her natural "ability," the extracurricular inputs provided by her parents (e.g., music lessons, extra tutoring in subjects), parental inputs (e.g., reading to their children, doing "educationally rich" activities at home), and her educational history (that is, her achievement level in fourth grade is not only a function of her current school, but also of her schooling in kindergarten, first, second, and third grade);[6] R_{ist} represents the resources under the control of school s in year t (e.g., class sizes, quality of teaching staff, and the curriculum); X_{ist} represents the school inputs that are not typically under the control of public schools (e.g., the quality of a student's "peers"), and e_{ist} is an error term that represents all of the other "stuff" that is not otherwise represented (e.g., measurement error).[7]

---

4. For example, in a recent review of curriculum-based interventions to improve middle school math achievement, the WWC staff found 77 studies. Of these 77 studies only 10 (studying five interventions) were found to have met the WWC standards for evidence, which place an emphasis on causal inference (or internal validity).

5. Parts of this section are drawn from Rouse (2005).

6. Why do we categorize a student's educational history as a "nonschool" input? Because we are attempting to distinguish between *contemporaneous* inputs under the control of the current school and inputs over which the current school has no control. Obviously, a school cannot change what happened to a student in the past.

7. Other researchers in the social sciences often represent this educational production function using hierarchical linear models (HLM) in which they explicitly account for more of the organizational structure, i.e., schools are made up of classes which are made up of individual students (Bryk & Raudenbush 1992). We address issues of identifying causal relationships in the framework commonly used in economics rather than in HLM; however, the issues of identification discussed later are also relevant to identification in the HLM framework. While HLM models allow for more nuanced and structured modeling of the parameters and error term, whether the coefficient estimates are unbiased continues to rest on whether the covariates included in the regression fully account for all confounding factors that might affect student achievement and are correlated with the school input in question. In this regard, HLM is similar to the ordinary least squares (OLS) estimation discussed later.

The function, f, represents the "production function" or the educational practices that transform the inputs into what a student actually learns. The formulation of the education production function depicted in Equation 1 also highlights some of the issues that complicate the design of methodologies for estimating the effectiveness of specific school resources—few of the measures that one would ideally include are observable. Take, for example, educational output, E_{ist}. We rely on our schools to help children learn academic subjects as well as to help them become fully functioning, happy adults by teaching democratic values, responsibility, cooperation, consideration, and other aspects of working well with others.[8] As such typical outcomes (such as test scores or labor market wages) clearly reflect only part of what we expect from schools. Further, standardized tests do not fully reflect the academic achievement of students. They typically focus on only a few subjects, and in order to keep the testing affordable and not too intrusive, are relatively short and mostly rely on multiple choice questions (which are less costly to score). Thus tests generally provide incomplete and noisy measures of educational output which make it much harder to detect the effectiveness of inputs.[9]

Because of nonschool factors and other inputs beyond the school's control, one cannot easily generate a causal estimate of the effect of school quality on outcomes.[10] For example, the test scores of more disadvantaged students (in School A) will likely be lower than the test scores of more advantaged students (in School B). If the quality of school resources in each school is correlated with the socioeconomic status of the students, it will be difficult to disentangle the role of school inputs from the influences of non-school factors. Suppose School B has a greater number of qualified teachers and more computers in the classroom than does School A. To study the effect of teacher quality and computers on school outputs, one must develop an analytical strategy that adequately controls for the nonschool factors. In many cases we suspect the school serving more advantaged students will also have higher quality school inputs. Since (in this example) more computers and a greater number of qualified teachers are positively correlated with student family background, education production function estimates will overstate the effectiveness of school resources if one does not adequately control for family background.[11]

Why is identification so important? From a policy perspective, if one implements a program based on estimates of school effectiveness that are overstated (or understated), then the benefits to society will be smaller (or larger) than anticipated by the research. If the misstatement (bias) is

---

8. That said, in this paper we often refer to the educational output as "student achievement" for ease of exposition.

9. More formally, a noisy measure of educational output (the dependent variable in a regression model) will increase the residual variance which will increase the size of the standard errors. As such, one will be less likely to reject the null hypothesis that an input has no effect on student outcomes.

10. In this regard, while economists refer to Equation 1 as a production function, in many respects it is not. In order to truly recover the parameters of a production function one would need to hold *everything* else constant. Thus if one were studying the effect of lowering class size on a student's achievement, one would require that all other educational inputs, such as teaching styles, curriculum, extracurricular activities, and nonschool factors remain constant. Because there are no data that allow the researcher to control for all such inputs, the literature typically asks a more general question: What is the effect of an exogenous decrease in, say, class size, on student achievement not requiring that all other inputs remain constant? In this example, teachers may change their teaching style in response to a smaller class size, or parents may ease up on complementary educational activities such as tutoring (believing their child is receiving a higher quality education while in school). This more systemic response is what one might expect from an exogenous change in educational policy. See Todd and Wolpin (2003) for a more in-depth discussion of this conceptual issue.

11. In some cases the bias may be negative. For example, special needs and English language learner classes tend to be much smaller than classes for regular or gifted students (Boozer & Rouse 2001). In this case, one may erroneously conclude that smaller class sizes lead to *worse* student outcomes.

small, this is not a big problem; however in many cases the bias could be quite large leading to no societal benefits, or worse, to adverse outcomes. (Or, in the case of understatement, a potentially beneficial program may not be adopted.)

The Ideal Way to Measure the Impact of Schooling Inputs

To identify the causal impact of school resources, ideally one would begin with a group of students and educate them during the year with the first educational input in question (or the status quo). At the end of the year, one would assess the students or administer an appropriate test, the results of which would perfectly reflect what the students know.[12]

Next, one would take the same group of students and revert them back to their initial conditions at the beginning of the *first* year. That is, they would be the same age, have the same living conditions, etc. This second year, one would then educate the students with the second educational input in question. (For example, in the first year the input might be teachers with regular teaching credentials, and in the second it might be teachers who have gone through an alternative certification program.) At the end of the year, one would again assess what each student knows.[13] The difference between the students' outcomes using the first input and those using the second would isolate the value of the second input relative to the first.

Why is this the ideal design for measuring the value of an input? First, because the same students are educated using each educational input starting from the same initial conditions, one has guaranteed that all background characteristics of the students are the same, including their prior exposure to high- and low-quality schooling, their family situation, and their innate ability. In other words, one has effectively controlled for X_{ist} and NS_{it}. Second, because the assessments perfectly reflect what students know, there is no measurement error. The combination of these two features means that one can isolate the relative influence of the educational inputs. The key is that by observing how students fare under both regimes one has a "counterfactual" outcome against which to compare the outcome using the main input of interest. Namely, we observe how much the students learn using the first input as well as how much they would have learned had we instead used the second input. As we will discuss, it turns out that establishing a credible counterfactual outcome is among the most difficult tasks faced by the analyst.

Clearly, the ideal evaluation is impossible to implement. No one can turn back time to assess the students under the exact same conditions in each year. In addition, there has not been an assessment devised that *perfectly* reflects what students know. Rather, existing tests reflect only a part of what students know, and there are permanent confounding factors (such as different test-taking abilities) and random confounding factors (such as some students not feeling well on the day of the test or not getting enough sleep before the test). The analyst's task is, nevertheless, to implement a methodology that comes as close to the ideal approach as possible.

One must also consider how generalizable the outcome of any evaluation would be—that is, whether the evaluation has "external validity" (Campbell & Stanley, 1963). If we started with a "representative" group of students, then the ideal evaluation would uncover the average rela-

---

12. Note that while we describe the ideal outcome as a test, in theory one could use any other outcome (such as adult wages or voting behavior).

13. In the ideal methodology one need not administer a test at the beginning of each school year because the students (and all of their characteristics) are identical in both years. If one were to administer a test at the beginning of the year, the difference between what the students know at the beginning of the year and the end of the year could (mostly) be attributed to the input used that year, since the students are the same in each testing period. This would constitute the input's "value-added" in each year.

tive effectiveness of the input even if the effectiveness of the input varies over the population. If it is the case that the first or second input is more effective for some students than others, the students in our study must be representative of the population of students in order to assess the effectiveness of each input on average. Consider the extreme example in which the first input is effective for teaching girls but not effective for teaching boys, and the second input is as effective for teaching boys as the first input is for teaching girls but not at all effective for teaching girls. Further, assume that 50 percent of the student population is female and 50 percent is male. In this extreme example, the two inputs are equally effective on average. However, if the students in the study were disproportionately female, we would incorrectly conclude that, on average, the first input is more effective than the second input. Thus, only by starting with a group of students who are representative of the population (in general, or the population of interest for the policy) can one guarantee that the exercise will uncover the true average treatment effect of the input. Of course, in this extreme but simple example with an ideal set-up in which one knows all of the characteristics of the students, one could estimate the effectiveness of the inputs for different subgroups of the population and discover, in fact, that the first input was more effective for girls and the second input was more effective for boys.

This issue of "heterogenous treatment effects" is part of the reason many in education cast a jaundiced eye toward randomized experiments (and many other quantitative methodologies). However, the average effect (even if there are different effects for different subpopulations or in different settings) is important for setting policy, especially if it is difficult for policymakers to target a policy narrowly or effectively. As such, the first-order question is whether an intervention works in general or for very broad categories of schools or students. Among the important subsequent questions is whether it is more effective for some groups or situations than for others.

In a related manner, one characteristic of many methodologies that emphasize causality is that the researcher does not delve into the intricacies of why the intervention may have mattered (or not mattered). For example, in the studies of class size reduction using the randomized Project STAR data from Tennessee, researchers have not identified *why* class size reduction mattered. Was it because there were fewer students in the class *per se* (i.e., a peer effect story) or because the teachers changed their teaching styles? It is important to note that this is not an inherent limitation of the randomization (or other methodologies which emphasize causality). Rather it follows from the researcher placing a greater emphasis on causality such that he or she will not attempt to address issues of which subcomponents of an intervention might have mattered, unless there was randomization along those dimensions as well. That is, unless the researcher randomly assigned teachers to teaching styles in addition to differing class sizes, he or she will worry that teachers who adopted certain styles may be different from those who did not in ways that are not observable. Using survey data (or other observational data) and applying ordinary least squares (OLS) regression will not solve this problem (unless, of course, they contain *all* of the relevant background variables).

In the next two sections we review methodologies researchers have used in their quest to study the effectiveness of school inputs.

METHODS USING OBSERVATIONAL DATA

Observational data are gathered from observing existing situations in schools. That is, they contain the existing input levels in schools (e.g., class sizes and teacher qualifications) as well as information on students attending the schools. These are "observational" because there is no attempt on the part of the analyst to manipulate the situation generating the data. Most of the literature on the effect of educational inputs on student outcomes relies on observational data typically because they are most readily available. However, the fundamental problem with observational data is that individuals and schools choose their situations, such that one must control for all factors that led the individual or school to their choice that might also be correlated with the outcome of interest. Each of the approaches discussed below attempts to address this fundamental problem in a different way.

Ordinary Least Squares Regression

Traditionally, researchers have used OLS to study the impact of school resources on outcomes (e.g., Coleman et al., 1966). In the cross-sectional case, the analyst relies on a specification such as the following equation.

$$E_{ist} = \alpha + \beta R_{ist} + \lambda NS_{it} + \delta X_{ist} + e_{ist} \tag{2}$$

Here the variables are the same as those in Equation 1, and α, β, λ, and δ are parameters to be estimated. If all of the other factors (NS_{it} and X_{ist}) are observed in the data set such that one can include them in the regression (thereby holding them constant), then one can generate an unbiased (causal) estimate of β. However, we know of no data that contain all of the other factors for which one must control. Rather, most cross-sectional data contain only limited information on important nonschool and school factors. For example, in school administrative data one rarely, if ever, has an accurate measure of family income. As a result, researchers control for whether the student was eligible for the National School Lunch Program, a proxy for income that is very crude at best.

Today many researchers believe that cross-sectional OLS estimates are likely inaccurate (i.e., they are statistically biased). As a result, they turn to data that follow a student over time—longitudinal data. With longitudinal data one can control for observed and unobserved student characteristics, particularly those that do not change over time. In addition, because these data have information on students over multiple years, one comes closer to the comprehensive data required in Equation 1. Because of accountability requirements in The No Child Left Behind Act of 2001, many states are beginning to collect such data on individual students statewide. This advance in data collection will be an invaluable resource for education researchers going forward.[14]

Since these data have not been readily available, one approach that researchers have used is known as a "value-added" specification (e.g., Summers & Wolfe, 1977). These equations take the form of the following.

$$E_{ist} - E_{ist-1} = \alpha' + \beta' R_{ist} + \lambda' NS_{it} + \delta' X_{ist} + e'_{ist} \tag{3}$$

Here E_{ist-1} is the student's outcome in the previous year. In this case, one estimates the effect of a (concurrent) resource R_{ist} on the change in a student's outcome. If E_{ist-1} fully captures the effect of all previous schooling and nonschooling inputs on the student's achievement, then one can generate an unbiased estimate of β', the effectiveness of the school input in question. However, it seems unlikely that a noisy measure of a student's performance in the prior year (as reflected in test scores) will fully control for all relevant factors.[15]

---

14. Texas, North Carolina, and Florida already have fairly rich databases and have provided researchers with access to them. That said, we know of no administrative data that contain all of the information that would be relevant for replicating the ideal research design.

15. See Todd and Wolpin (2003) for a more comprehensive discussion of what different empirical models using longitudinal data identify and under what assumptions.

In general, the basic problem with using OLS regression to estimate the effect of school resources on student achievement—using either cross-sectional or longitudinal data—is that one is uncertain whether or not one has controlled for all important factors[16] in the regression. As such, much of the latest and most compelling research on the impact of school resources on student achievement has moved away from simple OLS regression.

Regression Discontinuity

Imagine that an educational input is assigned to students based on the value of some measure. For example, suppose that a state imposes a maximum class size of 25 students per teacher. If the number of students exceeds 25 students, then the students are to have a teacher plus a teacher's aide. If there are more than 40 students, then the school must create two classes (each with one teacher). Because of the cutoffs imposed by the law, students in schools with 39 students in, say, the third grade will experience a much larger class size (39 students) than students in schools with 41 students in the third grade who will be educated in class sizes of 20 and 21. The key is that the variation in whether a school has 39 students in the third grade or 41 students likely occurs by chance. More specifically, it is unlikely there are other factors that determine whether there are 39 or 41 students in the third grade that also affect student outcomes. As such, one can compare the outcomes of students in schools with 39 students with those of students in schools with 41 students and attribute any difference to the effect of class size.

This basic methodology is known as a "regression discontinuity" design (Cook & Campbell 1979), and it has grown in popularity in research on education quality. More generally this design will work when the input in question (in this example, class size) is at least partly determined by a known discontinuous function[17] of an observed characteristic (in this example, third-grade enrollment). Because of the discontinuous relationship between the input in question and the observed characteristic, the researcher can control directly for the observed characteristic while still identifying the effect of the input in question on student outcomes, making the strategy much more compelling than typical OLS.[18]

An important disadvantage of regression discontinuity designs is that the range of values over which one gets identifying variation tends to be rather small. (For example, the most compelling comparison in the class size example is between schools with enrollments of 39 vs. 41; one can imagine that schools with 15 rather than 35 third-grade students also vary along other dimensions that may or may not be observable.) In addition, if the effect of class size on student achievement in the range for which one can generate unbiased estimates is different from that in other

16. Statistically "important factors" are those that influence the student's performance on the outcome measure and that are correlated with the resource in question.

17. That is, class sizes and enrollment do not simply increase one-for-one forever, but there is a change in the relationship at some point. In this example, class sizes increase one-for-one until there are 40 students in the class, and then class sizes abruptly (and discontinuously) decrease to 20 and 21 students.

18. In order for regression discontinuity design methods to provide credible estimates of the effect of educational inputs on student outcomes, the key individuals involved (e.g., parents, principals, teachers, students) must not have control over the exact value of the measure on which eligibility for the input will be based. Thus these key individuals must not have control over the exact size of the third-grade class in our example. If the underlying measure can be manipulated, then one could manipulate the school enrollment to engineer the desired class size. If the desired class size is correlated with other unobserved determinants of student outcomes, such as commitment to education, then the estimate of the effectiveness of class size will be biased. In this example, the methodology seems more credible when applied to public schools—which do not have complete control over their enrollment—than to private schools.

ranges, then the estimated parameters may not generalize.[19] However, because regression discontinuity provides a credible way to estimate a parameter with internal validity, it provides an invaluable tool for education research. Further, while it may not appear to be very practical, regression discontinuity is a candidate analytical design whenever there are cutoffs for program participation. Below, we discuss papers that use this design to study the effectiveness of professional development, smaller class sizes, and summer school and grade retention.

Natural Experiments (Instrumental Variables)

"Natural experiments" provide another approach for analyzing observational data in a way that comes closer to the ideal experiment than OLS. In this approach, researchers attempt to locate determinants of schooling inputs that would not be expected independently to alter their educational outcomes.

Here is the basic idea used in this methodology. Suppose we were interested in studying the effect of financial resources on student outcomes, and we knew of a determinant of financial resources, say a change in the state education financing formula, that would increase the amount of money allocated to one group of schools. Suppose further we were certain that this change in the financing formula did not have any direct effect on the students' outcomes, except through the impact on the schools' revenues.[20] We would then estimate the effect of state aid on outcomes in two steps. In the first step we would estimate the effect of the state aid on school revenue. In the next step we would measure the effect of the change in state aid on students' outcomes. If we found that the outcomes of the students improved, then we could be sure that increased revenues were the cause of the outcome improvement, since we would be certain that the change in state aid had no *direct* effect on outcomes. The ratio of the outcome improvement caused by the change in state aid to the change in the educational input caused by the state aid is a straightforward estimate of the causal effect of financial resources on student achievement. This instrumental variables (IV) estimator uses the "exogenous" event (a change in the state financing formula) as the instrumental variable.[21] This is, indeed, the approach taken in the recent paper by Jonathan Guryan (2003) to study the impact of "money" on student outcomes (see the section below on input studies).

---

19. For example, when class sizes vary by only 1 or 2 students—which may be the viable range for policy changes—teachers may not change their teaching styles significantly. However, when class sizes change a lot (e.g., 39 students vs. 20 students) then many other educational practices may change making it difficult to isolate the effect of class size, per se. Or the effect of class size reduction may matter for, say, classes with over 30 students but not for classes with 20–25 students.

20. Thus, for example, one would need to be careful with state aid formulas that were designed to be redistributive. In this case, schools in poor areas would likely receive more state aid and yet their students would likely perform worse on tests than students in wealthier areas. As such, one would not want to simply use the *level* of state aid as the outside determinant of resources. However, some *changes* in the formula may have been driven by factors that are uncorrelated with the characteristics of the districts such that these *changes* would be valid outside determinants of state aid.

21. Some investigators refer to the fact that schools use varying levels of a particular input as a "natural experiment." (For example, we have heard researchers propose studying the effect of a whole school reform model by "exploiting the natural variation" arising from the fact that some schools have adopted the model and others have not.) This is not what most economists would refer to as a "natural experiment," particularly since the method of analysis that follows is simply OLS (in which one relates whether or not a school uses the whole school reform model in question to student outcomes). One is still left with the question as to why some schools adopted the model and others did not, and whether this same (unobserved) factor that led them to adopt it is correlated with student outcomes.

As another example of how this estimation strategy works, consider the recent paper by Angrist and Lavy (2002) that studies the effect of technology on student achievement. Angrist and Lavy note that schools in Israel that received a technology grant were more likely to use computer-assisted instruction (CAI; again, see the section below on input studies). The grant program is a suitable instrumental variable so long as one can assume that any difference between schools that received funding through the program and those that did not is only the use of computers in the schools and not other observable characteristics of the schools (e.g., schools with more motivated principals were more likely to apply for the grant program and have better-performing schools). Angrist and Lavy study the correlation of participation in the program with other school environment characteristics (e.g., class size, hours of instruction, noncomputer technology) and conclude that the program increased CAI instruction without changing other characteristics of the schools. That said, this highlights the main empirical challenge in IV strategies: the researcher must make the claim that the instrumental variable only affects the outcome through its effect on the educational input (the endogenous variable) in question. As such, the researcher must make assumptions about unobservable factors—which are inherently difficult to prove or disprove.[22]

Another disadvantage of IV strategies is that like regression discontinuity designs, if there is heterogeneity in the effect of an input on student outcomes, the estimated effect may not generalize to other segments of the population. The reason is that IV identifies the effect of an input on student achievement among those students (or schools) that are induced to change their behavior because of the instrumental variable (Imbens & Angrist, 1994). Thus, in the case of the technology grant program in Israel, IV identifies an effect of CAI only for those schools that increased their intensity of CAI because of the grant program (there are others that may have received money from the program that would have increased their CAI intensity even without the program). If student achievement is particularly responsive to increases in CAI intensity in these schools, then the IV estimate of the effectiveness of technology will overstate the average effect across all schools. While this methodology is quite popular, especially among economists, it is extremely difficult to find credible instrumental variables so the methodology is unlikely to become a mainstay of education research.

METHODS USING EXPERIMENTAL DATA

Finally we come to what many describe as the "gold standard" in evaluation methodology: randomized designs. In this case, one group of students is randomly assigned to be educated with the input in question (the treatment group) and a second group of students is (randomly) assigned to be educated with the status quo or another input (the control group). One then tests the students at the end of the evaluation. The difference in student outcomes between those in the treatment group and those in the control group represents the effect of the input in question relative to an alternative. Why is this the ideal design for measuring the impact of school inputs on student outcomes? First, the random assignment of students to an educational input initially controls for all background characteristics of students, including their prior exposure to high- and low-quality schooling. That is, on average, both groups would have the same distribution of students along

---

22. In this regard, IV shares much in common with OLS. Both strategies rely on assuming that the error term is not correlated with either the input in question (in the case of OLS) or the instrumental variable (in the case of IV), conditional on the (other) observed covariates.

observable and unobservable dimensions such that one need not control for X_{ist} and NS_{it}.[23] Further, because a random event determined to which group (treatment or control) a student was assigned, one need not be concerned that students who expected to benefit more from an input were those likely to be educated using it (a concern under OLS), and the error term is uncorrelated with the input in question. Randomization makes the identification of causality in experiments more transparent than many other methodologies; thus experiments are quite compelling.

That said, experiments are not well suited to answering all questions. First, the more aggregated the unit of observation, the more "cumbersome" a randomized evaluation becomes. For example, to study the effect of districtwide open enrollment on student outcomes using an experimental design one must randomly assign *districts* to treatment and control groups. While there are more than 14,000 districts in the U.S. from which to choose, the logistics of getting a sufficient number of districts to cooperate, such that one would have a large enough sample from which to draw conclusions, would be quite daunting.

In addition, in an "ideal" experiment the random assignment process completely determines the status of individuals in the treatment and control groups. In many experimental settings involving human subjects, however, there is slippage between the random assignment status of experimental subjects and whether or not they actually receive the treatment.[24] For example, in the Tennessee Project STAR experiment some students randomly assigned to small classes ended up in larger classes and vice versa. In a randomized experiment, if one simply compares the outcomes of students *originally assigned* to the treatment group with those originally assigned to the control group (regardless of which treatment the student actually received), one estimates the "intention-to-treat" effect (Efron & Feldman, 1991; Rubin, 1974). While of interest, the intent-to-treat effect may be unsatisfying for those educators and policymakers who desire an estimate of the effects of a particular input for students who are educated actually using the input—the effect of "treatment on the treated." The estimated intent-to-treat effect does not establish whether the input in question—properly implemented—is better than an alternative. Note that the difference between the intent to treat and the treatment on the treated is "take-up" (or implementation). Students randomly assigned to the treatment group may actually choose to use another input (that is not the input in question), and students randomly assigned to the control group may actually use the input in the question (i.e., get "treated").

While the effect of treatment on the treated is important, we believe there are at least two reasons why we should also be interested in intention to treat. First, it is the only policy instrument available to policymakers. If the state of Tennessee decides to lower class sizes for all students, all that policymakers in Tennessee can do is mandate lower class sizes. If all schools comply with the new law, then one might expect results that follow from the treatment on the treated parameter. In reality, some schools may not be able to meet the new lower class size requirements. If so, any anticipated gains in student achievement will be diluted. Take the extreme case in which no schools are able to reduce class sizes (say, e.g., because of lack of building capacity). In this case, even if student achievement is much higher with smaller class sizes, there will be no achievement gains from the program because the program was not implemented. When consid-

---

23. While researchers will often also attempt to administer a pretest at the beginning of a randomized evaluation, it is not necessary to do so to generate an unbiased estimate of the effect of the input in question on student outcomes, if the randomization is conducted correctly. The reason is that the characteristics (both observed and unobserved) of the students in treatment and control groups are the same, on average, at the beginning of the evaluation. Hence, controlling for the student's pretest will not change the estimate of the effectiveness of the input in question. Controlling for the pretest can, at times, improve statistical precision (i.e., lower the standard errors).

24. This problem is exacerbated in multiyear studies.

ering a policy change, policymakers must consider both halves of the issue: both how the treatment affects the treated and whether the program can and will be implemented as desired.[25] Because it combines both halves of the issue, the intention-to-treat estimates reflect the overall potential gains from an educational policy change. Second, as in many experimental settings, the randomization only occurred in the intention to treat, and, as such, this estimate is the only unambiguously unbiased estimate that one can obtain from an OLS regression, assuming the initial selection was truly random. That said, one can estimate the effect of treatment on the treated by using an IV strategy in which one uses the random assignment as an instrumental variable for whether or not the student received the treatment (the input in question). This is a case in which, if the initial selection was truly random, the instrumental variable will not be correlated with the error term in the outcome equation and therefore will be valid.

Although experimental approaches probably come closest to the ideal evaluation design, they do have some analytical shortcomings which are worth highlighting. For example, they tend to be rather "blunt" instruments. One implements an experimental design out of concerns about obtaining an unbiased estimate of the effect of the input on student achievement. However, one can only truly get such an unbiased estimate from the point of random assignment, and unless the experimental design is sufficiently complicated, one can really only answer one question (whether those assigned to the treatment group fared differently from those assigned to the control group). Cost concerns (and complicated implementation) often preclude comparing the effectiveness of more than two or three different inputs in one study. Note, however, that one can ask whether the effect differs for subgroups identified on the basis of characteristics measured before random assignment takes place, provided sample sizes are large enough. Similarly, it is rare that researchers using experimental designs attempt to determine (at least causally) which dimensions of an intervention may have worked or not worked. Again, the reason is that unless random assignment also occurred along the "subdimensions," any such analysis will not necessarily yield causal estimates of the effectiveness of the subdimensions.

Keeping in mind these many empirical challenges, we now turn to a brief summary of what these methodologies suggest about the importance of schooling inputs on student outcomes.

DOES SCHOOL QUALITY MATTER?

Coleman, Hanushek, and Card and Krueger

The Coleman Report (Coleman et al., 1966) is credited with launching an explosion of studies estimating the relationships between educational outcomes and school inputs. Many papers were written criticizing the methodology used in the Coleman Report, including arguments that longitudinal studies or well-designed experiments were needed to make causal inferences (e.g., Sewell, 1967). Further, even the report's authors note that their cross-sectional analysis does not provide a strong basis for causal interpretation. However, the report was broadly interpreted to find that schools do not matter; instead, family background and peers explained most of the variation in education outcomes.

In the mid-1980s, Hanushek (1986) included 147 studies in a survey of the literature relating educational outcomes to school inputs. Ten years later, Hanushek (1996) found more than double the number of studies to survey. The reviews and conclusions of Hanushek's analyses

---

25. This discussion is analogous to the distinction between "efficacy" (i.e., how well a drug might work in theory) and "effectiveness" (i.e., how well a drug works in practice given the fact that patients may not follow the protocol exactly).

reinforced the findings of the Coleman Report, and by the early 1990s, many people were firmly convinced that "money does not matter," namely, that once family inputs into schooling were taken into account, school resources did not matter. As Hanushek (1997) writes, "Simple resource policies hold little hope for improving student outcomes." He further concludes, "Three decades of intensive research leave a clear picture that school resource variations are not closely related to variations in student outcomes and, by implication, that aggressive spending programs are unlikely to be good investment programs unless coupled with other fundamental reforms" (Hanushek, 1996).

Although Hanushek's meta-analyses have been extremely influential, researchers have criticized them along a number of dimensions. Hedges, Lain, and Greenwald (1994) note that many of the studies Hanushek has surveyed can be faulted for methodological reasons similar to those discussed above. For example, many of the surveyed studies are based on cross-sectional, observational data and do not have longitudinal data on student outcomes or natural experiment features. Further, Hanushek has relied on simple "vote counting" in his analysis. Using more sophisticated meta-analytical techniques, Hedges, Lain, and Greenwald conclude that among the studies surveyed in Hanushek (1989), per-pupil expenditures, teacher experience, and teacher–pupil ratios are positively related to student outcomes. They also find that the effect sizes for per-pupil expenditures are large and educationally important.

Krueger (2003) makes a more basic point in criticizing Hanushek for weighting all estimates equally and thus giving more weight to studies that publish more estimates. Focusing on the class size results included in Hanushek (1996), Krueger uses alternative weighting strategies, including giving equal weight to each study rather than equal weight to each estimate, and finds support for a positive relationship between smaller class sizes and better student outcomes.

Today, while researchers recognize the importance of family background and other non-school inputs in determining educational outcomes, many have come to question the findings of the Hanushek meta-analyses as well as the validity of many of the individual studies estimating education production functions. Card and Krueger (1992) perhaps marks the turning of the tide on the view that schools do not matter. Instead of focusing on direct education outcomes, Card and Krueger focus on how school quality affects the returns to schooling (i.e., the increase in earnings associated with an additional year of schooling). Assuming that school quality for men working in a given labor market varies exogenously by their state of birth and cohort, Card and Krueger find that men who were educated in states and years with higher-quality schools—schools with lower pupil-teacher ratios, longer school years, and higher relative teacher pay—earned more for an additional year of education than men educated in states and years with lower-quality schools. These results are consistent with earlier work finding positive relationships between school quality and earnings (e.g., Johnson & Stafford, 1973; Rizzuto & Wachtel, 1980) and work that attributes much of the closing of the Black–White wage gap to improvements in school quality for African American students (e.g., Smith & Welch, 1989). While some researchers challenged the assumptions used in Card and Krueger (1992), others began to consider that school resources may affect students' earnings after leaving school without having measurable effects on academic achievement while in school (Burtless, 1996).

Recent Studies

Since Card and Krueger (1992), there have been many new papers examining the effects of school inputs on student achievement, several of which use estimation strategies aimed at identifying the causal relationships between school inputs and student outcomes. In this section we review a few of the best studies in economics assessing school spending, class size, teacher quality, time in school, and technology.

Spending. Because some students may be more expensive to educate than others, and schools and districts differ in the types of students they serve, simply looking at the relationship between average student test scores and per-pupil spending may indicate that greater school spending is associated with lower student achievement. As a result, researchers rely on alternative strategies for identifying the causal relationship between spending and student outcomes. Barrow and Rouse (2004) and Guryan (2003) use changes in state school financing aid formulas as instrumental variables to isolate plausibly exogenous changes in school spending. Barrow and Rouse examine the general question of whether spending on schools is valued by the "market" by looking at the effects of increased school spending on local property values. Indeed, the authors find that school spending is valued, on average, since they estimate that property values increased by the expected amount in school districts that received an extra $1 per pupil in state school financing. If potential residents did not value the additional spending because school districts were viewed as spending excessively or wastefully, additional state aid should not have resulted in such large increases in property values.

Guryan (2003) looks more specifically at the relationship between school spending and student achievement in Massachusetts. He finds that additional state aid resulting from a change in the financing formulas led to a significant increase in math, reading, and science test scores for both fourth- and eighth-grade students. Specifically, he estimates that a $1,000 increase in per-pupil spending leads to a one-third to one-half of a standard deviation increase in average test scores. In sum, Barrow and Rouse (2004) and Guryan both suggest that money matters when it comes to public schools. Below we look at studies that examine more specifically whether different inputs matter.

Class size. Although the effect of class size on student achievement has most often been studied using observational data, Boozer and Rouse (2001) provide a clear demonstration of how estimates of class size effects can be misleading because of the relationship between class size and student ability and because school-level measures of pupil–teacher ratios can mask significant within-school variation in actual class size. Thus one should be suspicious of estimates that do not make use of more sophisticated estimation techniques to uncover the causal relationship between class size and student achievement. Fortunately, class size is one of the education topics that have been studied using a variety of estimation techniques, including regression discontinuity, instrumental variables, and randomized evaluation.

Angrist and Lavy (1999) use a regression discontinuity estimator to look at the effect of class size on student test scores in Israel. Public schools in Israel have a maximum class size of 40 pupils, which generates a nonlinear, nonmonotonic relationship between grade enrollment and class size. As discussed above, this will generate large differences in class size between grades with enrollment of 39 students and grades with enrollment of 41 students. For fourth- and fifth-grade students, Angrist and Lavy find that reductions in class size increase test scores by statistically significant and educationally important amounts. They do not find similar effects for third-grade students.

Two other papers have used regression discontinuity and/or instrumental variables as well. Hoxby (2000) uses class size minimums and maximums in Connecticut to look at the effect on student test scores of changes in class size driven by movements in enrollment populations that push schools over and under the class size thresholds. She finds mixed results on the relationship between class size and student performance. Boozer and Rouse (2001) use state class size maximums as an instrumental variable for student-level class size in the National Education Longitudinal Study of 1988 (NELS, p. 88) and find that smaller classes improve student achievement.

Perhaps the best known and most convincing evidence on the impact of class size comes from the Tennessee Student/Teacher Achievement Ratio experiment (Project STAR) in which

Tennessee kindergarten students were randomly assigned to small classes (13 to 17 students per teacher), regularly sized classes (22 to 25 students per teacher), or regularly sized classes with a teacher's aide (22 to 25 students per teacher). The experiment continued through the third grade, and then students were returned to regularly sized classes. Finn and Achilles (1990) and Krueger (1999) find that students in the smaller classes outperformed students in the larger classes on standardized tests. Additionally, in a longer-term follow-up of Project STAR, Krueger and Whitmore (2001) find that students who were randomly assigned to smaller classes were significantly more likely to take a college entrance exam and that this effect was greater for African American students.

At this point, many education researchers and policymakers have been convinced that smaller class sizes can improve student outcomes on average. However, many unanswered questions remain. For example, we need to know more about the cost of class size reduction relative to other interventions and whether it is cost-effective. In addition, California's experience with class size reduction in the 1990s highlighted that implementation—especially on a large scale—can go awry (Bohrnstedt & Stecher, 1999). Importantly, even the evidence from Project STAR suggests that the impact of class size reduction differs across schools and subpopulations of students (e.g., Krueger [1999] found the largest effects for African American and low-income students). Clearly we need to know more about the conditions under which reducing class sizes will be most fruitful.

Teacher quality. The preponderance of evidence suggests that teachers matter for student outcomes. Hanushek, Rivkin, and Kain (2005) use Texas data on elementary students linked to teachers at the school-grade level in order to estimate the effect of teachers on student learning, while Aaronson, Barrow, and Sander (2007) use Chicago Public Schools data on high school students linked to teachers at the classroom level to examine teacher quality. Both studies find large variation in teacher quality as measured by the effect of teachers on student test score gains. Hanushek, Rivkin, and Kain (2005) estimate that a one standard deviation increase in teacher quality at the grade level will increase student test scores by roughly 10 percent of a standard deviation, while Aaronson, Barrow, and Sander (2007) find that a one standard deviation improvement in ninth-grade math teacher quality for one semester is associated with a gain equal to 10 to 20 percent of the average math test score gain experienced in a typical school year.

When it comes to determining what makes a good teacher, the research is much less clear. Research by Clotfelter, Ladd, and Vigdor (2004) in North Carolina illustrates the great tendency for the most qualified teachers to teach in schools with the most advantaged students as well as for parents of more advantaged children to get their children into classes with more qualified teachers. This sorting of teachers and students makes it difficult to disentangle the causal effects of various measures of teacher quality. In addition, the characteristics of teachers available in the large administrative data sets are typically limited to those that determine compensation, such as whether or not a teacher has a master's degree and how many years she has been teaching in the school district.

Researchers have found some evidence that teacher quality improves sharply after one or two years of experience (e.g., Clotfelter, Ladd, & Vigdor, 2004; Hanushek, Rivkin, & Kain, 2005). However, new teachers exit teaching at fairly high rates, and Aaronson, Barrow, and Sander (2007) find that teachers in the lowest-quality decile in one year are 13 percent less likely to be teaching in the next year than teachers in the highest-quality decile, suggesting that some of the experience results may be driven by selection if only the higher-quality teachers stay beyond one or two years. Clotfelter, Ladd, and Vigdor also find evidence that teachers who score best on licensing tests are indeed higher quality teachers.

Using a regression discontinuity design, Jacob and Lefgren (2004a) take advantage of the nonlinear relationship between school-level student achievement in Chicago Public Schools and the assignment of schools to probationary status in order to examine the relationship between professional development and student achievement. In 1996, elementary schools in which fewer than 15 percent of students met national norms on a standardized test of reading were placed on probation and given resources (up to $90,000 in the first year) to purchase staff development services. Schools with more than 15 percent of students meeting national norms were not placed on probation and not given the additional resources. Jacob and Lefgren thus assume that whether a school has just fewer than 15 percent of students that met the reading norm or slightly more than 15 percent of students that met the norm is by chance.

The authors find that schools on probation primarily spent the additional resources on professional and staff development purchased from a wide variety of external sources including universities, nonprofit organizations, and independent consultants. The authors find that teachers report a 25 percent increase in the frequency of attending professional development programs, and others (e.g., Smylie et al., 2001) have reported a more substantial increase in the quality of the professional development teachers received. Unfortunately, however, the authors find no evidence that the increase in the quantity and quality of professional development induced by schools' probationary status translated into improved student achievement.

In sum, the best evidence suggests that teachers matter; however, we still have much to learn about how to identify quality teachers when making hiring decisions or how to increase teacher productivity with training or professional development.

Time in school. The length of the school year in the United States is a frequent target of criticism in discussions of why students in the United States score badly on standardized tests relative to other developed countries. Several studies document erosion of students' skills over the summer vacation (e.g., Cooper et al., 2000), and there is some evidence that summer school can improve student achievement (e.g., Jacob & Lefgren, 2004b).

Jacob and Lefgren (2004b) utilize regression discontinuity to look at the effect of summer school and grade retention on student achievement in Chicago. In 1996, Chicago Public Schools instituted a policy of requiring third- and sixth-grade students to attend summer school if they did not meet minimum test score thresholds. Students were then retained in grade if they did not achieve the minimum test score following summer school. The authors are able to use the discontinuity of the treatment rule in order to assess the benefits of the summer school and grade retention policy on student achievement. Namely, students scoring just below the minimum "passing" test score and students scoring just above the minimum passing test score are assumed to be quite similar except that those scoring just below the threshold are assigned to summer school. Jacob and Lefgren find that the net effect of summer school and grade retention was to increase student achievement among third-grade students. However, the authors find no similar achievement gains for sixth-grade students.[26]

Pischke (2003) specifically looks at the effect of school-year length by taking advantage of a natural experiment occurring in West Germany in the late 1960s. Adoption of a common fall

---

26. The authors also use regression discontinuity to look at the effect of grade retention alone using the post summer school test scores. Once again, they find that grade retention is beneficial to third-grade student achievement, but has no effect on sixth-grade student achievement.

start to the school year led students in most states to experience two short school years, equivalent to roughly two-thirds of the standard length school year. In contrast, students in West Berlin and Hamburg attended one long school year. Pischke finds that the shorter school year increased grade repetition among elementary school students, but that the shorter school year had no effect on the number of students attending the highest secondary school track or on subsequent earnings as adults. Thus there is little evidence of long-lasting negative effects of a shorter school year.

The Pischke (2003) results point to an important difficulty in estimating educational policy effects with observational data even in the presence of a natural experiment. Although we may believe that the natural experiment is valid in that it generated exogenous variation in the length of a school year and that it should only affect student outcomes through the experiment's effect on the length of a school year, it is quite likely that teachers changed their behavior to compensate for the temporarily shortened school year. Since the behavioral response to a short-term change in the school year may be different from the responses generated by a permanent change in the length of the school year, the results may lack external validity.

Technology. Research on the success of CAI has yielded mixed evidence at best. Some research using observational data has shown computers can offer highly individualized instruction, allow students to learn at their own paces, enhance assessment, and increase student motivation (e.g., Lepper, 1985; Means & Olson, 1997; Sandholz, Ringstaff, & Dwyer, 1997). In contrast, other research reports that computers are frequently poorly embraced by teachers, can disrupt classrooms, and fail to increase student achievement in any measurable way (e.g., Cuban, 2001; Becker, 2000; Angrist & Lavy, 2002; Rouse & Krueger, 2004).

A common critique of the literature is that both student outcomes and what constitutes "computer use" are poorly defined (Cuban, 2001). For example, while Angrist and Lavy (2002) are able to use an instrumental variables estimator to look at the effect of CAI on student test scores, the intensity of computer use is defined in their study by the teacher's response to a rather vague question about how often they used "computer software or instructional computer programmes." The authors find no evidence that greater use of CAI improved student test scores in math or Hebrew.

Borman and Rachuba (2001) and Rouse and Krueger (2004) have the advantages of being able to evaluate the effect of much more specific computer use—the use of a particular instructional software—and to implement random assignment of students to treatment and control groups. Both studies evaluate the popular *Fast ForWord*® (FFW) computerized reading instruction program using random assignment within schools in large urban school districts. The studies' findings are remarkably similar: both rule out large impacts of computerized instruction with estimated effects that are not statistically different from zero.

Although these studies suggest that CAI does not significantly improve student educational outcomes, one might find that different computerized reading programs were successful or that the use of CAI in other subjects significantly raised students' learning in those subjects. Further, one might find that FFW was effective when used in other settings. Both randomized evaluations of FFW were conducted in schools, but it may be that schools are not the best environment in which to implement the program (FFW is also often used by psychologists and reading specialists in private practice). While the schools and teachers in the studies did their best to engage students and keep them on task, the many disruptions that occur during the semester may have compromised students' ability to benefit from the program; the same students may have benefited from the program in a different setting. Currently, however, there is very little evidence that CAI is effective in schools.

CONCLUSION

Educators and policymakers are increasingly intent on using scientifically based evidence when making decisions about education policy. Thus education research today must necessarily be focused on identifying the causal relationships between education inputs and student outcomes. The good news is that the body of credible research on causal relationships is growing, and we have started to gather evidence that some school inputs matter while others do not.

As this body of knowledge grows, we can also get inside the "black box" of the inputs that work. Once we understand that an input improves student outcomes, on average, we can look at the next set of questions: Do all students benefit from a particular input? Who benefits most from a particular input? Which aspects of multidimensional programs are most beneficial? (A challenge will be to develop studies that also generate causal estimates of this next generation of questions!) As we develop a knowledge base regarding what works in education, we will also need a better understanding about how to implement appropriate policies using that knowledge.

In addition, policymakers need information with which to assess the trade-offs between different inputs to make sensible decisions. For example, Jacob and Lefgren (2004b) find a small, but statistically significant, positive effect of summer school and grade retention on student reading skills at a cost of about $750 per student.[27] This cost per student may be compared with other interventions, such as class size reduction, that have larger effects (more than three times as large) on student reading skills but also cost more than $2,000 per student (Krueger, 1999). As a result, requiring summer school and grade retention may be more cost-effective for some school districts than reducing class sizes. This conclusion could not be based on estimates of the effectiveness of grade retention and summer school alone. Clearly, more information on such trade-offs in educational practice is critical.

Policymakers must also understand that it is much more difficult to credibly evaluate the effectiveness of school policies *after the fact*. Rather, if research and evaluation are part of a new policy from the beginning, then researchers can collect the necessary data (which are often difficult—if not impossible—to collect after the policy has been implemented). Further, if a policy change is only to be implemented in a small number of locations, researchers can help policymakers design the selection of locations in a way that meets both political and research needs. Indeed, some of our best opportunities for learning more about the impact of education resources on student outcomes will come from just such partnerships between policymakers and researchers.

Finally we note that good policy is not based on the results of a single study, but rather on a pattern of results extending over time and across a number of settings. Let us take the evidence on small class sizes, as an example. The evidence from the Tennessee class size reduction experiment is important because it has been analyzed by multiple researchers, and the basic results have been found to be robust to alternative ways of analyzing the data. That said, without other credible evidence that smaller class sizes make a difference for students, one would not want to draw such conclusions. Another recent example of the caution with which one must approach a single study comes from the evidence on the FFW computerized language program. Results from Miller et al. (1999) suggest the program has a large and statistically significant effect on student

---

27. Authors' calculations based on the following assumptions. The current annual cost per pupil in the Chicago Public Schools is about $9,000. If the current school year is about 180 days, then the cost per pupil per day is $50. The summer school program for third graders was for six weeks for one-half day, or for 15 days. Thus, the cost per pupil for the summer school was about $750.

outcomes. However, as discussed earlier, this finding was not found to be robust in alternative settings. Indeed, the purpose of the federally funded WWC is to provide policymakers with summaries (or meta-analyses) of the best research on any particular topic. This effort reflects the fact that it is only by piecing together results from a variety of high-quality studies that we can begin to develop a picture of what does, and does not, work in education.

ACKNOWLEDGMENTS

We thank Brian Jacob, Jesse Rothstein, and Diane Whitmore Schanzenbach for helpful conversations, Helen Ladd and the editors for insightful comments, and Kyung-Hong Park for research assistance. Any errors in fact or interpretation are ours. The opinions in this paper do not reflect those of the Federal Reserve Bank of Chicago or the Federal Reserve System.

REFERENCES

Aaronson, D., Barrow, L., & Sander, W. (2003). Teachers and student achievement in the Chicago public high schools. *Journal of Labor Economics, 25*, 96–135.

Angrist, J. D. (2004). American education research changes tack. *Oxford Review of Economic Policy 20*, 198–212.

Angrist, J. D., & Lavy, V. (1999). Using Maimonides' rule to estimate the effect of class size on scholastic achievement. *Quarterly Journal of Economics 114*, 533–575.

Angrist, J. D., & Lavy, V. (2002). New evidence on classroom computers and pupil learning. *Economic Journal 112*, 735–765.

Barrow, L., & Rouse, C. E. (2004). Using market valuation to assess the importance and efficiency of public school spending. *Journal of Public Economics 88*, 1747–1769.

Becker, H. J. (2000). Who's wired and who's not. *The Future of Children 10*, 44–75.

Bohrnstedt, G. W., & Stecher, B. M., eds. (1999). *Class size reduction in California: Early evaluation findings, 1996–1999.* Palo Alto, CA: CSR Research Consortium.

Boozer, M. A., & Rouse, C. E. (2001). Intraschool variation in class size: Patterns and implications. *Journal of Urban Economics 50*, 163–189.

Borman, G. D., & Rachuba, L. T. (2001). Evaluation of the Scientific Learning Corporation's Fast ForWord computer-based training program in the Baltimore City Public Schools. Unpublished report prepared for the Abell Foundation, Baltimore.

Bryk, A. S., & Raudenbush, S. W. (1992). *Hierarchical linear models: Applications and data analysis methods.* London: Sage Publications.

Burtless, G. (1996). Introd. and summary to *Does money matter? The effect of school resources on student achievement and adult success*, G. Burtless (Ed.). Washington, DC: Brookings Institution Press.

Campbell, D. T., & Stanley, J. C. (1963). Experimental and quasi-experimental designs for research on teaching. In N. L. Gage (Ed.), *Handbook of Research on Teaching* (pp. 171–246). Chicago: Rand McNally.

Card, D., & Krueger, A. B. (1992). Does school quality matter? Returns to education and the characteristics of public schools in the United States. *Journal of Political Economy 100*, 1–40.

Clotfelter, C. T., Ladd, H. F., & Vigdor, J. L. (2004). Teacher sorting, teacher shopping, and the assessment of teacher effectiveness. Unpublished manuscript, Duke Univ.

Coleman, J. S., & Campbell, E. Q., with Hobson, C. F., McPartland, J., Mood, A. M., Weinfield, F. D., & York, R. L. (1966). *Equality of educational opportunity.* Washington, DC: U.S. Office of Education.

Cook, T. D. (2001). A critical appraisal of the case against using experiments to assess school (or community) effects. *Education Next Unabrigded Articles* 1 (3). Retrieved January 22, 2007, from http://www.educationnext.org/unabridged/ 20013/cook.html.

Cook, T. D., & Campbell, D. T. (1979). *Quasi-experimentation: Design and analysis issues for field settings.* Boston: Houghton.

Cooper, H., Charlton, K., Valentine, J. C., & Muhlenbruck, L. (2000). *Making the most of summer school: A meta-analytic and narrative review.* Society for Research in Child Development Monographs 65.1. Malden, MA: Society for Research in Child Development.

Cuban, L. (2001). *Oversold and underused: Computers in the classroom.* Cambridge, MA: Harvard University Press.

Efron, B., & Feldman, D. (1991). Compliance as an explanatory variable in clinical trials. *Journal of the American Statistical Association 86*, 9–17.

Finn, J. D., & Achilles, C. M. (1990). Answers and questions about class size: A statewide experiment. *American Educational Research Journal 27*, 557–577.

Guryan, J. (2003). Does money matter? Estimates from education finance reform in Massachusetts. Unpublished manuscript, Univ. of Chicago.

Hanushek, E. A. (1986). The economics of schooling: production and efficiency in public schools. *Journal of Economic Literature 24*, 1141–1177.

Hanushek, E. A. (1989). The impact of differential expenditures on school performance. *Educational Researcher 18*, 45–65.

Hanushek, E. A. (1996). Measuring investment in education. *Journal of Economic Perspectives 10*, 9–30.

Hanushek, E. A. (1997). Assessing the effects of school resources on student performance: An update. *Educational Evaluation and Policy Analysis 19*, 141–164.

Hanushek, E. A., Rivkin, S. G., & Kain, J. F. (2005). Teachers, schools, and academic achievement. *Econometrica 73*, 417–458.

Hedges, L. V., Laine, R., & Greenwald, R. (1994). Does money matter? A meta-analysis of studies of the effects of differential school inputs on student outcomes. *Education Researcher 23*, 5–14.

Hoxby, C. M. (2000). The effects of class size on student achievement: New evidence from population variation. *Quarterly Journal of Economics 115*, 1239–1285.

Imbens, G., & Angrist, J. (1994). Identification and estimation of local average treatment effects. *Econometrica 62*, 467–475.

Jacob, B. A., & Lefgren, L. (2004a). The impact of teacher training on student achievement: Quasi-experimental evidence from school reform efforts in Chicago. *Journal of Human Resources 39*, 50–79.

Jacob, B. A., & Lefgren, L. (2004b). Remedial education and student achievement: A regression-discontinuity analysis. *Review of Economics and Statistics 86*, 226–244.

Johnson, G. E., & Stafford, F. P. (1973). Social returns to quantity and quality of schooling. *Journal of Human Resources 8*, 139–155.

Krueger, A. B. (1999). Experimental estimates of education production functions. *Quarterly Journal of Economics 114*, 497–531.

Krueger, A. B. (2003). Economic considerations and class size. *Economic Journal 113*, F34–F63.

Krueger, A. B., & Whitmore, D. M. (2001). The effect of attending a small class in the early grades on college-test taking and middle school test results: Evidence from Project STAR. *Economic Journal 111*, 1–28.

Lepper, M. R. (1985). Microcomputers in education, motivational and social issues. American Psychologist *40*, 1–18.

Means, B., & Olson, K. (1997). *Technology and education reform.* Washington, DC: U.S. Department of Education, Office of Educational Research and Improvement.

Miller, S. L., Merzenich, M. M., Tallal, P., DeVivo, K., La-Rossa, K., Linn, N., Pycha, A., Peterson, B. E., & Jenkins, W. M. (1999). *Fast ForWord training in children with low reading performance.* Paper presented at the Netherlands Annual Speech-Language Association Meeting (NVLF Jaarcongres).

Pischke, J. (2003). *The impact of length of school year on student performance and earnings: Evidence from the German short school years.* NBER Working paper 9964. Cambridge, MA: National Bureau of Economic Research.

Rizzuto, R., & Wachtel, P. (1980). Further evidence on the returns to school quality. *Journal of Human Resources 15*, 240–254.

Rouse, C. E. (2005). Accounting for schools: Econometric issues in measuring school quality. In C. A. Dwyer (Ed.), *Measurement and research issues in a new accountability era*. Mahwah, NJ: Lawrence Erlbaum Associates.

Rouse, C. E., & Krueger, A. B., with Markman, L. (2004). Putting computerized instruction to the test: A randomized evaluation of a "scientifically-based" reading program. *Economics of Education Review 23*, 323–338.

Rubin, D. (1974). Estimating causal effects of treatments in randomized and non-randomized studies. *Journal of Educational Psychology 66*, 688–701.

Sandholtz, J. H., Ringstaff, C., & Dwyer, D. C. (1997). *Teaching with technology: Creating student-centered classrooms*. New York: Teachers College Press.

Sewell, W. H. (1967). Review of *Equality of educational opportunity*, by J. S. Coleman & E. Q. Campbell, with C. F. Hobson, J. McPartland, A. M. Mood, F. D. Weinfield, & R. L. York. *American Sociological Review 32*, 475–479.

Smith, J. P., & Welch, F. R. (1989). Black economic progress after Myrdal. *Journal of Economic Literature 27*, 519–564.

Smylie, M. A., Allensworth, E., Greenberg, R. C., Harris, R., & Luppescu, S. (2001). *Teacher professional development in Chicago: Supporting effective practice*. Chicago: Consortium on Chicago School Research.

Summers, A. A., & Wolfe, B. L. (1977). Do schools make a difference? *American Economic Review 67*, 639–652.

Todd, P. E., & Wolpin, K. I. (2003). On the specification and estimation of the production function for cognitive achievement. *Economic Journal 113*, F3–F33.

U.S. Department of Education. (2002). U.S. Department of Education awards contract for "What Works Clearinghouse." Press release. Washington, DC: Author. Retrieved January 22, 2007, from http://www.ed.gov/news/pressreleases/2002/ 08/08072002a.html.

8

The Elusiveness of Educational Equity: From Revenues to Resources to Results

W. Norton Grubb

A concern with equity flows throughout the history of the United States. In contrast to most European countries, with aristocracies and religious elites taken for granted, the debates around the Revolution were concerned with overthrowing old inequalities; in Pole's memorable phrase, the Revolution "introduced an egalitarian rhetoric to an unequal society" (1978, p.13). The Declaration of Independence declared that "all men are created equal," and the Constitution promised to "promote the general Welfare." Early legislation stressed political equalities, especially equality before the law—the right of all men to be represented in court—and equality of esteem, the ability of all citizens to address one another on equal terms. But equality itself remained elusive. Slaves and women were not granted citizenship until the 14th and the 20th amendments, and even then access to the vote remained contested; equality before the law did not mean equality of political influence; and the expansion of cities created new inequalities of wealth and earnings, contradicting any rhetorical commitment to equality.

In the intervening two centuries discussions about equality, and its normative cousin equity, have persisted. Early welfare programs were created after 1900, and then a welfare state, particularly between the 1930s and the 1960s. But the welfare state in the United States has always been comparatively weak and deferential to markets (Esping-Anderson, 1990), and it has been under attack for the past three decades—now with President George W. Bush's efforts to partially privatize Social Security, the mainstay of the welfare state. Inequality has been increasing; by 2000, the United States had the most unequal income distribution of any developed country.[1]

So too with public schooling, born of egalitarian impulses. The charity schools of the early 19th century were early versions of compensatory education, for children whose parents were too poor to pay. The common school created an image of public schooling incorporating all children, in the interests of socializing everyone in the values of an emerging democracy (Kaestle, 1983). The egalitarian impulse of the common school—if not its civic and moral purposes—lives

---

1. For comparative figures see www.lisproject.org/keyfigures/ineqtable.htm.

on in movements to provide access to groups left out, whether special education students, immigrant children, migrant children, or homeless children. A majority of the population (58 percent) now believes that schools are responsible for closing racial and ethnic gaps in educational achievement, even though only 17 percent believes that schools are mostly to blame for these gaps (Rose and & Gallup, 2005, Tables 19 and 21). Even antiegalitarians like President Bush have accepted equity through schooling; when he was asked about the widening gap between rich and poor, he responded with platitudes about education: "the No Child Left Behind Act [NCLB] is really a jobs act, when you think about it."[2]

But the common school ideal was not always translated into practice. The extension of the common schools to the high school was opposed by working class groups who could not afford to keep their children in school (Katz, 1968, part I). Only recently have women been able to assert rights to equal schooling; and the education of Black Americans, as well as of immigrant and language-minority children, has always been uneven. And so, despite rhetorical commitment to equal opportunity, the American system of schooling remains highly unequal, marked by enormous achievement gaps among White and Black and Latino students (Jencks & Phillips, 1998), and by enormous differences in attainment between high school dropouts and those (around 4 percent of each cohort) who earn postbaccalaureate degrees. Along with our unequal income distribution, we have among the most unequal educational outcomes.[3]

How has a country with such rhetorical commitment to equity simultaneously created a highly unequal system of schooling? The obvious answer lies in politics—both in the sense of values, since many Americans (especially the current administration) remain unconcerned about inequality, and in the sense of interest group politics, which has no effective ways of articulating the public good and of enhancing redistribution (Lowi, 1969; Truman, 1951). But this response isn't the entire explanation, since ideas have significantly shaped the politics of education (McDonnell, this volume). In addition, there are several problems with our ideas about equity in schooling. First, the simple conceptions of equity in the common schools were transformed into the much more slippery conception of equal opportunity, with many different variants; as I point out in the first section of this chapter, debates over equity reflect in part a lack of consensus about how equity is to be defined. There's additional uncertainty about whether equity should be applied to revenues and expenditures, or to the resources that money can (perhaps) buy, or to outcomes. With ambiguity in conceptions of equity and in how they should be applied, I develop a matrix of possibilities, a "landscape of equity," that clarifies how difficult it is to define equity.

Second, in a fragmented system of education with several levels of governance (McDonnell, this volume), there has been a problem of where equity efforts should be applied—whether to differences among states, among districts within states, among schools within districts, or among classrooms and students within schools. When I examine progress in equity, in the second section of the chapter, I show that most of the effort has gone into equalizing funding across districts within states, as well as into to the checkered efforts of the federal government in compensatory education. But these approaches address only a small region of the landscape of equity and have usually failed to address inequalities in resources or outcomes. So the dominant policy approaches to equity have been partial, and most inequities remain uncorrected.

A third problem is that extending conceptions of equity beyond funding requires better understanding of how to translate *revenues* (or expenditures) into those *resources* within schools that might matter to the *results* of schooling. But this process remains hotly disputed, even after

---

2. See the third presidential debate at www.debates.org/pages/trans2004d.html.

3. The PISA study of 15-year-olds showed that the United States has among the highest levels of inequality of reading and math of OECD countries. See Kirsch et al. (2002), Table 4.1, Table 4.15; OECD (2001), Table 3.1.

years of research. The dominant idea or narrative[4] remains the notion that money is inherently powerful, that "more money would buy more educational resources, which would create better education, which would enable more learning" (Cohen, Moffitt, & Goldin, this volume). But there are many reasons why this assumption is unwarranted. Instead a different approach I call the "improved" school finance recognizes a broader variety of school resources—simple, compound, complex, and abstract—as well as nonschool resources like parent effects and student behavior (Grubb, Huerta, & Goe, 2006). Only then can we identify the most important inequalities in schooling, as I do in the chapter's third section, and—potentially—develop more powerful approaches to equity.

CONCEPTIONS OF EQUITY: DEBATES OVER EQUAL OPPORTUNITY THROUGH SCHOOLING

The common school conception of equity was simple: all students should have access to a common curriculum and should complete the undifferentiated grammar school (to grade 8). As high schools developed, they were still dominated by a unitary curriculum. But shifts around 1900 associated with the spread of vocational purposes changed conceptions of equity (Grubb & Lazerson, 2004, ch. 7). Once schools were preparing youth to become professionals and businessmen, metalworkers and electricians, or (for girls) teachers and secretaries, a uniform education was irrelevant and inefficient (Elson & Frank, 1910):

> Instead of affording equality of educational opportunity to all, the elementary school by offering but one course of instruction, and this of a literary character, serves the interests of but one type of children and neglects in a measure the taste, capacity, and educational destination of all others, and of those, too, whose needs are imperative and to whom the future holds no further advantage. (p. 361)

The new conception of equal opportunity provided different experiences for students with different occupational goals: the academic track for middle class students bound for college and then professional and managerial work, industrial education for working class boys bound for factories, commercial education for working class girls heading for clerical positions, and home economics for future homemakers.

Another shift took place as the goals of schooling modulated from civic and moral purposes to occupational preparation: ideals surrounding schooling shifted from political to economic conceptions. Ideals of equality in the United States have applied much more to *political* equality—to equality before the law, equality of social and legal stature, and voting rights—than to *economic* equality. The only ideal of economic equality with any real power has been equality of opportunity (Pole, 1978). This promises equity in the race for success, not equality in results—and certainly not in an economy of growing inequality. Consistent with an older Protestant ethic of individual effort, it stresses the need for individuals to take advantage of opportunities offered, to earn their positions through diligence and hard work (now especially through schoolwork), and through merit rather than through compensatory efforts like affirmative action.

---

4. Policy in many countries is driven by narratives, or widely accepted "stories" about why certain approaches are worthwhile (Roe 1994). Once widely accepted, policy narratives—like the notion that money is inherently powerful—are resistant to change, especially by subtle empirical evidence like policy research. See also Baumgartner and Jones's (1993) conception of policy images.

As equal opportunity has been applied to schools, three reasons help explain why the concept has been so elusive (with a fourth discussed in the next section). First, several versions of equality of opportunity have developed historically, in addition to others that philosophers have dreamed up.[5] One was eloquently described by Noah Webster in 1793 (quoted in Pole, 1978):

> Here [in the United States] every man finds employment, and the road is open for the poorest citizen to amass wealth by labor and economy, and by his talent and virtue to raise himself to the highest offices of the State. (p. 118)

Outcomes may be unequal, then, because of difference in work, thrift, and talent, but there ought to be no barriers due to family background, race, or other artificial factors. However, eliminating overt barriers is a weaker version of equity than conceptions requiring more substantial action.

A stronger version of equal opportunity then emerged, requiring more than the elimination of obvious barriers. Andrew Jackson articulated a complaint about variation in what government provided (quoted in Pole, 1978):

> When the laws undertake to add to the natural and just advantages [of superior industry, economy, and virtue] artificial distinctions, to grant titles, gratuities and exclusive privileges, to make the rich richer and the potent more powerful, the humble members of the society—the farmers, mechanics and laborers—have a right to complain of the injustice of their Government. . . . If it would confine itself to equal protection, and, as Heaven does its rains, shower its favors alike on the high and the low, the rich and the poor, it would be an unqualified blessing. (p. 145)

Therefore any inequalities in what government provides to the rich and to the humble should be eliminated, implying a standard of equalization.

A recent variant of equalization has been adequacy, that each child should be provided an education in which no one falls below a minimum (Minorini & Sugarman, 1999). Adequacy is a weaker standard of equity than is equalization since it calls only for guaranteeing everyone some minimum, not a common level. Adequacy suffers a further ambiguity, since the level of adequacy must be defined. The common approaches have been to define adequacy as (1) the spending levels of districts or schools with high levels of performance; (2) the spending necessary for specific resources (qualified teachers, certain pupil:teacher ratios, sufficient textbooks, etc.) that professionals judge to be adequate; or (3) a level of spending sufficient to bring all students to some adequate level of outcomes, which itself needs to be defined. The first two of these *presume* that the levels of spending deemed adequate are sufficient to achieve strong outcomes, but the ways these adequate budgets are constructed do not link spending to outcomes. The third approach does examine explicitly the relation between inputs and outputs, but the empirical work (e.g., Duncombe & Yinger, 1999) relies on conventional production functions with low explanatory power and fails to recognize the uncertain connections between spending and outcomes (see, e.g., Grubb, forthcoming b). Adequacy has sometimes been viewed as an advance over equalization because of its potential to link spending to outcomes, but in practice it rarely does so.

---

5. Gutmann (1987) presents three persistent philosophical conceptions: maximization of life chances, equalization so that the life chances between the least and the most disadvantaged children are narrowed as much as possible, and a meritocratic conception in which the state distributes resources in proportion to a child's ability and willingness to learn. She then proposes a "democratic standard," a Rawlsian approach in which inequalities can be justified only if no child is deprived of the ability to participate effectively in the democratic process.

A fourth version of equal opportunity has emerged repeatedly, since simply equalizing the "gratuities and exclusive privileges" between the rich and the humble might ignore the different levels of preparation children bring to school. A still more active approach has asserted a governmental role in favoring to some groups or individuals (Pole, 1978, ch. 11). These "policies of correction" or compensatory efforts date at least from 19th-century charity schools for poor children, followed by the common schools and public funding. The compensatory version of equal opportunity has assumed that some children may be unable to take advantage of opportunities because of their impoverished family backgrounds or their unfamiliarity with the culture of schooling (Deschenes, Cuban, & Tyack, 2001). Along the way, "policies of correction" have suffered from the suspicion that the targets of such policies are deficient in fundamental ways.

A second reason for the elusiveness of equal opportunity is that it has never been clear what aspects of schooling it should address. Conceptions of equal opportunity might be applied to simple *access* to publicly funded schools, as in the efforts to include Black students in all-White schools or colleges, or handicapped students in schools from which they had been barred. They might also be applied to the *funding* of schools, for example in the conception of wealth neutrality (Coons, Clune, & Sugarman, 1970), where variations in property wealth would no longer determine levels of district funding, or the attempts to move toward greater equality of funding in the *Serrano* case and its progeny. Conceptions of equality might also apply not to funding but to *resources*, the personnel, materials, practices, and conditions that money might be able to buy; for example, the *Williams* case requires adequate textbooks, qualified teachers, and physical facilities. Both revenues and resources are generally classified as inputs; alternatively, conceptions of equity could apply to *outcomes*—test scores, graduation rates, attitudes and values developed—though the historical tendency to rely on equal opportunity as a *substitute* for equality of outcomes prevents this application from being popular. The goal in NCLB of having all students achieve "proficient" levels is a rare example of equity applied to outcomes.

If there are at least four different conceptions of equal opportunity, applied to three aspects of schooling, Figure 8.1 describes what I call the "landscape of equity," with some illustrative policies and court cases. Since most forms of equity are not systematically addressed, we might call this the "landscape of *in*equality." But the main point is that the different concepts of equity are inconsistent with one another. Wealth neutrality has required eliminating wealth differences among districts as barriers to funding (Figure 8.1, cell #1), eliminating only some of the variation that equal funding (cell #4) or adequacy definitions 1 and 2 (cell #7) have sought to eliminate. The efforts to provide compensatory funding or resources (cells #10 and #11), or smaller classes for English language learner (ELL) or special education students, often leads to the "politics of resentment" based on equity criteria of equal funding or resources (cells #4 and #5), where students and parents not so favored complain that others have unfair advantages. The court in the *Williams* case ordered minimally acceptable levels of textbooks, facilities, and teachers (cell #8), but left the funding up to the legislature; the principle of equal funding of students set by *Serrano* (cell #4) could weaken the *Williams* solution. When the Bush administration set targets in NCLB of minimum levels of proficiency for all students (cell #9), but failed to provide sufficient funding or technical assistance required to develop the most effective resources (cells #10 and #11), low-performing schools faced targets that they lacked the capacity to meet.

There has often been a dynamic process of shifts among different conceptions of equity. For example, to prevent charges of favoring middle class and White students, many districts have moved to a standard of equal funding (Figure 8.1, cell #4); but this leaves especially needy students with the same funding as less needy students, prompting shifts to compensatory funding (cell #10) via weighted student formulas providing additional revenues to low-income, special education, and ELL students. The problems with equality in *Serrano*-like cases (cell #4) led lawyers to develop adequacy lawsuits (cell #7), partly on legal grounds and partly in the hopes that this might lead to funding based on outcomes (cell #9); similarly the Williams case (cell #8) arose because of the ineffectiveness of the Serrano case (cell #4). Reformers thereby change the equity conceptions they use, as policies based on prior conceptions of equity prove ineffective— just as I argue in the next two sections to abandon equity based on funding in favor of equity based on effective resources. Policy analysts might be able to come up with rational ways to move through the landscape of equity—starting with access and moving to funding, then resources and outcomes, or worrying about eliminating favoritism (cell #4) before compensatory efforts (cells #10 and #11). But in practice, advocates for equity have argued for a variety of conceptions depending on what problems seem most pressing and on what legal approaches are most available.

A final difficulty is that equality of opportunity presents a never-ending series of evidentiary problems. Equality itself is easy to measure, if hard to achieve. But since opportunity is an abstract quality, it is hard to know when it has been achieved except when outcomes are equal, which is precisely the condition that equality of opportunity does *not* guarantee. It has been easier to know when equal opportunity fails to exist, and so the dominant approach has been to challenge the conditions that most obviously preclude educational opportunity. Exclusion has been the most obvious example, and challenges to exclusion (Figure 8.1, cells #1 and #2) have been prominent in the long struggles over racial segregation, the battles to include students with disabilities, the movements to provide equal access for women, the reforms eliminating tracking, and the debates over bilingual education.

Conceptions of equity:	Applied to funding	Applied to resources	Applied to outcomes
Webster: "no barriers"	1. Policies of inclusion; wealth neutrality.	2. Policies of inclusion.	3. Affirmative action.
Jackson: No "artificial distinctions"; equality	4. *Serrano*; equality of funding; district efforts to reduce favoritism; the "politics of resentment."	5. Kozol, *Savage Inequalities*; the "politics of resentment."	6. Radical egalitarians.
Adequacy	7. Adequacy 1 and 2.	8. *Williams*; class size reduction; "qualified teachers" in NCLB; state interventions for low-performing schools.	9. Adequacy 3, minimum standards exit exams.
"Policies of correction"	10. Compensatory education.	11. Compensatory education; early childhood programs.	12. Affirmative action; Vonnegut, *Player Piano*.[a]

[a]In *Player Piano* Kurt Vonnegut describes a world in which individual gifts are countered by social constraints: for example, especially intelligent individuals have their thoughts interrupted by electrical impulses every 30 seconds; especially graceful dancers are weighted down with sandbags. These egalitarian impulses effectively eliminate the effects of "labor and economy, talent and virtue" noted by Webster.

Figure 8.1.   Applications of Equity Concepts: "The Landscape of Equity"

Another barrier to equal opportunity has been underprovision of funding, on the *assumption* that money is inherently powerful. Educators began worrying about unequal funding shortly after 1900, with the "discovery" in 1905 by Cubberly (1905) that districts had differing capacities to finance schools (Figure 8.1, cell #4), and continuing with state aid and lawsuits related to equality and adequacy. Sometimes there has been some attention to equal resources rather than funding: some states (like California) and the federal government have enacted class size reduction, presumably creating maximum class sizes (cell #8); in NCLB the federal government has tried to require that all students have "qualified" teachers. But overall the attention to resources has been much less than the attention to funding, and—as I argue in the next sections—the focus on funding doesn't solve most of the real problems.

The focus on the obvious barriers to participation has made it difficult to engage in policies of correction, both because of the evidentiary burden as well as the politics of resentment. So we find ourselves in a vast landscape of conceptions of equity—inconsistent with one another, shifting over time, uneven in their application, and of unknown efficacy.

POLICY TOWARD EQUITY:
UNEVEN ATTENTION, UNEQUAL PROGRESS

A second prominent reason for the slipperiness of equal opportunity is that, in a fragmented system (Fuhrman, Goertz, and & Weinbaum, this volume), it remains unclear at what level of governance equity should be applied. It might be applied across states within the country, or to all districts within states—the latter being by far the most prevalent strategy. Equity might also be a goal of districts in allocating either funding or resources among individual schools. The allocation of resources and outcomes among students within a school might be the focus, as with concern over tracking, access to honors and Advanced Placement courses, or the allocation of experienced teachers to high-needs students. In theory, any conception of equity might apply equally to all children throughout the country, so that the real resources available to a rural child in Alabama might equal those of a high-income child in a wealthy Connecticut suburb. Different levels of the intergovernmental system would have to coordinate their efforts to achieve such an outcome, whereas the education each child now receives is a complex and uncoordinated admixture of federal, state, district, and school-level policies. In this section I briefly summarize equity efforts at different levels.

Inequality Among States

A substantial proportion of spending and resource variation among students results from differences among states. Spending per pupil corrected for cost differences in 2002 varied by about 2:1, from $9,907 in Vermont to $4,995 in Utah. The pupil:teacher ratio varied from 11.9 in Vermont to 21.5 in Utah; the proportion of secondary instructors teaching in their field of study varied from 80 percent in Minnesota to 48 percent in New Mexico and Louisiana; the beginning salaries of teachers corrected for price differences ranged from $35,481 in Delaware to $28,051 in Mississippi.[6] If these kinds of resources are effective, then obviously children in Alabama and Utah and California lack the opportunities of children in Connecticut and Delaware. And of course NAEP scores show enormous variation among states. Just to examine the 2003 eighth-grade

---

6. See *Education Week*, http://counts.edweek.org/sreports/qc04/article.cfm?slug=17sos.h23.

reading scores, the proportion of students considered proficient ranged from 20% in New Mexico to 43 percent in Massachusetts, and—to eliminate the effects of family background in a crude way—the proficiency levels for White students ranged from 25 percent in West Virginia to 49 percent in Massachusetts, again a 2:1 differential.

Some differences among states have diminished somewhat over time. The ratio of spending in the highest-spending state to the lowest-spending went from 2.72:1 in 1960 to 2.6:1 in 1970 to 2.2 in 1980 to 1.97:1 in 2000, as part of the convergence of state economies. However, the only other potential corrective for interstate inequalities would be federal redistribution among the states, and there's been no political support for that since federal revenue sharing in the 1960s. One potential mechanism forcing state convergence in educational opportunity might be the pressures of NCLB, forcing all states to assure "qualified teachers" (Figure 8.1, cell #8) and to meet proficiency standards (cell #9). But NCLB standards and definitions of "qualified teachers" are state-determined and cannot force greater interstate equality, and the federal government—preoccupied with the costs of war mongering, inequitable tax cuts, and now rebuilding the Gulf Coast—is unlikely to provide adequate funding. Narrowing interstate differences must wait for a federal administration with greater understanding of what school improvement requires.

Inequality Among Districts Within States

The intrastate dimension of inequality has been continuously attacked during the past thirty years, particularly in court cases following *Serrano* (Huang, Lukemeyer, & Yinger, 2004). However, the consequences in terms of funding are at best mixed: some states with strong court decisions and genuine legislative responses have reduced within-state inequalities, but differences have been essentially unchanged in many others (Thompson & Crampton, 2002). Within most states, variation among districts in expenditures per pupil remain substantial, with the coefficient of variation ranging from zero in Hawaii (a one-district state) and 5.7 percent in Florida, to a high of 19.5 percent in Vermont and 34.7 percent in Alaska, an outlier. Within states, expenditures per pupil are also correlated with income per pupil (U.S. General Accounting Office, 1997, Fig. 1); only 11 states have income elasticities close to zero (between –.1 and .1). We can look forward to continued lawsuits, and more legislative responses and nonresponses around intrastate differences.

Some states—Kentucky, Texas, and New Jersey prominent among them—have taken court challenges as an opportunity not only to equalize funding, but also to enact other reforms. The tactic of reshaping other policies while equalizing revenues potentially reflects the "improved" school finance: states in these cases have created planning procedures, incentives, and capacity-building mechanisms like special support for low-performing schools, which might enhance the effectiveness of spending. In theory, combining finance and other reforms makes sense because finance reform could provide the funds necessary to meet higher standards, whereas independent legislation might increase requirements without giving districts greater capacity to meet new demands (as NCLB has done). In practice, most states have established standards and accountability independent of any finance reform. Whether "integrated" legislation has had a greater effect on outcomes than fragmented efforts has never been examined.

What remains unclear is what any reductions in unequal *spending* (Figure 8.1, cell #4) have done for either *resources* (cell #5) or *outcomes* (cell #6). Because of the fixation of the "old" school finance on funding, analyses of changes after school finance lawsuits have usually failed to trace the effects on any real resources, never mind outcomes. One exception includes the five case studies in Yinger (2004), of Kansas, Kentucky, Michigan, Texas, and Vermont, all states with widely known court cases. Each case study finds that inequality in expenditures per student has decreased, but that outcomes—test scores, but also dropout rates in the case of Kansas—remain just as unequal after court cases. In the one case (Vermont) with information about resources, the variation in students per teacher, in average teacher salary, and in students per computer did not decrease. Even in states like Kentucky and Texas where the legislature did more than equalize funding, then, outcomes have not become more equal.

Furthermore, while there tends to be a drop in spending inequality right after legislation associated with litigation, greater equality then tends to be eroded by subsequent developments. Some states have had one lawsuit after another, as initial solutions prove inadequate (Huang, Lukemeyer, & Yinger, 2004). I conclude that the enormous energy put into school finance litigation over the past 30 years appears unsuccessful in equalizing resources or outcomes, though they have given some districts more money. But without clear conceptions of how to translate revenues into resources and results, all the equalization in the world cannot help low-performing students.

Inequality Among Schools Within Districts

At the beginning of the "modern" era of school finance litigation, a single case—*Hobsen* v. *Hansen* (1967, 1971)—successfully challenged funding *within* a district, charging that spending per pupil in older schools located in the poor and largely Black areas of Washington, DC, was lower than in newer schools in the wealthier, White northwest. However, intradistrict legislation did not catch on, perhaps because documenting spending or resource differences among schools is more difficult than documenting interdistrict differences. Despite inattention to inequalities among schools, they clearly exist. New buildings are usually found in fringe areas of a district, with the oldest and most dilapidated schools in the urban core. When teachers with seniority rights move to schools with vacancies, the most experienced (and most expensive) teachers tend to migrate to the schools that are more White and middle class, or to suburban schools (Ingersoll, 2004).

Within the past 10 years there's been greater attention to new mechanisms of allocating funds among schools, partly in order to eliminate any inequities that might exist. Starting with experiments in Edmonton, Canada, a few districts have moved to site-based funding (Odden, 1999; Cole & Grubb, 2006). Several use a weighted student formula, with more funds per student for low-income, ELL, and special education students, to direct resources to high-needs students. The approaches vary widely in what districts continue to control and in the weights for different levels of school and different groups of students. Usually site-based funding is accompanied by requirements for planning in advance of budgeting, where districts first set district-wide goals and then individual schools formulate more detailed mechanisms for achieving these goals, so that resources are tied to instructional plans—a nice illustration of the "improved" school finance. In these districts inequalities among schools have decreased (Roza & Miles, 2002). It's much less clear whether planning procedures have enhanced school-level resource allocation; an evaluation of New York's Performance-Driven Budgeting Initiative found some improved planning, but also the need for much more capacity building (Siegel & Fruchter, 2002). Site-based funding also supports the school-level reform communities that many reformers have championed (see, e.g., Ouchi, 2003; Carnoy, Elmore, & Siskin, 2003).

A different mechanism to mitigate inequalities among schools includes state programs to improve low-performing schools. Sometimes these have been prompted by finance reforms; for example, Kentucky's response to litigation included the STAR program of technical assistance to low-performing schools. In other cases such efforts have come from accountability legislation; California enacted the Immediate Intervention/Underperforming School Program (II/USP), which allocated up to $360 per student in low-performing schools and required a planning process. LaGuarda's review (2003) of nine such programs revealed a reliance on technical assistance from consultants, school assistant teams, or regional state agencies (like counties), with a few special grants. By and large there were no substantial increases in resources aside from technical assistance, and the amounts of money involved were trifling; the programs certainly did not address the substantial differences among schools in basic resources including well-qualified teachers. Similarly, evaluations of II/USP (O'Day & Bitter, 2003; Goe, 2003) clarified why substantial funds failed to have any overall effect: implementation problems included the competence of consultants, the resistance of schools to outside expertise, district restrictions on how schools spent their money, ill-advised reforms like reducing class size without modifying teaching strategies, using additional resources for "more of the same," and districts undermining the legislative intent of increasing expenditures. Overall, these state interventions need to be more carefully designed and implemented if they are to have the intended effects.

Many less systematic efforts focus on the improvement of individual schools, spearheaded by individual reform movements—small schools and accelerated schools, theme-based magnet schools and high schools using broad occupational clusters, specific curricula like Success for All and High Point, and efforts to incorporate external support like Comer schools and full-service schools. In a few cases these have been encouraged by legislation; for example, the Obey-Porter Comprehensive School Reform Demonstration Act of 1997 provided federal funds for so-called "proven practices," and some states have required particular curricular approaches in their underperforming schools. In practice implementation problems are serious, the "evidence" on outcomes is uneven and controversial, and different models are applied to random smatterings of schools across many states. These models may eventually provide suggestions of the elements necessary in successful schools, but the plethora of reform efforts does not represent a coherent effort that might eliminate inequalities among schools in either resources or outcomes.

Finally, the *Williams* case in California is a new kind of court case focused on *schools* and *resources*, not *districts* and *funding* as former lawsuits have. It sought to eliminate substandard levels of qualified teachers, textbooks, and physical facilities, an adequacy standard applied to these three resources (Figure 8.1, cell #8). The decision in the case currently provides inadequate sums of additional state revenue (cell #7) to fund these requirements, plus a procedure following Grubb and Goe (2002) that enables administrators, teachers, and parents in schools with inadequate resources to complain first to the district, and then to the county superintendent. (The initial results of this procedure are summarized in Allen, 2005.) The real hope of the *Williams* case is that it focuses directly on schools and on resources, rather than assuming that districts can correct inequalities among their schools and that funds will automatically be translated into the most useful resources.

Inequalities Within Schools

Inequalities in resources within schools also exist, certainly as a result of teacher allocation and of categorical programs for special education and ELL students, who have more resources (like more teachers per student) because of their greater needs (Miles & Darling-Hammond, 1998). However, whether these students have more *effective* resources is a different question, since special education, vocational education, and other practices like continuation schools may spend more per student but relegate them to ineffective practices and burned-out teachers. The case of intra-school inequalities is a good example where information about expenditure patterns is both technically difficult and not particularly useful, compared to information about effective resources.

Planning mechanisms, including those that districts require in site-based budgeting, might equalize effective resources within schools. If schools are accountable for the performance of low-achieving students, they face incentives to allocate resources within the school to the students who need them most. Similarly, schools that have developed mechanisms of "internal accountability" (Carnoy, Elmore, & Siskin, 2003)—accountability of teachers and administrators to one another, with widespread participation in decision making—are also better able to make decisions that are equitable as well as effective. But developing such schools requires leadership, teacher acceptance, stability, and a consensus on this alternative to top-down governance.

The allocation of resources within schools may also depend on the incentives embedded in state and federal accountability. Some accountability mechanisms contain incentives to "cream" by allocating the best teachers to high-performing students; conversely, California's Academic Performance Index gives more points for test-score gains at the lowest levels, providing incentives to focus resources on the lowest-performing students. States requiring pass rates (on high school exit exams, for example, or exams required before passing to subsequent grades) create incentives for triage solutions, focusing resources on students at the margin of passing. And all high-stakes tests create incentives to teach to the test and to narrow the range of subjects, a rational short-term strategy that fails to serve students' (and society's) long-run interests. The combination of intense accountability pressures and a lack of serious capacity building is lethal, often leading to narrow teaching, triage, and sometimes cheating (Anagnostopoulos, 2003; Woody et al., 2004; Kannapel, 1996; Diamond & Spillane, 2004; Benton & Hacker, 2004). An issue for future research is whether the internal allocation of resources is being made more or less equitable by the current mania for accountability.

Overall, only a few sources of inequality—particularly inequalities in spending among districts within states—have been the focus of systematic reform, and their effects on the distribution of resources or outcomes appear to be nonexistent. Other efforts, including reform "movements" and state interventions for low-performing schools, have been more limited and quixotic. And so the vast landscape of equity in Figure 8.1 has barely begun to be addressed.

SHIFTING FROM REVENUES TO RESOURCES TO RESULTS: APPLYING THE "IMPROVED" SCHOOL FINANCE

A third problem in efforts to enhance equity is that the dominant approaches and the "old" school finance have concentrated largely on revenues and expenditures—even where there is an intent to shift from funding to resources (see, e.g., Ladd & Hansen, 1999). However, there are many sources of dissatisfaction with confining the analysis of inequality to revenues. One comes from school finance researchers themselves, who have often noted that examining funding without understanding effects on resources is incomplete (see, e.g., Odden & Busch, 1998). Another comes from the moral texts and jeremiads that have galvanized public interest in school inequities, from Cubberly's 1905 diatribe to Kozol's attack (1992) on "savage inequalities" to various court cases with their litanies of miserable conditions.

In addition, anecdotal information about waste in schools—particularly in urban schools, which often suffer the paradox of limitless needs coinciding with enormous waste—indicates that it can take many forms: (1) Funds can be embezzled, or spent to hire incompetent friends and relatives. (2) Funds can be spent on ineffective inputs like incompetent teachers or salary increases without greater teacher effort or reduced turnover, or on resources like textbooks or computers unused by teachers who don't want them. (3) Resources may fail to change practices—

when staff development fails to change teaching, or when reforms fail to change practice—or may be spent on well-intentioned but ineffective practices like simple-minded forms of "technology" or the reform du jour. (4) Funds can be spent on purely symbolic practices like a new retention program or a new superintendent to assure parents that everything possible is being done. (5) Resources may be spent on long-run changes—improving school climate, or developing committed teacher-leaders—but are then wasted if other changes intervene like a new principal or superintendent, a different reform du jour. (6) Spending resources piecemeal usually fails to create any coherent change—for example, when schools spend money without an overall plan, when they spend year-end money quickly, or when categorical grants are used for peripheral changes without improving a school's core teaching. (7) Resources may be spent on changes that are necessary but not sufficient (NBNS)—computers without teacher training and maintenance, reducing chaos without improving teaching, or reducing class sizes without sufficient trained teachers.

Much of the policy research in this area has been unhelpful. The effective schools literature concluded that effective schools are those with strong administrative leadership, high expectations for student achievement, an orderly atmosphere conducive to learning, an emphasis on the acquisition of basic academic skills, and frequent monitoring of student progress (Edmonds, 1979; Purkey and & Smith, 1983); but in addition to controversy over its methods and conclusions, it failed to address the relationship between funding and these resources. The literature on production functions, relating school inputs to test scores, has generated quite uncertain results. Hanushek's infamous review (1989) concluded that expenditure per student was positively and significantly related to test scores in only 13 of 65 studies; only teacher experience was significant in more studies. But the technical rejoinders (like Hedges, Laine, & Greenwald, 1994) and the efforts to cite newer studies (summarized in Verstegen, 1998) with more positive results like Project STAR in Tennessee have not been satisfactory; they have continued to examine only a small number of resources, confined their analysis to test scores, and have failed to identify any strong effects that might counter the powerful influences of family background. The upshot has been the relatively weak statement that resources might matter under some conditions (Hanushek, 1997), but those conditions are not yet clear.

So there are many reasons indicating the need for an "improved" school finance, linking funding to resources at the school and classroom level, and disentangling effective from ineffective or wasted or "inert" resources. In our efforts to develop an alternative (Grubb, Huerta, & Goe, 2006), we have followed several precepts. It is first necessary to enter the classroom and the school—metaphorically, through classroom observation and measurement—to see how resources are used. Otherwise it is impossible to distinguish a skilled experienced teacher from someone who is burned out, to see what class size reduction (or staff development, or a new curriculum) has changed (if anything), or to see whether resources not typically measured—strong leadership, stability, or consistency of pedagogical approaches—are present. A second is to recognize the two-stage nature of effective spending: funding must result in changes in resources, *and* those resources must affect educational outcomes rather than being ineffective. This implies that funding affects outcomes indirectly, only by supporting effective resources. A third is to recognize that many resources are NBNS: class size reduction without an adequate supply of able teachers, computers without professional development, perhaps changes in teacher practices without changes in student conceptions of learning.

These precepts in turn lead to thinking of resources in much broader ways. Most of the time, production functions have included only what we call *simple* resources, which are components of expenditure per pupil and include the pupil:teacher ratio, average teacher salary (a function of credentials and experience), other expenditures like administrative costs, materials costs, capital outlays, and so on. However, if certain resources are NBNS, then it becomes necessary to identify *compound* resources: class size reduction with an adequate supply of able teachers, computers with professional development, and changes in teacher practices with efforts to change student conceptions of learning. Other resources might be termed *complex*, since they are not easily bought; pedagogical approaches are the most obvious of these. *Abstract* resources are often important, including stability, coherence of the curriculum (Newmann et al., 2001), trust (Bryk & Schneider, 2002), pedagogical consistency (Lampert, 2001, ch. 3), internal alignment (Debray, Parson, & Avila, 2003), distributed leadership (Spillane, Halverson, & Diamond, 2001), and alignment of views about reform. Often, abstract resources are embedded in relationships among many individuals in a school.

Once we amplify the conception of resources, several others must be considered. Schools provide noninstructional resources that may influence learning and progress, like extracurricular activities that keep students in school (Marsh & Kleitman, 2002) and student support services like guidance and counseling, or health and mental health services (National Research Council, 2003, ch. 6). Parents are obviously resources to their children's learning, and family background has been a powerful influence on virtually all schooling outcomes; but then we need to disentangle what parents as resources provide—and so the differences among such dimensions as parental education, income, occupation, and time demands become crucial (Grubb, forthcoming).

Finally, students are themselves resources to the schooling process (also emphasized by Cohen, Raudenbush, & Ball, 2003). They come to school with different personal and intellectual resources, reflecting differences in their prior preparation (whether at home or in school), in the expectations and financial resources provided by their parents, in their motivation and engagement, and in their approaches to discipline, schoolwork, and learning. Family background surely influences student ability to benefit from instruction, but it may also be enhanced by family literacy and family intervention efforts, early childhood programs, the quality of prior schooling, efforts to institute instructional practices (like constructivist and conceptual teaching) and organizational forms (like small schools) that might enhance motivation and engagement, the effects of peer groups and school composition, and various noninstructional services (National Research Council, 2003). And instructional resources may respond to a student's ability to benefit. For example, teachers may react positively to motivated students and negatively to those who are disruptive; student-centered teachers adjust their instruction to students with varying backgrounds and interests; and schools provide different resources through tracking or teacher assignments to students with lower levels of preparation—sometimes more and sometimes less.

From these ideas, we derive a model of schooling outcomes that looks like Figure 8.2, where the school and its internal processes are opened up rather than remaining a black box as in simple production functions. Only a few studies have used a variant of such a model (Raudenbush, Fotui & Cheong, 1998; Goldhaber & Brewer, 1997; Elliott, 1998), partly because the data necessary are often unavailable. However, the NELS:88 data, which followed eighth graders in 1988 to 10th grade, 12th grade, and then two years and eight years after graduation, are particularly appropriate for estimating such a model. They provide a great deal of information about family background, instructional and noninstructional conditions, and student ability to benefit from instruction, from sources including teachers, administrators, students, and parents. They can also be combined with other data on expenditures and revenue sources to provide the crucial link to funding. The data contain the usual test scores, but also many other outcome measures including progress through the grades, accumulation of credits in various subjects, student aspirations and values, and progress into two- and four-year colleges. These data can then be used to estimate all the relationships in Figure 8.1 (Grubb, 2006b).

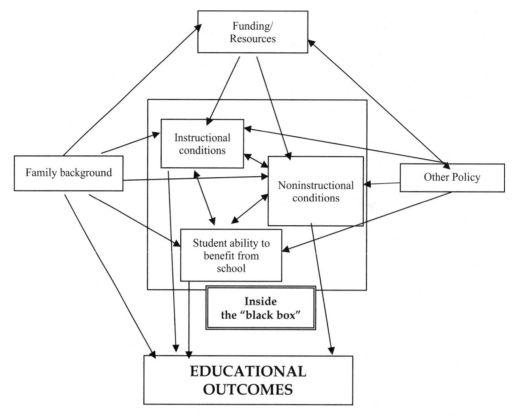

Figure 8.2.   An "Improved" School Finance Model of Student Achievement

To illustrate inequalities in spending and resources, I present findings about spending and resources that affect outcomes. As a working hypothesis, it seems likely that resources are more unequally distributed than are expenditures per pupil, if there are differences among schools or districts in how they allocate funds to resources. Compound resources should be more unequally distributed than simple resources almost by definition, since the variance of a weighted sum is generally greater than the variance of either component. Complex and abstract resources may be especially unequal, since they require a confluence of conditions that may be quite rare. Table 8.1 presents information on the inequality in various resources described by the coefficient of variation (the standard deviation divided by the mean) among *students*. The table also includes simple correlation coefficients between these resources and two measures of family background—maternal education and real family income per dependent—as well as real expenditures per pupil, to indicate the simple relationship of various resources to spending. What count in the "improved" school finance are *effective* resources, and so I have identified variables that are statistically significant in affecting some outcomes with positive or negative signs.[7]

_____

7. For technical details see Grubb (2006b). The variables for expenditures per student are corrected for cross-district variation in the costs of living; observations are weighted by PANELWT2 to compensate for nonrandom attrition, and the underlying regressions are estimated with Taylor series expansion to compensate for nonrandom sampling.

TABLE 8.1
Variation in Resources

	Coefficient of variation	Correlation with MED	Correlation with income	Correlation with exp/pupil
Funding				
Expenditure per pupil[c]	.282			
Instructional salaries[c]	.259	.090	.064	.881
Parental contributions[c]	2.903	.054	.029	.222
Instructional conditions:				
Simple resources				
(+) Years taught sec.	.386	.055	.025	.155
(−) Pupil–teacher ratio	.385	−.045	−.032	−.202
(+) Teacher salary base[c]	.146	.001	.028	.518
Certified teacher	.293	−.007	.010	.010
Complex resources				
Teacher in–field	.214	.039	−.005	.021
(+) Teacher prep. time	.298	.075	.026	.081
(+) Staff development	.378	.023	−.004	−.019
(−) Math teaching: rigid	.158	−.034	−.012	−.054
(+) Math teaching: creative	.134	.039	.003	.001
(−) Teaching conservative	.173	−.066	−.031	−.097
(+) Teaching progressive	.366	.183	.237	.000
(−) General track	1.239	−.110	−.032	−.030
(−) Vocational track	2.570	−.193	−.081	−.024
(−) Remedial education	1.609	−.100	−.072	−.039
Abstract resources				
(+) School climate (S)	.202	.082	.010	.004
School climate (A)	.449	−.103	−.053	−.025
(−) Negative school events	1.460	−.022	.002	.024
(+) School attendance rate	.051	.043	.044	−.040
School coherence (A)	.262	.051	.009	−.053
School changes (A)	.550	−.021	−.010	.027
Noninstructional conditions				
(+) Student use of couns.	.972	−.035	−.080	.007
(−) School help/referral	.898	.052	−.001	.086
(+) Extracurricular act.	1.267	.151	.064	.045
Student ability to benefit				
(−) Changed Schools	2.066	.001	−.020	−.043
(−) Has a child/expecting	4.636	−.117	−.051	−.033
(+) Outside activities	1.503	.208	.049	.050
(+) Hours outside reading	.878	.042	.015	.041
(−) Work hours/week	.919	−.097	−.033	−.025
(−) Television hours/week	.678	−.160	−.076	−.050
(+) Homework/week	.741	.093	.022	−.037
(−) Days absent	.715	−.103	−.055	.055
(−) Behavior problems	3.085	−.037	−.019	.013
(+) Friends pro–college	.341	.245	.102	.093
(−) Friends pro–dropout	3.117	−.113	−.047	−.023
(−) Involved with gangs	2.278	−.080	−.037	.028

(continued)

TABLE 8.1 *(continued)*

	Coefficient of variation	Correlation with MED	Correlation with income	Correlation with exp/pupil
Family Background				
(+) Income per dep.^{c}	.720			
(+) College savings	1.509	.322	.316	.092
(+) High parent ed.	1.515	.820	.224	.116
(−) Female–headed fam.	2.011	−.123	−.186	−.025
(−) Family instability	1.032	−.103	−.090	−.019
(−) Native language not English	3.418	−.154	−.099	.043
(−) Low parent expectations	1.775	−.268	−.098	−.050

Notes: MED = mother's education
c = corrected for cross–section price differences
S = student–reported
A = administrator–reported
(+) = positive effect on some outcomes, p ≤ .05
(−) = negative effect on some outcomes, p ≤ .05

Source: NELS88, second follow–up, calculations by author. National Center for Education Statistics. (1990). National Education Longitudinal Study of 1988, Second Follow–Up. http://nces.ed.gov/surveys/nels88/.

In these results, the coefficient of variation for real expenditure per student is .282, among the lowest levels of inequality in the table. Instructional salaries per pupil are also distributed relatively equally, though parental contributions per student—which seem to be increasing as a way of supplementing meager public resources—are highly unequal, since they are linked to unequal family incomes. Among simple resources, teacher experience and the pupil:teacher ratio are more unequally distributed than are expenditures, and as expected favor students of higher socioeconomic status (SES), in schools with higher spending.

Complex resources are more unequally distributed than expenditures per pupil; staff development, progressive teaching, and track placement are especially unequal. But these are not highly correlated with expenditure per pupil; funding is clearly NBNS since these resources need several different inputs. Similarly, the abstract resources that can be measured are generally unrelated to spending. A few—the likelihood of negative events (like fights, threats, drugs, and theft), school changes, and school climate perceived by administrators—are quite unequal.

Noninstructional conditions and measures of student ability to benefit are highly unequal, and generally have the expected correlations with SES. And inequality in measures of family background is also substantial, not surprisingly. Measures like maternal education and parental expectations have consistent and powerful effects on a variety of outcomes, and are much more unequally distributed than are funding or simple school resources. These results clarify why, in simple models of school outcomes, family background has such a powerful effect: the variations in family background, and in school resources associated with it like noninstructional conditions and student ability to benefit, are much larger than variation in instructional conditions; and the effects of family background, ability to benefit, and noninstructional conditions on various outcomes are also larger.

These preliminary results indicate that distinguishing among types of resources may explain, better than the "old" school finance can, why inequalities in outcomes are so large. The resources that count, in the sense that they affect outcomes of schooling, are more numerous and varied than expenditures or simple resources. In addition, many complex and abstract resources that affect outcomes (like progressive teaching, creative math and science teaching, staff development, and school climate) lack any significant relationship with expenditure (Grubb, forthcoming b). Money may be necessary, for example for staff development and release time, but it certainly isn't sufficient. Rather than being bought directly, as smaller classes can be, these resources must be *constructed* at the school and classroom levels, by principals and other leaders (see, e.g., Lemons, Luschei, & Siskin, 2003) and by teachers participating more actively in pedagogical developments (Little, 2005). In addition, the resources that show really large variation among students—noninstructional conditions and student ability to benefit—depend partly on parental and community influences, as well as on the long history of students' positive and negative contacts with schools. And some of these resources—like the negative effects of student mobility as they change schools (Rumberger & Larsen, 1998), and any component of attendance that is due to poor health—require social policies like subsidized housing, health care, and income support, all far beyond the reach of educational funding.

So the focus of champions for equity on expenditure differences among districts within states, valuable as that has been symbolically, does not even begin to address the kinds of inequality that matter to the outcomes of schooling. The vast landscape of inequality depicted in Figure 8.1 is barely touched by these efforts, particularly when we recognize the differences between funding and the many types of resources that affect outcomes. The implication is that the energy directed to funding reforms needs to be extended to a greater variety of resources before outcomes for students will be much different.

THE FUTURE OF EQUITY

There are, then, many reasons why equity in schooling has been so elusive, even in a country where equality of educational opportunity is widely accepted. These include political reasons, of course, especially in a period of concerted attacks on the welfare state, but they also include the variety of our historical conceptions of equity, the complexity of addressing equity consistently in a multilevel and complex system, and the sheer difficulty of understanding the ways that spending and school resources contribute to outcomes.

This leaves us with the question of how equity might be enhanced, and how policy research might contribute. In this effort, we're stuck with the country we have, the values we have, and the conceptions of equity that have emerged from our history. No amount of keening among egalitarians and reformers will generate the relatively egalitarian views that we see in Scandinavian countries, or in sects like the Quakers, the Shakers, the Amish, and educators. Equality of outcomes will remain a particularly elusive goal, since almost no one supports it. The various conceptions of equality of opportunity are probably the best we can hope for, since most Americans seem to believe that differences in effort, in native abilities, and in moral character—Webster's "labor and economy . . . talent and virtue"—are intrinsic to individuals rather than socially formed, and ought to be rewarded in the classroom as well as the labor market—or, in a vocationalized education system, in the classroom on the way to the labor market.

But there's enormous room for greater equity, even within the limits of equality of educational opportunity. In particular, the Jacksonian version of opportunity, eliminating "artificial distinction . . . to make the rich richer and the potent more powerful" and promoting "equal protection . . . shower[ing] its favors alike on the high and the low, the rich and the poor," is relatively widely accepted and embedded in various equal protection clauses at both state and federal levels. If it were possible to use this conception of equity, and then to shift from a concern with funding to a systematic focus on a broad variety of effective or active resources (and not just funding or simple resources), then it would be possible to eliminate some of the inequalities among students in outcomes as well as funding and resources.

This tactic in turn requires a shift from the "old" school finance to the "improved" school finance, with its concern for the ways that funds are used within schools and classrooms. It requires a continued search—through both quantitative methods and a variety of qualitative approaches as well—for ways of distinguishing effective or active resources from ineffective and inert resources. It suggests a change from lawsuits like the equality cases following *Serrano* and the more recent adequacy cases, all of which are expressed in funding, to efforts more like the *Williams* case, with its effort to express remedies in terms of resources rather than funding. The "improved" school finance also clarifies the potential value of weighted student formulas that a few districts have adopted, not just as a way of getting more funding to high-need schools but also as a vehicle for instructional planning at both the district and school levels, to help assure that resources are effectively spent. Finally, the "improved" school finance is at least a candidate to replace older and simpler narratives about spending. To existing preoccupations with spending levels and equity, it adds an emphasis on effectiveness consistent with the current interests in accountability and "what works"; it responds to the historical concern for efficiency (see, e.g., Callahan, 1967), since it explicitly links resources with results; and by focusing on instructional conditions within schools and classrooms, it is consistent with recent reforms emphasizing the pedagogies and cultures appropriate to enhanced learning.

Along the way, there are various ways that a clearer understanding of resources and equity can help clarify the equity agenda. One is to identify when conceptions within the vast "landscape of equity" conflict with one another. Probably the most pressing is to understand why NCLB, which appears to support proficient outcomes (Figure 8.1, cell #9), has no hope of doing so, because it fails to support sufficient compensatory funding or resources (cells #10 and #11). In addition, the way it has been implemented in every state constrains how both outcomes and resources have been defined, driving many schools toward rigid, behaviorist, and ineffective approaches to teaching—precisely the approaches that *depress* test scores (as results in Table 8.1 and Grubb, 2006 clarify). Other problems in current equity battles include the difficulty of providing more funding or resources to low-achieving students (cells #10 and #11)—the basis of all compensatory education—which inevitably conflict with the notions of equal treatment of all students (cells #4 and #5) and often lead to the politics of resentment. And of course Webster's "no barriers" conception (cells #1 or #2) is sufficient for many in our country, though it inevitably leads to perceptions that inequality in educational outcomes (cell #6) is the result of some students failing to take advantage of the opportunities available to them.

In the end, the purpose of "egalitarian rhetoric in an unequal society" is to remind us of our country's deepest values. Our political system can't always make good on these values, especially not at the present when the country is so bitterly divided and antidemocrats rule the land. But the principles embedded in constitutions and historical documents, and the hopes for all children revealed in the history of schooling, can always be resurrected as long as we continue to uphold the "landscape of equity" as a worthy goal.

REFERENCES

Allen, B. (2005). *The* Williams *v.* California *Settlement: The first year of implementation.* Los Angeles: ACLU Foundation of Southern California.

Anagnostopoulos, D. (2003). The new accountability, student failure, and teachers' work in urban high schools. *Educational Policy 17*(3), 291–316.

Baumgartner, F., & Jones, B. (1993). *Agendas and instability in American politics.* Chicago: University of Chicago Press.

Benton, J., & Hacker, H. (2004). Poor schools' TAKS surge raises cheating questions. *Dallas Morning News,* December 19.

Bryk, A., & Schneider, B. (2002). *Trust in schools: A core resource for improvement.* New York: Russell Sage Foundation.

Callahan, R. (1967). *Education and the cult of efficiency.* Chicago: University of Chicago Press.

Carnoy, M., Elmore, R., & Siskin, L. S., eds. (2003). *The new accountability: High schools and high-stakes testing.* New York: RoutledgeFalmer.

Cohen, D., Raudenbush, S., & Ball, D. (2003). Resources, instruction, and research. *Educational Evaluation and Policy Analysis 25*(2), 119–142.

Cole, A., & Grubb, W. N. (2006). *Equity and school control: The potential of recent district budgetary reforms.* Unpublished paper.

Coons, J., Clune, W., & Sugarman, S. (1970). *Private wealth and public education.* Cambridge, MA: Harvard University Press.

Cubberly, E. (1905). *School funds and their apportionment.* New York: Columbia University, Teachers College.

Debray, E., Parson, G., & Avila, S. (2003). Internal alignment and external pressure. In M. Carnoy, R. Elmore, & L. S. Siskin (Eds.), *The new accountability: High schools and high-stakes testing* (pp. 55–86). New York: RoutledgeFalmer.

Deschenes, S., Cuban, L., & Tyack, D. (2001). Mismatch: Historical perspectives on schools and students who don't fit them. *Teachers College Record 103*(4), 525–547.

Diamond, J. B., & Spillane, J. P. (2004). High-stakes accountability in urban elementary schools: Challenging or reproducing inequality? *Teachers College Record 106*(6), 1145–1176.

Duncombe, W., & Yinger, J. (1999). Performance standards and educational cost indexes: You can't have one without the other. In H. F. Ladd, R. Chalk, & J. S. Hansen (Eds.), *Equity and adequacy in education finance: Issues and perspectives* (pp. 260–297). Washington, DC: National Academy Press.

Edmonds, R. (1979). Effective schools for the urban poor. *Educational Leadership 37,* 15–24, 37.

Elliott, M. (1998). School finance and opportunity to learn: Does money well spent enhance students' achievement? *Sociology of Education 71*(3), 223–245.

Elson, W., & Frank, B. (1910). Different courses for elementary schools. *Educational Review 39,* 359–362.

Esping-Anderson, G. (1990). *The three worlds of welfare capitalism.* Princeton, NJ: Princeton University Press.

Goe, L. (2003). *An evaluation of California's Immediate Intervention/Underperforming Schools program (II/USP) in middle schools.* Ph.D. dissertation, University of California, Berkeley, School of Education.

Goldhaber, D., & Brewer, D. (1997). Why don't schools and teachers seem to matter? Assessing the impact of unobservables on educational productivity. *Journal of Human Resources 32*(3), 505–523.

Grubb, W. N. (2006a). When money might matter: Using NELS88 to examine the weak effects of school financing. *Journal of Education Finance 31*(4), 360–378.

Grubb, W. N. (2006b). *Multiple outcomes, multiple resources: Testing the "improved" school finance with NELS88.* Unpublished paper, submitted for publication.

Grubb, W. N. (Forthcoming). Families and schools raising children: The inequitable effects of family background on schooling outcomes. In J. D. Berrick & N. Gilbert (Eds.), *Raising children: Emerging needs, modern risks, and social responses,* Mahwah, NJ: Erlbaum.

Grubb, W. N., & Goe, L. (2002). The unending search for equity: California policy, the "new" school finance, and the *Williams* case. *Teachers College Record 106*(11), 2081–2101. Earlier version prepared for University of California, Los Angeles, Institute for Democracy, Education, and Access (IDEA). www.mofo.com/decentschools/expert_reports/grubb-goe_report.pdf.

Grubb, W. N., Huerta, L., & Goe, L. (2006). Straw into gold, resources into results: Spinning out the implications of the "renewed" school finance. *Journal of Education Finance 31*(4): 334–359.

Grubb, W. N., & Lazerson, M. (2004). *The Education gospel: The economic roles of schooling.* Cambridge, MA: Harvard University Press.

Gutmann, A. (1987). *Democratic education.* Princeton, NJ: Princeton University Press.

Hanushek, E. (1989). The impact of differential expenditures on school performance. *Educational Researcher 18*(4), 45–62.

Hanushek, E. (1997). Assessing the effects of school resources on student performance: An update. *Educational Evaluation and Policy Analysis 19*(2), 141–164.

Hedges, L.., Laine, R., & Greenwald, R. (1994). Does money matter? A meta-analysis of studies of the effects of differential school inputs on student outcomes. *Educational Researcher 23*(3), 5–14.

Huang, Y., Lukemeyer, A., & Yinger, J. (2004). A guide to state court decisions on education finance. In J. Yinger (Ed.), *Helping children left behind: State aid and the pursuit of educational equity* (pp. 317–330). Cambridge, MA: MIT Press.

Ingersoll, R. (2004). *Why do high-poverty schools have difficulty staffing their classrooms with qualified teachers?* Washington, DC: Center for American Progress and Institute for American's Future.

Jencks, C., & Phillips, M. (1998). The Black–White test score gap: An introduction. In C. Jencks & M. Phillips (Eds.), *The Black-White test score gap* (pp. 1–51). Washington, DC: Brookings Institution.

Kaestle, C. (1983). *Pillars of the republic: Common schools and American society, 1780–1860.* New York: Hill and Wang.

Kannapel, P., Coe, P., Aagaard, L., & Moore, B. (1996). *"I don't give a hoot if somebody's going to pay me $3600": Local school district reactions to Kentucky's high-stakes accountability program.* Paper presented at the annual meeting of the American Educational Research Association, New York.

Katz, M. B. (1968). *The irony of early school reform: Educational innovation in mid-nineteenth century Massachusetts.* Cambridge, MA: Harvard University Press.

Kirsch, I., de Jong, J., Lafontaine, D., McQueen, J., Mendelovits, J., & Monseur, C. (2002). *Reading for change: Performance and engagement across countries.* Paris: Organisation for Economic Co-operation and Development.

Kozol, J. (1992). *Savage inequalities: Children in America's schools.* New York: Harper.

Ladd, H., & Hansen, J., eds. (1999). *Making money matter: Financing America's schools.* Washington, DC: National Academy Press.

LaGuarda, K. (2003). *State-sponsored financial assistance to low-performing schools: Strategies from nine states.* Washington, DC: Policy Studies Associates.

Lampert, M. (2001). *Teaching problems and the problems of teaching.* New Haven, CT: Yale University Press.

Lemons, R., Luschei, T., & Siskin, L. S. (2003). Leadership and the demands for standards-based accountability. In M. Carnoy, R. Elmore, & L. S. Siskin (Eds.), *The new accountability: High schools and high-stakes testing* (pp. 99–128). New York: RoutledgeFalmer.

Little, J. W. (2005). *Professional development and professional community in the learning-centered school.* Paper presented at the annual meeting of the National Education Association, Los Angeles.

Lowi, T. (1969). *The end of liberalism: Ideology, policy, and the crisis of public authority.* New York: Norton.

Marsh, H., & Kleitman, S. (2002). Extracurricular school activities: The good, the bad, and the nonlinear. *Harvard Educational Review 72*(4), 464–511.

Miles, K. H., & Darling-Hammond, L. (1998). Rethinking the allocation of teaching resources: Some lessons from high-performing schools. *Educational Evaluation and Policy Analysis 20*(1), 9–29.

Minorini, P., & Sugarman, S. (1999). Educational adequacy and the courts: The promise and problems of moving to a new paradigm. In H. F. Ladd, R. Chalk, & J. S. Hansen (Eds.), *Equity and adequacy in education finance: Issues and perspectives* (pp. 175–208). Washington, DC: National Academy Press.

National Research Council, Committee on Increasing High School Students' Engagement and Motivation to Learn. (2003). *Engaging schools.* Washington, DC: National Academy Press.

Newmann, F. M., Smith, B., Allensworth, E., & Bryk, A. S. (2001). Instructional program coherence: What it is and why it should guide school improvement policy. *Educational Evaluation and Policy Analysis 23*(4), 297–321.

O'Day, J., & Bitter, C. (2003). *Evaluation study of the Immediate Intervention/Underperforming Schools program and the High Achieving/Improving Schools Program of the Public Schools Accountability Act of 1999.* Menlo Park, CA: American Institutes for Research.

Odden, A. (1999). School-based financing in North America. In M. Goertz & A. Odden (Eds.), *School-based financing* (pp. 155–187). Thousand Oaks, CA: Corwin Press.

Odden, A., & Busch, C. (1998). *Financing schools for high performance: Strategies for improving the use of educational resources.* San Francisco: Jossey-Bass.

Organisation for Economic Co-operation and Development (OECD). (2001). *Knowledge and skills for life: First results from PISA 2000.* Paris: Author.

Ouchi, W. (with Segal, L. G.). (2003). *Making schools work: A revolutionary plan to get your children the education they need.* New York: Simon and Schuster.

Pole, J. R. (1978). *The pursuit of equality in American history.* Berkeley, CA: University of California Press.

Purkey, S. C., & Smith, M. S. (1983). Effective schools: A review. *The Elementary School Journal 83*(4), 436–452.

Raudenbush, S. W., Fotiu, R. P., & Cheong, Y. F. (1998). Inequality of access to educational resources: A national report for eighth-grade math. *Educational Evaluation and Policy Analysis 20*(4), 253–267.

Roe, E. (1994). *Narrative policy analysis: Theory and practice.* Durham, NC: Duke University Press.

Rose, L., & Gallup, A. (2005). The 37th annual Phi Delta Kappa/Gallup poll of the public attitudes toward the public schools. *Phi Delta Kappan 87*(1), 41–57.

Roza, M., & Miles, K. (2002). *Moving toward equity in school funding within districts.* Providence, RI: Brown University. Annenberg Institute for School Reform, Annenberg Task Force on School Communities That Work.

Rumberger, R., & Larsen, K. A. (1998). Student mobility and the increased risk of high school dropout. *American Journal of Education 107*(1), 1–35.

Siegel, D., & Fruchter, N. (2002). *Evaluation of the performance-driven budgeting initiative of the New York City Board of Education.* New York: New York University, Institute for Education and Social Policy.

Spillane, J., Halverson, R., & Diamond, J. (2001). Investigating school leadership practice: A distributed perspective. *Educational Researcher 30*(3), 23–28.

Thompson, D. C., & Crampton, F. E. (2002), Winter. The impact of school finance litigation: A long view. *Journal of Education Finance 27*(3), 783–816.

Truman, D. (1951). *The governmental process: Political interests and public opinion.* New York: Knopf.

U.S. General Accounting Office. (1997). *School finance: State efforts to reduce funding gaps between poor and wealthy districts* (GAO-HEHS-97-31). Washington, DC: Author.

Verstegen, D. (1998). The relationship between school spending and student achievement. *Journal of Education Finance 24*(2), 243–262.

Woody, B., Buttles, M., Kafka, J., Park, S., & Russell, J. (2004). *Voices from the field: Educators respond to accountability.* Berkeley: University of California, Policy Analysis for California Education.

Yinger, J., ed. (2004). *Helping children left behind: State aid and the pursuit of educational equity.* Cambridge, MA: MIT Press.

Policy as Resource Allocation: Commentary

Helen F. Ladd

Policymakers are likely to be interested in at least four different but overlapping sets of questions about educational resources. As elaborated in the following discussion, these include questions about the *effects* of resources, the quantity of resources needed for *adequacy*, how resources can be made more *productive*, and how the distribution of resources affects *equity*. Each of these sets of questions has a large and growing research tradition associated with it. The chapters by Lisa Barrow and Cecilia Elena Rouse and by Norton Grubb do an excellent job of addressing the literature in the first and fourth categories but make only peripheral reference to the literatures related to resource adequacy or to making resources more productive.

WHAT IS THE IMPACT OF RESOURCES ON STUDENT ACHIEVEMENT OR OTHER OUTCOME MEASURES? (EFFECTS)

A large body of research, primarily by economists, addresses this question about the effects of resources within the context of a so-called education production function. As noted by Barrow and Rouse, this literature started with the Coleman Report in 1966 which concluded that variation in student achievement was better explained by variation in family background than by variation in school resources.

Though an education system generates many types of outcomes, much of the literature in this tradition treats student achievement as the main outcome of interest, with some studies using as the outcome measure a student's subsequent wages in the labor market. Typically, student achievement in year t would be specified as a function of the student's achievement in the previous year, school resources, and family background. The inclusion of prior-year achievement is designed to take account of the cumulative nature of learning. The model would then be estimated with data at the level of the individual student, which is the preferred approach, or, alternatively, aggregated to the school, district, and sometimes even the state level.

As noted by Barrow and Rouse, economists have typically been interested in the average effects of resources on achievement, where resources might be construed either as spending per pupil or as individual inputs that cost money, such as class size or experienced teachers. Because the typical model controls neither for practices within schools, such as whether teachers lecture or use more interactive teaching methods, nor for the institutional context in which the schools operate, such as whether there is a formal administrative accountability system, the effects of resources in such models may be confounded with the effects of practices and institutional contexts. Any estimated effects are best interpreted as the average effects of particular resources, given the distribution of practices and institutional contexts across the sample. If the institutional context were to change as a result, for example, of the introduction of an accountability system, or if practices within schools were to change, the average effects could well change. Importantly, within this research tradition, it is difficult for researchers to say much about the mechanism through which resources operate. For example, a finding that smaller class sizes on average have positive effects on student achievement does not answer the question of whether smaller class sizes are more effective in increasing achievement regardless of practice or because they facilitate more interactive teaching.

Barrow and Rouse's chapter clearly fits into this "effects" literature but is somewhat broader in that it deals with interventions that are not limited just to the spending of more money. Thus the discussion in principle includes changes in practice as well as in programs that make claims on the budget. In fact, though, most of the authors' examples are interventions that do cost significant amounts of money: reductions in class size, summer school programs, and some forms of computer-assisted learning. These interventions contrast with interventions within the classroom, such as tracking of students by ability, that might or might not involve additional resources.

The chapter specifically focuses on the methodological challenge of estimating relationships that are truly causal. Consistent with the production function literature, Barrow and Rouse pay far less attention to the mechanisms through which resources or interventions might operate than to the estimation of average effects. They make clear, though, that the estimation of average effects is just the first step. If the average effects are positive, then it would be reasonable to explore whether the magnitudes of the effects vary across students or across school contexts.

The first half of their chapter is a very nice discussion of the efforts, mainly by economists, to identify causal linkages between various inputs or other interventions on student outcomes. The authors begin by highlighting the shortcomings of cross-sectional studies for determining causal effects. They then describe various methods for countering those shortcomings, including regression discontinuity designs, natural experiments, instrumental variables, and full-fledged experiments.

The authors correctly highlight the trade-off between internal validity and the generalizability of results and note that this trade-off emerges most explicitly in connection with what many researchers view as the "gold standard" approach for determining causality, namely the use of random assignment design. The problem is that the experimental design puts such limits on the analysis that the results are hard to generalize to real-world policy applications. Another way of characterizing the problem is that the experiment, for example, random assignment of students to classrooms of different sizes, is, in the terminology of economists, a partial equilibrium analysis. It focuses on the change in one policy variable, namely class size, while holding everything else constant, including the quality of teachers. In fact, public policies to change class sizes have general equilibrium effects. Those include not only the direct effects of smaller class sizes on student outcomes assuming no change in teacher quality, but also the indirect effects that emerge through changes in teacher quality and in the distribution of quality teachers across districts and schools.

The second half of the chapter includes a nice summary of what has been learned from high-quality studies about the effects of spending, class size, teacher quality, professional development, summer school, and technology. Though some readers may be discouraged that the results are not more uniformly positive, even negative findings are important for policymakers. In addition, negative findings for certain interventions, for example, computer-assisted learning, highlight the importance of doing field-based research on pilot programs before spending large amounts of scarce resources on programs that are not likely to be effective.

WHAT RESOURCES WOULD BE NEEDED TO ACHIEVE A GIVEN SET OF EDUCATIONAL OUTCOMES? (ADEQUACY)

If we knew from the production function research the effects of various resources on student outcomes, we could then turn the "effects" question around and ask what resources would be needed to achieve some desired level of student outcome. This is the issue addressed in much of the growing empirical literate on educational adequacy (see discussion of adequacy in Ladd & Hansen, 1999, ch. 4).

Recent court rulings in various states have put pressure on state legislatures to make sure that all school districts within the state have sufficient resources for students to receive an adequate education. In making such rulings, the state courts have typically defined adequacy in broad terms. In the 1989 *Rose* v. *Council for Better Education* (790 S.W.2d 186) case in Kentucky, for example, the court specified that an adequate education would provide students with an opportunity to develop capabilities in areas such as communication skills, knowledge of economic and social systems, grounding in the arts, and preparation for advanced training. In responding to such rulings, however, state legislatures have often set for themselves a far more concrete task. That task is usually characterized as determining the specific dollar amount of resources that would meet the standard of adequacy, with attention both to the costs for an average district and for districts with differential costs attributable to factors outside their control. Those differential costs reflect differences across districts in the costs of inputs (caused, for example, by the need to pay high salaries to teachers because of a high local cost of living) or differences in the incidence of costly-to-educate students, such as those from poor families or who have learning disabilities.

In their quest to attach a dollar amount to educational adequacy, some states have relied on the professional judgment of experts. Such experts might begin by specifying appropriate class sizes, which in turn would determine how many teachers would be needed to serve a given number of students. Those teachers would then be added to other required resources, with each of them weighted by the relevant salaries or prices, to determine the per-pupil cost of providing an adequate education. Although the experts might base their judgments in part on the production function research just discussed, the results from that research are far from being sufficiently clear and concrete for the purposes of determining the cost of an adequate education. Hence, the professional judgment approach typically is not based solely on findings from research, and exactly what it is based on is not always clear. Hanushek (2005) argues that politics plays a major role.

An alternative approach for determining the costs of adequacy, advocated primarily by economists, begins with the estimation of an expenditure function. This type of research was developed initially for the purposes of determining the differential costs of educating students with differing needs across districts (Duncombe, Lukemeyer, & Yinger, 2004; Yinger, 2004). Specifically, an equation of the following form is estimated on the basis of district-level data: Expenditures = f (desired outputs, cost factors), where the desired outputs might include measures such as the percentages of students who are proficient on certain tests or who graduate from high school, and cost factors include both the determinants of differentials in input prices across districts, such as the local cost of living, and the characteristics of the district that determine the differential costs of educating specific groups of students, such as those who are poor or who are learning disabled. Once the equation is estimated, it is possible to simulate for each district the per-pupil cost of achieving a specified set of outcomes that can be held constant across all districts for the purposes of the simulation.

One putative advantage of the statistical approach is that is does not require the explicit estimation of an education production function. At the same time, however, the results should, at least in principle, be consistent with the production function literature. Thus if one interprets the production function literature as indicating little effect of resources on student achievement, one would expect the costs of achieving relatively high outcome levels to be very high, or perhaps even infinite. Stated differently, it could be that no amount of resources could compensate for economic disadvantage in the home.

One criticism of the approach is that because it is based on current spending patterns, the analysis cannot shed much light on the amount of resources that would be required if resources were being used productively. The literature includes a variety of ways of addressing the concern that districts may vary in the efficiency with which they use resources. Some researchers ignore the concern, and others try to control for it statistically using the technique of data envelopment analysis, some measure of interdistrict competition, or some other measure that might be correlated with efficiency. None of the studies in this genre are able to deal with the possibility that all districts may be operating in an unproductive manner. To address the productivity issue, one must turn to a third type of research literature.

HOW CAN A GIVEN AMOUNT OF RESOURCES BE USED MORE PRODUCTIVELY TO INCREASE STUDENT ACHIEVEMENT? (PRODUCTIVITY)

This third set of questions relates to the productivity with which resources are used. The issue here is what practices and institutional arrangements might best be used to make the existing resources more productive.

The "effective schools" literature of the early 1970s and 1980s can be interpreted as addressing this issue (see discussion in Ladd & Hansen, 1999, ch. 5). This body of research was initiated in response to the apparent conclusion of the 1966 Coleman Report that public schools do not make much difference, especially for disadvantaged children, and was used to identify characteristics of schools that do matter, such as the quality of school leadership. The effective schools literature differs from the standard education production function literature by its close attention to what goes on within the black box of schools, but it is subject to a number of methodological criticisms, not the least of which is its failure to determine causality. A more recent version of the effective schools literature is the work on "whole school reform" models. The idea behind such models is that it is not just the quantity of resources that matters, but it is how resources are put together within the school, more broadly defined in some models to include the families, that matters for student outcomes. Only now are careful studies being done to determine in a scientific manner how effective such models are.

Another major strand of research related to the issue of how to make educational resources more productive focuses on changes in the governance structure and the introduction of incentive systems designed to make money matter. Though that research is far too large to summarize here, suffice it to say that it includes extensive discussion and analysis of the effects of choice and competition on student achievement, and analysis of specific forms of parental choice, including intra- and interdistrict choice plans, charter schools, and voucher programs. In addition, it includes research on both the intended and unintended effects of external accountability systems designed to provide incentives for schools, teachers, and students to improve.

Such changes in governance might be justified as follows. If we had precise knowledge of the relationship between inputs and educational outcomes, we could presumably achieve educational outcomes by giving schools the resources they would need and directing them how to use them. In fact, however, we do not have precise knowledge of that type. Moreover, it could be that this lack of knowledge may reflect a broader reality, namely the absence of a stable relationship between educational inputs and outputs and/or the existence of a relationship that is so specific to the particular school or classroom that it is not useful for policy. Given this limited knowledge, the preferred strategy could well be for policymakers to focus on educational outcomes and then to promote governance structures designed to provide incentives for school officials and teachers to achieve objectives. Whether or not it is the preferred strategy is an empirical question that requires additional research.

HOW DOES THE DISTRIBUTION OF RESOURCES RELATE TO EQUITY? (EQUITY)

The final set of resource-related questions focuses on educational equity, which is the topic of Norton Grubb's chapter. As he correctly emphasizes, equity cannot simply be measured by how evenly or unevenly educational inputs are distributed among districts and schools. Instead, equity is a far richer concept that ultimately deals with educational outcomes.

Grubb highlights the various concepts of equity in what he calls the landscape of equity. One dimension of his landscape matrix identifies three potential objects of concern: per-pupil funding, specific resources such as class size or qualified teachers, and student outcomes, as measured, for example, by test scores or performance on exit exams. The other dimension of the matrix is conceptions of equity, including "no barriers," equality, adequacy, and a fourth category labeled "policies of correction" that perplexes me. The matrix is useful, first for depicting the complexities of the equity concept, and second for highlighting the limitations of the "old school finance" that focused narrowly on the inequality of funding across districts.

To replace the "old school finance," Grubb introduces what he refers to as "improved school finance." The key feature of this approach is that it shifts the focus to a broader concept of resources and to how they are distributed across not just districts but rather across schools and classrooms. He defines four sets of school resources: simple resources (inputs that cost money); compound resources (resources such as computers that are not useful without teachers who know how to use and maintain them); complex resources (things that do not show up in budgets, such as teacher preparation time); and abstract resources (such as school climate). In addition, he is cognizant of the well-known observation that family background contributes to student achievement in significant ways.

Grubb then uses this broader concept of resources to explain why inequalities in educational outcomes are so much larger than inequalities in educational spending. He does so by using data from NELS:88 to show that many of the "effective" resource variables exhibit higher variation than the simpler spending measure. For his purposes, he defines an effective resource as one that translates into higher educational outcomes on the basis of his previous research. Emerging from the empirical analysis that Grubb presents in his Table 9.1 is that per-pupil spending does not translate in any simple way into student outcomes and, therefore, that policymakers interested in promoting equity—defined with respect to the pattern of student outcomes—need to shift their attention away from spending to the variation across schools and classrooms in resources broadly defined. Thus Grubb argues that to promote educational equity, policymakers need to pay attention to the variation in all of the relevant resources across students—not just to the variation in spending across districts.

For policymakers to make use of this conclusion, however, they would need answers to the basic research questions discussed above. First is the question of effects. Which policy interventions—defined here to include not only those interventions that cost money but also those designed to enrich the more complex or abstract components of the education process—are likely to exert a causal impact on educational outcomes? Second is the adequacy question. What amount of resources—defined broadly to include more than simple monetary resources—would be needed to assure all students an adequate education? And last is the productivity question. What methods can be used to make resources of all types more productive toward the goal of higher educational outcomes for children? Not until we have better answers to these questions will policymakers be in a good position to promote greater educational equity.

CONCLUSION

Researchers should take steps to answer the questions by exploring effects, adequacy, productivity, and equity as suggested in this discussion. Research on effects should move beyond estimating average effects to examining whether the magnitudes of the effects vary across students or school contexts. Additionally, field-based research on pilot programs is needed to avoid committing resources to programs that are unlikely to be effective. Research on adequacy should continue to rely on professional judgment and estimation of the expenditure function, but should also be informed by production function research that indicates the high costs of achieving adequacy. Because productivity research itself is limited by the lack of precise knowledge about the relationship between inputs and educational outcomes, researchers should continue to explore methods that reveal the complexities of that relationship. Moreover, to achieve a better understanding of what is needed to promote educational equity, researchers should consider a broader range of resources than spending alone. In sum, the chapters discussed here suggest that our knowledge about educational resource allocation could be increased through research that considers in a more nuanced manner the many interacting factors that affect educational outcomes.

REFERENCES

Duncombe, W., Lukemeyer, A., & Yinger, J.. (2004). *Education finance reform in New York: Calculating the cost of a "sound basic education" in New York City* (CPR Policy Brief No. 28/2004). Syracuse, NY: Syracuse University, Center for Policy Research.

Hanushek, E. A. (2005). *The alchemy of "costing out" an adequate education.* Paper prepared for a conference, Adequacy Lawsuits: Their Growing Impact on American Education, Harvard University, Kennedy School of Government, Cambridge, MA.

Ladd, H. F., & J. Hansen, (1991). *Making money matter: Financing America's schools.* Washington, DC: National Academy Press.

Yinger, J., ed. (2004). *Helping children left behind: State aid and the pursuit of educational equity.* Cambridge, MA: MIT Press.

IV

ACROSS THE SECTORS

9

Boundaries With Early Childhood Education: The Significance of the Early Childhood Frontier for Elementary and Secondary Education

W. Steven Barnett and Debra J. Ackerman

Forty years ago, few children in this country attended school before the age of five, and only 60 percent of five-year-olds attended kindergarten. Today, 60 percent of children attend a preschool program at age four, and 40 percent attend at age three. Half of these preschoolers are enrolled in publicly funded programs. These percentages translate into roughly 4.2 million (52.4 percent) of three- and four-year-olds in the United States being enrolled in preschool programs in 2002.

Although these enrollment statistics suggest that the term "*preschool* education" is becoming an anachronism, the sector is limited in size by the total population in this age range. By comparison, nearly 55 million children enrolled in K–12 education in 2002. The preschool sector is only one-third larger than kindergarten at present levels of enrollment. Moreover, preschool is even smaller when compared in terms of funding. In 2002, expenditures for K–12 education exceeded $460 billion, with $430 billion of this amount public money, including $55 million in federal spending. Comparable data are not even collected on preschool expenditures, but states spent only about $2.5 billion on preschool programs (excluding preschool special education), and the federal government spent $6.5 billion on Head Start in 2002.

Given the small size and funding level of the preschool sector, to what extent can preschool policies influence K–12 education? From a policy perspective, is preschool education the rabbit in the proverbial horse–rabbit stew? We expect the influence of early childhood policy on elementary and secondary education to be limited by the preschool sector's small size and its structure, which is highly fragmented and not integrated with the K–12 system. Yet, as it continues to grow, some of preschool's unique aspects may impact K–12 education, nonetheless. We therefore predict modest influences on K–12, with the influence of K–12 on preschool education at least as large. Perhaps, more than anything else, we predict conflict as the two collide. To set the stage

187

for this discussion, we begin with an overview of the mixed public and private structure of preschool education.

OVERVIEW

Organization and Governance of the Preschool Sector

The organization and governance of preschool education are quite unlike that found in K–12. Whereas the latter sector is dominated by relatively uniform public schools and funded primarily by state and local government, the lines between private and public in the preschool sector are much less clear. Despite a long-term trend toward public funding, parental report suggests that about half (2.2 million) of all preschoolers are enrolled in private programs operated by a mix of for-profit, nonprofit independent, and religious organizations. In 2002, state preschool programs enrolled around 740,000 children, with the vast majority being four-year-olds. Roughly 70 percent of these enrollments were in public schools, 23 percent in private programs, and 7 percent in Head Start. Approximately 900,000 children were enrolled in Head Start, with about 85 percent attending programs run by private nonprofits, such as Community Action Agencies, and 15 percent attending public school programs. Preschool special education programs enrolled around 390,000 children. Some of these children are also served in private programs, but numbers are not reported for this nationally (Barnett, Hudstedt, et al., 2004). As many as 300,000 additional preschool children may be served by local public schools outside state and federal programs using federal (e.g., Title I) and local funds. When these figures are combined, it is evident that the vast majority of preschool enrollment is in privately owned programs. This amount is far higher than the usually cited 50 percent reported by parents, who may be attributing programs to the public sector if they are part of state-funded preschool or Head Start, even when they operate under private auspices.

The fragmented nature of the preschool sector means programs for young children have highly diverse goals, regulations, and funding mechanisms (Barnett & Masse, 2003; Holloway & Fuller, 1992; Mitchell, 1996). Such fragmentation often also means children's access to programs is uneven (Barnett & Yarosz, 2004). Yet the inclusion of a large private sector in many state preschool programs can provide various benefits. If school districts lack adequate facilities to house new programs for young children, utilizing already-existing, community-based programs can preclude the need for expensive and time-intensive construction initiatives. Working families also have increased access to both child care and preschool in the same facility (U.S. Government Accountability Office, 2004).

In addition, some in the early childhood field have argued that quality preschool education should reflect children's cultural heritage (Bredekamp & Copple, 1997). While secondary analyses of data from two large studies of children's experiences in community-based programs suggest that differences in teachers' and children's ethnicity and culture has little effect on children's cognitive and social outcomes (Burchinal & Cryer, 2003), the fact remains that over 75 percent of teachers in public school preschools are white (Saluja, Early, & Clifford, 2002). Therefore, if community-based preschool programs more closely represent "cultural congruence" (Fuller et al., 1996, p. 413) in terms of language, cultural goals for children, and beliefs about how they should be raised (Howes, James, & Ritchie, 2003; Liang, Fuller, & Singer, 2000), families may feel more comfortable enrolling their children in such programs. This may be particularly true if teachers and children share the same ethnic background (Wishard et al., 2003).

Potential Impact of Preschool on K–12 School Choice

Use of the private sector in many state preschool programs means privatization (private schools supported by public funds) is larger than in K–12 education. The preschool private sector is larger than the private high school sector and about half the size of the K–8 private sector (see Hill, this volume). Publicly financed private preschool dwarfs the K–12 voucher and charter school programs.

Reliance on the private sector can allow choice to play a much larger role in preschool than it currently does in K–12. For example, Florida's new universal preschool program for four-year-olds essentially appears to be a statewide voucher program where school districts are given the role of provider of last resort (Barnett & Ackerman, 2005). Clint Bolick, president of the Alliance for School Choice, has characterized Florida's program as "the largest private school choice program in the nation" (Alliance for School Choice, 2005). Private programs can reject (but not discriminate against) students, while public school preschool programs cannot. Georgia's universal program allows for substantial choice, though this is limited by the supply of good programs available at the price set by the state. Every year there are news stories on long lines of parents who camp out to sign up at some programs. In New Jersey's Abbott program (universal in 30 large districts), 70 percent of the children are enrolled in private programs, and parents are free to choose from programs operating within their specific district.

The degree of parental choice appears to vary from place to place, at least partly as a function of supply. Even when the private sector and funding programs are utilized at high levels, it takes time to bring new facilities and teachers into the sector. As choice has become prevalent, however, some private providers have also begun to look for political means to limit choice and public school expansion so that current providers do not lose enrollment. Some Head Start programs have experienced declining enrollment as eligible families choose other programs.

Currently the nation does not have enough experience with such programs to anticipate how they might influence K–12 education. Public preschool programs—like those in New Jersey and Florida—include for-profit and religious school sponsors that do not currently receive public funds for K–12 education in those states. However, it seems reasonable that parents who are satisfied with these choices might push to keep their children in the same schools for kindergarten and beyond at public expense. The business and religious organizations operating these programs could be expected to do the same. For-profits encompass a wide range of organizations, from small "mom and pops" to Knowledge Learning Corporation, which is the second largest child care management organization in the country and recently acquired one of its competitors, KinderCare Learning Centers (Neugebauer, 2005). Both small operators—representing many constituents—and big business are likely to get a sympathetic hearing in state capitols when they want to talk about the impact of state education policies on their businesses.

Potential Impact of Preschool on K–12 Curriculum Policy

Another area of potential influence is in K–12 curriculum. Preschool education has traditionally given a stronger emphasis than the elementary grades to social and emotional development and the importance of play for learning and development. Theories of constructivism are much more influential, as well. This difference is reflected in views about developmentally appropriate practice and the role it should play in preschool and kindergarten pedagogy and curriculum. Many in the preschool field are convinced that the push down of elementary school methods (and to some extent content) contributes to high rates of early school failure. As states have increasingly embraced both preschool and full-day kindergarten, there is a concurrent focus on providing the types of learning experiences that are cognizant of how young children best learn (Ackerman, Barnett, & Robin, 2005).

While there is a growing understanding of the need for curricular approaches that are responsive to children's individual abilities, K–12 schools face increasing pressure to meet state standards and accountability measures. Thus, kindergarten readiness criteria often are predicated on the supply of academic skills a child brings to school, rather than on how a school can be responsive to the needs of children. The emphasis on academic success has many parents, teachers, and policymakers advocating for more emphasis on literacy and numeracy skills in kindergarten (Ackerman & Barnett, 2005). Teachers may prefer to use a child-centered pedagogical approach that is more aligned with developmentally appropriate practice, but they may experience pressure to employ a one-size-fits-all, didactic approach for instruction (Wesley & Buysse, 2003).

Yet, preschool might affect K–12 curriculum because highly effective preschool programs can produce substantive improvements in the cognitive and social development of young children (Barnett, 2002). Although gains are likely to be largest for the most disadvantaged children, as preschool programs begin to saturate the population as is now happening in some cities and states, the average level of abilities in kindergartens may rise and the variance in abilities decrease. This could lead to changes in what is taught in kindergarten, and in turn result in curriculum content revisions on up the grades. There are anecdotal reports that this is happening in New Jersey's Abbott districts, where the preschool program requires well-trained, well-paid teachers and small classes. It might be expected in Oklahoma on the basis of on program characteristics and test results at kindergarten entry. To our knowledge, this question has not been systematically investigated.

Preschool also could impact what is taught in kindergarten by influencing state policy on the length of the kindergarten day. Forty percent of kindergartners still participate in a half-day, 2–3 hour daily program, but with most children starting "school" at or before age four and many attending up to 10 hours per day, such a schedule has come to be seen by many as antiquated. The literature on full-day (4.5–6 hours daily) kindergarten suggests a longer day may be educationally beneficial for children as well. Full-day kindergarten provides teachers with the opportunity to spend more time on reading, language arts, and math activities than in half-day programs. Children also have the chance for more time in self-selected activities. Many studies find modest benefits for children who attend full-day programs, particularly in terms of literacy and mathematics gains and reductions in retention rates (Ackerman, Barnett, & Robin, 2005). It is important to note, however, that long hours in preschool programs that do not adequately attend to social development may exacerbate behavior problems (Vandell, 2004), making it more difficult to teach kindergarten well.

Potential Effects on K–12 Standards and Assessment Policy

Increased state involvement in preschool education has led to the development of learning standards that have implications for K–12 policies. Almost every state that funds a preschool initiative—as well as some states without publicly financed programs—has a document specifying the information and skills children should learn in a preschool program (Neuman & Roskos, 2005). Most of these standards documents are broad, reflecting a traditional emphasis in preschool on both cognitive and social and emotional development. This emphasis has been reinforced by research finding that social and emotional outcomes are primary sources of the large social and economic benefits of preschool education for economically disadvantaged children (Boyd et al., 2005). Benchmarks in this domain, as well as those related to preschoolers' physical development, health, and safety and to the content areas of language and literacy, math, science, and the creative arts, are now being linked to K–12 outcome standards (Scott-Little, Kagan, and Frelow, 2003, 2005). Standards for the early grades often have been quite general in the past. These new preschool standards are likely to generate more carefully articulated standards through grade 3.

The much larger federal role in preschool education also has the potential to influence K–12 assessment policy. For example, the federal government has mandated testing for every Head Start four-year-old twice a year (Head Start Bureau, 2003). Head Start currently bypasses state government and relatively few state preschool programs are integrated with Head Start. Yet, if Head Start becomes integrated with state preschool programs, the federal government could mandate a national test with which state preschool standards would then have to be aligned. Testing and standards might then be bumped up the grades to meet up with No Child Left Behind (NCLB) standards and tests in third grade. As with other recent federal initiatives, there is a heavy emphasis on literacy skills and a tendency to neglect other aspects of learning and development. On its own, NCLB has not ventured below third grade, perhaps reflecting the widely held view in the early childhood field that assessing young children is a difficult endeavor due to their irregular and episodic development.

Although standardized assessment of young children is not prevalent in the field, the preschool sector has emphasized assessing the quality of educational contexts. These assessments have focused on the physical environment of classrooms, the learning activities children engage in, and the way a program is structured (e.g., Abbott-Shim & Sibley, 1987; Harms, Clifford, & Cryer, 2005). Such measures have not been as prevalent in K–12 settings (Lambert, 2003). If there is a greater movement in aligning the pedagogical approaches of early primary classrooms with the principles of developmentally appropriate practice, we might also see greater use of measures such as the *Assessment of Practices in Early Elementary Classrooms* (Maxwell et al., 2001), *A Developmentally Appropriate Practice Template* (Van Horn and Ramey, 2004), and the *Early Childhood Classroom Observation Measure* (Stipek & Byler, 2004). These assessments might provide useful models for "documenting the quality of educational programs . . . beyond tests scores obtained from measures of student achievement" (Lambert, 2003, p. 24).

Impacts of Preschool on K–12 Teacher Certification

Preschool also has the potential to impact the certification or endorsement K–12 teachers hold. Teachers in elementary school typically obtain a certification that spans kindergarten through grade 8 (Kaye, 2003), and only a few states require kindergarten teachers to have certifications that are specifically related to the early childhood field (Kauerz, 2005). Of the states that require teachers in their publicly funded preschools to be certified, however, the majority also require certification or an endorsement that is specifically related to teaching young children between the ages of three and eight (Barnett, Hustedt, et al., 2004). As the provision of preschool continues to expand within the public school sector, more early primary grade teachers, in particular, may be required to have endorsements focusing exclusively on children within this age range.

ARTICULATION BETWEEN PRESCHOOL AND K–12 POLICIES

Despite the increasing numbers of children served in both privately and publicly funded preschool programs, a more thorough investigation of these initiatives reveals that instead of being aligned or articulated with K–12, they often represent a case of preschool versus K–12 policy. This dichotomy reflects the historical tendency for programs focusing on young children to operate outside of the K–12 regulatory sector. This situation is further exacerbated by the fact that preschool programs themselves often have different goals, eligibility criteria, and funding mechanisms (Gallagher, Clifford, & Maxwell, 2004).

The expansion of publicly funded preschool as part of K–12 thus often involves the merger of two distinct systems of education, each with differing expectations for such variables as curriculum, teacher qualifications, and outcomes. As a result, the standards governing teacher training, scheduling, funding, and the outcomes programs are expected to achieve vary widely, making articulation between the two sectors difficult.

Teachers' Qualifications

Differences in standards for teachers' preservice qualifications are perhaps the most visible reminder that preschool has traditionally operated outside of the K–12 milieu. Every state requires public school kindergarten teachers to have a minimum of a bachelor's (BA) degree. While research has also found that teachers with a BA in early childhood education or a related field tend to have higher-quality preschool classrooms (Burchinal et al., 2002), the standards regarding publicly funded preschool teachers' qualifications are not consistently aligned with this research or K–12 policy.

For example, teachers working in the six states that offer publicly financed preschool solely through their K–12 systems are required to have a BA. An additional 12 states require teachers working in both public schools and private settings to have this degree. As can be seen in Table 9.1, however, nine states permit teachers working in private programs funded by the state to have a less stringent qualification, such as a Child Development Associate credential or an Associate's degree. An additional 12 states do not require teachers in public or private settings to have a BA (Barnett, Hustedt, et al., 2004).

Data collected during the 2003–2004 school year on the percentages of state-funded preschool teachers who have at least a four-year degree (Gilliam & Marchesseault, 2005) show a wide variation between states. In states requiring a BA, the vast majority have attained that credential. In the nine states that only require public school preschool teachers to have a BA, the percentages range from 47 to 99 percent, with those figures roughly mirroring the percentages of children served in that sector (Barnett, Hustedt, et al., 2004). The percent of teachers with a BA in those states that do not require it at all ranges from 34 to 79 percent. Here, too, states with higher percentages of degreed teachers tend to have larger enrollments in public schools. Finally, some states provide additional funding to Head Start programs, and the percentage of teachers in these programs with a BA ranges from 20 to 66 percent (Gilliam & Marchesseault, 2005).

Standards for Teacher Professional Development

Standards regarding in-service teacher professional development also differ between K–12 and preschool. These differences may reflect a misperception that educating young children requires little professional skill or knowledge (Ackerman, 2006). Yet, professional development is partic-

TABLE 9.1
Preservice Requirements for State-Financed Preschool Teachers

State-by-state preservice educational requirements, 2002–2003	Percentage of teachers with a BA or higher, 2003–2004*
Teachers in public or private settings must have a BA	
Alabama	96
Arkansas	77
Illinois	93
Kansas	98
Louisiana	98–100
Maine (excluding state-funded Head Start)	97
Maryland	100
Nebraska	94
Nevada	97
New Jersey	86–100
North Carolina	86
Oklahoma (excluding state-funded Head Start)	97
Pennsylvania	96
South Carolina	100
Tennessee	97
Texas	98
Vermont	83
West Virginia	100
Teachers in public schools only must have a BA	
Iowa	75
Massachusetts (excluding state-funded Head Start)	49
Michigan	96
Missouri	74
New York	91–99
Oregon	47
Virginia	92
Washington	47
Wisconsin (excluding state-funded Head Start)	99
No teacher in any setting needs to have a BA	
Arizona	56
California	39–45
Colorado	59
Connecticut (excluding state-funded Head Start)	58
Delaware	46
Florida	34
Georgia	77
Hawaii (excluding state-funded Head Start)	48
Kentucky	64
New Mexico (excluding state-funded Head Start)	42
Ohio (excluding state-funded Head Start)	79

Source: Data from Barnett, Hustedt, et al. 2004; Gilliam and Marchesseault 2005.

ularly critical for the preschool workforce. Teachers with a lesser amount of formal preparation will more likely need extensive in-service training to become highly effective teachers.

In 2002–2003, just nine states—Arkansas, Illinois, Maryland, New Jersey, New York, North Carolina, Oklahoma, South Carolina, and Wisconsin—required teachers in their state-funded preschool programs to participate in as much professional development as K–12 teachers. Seven of these states required all teachers to have a BA as well. In other states, the required annual amount was usually higher for K–12 teachers than for those working in state-funded preschools. For example, Arizona, Colorado, and Missouri required K–12 teachers to obtain between 90 and 180 hours of professional development or college credits over a specific time span. The preschool requirements in these same states ranged from 10 to 12 hours per year. In Iowa and Michigan, K–12 teachers were also required to obtain college credits as part of their in-service professional development, but teachers in their state-funded preschool programs were not required to participate in any in-service training (Barnett et al., 2004; Potts, Blank, & Williams, 2002).

Standards Regarding Group Size and Staff–Child Ratios

Two areas where standards might not be expected to converge are class size and staff–child ratios. Smaller group sizes and lower staff–child ratios in preschool increase the likelihood of individualized attention and more supportive interactions. Recent data (Barnett, Schulman, & Shore, 2004) suggest this is the case, with standards related to these two criteria in most state-financed preschool programs falling within the range recommended for quality by the National Association for the Education of Young Children (NAEYC; Barnett, Schulman, & Shore, 2004), the leading professional organization for those who work with children ages zero to eight. NAEYC recommends limiting four-year-old group sizes to 20 children or fewer and having staff–child ratios that are 1:10 or better. However, eight states do not limit their maximum class size for four-year-old programs. Three states have limits of 24 and 28 for all or some of their programs, making them more aligned with K–12. Four states also have staff–child ratios that allow one staff member to be responsible for 12 or more four-year-olds, and an additional three have no limits for their staff–child ratios (Barnett, Schulman, & Shore, 2004).

Interestingly, the Tennessee class size experiment suggests that it might be wise to reduce class size to 15 or fewer in the primary grades, particularly for disadvantaged students (Finn et al., 2001). This is a smaller class size than most states require at ages three or four.

Preschool Scheduling

Policies regarding the length of the school day differ among state-funded preschool programs and between those programs and K–12 overall. Sixty percent of kindergartners attend a full-day program, but state-funded preschool programs (in contrast to private programs) are much less likely to provide children with a similar schedule. As can be seen in Table 9.2, only eight states require all or some of their preschool programs to offer a full-day schedule over the course of an academic year. With the exception of New Jersey, which limits its full-day kindergarten funding to programs in its 30 Abbott districts, these states also provide all school districts with funding for full-day kindergarten programs (Ackerman et al., 2005).

Although many of the remaining states provide financial incentives for districts to offer full-day kindergarten programs (Ackerman et al., 2005), most do not do so for state-funded preschool programs (Barnett, Hustedt, et al., 2004). Effective preschool programs have utilized half-day schedules (Frede, 1998), but limiting such programs to a half day means that some parents will choose to send their children to child care with little or no educational effectiveness (Barnett, Hustedt, et al.,

TABLE 9.2
Preschool Schedules, 2002–2003

Schedule	States
Full day, five days/week, academic year	Alabama, Arkansas, Connecticut (in at least 60% of settings), Georgia, Louisiana (LA4 and Starting Points only), New Jersey (Abbott districts only), Tennessee, Texas (full-day programs only)
Half day, (2.0–3.5 hrs.), five days/week, academic year	California, Delaware (at least 160 days), Illinois, Kansas, Kentucky, Louisiana (NSECD only), Maryland, Missouri, Nebraska, New Jersey (ECPA districts only), New York (UPK), North Carolina, Oklahoma, Oregon (474 hours/year), Pennsylvania, South Carolina, Texas (half-day programs), Wisconsin (4K only; not required, but offered in most)
Half day, four days/week, academic year	Colorado, Michigan, Minnesota (Head Start), New York (EPK), Ohio, Washington, Wisconsin (Head Start)
Recommended	Arizona (12 hours/week)
No minimum operating schedule	Hawaii, Iowa, Maine, Massachusetts, Nevada, New Mexico, Virginia

Source: Data from Barnett, Hustedt, et al. (2004).

2001). These child care programs may also be publicly subsidized. The impacts of half-day preschool schedules should be examined more closely in terms of their effects on participation, as well as the direct educational consequences of a shorter or longer day for those who attend.

Per-Pupil Spending and Access

Even though few preschool programs are funded through K–12 formulas, states with preschool programs spend nearly as much on their share of preschool education costs as they do on their share of K–12 costs: $3,500 for preschool compared to $3,935 per pupil on K–12. As might be expected, vast disparities in per-pupil spending exist. For example, Maryland spends less than $1,000 per child, whereas New Jersey spends over $8,700. It is less clear to what extent state preschool programs have access to local and federal funding that would bring total expenditures up near the $9,295 total for grades K–12 (Barnett, Hustedt, et al., 2004).

The lower state funding levels and lack of access to federal and state funds are consistent with half-day offerings and programs that do not have any minimum operating schedule. Where programs can be provided by either local schools or private providers, the former may have some advantage based on access to local revenues. However, private programs might have an advantage in terms of lower costs, particularly where they are subject to lower standards for teacher qualifications.

As can be seen in Figure 9.1, lower per-pupil costs appear to be correlated somewhat with greater percentages of children served in state-funded preschool in 2002–2003. Of the five states that funded their preschool programs at $5,000 per pupil or more, just two served over 10 percent of four-year-olds in their states. Conversely, of the states that funded programs at a rate of less than $5,000 per pupil, 11 served between 20 and 60 percent of their four-year-olds.

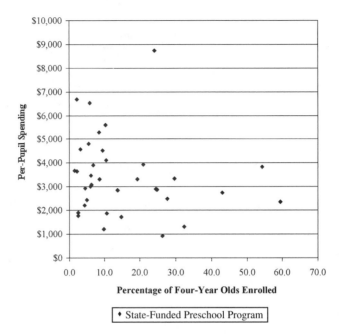

FIGURE 9.1.   Per-pupil state expenditures and percentage of children enrolled, 2002–2003.

It is plausible that programs targeting the most disadvantaged students would have higher per-pupil costs, because they must offer more intensive services to meet their students' needs. Also, programs serving a more general population can be expected to have greater local capacity to generate services for their programs. At the same time, however, 20 states spent less than $5,000 per preschool pupil and served less than 20 percent. In fact, the majority of this latter group enrolled less than 10 percent. As preschool programs that are either poorly or well funded by states relative to K–12 expand, these differences may generate attention to state funding formulas and perhaps add to pressures for change.

Learning Standards

Preschool's effectiveness relies on more than teacher qualifications and training, program scheduling, and funding. Standards regarding the skills and knowledge children should develop while in a preschool program are also important. Without such standards, teachers may rely on inappropriate beliefs or practices when deciding what and how to teach, what young children should learn, and how that learning might be assessed. This issue is particularly salient if teachers have not had specialized, college-level training in early childhood education. Even if teachers have participated in formal teacher preparation programs, the lack of clear expectations may result in the "sense of being 'rudderless' " (File & Powell, 2005, p. 4).

As noted earlier, most states have a document—often called "learning standards" or "content standards"—specifying the skills and knowledge children should attain in a preschool program. Given the early childhood field's emphasis on the whole child, it is not surprising that our review of the standards available in early 2005 found that almost all addressed children's literacy, math, and science skills, as well as their physical health, social and emotional development, and approaches to learning. Five states also had explicit standards related to the use of technology.

High-quality outcome standards documents do not merely encompass a wide variety of domains, however. Instead, they should also be clearly written so that they are understandable by teachers and other stakeholders (Neuman & Roskos, 2005). They should also contain enough information so that teachers and schools can document—in a nonstandardized, developmentally appropriate way—where children are in their progress toward achieving each of these outcomes (Bodrova, Leong, & Shore, 2004).

At the time of our review, these standards documents differed in terms of the amount of practical, "user-friendly" information they contained. In six states, standards documents focused solely on the outcomes or performance skills that children should be able to do upon completion of a preschool program. Although this is obviously the intent of these documents, the lack of additional information could be problematic for teachers without a formal educational background. For example, a language arts standard in Illinois' document states that children will "seek answers to questions through active exploration" (Illinois State Board of Education, 2002, p. 11). However, there is no accompanying information on what activities might demonstrate that a child is displaying "active exploration," and no information on what teachers might do to facilitate such a process.

Perhaps to help alleviate this potential problem, 14 states also provided examples of how children might demonstrate proficiency or competency in relation to a specific standard. For example, a math benchmark found in the document Arizona Early Childhood Education Standards (Arizona Department of Education, 2003) states that preschoolers will be able to "read and interpret displays of data using objects, pictures, and representations" (p. 72). This benchmark is then clarified by an example: a child can demonstrate proficiency when she "examines the graph of favorites and discusses which category has the most, the least, etc." (p. 72).

Twenty states have taken their standards one step further and offered strategies for how teachers might assist children in reaching them. For example, one of the math and science benchmarks for Arkansas's preschoolers is that children will make comparisons and show an awareness of cause–effect relationships (Brown & Wright, 1999). The state's standards document then advises teachers to involve children in simple science experiments such as investigating what materials sink or float, absorb water, or allow light to shine through, as well as examining what happens when two colors are mixed or when water is mixed with different liquids or solids. By providing these suggestions, teachers have concrete examples of the types of activities that can help children master these skills.

Despite the shortcomings of some standards, many of the state preschool standards are much more detailed, cover a broader range of learning and development, and provide more guidance to teachers than is typical of K–12 standards (Kendall & Marzano, 2000). To some extent, this reflects both "learning from experience" in developing K–12 standards and the strengths of the preschool field in these aspects of guiding learning and teaching. As states move to articulate preschool and early elementary standards (and assessments), these differences will become clear. One reasonable expectation is that early elementary standards will receive more attention and that they will become more detailed and specific at the very least. They might also be broadened.

Efforts might also arise to provide elementary teachers with more guidance, not necessarily in the standards, but in companion documents on what children should experience and how teachers should teach. Some states have done this for preschool programs in conjunction with standards. One possible advance stems from the combined influence of standards and the early childhood field's development of structured observation systems for evaluating teaching and classroom environments. Rather than the K–12 duality of standards and child assessment to influence teaching practices, the early childhood field appears to be moving toward a tripartite system of standards, child assessment, and teacher and classroom assessment. Could such a system migrate to the early elementary grades?

Ongoing formative research might aid in making informed program improvement decisions related to these variables. New Jersey's implementation of several evaluative feedback mechanisms as part of its state-funded Abbott preschool program may be particularly instructive in studying how such an approach might be implemented. For example, districts have engaged in a systematic self-appraisal that helped highlight their overall strengths and areas in need of improvement. The self-appraisal tool is aligned with the state's program implementation guidelines, as well as the field's standards regarding developmentally appropriate curriculum and assessment. The tool also provided districts with the opportunity to evaluate any improvements made. The New Jersey Early Learning Assessment System (ELAS) also uses teachers' observations and children's work samples both to evaluate children's emerging skills and to determine how the learning environment should be adjusted to enhance their development (Lamy et al., 2005).

An examination of policies and practices in state-funded preschool and the differences from K–12 suggests as much potential for clashes as for trade at the borders. What further research focusing on the interactions between early childhood and K–12 might be especially productive?

RESEARCH IMPLICATIONS

At present, most states have added preschool to their K–12 systems' arsenal of educational inputs. As noted by authors in this volume (e.g., Cohen, Moffitt, & Goldin; Barrow & Rouse; Grubb) among others, there has been a tacit assumption within the K–12 milieu that when schools have more resources and/or educational inputs, student achievement will also be greater. However, while resources certainly play a role, they are not "self-acting" (Cohen, Raudenbush, & Ball, 2003, p. 122). In short, resources do not directly promote outcomes unless they are effectively integrated into the daily practices within schools. Administrators, teachers, and policymakers therefore need to shift their focus from looking at merely acquiring resources to instead determining *which* specific inputs can make a difference in particular schools, how they influence children's outcomes, and under what circumstances.

Preschool education is the "Wild West," America's educational frontier. The larger K–12 establishment may view it as "the meeting point between savagery and civilization," echoing Turner's (1893) famous description of the American frontier. In Turner's view, the necessities of the frontier generated American virtues including democracy and an energetic and industrious individualism, with a distaste for centralized government. His critics argued that government, corporations, and local cooperation and communities were required to develop the frontier and integrate it into the nation.

Like the frontier, preschool education is fertile ground for experiments that examine the effects of changes in resources and their allocation on learning and development. The variations among state policies regarding funding and finance, eligibility, teacher education and development, class size and ratio, schedule, standards and assessment, and governance on preschool offer tremendous opportunities to learn. Much more may be learned if these variations can be harnessed in systematic experiments, rather than comparing "naturally" occurring differences (Boruch, 1997). What is learned could lead to substantial improvements in today's preschool programs, some of which would seem to have little hope of achieving their educational goals, while enlightening and enlivening K–12 reform (Barnett, 1998).

Research Related to the Transition Into K–12

Even where preschool is educationally effective, future research needs to investigate how K–12 programs might be realigned to build on the gains children acquire while enrolled in preschool, particularly for those students who are considered to be at risk of school failure. Past early childhood research indicates that transition into K–12 may play a role in sustaining any academic and developmental gains acquired in preschool (Pianta & Cox, 1999). Yet the transition is not always smooth. For example, Snow and Paez (2004) note that the oral language skills—and therefore the emergent literacy skills as well—of Head Start students who are also English language learners are placed at risk when they come from an English-only preschool setting, but are placed in a bilingual kindergarten or first-grade class. Conversely, some children may be able to speak their native language in preschool, but are effectively "silenced" by English-only policies in K–12 schooling (Smolkin, 1999).

In short, policymakers need to be aware not only of what types of kindergarten practices might undermine effective preschool programs, but also how to create "developmentally linked educational programs" that have unified academic and social goals (Sigel, 2004, p. 55). Future research should examine how K–12 schooling might minimize the cultural, linguistic, or contextual constraints that can make children's adjustment to kindergarten difficult. In addition, because children have participated in many different forms of preschool experiences before enrolling in kindergarten, research can examine the effectiveness of different K–12 instructional approaches in terms of being more responsive to individual children's needs.

Research Related to the Broader Policy Context

Once standards in both sectors are set, researchers also need to investigate the capacity of various stakeholders to implement new policies. For example, although requiring preschool teachers to obtain a BA is a key component in improving the quality of preschool, there are various "getting from here to there" issues that would also need to be considered, particularly if a policy's goals include increasing the credentials of the current workforce. These issues include the constraints facing preschool teachers in improving their credentials as well as the capacity of teacher preparation programs to support the policy and produce a more knowledgeable and effective workforce. States would also need to provide for newly degreed teachers to receive salaries that are comparable to those in K–12, or risk perpetual hiring and retention problems. Related ongoing, formative research is also needed to determine whether the supports intended to assist teachers in obtaining a BA actually work (Ackerman, 2005).

The policy implications of where—and how—preschool and subsequent K–12 schooling are offered also need to be investigated. If the majority of parents can choose between a wide variety of preschool initiatives, can program standards and subsequent academic goals be aligned? Although reducing choice might seem to promote more unified curricular approaches and academic goals, would this be for the best? What happens to access to effective education when programs like Florida's set minimal levels of state funding for a few hours of preschool, but let parents pay whatever they wish for the remaining hours each week? Research needs to examine the impact of choice—and the lack thereof—on the different populations of children served.

In conclusion, the boundary between early childhood and the K–12 sector at the preschool frontier seems unlikely to disappear into one seamless system of education any time soon. Given the focus on each component in the current public policy discourse, however, that boundary will be an exciting and changing place in the coming decade as it reflects the growing influence of each side.

REFERENCES

Abbott-Shim, M., & Sibley, A. (1987). *Assessment profile for early childhood programs*. Atlanta, GA: Quality Assist, Inc.

Ackerman, D. J. (2005) Getting teachers from here to there: Examining issues related to an early care and education teacher policy. *Early Childhood Research & Practice 7*(1). Retrieved september 1, 2005, from http://ecrp.uiuc.edu/v7n1/ ackerman.html

Ackerman, D. J. (2006). The costs of being a child care teacher: Revisiting the problem of low wages. Manuscript under review.

Ackerman, D. J., & Barnett, W. S. (2005). *Prepared for kindergarten: What does "readiness" mean?* New Brunswick, NJ: NIEER.

Ackerman, D. J., Barnett, W. S., & Robin, K. (2005). M*aking the most of kindergarten: Present trends and future issues and answers in the provision of full-day programs*. New Brunswick, NJ: NIEER.

Alliance for School Choice. (2005). *Florida Pre-K program an opportunity for choice*. News release, Jan. 3.

Arizona Department of Education. (2003). *Arizona early childhood education standards*. Phoenix, AZ: Author.

Barnett, W. S. (1998). Long-term effects on cognitive development and school success. In W. S. Barnett & S. S. Boocock (Eds.), *Early care and education for children in poverty: Promises, programs, and long-term results* (pp. 11–44). Albany: State University of New York Press.

Barnett, W. S. (2002). Early childhood education. In A. Molnar (Ed.), *School reform proposals: The research evidence* (pp. 1–26). Greenwich, CT: Information Age.

Barnett, W. S., & Ackerman, D. J. (2005). *Vouchers and other financing strategies: Effects on quality of early care and education.* Paper presented at the Conference on Ensuring Quality in Early Childhood Services—International Approaches and Perspectives, Berlin, Germany.

Barnett, W. S., Hustedt, J. T., Robin, K., & Schulman, K. L. (2004). *The state of preschool: 2004 state preschool yearbook*. New Brunswick, NJ: NIEER.

Barnett, W. S., & Masse, L. N. (2003). Funding issues for early childhood education and care programs. In D. Cryer & R. M. Clifford (Eds.), *Early childhood education and care in the USA* (pp. 137–165). Baltimore, MD: Paul H. Brookes.

Barnett, W. S., Schulman, K., & Shore, R. (2004). Class size: What's the best fit? *Preschool Policy Matters 9*. New Brunswick, NJ: NIEER.

Barnett, W. S., Tarr, J. E., Lamy, C. E., & Frede, E. C. (2001). *Fragile lives, shattered dreams: A report on implementation of preschool education in New Jersey's Abbott districts.* New Brunswick, NJ: Center for Early Education Research.

Barnett, W. S., & Yarosz, D. J. (2004). Who goes to preschool and why does it matter? *Preschool Policy Matters 8*. New Brunswick, NJ: NIEER.

Bodrova, E., Leong, D., & Shore, R. (2004). Child outcome standards in pre-K programs: What are standards; what is needed to make them work? *Preschool Policy Matters 5*. New Brunswick, NJ: NIEER.

Boruch, R. (1997). *Randomized experiments for planning and evaluation: A practical guide*. Thousand Oaks, CA: Sage Publications.

Boyd, J., Barnett, W. S., Bodrova, E., Leong, D. J., Gomby, D., Robin, K. B., & Hustedt, J. T. (2005). *Promoting children's social and emotional development through preschool.* New Brunswick, NJ: NIEER.

Bredekamp, S., & Copple, C. (1997). *Developmentally appropriate practices in early childhood programs.* (Revised edition). Washington, DC: National Association for the Education of Young Children.

Brown, D., & Wright, B. C. (1999). *Arkansas early childhood education framework: Benchmarks with strategies/activities for three and four year old children.* Little Rock, AR: Arkansas Department of Human Services, Division of Child Care and Early Childhood Education.

Burchinal, M. R., & Cryer, D. (2003). Diversity, child care quality, and developmental outcomes. *Early Childhood Research Quarterly 18*, 401–426.

Burchinal, M. R., Cryer, D., Clifford, R. M., & Howes, C. (2002). Caregiver training and classroom quality in child care centers. *Applied Developmental Science 6*, 2–11.

Cohen, D. K., Raudenbush, S. W., & Ball, D. L. (2003). Resources, instruction, and research. *Educational Evaluation and Policy Analysis 25*, 119–142.

File, N., & Powell, D. R. (2005). *Without standards to guide: Teachers' construction of learning goals in public school pre-kindergarten.* Paper presented at the annual meeting of the American Educational Research Association, Montreal, Quebec, Canada.

Finn, J. D., Gerber, S. B., Achilles, C. A., & Boyd-Zaharias, J. (2001). The enduring effects of small class sizes. *Teachers College Record 103*, 145–183.

Frede, E. (1998). Preschool program quality in programs for children in poverty. In W. S. Barnett & S. S. Boocock (Eds.), *Early care and education for children in poverty* (pp. 77–98). Albany: State University of New York Press.

Fuller, B., Eggers-Piérola, C., Holloway, S. D., Liang, X., & Rambaud, M. F. (1996). Rich culture, poor markets: Why do Latino parents forgo preschooling? *Teachers College Record 97*, 400–418.

Gallagher, J. J., Clifford, R. M., & Maxwell, K. (2004). Getting from here to there: To an ideal early preschool system. *Early Childhood Research and Practice 6*(1). Retrieved October 10, 2005, from http://ecrp.uiuc.edu/v6n1/clifford.html

Gilliam, W. S., & Marchesseault, C. M. (2005). *From capitols to classrooms, policies to practice: State-funded prekindergarten at the classroom level. Part 1: Who's teaching our youngest students? Teacher education and training, experience, compensation and benefits, and assistant teachers.* New Haven, CT: Yale University Child Study Center.

Harms, T., Clifford, R. M., & Cryer, D. (2005). *Early childhood environment rating scale.* (Revised edition) New York: Teachers College Press.

Head Start Bureau. (2003). *Information memorandum: Head Start national reporting system on child outcomes.* Washington, DC: U.S. Department of Health and Human Services.

Holloway, S. D., & Fuller, B. (1992). The great child-care experiment: What are the lessons for school improvement? *Educational Researcher 21*(7), 12–19.

Howes, C., James, J., & Ritchie, S. (2003). Pathways to effective teaching. *Early Childhood Research Quarterly 18*, 104–120.

Illinois State Board of Education. (2002). *Illinois early learning standards.* Springfield, IL: Author.

Kauerz, K. (2005). State kindergarten policies: Straddling early learning and early elementary school. *Beyond the Journal: Young Children on the Web*, March. Retrieved September 10, 2005, from http://www.journal.naeyc.org/btj/200503/ 01Kauerz.pdf

Kaye, A. E. (2003). *Requirements for certification: Of teachers, counselors, librarians, and administrators of elementary and secondary schools.* 68th ed. Chicago: University of Chicago Press.

Kendall, J. S., & Marzano, R. J. (2000). *Content knowledge: A compendium of standards and benchmarks for K–12 education.* 3rd ed. Aurora, CO: Mid-continent Research for Education and Learning.

Lambert, R. G. (2003). Considering purpose and intended use when making evaluations of assessments: A response to Dickinson. *Educational Researcher 32*(4), 23–26.

Lamy, C. E., Frede, E., Seplocha, H., Strasser, J., Jambunathan, S., Juncker, J. A., & Wolock, E. (2005). *Giant steps for the littlest children: Progress in the sixth year of the Abbott preschool program.* Trenton, NJ: Early Learning Improvement Consortium.

Liang, X., Fuller, B., & Singer, J. D. (2000). Ethnic differences in child care selection: The influence of family structure, parental practices, and home language. *Early Childhood Research Quarterly 15*, 357–384.

Maxwell, K. L., McWilliam, R. A., Hemmeter, M. L., Ault, M. J., & Schuster, J. W. (2001). Predictors of developmentally appropriate classroom practices in kindergarten through third grade. *Early Childhood Research Quarterly 16,* 431–452.

Mitchell, A. (1996). Licensing: Lessons from other occupations. In S. L. Kagan & N. E. Cohen (Eds.), *Reinventing early care and education: A vision for a quality system* (pp. 101–123). San Francisco: Jossey-Bass.

National Association for the Education of Young Children. (2004). *NAEYC accreditation criteria.* Retrieved October 10, 2005, from http://www.naeyc.org/accreditation/criteria98.asp

Neugebauer, R. (2005). Employer child care providers stalled, but optimistic: Fourteenth annual status report on employer child care. *Exchange* March/April, 66–68.

Neuman, S. B., & Roskos, K. (2005). The state of state pre-kindergarten standards. *Early Childhood Research Quarterly 20*, 125–145.

Pianta, R. C., & Cox, M. J., eds. (1999). *The transition to kindergarten.* Baltimore, MD: Brookes.

Potts, A., Blank, R. K., & Williams, A. (2002). *Key state education policies on PK–12 education: 2002. Results from the 2002 CCSSO policies and practices survey.* Washington, DC: Council of Chief State School Officers.

Saluja, G., Early, D. M., & Clifford, R. M. (2002). Demographic characteristics of early childhood teachers and structural elements of early care and education in the United States. *Early Childhood Research & Practice 4*(1). Retrieved August 5, 2005, from http://ecrp.uiuc.edu/v4n1/saluja.html

Scott-Little, C., Kagan, S. L., & Frelow, V. W. (2003). Creating the conditions for success with early learning standards: Results from a national study of state-level standards for children's learning prior to kindergarten. *Early Childhood Research & Practice 5*(2). Retrieved September 5, 2005, from http://ecrp.uiuc.edu/v5n2/little.html

Scott-Little, C., Kagan, S. L., & Frelow, V. W. (2005). *Inside the content: The breadth and depth of early learning standards.* Greensboro, NC: SERVE.

Sigel, I. E. (2004). Head Start—Revisiting a historical psychoeducational intervention. In E. Zigler & S. J. Styfco (Eds.), *The Head Start debates* (pp. 45–59). Baltimore, MD: Paul H. Brookes.

Smolkin, L. B. (1999). The practice of effective transitions: Players who make a winning team. In R. J. Pianta & M. J. Cox (Eds.), *The transition to kindergarten* (pp. 325–349). Baltimore, MD: Paul H. Brookes.

Snow, C. E., & Paez, M. M. (2004). The Head Start classroom as an oral language environment. In E. Zigler & S. J. Styfco (Eds.), *The Head Start debates* (pp. 113–128). Baltimore, MD: Paul H. Brookes.

Stipek, D., & Byler, P. (2004). The early childhood classroom observation measure. *Early Childhood Research Quarterly 19*, 375–397.

Turner, F. J. (1894). The significance of the frontier in American history. In *Annual report of the American Historical Association for the year 1893* (pp. 199–227). Washington, DC: American Historical Association.

U.S. Government Accountability Office. (2004). *Prekindergarten: Four selected states expanded access by relying on schools and existing providers of early education and care to provide services.* Washington, DC: Author.

Vandell, D. L. (2004). Early child care: The known and the unknown. *Merrill-Palmer Quarterly 50*, 387–413.

Van Horn, M. L., & Ramey, S. L. (2004). A new measure for assessing developmentally appropriate practices in early elementary school, A Developmentally Appropriate Practice Template. *Early Childhood Research Quarterly 19*, 569–587.

Wesley, P. W., & Buysse, V. (2003). Making meaning of school readiness in schools and communities. *Early Childhood Research Quarterly 18*, 351–375.

Wishard, A. G., Shivers, E. M., Howes, C., & Ritchie, V. (2003). Child care program and teacher practices: Associations with quality and children's experiences. *Early Childhood Research Quarterly 18*, 65–103.

10

Separation of K–12 and Postsecondary Education Policymaking: Evolution, Impact, and Research Needs

Michael W. Kirst

Over 85 percent of eighth graders want a postsecondary degree, and most realize there is an economic payoff to more years of schooling (Schneider, 2003). Although college enrollment rates have skyrocketed in the last 25 years, there has been little increase in the rate at which these students complete college (Bowen, Kurzweil, & Tobin, 2005). Some projections predict that the number of U.S. college graduates will decline by 2020 because of the increase in low-income minority high school students whose parents never attended college (Symonds, 2005). The chance of four-year degree completion (or vocational certificates) is less than 50 percent for students who attend nonselective four- and two-year institutions (Committee for Economic Development, 2005). Such broad-access institutions that accept most applicants comprise about 85 percent of all postsecondary schools and educate approximately 80 percent of the nation's first-year college students, and are the most seriously affected by the problems of student preparation discussed in this chapter. Most media and public attention, however, focuses upon the approximately 15 percent of students who attend the most selective four-year institutions that have the best prepared students, and have the most complicated methods to help sort and select applicants, such as Advanced Placement (AP) courses articulated with collegiate standards. Very few students at broad-access institutions have taken AP classes. Inadequate and inequitable preparation for college affects remediation and persistence rates—major problems in postsecondary institutions throughout the country. Remediation and college completion problems are the greatest in broad-access four-year institutions and community colleges. These institutions use placement exams as their key standards. Yet most standards-setting activities in K–12 systems stop at or before the 10th-grade level, well before students reach college placement standards. State high school exit exams typically send students the message that 10th-grade or lower skills comprise an adequate preparation for college.

This is only one indication that profound organizational, political, and cultural chasms persist in most states between the systems of K–12 and higher education, disjunctures that help create college preparation and completion problems. The two education sectors continue to operate in separate professional worlds. Within each state—and at the federal level as well—a division exists that is based on the historical and pervasive assumption that K–12 schools and colleges and universities should be guided by policies exclusive to each sector. As a result, the public policy "tools" that influence one sector—funding, accountability, assessment, and governance systems, for instance—have little in common with the policy tools that influence the other (Timpane & White, 1998). Moreover, there are separate state boards of education for each level, separate legislative committees, and boards that coordinate one level without involving the other.

The issues of sector disjuncture and related poor college preparation and low completion lack an immediate audience or constituency and remain largely invisible because they fall between the cracks of separate governance and policy systems (Kazis, Vargas, & Hoffman, 2004). Research indicates that only the two systems working together closely can improve college, preparation, readiness, and completion (Kirst & Venezia, 2004). But we have scant research showing how these fractured systems can overcome huge obstacles to policy integration. In recent years, a number of policymakers and educators have questioned why the policies and governance guiding K–12 schools and higher education ought to be totally distinct (Callan et al., 2005). They consider this assumption to be anachronistic and an impediment to educational improvement at both levels. In light of this questioning, this chapter focuses on the disjunctures between the K–12 and postsecondary sectors and on their effects on student success. The chapter examines elements of the disjunctures, the evolution of the disjunctures, and possible solutions through reforms in policy and governance.[1]

ELEMENTS OF THE K–16 DISJUNCTURES

Public Opinion

This section surveys important features of the education landscape that both contribute to and constitute effects of the disjunctures. An important one is the public's high approval rating for the current performance of postsecondary education, and its satisfaction with the higher education status quo. According to Immerwahr (1999) colleges and universities earned a respectable "B" in a 2001 nationwide random sample, while secondary schools were a full grade or more lower. The public's collective advice is that colleges and universities continue to focus on what they do best. Only 12 percent of the public would raise entrance standards for postsecondary education.

Although the public believes that college students are less prepared than a decade ago, only 11 percent hold postsecondary institutions responsible for students' failure to persist. Half of respondents in a national sample think that students are to blame, and another 40 percent think that it is a failure of high schools to prepare students for college level study that causes them to drop out. Very few respondents think the presence or absence of K–16 services such as better counseling or higher education working with public schools is a primary cause of student success or failure. Moreover, a majority of the public thinks students of color have about the same

---

1. There are many issues that affect student preparation for college and college completion. This research focuses solely on the role of policies and programs related to high school graduation, college admission, and college placement. I do not focus on issues related to financial aid or affordability. In addition, teacher preparation and professional development programs and policies play a major role in helping students transition successfully between high school and college. These issues warrant a separate study, and therefore they are not directly addressed in this chapter. College completion can also be impeded by family issues and lack of social integration with the campus.

opportunities as White, non-Latino students. This public opinion poll concluded that there is no mandate for change—or even a suggestion of what kind of higher education change would prove necessary (Immerwahr, 1999). It is unlikely, then, that elected officials will feel much public pressure to bring postsecondary education into greater alignment with K–12. A major public information campaign highlighting the lack of persistence and completion in broad-access postsecondary education might help shift opinion toward closing the gap between the sectors.

Standards

Another key element in the disjunctures is the standards movement that has swept across the United States. These reforms have focused only on K–12 and ignored the lack of coherence in content and assessment standards between K–12 and higher education. Until educators address this issue, secondary schools and their students will have no clear sense of what knowledge and skills constitute an adequate preparation for higher education. The current scene is a Babel of standards rather than a coherent strategy. This incoherence is clearly seen in the relationships of tests within and between the sectors. Tests at each level—K–12 achievement tests, standardized college entrance exams, and college placement assessments—use different formats, emphasize different content, and are given under different conditions; conditions vary from state to state. For example in 1995, universities in the southeastern United States devised 125 combinations of 75 different placement tests, with scant regard to secondary school standards. Texas has a statewide postsecondary placement test as part of the Texas Academic Skills Program (TASP), but many Texas universities also use their own placement exams. High school students in Texas are either confused by or ignorant of college placement standards (Venezia, 2000). High school assessments in Illinois and Florida rely heavily on written work, but ACT and some Florida college placement exams use multiple-choice tests to assess students' writing skills. Massachusetts's K–12 assessment also contains performance items that are dissimilar to the closed-ended multiple-choice format of the SAT and ACT. California's newly augmented Standardized Testing and Reporting (STAR) test includes math that is considerably more advanced and difficult than the SAT and ACT, but Alabama's high school assessment includes less algebra and geometry than the SAT. Some state K–12 assessments permit students to use calculators, but most college placement exams do not. In addition, because many state assessments do not go beyond 10th grade and do not test every pupil (they use a matrix sample), such scores cannot be used for college admissions or placement. Illinois is implementing a new state test given in grade 11 that combines a state standards-based assessment with the ACT, but such attempts to align tests across sectors are rare.

Universities provide some good arguments to explain why they pay little attention to K–12 standards or assessments. First, the universities emphasize that they are not involved in the creation or refinement of the K–12 standards. Second, the universities observe that both politics and technical problems lead to frequent changes in state K–12 standards. Third, they note that the K–12 assessments have not been evaluated to see how well they predict freshman grades (although such evaluations are not difficult to conduct). These arguments suggest a need for more active attempts to coordinate K–12 standards with freshman assessment and general education curriculum by involving universities in the making of standards policies.

Articulations

Attempts to remedy the disjunctures through formal secondary–postsecondary articulations largely fail to do so. One articulation concept is early college that blends the 11th and 12th grades with the freshman and sophomore years to form a coherent, accelerated learning opportunity. Although early colleges have the potential to serve bright students as well as at-risk students, separate governing boards affecting high schools and community colleges create different fiscal, accountability, and personnel systems that limit the potential for early colleges to be a widely available alternative to high schools (Maeroff, Callan, & Usdan, 2001). Moreover, financial disincentives often inhibit another articulation strategy, dual enrollment programs that expose high school students to college courses and standards. Policymakers object that "double dipping" ensues when the state has to pay for the same student twice, through both high school and community college funding. Further, systemic elements that could support articulations are lacking. Current data systems are not equipped to address issues across the sectors. Thus most states are not able to track students in articulations across sectors in order to address their academic needs and assess their outcomes. Also, accountability systems are not structured to motivate or monitor articulations.

Senior Year

The disjunctures are also characterized by the failure of either sector to use the senior year of high school for academic preparation for college. Most high school seniors who will attend broad-access institutions view their final months before graduation as an opportunity to take less demanding courses and enjoy nonacademic pursuits (Kirst, 2001). These students typically do not take any college preparatory mathematics during their senior year (Conley, 2005). The economic and social consequences of this "senior slump" are considerable. The de-emphasis on academic work in the senior year is reflected in the rising cost of remediation, as more college freshmen enroll in remedial writing, math, and science classes; the high dropout rates among those college students who are unprepared for college-level work; and poor academic skills among those high school graduates who move into the workforce or the military.

Senior slump stems in large part from the failure of both the K–12 schools and the colleges and universities to provide incentives for high school seniors to work hard. Indeed, senior slump appears to be the rational response of students to several gaps between K–12 and postsecondary education systems that leave academic preparation unaddressed, including K–12 assessments that evaluate performance only to grade 10 (only New York's state K–12 assessment includes the senior year), a college admissions calendar that provides few incentives for high school seniors to take rigorous academic courses, a lack of coherence and sequencing between the curriculum of the senior year and general education courses in college, the often contradictory assessments and standards, and finally the universal emphasis by high school counselors, college recruiters, college admissions and financial aid officers, students, and their parents on access and admission to college, with far less attention to the academic preparation needed.

College Knowledge

Another element of the disjunctures is the lack of combined efforts to increase knowledge about college going that is essential for K–12 student aspiration and preparation. College knowledge is acquired and possessed unequally among K–12 students and families of different social classes and racial/ethnic backgrounds. The college knowledge of secondary school students and parents should include knowledge of tuition, curricular requirements, placement tests, and admission procedures and selection criteria, but few high schools *or* colleges provide such knowledge in an easily accessible form to potential freshmen at broad-access institutions. Teachers can be a crucial source of college knowledge for students headed toward broad-access institutions, but students in non-honors courses receive less communication about college from their teachers than honors students (Venezia, Kirst, & Antonio, 2003). Moreover, the disadvantaged students who are likely to gain most from access to college knowledge typically receive it least often.

Career Education

The disjunctures also have a deleterious effect on career education. Career pathways, so vital to a volatile information-based economy, suffer from a lack of direction and commitment to career and technical education. Control is frequently diffused between and among institutions in both K–12 and higher education. Higher education generally is uninterested in vocational education issues, which have relatively little prestige. The secondary schools, for their part, are preoccupied with traditional academics and pressures to increase test scores in the current high-stakes assessment environment. Without coordinated policy, vocational/technical education will continue to float between K–12 and postsecondary levels, largely ignored except for turf battles between the sectors over which level should get most federal and state vocational categorical funds.

Student Problems

The disjunctures result in a set of major problems for students. Kirst and Venezia (2004), studying the transition from high school to college, identified several such problems, including the following:

- *Inequalities in education systems remain unaddressed.* Students who are in accelerated curricular tracks in high school receive clearer signals about college preparation than do their peers in other tracks. Many students in middle- and lower-level high school courses are not reached by postsecondary education outreach efforts, or by college counseling staff in their high schools. There is also an unequal distribution of such resources as college centers on high school campuses, opportunities to make college visits, and visits from college recruiters on high school campuses. Many economically disadvantaged parents often lack experience and information concerning college preparation, and the distribution of college preparation information to parents is inequitable. Forty-two percent, 44 percent, and 47 percent of economically disadvantaged parents in Illinois, Maryland, and Oregon, respectively, stated that they had received college information, as compared with 74 percent, 71 percent, and 66 percent of their more economically well-off counterparts (Kirst & Venezia 2004).

- *Student knowledge of collegiate curricular requirements remains sporadic and vague.* Less than 12 percent of the students surveyed in six states knew *all* the course requirements for the postsecondary institutions studied (Kirst and Venezia 2004). Students do appear to have considerable partial knowledge of curricular requirements; slightly more than one-half of the students knew three or more course requirements. But it is the lack of knowledge about content *within* course titles like "English" and "Algebra" that inhibits college readiness (Conley 2005). For example, a recent ACT study found that college instructors believe that grammar and usage skills are the most important writing skills needed by incoming students. The study also found that these skills are considered to be least important by high school teachers. Only 69 percent of high school teachers reported that they teach grammar and usage (ACT, Inc. 2003).

- *Teachers lack the resources they need to give students accurate information.* Teachers often play a greater role in helping students prepare for college than do counselors, but teachers lack connections with broad-access postsecondary institutions and up-to-date admission and placement information.
- *Students remain generally unaware of the content of postsecondary course placement exams.* Across all the studied states, less than one-half of the sampled students knew the specific placement testing policies for the institutions in the study. But failure of placement exams causes students to start in remedial noncredit college courses. A California high school student highlights a key issue: "I think they should prepare us better for the placement tests so that we don't get stuck in basic classes. I think we should have the opportunity to know, not necessarily what's on the test, but to have a good idea of it so that we know what to expect" (Venezia, Kirst, and Antonio 2003, p. 35).

Although the disjunctures cause major problems for students, research has found that clear and consistent K–16 signals are related to positive outcomes, such as less remediation and more completion of a student's desired postsecondary program (Henry & Rubenstein, 2002). But the obstacles to K–16 collaboration to improve secondary student preparation and college completion will be very difficult to overcome.

To understand the specific policy solutions that may help overcome these problems, a better grasp of the historical evolution of the K–16 disjunctures is useful. Examined are the evolution of curriculum, teacher preparation, community colleges, governance, and coordination across the sectors, including the New York Board of Regents.

EVOLUTION OF THE DISJUNCTURES

Curriculum

The origin of the fissure between lower and higher education in the United States stems, in part, from the laudable way the nation created mass education systems to deliver curriculum for both K–12 and higher education. In the 1890s there was no organized system or common standards for college admission. Nearly half the colleges had either low entrance requirements or none at all (Ravitch, 2000, p. 41). Some colleges accepted students from preapproved secondary schools or used their own exams. High school educators wanted a more uniform and less haphazard system. In 1892 the National Education Association appointed the nation's first blue ribbon education commission to recommend secondary school academic standards. The committee included five college presidents, three high school principals, a college professor, and the U.S. commissioner of education (Ravitch, 2000). This "Committee of Ten" was chaired by Charles W. Eliot, president of Harvard.

The committee envisioned only a tiny proportion of high school graduates going on to college. But the report recommended all pupils should be prepared for any path in life by "melding the objectives of liberal education (i.e. a curriculum of rich content) and mental discipline (i.e., the training of the mind)" (Ravitch, 2000, p. 43). The Committee of Ten supported adding subjects like history, the sciences, and classical languages (e.g., Latin) that would be taught through active learning instead of memorization. The report was attacked for its support of an academic education for all students, and some critics praised the European approach of different schools based on career choices of preteens.

The Committee of Ten's report influenced education policy and led to the College Board with its common college examination for diverse colleges. But by 1918 a new report with a very different vision appeared, called the Cardinal Principles of Secondary Education. High school enrollments were expanding, and many students were viewed as incapable of learning the traditional academic curriculum (Tyack & Cuban, 1995).

The Cardinal Principles were to be a blueprint for social efficiency, and the report recommended that students be offered vocational training and courses on family life, good health, citizenship, and ethical character. Students were to be given intelligence tests to put them in the appropriate academic track. The expanded and differentiated curriculum would retain more bored secondary students and better adapt them to a changing society.

Traditional academic subjects and pedagogy were deemphasized in the report. In its wake, courses multiplied to provide something practical and engaging that would retain students in high school. This influential report helped spawn a shopping mall high school that lacked coherence and was not focused upon adequate college preparation for most students (Powell, Farrar, & Cohen, 1985). A series of national commissions starting in the 1950s have tried to push the high school curriculum closer to the Committee of Ten's vision, with mixed results (Kirst & Venezia, 2004). In sum, the American comprehensive high school was designed for many—often conflicting—purposes, and did not focus primarily on college preparation. Today's comprehensive high school was designed to include vocational education, the worthy use of leisure, and many elective courses. High-quality college preparation could be reserved for a minority of students in a track of challenging courses that now feature AP and honors.

Over time, the chasm between secondary and postsecondary education in the United States has grown greater than that in many other industrialized nations (Clark, 1985), but before the development of comprehensive high schools, U.S. colleges and universities did play an important role in influencing high school curriculum. In 1900, for example, the College Board set uniform standards for each academic subject and issued a syllabus to help high school students prepare for college entrance subject-matter examinations. Soon after, the University of California began to accredit high schools to make sure that their curricula were adequate for university preparation. As the number of high schools grew rapidly, however, universities could no longer do accreditation. After the number of postsecondary institutions expanded greatly, the regional high school accrediting associations split from higher education accreditation to lessen the workload, but doing so de-emphasized K–16 alignment.

Moreover, in the years after World War II, the notion of academic standards shared across the sectors vanished. "Aptitude" tests like the SAT replaced subject-matter standards for college admission, and secondary schools placed more emphasis on elective courses in nonacademic areas. Today, K–12 faculty and college faculty may belong to the same discipline-based professional organizations, but they rarely meet to discuss curricular alignment. K–12 policymakers and higher education policymakers cross paths even less often. It was not until 1982 that the Carnegie Foundation organized the first national meeting ever held between K–12 state school superintendents and college presidents to discuss the growing chasm between them (Stocking, 1985, p. 258). Many groups mediate between high schools and colleges, but they have competing agendas that tend to work against curricular alignment. The number and influence of mediating groups, such as the College Board, Educational Testing Service (ETS), and American College Testing Program (ACT), is, for Stocking, an indicator of the "amount of disorder and confusion that has grown through the years in the relationship between the school and the university in America" (p. 263).

Today the only nationally aligned standards effort across the sectors is the AP program—a stalactite that extends from universities, which dictate the course syllabus and exam. The International Baccalaureate (IB) program attempts to align secondary and postsecondary curriculum, but its scope is limited. Better high school students are becoming more closely aligned with higher education through AP and IB, but the weaker students are becoming more disconnected. Beyond these programs, there are no major efforts to provide curricular coherence and sequencing across secondary schools (Conley 2005). Nor has anyone proposed a conception of liberal education that relates the academic content of the secondary schools to the first two years of college. Instead, students face an eclectic academic muddle in grades 10–14 (Orrill, 2000) until they select a college major.

Thus the high school curriculum remains unmoored from the freshman and sophomore college curriculum and from any continuous vision of liberal education that would help students prepare for college coursework. For example, in California, "literature" is the focus of high school English course work for college preparation. But the initial community college courses focus upon grammar and writing, while the University of California stresses rhetoric. Nationally, the policymaking for K–16 has been more concerned with access to postsecondary education than with the academic preparation and college knowledge needed to complete a postsecondary degree or certificate. Access, rather than preparation, is also the theme of many of the professionals who mediate between the high schools and the colleges, as discussed previously.

Teacher Preparation

Also important to the evolution of the disjunctures has been postsecondary teacher preparation, where the linkage of teacher education programs and the K–12 sector has weakened over time. Elementary teachers were originally prepared in two-year postsecondary normal schools—normal meaning according to rule, model, or pattern. In 1910, there were 264 normal schools enrolling 132,000 students (Dunham 1969). The next development was from a normal school for elementary teachers to a teachers college to prepare secondary teachers as well. These institutions were linked to K–12 schools, and interactions across K–16 levels were frequent.

But as demands for increasing higher education grew, teachers colleges expanded functions and enrollment to become multipurpose state colleges. This growth caused recruitment of arts and sciences professors who sought higher academic prestige. Education schools or departments were typically viewed by the colleges' more diverse faculties as having low prestige. The final step was for the former normal college to become a university lacking close contact with K–12 teachers and students except those enrolled in the education school. As institutions of higher education—including teacher education programs themselves—detached from K–12, secondary school students increasingly failed to receive clear signals about college placement exams and about what first-year university students need to know in order to be prepared. Western Michigan University is an example of this institutional evolution. Founded in 1903 as a normal school, it became Western State Teachers College in 1927, Western Michigan College of Education in 1941, and then Western Michigan University in 1957 with 18,500 students in 1969 served by 900 faculty members. The first doctoral degrees were conferred in 1968.

Thus many former normal schools have become broad-access institutions that typically admit all qualified applicants, but use placement tests for first-year students to preserve standards. Secondary school students know that it is easy to get in, but know little about placement tests and curricular demands (Kirst & Venezia, 2004). An historical irony of this evolution is that postsecondary institutions established to prepare teachers to follow standards no longer communicate their own standards to teachers at all.

Community Colleges

Just as teachers colleges moved away from K–12 education over the past century, community colleges have distanced themselves from secondary schools. Today, over 45 percent of undergraduates attend a community college, an increase of 10 percent in the last decade (Marcus, 2005). This number has been increasing because of the heavy use of community colleges in fast-growing states like California, Texas, and Florida. California, for example, enrolls two-thirds of its college freshmen in the community college system (Hayward et al., 2004).

Originally, community colleges were funded like public schools with mostly local support, state supplements, and no tuition. In California, community colleges originated as part of the local K–12 system and were considered 13th and 14th grades. For some students, however, the four-year systems dictated much of their curricula in order to facilitate transfer (Callan, 1997). It was not until 1950 that community colleges across the nation began to have their own governing boards, and some were termed junior colleges. Between 1950 and 1970, the number of community colleges more than doubled and enrollment increased from 217,000 to 1,630,000. Between 1969 and 1974, community college enrollment increased by 174 percent contrasted to 47 percent for four-year institutions (Callan, 1997).

This growth was accompanied by a much-expanded mission and a loss of interaction with and focus on secondary education. The colleges expanded their mission to vocational education and community service. New and neglected populations beyond recent high school graduates were added, including displaced housewives, immigrants, older adults, and laid-off industrial workers. The comprehensive community college sent fewer and less clear signals to high school students about necessary academic preparation and skills needed to obtain vocational certificates. The impact of this detachment from secondary education has been profound, with many students entering community college unprepared for its demands. For example, 95 percent of first-time students enrolled in Baltimore City Community Colleges (BCCC) in the fall of 2000 required remediation in math, English, and reading (Abell Foundation, 2002). Nationally, about 60 percent of students entering community colleges require remediation, a major risk factor for noncompletion of degree or certificate programs (Adelman, 1999). Of all the English and math courses offered at the community college, 29 percent and 32 percent, respectively, are remedial (Cohen & Brawer, 2003). The majority of the students enrolled in these remedial courses (60 percent) are of traditional college age and enter the college directly after high school. This implies that the high level of remediation is not just a result of having to refresh the skills of individuals who have been out of school for a while, but also of having to teach skills that were not received in high school. Increasingly, four-year institutions transfer their remediation to community colleges. Ten states currently discourage four-year universities from offering remedial education by not providing state funding (Jenkins & Boswell, 2002).

Compounding this remediation problem is the fact that many of the students who enter community colleges today fit the characteristics of those who are less likely to have access to college information and preparation. Community colleges serve a large proportion of low-income, ethnic minority, and first-generation college students (Bueschel, 2004). According to Stanford's Bridge Project, students from lower SES levels and ethnic minority students are less like to receive college counseling, be placed in college-preparation courses, and obtain information about college admissions and placement (Kirst & Venezia, 2004).

The lack of college preparation and information possessed by students entering community college is reflected in low transfer and degree completion rates. Although 71 percent of beginning community college students plan to obtain a bachelor's degree, only about 25 percent transfer to a four-year school (Bradburn & Hurst, 2001). Several studies demonstrate that students who enter community colleges and seek a four-year degree have much lower completion rates than students who proceed directly to a four-year school (Cabrera, Burkum, & La Nasa, 2005). Whereas 63 percent of students attending a four-year school earn a bachelor's degree, only 18 percent of those who begin at a community college do so (Wellman, 2002).

Despite low transfer and completion rates, community colleges continue to be an attractive option because of their proximity to students' residence, low enrollment fees, and "open door" policy with few entrance standards for admitting students. Unfortunately, students often mistake the open door policy to mean that the college has few academic standards. High school students often believe that they are free to enter any community-college-level courses they choose. (Rosenbaum, 2001). However, community colleges often use placement exams for specialties like nursing as well as for general subjects. Stanford's Bridge Project found that most secondary school students going to community colleges were unaware of college placement standards and thought their minimal high school graduation standards were adequate preparation (Kirst, Venezia, & Antonio, 2004). High school students view community college as a souped-up high school, even though community colleges must align their courses to four-year transfer standards. Most beginning students do not even learn that they need to take a placement exam until they enter the community college (Bueschel, 2004; Kirst & Venezia, 2004). High school counseling for prospective community college students is particularly weak. They are not told that their high school achievement may increase the amount of time it will take for them to finish transfer requirements, thus decreasing their chances of ever completing college. In short, the colleges that are closest to high school students have stepped as far away from them, with respect to academic preparation, as any four-year institution.

Governance

Agencies governing high schools and postsecondary institutions have evolved along with the institutions themselves. From 1950 to 1980, higher education grew so dramatically that the need for increased state coordination became a priority. In 1940, the majority of states did not have a higher education governing, coordinating, or planning agency with responsibility for all public higher education. By 1979 all states had such an agency (Richardson et al., 1999). In 1940, 70 percent of public campuses had their own board, but by 1976, only 30 percent did. State subsystems developed as branch campuses of major public universities, and as a way to govern former normal schools that had been under state boards of education. But these postsecondary statewide agencies were not linked with K–12 governance or policymaking. New higher education state bureaucracies operated in isolation from their K–12 counterparts as regulations grew from 1960 to 1980 at both levels. Richardson et al. state that a "1969 study of 12 large states found little political or budget conflict between K–12 and postsecondary education. The two levels basically ignored each other and proceeded in their separate ways" (p. 9).

In addition, the structure and organization of state legislative committees responsible for education traditionally reinforce the divide between K–12 and postsecondary education. Georgia and New York have separate K–12 and higher education committees in both houses, while Oregon and Florida have committees that oversee both (in both houses). Florida does have K–20 committees, and it will be important to learn from their work over time. Having separate bodies makes policymaking and appropriating funds across sectors very difficult. Appropriations committees are of crucial importance, and they usually have different subcommittees, making it virtually impossible to change the status quo. Higher education governance structures, in general, can be a major impediment to K–16 reform. The variation in state higher education governance is quite large. Some states, such as California, have three tiers, while Georgia has a single Board of

Regents governing community colleges through research universities. The ways these bodies interact with each other, and with K–12, depend on the history and culture of each state.

In the 1970s, several states, including Idaho, Massachusetts, Pennsylvania, South Dakota, and Virginia tried to bridge the K–16 gap through gubernatorially appointed secretaries of education. The positions were created with the expectation that centralized, state-level leadership for K–12 and higher education could better coordinate and integrate education policy, including such areas as teacher education. After 25 years, however, none of these states' K–16 system goals and policies are as aligned as they were originally intended. As an example, Oregon tried to improve K–14 educational pathways by placing the community colleges under the state board of education. But Oregon's state board makes policy for K–12 schools and community colleges separately. Oregon's promising competency-based exit exam, the Certificate of Advanced Mastery (CAM) for 11th- and 12th-grade students, is not fully developed, and the community colleges have not been enthusiastic about incorporating CAM in placement decisions. Once again, we find that more alignment of K–16 policy does not necessarily occur within a more consolidated governance structure.

Coordination Across the Sectors

Efforts to coordinate the sectors through legislation and voluntary alliances have also developed During the 1990s, several states attempted to coordinate the sectors through legislation and through voluntary councils. For example, in Florida the legislature passed implementing legislation in 1999 that established a unified, seamless, K–20 education system. This included creating a single, statewide K–20 board of education with broad authority. Meanwhile, a restructured Florida Department of Education is implementing a unified K–20 accountability system. The state is also integrating its extensive K–12 and postsecondary education student unit record systems. Policy analysis has improved in Florida since this unified system was created. With centralized student-unit records, the state board identified school districts where a disproportionately low number of students were enrolling in the state's four-year colleges or needed remedial education upon enrollment. The state analyzed high school and middle college course-taking patterns and recognized that students in these districts were not enrolling in a rigorous sequence of high school courses (Venezia et al., 2005).

In the wake of the failure of attempts to integrate the sectors through imposed systemic reform in the 1970s, several states established more voluntary K–16 linkages in the 1990s. These initiatives have made some incremental progress, but they depend for longevity on the next generation of committed leaders from both levels. The most ambitious of these efforts are the Maryland and Georgia P–16 councils (Kirst & Venezia, 2004). The goal of these councils is to profoundly change the ways in which schools and colleges operate, not just to add new "early-intervention-style" programs. In order to bring separately governed and financed systems together on issues of mutual interest, a voluntary P–16 council must have access to key leaders—including policymakers, communities, business and labor—and state policy levers (e.g., accountability provisions or shared student level data). While still evolving, Maryland's and Georgia's P–16 councils have put much more effort into improving teacher education than improving student pathways from secondary to postsecondary education. Recently, the Georgia statewide P–16 council began developing academic content standards for the first two years of college that are linked to the state's K–12 standards.

It is too early to reach a final verdict on these voluntary alliances in Maryland and Georgia. A major question is whether they will survive the statewide leaders who instigated them. Will ad hoc, voluntarily adopted institutional policies for admissions and placement lead to sustained changes and improved rates of postsecondary success? Richardson et al. (1999) raise the essential issue about whether governance structures will be effective apart from specific leaders:

> Certainly, leadership matters, but even good leaders should not be expected to achieve consistent results in the presence of a system design that inhibits institutional collaboration and system synergy. Leadership can make a system perform better or worse than its structural design, but it cannot compensate for badly designed systems or mismatched policy environments. (p. 17)

The evolution of governance leaves unanswered the question of what types of state and regional structures or arrangements will enhance K–16 deliberations, interaction, policy integration, and student outcomes. Clearly, policymakers, faculty, students, and parents across the K–16 spectrum need to be brought together. Given these lofty objectives, it is useful to examine the evolution of the most integrated education policy structure in the United States—the New York Board of Regents.

The New York Board of Regents was designed in 1784 to provide K–16 integration, and it is the broadest educational governance body in the nation. The Regents' scope of authority includes public and private elementary, secondary, and higher education; the licensed professions, including medicine, nursing, law, and accounting; libraries, museums, historical societies; and public television and radio stations. The New York Regents Exams began in the 19th century and have exerted a powerful K–16 influence. Regents are selected by the legislature for five-year terms, with each legislator having one vote. Consequently, the Regents are not an integral part of the governor's executive branch and lack independent fiscal powers. The legislative selection method provides some political insulation, but also a remoteness and inaccessibility from the rest of state government. In many ways, the Regents are a fourth branch of New York State government.

However, the birth of the State University of New York (SUNY) system in the 1960s led to a dramatic decline in the Regents' attention to, and impact on, higher education. All colleges and universities outside of the City University of New York (CUNY) system in New York City—public, nonprofit independent, and for-profit proprietary—are members of the SUNY system; SUNY has budget authority over the state's higher education appropriations. Every eight years, the Regents develop a Higher Education Plan that is subject to the governor's approval, but recently it has not been viewed as a K–16 policy that links the levels much more tightly. SUNY and CUNY are not tightly linked by the Regents plan (Bracco, 1997).

With its current disproportionate focus on K–12 issues, the Regents have retained one mechanism that aligns secondary and postsecondary education: the Regents Exams. When the exams were first conceived, student performance on these high school end-of-course-based exams was a factor in university admission and financial aid eligibility. But most New York financial aid is now need based. As the Regents exams' purpose evolved to certify minimum standards for high school completion—and the SUNY system's independence increased—Regents exams were used less frequently for SUNY admissions decisions. SUNY instead uses the SAT as an admissions factor. The Regents exams do still, however, provide high school students with information about postsecondary academic content standards. Regents' syllabi also provide a higher-education-oriented underpinning to high school course content in New York. Regents' exams include essays and open-ended questions that are closer to higher education standards than typical exams. Moreover, CUNY uses the K–12 Regents exams as its own placement exam, a policy that can reduce remediation by sending clear signals about college standards to high school students.

The lesson from New York's experience is that a consolidated K–16 governance structure can help align K–16 academic content standards, but structural consolidation does not necessarily lead to policy alignment (Callan et al., 2005). In particular, states need to pay attention to the authorities, particularly the budget authority, given to a K–16 consolidated structure in order to reach common goals of higher enrollment rates, lower remediation rates, and higher persistence rates.

If governance alone cannot bridge the K–12–postsecondary gap, what can? We surely cannot expect change to be effected spontaneously from within. The two levels of education have so little social contact among faculty, administrators, and policymakers that there is unlikely to be much social pressure to change the current condition. Perhaps K–16 governance mechanisms such as Florida's can bring K–12 and postsecondary education together in a way that will lead to social incentives to move forward. But most likely, we will have to rely on policy levers and governance to move toward closing the gap. The rest of this chapter recommends and explores possibilities for closing the gap and solving related problems.

NEW POLICY LEVERS AND GOVERNANCE TO OVERCOME THE DISJUNCTURES

Policy Levers

If K–16 reform is to establish common ground between K–12 and postsecondary education, it must extend well beyond local or regional collaborative efforts. It must reach farther than joint meetings, new memoranda of understanding, or statewide course numbering systems. And it must be more substantial than tinkering with the organization of schools on the one hand, or of colleges and universities on the other. Rigorous K–16 reform must change the public policy environment—the policies that currently create and reinforce the chasm between K–12 and postsecondary education—in ways that improve how students make the transition from high school to college-level education.

There are four crucial policy levers that can bring the systems together to enhance the college knowledge of secondary systems and enhance college completion.

1. *Alignment of coursework and assessments.* States need to align the content of their courses and assessments from the early grades through grade 14 or later.
2. *State finance.* Statewide goals for grades K–16 should be integrated into state education finance systems.
3. *Data systems.* States must create high-quality data systems that span the K–16 continuum.
4. *Accountability.* States need to connect their accountability systems for K–12 and postsecondary education.

Unfortunately, we know very little about how to improve these four policy levers. Better integrated K–16 governance can help stimulate these policies, but new incentives are also essential. Research needs to focus upon the four policy levers and how governance can assist these outcomes. Strong leadership will be needed to reframe the K–16 issue in order to build supportive public opinion. In the meantime, we can look to existing state policies to help us understand how these levers might work.[2]

---

2. The next four sections on the policy levers are derived from the collective work of Andrea Venezia, Pat Callan, Michael Usdan, Joni Finney, and Michael Kirst as part of a project at the National Center for Higher Education and Public Policy.

Alignment of curriculum and assessments. Curriculum and assessments need to be aligned from the early grades to at least the sophomore year of college, in order to improve students' college preparedness. California has attempted such alignment. The California State University (CSU) has worked extensively with California's K–12 school system to overcome bureaucratic, procedural, and political problems and to develop test items that will indicate to students whether or not they are ready for college-level work. The CSU's Early Assessment Program (EAP) is a collaborative effort between the CSU, the California State Board of Education (SBE), and the California Department of Education (CDE). EAP was established to provide high school students with information to measure their readiness for college-level mathematics and English in their junior year and to help them improve their skills during their senior year. The impetus for the program was the dismal remediation rate within the CSU; it was found that over 60 percent of the approximately 40,000 first-time freshmen admitted to the CSU require remedial education in English, mathematics, or both. The EAP's goal is to ensure that California high school graduates who enter the CSU are prepared to enroll and succeed in college-level courses. The criteria specifying that students admitted to CSU institutions must complete a college preparatory curriculum and earn a B or higher grade point average in high school were not working; clearly, true curricular and assessment alignment needed to occur. Representatives from the K–12 and CSU sectors worked together to augment the K–12 California Standards Test (CST) with mathematics and English items that measure college-ready knowledge and skills. In mathematics, the items assess whether students have a deep enough knowledge of algebra and geometry. In English, a 45-minute essay requirement was established to assess student readiness for college writing. Similarly, the K–12 English proficiency standards were aligned with the CST standards in English-language arts, but focused more attention on requiring students to demonstrate their reading and writing skills. To help students prepare better in English, K–12 and postsecondary educators developed a 12th-grade Expository Reading and Writing Course that high schools could pilot and adopt. It was aligned with California's content standards and geared toward preparing students for college-level English, focusing on analytical, expository, and argumentative reading and writing.

If this effort succeeds, students entering the CSU will be better prepared, will need fewer remedial classes, and will graduate in a timely fashion. In addition, the data generated will allow educators from both levels to understand students' progress from K–12 through the CSU system and analyze the effectiveness of the policy changes. Although this work is promising, its impact on California's public schools will be limited because the state's community colleges have not participated. A pilot study, however, is under way in community colleges in the Los Angeles area. The California experience should be studied, and similar attempts at alignment should be undertaken in other states.

State finance. Statewide goals for grades K–16 should be integrated into state education finance systems. State finance is a second necessary element of K–16 reform. Most current state finance systems perpetuate the divide between K–12 and postsecondary education by creating two separate funding streams. They lack incentives that would promote and support K–16 reform, and in many cases they undermine such reform.

Although no state has implemented this concept fully, Oregon is exploring the development of a K–20 finance model. The Oregon Business Council (OBC) described the state's education problems as follows: "Our current system is composed of four distinct sectors, budgeted and governed separately. There are no consistent [high school] exit and [postsecondary] entrance standards for students. Student movement through the system is organized by time rather than by achievement." The OBC concluded that "A unified and transparent budget linking funding to pupil need, progress, and attainment is the best tool for understanding key issues and changing system behavior" (Wyse, 2005; see also Oregon Education Roundtable, 2006). OBC staff analyzed both sectors' 2002–2003 expenditures of state and local funds as though they were all in one budget, and ranked those expenditures from high to low. The investments varied across grade and degree, with community colleges receiving the least state aid and K–12 receiving the most. The OBC consequently recommended to the governor that Oregon adopt a Pre-K–20 governing, budgeting, and management reform plan. Budgets would be based on per-student costs for the education level, or for the services provided. Similarly, pupil progress and outcomes would be established for every education level and service provided. Finally, the system would be transparent in terms of how schools spend the funds and how well students perform within each institution. The OBC and other state entities are working to develop a new education finance model; this is a work in progress. If Oregon succeeds with this model, it should be able to reduce financial inefficiencies and territorialism between the sectors, in addition to achieving the stated goals of improving student movement throughout the education pipeline and providing a more transparent system of financing. The state's efforts might provide a good model for other states to follow; policymakers should observe Oregon closely (Venezia et al., 2005).

A complementary issue is the state provision of funds to institutions or to students for financial aid as a leverage point for K–16 reform. Broad-access institutions do not usually provide incentives for students to complete their coursework or certificate programs. State attempts to establish such incentives, such as providing postsecondary institutions with additional funds for students who graduate, have not always succeeded because institutions that admit more students who are well prepared for college usually benefit more from such funding mechanisms than institutions that serve populations that are not as prepared. As a result, this type of funding system provides incentives to institutions to limit college access to those who are well prepared. In order to improve access, states should consider programs that address improved college readiness for all students as well as financial need.

Indiana's Twenty-First Century Scholars program is viewed as a national model for combining financial aid with precollege access intervention. Initiated in 1990, it was the first state program to provide college tuition costs for middle school students who qualify for the federal free and reduced lunch program. The Scholars Program targets students in the eighth grade and provides support services and a guarantee of grant aid to students who complete a pledge. The pledge requires that students finish high school, maintain at least a C grade point average, remain drug- and alcohol-free, apply for college and financial aid, and enroll in an Indiana postsecondary institution within two years of high school. In return, Indiana (1) pays tuition and fees for each Scholar (after other financial aid awards) at a public institution in Indiana (or contributes a similar portion for tuition at an independent college), (2) provides support services for the Scholars, and (3) disseminates additional information about postsecondary education to the Scholars and encourages them to pursue a college preparatory curriculum. A recent report describes how the program works for both the state and students:

> The Scholars program supplements the state grants Scholars receive as a consequence of their aid eligibility. Most students who received Scholars awards also had full need, so their normal state grants were high, and the additional award amounts were relatively modest. This pattern constrains the cost of the program for the state and provides an added incentive to fund other state grant programs. (Thomson, 2006, p. 7)

The Scholars program provides an incentive for students to complete a rigorous course of study in high school. It pays for at least 80 percent of the approved tuition and fees, but if a student has completed a more rigorous diploma—a Core 40 Diploma—that student receives

90 percent of the tuition and fees. All of the tuition and fees are covered if a student completes the most rigorous diploma pathway—the Academic Honors Diploma. Thus the program addresses financial needs and sends signals to students regarding academic preparation for high school. Overall, the Scholars Program succeeds in achieving its primary goal—to encourage low-income students to enroll in postsecondary education—and it has also had a positive impact on persistence and completion for students who earned two-year degrees.

Other initiatives to provide student financial incentives have been attempted in other states. In Georgia, the HOPE Scholarship provides funds for students who earn a B or better in the college preparatory track; the signal to students is clear, but the program has been criticized for primarily assisting economically well-off students. Along with integrated K–16 finance systems, such polices deserve more study and development in order to bridge the gap between the sectors.

Data systems. A third important element in K–16 reform is the development of data systems that can track student progress and the use of state funds from K–12 education to postsecondary education. Such a robust system is needed to determine the effectiveness of K–16 reforms in terms of student achievement, particularly since nearly 60 percent of undergraduates attend more than one institution, and one out of five goes to another state (Adelman, 2006). Currently, it is virtually impossible for most states to know if their efforts to improve student readiness for college are having an impact on college performance and completion. Although many states are working to improve their data systems, most are unable to link data from K–12 schools and postsecondary institutions. Eighteen states do not even collect data on high school students' course-taking patterns. In addition, community college data are generally not separated for traditional college-age students and older, returning students. Consequently, it is impossible to determine, as a measure of high school success, the degree-attainment rates of students who attend college right after high school. It is likewise impossible to identify and analyze success rates for students who enter college from the workforce. In short, without high-quality data systems that connect the education sectors, it is difficult—if not impossible—to assess needs accurately, identify where the most substantial problems are, gain traction for the work needed to find solutions, and evaluate ongoing reforms.

States do not have the data systems they need to support college success if they cannot answer the following kinds of questions:

- How do students who take college preparatory courses in high school perform in postsecondary education?
- How do students who pass (or earn a proficient score on) the state assessment perform in college?
- Considering those students who require remediation in college, what percentage took a college preparatory curriculum in high school?
- What happens to students who drop out of high school and try to reenter?
- What are the effects of precollege outreach programs on students' college readiness and success?
- What pedagogical approaches are common among teachers who consistently send well-prepared students to college?
- Given their students' performance in college, how can high schools change their curricula and instruction to improve student readiness for college?

Florida has developed a promising K–20 data system that will be able to answer some of these questions. It has a history of shared data on an ad hoc basis, but over the past several years, the State Department of Education has led the charge to connect formally all public databases using common student identifiers. The Office of K–20 Education's Information and Accountability Division oversees this work, which includes data on K–12 students; programs in all levels of postsecondary institution; assessment, financial aid, certification, facilities, and other systems across the K–20 spectrum; and employment and continuing education outcomes. By creating this linked data system, Florida hopes to work toward common standards, procedures, and quality assurance; eliminate duplicated functions and services; and establish a K–20 accountability system. In addition, Florida should be able to assess student needs throughout the pipeline as well as identifying and addressing problems in college preparedness. Other states need to begin to study the Florida example, and research is needed there to inform us on how well the data system is working.

Accountability. As a final policy lever, states need to connect their accountability systems for K–12 and postsecondary education. The public reporting of student progress and achievement across educational levels is crucial to the development of an effective educational system. Once a high-quality K–16 data system is in place, states can then start to hold systems and institutions accountable for student learning. This can begin to establish the incentives needed for all public education systems in every state to meet students' educational needs. Currently, accountability systems are usually focused on K–12 and rarely include postsecondary indicators. Simply requiring the reporting of K–16 data from educational institutions back to state departments of education will not suffice in creating effective accountability across the systems. High schools and postsecondary institutions need information about how to use the data to improve instruction, tracking, counseling, and many other variables to improve postsecondary attainment. From the K–12 perspective, high schools need to be able to use data about their graduates' performance in college to improve problematic areas, such as curricula, instruction, and grading. Effective and fair accountability systems, connected to positive incentives, can encourage the development of school cultures that are focused on results in order to make positive changes for students.

One of the most important, and difficult, accountability issues that states must tackle is creating the motivation and pay-off for systems, institutions, and people to change in ways that tie the systems together. As Haycock (2002) writes, there are two basic ways to create such incentives:

> The first, and probably the most popular, is to put dollars on the table for joint K–16 work . . . . This approach has the advantage of getting lots of activity underway quickly. But it has several disadvantages as well, not the least of which is that these activities tend to remain at the fringes of institutional life and institutional priorities. And when the dollars dry up . . . [author's ellipsis] the activity goes away.
>
> The alternative is to approach this issue through the lens of accountability. The core idea is simple: policymakers should design their accountability systems for both K–12 and higher education to include outcomes that each system cannot possibly deliver alone. K–12, for example, might be held accountable . . . for assuring that all of its secondary teachers have deep and substantial knowledge in the subject areas they are teaching. Similarly, higher education can be held accountable for decreasing the number of minority freshmen requiring remediation. (p. 16)

Although money helps motivate, the key is to avoid programmatic allocations that run into institutional resistance and keep K–16 reform on the edges of institutions and systems. There is little incentive, for example, for an institution of higher education to work with K–12 to reduce the number of students who require remediation, because those students bring with them valuable state and local funds. One strategy is to "use the 'push' of a reconstructed accountability system together with the 'pull' of recaptured funding for institutional or departmental priorities" (Haycock, 2002, p. 18). Moreover, accountability systems need to be designed to avoid problems currently found in many states' accountability systems, such as a focus on a single institution at the expense of systemic problems, a lack of a specific change agenda, and a lack of urgency. Designers of K–16 coordination policy should think carefully about crafting more integrated accountability systems with incentives that encourage the sectors to work with rather than against each other. Accountability mechanisms can be paired with financial inducements to work together as effective incentives for cooperation across the sectors.

In designing accountability systems across sectors, Florida is again leading the way. The state is developing a K–20 accountability system related to student achievement, seamless articulation and maximum access, a skilled workforce and economic development, and high-quality, efficient services. The system will measure return on investment, effectiveness of the system in educating students, effectiveness of the sectors in promoting student achievement, and effectiveness of schools and institutions in educating students. The elements of the system are statutory framework, mission and goals, measures and performance standards, public reporting, performance incentives, intervention and consequences, and linkages between the accountability plan and the budget. When the system is completely implemented, 10 percent of the education sectors' funding will be conditional on performance.

Ultimately, college persistence and graduation must be central outcomes for state accountability systems. Each state's system will be grounded in the unique and diverse educational needs of its population, the mix of educational institutions in the state, and the history and context of its educational enterprise. Developing the right systems for each state will require careful and informed collaboration across the sectors, the kind of collaboration that governance reforms can stimulate.

Governance Reforms

The development of K–16 governance commissions that include both K–12 and postsecondary leaders and that build upon the four policy levers discussed above can be an important step toward developing necessary reforms. These bodies, however, should be charged with specific responsibilities, provided the requisite resources, have enough influence and authority to make real change, and be held accountable for performance. State agency collaboration—both in terms of the content of work and the organizational structures supporting that work—is essential, and having components of K–16 reform in statute appears to be useful but not sufficient for creating change.

A K–16 entity, however, is in itself not sufficient to engage the depth of reform that is needed. In fact, state-level K–16 structures have sometimes deflected attention from policy changes; sometimes they have exacerbated tensions between school and college leaders, and sometimes they have become discussion forums rather than drivers of change. Likewise, some reform efforts in many states focus on technical issues, such as those involved in alignment. Some states are, for example, analyzing the relationships between their high school exit assessments and their college entrance and placement exams. While this is very important work, it is insufficient absent action to address the organizational, political, and finance issues that are often the real obstacles to alignment between the sectors.

In short, if states do not accomplish substantive changes in each of the four areas outlined above, they should not be surprised to find that their K–12 and postsecondary education systems continue to operate in separate orbits. Engaging in these kinds of reform necessarily involves political challenges; every state undertaking such reform will struggle with such issues as how to get the governor or the appropriate legislative committees involved in reform, and how to sustain the reform after leaders leave office. Each state's responses to these challenges must be unique. For example, a state with a K–16 structure in statute, and with a governor leading the charge, might have a greater ability to develop and implement necessary reforms than a state with ad hoc, grant-funded K–16 projects. In Georgia, Governors Miller and Barnes successfully used the bully pulpit and other public means to create state and regional P–16 councils and to charge them with specific duties. On the flip side, states with more entrepreneurial, project-based environments such as Oregon might be able to achieve more substantial changes than states that focus mostly on governance per se.

Current research does not provide a lot of guidance on effective K–16 structure, policymaking, or outcomes. There are several studies indicating that different organizational and governance forms do have an impact upon higher education politics and policy (Nicholson-Crotty & Meier, 2003; Knott & Payne, 2001). However, this research has not been extended to K–16 issues (McLendon & Heller, 2003). Such research should be encouraged as governance reforms designed to link the sectors emerge.

CONCLUSION

In sum, a profound organizational, political, and cultural chasm persists in most states between the governance systems of K–12 and higher education. The two sectors continue to operate in separate orbits and to live apart in separate professional worlds, associations, and networks. As a result, many students, particularly those entering broad-access institutions, are coming to college unprepared and at risk of failure. These issues lack an immediate audience or constituency and remain largely invisible, falling between the cracks of separate governance systems. Overarching governance entities might help to strengthen the multiple pathways to and through postsecondary education, and improve college success rates for a larger segment of the population. As has been shown, research needs to uncover more powerful interventions that address core incentives and the cultural separation of the sectors and that help states design more effective approaches.

REFERENCES

Abell Foundation. (2002). *Baltimore city community colleges at the crossroads.* Baltimore, MD: Author.

ACT, Inc. (2003). English and writing. In *Act research: ACT national curriculum survey* (pp. 7–19). Iowa City, IA: Author. Retrieved January 23, 2007 from http://www.act.org/news/releases/2003/pdf/intro.pdf.

Adelman, C. (1999). *Answers in the tool box: Academic intensity, attendance patterns, and bachelor's degree attainment.* Washington, DC: U.S. Department of Education.

Adelman, C. (2006). *Academic momentum to complete degrees.* Washington, DC: U.S. Department of Education.

Bowen, W. G., Kurzweil, M. A., and Tobin, E. M. (2005). *Equity and excellence in American higher education.* Charlottesville, VA: University of Virginia Press.

Bracco, K. R. (1997). New York politics and the funding of higher education. In P. Callan and J. E. Finney (Eds.), *Public and private financing of higher education* (pp. 198–228). Phoenix, AZ: Oryx Press.

Bradburn, E. M., and Hurst, V. (2001). Community college transfer rates to 4-year institutions using alternative definitions of transfer. *Education Statistics Quarterly 3*(3), 119–125.

Bueschel, A. (2004). The missing link: The role of community colleges. In M. Kirst and A. Venezia (Eds.), *From high school to college: Improving opportunities for success in postsecondary education* (pp. 252–284). San Francisco: Jossey-Bass.

Cabrera, A. F., Burkum, K. R., and La Nasa, S. M. (2005). Pathways to a four-year degree: Determinants of transfer and degree completion. In A. Seidman (Ed.), *College student retention: A formula for student success* (pp. 155–214). Boulder, CO: Praeger.

Callan, P. M. (1997). Stewards of opportunity: America's public community colleges. *Daedalus 126*(4), 95–112.

Callan, P. M., Venezia, A., Finney, J. E., Kirst, M. W., and Usdan, M. D. (2005). *Claiming common ground: Policymaking for improving college readiness and success.* San Jose, CA: National Center for Higher Education and Public Policy.

Clark, B. (1985). *The School and the university.* Berkeley: University of California Press.

Cohen, A. M., and Brawer, F. (2003). *The American community college.* San Francisco: Jossey-Bass.

Conley, D. (2005). *College knowledge.* San Francisco: Jossey-Bass.

Committee for Economic Development. (2005). *Cracks in the education pipeline: A business leader's guide to higher education reform.* Washington, DC: Author.

Dunham, E. A. (1969). *Colleges of the forgotten American.* New York: McGraw-Hill.

Haycock, K. (2002). Why is K–16 collaboration essential to educational equity? In *Gathering momentum: Building the learning connection between schools and colleges. Conference proceedings from the Learning Connection conference*, 8. San Jose, CA: Hechinger Institute on Education and the Media, Institute for Educational Leadership, and National Center for Public Policy and Higher Education.

Hayward, G. C., Jones, D. P., McGuinness, A. C., and Timar, A. (2004). *Ensuring access with quality to California's community colleges.* San Jose, CA: National Center for Public Policy and Higher Education.

Henry, G. T. and Rubenstein, R. (2002). Paying for grades. *Journal of Policy Management and Analysis 204*, 24–96.

Immerwahr, J. (1999). *Doing comparatively well: Why the public loves higher education and criticizes K–12.* San Jose, CA: National Center for Higher Education and Public Policy.

Jenkins, D., and Boswell, K. (2002). *State policies on community college remedial education: Findings from a national survey.* Denver, CO: Education Commission of the States, Center for Community College Policy.

Kazis, R., Vargas, J., and Hoffman, N. (2004). *Double the numbers: Increasing postsecondary credentials for underrepresented youth.* Cambridge, MA: Harvard Education Press.

Kirst, M. W. (2001). *Overcoming the high school senior slump: New education policies.* Washington, DC: Institute for Educational Leadership.

Kirst, M. W., and Venezia, A. (2004). *From high school to college: Improving opportunities for success in postsecondary education.* San Francisco: Jossey-Bass.

Kirst, M. W., Venezia, A., and Antonio, A. L. (2004). What have we learned, and where do we go next? In M. W. Kirst and A. Venezia (Eds.), *From high school to college: Improving opportunities for success in postsecondary education* (pp. 285–319). San Francisco: Jossey-Bass.

Knott, J. H., and Payne, A. A. (2001). *The impact of state governance structure on higher education resources* (IGPA Working Paper No. 93). Urbana-Champaign, IL: University of Illinois.

Marcus, J. (2005). CUNY sheds reputation as tutor U. *National Center for Public Policy and Education CrossTalk 13*(2), 1.

Maeroff, G. I., Callan, P. M., and Usdan, M. D., eds. (2001). *The learning connection.* New York: Teachers College Press.

McLendon, M. K., and Heller, D. E. (2003). High school to college transition policy: Barriers to conducting cross state comparisons. Paper presented at the annual meeting of the American Educational Research Association, New Orleans, LA.

Nicholson-Crotty, J., and Meier, K. J. (2003). Politics, structure, and public policy: The case of higher education. *Educational Policy 17*(1), 80–97.

Oregon Education Roundtable. (2006). *What cost, what results for PreK–20?* Portland, OR: Author.

Orrill, Robert. (2000). Grades 11–14: The heartland or wasteland of American education. Unpublished paper, Woodrow Wilson Institute, Washington, DC.

Powell, A., Farrar, E., and Cohen, D. K. (1985). *The shopping mall high school.* Boston: Houghton-Mifflin.

Ravitch, D. E. (2000). *Left back: A century of failed school reforms.* New York: Simon and Shuster.

Richardson, R. C., Bracco, K., Callan, P., and Finney, J. (1999). *Designing state higher education systems for a new century.* Phoenix, AZ: Oryx Press.

Rosenbaum, J. E. (2001). *College for all.* New York: Russell Sage.

Schneider, B. (2003). Strategies for success: High school and beyond. In D. Ravitch (Ed.), *Brookings papers on education policy* 2003 (pp. 55–93). Washington, DC: Brookings Institution Press.

Stocking, C. (1985). The United States. In B. Clark (Ed.), *The school and the university* (pp. 239–263). Berkeley: University of California Press.

Symonds, W. (2005). America the uneducated. *Business Week,* November 21, 120–122.

Thomson, S. C. (2006). Indiana's 21st century scholars. *National Center for Public Policy and Education CrossTalk 14*(1), 7.

Timpane, P. M., and White, L. S., eds. (1998). *Higher education and school reform.* San Francisco: Jossey-Bass.

Tyack, D., and Cuban, L. (1995). *Tinkering towards utopia.* Cambridge, MA: Harvard University Press.

Venezia, A. (2000). Connecting California's K–12 and higher education systems: Challenges and opportunities. In Barr, Elizabeth, and Kirst, Michael (Eds), *Crucial issues in California education 2000: Are the reform pieces fitting together?* 153–176. Berkeley: Policy Analysis for California Education.

Venezia, A. P., Callan, M., Finney, J. E., Kirst, M. W., and Usdan, M. D. (2005). *The governance divide: A report on a four-state study on improving college readiness and success.* San Jose, CA: National Center for Higher Education and Public Policy.

Venezia, A., Kirst, M. W., and Antonio, A. L. (2003). *Betraying the college dream: How disconnected K–12 and postsecondary education systems undermine student aspirations.* Stanford, CA: Stanford Institute for Higher Education Research.

Wellman, J.V. (2002). *State policy and community college-baccalaureate transfer.* San Jose, CA: National Center for Public Policy and Higher Education.

Wyse, D. (2005). Oregon state policy dimensions for K–16 reform. Paper presented at a conference, State Policy for K–16 Reform, Racine, WI.

Across the Sectors: Commentary

Border Crossings: On the Relations Between the Major Age-Graded Education Systems in the United States

J. Lawrence Aber

Policy research in education takes so many forms, from the purely descriptive through the rigorously analytic and comparative to the experimental. The two chapters in this section fall clearly in that methodological middle ground, aspiring to rigorous analysis within and comparison across the major age-graded education systems here in the United States.

The system of reference of course, by virtue of historical primacy and sheer size, is the K–12 system. Barnett and Ackerman trace features of the articulation between the preschool "system" (if I may use the term loosely) and the K–12 system over the last 40 years. Kirst traces the articulation between K–12 and postsecondary education over the last 100 years.

COMMON THEMES AND UNIQUE CONTRIBUTIONS

As the attentive reader has no doubt already noticed, both of these chapters share many common themes (thanks to thoughtful editors and responsive authors). These include major policy issues of governance, structure, funding, curricula, standards and assessment, and research. The two overarching messages of each chapter are these: how historically and politically determined are the disjunctures between major age-graded education systems; and how profoundly challenging it is to productively, efficiently, and creatively manage and/or transcend these disjunctures, these boundary conditions—or what I'll refer to as the "border crossings" throughout the rest of this commentary.

Although it is Barnett and Ackerman who offer the metaphor of managing borders, both chapters describe why this must be and how this could be done. Indeed, among the most interesting features of both chapters is how chockablock full they are of examples of states that have invented a rich array of best practices to try to overcome the dysfunctional disjunctures between major age-graded systems.

In addition to their commonalities of theme and foci, each chapter possesses unique strengths. For instance, Barnett and Ackerman emphasize the potential role of "true" and

"natural" policy experiments in shaping early education policy and the influence of early education policy on elementary and secondary education policy. I find their case convincing and, if anything, a bit understated or underdeveloped. On the one hand, true experiments like the Abecedarian Project and the Perry Preschool Project served as existence proofs in the early childhood
sector that high quality early intervention programs could positively impact not only the future
education of low-income children but also other features of their developmental trajectories. On
the other hand, the original Westinghouse Study evaluation of the intermediate-term impact of
Head Start and the evaluation of the Comprehensive Child Development Program have served
as sobering reminders that if the programmatic focus is too diffuse and sustained follow-up isn't
practiced, then early childhood investments don't necessarily produce positive results. This history of the role of true and natural experiments in evaluating the effects of early intervention
have brought to the fore policy issues of program quality, fidelity of implementation, generalizability, and scalability. Early Head Start has reinforced what Head Start research started: the
need for and value of adherence to program-quality standards; and the need to evaluate rather than
assume the generalizability/adaptability of various program features across communities and cultures. The growth of state pre-K programs has directly taken on problems of scalability that the
Head Start movement identified but didn't solve.

Experiments in early education policy have important implications for K–12 policy. If K–12
experiments on reform interventions took their cue from the high-quality early childhood experiments, they would draw attention to issues of implementation and alignment among standards
and assessments, including assessments of instruction. They would thus force us to look directly
at instruction in ways that policy research primarily focused on K–12 education has tended not to.

The Kirst chapter's unique strength is its fine analysis of such issues as challenges to policy
integration across the K–12 and postsecondary systems, the potential levers of policy change, and the
role of public opinion and straight-up politics. At the risk of drawing too sharp a distinction, I suggest
that the Barnett and Ackerman chapter entails a relatively more rational/structural analysis of the
disjunctures between the early childhood and K–12 systems, while the Kirst chapter entails more of
a political/functional analysis of the disjunctures between the K–12 and postsecondary education systems. I choose to make this distinction in this way to point out that the chapters confound somewhat
the systems under study and the analytic approach. Ideally, the political dimensions of the early child-
hood/K–12 disjunctures could be more fully developed, and the potential for true and natural policy
experiments to address some of the K–12/postsecondary junctures could be more fully developed.

ADDITIONAL PERSPECTIVES AND FUTURE DIRECTIONS

Taken together, these chapters represent marked progress in the analysis of disjunctures between
major age-graded systems in the United States. It is my hope that by calling out a few common
themes across and unique contributions of these two chapters, I will encourage both these authors
and other scholars of comparative educational policy to read each other's work and strive toward
a more integrative framework of disjunctures writ large. I believe that such a framework may
prove valuable not only to further scholarship in this field, but to the utility of the existing and
future research to policymakers, policy advocates, systems executives, and other actors in worlds
bridging policy research and policy practice. Said another way, wouldn't it be great if we could
create new understandings of the (dis)articulation between these systems that help more children,
youth, and jurisdictions manage and successfully negotiate these tricky border crossings?

I begin with the assumption that there will probably never be a single education system
that extends from birth through to emergent adulthood. Even if historically, politically, or

organizationally possible, it would probably not be desirable. Society, jurisdictions, families, and individuals ask something unique from each of these age-graded systems. In part, that is because the border spats between the systems have grown up around true quantum shifts in the human organism's cognitive, social, emotional, and physical competencies. I am arguing that at least a part of the borders are a response to phylogenetically influenced ontogenetic differences in the developing human being. I'm trying not to make a reductionist, overly simplistic argument that human biology is organizational and policy destiny. I am trying to assert that the "subjects" of our education policy efforts, developing human beings, on average reach important natural "transition points" at certain ages and that the quantum changes represent a significant enough organizational challenge that it will make more sense to have age-graded educational systems for quite some time. Based on this assumption, the challenge is not to so fully integrate these systems that they become one. The challenge is to effectively manage successful border crossings. While both chapters are replete with excellent concrete critiques of the existing border conditions and with good specific ideas for reform, there are several missing elements to the discussion that are needed, in my opinion, to make further progress.

Values, Goals, Objectives

To my way of thinking, neither chapter has set out to identify an overarching set of societal values or of government or family goals and objectives to guide the actions and investments of the multiple actors needed to ensure successful border crossings over the three major segments of our system. Without articulated values, goals, and objectives, it is hard for actors to identify and evaluate the linkages that should be made across systems. Please understand me; I don't think we can "values-clarify" our way out of the problems we currently face in improving border crossings from one system to the next. I do think that an overarching framework of what we want *all three systems* to contribute will very likely improve deliberation and decision making at local, state, and national levels. While there are several potential candidates for such a framework, I don't have the room or expertise to lay them out in this commentary. Rather, I will direct the reader to one, both by way of example and because it has the great advantage of already serving to facilitate cross-border planning and change at state (e.g., New Mexico) and local (e.g., Nashville, TN; Providence, RI) levels.

The framework, developed on the basis of both research and values analysis, was developed by a nonprofit, nonpartisan think-and-action tank called the Forum for Youth Investment (FYI; http://www.forumforyouthinvestment.org), and the framework is called Ready by 21™—Ready for College, Work, and Life. The framework clarifies a set of values, goals, and objectives for community systems of youth development that can be used to identify and solve disjunctures over time (stage) and across systems. For young people to be ready at 21, they have to be ready at 6, 14 and 18 as well, ready for each new developmental stage and its associated border crossing. There is a set of "developmental benchmarks" in cognitive/academic development (ready for college); physical, social-emotional, and civic development (ready for life); and vocational development (ready for work) that can and should be created by education systems and communities and monitored carefully for all children and youth, especially those at greatest risk of falling behind. To manage border crossings between the major education systems, leaders need to know whether children are on track all along the way. A detailed description of the Ready by 21™ framework is available at FYI's Web site, as well as detailed descriptions of the use of the framework for promoting the kind of cross-system policy changes that the Barnett and Ackerman and the Kirst chapters call for. (One note of fairness in advertising: I confess to be serving as the chair of the board of FYI currently; but all the credit for the Ready by 21™ framework goes to the staff of FYI and to the broader field of positive youth development on which FYI draws heavily for insight and inspiration.)

Conceptual and Theoretical Frameworks

Again, to my mind, neither chapter offers a sufficiently explicit, formal conceptual frame or theoretical perspective to support ongoing scholarship in this area. At a minimum, the analysis of disjunctures between major age-graded education systems would benefit from some sort of conceptual scaffolding on which to begin to arrange (if not yet integrate) the rich array of empirical observations offered in the two chapters. Without such a frame, it is very difficult to identify when the authors think X causes Y or when they think X is associated with Y largely because of selection processes. Similarly, nearly all the phenomena under scrutiny in these two chapters are "multilevel" in nature. To borrow the conceptual frame of "ecologies of human development" from Urie Bronfenbrenner (1979), the stories told include processes at the macro-level (political-economic and population dynamics factors), at the exo-level (institutional, organizational, and policy change factors), and at the meso- and micro-levels (small groups, households/families, individuals).

I'm probably asking too much, but as I read both chapters, I was constantly concerned about such questions as "what is the author's reason for thinking X caused Y rather than Y caused X, or both were caused by Z," and "why does the author believe that this feature of disjuncture emanates from the macro- or micro-levels of context rather than the reverse?"

This set of concerns sounds like egghead social science, not hard-headed policy analysis. But it's not. How are we going to draw on knowledge to repair the unproductive disjunctures, to improve the border crossings, if we don't have some kind of conceptual framework that helps us understand that "if we make these changes in policy A, it is likely to result in beneficial outcome B"? I fervently believe that this field of inquiry will benefit greatly from more formal definitions, measurements, and analyses of causal relations at multiple levels. Indeed, the incredibly high quality of description and of "hypothesizing" in the Barnett and Ackerman and the Kirst chapters make me even greedier for a more adequate overarching conceptual frame.

Toward an Experimenting Society

Finally, to surface my last bias in commenting on these splendid chapters, I believe that one productive path toward generating and testing the kind of conceptual framework I sketched above is through the design and conduct of theoretically driven, rigorously designed and conducted policy experiments. The early childhood/K–12 field has many examples of rigorous experiments testing the effects of early childhood interventions and policy changes on children's success in K–12. Over the last decade, the impact of secondary school interventions and policy changes on postsecondary success has increasingly become the object of study and experimentation. But very few of these studies simultaneously experiment or design intentional change strategies on both sides of the border. If we've learned anything, it's that we have to be thinking of both emigration and immigration, exits and entrances, as part of reciprocally influential systems if we are to develop a knowledge base adequate to guide changes in education policy that promote more successful border crossings.

REFERENCES

Bronfenbrenner, U. (1979). *The ecology of human development.* Cambridge, MA: Harvard University Press.

V

THE ROLE OF EDUCATION RESEARCH

11

Knowledge and Policy

Fritz Mosher

In this chapter[1] I will try to suggest what recent education policies require in the way of research-based knowledge, if they are to have a chance of achieving their stated goals, and also to assess what capacity exists or might have to be developed to meet these knowledge needs. For purposes of this discussion I will focus on policies set at the state and federal levels, though of course they are mirrored and/or implemented at the levels of districts and schools. The relevant policymakers are governors, chief state school officers, state legislators, state school board members, the president and federal education officials, and members of Congress. I probably also should include the federal and state branches of the judiciary and the lawyers and advocates who inevitably will become involved in forcing policy to confront what is and is not known.

It is my contention that we simply don't know enough now to attain what are widely asserted to be the goals of current education policy. Policies premised on the assumption that we do are likely at best to lead to frustration, and they could easily call the whole enterprise of public education into question. We would do better to pursue policies that would encourage the schools to learn over time what is required for improvement and the ultimate attainment of our newly ambitious goals—and to recognize that developing the knowledge needed and acting on it will in fact take time. We also need to pay more explicit attention to policy with respect to the management and funding of research relevant to education, since the education research, design, development, evaluation, and dissemination "system" lacks much of the infrastructure and incentives that will be required if it is to produce the knowledge and tools needed adequately to inform education policy and practice.

The goals of policy for American public schools underwent a remarkable sea change and took on a much greater focus over the last two or three decades. Spurred by the movements for civil and group rights and by the perceived demands of the new economy and of international economic competition, at all governance levels most of American education has adopted at least a rhetorical commitment to the goal that substantially all students should be enabled to meet or exceed specified standards of performance in core academic subjects and skills. Additionally,

---

1. I prepared an earlier draft of this chapter for a CPRE meeting in December 2003. It was to be written jointly with my late dear friend and colleague Tom Glennan. As it turned out, Tom did not have the time or energy to join in revising it for that meeting, but he kindly indicated that even though he might have framed and emphasized some things differently, he was not uncomfortable with the general argument. I am responsible for any mistakes or foolishness here, but if there is any wisdom, it stems in large part from my long and happy experience of working with Tom.

the rights and equity concerns have led to a commitment to end the achievement gaps between the performance of various disadvantaged groups and that of, presumably, White, not disadvantaged students—i.e., the distributions of achievement (scores) for all identified groups should be indistinguishable.

The standards movement of the 1990s took an expansive view both of the range of content that American students should be expected to cover and of the levels of performance with that content that they should be expected to reach. The standards looked beyond mere facts and rote learning to extend to understanding and the ability to transfer and apply knowledge, and they were to be "world class." As the standards movement has morphed into outcomes-based, high-stakes accountability, there has been a noticeable de-escalation of this rhetoric, moving toward a focus on a narrower range of content—primarily on the basic literacy areas of reading comprehension and writing, on mathematics, and in the near future on the content area of science—and less emphasis on demanding levels of performance and understanding. Nevertheless, in the use of such terms as "proficiency" to characterize the performance goals, there is still the implication that all students should at least reach levels that are well beyond "minimum competency" and that provide some ability to compete adequately in further education and the economy and to perform responsibly as good citizens.

So if these are the goals—substantially all students should reach or exceed proficiency in core subjects and skills, and the performance distributions of all relevant social groups should coincide—what policies will make them attainable? Presumably, the knowledge that policymakers need is the knowledge that would enable them to answer that question. There are two ironic points to make about the question: the first is that nobody knows an adequate answer to it, and the second is that most policymakers don't seem to know that nobody knows an adequate answer to it.

These goals are truly new. For most of the last century, school people did not expect to educate everyone to an adequate level. At best they expected a statistically normal or Gaussian distribution of achievement, including a substantial number at the low end of the distribution who would fail (and drop out, or receive some lesser form of certification). Schools were designed to select students according to how easy they were to educate (or how much external, family, or other support they had) and to hold high expectations for, and offer them only to, those who could relatively easily (or with external support) meet them. They did not think the society needed a high proportion of high achievers, and they were not particularly sensitive to the maldistribution of achievement by class, race, or other social background. At best, the equity standard applied was that each student should achieve up to his or her "potential," and achievement was often measured using tests that had the same psychometric properties as, and were highly correlated with, the aptitude tests that were used to assess potential. So most students proved to be doing about what should be expected of them (as were most groups, by extension, though that position was harder to defend, when it began to be confronted explicitly as Title I and the Civil Rights Movement began to take hold). Hence, now to expect our schools to bring all students to adequate levels of achievement regardless of their aptitudes represents a radically new challenge for them.

Having adopted these lofty goals, how do policymakers propose to ensure that the schools reach them? If we step back and try to take a broad look at what is going on, I would suggest the answer is that they are trying quite a wide variety of policies and interventions. In fact the perceived "crisis" in American public schools, particularly in those serving a high proportion of disadvantaged students, seems to have produced a massive exercise in trial and error. These "trials" have varying theories of action. With Elmore (2004a), Cohen and Ball (1999), and others I assume that in the end there can't be a change in the outcomes of schooling without changing what happens in instruction, defined as a three-way transaction among the student, the teacher (this can be taken broadly to include any resources that have an embodied intention to instruct), and the content/skills to be learned (as exemplified by curricula, texts, materials, activities, and so on).

I think that it is useful to make a crude distinction between (a) reform efforts that are mainly aimed at changing the context of instruction in ways that would provide both leeway and incentives to change instruction in more positive directions and (b) those that try somehow to affect instruction more directly. Obviously, there also can be mixed cases.

In the former category of reform efforts I would include such things as charter schools, school choice, vouchers, small schools, class size reduction, changing school funding to be more equitable or compensatory (including Title I, school finance reform, etc.), school-based management or other forms of decentralization, and outcomes-based accountability schemes with incentives or sanctions for schools, teachers, and/or students but without specific prescriptions about instruction. Surely there are others I am forgetting. (I suppose one could treat policies that emphasize choice as intending a direct effect on instruction, if you see them as being designed to match students with the instructional resources that would be most appropriate for them, but I think that the nature of such matching is so underprescribed or ill defined as to make it reasonable to leave choice in the camp of contextual interventions.)

In the more direct category I would include reform of the content of preservice teacher education; a focus on instructional leadership (where the leaders—district-level, principals, or "distributed" leaders—target what teachers do in instruction, targeted in turn on the students' needs and those most in need); district- and/or schoolwide, coherent curriculum; some forms of in-service professional development, when that is focused on approaches to instruction and/or teaching specific content knowledge and pedagogical content knowledge; teacher credentialing and compensation tied to measures of skill in instruction and of pedagogical and content knowledge; standards-based curricula, materials, activities, and classroom assessments; some comprehensive or whole school designs; a shift at the preschool and kindergarten level toward academics; "research-based" approaches to early reading instruction; detracking, algebra for all, and other approaches aimed directly at upgrading expectations and exposure to content; and thoroughgoing systemic reform with alignment running all the way to and through instruction. "Professionalization" and communities of learning and so on could fall on either side of this divide depending upon the degree of focus on content and content-related pedagogy, but I suppose they weigh more on the direct-impact side.

I am neglecting another set of even more contextually focused interventions having to do with such things as safety, security, and order; length of school and summer programs; after school; a focus on nutrition and/or health; early interventions with families and training in parenting; parental involvement and school–community relations; desegregation and integration; and probably many more.

Clearly what policymakers ought to want to know, and probably do want to know, is what of all this "works" and how well, in what mix, and for which particular situations or populations, and what it all costs—compared to what, in each respect. These are mostly evaluation-type questions which, in principle, might be answered with controlled studies that pit one or another of these policies or interventions or mixtures of them against others and with replications of such trials in differing settings. We in fact have some, but very few, such studies, and the obstacles to getting more are formidable. The reader will be familiar with most of the latter. It is politically and practically hard to introduce policies experimentally, and appropriate natural experiments are hard to find or control. In many instances it is hard to specify the policy or intervention well enough to know what you are testing, and doubly hard to know how to contrast it with quite different types of policy or intervention (say, one with a contextual focus versus one directly targeted on instruction, for instance, or some combination of the two) and weigh them on a common scale. Beyond that, the "field" of education research is desperately lacking in the range of kinds of researchers, the institutional infrastructure, and the access to actual schools and school systems required to carry out such research over the time, at the scale, and in the varied settings needed to provide answers of sufficient rigor and travel to be useful for answering the questions policymakers should want to ask. I will talk about these latter gaps a bit more below.

But first, it is important to recognize that evaluation research, particularly summative evaluation, is adapted at best to producing only one kind of knowledge—the knowledge of what works. It doesn't in itself tell you why something works or fails, and it is not particularly useful for explaining how things work in education, so that, for instance, you would have the knowledge needed to suggest and design new or alternative interventions or policies. I prefer to distinguish summative evaluation from what I would call "scientific" or disciplinary research intended to advance understanding and explanation of the phenomena of education, and I also would distinguish it from "design" or development, which (as in engineering) is meant to take advantage of the knowledge obtained from science but which inevitably extrapolates beyond it, on the basis of intuition, practical wisdom, or craft knowledge, to produce workable materials, approaches, or policies. These latter may be shaped by formative evaluation, and they presumably should provide the artifacts that can be subjected to summative evaluation.

Much of what we do as policy researchers involves descriptive and correlational studies that actually should be seen as falling on the side of trying to produce understanding and explanation of the phenomena of education. We look at the relationships we find in the natural variation in the real world, and in occasional experiments, and try to develop models and hypotheses about what is going on. These hypotheses do often form the base from which to argue for and design policies and interventions, but they seldom reach the status of well-warranted or "scientifically proven" models or theories of important relationships in education. In its current state our knowledge takes the form at best of identifying a number of factors or approaches that are probably necessary aspects of ensuring that all students succeed, but we do not know how they should be combined so that our efforts would be sufficient to ensure such success. This necessary but not sufficient (NBNS; see Grubb, this volume) state of our understanding poses a fundamental challenge to policy research and to education research more generally. Achieving sufficiency is likely to require varying many factors simultaneously, and doing that and studying the results in the real world of schools is hardly a simple task.

Under these circumstances, policymakers quite reasonably can feel they are free to pursue their own preferences and hunches based on political calculations, ideology, or whichever of the many arguably research-based hypotheses come to their attention and appeal to them. Very little of what we do would compel them to make any particular choice.

It looks to me as though the shift toward setting up systems of outcomes-based accountability is a quite reasonable response to these uncertainties. Policymakers seem to be saying, in effect: "We have these new goals for the schools. Nobody can tell us for sure how they can be achieved, and this being America, we are in any case not about to tell the schools exactly what to do in instruction. Instead, let's insist that the schools/states pick some reasonable way of measuring student proficiency in the most important subjects. Let's also insist that they tie incentives and sanctions to increasing the proportion of students in all relevant groups who meet these standards, in the case of schools, and to passing the standards as a condition of promotion or graduation, in the case of students. That way everyone will be motivated to try harder and to figure out how to do better, and the system may end up reaching the goals for all in some reasonable time." (I can hear echoes of the Deity saying, "Hey, why don't I start a world with an initial state and a rule like 'survival of the fittest' and see where it all comes out?")

As I have hinted above, however, there are some catches.

First, by focusing on incentives and sanctions and by not specifying much about instruction and/or building in systematic attention to it and to students' opportunities to learn the desired content, the actual systems seem to be assuming that the core problems are ones of motivation and effort (and the "soft bigotry of low expectations"), that somebody probably does know how to succeed with most students, that teachers and schools can find out how to do it if they try, and that students too can succeed if they just work harder. The systems don't build in the gathering of information that might help the schools learn how to succeed even if no one now knows how to.

Second, the truth is that as far as I know there are no examples of schools that succeed in getting substantially all of their students to achieve at what would be perceived as a reasonable level of proficiency, among schools that don't have a social-class segregated population and/or that serve a disadvantaged population and aren't somehow able to pre-select their student body on ability to learn or on the external supports available to them. There clearly are some schools and classrooms of this sort that do better than others, and there may be some that get most of their students over a low, minimum competency threshold, but I know of none whose students mostly meet a reasonable standard of proficiency. Similarly, we know quite a bit about the correlates of achievement. Interventions designed to affect individual, teacher, or school positions on those factors often do improve scores, but again, so far they do not shift the bulk of the score distribution above a reasonable proficiency threshold. So the idea that someone must know how to do it is a statement of hope, not a matter of evidence—so far.

Third, I think that the knowledge needed to enable schools and teachers to succeed with almost all students is going to have to include new basic knowledge about what underlies, and what kinds of experiences and instruction can change the distribution of, differences in students' ease of learning specific content and skills. The most compelling example of this kind of work is the long series of studies that ultimately identified phonological awareness as a key individual difference variable that influences the ease of developing fluent decoding in early reading and that can be affected by interventions involving explicit attention to, and direct instruction on, the alphabetic principle (Adams, 1990; Snow, Burns, & Griffin, 1998). I suspect that similar differences can be found at the level say of "syntactical awareness" affecting the development of reading comprehension, along with analogous dispositions to attend to mathematical aspects of experience that could underlie the ease with which students learn mathematics. Other basic work will be needed on such things as the relationship between differences in students' prior exposure to the linguistic registers and vocabulary used in school and how easily they learn, and on the ways in which these differences can efficiently be reduced, along with ways of taking advantage of aspects of disadvantaged students' experiences that might facilitate their appreciation of what school is asking them to learn (Hart & Risley, 1995; Hirsch, 2003; Lee, 2001; Moses & Cobb 2001).

Fourth, even if there are breakthroughs in research at these basic levels, there won't be much benefit unless there are explicit attempts to design materials, approaches, curricula, and activities that exploit them and that can be used in real schools. As an example, the early reading research still is in the stage of being turned into workable and tested designs, and there is a long way to go before we have warranted knowledge about which sequences and balances of experiences work with which kinds of kids. And we have a lot to learn about what teachers need to know about these things in order to use the materials to good effect—and about how to support their learning of these things (Moats, 1994; Torgesen, 2004).

Fifth, we need to be honest about, and to find a way to communicate to policymakers and the public, the fact that we do not now have adequate measures of achievement in the core subjects and skills that are being made the focus of accountability. Partly because of the inadequacy of our fundamental knowledge that I've already hypothesized, these measures don't now reflect a principled understanding of the key stages (or key alternative routes) in which knowledge and skill are acquired in these areas and/or the key ways that learning can go off track. The measures also do not provide any way of weighing the relative contribution to student scores of instruction in content and aspects of skills, which is what the schools tend to teach explicitly, and of students' status on subject-related aptitudes and dispositions, which the schools tend not to teach explicitly (Mosher, 2004). Because of these inadequacies, the measures are not very useful for providing feedback to schools about the success of what they are trying to do or the need to do other things (such as teach the relevant aptitudes and dispositions explicitly). They also are not structured in a way that would make it sensible to assert standards of proficiency of the sort the states now are trying to assert—i.e., threshold levels of progress in the acquisition of specific knowledge and skill that would justify the assertion that a student is adequately prepared to go to the next level or to graduate with a reasonable chance of performing adequately in what life may require next. Nor are they very useful for carrying out the kinds of research that might provide empirical evidence for such assertions about what levels of performance are "adequate"; for playing a role in summative or formative evaluation of interventions or policies; or for supporting teachers on a day-to-day basis in classroom instruction. I think that in this era of "a test is a test is a test," policymakers are simply unaware of this fundamental weakness of current assessments, and the profession has utterly failed to find a compelling way to communicate it to them, perhaps because we are also hiding it from ourselves.

Sixth—and this is my basic message—the odds that such fundamental work and the related, principled design and evaluation of policies, interventions, and assessments will actually happen in such a way as to develop the knowledge needed to give the schools a chance of succeeding with substantially all students are extremely slim unless education research and education-relevant work in the disciplines are managed and funded in a much more strategic way (Burkhardt & Shoenfeld, 2003).

The policymakers that should be of most immediate concern to us are the ones who manage and fund education research and development and the training of people who go into the relevant research and development fields. Research funders and managers need to recognize that much too high a proportion of education-related research, particularly doctoral research, is now carried out on a small scale with a focus on generating insights and hypotheses about a very wide range of the phenomena of education. Much of the research is designed to amplify the critical point that the system tends to produce the very disadvantage that it deplores, rather than focusing on what might be done to change that (I am pleased that "policy researchers" in general are less guilty of this, but the "field" as a whole certainly is). I think that funders need to shift the balance toward being more self-consciously "strategic" in the sense of picking a few large goals (such as that the schools should succeed with substantially all students in the core subjects and skills) and then orchestrating research planning and support to identify the key impediments to success, both in terms of the fundamental knowledge needed and in terms of principled development or design and evaluation of policies and tools based as much as possible on fundamental knowledge. I think that the balance should shift toward, in Stokes's (1997) terms, "use-oriented basic" work supported programmatically (i.e., over sustained periods of time with careful periodic reviews carried out in close collaboration with the relevant scholars in the field about where each relevant subfield is heading and whether and how it is paying off). The balance should also shift toward a much greater emphasis on principled design, evaluation, and replication over real settings, of promising approaches based on the best available disciplinary and scientific understanding. The results should be fed back to influence the further development of basic understanding when what we have now proves to be inadequate.

As funders begin to move in this direction (and as the Institute of Education Sciences now seems to have begun to, albeit with a surprisingly heavy focus on the summative end stage of the basic-research-to-formative-design-to-summative-evaluation cycle, rather than on the basic work and design needed to get to that stage), they are certain to find that the field is not ready to give them very many of the kinds of proposals they want, nor are there very many settings in which rigorous long-term design and evaluation can be carried out. They also will find that current graduate training programs are not well designed to provide graduate students with the experiences and skills that would expose them to, and ready them to participate in, either long-term programmatic basic work or design and evaluation at the scale and over the periods of time required to make a dent in education's knowledge requirements. University tenure incentives also seem to discourage younger faculty from engaging in the kinds of larger scale and practice-oriented efforts that are likely to be most useful. There are some exceptions, particularly in areas concerning the application of technology to education, and these should be mined for lessons to be applied more broadly, but it is clear to me that both the management and funding of education research and development and the organization of training for entering the field represent massive policy design problems in their own right.

Any strategic effort to produce warranted knowledge about what is required to enable schools and teachers to succeed at ambitious levels with substantially all students would certainly have to come to terms early with the fact that the tools we need to carry out such research are inadequate to the task.

We don't really have clear agreement on what we mean by standards of proficiency specific to the core subjects and skills for which we want to assert such goals. We don't have measures of attainment of any of these standards that are validated by independent observations of students' performances to determine whether those who meet the standards on the assessments can also perform in ways, over a range of settings, that would match any reasonable interpretation of what proficiency might mean. We don't have detailed conceptions of the ways student performance advances (and/or goes off track) on the way to proficiency that would allow us to develop assessments or observation protocols that could inform teacher and researcher judgments about each student's progress in each subject or skill and allow us to respond appropriately to keep or get the student on track.

We also have only the beginnings of agreed and validated ways of defining, observing, and recording what happens between teachers and students in instruction that could be used across research and development projects and interventions and provide some basis for comparing them and building cumulative knowledge. Unless there is some common currency for valuing instructional change, there can hardly be a basis for arraying, comparing, and explaining the effects of wildly differing direct and indirect approaches to reform.

Without these bedrock tools for measuring instruction and student achievement it is unlikely that education research and development will converge on any kind of agreement about how to improve instruction. Further, it also is the case that giving priority to the development of these tools might itself help focus the dialogue in ways that would increase the chances of cumulative work, rather than mere accumulation of results (Cohen, 2003). Another virtue of this work would likely be that much of it would of necessity involve collaboration between practitioners and researchers in ways that may help to reground education research and discipline it by refocusing it on its obligations to inform practice.

On the policy side, it seems clear that if policymakers enact policies based on the false assumption that schools ought now to know how to succeed with every student, and if they establish rewards and punishments based on that assumption, something—in fact many things—will have to give. As Cohen, Moffit, and Goldin (this volume) point out, there may be open conflict between levels of the system, or evasion or cheating, or a lowering of standards to levels that seem attainable, whether or not they leave students in a position to function well in the world. It seems reasonable to hold schools, teachers, and students accountable by paying attention to outcomes for each student, by setting goals in ambitious terms, and by requiring evidence of improvement, but there needs to be recognition that, as Elmore has argued (2004b), improvement comes in uneven stages, often with plateaus while school people figure out what is involved in moving to the next level, and so far there are no schools that seem to have made it all the way. Clearly one of the things we have to learn from research is how to strike a balance between pressure to improve and recognition of the need to make provision for learning how to improve— provision that would have to apply to all levels of the system and its governance.

Perhaps the greatest test for the policy research community is whether we can meet our responsibility to teachers and students to speak these truths to power. It would be naïve to expect knowledge to prevail even if it were to improve—it inevitably will continue to be complex and tentative—but we have an obligation to try to be clear about what we do, and don't, know.

REFERENCES

Adams, M. J. (1990). *Beginning to read: Thinking and learning about print.* Cambridge, MA: MIT Press.

Burkhardt, H., and Shoenfeld, A. (2003). Improving educational research: Toward a more useful, more influential, and better-funded enterprise. *Educational Researcher 32*(9), 3–14.

Cohen, D. K. (2003). Remarks at a workshop on understanding and promoting knowledge accumulation in education: Tools and strategies for education research. Committee on Research in Education of the Center on Education of the National Research Council, National Academies, Washington, DC, June 30–July 1. Retrieved January 23, 2007, from http://www7.nationalacademies.org/core/Remarks%20by%20David%20Cohen.html

Cohen, D. K., and Ball, D. L. (1999). *Instruction, capacity, and improvement* (CPRE Research Report No. RR–43). Philadelphia: University of Pennsylvania, Consortium for Policy Research in Education.

Elmore, R. F. (2004a). Change and improvement in educational reform. In *School reform from the inside Out: Policy, practice, and performance* (pp. 211–226). Cambridge, MA: Harvard Education Press.

Elmore, R. F. (2004b). Doing the right thing, knowing the right thing to do. In *School reform from the inside out: Policy, practice, and performance* (pp. 227–258). Cambridge, MA: Harvard Education Press.

Hart, B., and Risley, T. R. (1995). *Meaningful differences.* Baltimore, MD: Brookes.

Hirsch, E. D. (2003). Reading comprehension requires knowledge—of words and the world: Scientific insights into the fourth-grade slump and the nation's stagnant reading comprehension scores. *American Educator 27*(1), 10–22, 28–29, 48.

Lee, C. D. (2001). Is October Brown Chinese? A cultural modeling activity system for underachieving students. *American Educational Research Journal 38*(1), 97–142.

Moats, L. C. (1994). The missing foundation in teacher education: Knowledge of the structure of spoken and written language. *Annals of Dyslexia 44*, 81–102.

Moses, R., and Cobb, C. (2001). *Radical equations: Math literacy and civil rights.* Boston: Beacon Press.

Mosher, F. A. (2004). What NAEP really could do. In L. V. Jones and I. Olkin (Eds.) *The Nation's report card: Evolution and perspectives* (pp. 329–340). Bloomington, IN: Phi Delta Kappa Educational Foundation in cooperation with the American Educational Research Association.

Snow, C. E., Burns, M. S., and Griffin, P., eds. (1998). *Preventing reading difficulty in young children.* Washington, DC: National Academy Press.

Stokes, D. E. (1997). *Pasteur's quadrant: Basic science and technical innovation.* Washington, DC: Brookings Institution Press.

Torgesen, J. K. (2004). Preventing early reading failure—and its devastating downward spiral: The evidence for early intervention. *American Educator 28*(3), 6–9, 12–13, 17–19, 45–47.

12

Learning, Teaching, and Keeping the Conversation Going: The Links Between Research, Policy, and Practice

Barbara Neufeld

Education Matters, Inc. is a firm that conducts formative evaluations using qualitative methods. We use qualitative methods because they include the tools with which we can gain insight into how and under what circumstances programs and practices influence teaching, learning, and other aspects of educational practice. We conduct formative evaluations because such studies are designed to provide ongoing feedback that can be used to make program and implementation adjustments. As a firm, we strive to provide school districts and schools with knowledge they can use to improve the education they provide to students. We try to learn from the formative evaluations we conduct and then teach those directly involved in the work how they might improve on their efforts. In this regard, Education Matters is a learning and teaching organization.

Like most people who teach, we think we have something of value to share. Therefore, although most of my colleagues and I have formal training as researchers and we do carefully planned, external evaluations, our goal is to become part of the process of school improvement by helping practitioners—whether in district offices, schools, or intermediary organizations—consider the progress of their work and, if necessary, take new steps in light of evaluation findings. Our purpose is to help local practitioners use the knowledge we produce to achieve their goals.

Construing the work as learning and teaching requires us to develop genuine relationships with the practitioners we study. We cannot merely come and go in the process of collecting data. Rather, we need to become colleagues with our school improvement district partners, colleagues who do different work, but who respect and trust one another, and share common goals. It is only in an honest, trusting relationship that learning and teaching can occur in any educational context. It is only in such a relationship that we can remain in the conversation, remain a part of the process. In the end, like our partners, we are motivated by the desire to improve schools so that children achieve high-quality academic and social outcomes.

Our success depends primarily on the extent to which we produce valid, compelling, persuasive conclusions and recommendations that have clear implications for practice. Still, whether that knowledge is used depends on factors beyond our control, for example, practitioners' prior knowledge and motivation for learning what we want to teach, their time to reflect on and use the findings, organizational structures in which to consider what we report, budget constraints, and factors such as local policies, politics, and practices that may be more pressing than the work we have presented. As a result, providing usable knowledge does not guarantee that it will be used.

Given our purpose, I want to address two questions in this chapter: (1) What features of Education Matters' work seem to make it useful at the local level? (2) Under what circumstances and how does Education Matters' work contribute to the development and/or improvement of local policy and practice?

I will address these two questions by focusing primarily on Education Matters' multiple evaluation studies in the Boston Public Schools (BPS) which began in the 1996–1997 school year and are ongoing. I will contrast our experiences in Boston with those in San Diego City Schools (SDCS), San Diego, CA; in the Jefferson County Public Schools (JCPS), Louisville, KY; and in the Corpus Christi Independent School District (CCISD), TX, between 1993 and 2003 in order to draw tentative conclusions about factors that led to more and less use of ostensibly usable evaluation findings.

I begin with three conclusions I have drawn from our work in these school districts. They are conclusions that suggest there will always be limits on the extent to which evaluation research will be used to inform policy and practice regardless of its quality and potential utility. The conclusions should not be surprising.

1. The districts in which we have worked vary considerably in their desire for and/or capacity to use new knowledge. They rarely seek evaluation data. Most of the time, evaluations are a required component of program grants. As such, it is compliance, more than a quest for knowledge, that drives districts to seek evaluators.

2. The extent to which our findings are used seems to have a great deal to do with their implications for the normal functioning of the school district. *First*, school districts are not organized for or familiar with using formative evaluation findings. *Second*, school district administrators, tend to focus on improving others—schools, principals, teachers—and not on examining their own knowledge, skill, and practice. *Third*, perhaps as a result of this, findings that can be accommodated with superficial changes in practice and/or at the school rather than at the district level are more likely to be used or at least supported than are those that require deeper changes in how the schools or school district functions. This is disappointing in light of current efforts to achieve district-wide school improvement and increase the capacity of district offices to support their schools.

3. Without a local, influential champion, an individual who genuinely seeks knowledge with which to consider the progress of ongoing school improvement efforts, there is little chance that the evaluation findings will lead to changes in either policy or practice. Local, influential champions, in Education Matters' experience, are scarce. Ellen Guiney, Executive Director of the Boston Plan for Excellence (BPE), is such a champion in Boston.[1]

When I consider the amount of work Education Matters has completed over the last 10 to 12 years and the extent to which that work has had any noticeable impact on local practice, I cannot be optimistic about claiming a significant role for our evaluations regardless of how well

---

1. For a full discussion of the BPE and its role working with the BPS to design and support its whole-school improvement agenda as well as a brief discussion of the role that Education Matters has played in the BPE's work, see Neufeld and Guiney (2003), available at www. annenberginstitute.org.

they were conducted and written. Evaluation findings, like any form of information and data, exist among a host of competing claims for attention. The best we can hope is that we are compelling enough to garner attention and remain part of the conversation. Nonetheless, I want to explore what it takes to conduct work that has the potential to be useful and which, at times, has been used.

I turn next to a discussion of the methods we employ to design evaluation studies, gather data, conduct the analyses, and write our reports. After all, it is only if we and our clients have confidence that we are conducting high-quality studies that we can suggest they use the findings to make changes. As part of this discussion, I will present the range of "products" that result from our work. At the most obvious level, formal reports represent our work and suggest implications for practice. But there are other products such as memos, conversations, and even negotiations that can lead to the use of our findings or can be considered useful in and of themselves.

Following this discussion, I will present examples of how our work has been used. In developing this discussion, I will rely heavily on examples from Education Matters' ongoing work in Boston and compare them with examples from work we completed in the previously mentioned districts over a 10-year period for the Edna McConnell Clark Foundation (EMCF). My purpose in making comparisons is to identify factors that seem to be associated with greater and lesser use of the findings. As part of this discussion, I consider what we have learned about how school districts do their work that may influence their capacity to use evaluation findings.

The final section of the chapter will focus on the challenges Education Matters faces as an organization in conducting long-term, district-focused, qualitative evaluation studies. Challenges include (a) developing a predictable funding and staffing stream and (b) attempting to make a difference without getting fired.

WHAT IS THE NATURE OF EDUCATION MATTERS' WORK?

There is little in the design, data collection strategies, document review, or analysis techniques that sets Education Matters apart from other evaluators or from researchers whose purposes are other than local use. We develop targeted, researchable questions that address key variables. Given that our work is evaluative, we include questions that focus on how well, to what extent, in what ways, and under what circumstances some intervention looks promising.[2] We select samples of schools, teachers, principals, and others with a clear focus on representing the variation relevant to the evaluation questions in the district context. And we (a) design interview and observation instruments, (b) develop and implement data collection schedules, (c) tape record interviews and script observations, (d) transcribe interviews and write observation and analytical field notes, (e) systematically code and analyze the data, and (f) write reports. What we can do, how large our sample can be, and for how long the work continues depends, as does all research, on the limits of budget and on the reasonable demands we can place on teachers, administrators and others who become part of our sample.

Overall Design Principles

We design each evaluation study to answer questions about specific components of practice, as requested, but our designs include attention to a range of variables we consider relevant to

---

2. Since we do not conduct summative evaluations, we are not able to provide districts with conclusions about the effectiveness of their programs and practices.

implementation. For example, when studying classroom implementation of the reading comprehension curriculum for grades K–6, Making Meaning™, we included a focus on the role principals took with respect to supporting that implementation. We did this because we know how important school-based leadership is to successful implementation of new teaching practices. When designing the study of the school-based implementation of Boston's Essentials of Whole-School Improvement, we included a focus on the deputy superintendents because they both support and evaluate principals. We wanted to understand whether, how, and to what extent their work influenced the quality of implementation. Similarly, when studying the implementation of the Literacy Framework in San Diego's middle schools, we did not limit our inquiry to the schools. Rather, we also focused on (a) the role of the central office instructional leaders as they helped principals learn how to support their teachers, and (b) the professional development provided to the literacy coaches who supported teachers' learning. Our direct focus was on changes in classroom instruction; our evaluations were designed to capture the system of support in place to influence classroom practice.

Unpredictable Flow of Work

The evaluations we conduct may continue over a long period of time, but it would be an error to conclude that we operate with a formal, longitudinal research agenda. Rather, we achieve longevity when local districts, foundations, and intermediary organizations such as the BPE keep hiring us to focus on different aspects of their improvement efforts as they are developed. In the case of the middle school-focused work we conducted for the EMCF, our evaluations were shaped by the focus of the foundation's initiative and by the ways in which each of the districts developed their local response to the foundation's multiple requests for proposals (RFPs). We wrote new funding proposals approximately every $2\frac{1}{2}$ years over a 10-year period that began in 1993.[3]

In Boston, we began our work during the 1996–1997 school year with a focus on coaching at the request of the BPE. At the same time, also at the request of the BPE, we wrote an evaluation proposal with the BPE and another firm, Policy Studies Associates (PSA), to study the work of the first cohort of reforming schools. That proposal provided four years of financial support for evaluation. The parameters of the evaluation were vaguely specified in light of the evolving character of the program development work. Subsequent funding from the Boston Annenberg Challenge and from a Comprehensive School Reform Development Grant from the federal Department of Education provided support for additional evaluations that focused on school-based, whole-school improvement efforts and the development and implementation of the district's literacy-focused instructional coaching effort.

More recently, Education Matters has been asked to evaluate (a) the pilot phase of the implementation of Making Meaning (spring 2004); (b) high school renewal, the conversion of the district's comprehensive high schools into small high schools and small learning communities (October 2003–June 2007); (c) the Boston Teacher Residency Program (BTR), Boston's program to prepare teachers to work in the district's elementary and secondary schools (October 2004–September 2006); (d) the pilot phase of the BPE's formative assessment project (spring 2004), and the scale-up of what is now called the BPE's Formative Assessment of Student Thinking in Reading (FAST-R; October 2005–August 2006); and (e) four cases of Collaborative Coaching and Learning (CCL) in a selected sample of one elementary, one middle, and two high schools

---

3. For more detail on the trajectory of our work in these districts, see reports about San Diego, Louisville, and Corpus Christi at www.edmatters.org.

(October 2005–January 2006). We were chosen to evaluation the School Leadership Institute (SLI), Boston's program to prepare principals for the district and provide them with support during their first two years on the job (August 2004–July 2007) after a competitive bidding process. We were asked to join the BPS in what was a successful proposal to the federal Department of Education for Phase II of the SLI, and we anticipate beginning our evaluation of Phase II shortly.

The point of generating this list is to indicate that Education Matters' span of work in the BPS has been broad and, in some instances such as our focus on coaching, quite deep. What we have not had is a traditional research agenda in which we identified the areas in which we wanted to work. Rather, we have followed components of the district's reform work as they have become funded and/or as the district or the BPE has determined that it needs new data with which to refine its practice. On the problematic side, this means that we do not get to follow the district's work over time until some point at which it is considered "finished." Rather, we move from project to project as a function of funding for district initiatives. On the advantageous side, we learn about a great many facets of the district's work, and we are privy to patterns in that work that develop across the multiple initiatives and interventions. Within these parameters, we have carved out areas important to school improvement—school-level and district leadership, for example—and studied them when we could.[4]

Evaluation Products

The products of our work are formal reports, short "anticipatory" memos, negotiations, private conversations, and, from time to time, presentations. To be useful, we need to conduct our analyses and write our reports very quickly after finishing data collection. Most of the time, this means finishing data collection in May or June of a school year and producing reports during July, August, and September of the same year. The work we completed for the EMCF required midyear as well as annual evaluation reports.

With respect to reports, we strive to write to a broad, local audience with the goal of making the findings and their implications accessible to educators at all levels of the system. Decisions about how to frame a convincing argument from the data, therefore, include a good deal of imagining the different practitioners who might read the report and what we must do to make it comprehensible to them. This is not a matter of "dumbing down" reports, but rather of thinking of the readers and scaffolding appropriately.

For example, in developing our report about the initial implementation of the Making Meaning curriculum, we considered that few educators in the district were genuinely familiar with it given its pilot status. Therefore, we chose to include a detailed description of the program and the purposes of its components. To do this, we quoted salient passages from the Teacher's Manual. And, in order to allow readers to "see" how teachers used it, we presented two detailed lesson segments (Neufeld & Sassi, 2004).[5] Similarly, in developing our first report on CCL, *Off to a Good Start: Year I of Collaborative Coaching and Learning in the Effective Practice Schools* (Neufeld & Roper, 2002), we began the paper with an in-depth description of the coaching model and then provided narrative examples of its use in order to help readers understand this novel approach to literacy coaching.

---

4. I will return to the implications of this way of working for funding and staffing Education Matters later in the chapter.

5. This report is available at www.edmatters.org, as are all of the Education Matters reports cited in this chapter.

Over the years, to achieve this goal of accessibility we have come to write many of our reports in somewhat of an essay format in which we lay out the findings early, set the context for understanding them, establish an argument based on the data, and then use the data to develop that argument. We use this format because we have learned that what clients value is what we make of the data. In reality, we are often reporting what key practitioners know in part or in full because of their daily involvement in the districts and schools. Therefore, it is in the framing of the data, in the argument we provide, that clients identify the value-added component of our work.[6]

In addition to formal reports, we develop what might be called "anticipatory memos" to provide clients and primary stakeholders with timely feedback on what we have learned and what will be presented in long reports that are not yet ready.[7] We write these memos most often to report findings that we anticipate (a) need attention and/or (b) will be unwelcome even if they are construed as valid. For example, we provided such a memo to the High School Renewal Work Group in Boston, the set of partners that guides the district's high school renewal efforts, to alert them to troubling findings about school climate and culture in our sample of small high schools and small learning communities. We have prepared such memos several times for Boston's super-intendent of schools. Each memo has been followed by a face-to-face conversation with relevant stakeholders. In addition to preparing people for the focus and findings of the full report, memos like these serve as a check on Education Matters' initial analyses and they alert us to findings that may generate what is called, euphemistically, "pushback" from districts.

We also have informal conversations with key stakeholders when we do not have the time to write an anticipatory memo or do not think it would be necessary. Whether, when, and with whom to have such conversations is a matter of professional judgment. When they occur, such conversations might take the form of our asking, Would you be surprised to know that . . . ? or proposing, In light of your work at the moment, you might want to know that . . . . Initiating these conversations depends on having developed a high level of trust with specific stakeholders. Providing this kind of feedback, however, can increase the likelihood that our work will be useful.[8]

There are additional factors related to Education Matters' stance towards its work and its clients that make it possible for us to increase the odds that our work and evaluation products will be taken seriously even if it does not lead to immediate, noticeable changes.

First, we are not allied with any special interests in the district or among its partners. For example, in Boston, we are not seen as having a position on whether small high schools, small learning communities, or comprehensive high schools are the appropriate organizational structure in which to improve teaching, learning, and students' engagement with school. We do not have a position with respect to whether Readers' and Writers' Workshop should be the district's approach to literacy instruction or whether the district should be basing early literacy instruction on a phon-

---

6. We consider the organizations we work with as our clients. As such, we are accountable to them for producing work they value. We consider the leaders of the different programs and initiatives we study as primary stakeholders in the work. And we also consider those who are at the forefront of implementing new practices, be they teachers, principals, or other administrators, as stakeholders. When conducting our work, we are aware of the relationship and responsibility we have to clients and to stakeholders, and we recognize that these categories can overlap.

7. In working with the EMCF, we used telephone conversations more often than such memos to inform Hayes Mizell, program officer, of critical conclusions we had formed about each of the districts in which we were working. We did this in the interest of speed and because it was the program officer, rather than the districts, that used our evaluation findings.

8. Clients may also ask us for early feedback, and when we deem it appropriate, we report what we can in light of the stage of our data analyses. We do not provide feedback that would violate our agreements about confidentiality.

ics-based system. As a result, we are viewed as nonpartisan. Our goal is to help the district improve the effectiveness of what it has chosen to do.

Nonetheless, given the emotion and contentiousness that surround improvement efforts in school districts, from time to time we are perceived as having taken a stand for one reform over another. When this occurs, we need to correct the perception immediately. When we wrote in our baseline high school report that scheduling was extremely difficult in Boston's new small high schools and that it might be worthwhile for the district to consider how it might provide electives like music and art to its students, we were accused of being advocates for large, comprehensive high schools and, as a consequence, of undermining district policy. We rephrased sections of the report to make clear that these were the findings and did not represent a policy suggestion from Education Matters.

Second, from time to time we have taken the initiative to develop small areas of focus that are not specified in our work plan but that we have come to judge as salient to the district's work. For example, early in our work in Boston, we noted challenges associated with the implementation of a teacher leader role developed out of contract negotiations with the Boston Teachers Union (BTU). We were not studying this role directly, yet we began to conclude that it was relevant to the implementation of the district's whole-school improvement agenda. As a result, we took a bit of time to study the role in the schools in our sample and attend some of the related district-provided professional development. Then we wrote a memo to key central office administrators describing our findings and our concerns. Later in our tenure in the district, we wrote a memo to the superintendent about how high-level BPS administrators viewed the role of the BPE. The information for this memo arose out of interviews we were conducting on a related topic.

We do not know what those who received these memos thought of the fact that we had chosen to develop them. No one questioned us or objected. No one may have considered whether the reports were part of our work plan. Whatever the reality, in my view, taking this kind of initiative may have increased the district's perception that we are genuinely interested in their work and want to help it succeed.[9]

Third, I have agreed to participate in discussions of the district's work and the work of the BPE that could not be construed as part of our formal evaluation role. For example, several years ago the district was engaged in developing expectations for principals with respect to implementation of the district's Essentials for Whole-School Improvement. The expectations were being written to make clear to principals what their deputies would look for when they made evaluative visits to their schools. I was asked by the BPE, as it collaborated with the BPS in this work, to review the expectations and offer my thoughts on whether they were complete. As part of my involvement, I attended a meeting with the deputy most involved in developing the expectations and with Ellen Guiney, the executive director of the BPE, to discuss the document that was being developed.

In the context of having been asked my opinion, I offered the unsolicited suggestion that the district ought also to develop expectations for central office administrators so that (a) there would be clarity and agreement about central office administrators' responsibilities to the schools, and (b) principals could understand the work for which those who supervised them would be held accountable. When asked for examples, I provided some suggestions that grew out of knowledge I was accumulating as Education Matters worked in Boston. Making the suggestion was not part of the formal evaluation process, and indeed, it may have meant I crossed the line

9. Whether to do this sort of report is a matter of professional judgment. I recognize that Education Matters has worked in districts where such initiative would not have been welcome and we would have been, at best, asked to mind our own business.

from outside evaluator to consultant. In long-term work, however, the role parameters can get blurred. Experience has led me to believe that, given a strong knowledge base with respect to the district and issue under consideration, taking the initiative can be seen as helpful and can increase our value to the district.[10]

Fourth, we think carefully about how to frame the recommendations or suggestions we include at the end of most reports.[11] Despite the depth of our inquiry and the confidence we have in our analyses, we know that we cannot be aware of all factors that might go into making a decision about "next steps." After all, no matter how closely we observe and how well we interview, in the end, we experience educators' work from the outside. Therefore, we frame our recommendations differently in light of the project we are studying and our knowledge of it. In the case of interventions and programs we have studied in their pilot phases, for example, Making Meaning and the Formative Assessment Pilot (FAP) of FAST-R, we might find ourselves able to make specific suggestions about concrete implementation issues or program design factors that arise repeatedly in the data.

For example, virtually every participant in our FAP sample reported a desire for more question sets and for continued support from the data coaches. Therefore, we felt confident in recommending,

- Increase the number of question sets and the number of genres included. Make them available to the schools at the start of the school year.
- Continue to provide high-quality support, facilitation, and technical assistance to schools using the Formative Assessments. To this end, explore the ways in which coaches and/or teacher leaders and Directors of Instruction might be involved with the FAP and its future iterations. (Neufeld & Schwartz, 2004, pp. 24, 26)

In contrast, while we knew that the BPE was interested in connecting the use of formative assessments to CCL cycles, we were not sure of how or whether that link should be made in light of what we had learned from the evaluation. Therefore, we suggested that the BPE look further into the possibility of linking the assessments to coaching cycles and wrote,

- Consider how and whether to use the question sets as part of a coaching cycle. (p. 27)

As a result of our study of the pilot phase of Making Meaning (Neufeld & Sassi, 2004), we focused on the program's use in the context of Readers' Workshop, the district's approach to literacy instruction, and couched our recommendations as "reminders." We wrote, for example,

> In the context of implementing Making Meaning, the district should not lose sight of the fact that there are other components of Workshop that need considerable attention. We noted the tendency for Making Meaning lessons to take most of the time available for reading. This particular challenge can be readily overcome. But, we also noted that many teachers were neither developing and instructing guided reading groups nor implementing independent reading and its associated con-

---

10. On this point, it is important to remember that no one has to accept the recommendation of an evaluator. We have no authority. Therefore, I do not worry too much about becoming a significant intervention in district policy and practice by muddying my role from time to time.

11. On occasion, we have been asked to present findings without making suggestions or recommendations. Nonetheless, we continue to include recommendations in our reports because we consider them to be the final phase of our analysis. As we noted earlier, no one has to accept or act on our suggestions.

ferences. Teachers readily admit that they need help implementing these components of Workshop. They should get that help so that they can develop reading blocks that fully develop students reading skills. (p. 47)

The form and focus of our recommendations, then, depend on our judgments about (a) how certain we are about what will most improve the next phase of the district's work and (b) how we can best frame the recommendation in light of our understanding of the district context and the positions of key stakeholders.[12]

Fifth, we include a review process for reports which involves sharing them confidentially with key stakeholders before they are distributed more broadly within the district. The review process is a period of fact checking and negotiation. The fact-checking component is the least troublesome and the quickest. What takes time is (a) negotiating phrases that might suggest that we have become advocates for one position or another, as noted earlier; (b) formulating language that softens a contentious point so that stakeholders are comfortable with leaving it in the report; and, in a few instances, (c) making the decision to delete a piece of text without unduly compromising the report in the interest of maintaining a viable role with a district or other client.

One example will make the last point clear. In Education Matters' draft baseline report on high school renewal, we made the following suggestion to the BPS:

Consider whether it would be sensible to allow some schools to house more than 400 students. If they must remain under 400, then consider allocating additional teachers to the schools so that they have a measure of staffing flexibility. (no page number)

As part of this consideration, we elaborated its advantages for implementing other aspects of the district's instructional improvement agenda. All the while, we knew that the district would not increase the number of students in these schools because of conditions associated with funding from the Gates Foundation. And we knew that the district would not allocate additional teachers to the schools, given the fact that the changes in high school organization were required to be budget neutral. Nonetheless, in light of the high schools' scheduling dilemmas that were associated with trying to meet the educational needs of the student population, we felt compelled to emphasize the issue by making the recommendation even while using the mild verb "consider."

As part of the negotiation process that focused on this and a few other "considerations," we spent several months negotiating the final text with the High School Renewal Work Group and with the superintendent. In the end, we agreed to remove this and one other "consideration." We were never asked to remove the data in the body of the report that highlighted teachers' and administrators difficulties in developing workable schedules given school size, student population, and staffing allocations.

The time we spend negotiating the public version of reports may be stressful, but it is an opportunity to engage district leaders with our findings, an opportunity to teach and to learn. We try to teach more about what we have learned and why we have written the reports as we have written them. And, through such negotiations, we have the opportunity to deepen our understanding of stakeholders' experience of policy and practice. In a sense, negotiations over reports are opportunities to collect additional data as well as be responsive to the educators with whom we are working. If we conclude the negotiations successfully, meaning both the client and

---

12. We discuss next the challenges that can arise with respect to recommendations even when we think we are being (a) responsive to the data and (b) cautious in our conclusions.

Education Matters are satisfied with the outcome, then we maintain our relationships and we will likely have the opportunity to return to significant, problematic issues that remain unaddressed.[13]

Sixth, we try to have our evaluation reports circulate broadly in the district and beyond. To this end, we share our reports with all of the educators who contributed to them through granting us interviews and observations. By doing this, we keep the knowledge we are generating visible, and we open our analysis to scrutiny by those who have the most to gain or lose from our work. In addition, we demonstrate to members of our sample (a) that we value their contributions to the work and use what they know from their practice to improve teaching, learning, and leadership in the district and its schools and (b) that we are not writing reports in ways that put them in jeopardy by revealing their identities.

HOW HAS EDUCATION MATTERS' WORK BEEN USED?

Use of evaluation findings does not have to be visible to be real, but most of the time, it is only the visible, formal use that we can document. In Boston, the BPE has made both more and less visible use of our evaluation reports, and we have examples of both. First, the organization has used our findings to inform its next steps in program development. Second, the BPE has used our work to inform publications it developed for teachers and school leaders. And third, at the less visible level, the BPE has used what it learned from our cumulative reports, memos, and informal conversations to engage the district in discussions of "next steps" it might need to consider in supporting its improvement agenda.

With regard to program development, the BPE has written that Education Matters' early reports on the implementation of on-site coaching led the BPE to understand that coaches needed ongoing professional development in order to implement their roles effectively. "Education Matters' reports," wrote Executive Director Ellen Guiney, "led to the creation of weekly professional development for coaches and far greater co-construction of the work. Ultimately, the reports led to the BPE completely redesigning its on-site coaching model and increasing its effectiveness" (Neufeld & Guiney 2003, p. 53).

As a result of that redesign, the BPE launched its CCL model in September 2002. Education Matters studied CCL implementation during the 2002–2003 school year and submitted a report to the BPE in July 2003. The BPS, while observing CCL during the pilot year, had decided to implement CCL in all district's schools beginning in September 2003.

In light of the scale-up, early in the fall of the 2003–2004 school year, the BPE developed *Straight Talk*, a newsletter sent to all BPS school leaders—principals, headmasters, and directors of instruction—and *Plain Talk*, a newsletter sent to all teachers. The newsletters were designed to help teachers and school leaders get started effectively with CCL. Both newsletters included numerous references to and suggestions from Education Matters' evaluation report.[14] For example, *Straight Talk* included the following:

> Research and experience also show, however, that transitioning to more learning-centered workshop instruction is challenging professional work, difficult for even the most skilled teacher to do

---

13. We took the opportunity to return to one such issue in our second high school renewal report. We were not asked to remove it.

14. *Plain Talk* (Boston Public Schools and Boston Plan for Excellence 2003a) and *Straight Talk* (Boston Public Schools and Boston Plan for Excellence 2003b) are available at www.bpe.org.

alone. To help, BPS has created a school-based professional development approach—Collaborative Coaching and Learning (CCL)—in which teachers learn about workshop instruction and analyze their classroom practice together.

> This collaboration about instruction is particularly important. Education Matters, the district's independent evaluator, has identified four factors that best indicate whether a school is likely to make rapid progress improving instruction and school organization: all four relate to whether the school has a collaborative culture focused on instruction. Education Matters has found that where such a culture is absent, a school may have pockets of progress, but is unlikely to have school-wide improvement in instruction or student proficiency. (Boston Public Schools and Boston Plan for Excellence, 2003b, p. 3)

A sidebar described four findings from our cumulative set of reports that the BPE thought were relevant to the implementation of CCL. The text in the sidebar reminded readers,

> In schools that are improving instruction: (1) teachers understand that professionals never stop learning and are willing to work with one another and the principal to meet their student learning goals; (2) the principal/headmaster is willing to share leadership with teachers and others; (3) principals/headmasters, teachers, and coaches recognize one another's expertise and learn from the knowledge and skill each brings to their shared work; (4) teacher-leaders are willing to take the lead in adopting new instructional strategies and making their practice public (Education Matters, various reports). (p. 3)

More recently, at the start of the 2004–2005 school year, the BPE devoted an issue of FOCUS, a newsletter for Boston teachers produced by the BPE in collaboration with the BPS, to highlight Making Meaning and how it could be used on the context of Boston's literacy efforts. Page 8 of FOCUS reviews recommendations from Education Matters' evaluation with a section headed "What principals need to do" and another headed "What 'Court Street' [district office] needs to do." (Boston Plan for Excellence, 2004–2005)[15]

Finally, the BPE has publicly identified one instance in which it used the findings from Education Matters' reports to address a significant issue: the official status of the BPE in its relationship with the BPS. As the BPE's executive director wrote:

> BPE's outside organization status means that it has very little authority and influence with schools that do not want to undertake reform work. After a four-year struggle with this issue, Education Matters' reports helped both the superintendent and the BPE recognize that they had to address the BPE's status directly. (Neufeld and Guiney, 2003, p. 53)

The BPE has also used our reports as texts around which to base discussions of its innovations. For example, the set of principals involved with the development and use of FAST-R were asked to read our pilot report and respond to it as part of an Effective Practice Schools principal meeting. More recently, we observed a segment of our report on the BTR program being used as part of a discussion at a professional development session of the program's site directors.

These are not the only examples of how the BPE has used Education Matters' evaluation reports, but they serve the purpose of demonstrating that there are ways in which our work has proven useful to an organization that (a) seeks formative feedback on its work and (b) is directly involved with a school district's reform agenda.

---

15. FOCUS is available at www.bpe.org.

It is more difficult for the BPS to make such direct use of our work even when it sees the potential for such use and chooses to act. For example, the BPS determined that our report on the pilot phase of Making Meaning had value for the district, and it wanted the findings shared with principals and literacy coaches who would support further implementation. To that end, early in the school year, the BPS attempted to organize a full-day meeting of principals and coaches from schools that had opted to use the program. I was asked to present the evaluation findings and their implications during one segment of the day's program.[16]

Once the school year began, however, it was difficult for the district to find a common time when the relevant set of district administrators, principals, and literacy coaches would be available to spend a day together. It took several months to arrange the meeting. In the interim, schools were doing the best they could to use Making Meaning appropriately. Ideally, the meeting would have been held at the start of the school year. Realistically, the BPS, like most school districts, could not interfere with previously scheduled work to call a special meeting. And the district had other tasks to accomplish as the school year began, tasks that understandably took precedence over calling an instructionally focused meeting.[17]

In providing this example we are not faulting the BPS. We are merely stressing the advantages that an organization such as the BPE has over a school district when it comes to making swift use of new knowledge. A school district has many essential jobs to accomplish on any day. It is a large, complex, hierarchical organization. In contrast, the BPE is a small organization that does not run a school system. Even when it implements a district-based initiative such as CCL or FAST-R, the BPE does not operate as a unit of the district. It need focus only on the work it is doing with schools that have agreed to work with it. Unlike the district, it can choose its work and can staff itself in light of changing patterns of work.

As a result, the BPE has the capacity to turn its resources to a new task quickly if it chooses to do so. The BPE had the flexibility to focus and act swiftly over a period of a few months to reconfigure its coaching model. It had the flexibility and human capacity to quickly develop *Plain Talk* and *Straight Talk*. School districts will never have this degree of flexibility. Thus it is important to stress that there are limits to what the BPS or any other district can do with evaluation data given the range and complexity of its primary obligations. This fact has implications for the use of formative evaluations in school districts regardless of the quality and usefulness of the data reported and regardless of the district's desire to use the new knowledge. It may be that school districts, particularly large, urban districts, need a partner like the BPE to take on the task of considering evaluation findings and, in collaboration with the district, of making use of them.[18]

In making this comment, I want to return to a point I made earlier in the chapter: evaluators need a local, influential champion if their work is to be used. In the instance of the BPE, that champion is an active player in the district's school improvement agenda. The organization's

---

16. Formal evaluation reports have limited value to teachers and principals. They need to be translated into more directly usable forms if they are to guide practice. *Plain Talk* and *Straight Talk* are examples of such translations. So are direct presentations of findings to relevant practitioners.

17. As we continue to collect data in Boston, we hear about other ways in which our reports have become part of the discussion of the district's whole-school improvement agenda. One principal recently remarked during an interview that our reports have been discussed at cluster meetings, meetings of geographically organized groups of BPS schools. Others have commented that they have used our reports to persuade teachers that it is worthwhile to donate their time to our evaluations.

18. I thank Tony Bryk for making this point during a meeting of the Good Beginnings, and Second Chances: Improving Elementary and Secondary Education initiative of the John D. and Catherine T. MacArthur Foundation, held from November 30 to December 1, 2000, in Los Angeles, CA.

role and relationship gives it considerable leverage with the district. Other champions rarely have the set of characteristics present in the BPE.[19]

For example, Hayes Mizell was certainly an activist program office for the EMCF's Program for Student Achievement. He was in constant communication with district leaders and visited frequently to observe the progress of the work. He valued the evaluation reports we produced and prodded the districts to learn from them. It was an uphill struggle. In a letter that accompanied one of our evaluation reports, Mizell went so far as to tell the superintendent that he should consider it a "luxury" to have the information provided by Education Matters. On other occasions, he and I met with district leaders to discuss the evaluation reports and their implications for practice. But regardless of this level of effort and commitment, districts appeared to view evaluation as a matter of compliance. Our impact was negligible at best.

Although a sample of two cases does not allow me to draw clear conclusions about what it would have taken to make evaluation more salient to the districts involved in the Program for Student Achievement, what was clear was that no one on the local scene came close to taking the role of the BPE in engaging with the district in its work and in encouraging it to learn from the enterprise. There were not local, influential evaluation champions on the scene in these districts.

CHALLENGES

District Challenges

Participating in long-term evaluation studies in Boston and in the districts funded by the EMCF, both over a 10-year period, has led me to conclude that there are endemic features of school districts that (a) go beyond the challenges posed by their primary obligations and (b) make it unlikely that they will use the results of formative evaluations to improve their programs and practices.

Districts generally lack a formal process by which high level administrators learn from their school improvement efforts and, as a result of that learning, make adjustments where they are needed. There are no formal organizational structures and there is no set-aside time in which key stakeholders sit together to consider data that provide them with feedback on implementation. Teachers may increasingly look at student work to determine the impact of their instruction. District leaders do not yet examine their own work to determine its impact. In such contexts, even if they might value the provision of formative feedback, they do not know what to do with it.

Philosophy and deeply held beliefs are often valued more than evidence in district-level discussions.[20] Research findings, if they are used at all, are typically assembled to support individuals' extant positions. Beliefs can be imposed on a district by external funders, as exemplified, for example, by the Gates' Foundation's explicit specification of what they will fund with respect to small high school development. Philosophy can dominate internally, emanating from powerful individuals who purport to "know" what is required to improve schools and, as a

---

19. Neufeld and Guiney (2003) point out that there is great trust between the superintendent and the executive director of the BPE. This is likely of considerable importance in understanding the BPE's role in program development in the district as well as with its championship of evaluation findings.

20. I thank Tom Corcoran for making this point during the discussion of an early draft of this chapter.

result, reject the need for further inquiry. When philosophy and belief trump evidence, formative evaluations are beside the point.

Central office administrators may have competing views about what constitutes good instruction, and the differences remain unresolved over time.[21] The differences remain unresolved for any number of reasons, including (a) the absence of a framework within which to discuss them, (b) the fact that they are based on unresolvable philosophical differences, and/or (c) those at the top of the organization do not recognize that the differences exist, think such differences are healthy, and/or do not want to create a situation in which some individuals have to give up their views in favor of others. Whatever the reasons, the result is lack of opportunity to create coherence around what constitutes high-quality practice and a context in which it would be productive to discuss evidence.

The superintendent and other central office administrators may believe that hiring the right person is the way to succeed with instructional improvement. While the character, knowledge and skill of individuals matter tremendously, this approach to staffing minimizes the need for districts to spend time teaching its leaders to do their jobs in the context of the district's improvement agenda. It precludes their spending time developing a coherent set of beliefs and strategies, a common knowledge base among senior administrators, an associated implementation process, and an accountability system. The belief in the power of individuals, in my experience, results in leaders who may acknowledge disappointing implementation findings but identify their source incorrectly. We have frequently proposed explanations for findings that identified factors other in individual failures. Sometimes, these explanations were rejected in light of a superintendent's prevailing belief structure about the power of individuals. At other times, if our explanations were accepted, the superintendent reported confusion about what next steps to take. In the latter instance, evaluation findings will not be used unless a school district leader chooses to adopt a new set of ideas with respect to leadership.

Central office administrators too often have little opportunity to learn what they need to know to foster instructional improvement. It is not clear who is available to teach them. With rare exceptions, we have found that deputy or assistant superintendents, leaders of central office curriculum and instruction units, and even those who head professional development units in districts have little or no opportunity to fully understand the instructional reforms they are supporting prior to developing the infrastructure for those supports. As a result, the initial required workshop on a reading program, for example, may misrepresent the program's philosophy and practices. Principals' translation of district instructional practices at their schools may fall short of what the program developers had in mind. Lack of understanding makes it difficult for these educators to lead the implementation of instructional improvement efforts and it makes it challenging for them to make sense of evaluation findings.

If districts have usable evaluation findings and are inclined to use them, there are structural, time-related factors that stand in the way of their use. First, regardless of the ways in which high-level central office administrators are brought together to talk about their work, immediate issues and crises tend to dominate the discussions. Time set aside to discuss

---

21. I include superintendents, deputy superintendents, instructional leaders, and those who lead and staff different units in the central office, for example curriculum and instruction, when I use the phrase "central office administrators."

school-based instructional practices, we are told, is often lost to discussions about operations. *Second,* the budget cycle and, therefore, decisions about how to allocate and spend instructional resources do not often coincide with the availability of data that might inform decisions. For example, a program evaluation may be available in the summer; decisions about whether to fund the program for another year may have had to be made the previous February. *Third*, many districts have a short attention span; administrators and school board members may want results far too soon. As a result, programs that may have promise are terminated too soon. While the factors identified earlier may be more important to the overall capacity of the central office to support instructional improvements, these time-related issues also play a real role.

In ending this section on challenges to the use of evaluation findings, I want to make another comment about the nature of evaluation findings and their subsequent use: much of the time, findings cannot be neatly packaged into steps that policymakers or practitioners should take. Despite the fact that our data are collected locally and are place specific, in order to use them, users have to translate the findings so that they have practical implications for their work. In the case of the BPE, it is important to note that although it found our reports on coaching instructive, we did not recommend the CCL model. We never thought of an alternate model. What the BPE did was take our findings and use them to develop something new, something they thought would be responsive. Then they asked us to help them determine whether and to what extent the transformation was an improvement over the previous practice and, if so, what might improve the new practice. Much of the time, use involves complicated work. It does not lend itself to simple solutions.

In a similar vein, in our *Taking Stock* report we identified and described levels of implementation with respect to features of the district's whole-school improvement agenda (Neufeld & Woodworth, 2000). With respect to the low-implementing schools, we noted that they were not all low-implementing for the same reasons. It took over two pages of text for us to sufficiently elaborate the range of reasons we identified. What follows is one excerpt from that text.

> For example, one school might have a principal who refuses to change her interaction patterns with teachers in order to enable them to take leadership roles on the ILT [Instructional Leadership Team]; another might have a principal who wants to change her ILT interaction patterns, but, despite coaching, does not know how to do so; and/or another school might have a principal who does not value the basic ideas of the reform and/or considers too great the personal costs of making the requisite changes. A few principals, whether by disposition or level of leadership skill, have no strategies with which to address teachers who refuse to participate in the whole-school change effort. This absence of principal leadership prevents the entire school from moving forward. (p. 113)

At the end of the section we recommended a set of actions that included the following.

- Carefully collect data that will identify the factors influencing each school's implementation status.
- Develop intervention strategies that are targeted to the factors identified by the data collection.
- Resist the urge to develop more prescribed, "dumbed-down" interventions that eviscerate the core components of the Essentials. (pp. 114–115)

We elaborated what we meant by each of the actions, and we suggested that the BPS and the BPE might collaborate on this challenging work. Subsequent data collection led us to conclude that little happened to change conditions at the schools that were associated with low implementation other than replacing principals when that was an option.

With hindsight, I remain convinced that these were appropriate recommendations that provided a strategy with which to increase school-based capacity. But they implied the need for a great deal of work on the part of those who supervised principals. Therefore, these recommendations were not helpful to the district because it did not have the resources with which to address the problems in this way. At the time, there were approximately 130 schools in Boston and too few supervisors who could have devoted the requisite time to the work we suggested without making major changes in district operations.

Given the size and complexity of school districts as well as their standard operating procedures, it is difficult to know how to be helpful even if the data are valid and the reports compelling. In thinking about how districts use or do not use evaluation findings, it is essential to keep in mind the complexity of their organization, the multiple goals they need to achieve, and the limited resources they may have on hand. I do not present this as an excuse; I present it as a set of conditions in which Education Matters does formative evaluation and the superintendent and deputies run the school district.

Challenges for Education Matters

There are challenges for Education Matters as an organization associated with engaging in long-term work of the sort we do in Boston. We have had little control over the ebb and flow of the work. While several of the grants covered multiple years, the focus of our evaluation work shifted as the district's and BPE's work shifted. In addition, the BPE and BPS frequently ask us to take on additional, small, short-term studies with little notice. This is rewarding, but small, short-term projects are difficult to staff because they do not warrant hiring either full-time staff or long-term, part-time staff.

Making Meaning, for example, required intensive data collection over a three-month period, followed by a written report. The total funding available for the work was $15,000. The FAP had a slightly longer data collection period but similar financial parameters. For me, as the president of Education Matters, the first questions I must answer in deciding whether to accept such evaluation studies, even when I want to do them, are (a) Can I find a qualified researcher? and (b) Can I afford to have us do the work?[22]

My response to the exigencies of funding and the uncertain flow work has been to depend heavily on the availability of high-quality, part-time graduate students who are interested in working as research assistants. These research assistants have made invaluable contributions to the work, and some were able to develop dissertations related to their Education Matters studies. But their stay at Education Matters was short, never lasting more than a few years. As a result, we have had frequent turnover in staff.[23]

In a long-term evaluation relationship, such as the one we have with the BPS and the BPE, the staff turnover and the reliance on graduate students has meant that, for the most part, I am the only one who carries the collective knowledge derived from our Boston-based work. I am the only one who has sufficient knowledge of individuals and of the organizations to make

---

22. This chapter focuses primarily on our long-term work in Boston, but these factors are relevant to the other work we do, as well.

23. The funding available on longer-term evaluations in Boston has not been sufficient to support a full-time, senior research associate. And, it is not feasible to construct a full-time job out of the accumulated work of three or four distinct, small projects. This, too, limits the potential of developing a set of staff members who share collective knowledge.

judgments about how and what to negotiate, for example, when we face challenges from the BPS or BPE. In the end, the absence of anyone else with the collective knowledge necessary to carry on the conversation means that (a) I need to have a role in most of the work we do in Boston and (b) when I reach the limit of my capacity, we cannot take on additional work.[24] Had I been more prescient when I began the organization, or had I had an interest in developing a larger organization, I might have been able to create a firm that was not limited in these ways.

There is another issue that contributes to the difficulty of staffing projects and producing high-quality, usable reports: the need for researchers who can analyze data and write on an extremely short time line. As I noted earlier in the chapter, our reports must be completed within two or three months of completing the data collection. We cannot ruminate on our data for even six months, let alone a year. Yet we must not take shortcuts in data analysis that would lead to weaknesses in our conclusions. As a result, I take the lead in writing most of the reports we produce. The limits of my ability to analyze and write quickly constrain what we can do.

We may have entered a new phase, in this regard, quite recently. As a result of her work as an Education Matters research assistant on the FAP, and her subsequent success in conducting the second evaluation of FAST-R as an independent consultant to the BPE, Sara Schwartz Chrismer, now a research associate, is leading the evaluation of FAST-R at Education Matters and has a research assistant working with her. And Annette Sassi, a senior research associate who began her tenure with Education Matters by working on the study of Making Meaning, has taken responsibility for the firm's study of the BTR Program. I serve as an advisor to both of these studies.

These challenges for Education Matters are real and important. But it is essential to remember that they arise because we have been able to do the kind of work we think matters. We have been able, in many respects, to work as external evaluators and as partners in the important school improvement work that is ongoing in Boston.

If those of us who work at Education Matters wanted to assess our value to the districts and schools with which we work by measuring the improvements that followed the presentation of our reports, we would be despondent most of the time. Certainly, we have our moments of doubt and of extreme frustration. Sometimes an immediate change that from our perspective would be simple and meaningful does not occur. Like anyone else, we wonder what we are doing and whether it matters.

But most of the time, we know that we are engaged in a complicated line of work, as are all of the others who are trying to improve teaching, learning, and leadership in the nation's urban schools. We know that there are no simple solutions to the challenges these districts face. As an external, qualitative evaluation firm, we have a role to play, and we play it as best we can. We keep our voice in the conversation. We remain on the scene as long as we can, and we believe that our contribution is meaningful. It will be for others to evaluate the validity of this belief.

REFERENCES

Boston Plan for Excellence. (2004–2005). *FOCUS: Making Meaning.* Boston, MA: Author.
Boston Public Schools and Boston Plan for Excellence. (2003a). *Plain talk about CCL: Crafting a course of study.* Boston, MA: Author.

---

24. In this regard, it is necessary to note that my evaluation portfolio includes a significant percentage of work that is not focused on school improvement in Boston.

Boston Public Schools and Boston Plan for Excellence. (2003b). *Straight talk about CCL: A guide for school leaders.* Boston, MA: Author.

Neufeld, B., & Guiney, E. (2003). Transforming events: A local education fund's efforts to promote large-scale urban school reform. In *Research perspectives on school reform: Lessons from the Annenberg Challenge* (pp. 51–68). Providence, RI: Brown University, Annenberg Institute for School Reform. Available on line at www.annenberginstitute.org.

Neufeld, B., & Levy, A. (2004). *Baseline report: High school renewal in Boston.* Cambridge, MA: Education Matters, Inc.

Neufeld, B., & Roper, D. (2002). *Off to a good start: Year I of collaborative coaching and learning in the effective practice schools.* Cambridge, MA: Education Matters, Inc.

Neufeld, B., & Sassi, A. (2004). *Getting our feet wet: Using Making Meaning™ for the first time.* Cambridge, MA: Education Matters, Inc.

Neufeld, B., & Schwartz, S. (2004). *Formative assessment pilot implementation: Final report.* Cambridge, MA: Education Matters, Inc.

Neufeld, B., & Woodworth, K. (2000). *Taking stock: The status of implementation and the need for further support in the BPE-BAC cohort I and II schools.* Cambridge, MA: Education Matters, Inc.

13

Research In, Research Out: The Role of Research in the Development and Scale-Up of Success for All

Robert E. Slavin, Nancy A. Madden, and
Amanda Datnow

Success for All (SFA; Slavin & Madden, 2001) is a comprehensive reform program for elementary schools. Intended to ensure students' success in reading by preventing them from falling behind in the early grades, SFA provides schools with extensive professional development in reading instructional methods with strong evidence of effectiveness, as well as student reading materials designed to facilitate daily use of research-based instruction. The program also includes cross-grade grouping strategies, parent involvement programs, and one-to-one tutoring for struggling students. Table 13.1 summarizes the main elements of the approach.

Since it began in 1987, SFA has been the subject of more than 50 matched experimental-control comparison studies, carried out by researchers throughout the United States. Borman et al. (2003), reviewing research on comprehensive reform models, identified 46 studies of SFA and an essentially identical program called Roots and Wings, and found a combined effect size of +0.20. This number of well-controlled studies was somewhat more than those on the Direct Instruction program (Adams & Engelmann, 1996), and far more than those for all other comprehensive reforms. A longitudinal follow-up study found that students who had begun SFA in the early elementary grades and continued no later than grade 5 were still reading significantly better than former control students in the eighth grade, and were about half as likely to have been retained or assigned to special education (Borman & Hewes, 2003). Currently, a randomized evaluation of SFA is under way, involving 41 schools across the country. Using hierarchical linear analyses, results show significant positive effects of the program on reading measures (Borman et al., 2005; Borman et al., in press).

The SFA elementary reading program is currently being implemented in more than 1,100 schools in 47 states. Current SFA schools have used the program for a median of five years (Slavin & Madden, 2004). These schools are mostly high-poverty Title I schools serving many African American, Hispanic, and White students in urban and rural districts. Until 1998, the program was part of Johns Hopkins University, but at that time it was moved to a nonprofit organization, the Success for All Foundation (SFAF).

TABLE 13.1
Major Elements of Success for All

Success for All is a schoolwide program for students in grades pre-K to eight which organizes resources to attempt to ensure that virtually every student will acquire adequate basic skills. The main elements of the program are as follows:

A Schoolwide Curriculum. Success for All schools implement research-based reading, writing, and language arts programs in all grades, K–8. The reading program in grades K–1 emphasizes language and comprehension skills, phonics, sound blending, and use of shared stories that students read to one another in pairs. The shared stories combine teacher-read material with phonetically regular student material. In grades 2–8, the program emphasizes cooperative learning and partner reading activities, comprehension strategies such as summarization and clarification built around narrative and expository texts, writing, and direct instruction in reading comprehension skills. At all levels, students are required to read books of their own choice for 20 minutes at home each evening. Cooperative learning programs in writing/language arts are used in grades 1–8.

Tutors. In grades 1–3, specially trained tutors work one-to-one 20 minutes each day with struggling students. Tutorial instruction is closely coordinated with regular classroom instruction.

Quarterly Assessments and Regrouping. Students in grades 1–8 are assessed every quarter to determine whether they are making adequate progress in reading. This information is used to regroup students for instruction across grade lines, so that each reading class contains students of different ages who are all reading at the same level.

Solutions Team. A Solutions Team works in each school to help support families in ensuring the success of their children, focusing on parent education, parent involvement, attendance, and student behavior. This team is composed of existing or additional staff such as parent liaisons, social workers, counselors, and assistant principals.

Facilitator. A program facilitator works with teachers as an on-site coach to help them implement the reading program, manages the quarterly assessments, assists the Solutions Team, makes sure that all staff are communicating with each other, and helps the staff as a whole make certain that every child is making adequate progress.

THE IMPORTANCE OF RESEARCH IN SUCCESS FOR ALL

One of the key policy objectives of SFA has been to move educational practice toward a focus on evidence. Since 1986, the first author of this chapter has written and revised an educational psychology textbook (Slavin, 2006), reviewing research on all of the major topics that relate to effective practices in education: learning, instruction, grouping, motivation, classroom management, assessment, school organization, parent involvement, leadership, provisions for struggling students and for English language learners, and so on. Many principles of effective practice have long been accepted by most researchers, and are included in all educational psychology texts. Yet they are unknown, unused, or misused by educators.

The researchers who developed SFA and have worked on it for many years share a belief that educational outcomes will never change on a serious scale until the core technology of teaching, down to daily lessons and teacher behaviors and up to school and district organization, comes to embody well-validated principles of practice. We contrast the constant progress of evidence-based fields such as medicine, agriculture, and technology to the faddishness of education (Slavin, 2003).

SFA was intended to be an example of what education reform would be like if it were based on evidence and then continually evaluated itself to progressively improve. It was also designed to demonstrate how research-based practices could scale up to serve a meaningful number of students, as a direct challenge to the famous Rand Change Agent Study (Berman & McLaughlin, 1978) that for more than 35 years has served as the touchstone for those who believe that externally developed programs cannot be replicated in schools, that each school must find its own unique path to reform.

USES OF RESEARCH IN SUCCESS FOR ALL

Since it was first conceived, SFA has been designed as a means of creating conditions in which teachers would use the results of rigorous research every day. Each of the major components of the program was designed to operationalize practices known from research to increase the achievement of students at risk. At the outset, and again as the program developed, SFA researchers have carried out reviews of research in many areas relevant to practice to inform us about effective strategies.

As the program developed, we continued to focus on using research to learn from the teachers and principals implementing it and, most importantly, to learn how program implementation, variations, and conditions affect student outcomes.

Finally, we have carried out a large number of studies to evaluate program outcomes, and have encouraged third party organizations and individuals to do such studies. There are now more than 50 matched experimental-control comparisons (and one large randomized study) evaluating SFA. These have involved at least 40 researchers throughout the world, in many different institutions.

The following sections discuss each of these uses of research in the SFA program of research.

EVIDENCE BASES FOR SUCCESS FOR ALL COMPONENTS

Each of the components of SFA was incorporated into the program after a review of the literature in the area involved. The following subsections briefly present the evidence base for the main SFA components.

Cooperative Learning

Cooperative learning, or peer-assisted learning, refers to a set of instructional methods in which students work in small groups to help one another master academic content. Cooperative learning methods are central to SFA at all levels, from prekindergarten to grade 8.

Research on the achievement effects of cooperative learning finds that cooperative methods are effective if there is a group goal that students can achieve only if all group members make academic progress. A review of this research (Slavin, 1995) found a median effect size of +0.32 (+0.21 for standardized tests) for studies of cooperative methods that incorporated group goals and individual accountability. These studies involved grades 2–12, a wide variety of subjects, and a wide variety of investigators. Other reviewers (e.g., Rohrbeck et al., 2003; Johnson & Johnson, 1999; Webb & Palincsar, 1996) came to similar conclusions about the effectiveness of cooperative learning if it incorporates these essential elements.

Cognitive Strategy Instruction

In addition to cooperative learning, the upper elementary and middle school components of SFA make extensive use of cognitive strategy instruction, teaching students to use specific skills to enhance their comprehension of narrative and expository texts. The key strategies emphasized, and their research bases, are as follows.

Summarization. Having students summarize information they have read is one of the most consistently supported of all cognitive reading comprehension and study strategies (Brown & Day, 1983; Taylor & Beach, 1984). Armbruster, Anderson, and Ostertag (1987) successfully evaluated a particular form of summarization in which fifth graders analyzed social studies content into three boxes: statement of a problem, actions taken to solve the problem, and results of the actions. Malone and Mastropieri (1992) found that summarization was made more effective if students with learning disabilities were also taught to monitor their own summaries using a checklist.

Graphic organizers. A particularly promising form of summarization is having students represent ideas and connections among ideas in graphic forms. For example, Berkowitz (1986) had sixth graders write the title of a passage in the middle of a sheet of paper, and then add main ideas and supporting details around the passage title as they encountered them in the text. This strategy increased comprehension and retention of the content. Similarly, Baumann (1984) had sixth graders conceptualize the main idea of a paragraph as a tabletop, and then identify supporting details as the table's legs. "Web" strategies, in which students link concepts as they read, have been widely used and generally found to be effective.

Story grammar. Another form of facilitated summarization that has been successfully evaluated is having students identify story grammar in narratives. That is, students identify the main characters, setting, problem, attempted problem solutions, and final solutions. Short and Ryan (1984) found this strategy to help fourth graders understand text. Idol (1987; Idol & Croll, 1987) had upper elementary children use a "story map" that focused on the same story grammar elements, and this helped poor readers (but not proficient readers) to comprehend the content.

Imagery. Gambrell and Bales (1986) had poor readers in fourth and fifth grades make pictures in their minds to understand the content of stories. For example, in reading a story about pigeons they visualized how pigeons who were blindfolded might find their way home. Imagery has also been extensively studied as a mnemonic device for learning paired associates, as in learning names in other languages for objects (Hattie, Biggs, & Purdie, 1996; Pressley, Levin, & Delaney, 1982).

Question generation. Another robust strategy for comprehension and vocabulary development is teaching children to generate their own questions about material they are reading. For example, Davey and McBride (1986) taught sixth graders to develop "think-type" questions as they read. This strategy helped students understand and recall the key ideas. King (1994) successfully used a similar strategy, and question generation is a central feature of reciprocal teaching, described below. A variant focused in particular on vocabulary development is "question the author" (Beck & McKeown, 2001), in which children are taught a strategy for expository text in which they ask why an author included certain information or explanations.

Activating prior knowledge. Good readers automatically bring prior knowledge to bear on new, related content, but poor readers may not do so. Several studies have found that children can be successfully taught to ask themselves what they already know about a given topic and then relate this to the current text, and that this increases comprehension (e.g., Hansen & Pearson, 1983; Dewitz, Carr, & Patberg, 1987). This strategy is widely used as part of the common KWL strategy, in which students are asked before reading what they already know about a topic (K), what they want to learn (W), and later, what they learned (L).

Peers as strategy partners. A variety of cooperative learning methods have been used to develop students' comprehension skills. For example, Dansereau (1988) and O'Donnell (1996) have studied "cooperative scripts," in which students take turns summarizing and evaluating each other's summaries. Meloth and Deering (1992, 1994) found that peers could help each other acquire cognitive strategies. Fantuzzo, Polite, and Grayson (1990) developed and evaluated reciprocal peer tutoring strategies to help students study complex material. In each of these methods, students are given specific guidance in how to help a partner or teammate learn the content and develop a strategy.

Vocabulary strategies. Vocabulary development strategies are of importance for all students, but especially for English language learners (Blachowicz & Fisher, 2000; Coady & Huckin, 1997; Fitzgerald, 1995; García, 2000). Particularly promising vocabulary strategies include those described by Chamot and O'Malley (1996), Calderón (2001), and Padrón (1992). Neuman and Koskinen (1992) found that use of captioned television related to books students were reading significantly improved their vocabulary and comprehension performance.

Self-regulation. Metacognitive strategies typically grouped under the term self-regulation can be taught and used as reading comprehension strategies (Paris & Paris, 2001). A large body of research has shown the achievement benefits of self-regulatory strategies such as goal setting (Schunk & Scwartz, 1993), using self-verbalization to talk oneself through a problem (Schunk & Cox, 1986), and self-monitoring by recording one's progress (Zimmerman, Bonner, & Kovach, 1996).

Vocabulary Strategies Instruction

Perhaps the most robust findings in the field of literacy is the high correlation between vocabulary and reading comprehension (Cunningham & Stanovich, 1997; Dickinson & Tabors, 2001; Stahl, 2003). This is particularly true for English language learners (Calderón et al., 2004; Saville-Troike, 1984). Garcia (1991) found that vocabulary knowledge was more important than prior knowledge, when examining the factors that influenced reading test performance for a sample of fifth- and sixth-grade Latino students. For this reason, SFA emphasizes vocabulary development strategies throughout the grades.

Findings from the National Reading Panel (2000) indicate that various methods improve students' vocabulary. For example, promising vocabulary strategies include those described by Beck and McKeown, (2002), Scott and Nagy (1997), Stahl (2003), Carlo et al. (2004), Calderón (2001), and Padrón (1992). In a longitudinal study (Calderón et al. 2004), the reading performance of Latino students transitioning from Spanish to English instruction was enhanced by a combination of high frequency and multiple, repeated exposures; rich instruction of vocabulary in which words are applied to multiple contexts; preinstruction of vocabulary to facilitate text comprehension; and restructuring of materials or procedures to bolster comprehension.

Preschool and Kindergarten

The SFAF created Curiosity Corner and KinderCorner, comprehensive preschool and kindergarten programs based on recent brain research and research on cognitive development indicating that early education is crucial in getting children off to a good start in life (Bowman, Donovan, & Burns, 2001; National Research Council and Institute of Medicine, 2000; Magnuson et al., 2003). In addition to short-term effects on academic achievement, long-term effects of several early childhood programs include fewer arrests, fewer teen pregnancies, and higher employment (Gilliam & Zigler, 2000).

Many studies have shown short- and long-term impacts of participation in high-quality preschool programs in comparison to no preschool experience (see, e.g., Barnett et al., 1987; Berreuta-Clement et al., 1984). Further, there is evidence that center-based preschool programs are more effective and cost-effective than programs that only intervene with the child's family (Bryant & Ramey, 1987; White, Taylor, & Moss, 1992).

Curiosity Corner and KinderCorner support teachers in their efforts to achieve the specific emerging literacy skills outlined by the National Reading Panel (2000) and the National Research Council (2000). The programs include specific research-proven strategies for promoting young children's vocabulary and oral language development, phonemic awareness, letter recognition, understanding of narrative, and conventions of print (Neuman, Copple, & Bredekamp, 1999; Snow, Burns, & Griffin, 1998; Whitehurst et al., 1994).

Each classroom has Learning Labs set up with developmentally appropriate, high-quality children's books, manipulatives, a variety of papers and writing tools; meaningful environmental print; and concrete directions for teachers on how to facilitate learning in these learning centers (Burns, Griffin, & Snow, 1999).

Dynamic Assessment Portfolios provide snapshots of the child at particular times, indicate how the child is continually growing and changing, and include information across the domains of the child's development. The portfolio assessment that Curiosity Corner teachers are trained to use is a tool that organizes an array of assessments to provide a broad picture of the child.

Studies of the Abecedarian Project (Ramey & Ramey, 1998) and of the Chicago Child-Parent Centers (Reynolds, 1998; Reynolds & Temple, 1998), among others, find that sustained interventions beyond the preschool years have a substantially greater longitudinal impact on children's reading and other measures of school success than preschool alone. These studies imply that a quality preschool experience is necessary but not sufficient for substantial and lasting achievement benefits.

The Curiosity Corner curriculum and objectives directly align with KinderCorner and Reading Roots, the first-grade reading program, in a way that enables teachers to continuously scaffold conceptual knowledge, oral language, vocabulary, phonological awareness, and mastery of the shapes and sounds of the alphabet. Emergent skills fostered in Curiosity Corner are the basis for early reading skills taught in KinderCorner and Reading Roots.

Beginning Reading Instruction

SFA beginning reading instruction incorporates all of the critical elements outlined by the National Reading Panel (2000): phonemic awareness, phonics, vocabulary, fluency, and comprehension. Literacy instruction begins with phonemic awareness, in which students isolate initial, final, and medial sounds; blend sounds to make words; and segment words into their separate sounds, based on the work of Adams et al. (1998). The systematic phonics instruction uses mnemonic key pictures, alliterative phrases, letter writing cues, and animations to help children learn letter sounds. Initial instruction focuses on letter sounds and only after they have been introduced, letter names are taught. As soon as a few phonemes have been taught, students begin blending them together to read consonant-vowel-consonant (CVC) words. Video segments with puppets model blending simple words.

The program then introduces simple decodable stories in which every word (other than a handful of sight words) is composed of letters that the children have already learned. Students engage in discussions about the stories to enhance their comprehension. They learn about purposes of reading, making predictions, summarizing, and about the elements of narratives. This approach was developed from research on effective practices in beginning reading by Adams (1990). Video skits introduce the vocabulary of the stories to the children before they read the stories to increase their comprehension of them. Neuman and Koskinen (1992) used captioned television to helped English language learners learn key vocabulary and comprehension skills.

The multimedia segments used in the program, the phoneme animations, puppet blending segments, and vocabulary skits, are based on research on the effectiveness of multimedia (Mayer, 2001; Mayer & Moreno, 2003). Research on educational programs such as *Sesame Street* (Fisch & Truglio, 2000; Rice et al., 1990) and *Between the Lions* (Linebarger et al., 2004) has shown positive effects of educational television for the reading and language development of young children.

Upper Elementary and Middle School Reading

The upper elementary reading program used in SFA, called Reading Wings, and the middle school reading program, The Reading Edge, are based on the research cited above on cooperative learning and cognitive strategy instruction, but also on an earlier program called Cooperative Integrated Reading and Composition (CIRC). Several studies at the elementary level (Stevens et al., 1987; Stevens & Slavin, 1995) and at the middle school level (Stevens & Durkin, 1992) have found positive effects of CIRC on reading comprehension. A bilingual form of CIRC designed to help English language learners transition from Spanish to English reading has also been found to be effective (Calderón, Hertz-Lazarowitz, & Slavin, 1998).

Writing

SFA uses a process writing approach, called Writing Wings, based on the work of Graves (1983) and Calkins (1986). That is, students work together in small teams to help each other plan, draft, revise, edit, and "publish" compositions in various genres. SFA adds to this specific instruction in cognitive writing strategies, such as use of graphic organizers and visualizations.

Research has supported the effectiveness of writing process models in general (Harris & Graham, 1996; Hillocks, 1984). More specifically, the SFA writing programs for grades 1–8 are based on a program called Cognitive Strategy Instruction in Writing (CSIW; Englert et al., 1991). In the context of a process writing model, CSIW provides explicit instruction on writing structures (e.g., comparison/contrast), "Think Alouds" to verbally model thinking about composition, and construction and revision of text. Research on CSIW has found it to significantly enhance the development of proficient writers (Englert et al., 1991).

Classroom Management

Throughout grades K–8, SFA uses a preventive approach to classroom management that emphasizes cooperative learning, a rapid pace of instruction, high success rates among children, and means of making certain that students always have meaningful work to do. This approach is based on the work of Good, Grouws, and Ebmeier (1983); Emmer, Evertson, and Worsham (2003); and Hawkins, Doueck, and Lishner (1988).

Grouping

The grouping strategy used for SFA in grades 1–8 is an adaptation of the Joplin Plan, in which students are placed in reading classes according to their reading level, not their age. That is, a 2–1 reading class may contain some advanced first graders, a lot of on-level second graders, and a few third graders. Research on this approach has found it to enhance student reading achievement (Gutiérrez & Slavin, 1992; Slavin, 1987).

Tutoring

One-to-one tutoring is the most effective form of instruction known. A review of research on this topic by Wasik and Slavin (1993) found effect sizes approaching +0.75 for tutoring programs using certified teachers. Smaller but still impressive effects have been found in studies of tutoring done by paraprofessionals (Morris, Shaw, & Perney, 1990). SFA provides tutoring to struggling students in grades 1–3 using a model patterned on Reading Recovery, the most extensively evaluated tutoring program (see Pinnell et al., 1994).

English Language Learners

From its early days, SFA has had a strong emphasis on teaching children who are acquiring English (Cheung & Slavin, 2005; Slavin & Madden, 1999). Two formats are available. A Spanish bilingual program provides instruction in Spanish, with a transition to English completed by third grade for most students. The other is an English language development approach, which emphasizes vocabulary development, oral language, and assistance for English language learners. We have not taken a position on which of these is best, although a recent review (Slavin & Cheung, 2004a, 2004b) suggests that paired bilingual models, in which children are taught in English and Spanish, may be optimal.

The SFA approaches to programming for English language learners build on children's strengths in their native language, using vocabulary development strategies adapted from those of Carlo et al. (2004), Fitzgerald (1995), Calderón (1999), and many others, as described previously.

RESEARCH ON OUTCOMES OF SUCCESS FOR ALL

It is not enough that programs be based on well-validated principles. The program itself must be rigorously evaluated in comparison to similar control groups. SFA researchers have carried out many large-scale, longitudinal studies of the program, as have many others. As noted earlier, Borman et al. (2003) identified a total of 46 experimental-control comparisons evaluating SFA, of which 31 were carried out by third-party investigators. A mean effect size of +0.20 (combining SFA and Roots & Wings) was obtained across all studies and measures. A longitudinal study by Borman and Hewes (2003) found that students who had been in SFA elementary schools were, by eighth grade, still reading significantly better than former control group students and were about half as likely to have been retained or assigned to special education.

Since the Borman et al. (2003) review, a number of additional studies of SFA have been carried out. Most importantly, a national randomized evaluation of SFA is under way. A total of

41 schools were randomly assigned to use SFA either in grades K–2 or in grades 3–5. The primary grades in 3–5 schools were used as controls, as were the intermediate grades in K–2 schools. First-year results found positive effects for students in kindergarten and first grade on measures of word attack (Borman et al., 2005). Second-year analyses found significant impacts on three of the four reading measures used (Borman et al., 2005). This first large-scale randomized evaluation is particularly important in today's policy environment, which is strongly supporting randomized experiments (Whitehurst, 2002). Taken together, there are now more than 50 experimental-control studies of SFA involving more than 200 schools throughout the United States.

THE CULTURE OF DATA-DRIVEN DECISION MAKING IN SUCCESS FOR ALL

In addition to the formal research efforts described above, the entire culture of SFA is one that revolves around the continuous use of student achievement data as the basis for decision making, both at the school and Foundation levels. Schools are expected to conduct their own informal research on their practice with SFA by collecting and analyzing student data. At each school, educators examine the 8-week and quarterly assessments of their students' progress and make changes in practice accordingly. SFA schools now also have available to them additional assessments, called 4Sight (Slavin et al., 2005), that are benchmarked to their particular state standards. As one teacher in an SFA school explained: "We have ongoing data collection. . . . If we see, oh my gosh, half of my kids aren't really getting this, then even within the program they give us reteaching lessons. . . ." (Datnow & Park, 2005, p. 15).

In addition to informing their practice, school-level assessment data are used by educators to support SFA's effectiveness and continuation, particularly in the face of political challenges from district staff or from skeptical teachers. A facilitator in one SFA school stated, "one of the things they cannot deny is that it's working for our children and because the data is there and they can see it . . . it's not just us talking, it's the numbers and the database that we have." At this school, having data on students' progress enabled the school to validate their commitment to SFA (Park, 2005, p. 16).

From Program Monitoring to Goal-Focused Implementation

A common misperception about SFA is that it is a completely "scripted" program that does not allow for flexibility on the part of local educators. Indeed, early qualitative studies on SFA found that even though most teachers found the program beneficial for students, some still complained about the constraints on their autonomy (Datnow & Castellano, 2000; Datnow, Hubbard, and Mehan, 2002). Historically, SFA has in fact had a strong focus on fidelity to the model and, as one SFA staff member explained, earlier on there was more of an emphasis on "*doing* the program." This was particularly the case for the new SFA schools that were just learning the mechanics of the model.

However, after years of experience with the model and with working with mature implementation sites (which comprise most of the SFA schools), SFA allows adaptations to the model if they are aimed toward improving student outcomes and meeting the individual school's goals. This shift in stance toward fidelity to implementation allows the schools greater freedom in making adaptations that are geared toward student outcomes. SFA calls the new approach "goal-focused implementation."

To be sure, program fidelity is still expected on a number of key dimensions (e.g., the reading curriculum, cross-grade grouping, full-time facilitator). However, SFA's measure of the quality of implementation differs as it now provides space for some innovative practices arising from the needs of specific schools. The theory is that program fidelity should serve program effectiveness rather than fidelity for its own sake. In a study by Datnow and Park (2005), an SFA facilitator explained how the relationship between trainers and teachers had become one characterized by support:

> When we first started . . . they would come in and watch the teachers, "are you following the schedule? Are you doing Adventures in Writing on Day 3?" . . . And they've lightened up on it. Now they come in and they are looking and listening to the kids and seeing, "Okay, what's the conversation the kids are having? Are they using the strategies?" . . . Not so much, "Here's a schedule." And I think it has been beneficial for the teachers and for them. It lets teachers have some flexibility. . . . But I think they are more focused on what the student outcomes are and supporting teachers so that those kids have those outcomes. (p. 14)

A teacher at an SFA school reiterated: "They trust our judgment that we are doing the program, that we are following the components, and if we add something, if we lengthen it, if we shorten something, if I do it on the wrong day, it's not taking away from the overall comprehension of the program." An SFA staff person confirmed: "If you can do meaningful sentences this way and still get the same outcome, then all the more power to you, but it really takes an understanding and an acceptance of what the rationale is behind the activity" (p. 17).

This shift from a focus on pure fidelity—which was heavily based on feedback received from schools—to a focus on schools' needs appears to have substantially changed the relationship between the SFA staff and the educators in the schools they work with (Datnow & Park, 2005). Previously, SFA trainers were seen as "SFA police" focused on visible details of implementation (e.g., Are the "Word Walls" posted in the classrooms?), but now they are seen as valuable sources of instructional support. Another change is that whereas in the past, trainers would meet only with administrators or with whole staffs to share the results of their "implementation checks," they now meet one-on-one with teachers to help them improve their practice. Overall, as a result of this change, the relationship between educators and the SFAF appears to be more collaborative than evaluative. The shift to "goal-focused" rather than simply fidelity-focused implementation is a significant exemplar of a change in the program that is the result of the valuing of practitioners' experiences with SFA.

Feedback Loops between Schools and the Success for All Foundation

As the above discussion implies, there is a frequent exchange of information between and among staff in the SFAF and educators in SFA schools. Several processes have been put into place to enable feedback loops and ongoing dialogues between school educators, trainers, other SFAF staff, and the SFA directors. The topics of these discussions range from implementation issues, successes or problems with particular program components, and the degree to which SFA is helping meet schools' goals. At the most simple level, trainers gather information about how the program is working when they visit local schools, and they share this knowledge with other foundation staff on a regular basis. At one school in Datnow and Park's study (2005), the principal, teachers, and SFA facilitator all mentioned taking part regularly in this type of dialogue. A teacher observed:

It's kind of like formal versus informal research, because some of the component meetings we have with our trainers. . . . We sit down and she asks us questions, "Are you comfortable? Do you need more training? What do you like? What don't you like?" And so she's kind of doing informal research. (p. 18)

This "informal" research leads to both changes at the local level and changes ultimately in the overall program. Undoubtedly, the SFAF has more interaction with some schools than others, depending on their maturity in program implementation and on the number of days that schools contract with the SFAF for training. Some schools, particularly those that are involved in research studies related to SFA, might experience an even tighter feedback loop with the foundation (Datnow & Park, 2005).

In any event, SFA has instituted several new efforts to enhance feedback loops between the foundation and all of its member schools. First, SFA trainers can be available on speaker phone to address questions and gather feedback during teachers' monthly "teacher learning community" meetings that occur in each school. Second, phone interviews with educators in particular schools take place, particularly when the foundation staff is interested in finding out how a new component of SFA is working. A teacher in Datnow and Park's study (2005) explained:

We've been on conference calls to Maryland in the past, just talking. They want to know how the questioning is going. . . . So they are listening to us, and they want to know. . . . So you feel like they are going into classrooms, talking to teachers to find out what is working and what is not. So I really feel like the research is coming from us. (p. 18)

The SFAF also holds focus groups among teachers at the annual SFA "experienced sites" conferences, giving practitioners an opportunity to share the knowledge they have gained in working with the model. All of these processes are designed to achieve a smooth feedback loop between schools and the SFA Foundation.

Support to Success for All Schools and the Role of Trainers

Understanding how the SFAF is structured with respect to the training and support of schools is important to further making sense of the links between research and practice and the feedback loops within the organization. In the period of 1995–1998, the total number of schools using SFA quadrupled, having sextupled in the three years prior (Slavin & Madden, 1998). During this period, the number of SFA schools grew so significantly that developers felt they could no longer efficiently support schools from their original location at Johns Hopkins University. The goal was to maintain quality of support as the quantity of schools grew. The decision was then made to launch the SFAF, a nonprofit organization (Slavin & Madden, 1998). At the same time, the SFAF added layers of organizational complexity and morphed into a new structure.

As of 2005, there were approximately 150 SFA regionally based trainers across the country, most of whom work out of their homes. This arrangement, as Slavin and Madden (1998, p. 14) explain, "gives us far more control and assurance to fidelity than does engaging regional training sites in universities or other existing agencies, which may have their own agendas and constraints." Trainers work with anywhere from 5 to 20 schools each, depending on the number of contracted days per school. The SFAF recruits trainers from schools, usually former SFA teachers and facilitators, who have expert knowledge in how the model works in a particular local context. Overseeing the 120 trainers are 15 area managers, who also deal with district relations and respond to trainers' questions regarding school adaptations of SFA. Area managers are supported by a team of expansion and outreach staff. Two "implementation officers" oversee the area managers and outreach personnel. While some staff members are located at the foundation offices in Baltimore, others are spread around the country.

Training has always been seen as strength of the SFA program, especially in comparison to that provided with other comprehensive school reform models (Bodilly, 1998; Datnow, Hubbard, & Mehan, 2002). Efforts have been made to continually improve training support to schools. In keeping with the commitment to goal-focused implementation, professional development is now based on school self-identified areas of need, rather than generic support. As one SFA facilitator in Datnow and Park's study (2005) explained, "When [our trainer] comes in to sit with [the principal], she asks us, 'what are the needs of your school? What training do you want from us? What support?' So it's not just them dictating what support it's going to be" (p. 20). This statement by a principal also gives insight into the level of collaboration between SFAF trainers and educators in her school: "I think we have always felt a give and take and that we are accepted as peers and colleagues . . . that they are interested in what we say and that there's a response to that" (p. 20). Efforts are also made to match schools to trainers with relevant expertise and background. As one administrator explained, "They're like a perfect match for our school. The people, their personalities, their backgrounds in bilingual [education] you know, for ELD [English language development]. . . . I think they tried to match the person to the school because they are just perfect for us" (p. 21).

In addition to providing support in the implementation of SFA, the advent of the No Child Left Behind (NCLB) Act has meant that trainers now serve as policy mediators, helping schools gain the knowledge to meet state and federal mandates. Trainers help schools understand how they can meet NCLB mandates, providing them with knowledge that some districts do not. Trainers also work with educators to help them use SFA to meet state curriculum standards. This process is very localized, based on individual school needs. The SFAF has also recently developed benchmark SFA assessments that schools can use five times a year. These benchmark assessments are linked to state assessments. While obviously reflecting a change in response to the policy climate, this change was also made very much in response to the requests of educators, who wanted assessments that related better to state measures.

The role of SFA trainers in the continual development of the model is also important to consider, especially with respect to feedback loops. Annual conferences are held for trainers where they convene to share strategies for working with schools and to discuss successful and unsuccessful program adaptations they have observed. During these conferences, trainers also engage in discussion about current research that is related to SFA, but not on SFA per se. For example, trainers might learn about new research on strategies for teaching English language learners. Trainers then use this research when they are meeting with school educators to help them understand why particular program components are necessary. Information is also shared among SFAF staff on a continual basis through phone and e-mail communication.

Summary

Essentially, the continual development of SFA is a story of how developers, trainers, researchers, and practitioners work together. There is considerable formal research informing the program and its continual development. However, while there is a reliance on rigorous, quantitative research methods in informing model development, there is also a very strong commitment to learn from teacher practice. SFA seeks a constant interplay between teachers' practice and research. The knowledge of SFA trainers, many of whom were former SFA teachers, is also integral to the continual development of the model and its implementation strategies.

POLICY IMPLICATIONS OF RESEARCH
ON SUCCESS FOR ALL

The policy implications of research on SFA go far beyond a recommendation that educators use this program. The process by which SFA was developed, evaluated, and disseminated is one that should be applied to develop programs at all levels of education, in all subjects, and to solve all kinds of problems. Educational policies need to change substantially to support the continued development of SFA itself and, more importantly, other programs that may have even greater impacts.

1. Substantially increase support for research and development.

SFA has benefited from sustained (though modest) funding for research and development over its 18-year history. If evidence-based reform is to take hold, there must be funding available for many more such efforts. Given its potential importance, funding for research in education is shockingly low, and much of what is spent goes for routine data collection, technical assistance, and other activities that are not research. It is difficult to separate out, but funding for development, evaluation, and dissemination of programs and practices for K–12 education is surely less than $100 million per year across all agencies, and may be less than $50 million. In contrast, the U.S. Department of Education spends about $1 billion per year just on support for after-school programs. For half this amount, $500 million per year, researchers and developers could substantially advance knowledge about practical, effective programs for all types of schools.

2. Fund development of new programs.

There are still too few promising programs in the pipeline. Researchers and developers need funding to develop new replicable programs based on current understandings of how children learn, current technologies, and current needs. In particular, the Department of Education should hold "design competitions" in which developers are challenged to create programs of all kinds to solve central problems of American education: reading, math, science, and social studies programs at all grade levels; programs for English language learners; solutions for children with reading disabilities; dropout prevention programs; school-to-work programs; classroom management programs; assessment methods; schoolwide reform models for preschool, elementary, and secondary schools; and much more. In each case, a number of developers should be supported to create, pilot, and ultimately evaluate promising models. As the work progresses, additional projects should be added and ones that are not working as hoped winnowed out. As part of the development process, there is a need for basic research, including correlational, descriptive, and small-scale experimental research, to provide a base for development of research-based programs.

3. Fund evaluation of existing and new programs.

IES is now funding an impressive array of rigorous evaluations of educational programs and practices, but much more remains to be done. Ideally, developers should have funding to do their own evaluations as they are preparing to scale up their programs, but then independent, third-party evaluators need support to do their own high-quality evaluations. In today's context, a "rigorous evaluation" means one in which schools are assigned at random to use a given program or to use an alternative control program, with measurement of achievement at pre- and post-test and of implementation throughout the experiment.

4. Provide incentives for schools to participate in research.

One cost-effective way to carry out randomized experiments evaluating educational programs would be to provide a competitive preference in school funding programs for schools willing to be assigned at random to use a given program immediately or one year later. For example, schools applying for funding to implement comprehensive school reform programs, secondary reading programs under the new Striving Readers initiative, K–3 reading programs under Reading First, or after-school programs under 21st Century Community Learning Centers would be given a better chance of success if they agreed to participate in randomized evaluations. In this way, the cost of the research would just be the data collection and analysis, not the program implementation (which usually consumes the majority of the funding for randomized field research).

5. Provide incentives for schools and districts to use programs validated in rigorous research.

SFA is one of a small set of replicable programs with strong evidence of effectiveness, and many more will be validated in the coming years. District and school leaders need clear information on the findings of this research, but information alone will not suffice, as large textbook and technology companies will continue to demonstrate that marketing is more powerful than evidence. Yet the federal government has many levers it can use to promote adoption of programs validated in rigorous research. For example, it can give competitive preferences to schools that use proven programs in discretionary grants. It can insist that schools failing to meet adequate yearly progress (AYP) standards for three years choose a proven model. It can ask schools not meeting AYP to explain in their Title I plans why they feel it is important to continue to use programs with no evidence of effectiveness when well-validated alternatives exist. The necessary language for this policy already resides in No Child Left Behind, but it would be necessary to redefine programs and practices "based on scientifically based research" as ones that have been evaluated in comparison to control groups and found to be effective in increasing student achievement.

6. Maintain the integrity of proven programs.

If evidence-based programs are emphasized in educational policy, there needs to be some oversight to ensure that the programs being adopted are essentially the same as the ones that were proven to be effective. For example, a program that was successful with extensive training and follow-up could not be considered "evidence-based" if it were later disseminated with minimal professional development.

7. Encourage states to base policies on research.

So far, the evidence-based policy movement has been almost entirely a federal initiative. State departments of education need to embrace this dynamic if it is to take hold on a wide scale. For example, the states now control a fund that amounts to 4 percent of their Title I funding to help schools meet AYP standards. No Child Left Behind encourages them to use this money to help schools adopt proven programs, but this is unlikely to happen unless the states dedicate themselves to evidence-based policies.

CONCLUSION

The solutions to America's educational problems must draw on our nation's greatest strength: the ingenuity, inventiveness, and technological capacity of the American people. America leads the world in medicine, agriculture, and technology because of its unequaled national capacity to create new solutions. This dynamic has not taken hold in education, but there is no reason that it cannot do so. The research, development, and dissemination of SFA provides one example of how research could ultimately transform educational practice. Educational policies at all levels should encourage the use of proven programs that already exist and help develop and evaluate many more. With a modest investment of, say, $500 million per year in research and development, our country can bring about a revolution in education. This will be beneficial to all children, but especially to those who are least well served by today's schools.

REFERENCES

Adams, G. L., & Engelmann, S. (1996). *Research on Direct Instruction: 25 years beyond DISTAR.* Seattle: Educational Achievement Systems.

Adams, M. J. (1990). *Beginning to read: Thinking and learning about print.* Cambridge, MA: MIT Press.

Adams, M. J., Foorman, B. R., Lundberg, I., & Beeler T. (1998). *Phonemic awareness in young children.* Baltimore, MD: Paul H. Brookes.

Armbruster, B. B., Anderson, T. H., & Ostertag, J. (1987). Does text structure/summarization instruction facilitate learning from expository text? *Reading Research Quarterly 22*(3), 331–346.

Barnett, W. S., Frede, E. C., Mosbasher, H., & Mohr, P. (1987). The efficacy of public preschool programs and their relationship of program quality to efficacy. *Educational Evaluation and Policy Analysis 10*(1), 37–49.

Baumann, J. E. (1984). The effectiveness of a direct instruction paradigm for teaching main idea comprehension. *Reading Research Quarterly 20*(1), 93–115.

Beck, I. L., & McKeown, M. G. (2001). Inviting students into the pursuit of meaning. *Educational Psychology Review 13*(3), 225–242.

Beck, I. L., & McKeown, M. G. (2002). *Increasing young children's oral vocabulary repertoires through rich and focused instruction.* Paper presented at the annual meetings of the American Educational Research Association, New Orleans.

Berkowitz, S. J. (1986). Effects of instruction in text organization on sixth-grade students' memory for expository reading. *Reading Research Quarterly 21*(2), 161–178.

Berman, P., & McLaughlin, M. W. (1978). *Implementing and sustaining innovations.* Vol. 8 of Federal programs supporting educational change. Santa Monica, CA: RAND.

Berrueta-Clement, J., Barnett, W., Schweinhart, L., Epstein, A., & Weikart, D. (1984). Changed lives: *The effects of the Perry Preschool Program on youths through age 19.* High/Scope Educational Research Foundation Monograph 8. Ypsilanti, MI: High/Scope Press.

Blachowicz, C. L. Z., & Fisher, P. (2000). Vocabulary instruction. In M. L. Kamil, P. B. Mosenthal, P. D. Pearson, & R. Barr (Eds.), *Handbook of reading research*, vol. 3 (pp. 503–523). Mahwah, NJ: Lawrence Erlbaum Associates.

Bodilly, S. J. (1998). *Lessons from New American Schools' scale-up phase: Prospects for bringing designs to multiple schools.* Santa Monica, CA: RAND

Borman, G. D., & Hewes, G. M. (2003). Long-term effects and cost effectiveness of Success for All. *Educational Evaluation and Policy Analysis 24*(2), 243–266.

Borman, G. D., Hewes, G. M., Overman, L. T., & Brown, S. (2003). Comprehensive school reform and achievement: A meta-analysis. *Review of Educational Research 73*(2), 125–230.

Borman, G. D., Slavin, R. E., Cheung, A., Chamberlain, A., Madden, N. A., & Chambers, B. (2005). Success for All: First year results from the National Randomized Field Trial. *Educational Evaluation and Policy Analysis 27*(1), 1–22.

Borman, G. D., Slavin, R. E., Cheung, A., Chamberlain, A., Madden, N. A., & Chambers, B. (in press). The National Randomized Field Trial of Success for All: Final outcomes. *American Educational Research Journal.*

Bowman, B. T., Donovan, M. S., & Burns, M., eds. (2001). *Eager to learn: Educating our preschoolers.* Washington, DC: National Research Council.

Brown, A. L., & Day, J. D. (1983). Macrorules for summarizing texts: The development of expertise. *Journal of Verbal Learning and Verbal Behavior 22*(1), 1–14.

Bryant, D. M., & Ramey, C. T. (1987). An analysis of the effectiveness of early intervention programs for environmentally at-risk children. In M. J. Guralnick & F. C. Bennett (Eds.), *The effectiveness of early intervention for at-risk and handicapped children* (pp. 33–78). Orlando, FL: Academic Press.

Burns, S., Griffin, P., & Snow, C. (1999). *Starting out right: A guide to promoting children's reading success.* Washington, DC: National Academy Press.

Calderón, M. (1999). Teacher learning communities for cooperation in diverse settings. *Theory into Practice 38*(2), 94–99.

Calderón, M. (2001). Curricula and methodologies used to teach Spanish-speaking limited English proficient students to read English. In R. Slavin & M. Calderón (Eds.), *Effective programs for Latino students* (pp. 251–306). Mahwah, NJ: Lawrence Erlbaum Associates.

Calderón, M., August, D., Slavin, R. E., Durán, D., Madden, N. A., & Cheung, A. (2004). The evaluation of a bilingual transition program for Success for All. Baltimore, MD: Johns Hopkins University, Center for Research on the Education of Students Placed at Risk.

Calderón, M., Hertz-Lazarowitz, R., & Slavin, R. E. (1998). Effects of Bilingual Cooperative Integrated Reading and Composition on students making the transition from Spanish to English reading. *Elementary School Journal 99*(2), 153–165.

Calkins, L. M. (1986). *The art of teaching writing.* Portsmouth, NH: Heinemann.

Carlo, M. S., August, D., McLaughlin, B., Snow, C. E., Dressler, C., Lippman, D., Lively, T., and White, C. (2004). Closing the gap: Addressing the vocabulary needs of English language learners in bilingual and mainstream classrooms. *Reading Research Quarterly 39*(2), 188–215.

Chamot, A. U., & O'Malley, J. M. (1996). The Cognitive Academic Language Learning Approach (CALLA): A model for linguistically diverse classrooms. *The Elementary School Journal 96*(3), 259–273.

Cheung, A., & Slavin, R. E. (2005). Effective reading programs for English language learners and other language minority students. *Bilingual Research Journal 29*(2), 241–267.

Clark, J. M., & Paivio, A. (1991). Dual coding theory and education. *Educational Psychology Review 3*(3), 149–210.

Coady, J., & Huckin, T., eds. (1997). *Second-language vocabulary acquisition: The rationale for pedagogy.* Cambridge: Cambridge University Press.

Cunningham, A. E., & Stanovich, K. E. (1997). Early reading acquisition and its relation to reading experience and ability ten years later. *Developmental Psychology 33*(6), 934–945.

Dansereau, D. F. (1988). Cooperative learning strategies. In C. E. Weinstein, E. T. Goetz, & P. A. Alexander (Eds.), *Learning and study strategies: Issues in assessment, instruction, and evaluation* (pp. 103–120). Orlando, FL: Academic Press.

Datnow, A., & Castellano, M. (2000). Teachers' responses to Success for All: How beliefs, experiences, and adaptations shape implementation. *American Educational Research Journal, 37*(3), 775–799.

Datnow, A., Hubbard, L., & Mehan, H. (2002). *Extending educational reform: From one school to many.* London: RoutledgeFalmer.

Datnow, A., & Park, V. (2005). *How does Success for All create knowledge for school improvement?* Paper presented at the annual meeting of the American Educational Research Association, Montreal.

Davey B., & McBride, S. (1986). The effects of question generation training on reading comprehension. *Journal of Educational Psychology 78*(4), 256–262.

Dewitz, P., Carr, E. M., & Patberg, J. P. (1987). Effects of inference training on comprehension and comprehension monitoring. *Reading Research Quarterly 22*(1), 99–121.

Dickinson, D. K., & Tabors, P. O., eds. (2001). *Beginning literacy with language: Young children learning at home and school.* Baltimore, MD: Paul H. Brooks.

Emmer, E., Evertson, C., & Worsham, M. (2003). *Classroom management for secondary teachers,* 6th edition. Boston: Allyn and Bacon.

Englert, C. S., Raphael, T. E., Anderson, L. M., Anthony, H. M., & Stevens, D. D. (1991). Making strategies and self-talk visible: Writing instruction in regular and special education classrooms. *American Educational Research Journal 28*(2), 337–372.

Fantuzzo, J. W., Polite, K., & Grayson, N. (1990). An evaluation of reciprocal peer tutoring across elementary school settings. *Journal of School Psychology 28*(4), 309–323.

Fisch, S., & Truglio, R. (2000). *G is for growing: 30 years of research on Sesame Street.* Mahwah, NJ: Lawrence Erlbaum Associates.

Fitzgerald, J. (1995). English as a second language instruction in the United States: A research review. *Journal of Reading Behavior 27*(2), 115–152.

Gambrell, L. B., & Bales, R. J. (1986). Mental imagery and the comprehension-monitoring performance of fourth- and fifth-grade poor readers. *Reading Research Quarterly 21*(4), 454–464.

Garcia, E. E. (1991). Bilingualism, second language acquisition, and the education of Chicano language minority students. In R. R. Valencia (Ed.), *Chicano school failure and success: Research and policy agendas for the 1990s* (pp. 93–118). New York: Falmer.

García, G. E. (2000). Bilingual children's reading. In M. L. Kamil, P. B. Mosenthal, P. D. Pearson, & R. Barr (Eds.), *Handbook of reading research*, vol. 3 (pp. 813–834). Mahwah, NJ: Lawrence Erlbaum Associates.

Gilliam, W. S., & Zigler, E. F. (2000). A critical meta-analysis of all evaluations of state funded preschool from 1977 to 1998: Implications for policy, service delivery and program evaluations. *Early Childhood Research Quarterly 15*(4), 441–473.

Good, T., Grouws, D., & Ebmeier, H. (1983). *Active mathematics teaching.* New York: Longman.

Graves, D. (1983). *Writing: Teachers and children at work.* Portsmouth, NH: Heinemann.

Gutiérrez, R., & Slavin, R. E. (1992). Achievement effects of the nongraded elementary school. A best-evidence synthesis. *Review of Educational Research 62*(4), 333–376.

Hansen, J., & Pearson, P. D. (1983). An instructional study: Improving the inferential comprehension of good and poor fourth-grade readers. *Journal of Educational Psychology 75*(6), 821–829.

Harris, K. R., & Graham, S. (1996). *Making the writing process work: Strategies for composition and self-regulation.* Cambridge, MA: Brookline Books.

Hattie, J., Biggs, H. J., & Purdie, N. (1996). Effects of learning skills interventions on student learning: A meta-analysis. *Review of Educational Research 66*(2), 99–136.

Hawkins, J. D., Doueck, H. J., & Lishner, D. M. (1988). Changing teaching practices in mainstream classrooms to improve bonding and behavior of low achievers. *American Educational Research Journal 25*(1), 31–50.

Hillocks, G. (1984). What works in teaching composition: A meta-analysis of experimental treatment studies. *American Journal of Education 93*(1), 133–170.

Idol, L. (1987). Group story mapping: A comprehension strategy for both skilled and unskilled readers. *Journal of Learning Disabilities 20*(4), 196–205.

Idol, L., & Croll, V. J. (1987). Story-mapping training as a means of improving reading comprehension. *Learning Disability Quarterly 10*(3), 214–229.

Johnson, D. W., & Johnson, R. T. (1999). *Learning together and alone: Cooperative, competitive, and individualistic learning.* Boston: Allyn and Bacon.

King, A. (1994). Guiding knowledge construction in the classroom: Effects of teaching children how to question and how to explain. *American Education Research Journal 31*(2), 338–368.

Linebarger, D. L., Kosanic, A. Z., Greenwood, C. R., & Doku, N. S. (2004). Effects of viewing the television program *Between the Lions* on the emergent literacy skills of young children. *Journal of Educational Psychology 96*(2), 297–308.

Madden, N., Livingston, M., & Cummings, N. (1998). *Success for All, Roots and Wings principal's and facilitator's manual.* Baltimore, MD: Johns Hopkins University.

Magnuson, K., Meyers, M., Ruhm, C., & Waldfogel, J. (2003). *Inequality in preschool education and school readiness.* New York: Columbia University.

Malone, L. D., & Mastropieri, M. A. (1992). Reading comprehension instruction: Summarization and self-monitoring training for students with learning disabilities. *Exceptional Children 58*(3), 270–279.

Mayer, R. E. (2001). *Multimedia learning.* New York: Cambridge University Press.

Mayer, R. E., & Moreno, R. (2003). Nine ways to reduce cognitive load in multimedia learning. *Educational Psychologist 38*(1), 43–52.

Meloth, M. S., & Deering, P. D. (1992). The effects of two cooperative conditions on peer group discussions, reading comprehension, and metacognition. *Contemporary Educational Psychology 17*(2), 175–193.

Meloth, M. S., & Deering, P. D. (1994). Task talk and task awareness under different cooperative learning conditions. *American Educational Research Journal 31*(1), 138–166.

Morris, D., Shaw, B., & Perney, J. (1990). Helping low readers in grades 2 and 3: An after-school volunteer tutoring program. *Elementary School Journal 91*(2), 132–150.

National Reading Panel. (2000). *Teaching children to read: An evidence-based assessment of the scientific research literature on reading and its implications for reading instruction.* Rockville, MD: National Institute of Child Health and Human Development.

National Research Council and Institute of Medicine. (2000). *From neurons to neighborhoods: The science of early childhood development.* Washington, DC: National Academy Press.

Neuman, S. B., Copple, C., & Bredekamp, S. (1999). *Learning to read and write: Developmentally appropriate practices for young children.* Washington, DC: National Association for the Education of Young Children.

Neuman, S. B., & Koskinen, P. (1992). Captioned television as comprehensible input: Effects of incidental word learning from context for language minority students. *Reading Research Quarterly 27*(1), 241–259.

O'Donnell, A. M. (1996). Effects of explicit incentives on scripted and unscripted cooperation. *Journal of Educational Psychology 88*(1), 74–86.

Padrón, Y. (1992). The effects of strategy instruction on bilingual students' cognitive strategy use in reading. *Bilingual Research Journal 16*(3–4), 35–51.

Paris, S. C., & Paris, A. H. (2001). Classroom applications of research on self-regulated learning. *Educational Psychologist 36*(2), 89–101.

Park, V. (2005). *Understanding the research-to-practice gap: Teachers' perceptions of research on Success for All.* Working paper, Rossier School of Education, University of Southern California, Los Angeles.

Pinnell, G. S., Lyons, C. A., DeFord, D. E., Bryk, A. S., & Seltzer, M. (1994). Comparing instructional models for the literacy education of high risk first graders. *Reading Research Quarterly 29*(1), 8–39.

Pressley, M., Levin, J. R., & Delaney, H. (1982). The mnemonic keyword method. *Review of Educational Research 52*(1), 61–92.

Ramey, C. T., & Ramsey, S. L. (1998). Early intervention and early experience. *American Psychologist 53*(2), 109–120.

Reynolds, A. J. (1998). The Chicago Child-Parent Center and expansion program: A study of extended early childhood intervention. In J. Crane (Ed.), *Social programs that work* (pp. 110–147). New York: Russell Sage Foundation.

Reynolds, A. J., & Temple, J. A. (1998). Extended early childhood intervention and school achievement: Age thirteen findings from the Chicago Longitudinal Study. *Child Development 69*(1), 231–246.

Rice, M. L., Huston, A. C., Truglio, R., & Wright, L. C. (1990). Words from *Sesame Street*: Learning vocabulary while viewing. *Developmental Psychology 26*(3), 421–428.

Rohrbeck, C. A., Ginsburg-Block, M. D., Fantuzzo, J. W., & Miller, T. R. (2003). Peer-assisted learning interventions with elementary school students: A meta-analytic review. *Journal of Educational Psychology 94*(2), 240–257.

Saville-Troike, M. (1984). What really matters in second language learning for academic achievement? *TESOL Quarterly 18*(2), 199–219.

Schunk, D. H., & Cox, P. D. (1986). Strategy training and attributional feedback with learning disabled students. *Journal of Educational Psychology 78*(3), 201–209.

Schunk, D. H., & Swartz, C. W. (1993). Goals and progress feedback: Effects of self-efficacy and writing instruction. *Contemporary Educational Psychology 18*(3), 337–354.

Scott, J. A., & Nagy, W. E. (1997). Understanding the definition of unfamiliar verbs. *Reading Research Quarterly 32*(2), 184–200.

Short, E. J., & Ryan, E. B. (1984). Metacognitive differences between skilled and less skilled readers: Remediating deficits through story grammar and attribution training. *Journal of Educational Psychology 76*(2), 225–235.

Slavin, R. E. (1987). Ability grouping and student achievement in elementary schools: A best-evidence synthesis. *Review of Educational Research 57*(3), 347–350.

Slavin, R. E. (1995). *Cooperative learning: Theory, research, and practice.* 2nd ed. Boston: Allyn & Bacon.

Slavin, R. E. (2003). Evidence-based education policies: Transforming educational practice and research. *Educational Researcher 31*(7), 15–21.

Slavin, R. E. (2006). *Educational psychology: Theory and practice.* 8th ed. Boston: Allyn & Bacon.

Slavin, R. E., Chambers, B., Holmes, G., & Madden, N. A. (2005). *A pulse, not an autopsy: Benchmark assessments and education reform.* Manuscript submitted for publication.

Slavin, R. E., & Cheung, A. (2004a). Effective early reading programs for English Language Learners. In O. Saracho & B. Spodek (Eds.), *Contemporary perspectives on language policy and literacy instruction in early childhood education* (pp. 119–152). Greenwich, CT: Information Age Publishing.

Slavin, R. E., & Cheung, A. (2004b). How do English language learners learn to read? *Educational Leadership 61*(6), 52–57.

Slavin, R. E., & Madden, N. A. (1998). *Disseminating Success for All: Lessons for policy and practice.* Baltimore, MD: Center for Research on the Education of Students Placed at Risk, Johns Hopkins University.

Slavin, R. E., & Madden, N. A. (1999). Effects of bilingual and English as a second language adaptations of Success for All on the reading achievement of students acquiring English. *Journal of Education for Students Placed at Risk 4*(4), 393–416.

Slavin, R. E., & Madden, N. A., eds. (2001). *One million children: Success for All.* Thousand Oaks, CA: Corwin.

Slavin, R. E., & Madden, N. A. (2004). Scaling up Success for All: Lessons for policy and practice. In T. Glennan, S. Bodilly, J. Galegher, & K. Kerr (Eds.), *Expanding the reach of education reforms: Perspectives from leaders in the scale-up of educational interventions* (pp. 159–198). Washington, DC: RAND.

Snow, C. E., Burns, M. S., & Griffin, P. (1998). *Preventing reading difficulties in young children.* Washington, DC: National Academy Press.

Stahl, S. A. (2003). How words are learned incrementally over multiple exposures. *American Educator*, Spring, 18–19.

Stevens, R. J., & Durkin, S. (1992). *Using Student Team Reading and Student Team Writing in middle schools: Two evaluations.* CDS Report No. 36. Baltimore, MD: Johns Hopkins University, Center for Research on Effective Schooling for Disadvantaged Students.

Stevens, R. J., Madden, N. A., Slavin, R. E., & Farnish, A. M. (1987). Cooperative Integrated Reading and Composition: Two field experiments. *Reading Research Quarterly 22*(4), 433–454.

Stevens, R. J., & Slavin, R. E. (1995). Effects of a cooperative learning approach in reading and writing on handicapped and nonhandicapped students' achievement, attitudes, and metacognition in reading and writing. *Elementary School Journal 95*(3), 241–262.

Taylor, B. M., & Beach, R. W. (1984). The effects of text structure instruction on middle-grade students' comprehension and production of expository text. *Reading Research Quarterly 19*(2), 134–146.

Wasik, B. A., & Slavin, R. E. (1993). Preventing early reading failure with one-to-one tutoring: A best-evidence synthesis. *Reading Research Quarterly 28*(2), 178–200.

Webb, N. M., & Palincsar, A. (1996). Group processes in the classroom. In D. C. Berliner & R. C. Calfee (Eds.), *Handbook of educational psychology* (pp. 841–876). New York: Macmillan.

White, K. R., Taylor, M. J., & Moss, V. D. (1992). Does research support claims about the benefits of involving parents in early intervention programs? *Review of Educational Research 62*(1), 91–125.

Whitehurst, G. J. (2002). Charting a new course for the U.S. Office of Educational Research and Improvement. Paper presented at the annual meeting of the American Educational Research Association, New Orleans.

Whitehurst, G. J., Epstein, J. N., Angell, A. C., Payne, A. C., Crone, D. A., & Fischel, J. E. (1994). Outcomes of an emergent literacy intervention in Head Start. *Journal of Educational Psychology 86*(4), 542–555.

Zimmerman, B. J., Bonner, S., & Kovach, R. (1996). *Developing self-regulated learners: Beyond achievement to self-efficacy.* Washington, DC: American Psychological Association.

The Role of Education Research: Commentary

Can We Influence Education Reform Through Research?

Carol Hirschon Weiss

In a time of rampant discontent with the educational enterprise, research is often called on to give practical aid. How much does research actually help improve education in these parlous times?

The three sophisticated chapters on the uses of research in this volume address the question from different perspectives. They agree that research has a useful role to play. For Slavin and his colleagues and for Neufeld, the contribution is obvious now. For Mosher, the main contribution lies in the future. But they are all aware of the difficulties that beset the linking of good research to good practice.

Slavin, Madden, and Datnow write primarily as program developers who use research as they go about developing a program. Slavin's program, Success for All (SFA), has drawn upon decades of research in a variety of areas: cooperative learning, cognitive strategy instruction, vocabulary strategies instruction, beginning and upper-level reading instruction, writing, classroom management, grouping, and tutoring. It was from knowledge gathered by research that Slavin and his colleagues fashioned their program, and as of this writing, more than 50 quasi-experimental evaluations have found the program (and its twin, Roots and Wings) to be effective.

Their perspective is the classroom. They are concerned with research that helps them craft effective practices and materials. They are also concerned with the school district, the level at which decisions are made to adopt SFA. It is for the edification of the district that Slavin and his colleagues support summative evaluations of their program. They are currently involved in a national randomized evaluation to provide rigorous data on the effectiveness of SFA. Early signs, they say, are hopeful.

Neufeld writes as a doer of research. She is a qualitative researcher who works in partnership with school people to improve the success of their current reform efforts. She calls what she does "formative evaluation." Because she has had a long relationship with the Boston Public Schools, doing numbers of studies over the years, she has had the opportunity to feed back to the district and to the schools acute observations on what is happening in the course of school reform (or rather, a rather haphazard succession of reforms).

Neufeld is concerned with the district level. She provides information to the superintendent and his staff, as well as to principals and schools, to help them make midcourse corrections as they set about reform.

Mosher comes through as a critic of research. He surveys current research knowledge and bemoans its inability to show us the way to improve educational practice and policy. He finds research lacking in terms of both the knowledge it currently provides and its funding apparatus. The structures and procedures of research funding yield fragmentary and partial lessons.

Mosher bases his critique largely at the federal level, but he believes it applies to states as well. He wants to talk to legislators, executive agencies, foundation executives, and other funders of education research. He particularly wants policymakers to understand the limits of what education research can currently tell them.

This collective picture of the variegated and multilayered connection between research and practice captures some of the key features of the relationship. From the three different vantage points, the authors highlight different aspects of the subject, as described in what follows.

SLAVIN, MADDEN, AND DATNOW

About half of the Slavin et al. chapter summarizes research on curriculum and teaching strategies that the developers of SFA have drawn on. An example is research on the effectiveness of multiple media in teaching reading. The second half of their chapter discusses other data that they bring into play. SFA makes use of testing data—and expects schools to do so too—to analyze how well students are learning each element in the curriculum. SFA includes lessons to reteach segments of curriculum that tests show students have not grasped, when this becomes necessary.

Other data are more informal, what has been called "colloquial forms of evidence" (Canadian Health Services Research Foundation, 2005). SFA collects opinions from schools and teachers, from its regionally based trainers across the country, and from area managers. Feedback from the field is a vital part of the ongoing development of SFA. The authors emphasize "a very strong commitment to learn from teacher practice."

In the end, they are very satisfied with their experience. They offer it as a model that other reform efforts can follow. They believe that a basic research base is essential (and needs more funding), that evaluation will winnow out those programs that work from those that do not, that replicability is vital and the integrity of "proven" programs has to be maintained, and that federal and state agencies should provide funding incentives to schools and districts for using proven programs. (Despite the obvious sense of this last recommendation, the lists of model programs are not always carefully developed. See Gandhi et al., forthcoming.)

NEUFELD

Neufeld runs a firm with the charming name of Education Matters. It does research with schools and school districts that are implementing innovative programs and practices. She and her colleagues collect qualitative data during the time the program is being conducted and give quick feedback to school people and district people about what is happening, what is going well, and what is not going well. The people in the schools have time to take corrective action to improve the efficacy of what they are doing.

Neufeld gets to know some of the people in the districts well over lengthy periods of time. She studies many different programs as the popularity of reform ideas wax and wane. Through her work with Boston Public Schools, she knows the people, their idiosyncrasies, what they listen to and what they know how to do. She can tailor her reports, and her informal conversations, to appeal to their interests and their capabilities. She works with other school districts too, and has opportunities for comparison and for trying out new sets of relationships.

There are disadvantages to the ways that Neufeld works. She accepts short-term projects, and her schedule is uncertain. Her reports are due in very short order. Because of the difficulties of staffing shifting projects, she winds up doing much of the work herself. But she has great advantages, especially in Boston, because a local foundation, the Boston Plan for Excellence, champions her work. It is a powerful intermediary between research and policy. In other districts that lack such a go-between, Neufeld finds less receptivity to her findings. Enmeshed as they are in the day-to-day-ness of running districts and schools, even appreciative and well-intentioned school people appear to make less use of the evidence that her research provides.

Neufeld's chapter starts as an upbeat survey of her work. Her formative evaluations are timely. She interacts formally and informally with her audience and has many occasions to transmit her messages. Her long-term relationship with the Boston Public Schools has developed respect and rapport. She writes with no fancy lingo and no statistics, and school people understand what she says. She has the Boston Plan for Excellence as a support and champion.

But by the end of the chapter, she acknowledges that it is not common to see any immediate use of her work in school practice. She writes, "If those of us who work at Education Matters wanted to assess our value . . . by measuring the improvements that followed the presentation of our reports, we would be despondent most of the time." An optimistic beginning to the chapter gives way to a downbeat, if realistic, end. She concludes with the reassuring thought that "We remain on the scene as long as we can and we believe that our contribution is meaningful."

MOSHER

On the other hand, Mosher starts out with a pessimistic roar and comes around to a glow of optimism at the end. His initial position is that current research and evaluation have not been able to yield sufficient knowledge to assist with federal and state policy, The main reason is that today's policy goals outstrip any experience the country has yet had, and therefore evaluating what is or has been is largely irrelevant. Nobody before has ever tried to educate *all* children to levels of proficiency and at the same time eradicate the differences in the achievement of racial and economic groups. He acknowledges the difficulties inherent in summative evaluation of shifting programs in shifting settings, but the key point is that no models exist of what an effective school should be.

The goals of contemporary education in the United States are to see that all students reach or exceed proficiency in core subjects and skills, and that all the main social groups attain the same level of achievement. Nobody has ever done these things, and (here is the kicker) *nobody knows how to do them*. Research can't help, because research has not shown how such accomplishment can be reached.

I find this a persuasive argument. Slavin et al., as we have seen, believe that they have gleaned enough from research about such elements as grouping, motivation, classroom management, assessment, and so on to craft a successful reading program. Their program, SFA, and others like it, can combine these ingredients to improve the achievement of students—presumably to a high enough level to meet the goals of proficiency for all.

But Mosher is skeptical—more than skeptical, disbelieving. He has looked and doesn't find a single school dealing with a general student population that has reached the goals of the No Child Left Behind (NCLB) policy. He foresees continued experimentation in schools around the country on a massive scale but little chance of identifying what works with whom and how.

The solution that he proposes is a major reorganization of the research enterprise. He advocates more targeted basic research aimed at the central issue of contemporary education, viz., to identify specific elements of effective education for specific groups of students. He finds current research to be fragmented and all over the lot, using disparate methods and measures, lacking common theories and metrics, and therefore yielding noncumulative information. The result is that research is unlikely to yield the kind of information that policymakers need and assume research now can provide. The Department of Education's Institute of Education Sciences, he says, has made a start at principled research design and replication in real settings, but its focus has disappointingly been on summative evaluation—a focus that he sees as unwarranted.

Instead Mosher suggests that researchers build up the knowledge bit by bit upon which developers, teacher educators, school boards, and the rest of the education community can build effective strategies to achieve current goals. The incentive system embodied in NCLB motivates teachers and students to work harder and thus do better (and punishes those who do not improve). But nobody truly knows *how* to improve, at least on all the dimensions required by NCLB (and its state and local kindred). Research has to supply better direction so that educators are able to achieve today's ambitious goals.

Mosher, who is skeptical about the utility of current research findings, appears to have considerable hope for the utility of future research. He urges policymakers to reconfigure research funding and structure, support training for researchers, and promote adoption of common methods and emphases. If we can accomplish those reforms, then research will contribute to policy and practice in ways that enable evidence to "speak these truths to power." Mosher acknowledges that knowledge may not prevail, but at least researchers will provide the basis on which achievement is possible.

I appreciate Mosher's message and have a great deal of sympathy with his position. But just as I find his judgment of the irrelevance of current research findings a bit too sweeping, so too do I find his expectations for the future too rosy. The changes he proposes in the research enterprise are profound, and even should they come to pass, it is hard to have high hopes for the authoritativeness of research findings on a topic as multidimensional and mutable as effective education practice. Education research certainly can (and does) contribute to the development of structures, practices, and materials that enhance student learning, but it is unrealistic to expect research to identify features and combinations of features that maximize learning for each type of student in each type of setting.

Moreover, research does not produce hard-and-fast findings once and for all. Even researchers in the harder sciences have seen big differences in research results on topics as varied as the health effects of low-fat diets, the consequences of low-intensity aerobic activity, the effects of hormone replacement therapy, and the pace of global warming. As a newspaper columnist summarized the recent turnabouts in scientific research, "the rest of us have to remember that contradiction, confusion, and changing opinions have always been a part of the scientific process" (Jacoby, 2006).

When we have good research, how many decision makers pay attention? While Slavin et al. will be a ready audience for findings on effective educational practices, policymakers at federal, state, and local levels have not displayed concerted eagerness to be guided by research. Neufeld has given us an explanation for some of the neglect of research by district-level decision makers: they are too busy doing their daily tasks to take on the burden of translating—or even listening to—research, however local and relevant it may be. Their motto is "Just do it." They have to get on with the job. Under current rules and regulations, they have to avoid such outright dereliction that they become subject to penalties. But they do not have the time or the job description to seek out the *best* way to "do it."

Slavin et al. add another limitation on school people's receptivity to research. They write, "large textbook and technology companies will continue to demonstrate that marketing is more powerful than evidence." Other researchers over the decades have identified a host of further constraints. Only some decision makers at some junctures will be on the *qui vive* for new ideas and evidence-based ways of work.

It is tempting to blame policymakers and practitioners for their frequent inattention to research evidence. But consider the stance of researchers themselves. Imagine the reception that the education research community will give to suggestions that research be supported on only a limited number of topics; that all researchers on those topics adopt common data collection methods, measures, and assessments; and that research funders institute, in Mosher's words, "periodic reviews . . . about where each relevant subfield is heading and whether and how it is paying off" (with the implication of termination of funds if the payoff is scanty). I sat on a committee at the National Academies that tried to develop a short list of research topics that were worthy of 15 years of large special funding. Our task was to limit the number of topics to three, or at most four. Even when we defined the topics in terms so wide and spraddling that they lost coherence, the only way we could limit the list to four was by horse trading. When our own turf is in jeopardy, researchers respond with much the same protective resistance as any other practitioners.

CONCLUSION

I do not believe that there are inevitable intransigent obstacles to the use of research in policy and practice. Examples abound of the influence of research on what practitioners do and on the direction of policies in many fields, including education. But research alone is not and cannot be the only basis of policy. Research is not enough. Figure 1 (modified from Davies, 2004) is a cartoon that shows a puzzled decision maker surrounded by eight bubbles, many of them pointing in different directions. The sources of influence in the bubbles are habits and traditions, values, resources, judgment, experience and expert opinions, pragmatics and contingencies, public opinion and pressure groups, and evidence. I find it hard to say that decision makers should ignore any of these factors. "Habits and traditions" are now called "culture," and management gurus have impressed on us that it is essential to take organizational culture into account. "Values" are absolutely necessary for decision making. I have lately been volunteering in the office of my state representative, and I have learned that many of the bills that come up for decision hardly depend on data or evidence at all but almost exclusively on values. Should health become a core subject in the high school curriculum? Should undocumented aliens who graduated from state high schools be charged the in-state tuition rate in state colleges? Other than the experience of any states that have already initiated such policies, it is difficult to think of evidence that would help state legislators in deciding such issues. When the policy is new and there is no prior experience to draw on, values tend to be the guide.

It is similar with the importance of judgment, experience and experts' opinions, resources, pragmatics and contingencies, and public opinion and pressure groups. All these elements have a place in decision-making systems at federal, state, district, and school levels. Obviously, when research supports the position favored by other pressures in the system, it is more likely to make

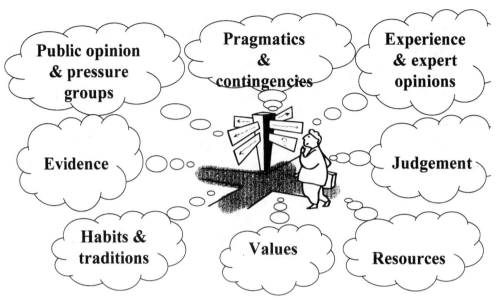

Source: Reproduced and modified, by Merete Konnerup, from Davies (2004).

FIGURE 1.1 Decisions—What Are They Based On?

headway. Research may be consonant with other forces because it derives from common experiences and evidence. It may happen to line up with current resources, values, and contingencies. Or it may have been persuasively disseminated to other groups and managed to infiltrate expert opinion, public opinion, and pressure groups. Ongoing dissemination on many levels can amplify the influence of research findings.

Research has a much harder time getting heard when its findings are out of sync with prevailing values and accepted knowledge. But sometimes that is the kind of research that is most important of all. What do we do then?

Research that punctures prevailing myths can lead to new ways of perceiving and acting. When such "creative destruction" is replicated and shown to have persuasive theoretical underpinnings, its counterintuitive findings can be a significant basis for policy change. But it will usually be a hard sell. Those who produce and promote the findings of such research may need energetic efforts and committed champions to gain a hearing for the results. Repeated communication of repeated studies will be in order. Advocates of research evidence may have to go beyond the presentation of data or even of generalizations to engage in the rough-and-tumble of political argument.

In the meantime, research with smaller-bore, cumulative additions to the current knowledge base is likely to be more readily picked up. There is an audience in program developers like Slavin, foundation people like Neufeld's colleagues in the Boston Plan for Excellence, the school principals in Biddle and Saha's (2005) study, the legislative staffers in Weiss's study (1989), and hundreds of others who hold allegiance, at least in some degree, to the idea of evidence-based policy and practice. "Evidence-based practice" is a popular watchword these days, and researchers with well-supported findings can carry its banner into the decision arena. Given the thousands of decision points in the U.S. educational system, some of them are no doubt receptive to relevant research results.

REFERENCES

Biddle, B. J., & Saha, L. J. (2005). *The untested accusation: Principals, research knowledge, and policy making in schools.* Lanham, MD: Scarecrow Press.

Canadian Health Services Research Foundation. (2005). *Conceptualizing and combining evidence for health system guidance.* Ottawa, ON, Canada: Author.

Davies, P. (2004). Is evidence-based government possible? Jerry Lee lecture, 4th Annual Campbell Collaborative Colloqium (PowerPoint presentation). http://www.odi.org.uk/RAPID/Meetings/Impact_Insight/docs/Jerry_Lee_Lecture.ppt

Gandhi, A. G., Murphy-Graham, E., Petrosino, A., Schwartz, S., & Weiss, C. H.. (Forthcoming). The devil is in the details: Examining the evidence for "proven" school-based drug abuse prevention programs. *Evaluation Review.*

Jacoby, J. (2006). You bet I want fries with that. *Boston Globe*, February 12, 10.

Weiss, C. H. (1989). Congressional committees as users of analysis. *Journal of Policy Analysis and Management 8*(3), 411–431.

VI

POLICY AND PROFESSIONALS

14

Misdiagnosing the Teacher Quality Problem

Richard M. Ingersoll

Few educational issues have received more attention in recent times than the problem of ensuring that our nation's elementary and secondary classrooms are all staffed with quality teachers. Concern with the quality of teachers is neither unique nor surprising. Elementary and secondary schooling are mandatory in the United States, and children are legally placed into the care of teachers for a significant portion of their lives. The quality of teachers and teaching is undoubtedly among the most important factors shaping the learning and growth of students. Moreover, the largest single component of the cost of education is teacher compensation. Especially since the publication of the seminal report *A Nation at Risk* (National Commission on Excellence in Education, 1983), a seemingly endless stream of studies, commissions, and national reports has targeted teacher quality as one of the central problems facing schools. Such critics have blamed the performance of teachers for numerous societal ills—the erosion of American economic competitiveness and productivity, the decline in student academic achievement, teenage pregnancy, juvenile delinquency and crime, the coarsening of our everyday discourse and culture, a decline in morals, gender and racial discrimination, and on and on.

As a result, in recent years reformers at the federal, state, and local levels have pushed a host of initiatives and programs seeking to upgrade the quality of teachers. These include a variety of teacher recruitment initiatives, increased teacher training and retraining requirements, improved teacher licensing examinations, performance standards, more rigorous teacher evaluation, merit pay programs, and most recently, state and national accountability mechanisms.

Although ensuring that our nation's classrooms are all staffed with quality teachers is a perennially important issue in our schools, it is also among the most misunderstood. This misunderstanding centers on the supposed sources of the problem—the reasons behind the purportedly low quality of teaching in American schools—and has undermined the success of such reform efforts. Underlying much of the criticism and reforms is a series of assumptions and claims as to the sources of the problems plaguing the teaching occupation. In this chapter I will focus on three of these.

The first is that the teaching occupation is plagued by unusually restrictive and unnecessary entry barriers—state teacher preparation and teacher licensing requirements, in particular. In this view, as a result of these rigid bureaucratic regulations, large numbers of high-quality candidates are discouraged from getting into the occupation.

The second is that severe teacher shortages are confronting our elementary and secondary schools and our traditional teacher preparation sources are simply not producing sufficient numbers of teachers to meet the demand. Restrictive entry requirements may exacerbate this situation, but the root of this school staffing crisis, according to this view, are two converging macro demographic trends—increasing student enrollments and increasing teacher attrition due to a "graying" teaching force. The resulting shortfalls of teachers, the argument continues, are forcing many school systems to resort to lowering standards to fill teaching openings, inevitably resulting in high levels of underqualified teachers.

The third and final claim I will examine is that the teaching force is inadequately trained and prepared. Unlike the first view, this perspective argues that entry into the occupation is not restrictive enough. In this view, the preservice preparation of teachers in college or university preparation programs, and state certification standards, all too often lack adequate rigor, breadth, and depth, especially in academic and substantive coursework, resulting in high levels of underqualified teachers.

These three claims are, of course, not the only explanations given for the problem of low-quality teachers and teaching. Nor are these views universally believed—indeed each is the subject of much contention—and proponents of some are opponents of others. But all are prominent views, all are part of the conventional wisdom as to what ails teaching, and all have had an impact on reform and policy.

The thesis of this chapter, however, is that each is largely incorrect. My theoretical perspective is drawn from the sociology of organizations, occupations, and work. My operating premise, drawn from this perspective, is that fully understanding issues of teacher quality requires examining the character of the teaching occupation and the social and organizational contexts in which teachers work. A close look at the best data available from this perspective, I argue, shows that each of these views involves a wrong diagnosis and a wrong prescription. In the following sections I review each of the above views and explain why I believe each provides an inaccurate explanation of, and solutions to, the quality problems plaguing the teaching occupation. For each, I suggest implications for future education research to help clarify these misunderstandings and issues.

OVERLY RESTRICTIVE OCCUPATIONAL ENTRY

Entry into many occupations and professions is regulated. That is, entry into many kinds of work typically requires a license, which is obtained only after completion of an officially sanctioned training program and passage of examinations. Indeed, it can be illegal to do many kinds of work, from plumbing or hairstyling to law or medicine, without a license. These credentials serve as screening or "gatekeeping" devices. Their official rationale is protection of the interests of the public by assuring that practitioners hold an agreed-upon level of knowledge and skill, and by filtering out those who are unable to pass over these "bars" and "hurdles."

Rigorous entry requirements are one of the hallmarks of the traditional or established professions, such as law, medicine, academia, engineering, and science. Among those who study work and occupations, the underlying and most important quality distinguishing professions from other kinds of occupations is the degree of expertise and complexity involved in the work itself. In this view, professional work involves highly complex sets of skills, intellectual functioning, and knowledge that are not easily acquired and not widely held. For this reason, professions are often referred to as the "knowledge-based" occupations. Accordingly, professions are usually more selective and characterized by higher training bars and narrower entry gates than nonprofessional occupations (Hall, 1968; Hodson & Sullivan, 1995). The importance of entry requirements is evidenced by the practice, especially common among those employed in the traditional professions, such as physicians, dentists, architects, and attorneys, of prominently displaying official documentation of their credentials in their offices.

Given the importance of credentials, especially in the traditional professions, the content and rigor of the licensing and certification requirements for new teachers has been an important issue in school reform. But it has also been a source of contention. On one side are those who argue that entry into teaching should be more highly restricted, as in the traditional professions. From this viewpoint, upgrading the qualifications and certification standards required of new teachers will upgrade the quality of teaching (see, e.g., National Commission on Teaching and America's Future, 1996, 1997)—a perspective to which I will return.

On the other side are those who argue that entry into the teaching occupation is already plagued by unusually restrictive and unnecessarily rigid bureaucratic entry barriers (e.g., Ballou, 1996; Finn, Kanstoroom, & Petrilli, 1999; Hanushek & Rivkin, 2004). From this viewpoint, traditional teacher preparation and state certification requirements, in particular, are akin to monopolistic practices. These critics argue that there is no solid empirical research documenting the value of such entry requirements. These regulations, they charge, are motivated less by an interest in protecting the public than by a desire to protect the interests of those in the occupation. As a result, this view holds, large numbers of high-quality candidates are discouraged from getting into the occupation. By doing away with these impediments, this argument concludes, schools could finally recruit the kinds and numbers of candidates they deem best, and this would solve the quality problems that plague teaching.

There are a number of different variants of the anti-restrictive-entry perspective. One of the more popular variants favors a training model analogous to that dominant in higher education. The preservice preparation of professors often includes little formal training in instructional methods. Similarly, from this viewpoint, having an academic degree in a subject is sufficient to be a qualified secondary school teacher in that subject. From this viewpoint, content or subject knowledge—knowing what to teach—is considered of primary importance for a qualified teacher. Formal training in teaching and pedagogical methods—knowing how to teach—is considered less necessary (e.g., Finn, Kanstoroom, & Petrilli, 1999).

Another variant of the anti-restrictive-entry perspective is motivated by concern for the demographic diversity of the teaching force. From this viewpoint, teaching's entry requirements result in reduced numbers of minority candidates entering the occupation, either because the requirements are themselves racially or ethnically biased, or because they screen out otherwise worthwhile candidates who are unable to pass over particular hurdles because of an underprivileged background (see, e.g., Villegas & Lucas, 2004).

Proponents of the anti-restrictive-entry perspective have pushed a range of initiatives, all of which involve a loosening of the traditional entry gates. Examples include alternative certification programs, whereby college graduates can postpone formal education training, obtain an emergency teaching certificate, and begin teaching immediately; and Peace Corps-like programs, such as Teach for America, which seek to lure the "best and brightest" into understaffed schools. It is important to note that proponents of these alternative routes into the occupation claim the same rationale as those who propose to upgrade existing entry standards and programs—enhanced recruitment of high-quality candidates into teaching.

To be sure, there are at least two problems with existing elementary and secondary teaching entry requirements. First, such requirements sometimes keep out quality candidates. Not everyone needs such qualifications to be a quality teacher. There are no doubt some individuals who are able to teach anything well, regardless of how few credentials they have. Moreover, especially in the absence of subsequent commensurate rewards, otherwise qualified candidates might be discouraged by the initial commitment and costs incurred by these entry hurdles. According to some, historically this has been the case in teaching. Attempts to upgrade the status of the occupation through more rigorous preparation and licensing standards or more selective entry gates appear to have often resulted in decreases in male entrants to teaching, who were eligible for, and more attracted to, occupations with better rewards (Strober & Tyack, 1980).

The second, and converse, problem with occupational entry barriers is that they sometimes do *not* keep out some who ought not be in a particular line of work. Entry selection criteria and screening mechanisms can sometimes fail. Moreover, the training itself can be flawed or of low quality. Having obtained credentials and completed exams does not, of course, guarantee that an individual is a quality teacher, nor even a qualified teacher. There are no doubt some individuals who are unable to teach anything well, regardless of how many hurdles they have passed and credentials they have obtained.

But these two problems exist in all occupations and professions. There are no doubt otherwise qualified individuals who cannot practice law because they did not complete a law school program and pass a state bar exam. Conversely, there are no doubt individuals who did complete law school and did pass a bar exam, but who ought not be practicing lawyers. Indeed, a major criticism of the traditional professions, like medicine and law, is that they have become monopolistic and have too little accountability to their clients. For example, critics of medicine hold that doctors do not adequately police their own ranks, and the public has few mechanisms to monitor or sanction incompetent doctors (Freidson, 1986). It is useful to place elementary and secondary teaching's entry requirements, and the criticisms of them, in this larger context. The restrictiveness of occupational entry requirements is relative, and when evaluating the rules governing a particular occupation one must always pose the question—compared to what?

An Easy-In/Easy-Out Occupation

Compared with that in some other developed nations, entry into the teaching occupation in the United States does not appear to be especially restrictive. Recent cross-national data indicate that the filters and requirements embedded in the process of becoming a teacher in the United States are less rigorous, less arduous and less lengthy than those in a number of other countries, including Australia, England, Japan, Korea, the Netherlands, Hong Kong, and Singapore (Wang et al., 2003). Moreover, the argument that entry into teaching is unusually restrictive stands in contrast to the perspective long held by organization theorists and among sociologists who study work, organizations, and occupations in general. From a cross-occupational perspective, teaching has long been characterized as an easy-in/easy-out occupation. Compared with other occupations, and in particular compared to the traditional professions, teaching has a relatively low entry bar and a relatively wide entry gate (Etzioni, 1969; Ingersoll, 2001). There are some occupations, such as journalism, that do not require specialized training at either the undergraduate or graduate levels. However, many do require specialized training and often at an advanced level. Becoming a professor, lawyer, or dentist, for example, requires graduate-level training. This is also increasingly true for becoming an architect or engineer. Others such as accounting do not require graduate-level training, but do have relatively rigorous entry exams.

In his classic study of the teaching occupation, Lortie (1975) drew attention to a number of mechanisms that facilitate ease of entry. First, teacher training is relatively accessible. Beginning in the early part of the 20th century, the states created large numbers of low-cost, dispersed and non-elitist teacher training institutions. Another aspect that facilitates entry is what Lortie calls "contingent schooling"—training programs geared to the needs of recipients and accessible to those already teaching. Persistors can increase their investment in occupational training, while others can choose to restrict their commitment to the minimum required. Teaching also has a relatively wide "decision range"—individuals can decide to become teachers at any number of points in their life span. Finally, most of those who desire to enter the teaching occupation are free to do so—individuals choose the occupation, not vice versa—a characteristic Lortie labeled the "subjective warrant." In contrast, the opposite prevails in many occupations and most traditional professions. Especially in the latter, occupational gatekeepers have a large say in choosing new members, and not all who desire to enter are allowed to do so.

In recent years, there has been a movement in a number of states to strengthen teacher certification standards. In the 2003–2004 school year, about 91 percent of public school teachers held a regular or full state-issued teaching certificate. Another 7 percent held only a temporary, emergency or provisional certificate. About 2 percent of public school teachers held no teaching certificate of any type (Ingersoll, 2004a). Moreover, although in many states they are not required to be, a majority of private school teachers also are certified. In the 1999–2000 school year, about 59 percent of private school teachers held a regular or full teaching certificate. Another 4 percent held only a temporary, emergency, or provisional certificate. About 37 percent of private school teachers held no teaching certificate of any type. By 2000, 74 percent of states required written tests of basic skills for those teachers entering the occupation, 58 percent had tests of content knowledge, and 48 percent had written tests for subject-specific pedagogy (Edwards, 2000). But the requirements to become an elementary- or secondary-level teacher are still neither uniform nor considered rigorous. While some states have implemented more rigorous certification criteria, others have passed legislation that waives requirements to meet certification criteria— an ambivalence reflecting the two opposing views described above.

Ironically, although teaching's entry training and licensing requirements are lower than those for many other occupations in the United States and lower than in some other nations, they appear to be subject to far more scrutiny than those in other occupations. There is an extensive body of empirical research, going back a couple of decades, devoted to evaluating the effects of teacher qualifications on teacher performance. Typically such studies try to assess the relationship between various measures of teacher education and various measures of student performance (for an earlier review see, e.g., Murnane & Raizen, 1988). A number of studies have indeed found teacher education and training, of one sort or another, to be significantly related to increases in student achievement. For example, in a review of 60 empirical studies on the effects of teacher education, Greenwald, Hedges, and Laine (1996) concluded that teachers' degree levels consistently showed "very strong relations with student achievement" in "a wide variety of studies over a three decade period" (284–285). Some studies look closely at the amount and effects of subject-specific teacher education. For example, in a multilevel analysis of 1992 National Assessment of Educational Progress (NAEP) data, Raudenbush, Fotiu, and Cheong (1999) found teacher education in mathematics (as measured by a major in math or in math education) to be consistently positively and highly significantly related to math proficiency in eighth-grade students. Similarly, a recent analysis of 2000 NAEP data found that eighth-grade students whose math teachers had a regular teaching certificate in math, or had a major or minor in math or math education scored significantly higher on the eighth-grade math test (Greenberg et al., 2004).

However, accurately isolating and capturing the effects of teacher's qualifications on their students' achievement is difficult, and not surprisingly, the results from this literature are often contradictory. There are also large gaps in this research (for a recent review, see Allen, 2003), and also, not surprisingly, there is currently a large interest in further pursuing this line of research.

Education policy research could play an important role in trying to carefully sort out and test the contrary hypotheses concerning the relative benefits and costs of different entry routes into teaching and different types and amounts of preservice preparation. Given the current variety of routes into the occupation, it should be possible to compare the relative value of these various alternatives. Which kinds of preparation and training and which routes into the occupation have which impacts on which outcomes?

Policy research could also provide a useful function by placing teaching's entry and training requirements, and the arguments for and against, in context. One useful comparison, already mentioned (see Wang et al., 2003), is cross-national. Compared to the United States, how restrictive and rigorous is entry into the teaching occupation in a wide range of developed nations? This line of inquiry could be further pursued.

Another useful comparison is cross-occupational. Policy research might provide a useful context for the current debates by systematically comparing teaching's entry requirements and routes to those of other occupations. Research could also look closely at how the complexity and character of the work itself compares to that in other occupations. Sociologists of work and occupations have traditionally classified teaching as a relatively complex form of work, characterized by uncertainty, intangibility, and ambiguity and requiring as high a degree of initiative, thought, judgment and skill to do well (e.g., Bidwell, 1965; Lortie, 1975). For example, in a classic comparative study of a number of occupations, Kohn and Schooler (1983, p. 68) concluded that secondary teaching involved greater substantive complexity than the work of accountants, salespersons, machinists, managers, and officials in service industries and in the retail trade. This line of inquiry could also be further pursued.

Finally, cross-occupational comparisons could contextualize the research itself. Is there as much concern with empirically documenting and justifying the training requirements in other occupations? In preliminary searches I have been unable to find analogous evaluative research—an effects literature—for a number of other occupations and professions. To be sure, there does appear to be interest in determining the best form of preparation of engineers, for example, or lawyers. But typically for most occupations there is little empirical research done assessing the value added of practitioners having a particular credential, license or certification (American Educational Research Association, American Psychological Association, and National Council on Measurement in Education, 1999; Kane, 1994). Such research can be difficult to undertake; if licensure is mandatory in an occupation, it is impossible to compare the performance of those licensed with those unlicensed. Nevertheless, occupational entry requirements, whether by precedent or by law, are common. For example, almost all universities require a doctorate degree for full-time academic positions. There is, of course, a growing secondary labor market in academia in which those without doctoral degrees are hired for various instructional or research positions, usually as non-tenure-track employment. However, there are very few examples of a "professor effects" literature that examines whether professors' qualifications have a positive effect on student achievement or on research quality (for a review, see, e.g., Pascarella & Terenzini, 1991). In other words, in academia as in most occupations and professions, it appears that typically it is taken as a given that particular credentials are necessary to practice particular kinds of work.

Hence, from an occupational and organizational perspective, the interesting research question is not solely, do qualifications matter for teachers? but also, why do so many find this an important question? Is teaching held to up to more scrutiny and skepticism than other occupations, and if so, why? Is there a double standard, and if so, is it justified?

Research could also investigate the consequences of the anti-restrictive-entry reforms, where implemented. Does a loosening of the entry gates to teaching increase the entry of quality candidates? Would such deregulation also shift some burden onto schools themselves to provide whatever practical training is needed to function on the job, if the latter has been neglected by the new standards and requirements?

Regardless of their impact on recruitment, the data suggest this kind of occupational deregulation and gate loosening, alone, will not solve the problem of ensuring a quality teacher in every classroom if it does not also address the issue of retention—the subject of the next section.

SEVERE TEACHER SHORTAGES

A second and related explanation for the problem of low-quality teaching in U.S. schools is teacher shortages. In this second view, the problem is that the supply of new teachers is insufficient to keep up with the demand. Restrictive entry requirements may exacerbate this condition, but the root of this gap, it is widely believed, is a dramatic increase in the demand for new teachers primarily resulting from two converging demographic trends—increasing student enrollments and increasing teacher retirements due to a "graying" teaching force. Shortfalls of teachers, this argument continues, have meant that many school systems have not been able to find qualified candidates to fill their openings, inevitably resulting in the hiring of underqualified teachers, and ultimately lowering school performance. Teacher shortage crises are not new to the K–12 education system. In the early and mid-1980s also a series of highly publicized reports warned of an impending shortage crisis for the teaching occupation (see, e.g., National Commission on Excellence in Education, 1983; Darling-Hammond, 1984; National Academy of Sciences, 1987; for reviews of this issue, see Boe & Gilford, 1992). Indeed, teacher shortages have been seen as a cyclic threat for decades (Weaver, 1983).

The prevailing policy response to these school staffing problems has been to attempt to increase the supply of teachers through a wide range of recruitment initiatives. Some of these involve a loosening of entry requirements, some do not. There are career-change programs, such as the federally funded Troops-to-Teachers program, which aim to entice professionals to become teachers. Some school districts recruited teaching candidates from other countries. Financial incentives, such as signing bonuses, student loan forgiveness, housing assistance, and tuition reimbursement have all been used to aid recruitment (Hirsch, Koppich, & Knapp, 2001).

The best data for understanding teacher supply and demand issues come from the nationally representative Schools and Staffing Survey (SASS) conducted by the National Center for Education Statistics (NCES), the statistical arm of the U.S. Department of Education. Begun in the late 1980s, this is the largest and most comprehensive data source available on teachers and school staffing. Indeed, it was originally created because of a dearth of information on these very problems and issues. Over the past few years I have undertaken a series of analyses of these data to examine what is behind the teacher shortage. Below I will summarize the results of this research (the data and discussion below are drawn from Ingersoll, 2001 and 2003b). From these analyses, I have concluded that the above reform efforts will not, alone, solve the problem schools have staffing classrooms with qualified teachers.

The data show that the conventional wisdom on teacher shortages is partly correct. Consistent with shortage predictions, demand for teachers has increased over the past two decades. Since the mid-1980s student enrollments have increased, teacher retirements have also increased, most schools have had job openings for teachers, and the size of the elementary and secondary teaching workforce has increased. Most important, the data tell us that substantial numbers of schools have experienced difficulties finding qualified candidates to fill their teaching position openings.

After that the data and conventional wisdom begin to diverge. National data on the supply of teachers trained, licensed, and certified each year are difficult to obtain. One of the best sources is NCES's Integrated Postsecondary Educational Data System (IPEDS). This source collects national data on the numbers of postsecondary degree completions by field and by year. These data suggest that, contrary to the conventional wisdom, there are overall more than enough prospective teachers produced each year in the United States. But there are also some important limitations to these data. An overall surplus of newly trained teachers does not, of course, mean there are sufficient numbers of graduates produced in each field. A large proportion of education degree completions are in elementary education. The data are unclear on whether a sufficient quantity of teachers are produced each year in such fields as math, science, and special education.

On the other hand, the IPEDS data on degree completions underestimate the supply of newly qualified teachers, because this database does not include recipients of undergraduate degrees in fields other than education who also completed the requirements for certification. Moreover, newly qualified candidates, as counted in the IPEDS data, are only one source of new hires in schools. Far more of those newly hired into schools each year are from what is often referred to as the "reserve pool." These include delayed entrants, those who completed teacher training in prior years but who have never taught, and re-entrants, former teachers who return to teaching after a hiatus. The addition of these other types and sources of teachers lends support to the argument that there are more than enough teachers supplied each year.

However, the key question is not whether the overall national supply of teachers is adequate or inadequate, but rather which schools have staffing problems and teacher supply and demand imbalances. Even in the same jurisdiction, the degree of staffing problems can vary greatly among different types of schools, and sites ostensibly drawing from the same teacher supply pool can have significantly different staffing scenarios. Some analysts have found, for example, that in the same metropolitan area in the same year some schools have extensive waiting lists of qualified candidates for their teaching job openings, while other nearby schools have great difficulty filling their teaching job openings with qualified candidates (National Commission on Teaching and America's Future, 1997). This suggests that imbalances between demand and supply must be examined at the organizational level to be fully understood—an issue to which I will return.

There is also another large problem with the conventional wisdom on shortages. The SASS data show that the demand for new teachers and subsequent staffing difficulties confronting schools are not primarily due to student enrollment and teacher retirement increases, as widely believed. Most of the demand for teachers and hiring is simply to replace teachers who have recently departed from their teaching jobs, and most of this teacher turnover has little to do with a "graying" workforce.

The Revolving Door

The data tell us that large numbers of teachers exit their schools each year. I have found that, as an occupation, teaching has higher turnover rates than a number of higher-status professions (such as professors and scientific professionals), about the same as other traditionally female occupations (such as nurses), and less turnover than some lower-status, lower-skill occupations (such as clerical workers). But teaching is also a relatively large occupation. Teachers represent 4 percent of the entire civilian workforce. There are, for example, more than twice as many elementary and secondary teachers as there are registered nurses, and there are five times as many teachers as there are either lawyers or professors. The sheer size of the teaching force combined with its levels of annual turnover means that there are large numbers of teachers in some kind of job transition each year. For example, the data show that over the course of the 1999–2000 school year, well over a million teachers—almost a third of this large workforce—moved into, between, or out of schools. The image that these data suggest is one of a "revolving door." The latter is a major, but unheralded, factor behind the difficulties many schools have ensuring that their classrooms are staffed with qualified teachers.

Of course, not all teacher turnover is negative. Some degree of employee turnover is normal and beneficial in any workplace. Too little turnover of employees is tied to stagnancy in organizations; effective organizations usually both promote and benefit from a limited degree of turnover by eliminating low-caliber performers and bringing in "new blood" to facilitate innovation. But a "revolving door" is costly. In the corporate sector it has long been recognized that high employee turnover means substantial recruitment and training costs and is both the cause and effect of productivity problems (e.g., Bluedorn, 1982; Hom & Griffeth, 1995; Mobley, 1982; Price, 1977, 1989). In contrast to the corporate sector, however, there has been very little attention paid to the impact of employee turnover in education. One notable exception was a recent preliminary attempt to quantify the costs of teacher turnover in Texas. This study estimated that teacher turnover costs the state hundreds of millions of dollars each year (Texas Center for Educational Research, 2000).

Some of the costs and consequences of employee turnover are probably more easily measured than others. One type of cost that could be difficult to quantify concerns the negative consequences of high turnover for organizational performance in work sites, like schools, requiring extensive interaction among participants. Much research has shown that the good school, like the good family, is characterized by a sense of belongingness, continuity, and community (e.g., Coleman & Hoffer, 1987; Durkheim, 1925/1961; Grant, 1988; Kirst, 1989; Parsons, 1959). Moreover, continuity and coherence are also important for long-term school improvement efforts. The capacity of schools to carry out successful reform often depends on the continuing presence of sufficient numbers of staff committed to the change (Fullan, 1991; Smylie & Wenzel, 2003). Hence, from an organizational perspective, teacher turnover is of concern not simply because it may be an indicator of sites of so-called shortages, but because of its relationship to school cohesion and, in turn, school performance.

The data also show that turnover varies greatly among different kinds of teachers. Teaching is an occupation that loses large numbers of its new members very early in their careers—long before the retirement years. A number of studies have found that after just five years, between 40 and 50 percent of all beginning teachers have left teaching altogether (Hafner & Owings, 1991; Huling-Austin, 1990; Murnane et al., 1991). A number of studies have also found that the "best and brightest" among new teachers—those with higher test scores, such as on the SAT and the National Teacher Exam—are the most likely to leave (e.g., Henke, Chen, & Geis, 2000; Murnane et al., 1991; Schlecty & Vance, 1981; Weaver, 1983). Moreover, the SASS data show that turnover also varies greatly among different kinds of schools. High-poverty public schools have far higher teacher turnover rates than do more affluent schools. Urban public schools have more turnover than do suburban and rural public schools.

These data raise two important questions: why is there so much teacher turnover, and why are these rates so dramatically different between schools?

Contrary to conventional wisdom, the SASS data show that retirement accounts for only a small part—about one-eighth—of the total departures. Far more significant are personal reasons for leaving, such as pregnancy, child rearing, health problems, and family moves. These are a normal part of life and common to all workplaces. There are also two other equally significant reasons for teacher turnover—job dissatisfaction and the desire to pursue a better job inside or outside of the education field. Together, these latter two reasons are the most prominent source of turnover and account for almost half of all departures each year. Of those who leave because of job dissatisfaction, most link their departures to several key factors: low salaries, lack of support from the school administrators, lack of student motivation, student discipline problems, and lack of teacher influence over school decision making.

What are the implications for policy? The data tell us that the sole root of the problem is not shortages, in the sense of too few teachers being produced, but rather also includes turnover— too many teachers departing prior to retirement. Thus, the solution is not solely recruitment, but retention. In plain terms, recruiting thousands of new candidates into teaching, alone, will not solve the teacher crisis if 40 to 50 percent of these new recruits leave the occupation in a few short years, as the data tell us they do. The image that comes to mind is that of a bucket rapidly losing water because there are holes in the bottom. Pouring more water into the bucket will not be the answer if the holes are not first patched.

Of course, nothing in the data suggests that plugging these holes will be easy. But the data do make clear that schools are not simply victims of inexorable societal demographic trends, and there is a significant role for the organization of schools as workplaces and the treatment of teachers as employees in these workplaces. Improving the workplace conditions in our schools, as discussed above, would contribute to lower rates of teacher turnover, which in turn would slow down the revolving door, help ensure that every classroom is staffed with qualified teachers, and ultimately increase the performance of schools.

These findings also have implications for policy research. There is a need for better data and research on the supply side. One of the best sources of information on the number of newly produced teachers is NCES's IPEDS. But, as mentioned, there are important limitations to these data. Information on all of the types and sources of new teachers is necessary to discern if there are or are not enough teachers produced each year.

There is also a need for research on the demand side. The data suggest that schools are not simply victims of inexorable societal demographic trends, and there is a significant role for the management and operation of these workplaces in both the genesis of and the solution to their staffing problems (Ingersoll, 2001; Johnson & Birkeland, 2003). From a policy perspective it is essential to understand what about districts and schools impacts turnover and school staffing problems, because it those are the things that are most often policy amenable. But currently, however, there is a dearth of research on which aspects, conditions, and characteristics of districts and schools impact turnover, retention, and the revolving door (for a recent review of the empirical literature on teacher recruitment and retention, see Allen, 2005).

A final useful role research might play is to examine the costs, benefits, and consequences to schools and districts of teacher turnover. These could include both "hard" financial costs and "soft" impacts. Research could examine the relationship between teacher turnover and school cohesion and, in turn, performance. Such research could address vital questions: What effects does turnover have on the community and performance of schools? How well are schools able to cope with a recurring loss of staff and a recurring need to rehire? What does continual turnover mean for the ability of the teaching staff to establish teamwork and continuity of curricula and programs? How does the loss of teachers affect ties to parents, students, and the community?

TOO MANY UNDERQUALIFIED TEACHERS

A third prominent explanation of the low quality of teaching focuses on the qualifications, training, and licensing of prospective teachers. Rather than too many requirements, as in the earlier anti-restrictive-entry perspective, this third view argues the opposite. In this view, a major source of low-quality teaching is inadequate and insufficient preservice training and certification standards. In response, reformers in many states have pushed tougher certification requirements and more rigorous coursework requirements for teaching candidates. However, like many similarly worthwhile reforms, these efforts alone will also not solve the problem, because they do not address some key causes.

One of the least recognized of these causes is the problem of out-of-field teaching—teachers being assigned to teach subjects that do not match their training or education. This is a crucial issue, because highly qualified teachers may actually become highly unqualified if they are assigned to teach subjects for which they have little training or education. Until recently there has been little recognition of this problem, however, largely because of an absence of accurate data—a situation remedied with the release of the SASS data in the early 1990s.

In analyses of these data, summarized below, I have found that out-of-field teaching is a chronic and widespread problem (the data and discussion below are drawn from Ingersoll, 1999, 2004a). The data show, for example, that about one-third of all secondary (7th–12th grades) math classes are taught by teachers who do not have either a major or a minor in math or in related disciplines such as physics, statistics, engineering, or math education. Almost one-quarter of all secondary school English classes are taught by teachers who have neither a major nor a minor in English or in related disciplines such as literature, communications, speech, journalism, English education, or reading education. The situation is even worse within such broad fields as science and social studies. Teachers in these departments are routinely required to teach any of a wide array of subjects outside of their discipline, but still within the larger field. As a result, over half of all secondary school students enrolled in physical science classes (chemistry, physics, earth science, or space science) are taught by teachers who do not have either a major or a minor in any of these physical sciences. Moreover, more than half of all secondary school history students in this country are taught by teachers with neither a major nor a minor in history. The actual numbers of students affected are not trivial. For English, math, and history, several million secondary school students a year in each discipline are taught by teachers without a major or minor in the field.

Out-of-field teaching also varies greatly across teachers and schools. For instance, recently hired teachers are more often assigned to teach subjects out of their fields of training than are more experienced teachers. Low-income public schools have higher levels of out-of-field teaching than do schools in more affluent communities. Particularly notable, however, is the effect of school size; small schools have higher levels of out-of-field teaching. There are also differences within schools. Lower-achieving classes are more often taught by teachers without a major or minor in the field than are higher-achieving classes. Junior-high-level classes are also more likely to be taught by out-of-field teachers than are senior high classes.

The data clearly indicate that out-of-field teaching is widespread. Some of it takes place in over half of all secondary schools in the United States in any given year—both rural and urban schools and both affluent and low-income schools. Each year over one-fifth of the public 7th–12th grade teaching force does some out-of-field teaching. No matter how it is defined, the data show that levels of out-of-field teaching are alarming. I found, for example, that similarly high numbers of teachers do not have teaching certificates in their assigned fields. Indeed, when I upgraded the definition of a qualified teacher to include only those who held *both* a college major and a teaching certificate in the field, the amount of out-of-field teaching substantially increased. Moreover, out-of-field teaching does not appear to be going away; I found that levels of out-of-field teaching have changed little over the past decade.

The crucial question, and the source of great misunderstanding, is why are so many teachers teaching subjects for which they have little background?

The Sources of Out-of-Field Teaching

Typically, policymakers, commentators and researchers have assumed two related explanations for the continuing problem of out-of-field teaching. One involves the adequacy of teacher training; the other involves the adequacy of teacher supply. The first blames teacher preparation programs or state certification standards (e.g., American Council on Education, 1999; Committee for Economic Development, 1996; Darling-Hammond, 1999). One subset of this view argues that the problem can be remedied by requiring prospective teachers to complete a "real" undergraduate major in an academic discipline.

It certainly may be correct that some teacher preparation programs and teacher certification standards suffer from shortcomings, but these problems do not explain the practice of out-of-field teaching. The SASS data indicate that most teachers have completed basic college education and teacher training. Ninety-nine percent of public school teachers hold at least a bachelor's degree, and almost half hold a master's degree or higher. Moreover, as mentioned earlier, in the 2003–2004 school year about 91 percent of public school teachers held a regular or full teaching certificate. Another 7 percent held only a temporary, emergency, or provisional certificate. About 2 percent of public school teachers held no teaching certificate of any type.

These data appear to conflict with conventional wisdom. In recent years, much attention has been focused on the plight of school districts, especially those serving low-income, urban communities that according to popular belief have been forced to hire significant numbers of uncertified teachers to fill their teaching vacancies. The national data suggest, however, that the numbers of teachers without a full certificate actually represent only a small proportion of the K–12 public teaching force.

My main point, however, is that the assumption that out-of-field teaching is due to teacher training deficits confounds and confuses two different sources of the problem of underqualified teaching; it mistakes teacher preservice education with teacher in-service assignment. The data show that those teaching out of field are typically fully qualified veterans with an average of 14 years of teaching experience who have been assigned to teach part of their day in fields that do not match their qualifications. At the secondary level, these misassignments typically involve one or two classes out of a normal daily schedule of five classes.

Why then is there so much misassignment? The second explanation of the problem of out-of-field teaching offers an answer—teacher shortages. This view holds that shortfalls in the number of available teachers have led many school systems to resort to assigning teachers to teach out of their fields (see, e.g., National Commission on Teaching and America's Future, 1996, 1997).

School staffing difficulties clearly are a factor in the degree of misassignment, but the data show that there are two problems with the shortage explanation for out-of-field teaching. First, it cannot explain the high levels of out-of-field teaching that the data indicate exist in fields, such as English and social studies, that have long been known to have surpluses. Second, the data also indicate that about half of all misassigned teachers in any given year were employed in schools that reported no difficulties finding qualified candidates for their job openings that year.

The implications of these misdiagnoses for reform are important. The efforts by many states to recruit new teachers, to enhance their training, to enact more stringent certification standards, and to increase the use of testing for teaching candidates, although perhaps highly worthwhile, will not eliminate out-of-field teaching assignments and hence will not alone solve the problem of underqualified teaching in our nation's classrooms. In short, bringing in thousands of new candidates and mandating more rigorous coursework and certification requirements will help little if large numbers of such teachers continue to be assigned to teach subjects other than those for which they were educated or certified.

Human Resource Management

Rather than to deficits in the qualifications and quantity of teachers, the data point in another direction. Decisions concerning the allocation of teaching assignments are usually the prerogative of school principals (Ingersoll, 2003a). These administrators are faced with resolving the tension between the many expectations and demands state and federal governments place on schools and the limited resources school receive. School managers are charged with the often difficult task of providing a broad array of programs and courses with limited resources, limited time, a limited budget, and a limited teaching staff (Delany, 1991). Principals' staffing decisions are further constrained by numerous factors, such as teacher employment contracts, which among other things typically stipulate that full-time secondary school teaching staff must teach five classes per day. But within those constraints, principals have an unusual degree of discretion in these decisions. There has been little regulation of how teachers are employed and utilized once on the job. Teacher employment regulations have been weak or rarely enforced, and finally, most states have routinely allowed local school administrators to bypass even the limited requirements that do exist (Edwards, 2000; Robinson, 1985). In this context, principals may find that assigning teachers to teach out of their fields is often more convenient, less expensive, and less time-consuming than the alternatives.

For example, rather than finding and hiring a new part-time science teacher to teach two sections of a newly state-mandated science curriculum, a principal may find it more convenient to assign a couple of English and social studies teachers to each "cover" a section in science. If a teacher suddenly leaves in the middle of a semester, a principal may find it faster and cheaper to hire a readily available, but not fully qualified, substitute teacher, rather than conduct a formal search for a new teacher. When faced with the choice between hiring a fully qualified candidate for an English position and hiring a less-qualified candidate who is also willing to coach a major varsity sport, a principal may find it more convenient to do the latter. When faced with a tough choice between hiring an unqualified candidate for a science teacher position and doubling the class size of one of the fully qualified science teachers in the school, a principal might opt for the former choice, resulting in a smaller class, but one taught by a less-qualified teacher. If a full-time music teacher is under contract, but student enrollment is sufficient to fill only three music classes, the principal may find it both necessary and cost-effective in a given semester to assign the music teacher to teach two classes in English, in addition to the three classes in music, in order to employ the teacher for a regular full-time complement of five classes per semester. If a school has three full-time social studies teachers, but needs to offer 17 social studies courses, or the equivalent of 3 2/5 full-time positions, and also has four full-time English teachers, but needs to offer only 18 English courses, or the equivalent of 3 3/5 full-time positions, one solution would be to assign one of the English teachers to teach three English courses and two social studies courses.

All of these managerial choices to misassign teachers may save time and money for the school, and ultimately for the taxpayer, but they are not cost free. They are one of the largest sources of underqualified teachers in schools.

These findings have implications for both policy and research. They suggest that rather than simply examining inadequacies in the supply or training of teachers, it is also necessary to examine the way schools are organized and teachers are managed. The data tell us there are large cross-school differences in out-of-field teaching, but we know little of why this is so. In a series of exploratory multivariate analyses, I have found that, after controlling for school recruitment and hiring difficulties and after controlling for school demographic characteristics, factors such as the quality of principal leadership, average class sizes, the character of the oversight of school hiring practices provided by the larger district, and the strategies districts and schools use for teacher recruitment and hiring are all significantly related to the amount of out-of-field teaching in schools (Ingersoll, 2004a). Such findings are suggestive of lines of further inquiry. But analyses of large-scale survey data have obvious limits for understanding the processes behind school staffing. Field investigations could better illuminate the decision-making processes surrounding the hiring, assignment, and utilization of teachers in particular kinds of schools. What are the hidden incentives systems within which administrators make staffing decisions? How do particular teachers come to be teaching particular classes? What are the reasons behind the misassignment of teachers?

Finally, besides cross-district and cross-school comparisons, another potentially illuminating comparison might be cross-national. As yet unanswered is a large question: Why is out-of-field teaching prevalent across the American K–12 education system as a whole? Anecdotal data suggest there are large differences across nations in their teaching force management practices. Compared to that in the United States, how much out-of-field teaching exists in classrooms in other developed nations?

ACKNOWLEDGMENTS

This chapter draws from an earlier paper (Ingersoll, 2004b).

REFERENCES

Allen, M. (2003). *Eight questions on teacher preparation: What does the research say?* Denver, CO: Education Commission of the States. Retrieved January 22, 2007, from http://www.ecs.org/tpreport.

Allen, M. (2005). *Eight questions on teacher recruitment and retention: What does the research say?* Denver, CO: Education Commission of the States. Retrieved January 22, 2007, from http://www.ecs.org/trrreport.

American Council on Education. (1999). *To touch the future: Transforming the way teachers are taught.* Washington, DC: Author.

American Educational Research Association, American Psychological Association, and National Council on Measurement in Education. (1999). *Standards for educational and psychological testing.* Washington, DC: Author.

Ballou, D. (1996). Do public schools hire the best applicants? *Quarterly Journal of Economics 111*(1), 97–133.

Bidwell, C. (1965). The school as a formal organization. In J. March (Ed.), *Handbook of organizations* (pp. 973–1002). Chicago: Rand McNally.

Bluedorn, A. C. (1982). A unified model of turnover from organizations. *Human Relations 35,* 135–153.

Boe, E., & Gilford, D. (1992). *Teacher supply, demand, and quality.* Washington, DC: National Academy Press.

Coleman, J., & Hoffer, T. (1987). *Public and private schools: The impact of communities.* New York: Basic Books.

Committee for Economic Development. (1996). *American workers and economic change.* New York: Author.

Darling-Hammond, L. (1984). *Beyond the commission reports: The coming crisis in teaching.* Santa Monica, CA: Rand Corporation.

Darling-Hammond, L. (1999). *Teacher quality and student achievement: A review of state policy evidence.* Seattle, WA. University of Washington, Center for the Study of Teaching and Policy.

Delany, B. (1991). Allocation, choice and stratification within high schools: How the sorting machine copes. *American Journal of Education 99*(2), 181–207.

Durkheim, E. (1925/1961). *Moral education: A study in the theory and application of the sociology of education* (E. K. Wilson & H. Schnurer, Trans.). Reprint. New York: Free Press.

Edwards, V. B., ed. (2000). *Quality counts 2000: Who should teach?* Special issue. *Education Week 19*(18).

Etzioni, A., ed. (1969). *The semiprofessions and their organizations: Teachers, nurses and social workers.* New York: Free Press.

Finn, C., Kanstoroom., M., & Petrilli, M. (1999). *The Quest for better teachers: Grading the states.* Washington, DC: Thomas B. Fordham Foundation.

Freidson, E. (1986). *Professional powers: A study in the institutionalization of formal knowledge.* Chicago: University of Chicago Press.

Fullan, M. (1991). *The new meaning of educational change.* New York: Teachers College Press.

Grant, G. (1988). *The world we created at Hamilton High.* Cambridge, MA: Harvard University Press.

Greenberg, E., Rhodes, D., Ye, X., & Stancavage, F. (2004). *Prepared to teach: Teacher preparation and student achievement in 8th grade mathematics.* Paper presented at annual meeting of the American Educational Research Association, San Diego.

Greenwald, R., Hedges, L., & Laine, R. (1996). The effect of school resources on student achievement. *Review of Educational Research 66*(3), 361–396.

Hafner, A., & Owings, J. (1991). *Careers in teaching: Following members of the high school class of 1972 in and out of teaching* NCES Report No. 91-470. Washington, DC: U.S. Department of Education, National Center for Education Statistics.

Hall, R. (1968). Professionalization and bureaucratization. *American Sociological Review 33*, 92–104.

Hanushek, E., & Rivkin, S. (2004). How to improve the supply of high quality teachers. In D. Ravitch (Ed.), *Brookings papers on education policy 2004* (pp. 7–44). Washington, DC: Brookings Institution Press.

Henke, R., Chen, X., & Geis, S. (2000). *Progress through the pipeline: 1992–93 college graduates and elementary/secondary school teaching as of 1997.* Washington, DC: U.S. Department of Education, National Center for Education Statistics.

Hirsch, E, Koppich, J., & Knapp, M. (2001). *Revisiting what states are doing to improve the quality of teaching: An update on patterns and trends.* Seattle: University of Washington, Center for the Study of Teaching and Policy.

Hodson, R., & Sullivan, T. (1995). Professions and professionals. In R. Hodson & T. Sullivan (Eds.), *The social organization of work* (pp. 287–314). Belmont, CA: Wadsworth.

Hom, P., & Griffeth, R. (1995). *Employee turnover.* Cincinnati, OH: South-Western College Publishing.

Huling-Austin, L. (1990). Teacher induction programs and internships. In W. R. Houston (Ed.), *Handbook of research on teacher education* (pp. 535–548). Reston, VA: Association of Teacher Educators.

Ingersoll, R. (1999). The problem of underqualified teachers in American secondary schools. *Educational Researcher 28*, 26–37.

Ingersoll, R. (2001). The status of teaching as a profession. In J. Ballantine & J. Spade (Eds.), *Schools and society: a sociological perspective* (pp. 115–129). Belmont, CA: Wadsworth Press.

Ingersoll, R. (2001). Teacher turnover and teacher shortages: An organizational analysis. *American Educational Research Journal 38*(3), 499–534.

Ingersoll, R. (2003a). *Who controls teachers' work?: Power and accountability in America's schools.* Cambridge, MA: Harvard University Press.

Ingersoll, R. (2003b). *Is there really a teacher shortage?* Philadelphia: University of Pennsylvania: Consortium for Policy Research in Education. http:// www.gse.upenn.edu/faculty_research/docs/ Shortage-RMI-09-2003.pdf.

Ingersoll, R. (2004a). Why some schools have more underqualified teachers than others. In D. Ravitch (Ed.), *Brookings Papers on Education Policy 2004* (pp. 45–88). Washington, DC: Brookings Institution Press.

Ingersoll, R. (2004b). Four myths about America's teacher quality problem. In M. Smylie & D. Miretzky (Eds.), *Developing the teacher workforce: The 103rd yearbook of the National Society for the Study of Education, part 1* (pp. 1–33). Chicago: National Society for the Study of Education.

Johnson, S., & Birkeland, S. (2003). Pursuing "a sense of success": New teachers explain their career decisions. *American Educational Research Journal 40*(3), 581–617.

Kane, M. (1994). Validating interpretive arguments for licensure and certification examinations. *Evaluation & The Health Professions 17*(2), 133–159.

Kirst, M. (1989). Who should control the schools? Reassessing current policies (pp. 62–68). In T. J. Sergiovanni & J. Moore (Eds.), *Schooling for tomorrow: Directing reforms to issues that count.* Boston: Allyn and Bacon.

Kohn, M., & Schooler, C. (1983). *Work and personality.* Norwood, NJ: Ablex

Lortie, D. (1975). *School teacher.* Chicago: University of Chicago Press.

Mobley, W. (1982). *Employee turnover: Causes, consequences and control.* Reading, MA: Addison-Wesley.

Murnane, R., & Raizen, S. (1988). Indicators of teaching quality. In R. Murnane & S. Senta (Eds.), *Improving indicators of the quality of science and mathematics education in grades K–12* (pp. 90–118). Washington, DC: National Academy Press.

Murnane, R., Singer, J., Willett, J., Kemple, J., & Olsen, R., eds. (1991). *Who will teach?: Policies that matter.* Cambridge, MA: Harvard University Press.

National Academy of Sciences. (1987). *Toward understanding teacher supply and demand.* Washington, DC: National Academy Press.

National Commission on Excellence in Education. (1983). *A nation at risk: The imperative for educational reform.* Washington, DC: Government Printing Office.

National Commission on Teaching and America's Future. (1996). *What matters most: Teaching for America's future.* New York: Author.

National Commission on Teaching and America's Future. (1997). *Doing what matters most: Investing in quality teaching.* New York: Author.

Parsons, T. (1959). The school class as a social system: Some of its functions in American society. *Harvard Educational Review 29*, 297–318.

Pascarella, E., & Terenzini, P. (1991). *How college affects students: Findings and insights from twenty years of research.* San Francisco: Jossey-Bass.

Price, J. (1977). *The study of turnover.* Ames: Iowa State University Press.

Price, J. (1989). The impact of turnover on the organization. *Work and Occupations 16*, 461–473.

Raudenbush, S., Fotiu, R., & Cheong, Y. (1999). Synthesizing results from the trial state assessment. *Journal of Educational and Behavioral Statistic 24*(4), 413–438.

Robinson, V. (1985). *Making do in the classroom: A report on the misassignment of teachers.* Washington, DC: Council for Basic Education and American Federation of Teachers.

Schlecty, P., & Vance, V. (1981). Do academically able teachers leave education? The North Carolina case. *Phi Delta Kappan 63*, 105–112.

Smylie, M. A., & Wenzel, S. A. (2003). *The Chicago Annenberg Challenge: Successes, failures, and lessons for the future. Final technical report of the Chicago Annenberg Research Project.* Chicago: University of Chicago, Consortium on Chicago School Research.

Strober, M., & Tyack, D. (1980). Why do women teach and men manage? *Signs 5*, 499–500.

Texas Center for Educational Research. (2000). *The cost of teacher turnover.* Austin, TX: Texas State Board for Educator Certification.

Villegas, A., & Lucas, T. (2004). Diversifying the teacher workforce. In M. Smylie & D. Miretzky (Eds.), *Developing the teacher workforce: The 103rd yearbook of the National Society for the Study of Education, part 1* (pp. 70–104). Chicago: National Society for the Study of Education.

Wang, A., Coleman, A., Coley, R., & Phelps, R. (2003). *Preparing teachers around the world.* Princeton, NJ: Educational Testing Service.

Weaver, T. (1983). *America's teacher quality problem: Alternatives for reform.* New York: Praeger.

15

The Changing and Chaotic World of Teacher Policy

Thomas B. Corcoran

A growing body of evidence is confirming what common sense has suggested all along: that the quality of teaching in the public schools matters for how well students learn. This statement reminds me of a conversation that I had with my great-aunt in the 1970s. A graduate of a normal school in Indiana who retired after teaching for over 35 years in a Cincinnati high school, she was interested in what I was doing. I told her about a study examining the importance of time on task in the classroom. "And how much did you spend to discover that?" she asked. "You could have just asked a teacher." Obvious or not, the dictum that teachers and teaching matter is now widely heralded as a discovery in the policy community. A more important, but less heralded, corollary is that poor children, minority children, and children from non-English-speaking homes are even more dependent on the quality of their teachers than are more affluent, English-speaking White children.

The evidence supporting these propositions is piling up. A 1991 study of student performance in Texas (Ferguson, 1991) found that the ability of teachers was the most influential factor, outside of home and family circumstances, in student academic success. Repeated and oft-cited studies conducted in Tennessee (Sanders & Horn, 1998; Sanders & Rivers, 1996) using value-added analysis found that students who had good teachers three years in a row showed significant increases in their percentile rankings on state assessments—regardless of their socioeconomic background. Conversely, students who had a series of ineffective teachers during that same period showed significant decline in their rate of academic growth. Goldhaber and Liu (2003) and Rivkin, Hanushek, and Kain (2005) estimated that teacher characteristics account for 7.5 percent or more of the variance in student achievement—a larger share than other school variables, but still dwarfed by the 60 percent of the variance both studies reported was explained by student and family characteristics. Using national data, Darling-Hammond (2000) found that state investments in teacher quality predicted statewide gains on the National Assessment of Educational Progress (NAEP). In a recent comparison of various methods of calculating these effects, more sophisticated methods were found to result in even higher estimates of teacher effects (Rowan, Correnti, & Miller, 2002).

This accumulating evidence, along with appeals to common sense, has led to demands that local, state, and federal policymakers ensure that skilled, caring, and effective teachers are provided for all children. Pressures to improve teacher quality stem both from state efforts to raise academic performance standards and from the requirements of the No Child Left Behind Act (NCLB) as well as from other factors such as class-size reductions and changing student demographics. But teacher quality is not a new issue. In fact, it has been at the top of the policy agenda in many states and districts since civil rights laws and changes in employment patterns began to provide more varied and more lucrative opportunities for women in the United States and negatively impacted the quality of the pool entering teaching. Prior to the 1960s, teaching was one of the best employment options that college-educated women had, and for decades a steady supply of highly qualified women had met the needs of most public schools. In the 1960s this source of good teachers began to decline, and this happened at the same time that policymakers discovered that the public schools could not fully compensate for the disadvantages of growing up in poverty. McDonnell (1989) reported that during the 1980s virtually every state made changes in the way teachers were trained, licensed, and compensated.

WHAT CAN THE STATES DO?

In this chapter, I focus on state policy because of its salience in shaping the quality of the teaching force, and I address three key questions: What are the primary policy levers through which state policymakers can improve the quality of teachers and teaching? What are the debates and options with regard to those policy mechanisms? And what guidance does research offer to policymakers as they attempt to resolve difficult questions such as these:

- Are state standards for entering the teaching profession appropriate and adequate? What would be gained or lost by raising them or eliminating them?
- How effective are traditional teacher education programs provided by institutions of higher education? How can they be strengthened?
- How does the quality of teachers provided by alternate pathways compare to that of those from traditional teacher education programs?
- What support(s) do new teachers need to be successful and remain in teaching?
- What should teachers be held accountable for, and how should we ensure their accountability?
- Can teacher compensation be linked to performance in ways that raise both individual and organizational productivity?
- What kind of learning opportunities do teachers need? What incentives are most effective at getting teachers to improve their knowledge and skills?

And a fourth question addressed at the end is this: What are the critical questions that the policy research community should be addressing to support the efforts of policymakers to improve the quality of teachers and teaching?

The key policy domains through which state policymakers can affect the quality of teachers and teaching provide the basic organizational structure of the chapter. In a meeting of policy researchers supported by the Carnegie Corporation of New York, we identified 14 such domains. They are the following:

- teacher licensure standards and assessments
- teacher education program requirements/accreditation standards
- funding of teacher education programs

- financial support for teacher candidates
- teacher compensation
- monitoring of local staffing practices (NCLB high-quality teacher requirements)
- teacher induction requirements
- recertification requirements
- professional development
- teacher evaluation
- collective bargaining laws and the scope of bargaining
- state accountability systems
- state data policy and data systems
- teacher recruitment and distribution strategies and incentives

Attempting to address all of the complex issues embedded in these domains in a single chapter would be foolhardy. Here I have focused on six of them that seem to me to be most salient in today's policy environment: licensure, teacher preparation, compensation and evaluation, induction, professional development, and state data systems. These are among the issues addressed by the National Commission on Teaching and America's Future (NCTAF, 1997) and the more recent Teaching Commission (2004). Teacher recruitment and distribution issues are also of critical importance but they have been addressed in Richard Ingersoll's chapter in this volume. These six issues are compelling to me because logic and evidence argue that policies adopted in these domains can have significant effects on the quality of the workforce, and because higher retirement rates and simultaneous pressures to improve the workforce will provide both incentives and opportunities for policymakers to act in these areas.

In the following sections, I will examine the issues facing state policymakers in each of these six domains, the policy instruments that they are using to address them, and the evidence available to guide them. I am relying heavily on existing reviews of the research literature where they exist, and where they do not, I have focused on the major studies available in the domain.

TEACHER LICENSING STANDARDS

The states determine the qualifications individuals must possess to obtain licenses to work as teachers in public schools in their jurisdictions. While all states require teachers to hold licenses to gain permanent employment as teachers, both the nature and the quality of their licensing standards and assessments vary. All of the states require teachers to hold college degrees, but beyond these requirements are varied mixes of college courses taken, clinical experiences, and scores on assessments measuring general knowledge, subject matter knowledge, and pedagogical knowledge. In the past decade, testing has gained in popularity, and in 2005, 48 states required teachers to pass one or more tests to obtain a teaching license (Goldhaber, 2006). Most of the states are using a test developed by the Educational Testing Service (ETS), but set different standards—cut scores—for passing it. The American Board for Certification of Teacher Excellence (ABCTE) is developing a national test battery that would provide a common standard for states that adopted it, and a more portable license for teachers—again, in the states that adopted it.

In recent years, there have been other shifts in state licensing policies. There is a trend towards requiring specialized licenses for different levels of public schooling—preschool, elementary, middle, and high. Policy also has shifted towards requiring candidates for licenses to

- possess majors in a discipline;
- pass tests of their general knowledge, subject matter knowledge, and pedagogical knowledge;
- obtain a probationary license and demonstrate their efficacy as a teacher prior to obtaining a professional license;
- demonstrate skills as a teacher through success on performance assessments; and
- demonstrate evidence of continued learning to periodically renew professional licenses.

Some states have collaborated in a national project, the Interstate New Teacher Assessment and Support Consortium (INTASC), to develop and test new assessment procedures for licensing. States have also tried system-changing strategies to strengthen licensing procedures, and in a minority of states licensing standards are now set by independent professional boards. In most states, however, these policies are still determined by legislation or by regulations adopted by state boards of education.

These changes on the margins of licensing policy have not satisfied those who feel that the current supply of teachers lacks the knowledge and skills required to solve the problems of performance that plague the public schools. Competing groups of reformers are advocating at least four different models for determining who is qualified to teach. The one model supported by most of the education establishment is called a professionalization model, and it calls for more state regulation of teacher preparation, improved graduate-level preparation programs, and higher licensing standards. Another group of reformers advocates an alternative pathways model that would permit a wider variety of training programs operating under some state regulation. This actually approximates the emerging situation in most states. A third group argues for abandonment of program regulation altogether; it wants to abandon regulation of preparation and specific preparation requirements and place the focus on the assessment of the knowledge and skills of candidates. This would operate like entry into the legal profession in those states where any candidate can take the bar examinations. Finally there are those who argue for full deregulation and who would permit schools to hire anyone who meets some minimum set of qualifications like possessing a degree and having no criminal record. What all of these reformers share is a conviction that the "traditional approach" to teacher training is badly flawed and major changes are needed.

These competing visions of reform have shifted the policy talk in the states from the benefits of raising licensure standards to an increasingly contentious debate over whether licensing is a good idea at all. The professionalization reformers want to define standards more precisely, make them more performance based, and assess them over time in the workplace (Darling-Hammond, Wise, & Klein, 1999; National Commission on Teaching and America's Future, 1997). Certainly a licensure policy would be more effective if it rested on a clear understanding of the knowledge and skills needed to perform well. Unfortunately there is only partial agreement about what this knowledge and these skills are, and mixed evidence about their importance. Differences in educational philosophy and beliefs about teaching lead to differing definitions of the critical knowledge and skills. Advocates of deregulation see licensing as an ineffective quality-control mechanism that constrains market forces and keeps many intellectually qualified people from pursuing teacher careers (Ballou & Podgursky, 1998; Finn & Madigan, 2001). These differences have led to allegations on both sides of misrepresentation of evidence; for example, see the exchange between Ballou & Podgursky (2000) and Darling-Hammond (2000) in the *Teachers College Record*. It is hard to sort out these arguments because much of the research evidence presented by both sides to support their cases suffers from conceptual and methodological problems, and because the two sides differ over the outcomes being sought and the public interest that is at stake (Cochran-Smith & Fries, 2001).

The conflict between professionalization and deregulation also surfaces in clashes over the approval of alternative pathways to licensure that require little or no formal preparation for teaching. These pathways first emerged in the 1980s in response to teacher shortages, the difficulties of staffing schools in high-poverty areas, and concerns over the heavy reliance of some districts on teachers with emergency certification. Forty-eight states and the District of Columbia provide alternatives to traditional teacher education programs. Use of alternate pathways has expanded dramatically in the past two decades, and in 2004–2005 between a quarter and a third of newly licensed teachers utilized them. The alternatives take many forms, varying from programs run by universities that provide training to new teachers after they begin to work to similar programs run by school districts and nonprofit organizations to programs that are little more than test prep courses for state licensing examinations. Perhaps the best known of these alternate route programs is Teach for America (TFA), which by 2005 provided nearly 2,000 new teachers a year to high-poverty schools across the nation (Humphrey & Wechsler, 2005). But there are numerous state, local, and university programs that are less well known but larger, and perhaps holding more significant implications for the composition of the teaching force in the long run. For example, the state-approved alternate route program in New Jersey provides nearly a quarter of the state's new teachers each year. And the New York Teaching Fellows program provides over a quarter of the new teachers for the city.

The Evidence

Can examination of research findings help policymakers sort out the question of whether teacher licenses matter? In a 1985 review of research on teacher certification, Evertson and colleagues reported that 11 of 13 studies found certified teachers outperformed those holding provisional or emergency certificates. But the methodologies were weak in most of these studies. Darling-Hammond (2000) examined trends in state-level assessment data and concluded that the proportion of teachers with full certification and majors in their teaching field was the best predictor of statewide gains in student achievement. But her methodology was also severely criticized. Goldhaber and Brewer (2000) found that teachers with standard certification outperformed those who were not certified, but did not appear to be more effective than individuals holding emergency certificates. What can we conclude from these studies about the importance of licensing? Only that the research evidence is weak and that the best argument for licensing seems to be that it protects the public from poor local hiring decisions, but by itself it does not guarantee a high-quality teaching force.

Are scores on licensing tests effective signals of teacher quality? A recent National Research Council committee (2001) reported finding little evidence of a relationship between teacher performance on licensure examinations and the performance of their students. Goldhaber (2003) reviewed the research literature on licensing, and finding few studies that met minimum standards of rigor, reported that we do not know much about their effects. He subsequently conducted a study (Goldhaber, 2006) of licensing tests in North Carolina and reports a weak, but positive link between teachers' scores on the licensing exams and the performance of their students on state assessments, but warns that there are many false positives and false negatives. He also found that raising the standard on the licensing exam would dramatically increase the false negatives. He concludes the examinations are a useful screen, but that districts need to be aware of the limitations of licensing procedures, be selective when hiring, and shape their work forces by observing actual effectiveness in classrooms.

What about the efficacy of the increasingly popular alternate pathways to licensing? There have been several studies of TFA. The most rigorous of these studies found that TFA teachers produced higher gains in mathematics than other new teachers, but there were no differences found in reading scores (Decker, Mayer, & Glazerman, 2004). The former finding suggests that the better undergraduate academic preparation of the TFA teachers was a major advantage in fields requiring specific disciplinary knowledge. It seems safe to surmise that similar results would be found in science or foreign language. Susan Moore Johnson and her colleagues (2003) followed the experiences of adults who entered 11 "fast-track" alternate programs which delivered all of their preservice preparation in the summer before employment. They found that the programs were successful in attracting a pool of able candidates, but that their preparation varied in quality. The better programs provided sufficient preparation to get these new teachers through the first few months, but significant continuing support was needed to sustain them through the first year and to help them become competent teachers. The authors noted "the introduction of fast-track alternative certification programs has not resolved the issue of who is responsible for the effective preparation and induction of teachers" (p. 35).

There have been two recent reviews of the research on alternative certification programs, and they have reached similar conclusions. Wilson, Floden, and Ferrini-Mundy (2001) reviewed the evidence on alternate route programs and concluded that alternate routes had been successful in recruiting a more diverse pool of teachers, but had a mixed record in terms of the quality of the teachers supplied. They also identified the characteristics of strong alternate programs, which seemed surprisingly similar to those of effective traditional teacher education programs. Two years later, Michael Allen (2003) conducted a rigorous review and concluded that there was only limited support for the contention that there were alternate route programs that "produced cohorts of teachers who were as ultimately effective as traditionally trained teachers" (p. 59). Allen noted that it was hard to review this research because definitions of alternate route programs varied, there were no studies looking at long-run effects, and results were confounded by selection bias. Indeed, as he notes, alternate route programs often are created to attract a more select pool of candidates and to place them in hard-to-staff schools, making it hard to compare outcomes. The broad question about the effectiveness of alternate routes may not be worth asking, given the growing variation in types of alternate routes and whom they serve. Feistritzer's annual reports of statistics about alternate pathways identify 10 different types.

Since the two reviews just discussed were conducted, reports have been issued from two well-designed studies of alternate pathways into teaching that are ongoing. One, conducted by SRI, is comparing the effectiveness of a number of different types of alternate route programs. The other, being conducted by university researchers, is examining the effectiveness of the many pathways taken to obtain teaching positions in New York City. While neither of these studies has been completed, they have issued preliminary results that support and perhaps strengthen Allen's conclusions. The first study, by Humphrey and Wechsler (2005), reports enormous variation in the characteristics of those who seek licensure through alternate routes and in their experiences in the programs. They found that large numbers of the participants had prior teaching experience, that the quality and amount of clinical experience varied, that the value of on-the-job training varied widely and was a function of the school context, and that the quality of mentoring was unpredictable. They conclude that gross comparisons among alternate programs and between alternate programs and traditional pathways are simply not useful, and they argue for research that examines the experiences and performance of similar groups of candidates.

The second study, the Teacher Pathways Project, is an ambitious multiyear study of pathways into teaching being conducted in New York City by researchers from the State University of New York at Albany and Stanford University. The study is examining the characteristics of conventional higher-education-based teacher education and other pathways into teaching and seeking to identify the attributes of these programs that impact student outcomes in New York City schools (Boyd et al., 2005). The researchers report that the alternate route teachers are largely replacing individuals with emergency certificates, and are having only a small effect on the number of teachers hired from traditional training institutions. They describe a complex and varied pattern of effects on student achievement, but overall conclude that the teachers hired through alternate routes generally do less well in their first year, but largely close gaps between their performance and that of teachers from traditional college programs by their third year (Boyd et al., 2005). They contend that the observed patterns of performance might be explained by differences in experiences working with children prior to employment (conventionally trained teachers have more), differences in coursework prior to employment (conventionally trained teachers have more job-relevant training), differences in the content knowledge of the teachers (teachers from some alternate programs like TFA have higher scores), and also differences in their initial teaching positions (alternate route teachers tend to be placed in harder-to-staff schools). They conclude that the city needs all of these programs to meet the requirements of NCLB and that the different pathways bring different strengths to teaching. This is not a finding that helps clarify the choices facing state policymakers.

In sum, the evidence about the benefits and essential characteristics of licensing is not compelling. The debate between the regulationists and the free market advocates cannot be resolved by appeals to research evidence. Raising standards for entering teaching is an expensive proposition because of its implications for preparation programs, its effects on the candidate pool and the implications for recruitment, and the likelihood that more complex, costly assessments would be needed. The available evidence certainly justifies some experiments with new licensing policies—including policies that focus on individual competence—but it does not justify making systemwide or large-scale change or making large investments in new licensing procedures. Policymakers would be well advised to stick with the systems they have in place until we have better evidence of the consequences of raising or eliminating standards and about who suffers those consequences. Perhaps field tests of the new national assessment under development by ABCTE will shed some light on this issue. Clearly we need some well-designed experiments with different licensing regimes to help state policymakers decide which direction to take.

The related evidence about the effectiveness of alternative routes to certification is somewhat stronger. We know that some alternative route programs are as effective as more traditional campus-based programs. We also know something about the characteristics of the more effective alternative route programs. Policymakers would be well advised to act on this evidence to improve the quality of the alternative pathways in their states. This should be monitored carefully to ensure that particular pools of candidates are not losing access to credentials. Better evidence may be available in the near future, and until then policymakers would be wise to live with the licensing standards they have and the chaos of many alternative pathways.

TEACHER EDUCATION POLICIES

It might be argued that the states do not have coherent policies about teacher education. While researchers and policymakers often refer to college-based training programs as "traditional" teacher education programs, and speak of them as though they were the norm, there is actually enormous variation in the pathways students pursue to achieve certification and employment as teachers. And there is also great variation among and within "traditional" training programs in terms of their visions of good teaching, standards for admission, rigor and amount of subject matter preparation, clinical experiences provided, and quality of assessments. Compared to the preparation of other professions, the preparation of teachers is chaotic. There is no coherent system; there are simply many pathways into teaching. And if one wanders through a bookstore on any campus and examines what teacher candidates are being asked to read, one immediately realizes that the trainers of teachers have not yet embraced evidence-based practice. It seems to me that in other professions such as law, engineering, medicine, nursing, or the clergy, curricula, standards, and assessments are far more regulated, standardized, and evidence based, but that is another one of the many empirical questions that we cannot answer. Critics take note of the chaos in the preparation of teachers and conclude that it doesn't matter how teachers are prepared.

This chaos is the product of the interaction of state policy, collegiate institutional autonomy, the academic freedom claimed by the faculties who prepare teachers, and the layers of reforms that have accumulated. Here we focus on the policy parameters. The states determine who is permitted to offer a teacher education program in their jurisdictions, and they set standards for teacher education programs offered by public and private institutions and, one should add, by nonprofit and for-profit organizations. However, these standards vary from highly specific course and clinical requirements to broad program requirements. They rest loosely on general understandings of what teachers need to know and be able to do rather than on a body of empirical evidence linking them to teacher performance on the job.

Even as researchers acknowledge the crucial importance of teachers, there is growing disagreement about the best way to prepare them. As suggested in the previous section, some argue that easing entry into teaching by eliminating requirements is the best way to attract strong candidates (U.S. Department of Education 2002), whereas others argue that investing in the development of higher-quality teacher preparation programs will better serve our nation's children (National Commission on Teaching and America's Future, 1997). The latter group of reformers is stressing strengthening the role of arts and science faculty in teacher training and strengthening requirements for disciplinary study, arguing for expanded and higher-quality clinical experiences for preservice teachers and a role for universities in supporting new teachers, and attempting to build stronger internal accountability for teacher education programs that examines the performance of their graduates. A foundation-funded initiative based on these principles is under way in 11 universities to design programs (Carnegie Corporation of New York, 2001).

The states also decide whether teacher education programs will be approved by the state or must meet national accreditation standards. Every state except Arizona requires some form of accreditation process (Allen, 2003). One major policy issue has been how to evaluate and accredit teacher education programs. The program approval processes used by the states are widely regarded as weak and the evidence presented to support this contention is that very few programs have been closed by state action. So the trend has been towards the adoption of national accreditation standards and processes. There are two national organizations that accredit teacher education programs—the National Council for the Accreditation of Teacher Education (NCATE) and a newer rival, the Teacher Education Accreditation Council (TEAC). Both are pressuring institutions to collect data on the performance of their graduates and to develop internal accountability systems—and norms—that help them improve.

Some states face major problems of articulation and coordination in teacher education because high percentages of their teacher candidates attend the first two years of college in community colleges and receive most of their disciplinary training in these institutions. These programs often lack coherence, particularly as individuals may take several years to complete the requirements and attend different institutions in the process. It is also difficult to develop courses that provide future teachers with deep knowledge of the content of the public school curriculum rather than surveys of a field. As college tuition rises, more and more students seek less expensive options, and this compounds the problems of college administrators and state policymakers.

Another major policy issue has accompanied the rise of web-based education. Numerous for-profit organizations now offer virtual teacher education programs at much lower cost to students than conventional universities. State policymakers must decide whether the credentials offered by these programs will be recognized and whether these programs will be permitted to operate within their jurisdictions. There is often considerable political pressure exerted to keep these new providers out, but they are expanding, and their low costs and public acceptance of web-based programs are fueling their expansion. It is hard for policymakers to object because in many instances, they have permitted similar programs to be offered by state institutions to save money and serve nontraditional clients. These programs raise new questions about program standards. Does a program have to have a physical campus? Does it need a library? Do staff–student ratios make any sense? This issue is closely related to the question of alternate routes to licensure, but raises broader questions about the forms of education recognized as legitimate preparation.

The Evidence

What do we know about the characteristics of effective teacher education programs? There appears to be general agreement that the knowledge base underlying teacher education is weak. There have been three major reviews of research on teacher education conducted in the past three years, and they all reached this conclusion (Allen, 2003; Cochran-Smith & Zeichner, 2005; Wilson, Floden, & Ferrini-Mundy, 2001). While hundreds of studies have been published on specific aspects of teacher training and their effects on teacher knowledge, beliefs, practices, and, more rarely, performance, the quality of this work is low according to the reviewers. The studies tend to be small in scale, and employ weak methodologies that make it difficult to establish causation. In general these three reviews report that

- subject matter preparation is important for teachers, but there is little research on how much or what kind is needed, the research is heavily focused on mathematics, and it is inconclusive about the value of subject matter majors;
- pedagogical preparation is valuable, but it is not clear what skills are critical or how they are most effectively acquired;
- clinical experiences are important, but it is not clear how much is needed or how best to provide it, and these experiences are often poorly designed and managed;
- the effects of state program approval and national accreditation are unclear; and
- more research is needed.

In sum, the research literature on teacher education and accreditation of teacher education programs provides little guidance for policymakers, beyond the conventional wisdom of requiring more content courses and more clinical experience. This is especially true if they are concerned about cost-effectiveness, cost to the participants, and meeting the needs of the most performance-stressed schools and districts. There is little research available on the costs of high-quality teacher education. However, conducting this research depends in part on policymakers' willingness to invest in the development of comprehensive data systems that link teachers and students (see the later section on data policy and systems) and supports value-added studies. The Teaching Commission (2006) has called for states and institutions to assess the results of teacher education programs and to act on those results to improve, or close, ineffectual programs. The new national Data Quality Consortium formed by a number of education organizations is encouraging the development of such data systems, and the U.S. Department of Education is investing in their development. So better information and more useful research may be just around the corner.

TEACHER COMPENSATION AND EVALUATION

I have combined these two policy domains because they are linked in policy debates over how to strengthen incentives for improving productivity in the teaching force and improve the quality of teaching. First, let's describe the status quo for each. For the most part, teachers are paid according to state or local salary schedules which pay teachers on the basis of experience and credentials or college credits earned, but treat all teachers the same regardless of their assignments, skills, or performance. The highest salaries paid in a jurisdiction tend to be about twice the starting salaries, so there is little growth across a career in teaching.

Beyond this general pattern, there is some variance in teacher compensation policies among the states. The three major dimensions of variance are the levels of pay—higher in the Northeast and West, lower in the South and upper Midwest; who decides teachers salaries—state or local policymakers; and the process for deciding—legislation, collective bargaining, or meet and confer processes. There is a considerable literature on the question of how much teachers are paid, and not surprisingly advocates of professionalization and supporters of unions often contend that teachers are paid too little, and free market advocates and those opposed to bargaining complain that they are paid too much or paid for the wrong things (Temin, 2003; Vedder, 2003). Compensation is determined at the state level in some states, and locally in the others. Thirty-three states require or permit collective bargaining. Twenty-one states have "right-to-work" laws that prevent collective bargaining agreements from requiring workers to support and share the costs of union representation. Here another dimension of variance appears—the scope of bargaining. Some states permit bargaining on a wide range of issues including matters of policy such as class size and professional development; others restrict bargaining to wages and benefits and conditions of employment. These matters have often been the subject of heated policy debates in the past, and much has been written about them—most of it polemical. I want to pass over these policies that clearly affect compensation to focus on what is common across these varied settings—the use of uniform salary schedules and the absence of any link between salary increments and performance. These are the issues that are currently being debated.

Two major policy debates are under way over how to compensate teachers. The first debate is over paying teachers for their performance. On the first question, reformers appear to be divided into at least three camps: those who want to pay teachers according to gains in student achievement (Ballou, 2001); those who advocate granting pay increases for observed improvements in practice—knowledge- and skill-based pay (Odden, 2001); and those who argue for compensation systems that use multiple approaches and measures (Koppich, 2005). These approaches do share some common goals, however. They all want to tighten the connection between teacher compensation and student achievement gains, although some want to do it indirectly. Given rising standards and increased accountability, this is compelling for many policymakers. Some of the proposals for reform in compensation are designed to recruit higher-quality teachers to high-poverty schools, and to retain them, or to recruit more candidates in areas of shortage such as mathematics and science. Most of the reformers also want to use redesigned compensation plans to stimulate more productive professional development for teachers that is related to their job assignments. Single salary schedules tend to reward teachers for the amount, and not the quality or relevance, of professional development, so they do not provide the desired incentives (Odden & Kelley, 1997; Stout, 1996). To get around this, some states have allowed school administrators to prescribe parts of teachers' professional development programs when either individual or school performance was judged to be inadequate.

Prior to the 1990s, most efforts to change teacher compensation experimented with various versions of merit pay (Hatry, Greiner, & Ashford, 1994; Murnane & Cohen, 1986) or career ladder programs (Freiberg & Knight, 1991; Schlechty, 1989), very few of which worked or lasted. Today's strategies are both different and more varied, and include signing bonuses; housing supplements; higher pay levels for teachers in shortage areas like mathematics, science, and technology, or for teachers in hard-to-staff or low-performing schools; salary incentives for teachers who earn certification from the National Board for Professional Teaching Standards (NBPTS); more elaborate knowledge- and skill-based pay incentives (Milanowski, 2003); as well as school-based performance-award programs that provide cash bonuses to everyone in a school for improved student performance.

Reforms in how teachers are paid—and in particular, basing at least part of their pay on some measure of performance—are gaining political traction as mechanisms for improving teaching and learning and holding teachers more accountable for their work. They are also seen as vehicles for addressing the needs of hard-to-staff schools. Schools, districts, and states are experimenting with pay schemes that focus on the acquisition and demonstration of increased knowledge and skill, individual performance pay, and school rewards based on student performance gains. The Education Commission of the States (Azordegan et al., 2005) reports that 20 governors outlined teacher compensation as one of their major education issues in their 2005 state of the state addresses, and nine specifically spoke of some sort of merit pay. However, so far the experimentation appears to be producing slow and mixed results. In a few districts, compensation has been linked to the performance of teachers. In others, ambitious experiments have been abandoned or watered down. Putting performance pay into practice turns out to be as difficult as creating career ladders or differentiated pay schemes. However, the central idea is appealing: define what is meritorious and then pay extra for it to increase teacher responsiveness and accountability.

There are several forms of merit or performance pay. In knowledge- and skill-based pay systems, teachers are evaluated on the basis of a vision of good practice. In value-added plans, complex statistical analysis of gains in the performance of their students, usually measured by standardized tests, would be used to determine pay increases. In a softer, less rigorous variation, teachers and administrators mutually determine the performance assessments to be used and set the performance targets. And, finally there are school-based performance-pay systems in which entire faculties or staffs are rewarded for improved test scores in their schools. Finally, career ladders or leadership models offer teachers higher salaries for assuming extra responsibilities presumably because they have demonstrated special knowledge and skill. This approach fits nicely with current instructional-support strategies that utilize "coaches" to assist teachers and it also has been used to reward teachers who have achieved NBPTS certification.

States have encouraged experimentation with compensation reforms. Some like Kentucky have tried school-level performance rewards. Others like Colorado, Kentucky, and Minnesota have used inducements to stimulate local experiments with performance-based pay. A number have provided salary increases for teachers achieving NBPTS certification. Quite a few districts use modest versions of the career ladder design, modest because they are not perceived as threats to the single salary schedule, either because the stipends are small or small numbers of teacher are affected or both. But there are only a handful of districts that have successfully implemented pay for performance designs.

The second major policy debate concerns differentiated pay, which is also controversial. Leaders of national and local teacher unions seem committed to the defense of the single salary schedule in spite of evidence of unequal assignments (Corcoran, Walker, & White, 1988) and systematic scarcities in specific teaching fields. States and districts have offered signing bonuses, loan forgiveness, assistance with housing, reimbursement of moving expenses, and tuition reimbursement to attract teachers in hard-to-fill positions in mathematics, science, bilingual education, and special education, but they have not touched the uniform salary schedule.

All of these new compensation plans require reliable and fair evaluation procedures. Some states have adopted specific regulations prescribing the conduct of teacher evaluations. Others simply require that local districts conduct evaluations and mandate who does them and how often. For experienced teachers, evaluations are generally based on one to three observations by an administrator or supervisor. There is general agreement that these evaluation systems are weak and often conducted in a pro forma manner except in cases of egregiously poor performance. Teacher unions have initiated peer-evaluation strategies in some districts, and once accepted, these have proved to be productive means of improving classroom teaching. Neglected by most policymakers for a long time teacher evaluation has become a matter of greater interest because some reformers want to link teacher performance to compensation, and therefore they need more robust and reliable forms of evaluation.

For several reasons, it seems prudent for state policymakers to avoid the more extreme forms of performance pay. First, value-added models may be subject to measurement errors that could lead to costly legal proceedings, and knowledge- and skill-based pay systems depend on the creation of reliable, valid, and legitimated local evaluation systems. Second, even if local administrators wanted to protect teachers and use the data to help them improve, there is a risk that results will become public, leading to conflicts with parents and pressures for unfair actions. Indeed in some jurisdictions, the media have indicated that they would use freedom of information provisions to obtain the results of value-added analysis. Third, monetary incentive programs have not proved to be very effective in improving teachers' behaviors in the long run (Heneman & Milanowski, 1999). Fourth, teachers' unions are likely to bitterly oppose performance pay—although there have been some interesting exceptions—and the resulting conflicts with administrators and policymakers will engender long-term costs that might offset any productivity gains. Finally, in most states, salary schedules are determined locally, and neither local policymakers nor local teachers' unions will welcome interference from the state.

The Evidence

What do we know about the effects of various forms of performance pay on teacher behavior, student performance, or district budgets? The answer is "not much." Efforts to move away from the single salary schedule are still in early stages of experimentation, and the results are not clear. Researchers are learning about what it takes for such plans to succeed, and this work may lead to better-designed and more successful efforts to reform compensation. Meanwhile, policymakers, reacting to pressures for improved performance and more accountability, and hearing about the experiments, are likely to begin to examine options for restructuring teacher compensation in their districts and states without being guided by research findings.

So what do we know? First, it is generally believed that teachers earn smaller salaries than those holding similar jobs in other professions, and there is a large literature on this subject. The results are mixed and confusing. Some analysts confirm the proposition (Allegretto, Corcoran, & Mishel, 2004; Temin, 2003) and others dispute it, arguing that when benefits and hours of employment are considered, teacher salaries are competitive (Vedder, 2003). Second, some believe that higher salaries will attract better candidates and improve student performance, so they advocate across-the-board salary increases. This is one of the recommendations of the Teaching Commission (2006). And some studies do report that higher salaries lead to improved teacher quality and student achievement (Figlio, 1997; Loeb & Page, 2000), while others show that across-the-board salary increases—an expensive policy option—have a negligible effect on teacher mobility and student performance (Ballou & Podgursky, 1996; Hanushek, Kain, & Rivkin, 2004).

What about years of experience and college credits—the cornerstones of the uniform salary schedule system that is now used? A number of studies have reported the relationship between teacher quality and years of teaching experience to be weak or nonexistent after the first five years, and some report negative relationships after 20 years (Darling-Hammond, 2000; Ferguson & Ladd, 1996; Hanushek, 1997; Murnane, 1983; Plecki, 2000). However, Rice (2003) points out these studies often use flawed data, relying on the number of years a teacher has worked in a specific district rather than their total teaching experience. Reviewing this literature carefully, she concludes that the value of experience is evident in the first few years of elementary teaching but has sustained effects for high school teachers that continue later into their careers. In addition, these studies rely on standardized tests which typically measure student knowledge of basic skills and facts. It is possible that the value added by experience shows up in deeper student understanding and higher-order skills. It also seems likely that the value of experience is highly dependent on the professional culture of the school in which the teacher works. More sophisticated studies of the value of experience are obviously needed.

Studies linking teaching quality to the accumulation of college credits, particularly graduate coursework in education, have generally produced inconclusive results (Ferguson and Ladd, 1996; Hanushek, 1994; Murnane, 1983; Rivkin, Hanushek, & Kain, 2005). However, using more refined measures of coursework, Monk (1994) found that the amount of content preparation teachers have is positively related to student achievement in high school mathematics and science, but the relationship is curvilinear and the benefits decline after five courses. He also found positive effects for courses in pedagogy. Rice (2003) reviewing a number of studies of the relationship between coursework in content and pedagogy and student achievement, concludes that both content courses and pedagogical courses contribute to positive outcomes, but the impact of content coursework is greater for secondary teachers, and even for them, diminishes over time.

What do we know about the alternative compensation schemes discussed previously? As I indicated, there is not persuasive research evidence about the impact of the various alternative compensation arrangements under consideration, but there has been some research. Earlier efforts to put merit-pay plans in place suffered from weak evaluation systems and, in some cases, weak fiscal incentives, so it is not surprising that researchers found that these programs had little impact on teacher quality (Mohrman, Mohrman, & Odden, 1996; Murnane and Cohen, 1986). The career-ladder systems introduced in the 1980s seemed to hold greater promise. These programs provided advancement opportunities for high-performing teachers, including mentoring and administrative responsibilities, accompanied by stipends or additional steps in single salary schedules. In some sites career ladder programs were associated with improvements in student achievement, but many of these programs lost funding before significant impacts could be demonstrated (Odden & Kelley, 1997). States and districts abandoned these programs due to high costs, teacher opposition, and the lack of clear results, but also because many states began to experience revenue problems at the end of this period and cut nonessential programs from their budgets (Cornett & Gaines, 1994; National Association of State Boards of Education, 2002).

Knowledge- and skill-based pay systems focus teachers on the use of "best practices" and promote professional development, and proponents argue that they create more direct relationships between teacher compensation and teacher quality (Milanowski, 2003; Odden et al., 2001). They are being tried in a small number of districts, and early reports show that teachers view these programs more favorably than early attempts at merit pay or career ladder systems (Milanowski, 2003), and some districts report higher rates of retention of highly qualified teachers (Reichardt & Van Buhler, 2003). However, several major efforts to introduce these plans were abandoned due to teacher opposition and their costs.

The use of performance awards has also been examined. These plans seek to reward teachers for the academic performance gains of their students, in hope of motivating higher levels of productivity. The designs being used vary along two critical dimensions. The first is the unit of performance—whether the outcome measure focuses on the students taught by an individual teacher or the performance of students in a school. There has been some research on group rewards. Group-based or school-based performance awards offer greater appeal to some by explicitly encouraging the collaborative nature of teaching, though advocates note that individual-based awards may indirectly encourage collaboration, as the awards are available to all teachers and thus not zero-sum systems (Solmon & Podgursky, 2000). Further, group-based awards may encourage teachers to address broader goals that match community and school expectations (Firestone, 1994; Kelley, Heneman, & Milanowski, 2000). Studies generally find that teachers working in systems providing group rewards for performance exhibit greater motivation towards improved student performance, with motivation varying based on the teachers' perception of the award system's fairness (Heneman & Milanowski, 1999; Kelley, Heneman, & Milanowski, 2000).

Considerable work is being done on the development of value-added models, and these analyses are being used in Tennessee and elsewhere to identify high- and low-performing teachers. They are not yet being used to determine teacher compensation. Critics of individual-based performance awards like these contend that there is too much error in current testing systems to accurately assess the progress made by students, and that too often results in inaccurate measures of teacher performance (Milanowski, 1999; Odden & Kelley, 1997). Advocates for individual-based awards argue that when carefully incorporated into a sophisticated model of teacher quality, gains on student achievement tests can provide an independent measure for teacher performance, and can be included as one part of a teacher's evaluation (Solmon & Podgursky, 2000). Similar to skill-based pay systems, performance systems focusing on individuals appear to have positive effects on the retention of highly qualified teachers, but no clear effects on teacher recruitment (Reichardt & Van Buhler, 2003).

Despite the potential offered by these new systems for teacher compensation, there are still significant problems blocking their general implementation. The primary obstacle is the opposition of national and local union leaders to giving up the single salary schedule. And even well-designed systems may face suspicion or opposition from teachers and their unions, based on concerns about both the effectiveness of existing evaluation systems and teachers' abilities to meet continually higher standards for student performance or skill acquisition (Hatry, Greiner, & Ashford, 1994; Heneman, 1998; Kelley, Heneman, & Milanowski, 2000; Milanowski, 2003). These problems of accuracy and perceived fairness in measurement of performance arise whether the standard is the teacher's performance against some model of good practice or student gains on some assessment. Critics also argue that performance-award systems may encourage higher test scores; however, if tests are not aligned with broader goals of education, such improvements may not correlate with improvements in actual learning (Cohen, 1996). Successful programs also have the potential to become expensive, as a high percentage of teachers qualify for higher salaries through skill development or high performance (Milanowski, 2003).

In light of the limited evidence, larger, perhaps regional, experiments with the Teaching Commission's recommendations to raise base pay, provide new advancement pathways, and pay extra for assignments to hard-to-staff schools seem in order. These experiments would have to be conducted in a large geographic area, a regional labor market, for example, in order to avoid simply encouraging teachers to move across district lines and shift the location of the labor problems.

TEACHER INDUCTION

The National Commission on Teaching and America's Future and the Teaching Commission have both strongly recommended that all states develop and adequately fund beginning teacher support programs for all new teachers. Well-designed supports for new teachers help them to continue their learning during a critical period, one which makes a tremendous difference in the kind of teachers they eventually become and the kind of experience their students have. Beginning teacher support programs are intended to provide novice teachers with the support and guidance needed to facilitate a successful transition into the classroom, thereby increasing teacher retention and building a solid foundation for the development of teaching competence and professionalism. Within this framework, these programs typically provide personal support and professional guidance from a mentor, additional skills training, regular feedback on performance, and a summative assessment that may be connected to licensing.

This is not a new idea, as states have been experimenting with induction programs since the 1970s. While only eight states reported having induction programs in 1984, the number had increased to 31 by the early 1990s, and nearly two thirds of states required some kind of teacher induction programs by the end of the decade (Weiss & Weiss, 1999). However, the number fluctuates as states add and drop programs in response to changes in their fiscal circumstances. Unfortunately, many of these programs are simply unfunded mandates that leave it up to local districts to decide what supports should be provided. A number of states provide more specific guidance about induction, and some also provide training for the mentors who work with new teachers. But only a handful of states provide well-funded, multifaceted induction programs. These programs have not proved to be stable over time, as legislators faced with fiscal problems have often cut support for induction programs, viewing them as a luxury rather than a necessity.

During the first few years, new teachers must learn how to apply their content and pedagogical knowledge in the classroom; form relationships with students, parents, and colleagues; and master the art of "good teaching." This process can often be difficult, especially given that many new teachers are left to choose or create their curriculum, find instructional materials, develop their lesson plans, and manage their classroom without any assistance from administrators or fellow teachers (Johnson et al., 2001). Teachers gain experience and hone their craft through these early trials, which ultimately provide them with the experience that allows them to greatly affect the achievement of their students. This process of "baptism by fire," however, often causes new teachers to leave the profession before they have the chance to establish themselves in their position. The nation's public schools, as a result, have been burdened with a serious problem of teacher attrition, a problem that only will only worsen as student enrollment increases, class sizes decrease, and many aging teachers retire in the coming decade (Weiss & Weiss, 1999). This problem disproportionately affects poor children whose learning is more dependent on teacher quality There are a number of potential policy solutions available to help decrease the attrition rate of new teachers, including salary increases and loan forgiveness, but the support provided by teacher induction programs may represent the best option for retaining new teachers and, consequently, increasing student achievement over time.

Although some attrition is inevitable and, in cases where teacher quality is low, even beneficial, there comes a point where attrition hurts the overall quality of the product put forth by an organization, whether it be a business and a traditional commodity, or a school community and the quality of education offered. Ingersoll and Smith note, however, that unlike other professions, "teaching has long had alarmingly high rates of attrition among newcomers" (Ingersoll & Smith, 2004). Those alarmingly high rates, in some studies, have translated into as many as 50 percent of new teachers leaving within their first five years in the profession (Ingersoll & Smith, 2004). Even more unsettling is the fact that 30 percent of new teachers either move to another school or leave the profession after their first year. The side effects of this trend of high teacher attrition, though, are just as disturbing as the numbers themselves. Teachers with high scores on exams like the SAT, those considered "the best and the brightest," are more likely to leave during their early years on the job (Ingersoll & Smith, 2004). Recent research has also supported the belief that high rates of attrition among new teachers can be linked to the teacher shortages currently affecting education in the United States, in the sense that a "revolving door" in schools has caused many teachers to leave early in their careers (Ingersoll & Smith, 2004, p. 29). While efforts to increase salaries or provide greater amounts of loan forgiveness could potentially serve to alleviate this problem of teacher attrition, induction programs for new teachers represent the best overall option in the fight to retain new teachers.

Teacher induction programs have distinct advantages over other initiatives aimed at the retention of teachers, such as increased salaries and loan forgiveness. While salary increases and loan forgiveness money can attract new teachers and retain them for a certain amount of time, they do not provide any support for teachers that can help them through their difficult early years. Teacher induction programs can also be used to help teachers improve their teaching, in terms of pedagogical knowledge, teaching style, and overall knowledge of the core curriculum. Besides the general features described previously, the specific features of induction programs include, but are not limited to, the following:

- new teacher workshops,
- formal assignment of a mentor and preparation for mentors,
- the use of case studies and videos,
- journal writing,
- ongoing assessment,
- participation in team teaching situations, and
- providing a support team or a network of new and experienced teachers with whom to share concerns and discuss issues (Torres et al., 2004).

Although all of these aspects of induction programs can aid in reducing the overall attrition of new teachers, it is important to differentiate among them and determine which ones are most effective in the retention of new teachers. Determining which features are most important has cost implications. States must also make important decisions about the characteristics of teacher induction programs, such as their duration, their availability, and their intensity, and these decisions also have cost implications.

The Evidence

In recent years there have been a number of reviews of the research literature on teacher induction. The most rigorous and complete reviews to date have been conducted by SRI International (2004), the EPPI-Centre (2004), and Ingersoll and Kralick (2004). All three reviews describe the research on induction and mentoring as weak and eliminate many studies from consideration. The EPPI-Centre review examined 51 studies of the effects of induction on newly qualified teachers and found only two worthy of in-depth review. SRI concluded that they simply could not conclude that induction works, because of the weakness of the research. They pointed to inadequate and varying definitions of key constructs, reliance on self-report, reliance on a single outcome measure, and lack of comparison groups as major problems in the literature. They were also unable to identify the most effective induction practices because of the lack of experimental data. Ingersoll and Kralick came to a somewhat different conclusion. From 150 empirical studies reviewed, they found 10 that had reliable quantitative measures of the effects of mentoring and induction and used comparison groups to determine the value added. They concluded that there was empirical support for the claim that such assistance has a positive effect on teachers and their retention. However, they also noted that more rigorous studies were needed to answer basic questions about the design of induction programs, such as which elements were most helpful.

To answer some of these questions, Ingersoll and Smith (2004) used data from the 1999–2000 Schools and Staffing Survey (SASS) and the 2000–2001 Teacher Follow-Up Survey to examine the effects of teacher participation in induction or mentoring programs. From the analysis of these data, they concluded that teacher induction programs were effective in reducing attrition among new teachers, and they also were able to reach some broad conclusions about the importance of various program features. The SASS data from 1990–1991, 1993–1994, and 1999–2000 show that the number of new teachers receiving support through induction has almost doubled in a 10-year period (Ingersoll & Smith, 2004). After controlling for confounding factors like the background characteristics of the teachers and schools, Ingersoll and Smith found an association between beginning teachers receiving induction and mentoring support and their likelihood of turnover. This likelihood, however, depended on the type and number of supports. Teachers with a mentor from the same field, with common planning time with other teachers in the same subject, with regularly scheduled collaboration with other teachers, and with membership in an external network of teachers were less likely to leave the profession. Not all of the components of the induction programs that they observed had such a profound effect. Supports with weaker effects on the retention of new teachers included "a reduced teaching schedule, a reduced number of preparations, or extra classroom assistance" (p. 34).

Ingersoll and Smith (2004) found that, among teachers who entered the profession in the 1999–2000 school year, 16 percent received no induction supports, and they had a 40 percent probability of attrition by the end of their first year. Twenty-two percent of the teachers took part in programs offering three induction supports, and they had a 28 percent chance of not returning after their first year. Teachers who received six induction supports represented only 13 percent of the sample, and they had a turnover probability of 24 percent. A very small percentage of the teachers (less than 1 percent) took part in programs that offered eight induction supports, but the probability of attrition among these subjects was "less than half of those who participated in no induction activities" (p. 37).

While there is a need for more research on induction, particularly on the value of various program components, the effects of different funding mechanisms, and the duration and timing of various forms of support, there does seem to be modest evidentiary support for investing in these programs.

In this domain, we have the evidence, but we have been unable to convince most state policymakers to make the required investments. State policymakers have often tried to have their cake and eat it too by adopting regulations requiring induction supports and then passing the costs on to local school districts. We do need to help them find ways to deliver these services at reasonable costs while maintaining their quality. One possible solution that would also contribute to the improvement of teacher education would be to encourage collaboration between school districts and higher education and utilize the resources of both institutions. Other promising strategies are to make more use of web-based services and retired teachers to support beginning teachers. Again, we need to conduct well-designed experiments here to understand the relationships between costs and quality.

PROFESSIONAL DEVELOPMENT

Professional development for teachers in the United States is primarily funded, designed, and delivered by local school districts. The menu of professional development for teachers consists primarily of three sets of activities: (1) formal supervision, (2) in-service training, and (3) collegial learning. Although there are some notable exceptions, most teachers do not receive professional development that is tightly connected to their job assignments or beneficial to their practice. Corcoran (1995) asserts that commonly practiced design flaws result in professional development approaches that lack focus and continuity, consider only short-run needs, fail to involve teachers and respect their expertise, and neglect subject matter knowledge. Studies have exposed problems and concerns with the conventional approaches to professional development, citing most often their ineffectiveness in changing teaching practices (Guskey, 1986; Slavin, 1989).

States could play leadership roles in building the kind of professional development systems we need. State policymakers could alter the incentives for teachers by changing recertification requirements. They could support regional or intermediate units and demand that they deliver professional development that meets the consensus standards. States could provide more guidance for local professional development activities. Most states have shown little concern about the character or content of the learning opportunities provided by their regional or intermediate-unit structures. More than half of the states support some type of intermediate unit, but few have seriously attempted to influence their priorities, monitor the quality of their offerings, or evaluate their impact. States still provide little guidance or oversight to local districts and (increasingly) schools where most key decisions about professional development are made.

As of 2000, fewer than 20 states provided funds for local professional development other than the federal categorical aid available for this purpose. Eleven states had set time requirements (ranging from two to 10 days) for professional development. Thirty-six states required district plans for professional development, and 17 states also required school plans, but there was generally no meaningful review of these plans by the responsible state agencies. The states did not require that districts justify investments in professional development with evidence that the content would be useful or that the learning opportunities would lead to changes in practice.[1]

---

1. Unpublished data from my 2001 analysis of the state professional development policy profiles developed by the Consortium for Policy Research in Education (CPRE) with the support of the Carnegie Corporation of New York.

Ten states had set quality standards for professional development by 2000, but only a few states were using these standards to review local plans or state programs. Several states—Kentucky, Massachusetts, Michigan, and New Jersey—had attempted to review the quality of providers of professional development to provide better information to the districts and schools that used their services. Still, all in all, the state role in shaping and improving professional development remained weak.

Total expenditures, both direct and indirect, by state and local districts on professional development for teachers represent a significant portion of education expenditures. We lack nationwide or even statewide data on expenditures, but a set of well-designed studies in large urban districts found that professional development expenditures ranged from 2.2 to 6.9 percent of the operating budgets (Miles et al., 2004). These estimates are somewhat higher than results reported in previous studies which ranged between 2 to 4 percent of operating budgets. This may be because urban districts have greater needs or more funds targeted at professional development. Or it may be because the studies in urban districts were based on a more carefully defined cost structure. Most of the funds came from local revenues, with the states providing between 2 and 13 percent, the federal government between 18 and 37 percent, and private sources between 0.1 and 17 percent (Miles et al., 2004). The limited amount of state funding sheds light on why states have been so reluctant to try to shape the character and quality of professional development.

Stimulated in part by new accountability policies, states and districts have been encouraging teachers to participate in professional development through certification renewal requirements, salary schedules and stipends, intermediate units, dedicated days, and other inducements. As a consequence, a large industry of professional development service providers has developed. While professional development traditionally has been provided by local districts, state-supported regional education service centers, and college and university faculty, districts, schools, and teachers are now bombarded with solicitations from private training firms and independent consultants vying for the growing pool of professional development dollars. For the most part, these providers compete in an unregulated market where the quality of professional development programming varies greatly.

The Evidence

What defines quality professional development? A great deal is known about what works in professional development, and a consensus has emerged among some researchers and many teacher development advocates about the elements and structural components that are key to increasing the likelihood that professional development will result in changed teacher behavior and improved student learning. On the basis of this general consensus, a number of organizations (and some states) have developed standards of quality for professional development (American Federation of Teachers, 1999; Hawley & Valli, 1999; Knapp, McCaffrey, and Swanson, 2003; National Commission on Teaching and America's Future, 1996; National Staff Development Council, 2001). A good summary of this emerging consensus was produced by Elmore (2002), who compiled a set of principles for the design of effective professional development programs. But many policymakers and education leaders choose to ignore these standards. Why have they not been persuaded to make the needed investments in professional development that is designed according to the consensus standards? Why do districts and even many professional development providers continue to invest resources in learning opportunities for teachers that are poorly designed and have weak effects at best?

There are a number of reasons. First, the consensus standards are not entirely consistent with the body of research literature, and there is not compelling empirical evidence that meeting all of these standards is essential to the effectiveness of professional development. The consensus view is that job-embedded professional development that is led by, designed by, and provided by teachers is the best model. But the research findings seem to suggest a slightly different vision—intensive, extended, curriculum-based training that is usually provided outside the workplace combined with on-site, job-embedded implementation support (e.g., see Cohen & Hill, 1998; Corcoran, McVay, & Riordan, 2003; Elmore & Burney, 1997; Garet et. al., 1999; Kennedy, 1999; Miller, Lord, & Dorney, 1994; Supovitz, Mayer, & Kahle, 2000; and Wilson & Berne, 1999).

Like many other school reform proposals, the consensus standards are viewed by many policymakers as reflections of the personal philosophies and reform agendas of their creators and advocates rather than as compelling, scientifically supported prescriptions for policy and practice. Education has been a field dominated by philosophy, theory, and political preferences, and evidence has had less standing. In this sense, professional development is no different than other areas of activity in education. Only in the past decade have we seen the emergence of pressures for improving the quality of the evidence collected and more evidence decision making. Even now, educators are more inclined to argue over the merits of varying kinds of evidence than to consider the implications of the evidence we possess.

Furthermore, much of the research has lacked rigor. It must be noted that researchers who study the effects of professional development do face some serious challenges. We lack cost-effective tools for measuring changes in classroom practice. We have relied heavily on self-reports about practice collected through surveys that tend to produce overestimates of reformed practice. Alternative methods such as observations, logs, and videos are available but are more expensive and intrusive. We have lacked cost-effective tools for assessing changes in teachers' disciplinary knowledge and pedagogical content knowledge. And we are often not sure what we are looking for. Is it implementation of a mandated curriculum? Compliance with someone's vision of reformed practice? Changes in professional norms and adoption of continuous improvement strategies? Recent discussions of what is meant by inquiry in science reveal how difficult it is to reach agreement on measures of practice.

Researchers also face serious problems when they attempt to link professional development to student performance. The available achievement measures are not always sensitive to the learning outcomes that are being sought through the changes in curriculum or instructional practice. Local and state testing policies and data management make it difficult to link individual student gains to individual teachers.

What then can we say to policymakers? First, we must convince them that effective professional development is that which produces the desired changes in teachers' classroom practices and enhances their capacity for continued learning and professional growth, which in turn contribute to improvements in student learning. There are a number of studies that have linked program strategies to changes in teachers' instructional practice, and sometimes but less frequently to gains in student achievement. These studies include the longitudinal analysis of efforts to improve mathematics in California (Cohen & Hill, 1998, 2001; Wilson, 2003); the studies of District #2 in New York City (Elmore & Burney, 1997; Stein & D'Amico, 1998); the Consortium for Policy Research in Education (CPRE) longitudinal study of sustained professional development provided by the Merck Institute for Science Education (Corcoran, McVay, & Riordan, 2003); the studies funded by the National Science Foundation of professional development to improve teaching and learning in mathematics and science (Supovitz & Turner, 2000; Weiss et al., 2003); and evaluations of the federal Eisenhower mathematics and science professional development program (Garet et al., 1999).

Drawing heavily upon two recent summaries of this literature (Elmore, 2002; Odden et al., 2002), I offer the following nine critical features of effective professional development.

- A clear *focus* on the improvement of student learning in a specific content area and in a specific setting. Effective professional development is designed to help teachers meet the needs of real students in real classrooms and addresses real problems that educators are facing with these students.
- The *form* of the activity—that is, whether the activity is organized as a summer institute, university course, study group, teacher network, or mentoring collaborative. Research suggests that effective professional development often combines intensive off-site learning experiences with school-based and job-embedded opportunities to learn.
- The *duration* of the activity, including the total number of hours that participants are expected to spend in the activity, as well as the span of time over which the activity takes place. Research has shown the importance of intensive immersion in new content combined with continuous, ongoing, long-term experiences that total a substantial number of hours each year. Some researchers have found that teachers often take two to three years to fully incorporate new approaches into their practice.
- The degree to which the activity emphasizes the *collective participation* of groups of teachers from the same school, department, or grade level and contributes to the development of their collaborative practice. Research suggests that the most effective professional development is organized around groups of teachers from a school who share responsibility for the same children and/or subject.
- The degree to which the activity is *content-based*—improving and deepening teachers' knowledge of the content of the curriculum they teach. Research concludes that teachers need to know well the content they teach, need to know common student miscues or problems students typically have learning that content, and need to know effective instructional strategies linking the two.
- An emphasis on *active learning*, as suggested by research on adult learning. Teachers are engaged in the meaningful analysis of teaching and learning, for example by scoring student work or developing and "perfecting" a standards-based curriculum unit or by observing a lesson and reflecting on it.
- The use of *evidence* in design. Evidence of the strengths and needs of learners in the setting and evidence of what works drawn from research and clinical experience enhances the likelihood that the professional development will contribute to better learning outcomes. It is important to provide teachers with models of effective practice, but even more important to improve their skills as diagnosticians and developers and users of knowledge about their practice.
- The creation of *coherence* by helping teachers see connections among student content and performance standards, instructional materials, local and state assessments, school and district goals, and the development of a professional community. Research supports tying professional development to a comprehensive, interrelated change process focused on improving student learning.
- The active support of *school and district leaders*. School leaders participate in these activities as appropriate in order to be able to support the use of the new knowledge and skills by teachers.

These features provide a frame for describing, comparing, and analyzing professional development. They imply a purpose and rigor to the activity. They suggest that it is serious business, a product of thoughtful design, and that the rationale for participation and learning is clear and compelling. Thus teachers should be expected to incorporate new knowledge and skills into their practices.

Professional development is another instance where we have rather compelling evidence about what works in most situations, but we have experienced enormous difficulty persuading either state or local policymakers to adopt effective strategies or make the necessary investments. Part of the problem is that decision making about professional development is so decentralized, but another aspect of the problem is that there are so many small providers who lack the capacity to create programs that meet the criteria listed above, but who benefit from the tendency of local decision makers to follow the fads. This is an instance where the market does not work. There are also large membership organizations with vested interests in particular approaches to professional development that advance their positions as being based on research when they are really based on ideology or the interests of their members. So we have "national" standards being promoted that are not wholly consistent with the research findings. We need state policymakers to recognize the importance of professional development, consider the amount of money that is being spent, and take action to improve the quality of what is provided for teachers, either by providing high-quality options as the California Subject Matter Projects did, or by enforcing standards and monitoring district and school expenditures.

STATE DATA POLICY AND DATA SYSTEMS

In order for state policymakers to test alternative pathways to licensure, improve teacher education and professional development, make cost-effective investments in teacher induction, and test reforms in compensation, they will need access to better data on teachers and teaching. If they want to know how many candidates pursue different pathways to licenses, the characteristics of those candidates, how they perform on licensing exams, where they are employed, how long they stay in teaching, and how effective they are, they will need to invest in better data systems. If they are interested in which higher education institutions or which programs produce candidate qualified in particular fields, where the teaching vacancies are, how professional development funds are being spent, and answers to dozens of similar questions, they will need to create better data systems. At present most states have little data on teachers besides their licensing scores and their credentials. And most cannot link even these limited data about teachers to data on the students whom they teach, so researchers cannot conduct value-added studies to inform legislators, teacher training programs, and school districts. And in some of the states where such links can be made, they are not, because of concerns about harming teachers or being forced to release the data to the public. Only Florida, North Carolina, Tennessee, and Texas have the data elements needed to longitudinally link students and teachers; and only these states have begun to build the comprehensive, integrated databases needed to answer the critical questions facing policymakers (Berry, 2005). Barnett Berry writes:

> Universities, state departments of education, higher education agencies, professional standards commissions, and retirement boards have built most of the current data systems separately, such that they function as discrete and isolated silos of information only to make sure teachers have met minimal licensing standards and completed that particular state's prescribed coursework. New policy questions and demands for accountability from students, teachers, and the institutions that prepare them require data to be gathered and housed in new ways, but most states still rely on these antiquated systems.

Without access to better indicators and better data systems, policymakers are not likely to improve the quality of teachers and teaching, as they lack the information needed to define problems correctly or evaluate the effectiveness of the policy options available to them.

Since the late 1970s, the states have been building databases on students to support their school accountability systems and provide comparable data on student, school, and district performance to policymakers and the public, but only recently has there been much interest in data on teachers. The Higher Education Act requires states to rank teacher preparation programs in quartiles based on the performance of their graduates on state licensing tests. Some states such as Georgia, Kentucky, New York, and Texas have linked program approval to pass rates on these tests. However, state student achievement cannot be used as a measure of the effectiveness of teacher preparation programs, because no state has a system that seamlessly links teachers with the assessment results of their students and also with information on where and how they were prepared.

NCLB requires the states to ensure that students are taught by "highly qualified" teachers. A 2003 U.S. General Accounting Office report concluded that the states do not have the data systems needed to track teacher qualifications for the subjects they are teaching. Most states have to rely on districts to report on the qualifications of their staffs. The states are using different definitions as well as different methods of determining whether teachers are qualified, so their data are not comparable. In 2005, Alabama and Tennessee reported that approximately one third of classes were taught by highly qualified teachers, whereas Georgia and North Carolina claimed about 90 percent (U.S. Department of Education, 2005). These discrepancies are at least partly due to differences in state definitions, measurements, reporting processes, and data checking and cleaning procedures. Cross-state comparisons are not meaningful given the quality of the data available and the lack of common definitions and data collection procedures.

With NCLB as a stimulus, state policymakers are beginning to address these data system problems. To assist them, the federal government has initiated a grants program to support the design and development of new comprehensive state data systems. Grants were awarded in 2005 to 14 states to begin this work. Second, the Carnegie Corporation of New York's Teachers for a New Era (TNE) is reaching out to policymakers in the 10 states in which it has awarded grants to institutions of higher education for the purpose of redesigning their teacher education programs. These institutions need access to teacher data systems that allow them to track their graduates, as Carnegie is asking these institutions to use evidence, particularly evidence of student learning, to examine the effectiveness of their graduates and improve their programs. CPRE has conducted reviews of teacher policy in these states and discovered that the quality of state data systems, the lack of links between teacher and student databases, and problems gaining access to these data are major barriers to the TNE institutions in all 10 states (Corcoran et al., 2006). At present, these institutions are unable to track their graduates, even those teaching locally, let alone those who go to a different state or do not enter the profession. Without this information, the institutions cannot judge the success of their programs, and cannot set priorities for improvement. State policymakers face the same dilemma on a larger scale.

There also is growing interest among state policymakers in the use of value-added analysis to measure teacher effectiveness and to assess the effectiveness of teacher education programs, alternative routes, and the impact of teacher licensing tests and advanced certification. The publicity given to the studies in Tennessee has led other states to explore the possibilities of using this methodology to inform policymakers and guide state decisions. This draws attention to the need for the development of better databases in order to support this kind of analysis.

The Evidence

There is clear evidence that the states have highly fragmented and inadequate databases (Southeast Center for Teaching Quality, 2004). Berry and his colleagues found that key state leaders did not recognize the potential value of comprehensive data systems and state agencies were understaffed. But we really have little evidence that better databases will produce better policies. In fact, we have some contrary evidence in the cases of teacher induction and professional development, where most state policymakers have been slow to respond to accumulating evidence about the impact of particular strategies. But some states have responded. If only they had good data systems, that would allow them to demonstrate the value of what they had done. But it is clear that providing data is not sufficient; the culture of policymaking also would have to change to place more value on evidence and less on the preferences of interest groups and the distribution of benefits to their constituencies. But there are signs that the federal-led efforts to improve the quality of evidence and to insist that it be used are paying some dividends. Publishers say that school district leaders are asking for evidence of effectiveness when they purchase textbooks and curricular programs. As a consequence, publishers are investing in field trials of their primary products. Perhaps state policymakers will follow suit.

SUMMING UP: THE EVIDENCE, THE PROFESSION, AND POLICY

Do we have the kind of research evidence we need to guide the development of policy in these six critical domains that affect the quality of teachers and teaching? The answers are mixed. We have very compelling evidence about the effects of induction and less compelling, but still useful, evidence about the qualities of effective alternative route programs and professional development opportunities. We lack compelling evidence about teacher licensing, teacher education, and teacher compensation reforms.

The development of statewide data systems linking student and teacher data should lead to studies that will fill in some of these gaps. But even this development begs the larger question of whether policymakers will use the results of these studies to guide their decisions. At present, policymakers appear to be ignoring the research evidence that is available. Yes, they are supporting teacher induction programs and to a lesser degree professional development for teachers. However, the devil is in the details. Requiring induction programs is a good idea, but the potential gains will not be realized if the specific qualities related to their effectiveness are ignored. And this requires consistent state support and investment in strong systems of induction. Simply adopting broad regulations requiring districts to provide mentors is unlikely to produce the benefits associated with the multifaceted, well-designed programs adopted in Connecticut or California or piloted in Texas and New Jersey. More professional development is also a good idea, but not if state recertification requirements are used to encourage teachers to accumulate "hours" and participate in many fragmented, low-quality activities, or if annual accountability cycles drive schools to seek quick fixes.

Some of the policy debates are really normative, and are hard to resolve with appeals to evidence. The professionalizers who seek higher licensing standards and stronger teacher preparation programs hold different visions of good teaching than the deregulation, free market crowd. These issues cannot be fully mediated through better empirical research.

Clearly there are many important questions here that can be addressed through better designed research. To name a few in the domain of teacher education: Would raising entrance requirements for teacher education programs or conducting more selective screening ensure that graduates would be more likely to take jobs as teachers and be more effective? Do candidates have adequate subject matter preparation? What do institutions of higher education do to ensure this? What could they do? Why do so many who enter preservice programs choose not to become teachers?

We could go on to list similar questions in each of the six domains. The more pressing question is how we convince policymakers to pay attention to findings when they are compelling. Yes, some do already, and others do it selectively when it suits their agendas and their constituents. But we need only look at the case of teacher induction to see how whimsical policymakers are about attending to research findings.

We need to think harder about how research findings are disseminated and to whom they are disseminated. It seems clear that policymakers pay attention to public and institutional pressures for action. Perhaps it is a mistake to try to directly address the concerns of policymakers and to provide them with research findings. Perhaps the policy research community needs to become more media wise, and to learn from the social marketing efforts that affected public health, conservation, driving habits, and other areas of social behavior and social policy. We have convinced the public of the value of the comprehensive high school, class size, Advanced Placement, and other education policies. And when we convinced them, they demanded action by policymakers. We need to find better ways to get research findings directly to the public and to enlist their support in pressuring state policymakers to take action. In short, the policy research community needs to trust, and to use the democratic process.

REFERENCES

Allegretto, S. A., Corcoran, S. P., & Mishel, L. (2004). *How does teacher pay compare? Methodological challenges and answers.* Washington, DC: Economic Policy Institute.

Allen, M. B. (2003). *Eight questions on teacher preparation: What does the research say?* Denver, CO: Education Commission of the States.

American Federation of Teachers. (1999). *Principles for professional development: AFT's guidelines for creating professional development.* Washington, DC: Author.

Azordegan, J., Byrnett, P., Campbell, K., Greenman, J., & Coulter, T. (2005). *Diversifying teacher compensation* (ECS Issue Paper). Denver, CO: Education Commission of the States.

Ballou, D. (2001). Pay for performance in public and private schools. *Economics of Education Review 20*, 51–61.

Ballou, D., & Podgursky, M. (1996). *Teacher pay and teacher quality.* Kalamazoo, MI: Upjohn Institute for Employment Research.

Ballou, D., & Podgursky, M. (1998). The case against teacher certification. *The Public Interest 132*, 17–29.

Ballou, D., & Podgursky, M. (2000). Reforming teacher preparation and licensing: What is the evidence? *Teachers College Record 102*(1), 5–27.

Berry, B. (2005). *Taking action to improve teaching quality: Addressing shortcomings in the Teaching Commission report.* Chapel Hill, NC: The Center for Teacher Quality.

Boyd, D., Grossman, P., Lankford, H., Loeb, S., & Wyckoff, J. H. (2005). *How changes in entry requirements alter the teacher workforce and affect student achievement* (NBER Working Paper No. W11844). Cambridge, MA: National Bureau of Economic Research.

Carnegie Corporation of New York. (2001). *Teachers for a New Era: A national initiative to improve the quality of teaching.* New York: Author.

Cochran-Smith, M., & Fries, M. K. (2001). Sticks, stones, and ideology: The discourse of reform in teacher education. *Educational Researcher 30*(8), 3–15.

Cohen, D. K. (1996). Rewarding teachers for student performance. In S. H. Fuhrman, and J. A. O'Day (Eds.), *Rewards and reform: Creating educational incentives that work* (pp. 60–112). San Francisco: Jossey-Bass.

Cohen, D. K., & Hill, H. C. (1998). *Instructional policy and classroom performance: The mathematics reform in California* (CPRE Research Report No. RR-39). Philadelphia: University of Pennsylvania, Consortium for Policy Research in Education.

Cohen, D. K., & Hill, H. C. (2001). *Learning policy.* New Haven, CT: Yale University Press.

Corcoran, T. B. (1995). *Helping teachers teach well: Transforming professional development* (CPRE Policy Brief No. RB-16). New Brunswick, NJ: Rutgers University, Consortium for Policy Research in Education.

Corcoran, T., Goertz, M., Robinson, M., & Riordan, J. (2006). *Teachers for a New Era: Final report.* Philadelphia: University of Pennsylvania, Consortium for Policy Research in Education.

Corcoran, T., McVay, S., & Riordan, K. (2003). *Getting it right: The MISE approach to professional development* (CPRE Research Report No. RR-055). Philadelphia: University of Pennsylvania, Consortium for Policy Research in Education.

Corcoran, T. B., Walker, L. J., & White, J. L. (1988). *Working in urban schools.* Washington, DC: Institute for Educational Leadership.

Cornett, L. M., & Gaines, G. F. (1994). *Reflecting on ten years of incentive programs: The 1993 SREB Career Ladder Clearinghouse Survey.* Atlanta, GA: Southern Regional Education Board.

Darling-Hammond, L. (2000). Reforming teacher preparation and licensing: Debating the evidence. *Teachers College Record 102*(1), 28–56.

Darling-Hammond, L., Wise, A., & Klein, S. (1999). *A license to teach: Raising standards for teaching.* San Francisco: Jossey-Bass.

Decker, P. T., Mayer, D. P., & Glazerman, S. (2004). *The effects of Teach for America: Findings from a national evaluation.* Princeton, NJ: Mathematica Policy Research.

Elmore, R. F. (2002). *Bridging the gap between standards and achievement: The imperative for professional development in education.* Washington, DC: Albert Shanker Institute.

Elmore, R. F., & Burney, D. (1997). *Investing in teacher learning: Staff development and instructional improvement in community school district #2, New York City.* New York: Columbia University, Teachers College, National Commission on Teaching and America's Future; Philadelphia: University of Pennsylvania, Consortium for Policy Research in Education.

EPPI-Centre. (2004). *The impact of newly qualified teachers (NQT) induction programmes on the enhancement of teacher expertise, professional development, job satisfaction or retention rates: A systematic review of research literature on induction.* London, England: University of London, Institute of Education, Author.

Evertson, C., Hawley, W., & Zlotnik, M. (1985). Making a difference in educational quality through teacher education. *Journal of Teacher Education 36*(3), 2–12.

Ferguson, R. (1991). *Paying for public education: New evidence on how and why money matters.* Cambridge, MA: Harvard University, John F. Kennedy School of Government.

Ferguson, R., & Ladd, H. (1996). How and why money matters: An analysis of Alabama schools. In H. Ladd (Ed.), *Holding schools accountable* (pp. 265–298). Washington, DC: Brookings Institution.

Figlio, D. N. (1997). Teacher salaries and teacher quality. *Economic Letters 55*(2), 267–271.

Finn, C. E., & Madigan, K. (2001). Removing the barriers for teacher candidates. *Educational Leadership 58*(8), 29–31, 36.

Firestone, W. A. (1994). Redesigning teacher salary systems for educational reform. *American Educational Research Journal 31*(3), 549–574.

Freiberg, H. J., & Knight, S. L. (1991). Career ladder programs as incentives for teachers. In S. C. Conley and B. S. Cooper (Eds.), *The school as a work environment: Implications for reform* (pp. 204–235). Boston: Allyn & Bacon.

Garet, M. S., Birman, B. F., Porter, A. C., Desimone, L., Herman, R., & Yoon, K. S. (1999). *Designing effective professional development: Lessons from the Eisenhower Program.* Washington, DC: American Institutes for Research.

Goldhaber, D. (2003). *Why do we license teachers?* Seattle: University of Washington.

Goldhaber, D. (2006). *Everybody's doing it, but what does teacher testing tell us about teacher effectiveness?* Seattle: University of Washington, Center on Reinventing Public Education.

Goldhaber, D., & Brewer, D. J. (2000). Does teacher certification matter? High school teacher certification status and student achievement. *Educational Evaluation and Policy Analysis 22*(2), 129–145.

Goldhaber, D., & Liu, A. (2003). Occupational choices and the academic proficiency of the teacher workforce. In W. Fowler (Eds.), *Developments in school finance 2001–02* (pp. 53–75). Washington, DC: National Center for Education Statistics.

Guskey, T. (1986). Staff development and the process of teacher change. *Educational Researcher 15*(5), 5–12.

Hanushek, E. A. (1994). *Making schools work: Improving performance and controlling costs.* Washington, DC: Brookings Institution.

Hanushek, E. A. (1997). Assessing the effects of school resources on student performance: An update. *Educational Evaluation and Policy Analysis 19*(2), 141–164.

Hanushek, E. A., Kain, J. F., & Rivkin, S. G. (2004). Why public schools lose teachers. *Journal of Human Resources 39*(2), 326–354.

Hatry, H. P., Greiner, J. M., & Ashford, B. G. (1994). *Issues and case studies in teacher incentive plans.* Washington, DC: Urban Institute.

Hawley, W., & Valli, L. (1999). The essentials of effective professional development: A new consensus. In L. Darling-Hammond and G. Sykes (Eds.), *Teaching as the learning profession: Handbook of policy and practice* (pp. 127–150). San Francisco: Jossey-Bass.

Heneman, H. G., III. (1998). Assessment of the motivational reactions of teachers to school-based performance award programs. *Journal of Personnel Evaluation in Education 12*(1), 43–59.

Heneman, H. G., III, and Milanowski, A. (1999). Teacher attitudes about teacher bonuses under school-based performance award programs. *Journal of Personnel Evaluation in Education 12*(4), 327–342.

Humphrey, D. C., & Wechsler, M. E. (2005). Insights into alternative certification: Initial findings from a national study. *Teachers College Record* (September 2, ID No. 12145). Retrieved January 23, 2007, from http://www.tcrecord.org

Ingersoll, R., & Kralik, J. (2004). *The impact of mentoring on teacher retention: What the research says.* Denver, CO: Education Commission of the States.

Ingersoll, R. M., & Smith, T. M. (2004). Do teacher induction and mentoring matter? *NASSP Bulletin 88*(638), 28–40.

Johnson, S. M., Birkeland, S. E., Kardos, S. M., Kauffman, D., Liu, E., & Peske, H. G. (2001). Retaining the next generation of teachers: The importance of school-based support. *Harvard Education Letter.* July/August. Retrieved January 23, 2007, from http://www.edletter.org/past/issues/2001-ja/suport.shtml

Johnson, S. M., Birkeland, S. E., & Peske, H. (2003). *Fast-track alternative certification programs: Opportunities and challenges for participants and state officials.* Paper prepared for the annual meeting of the Public Policy Analysis and Management Conference, Washington, DC.

Kelley, C., Heneman, H., & Milanowski, A. (2000). *School-based performance award programs, teacher motivation, and school performance: Findings from a study of three programs.* Philadelphia: University of Pennsylvania, Consortium for Policy Research in Education.

Kennedy, M. M. (1999). *Form and substance in mathematics and science professional development* (NISE Brief Vol. 3, No. 2). Madison, WI: University of Wisconsin–Madison, National Institute for Science Education.

Knapp, M. S., McCaffrey, T., & Swanson, J. (2003). District support for professional learning: What research says and has yet to establish. Paper presented at the annual meeting of the American Educational Research Association, Chicago.

Koppich, J. E. (2005). All teachers are not the same. *Education Next 5*(1), 13–15.

Loeb, S., & Page, M. E. (2000). Examining the link between teacher wages and student outcomes: The importance of alternative labor market opportunities and nonpecuniary variation. *Review of Economics and Statistics 82*(3), 393–408.

McDonnell, L. M. (1989). *The dilemma of teacher policy* (Joint Report Jre–03). Santa Monica, CA: RAND.

Milanowski, A. T. (1999). Measurement error or meaningful change? The consistency of school achievement in two school-based performance award programs. *Journal of Personnel Evaluation in Education 12*(4), 343–363.

Milanowski, A. T. (2003). The varieties of knowledge and skill-based pay design: A comparison of seven new pay systems for K–12 teachers. *Education Policy Analysis Archives 11*(4).

Miles, K. H., Odden, A., Fermanich, M., & Archibald, S. (2004). Inside the black box of school district spending on professional development: Lessons from five urban districts. *Journal of Education Finance 30*(1), 1–26.

Miller, B., Lord, B., & Dorney, J. (1994). *Staff development for teachers.* Newton, MA: Educational Development Center.

Mohrman, A. M., Mohrman, S. A., & Odden, A. R. (1996). Aligning teacher compensation with systemic reform: Skill-based pay and group-based performance awards. *Educational Evaluation and Policy Analysis 18*(1), 51–71.

Monk, D. H. (1994). Subject area preparation of secondary math and science teachers and student achievement. *Economics of Education Review 13*(2), 125–145.

Murnane, R. J. (1983). The uncertain consequences of tuition tax credits: An analysis of student achievement and economic incentives. In T. James and H. M. Levin (Eds.), *Public dollars for private schools* (pp. 210–222). Philadelphia: Temple University Press.

Murnane, R. J., & Cohen, D. K. (1986). Merit pay and the evaluation problem. *Harvard Educational Review 56*(1), 1–17.

National Association of State Boards of Education. (2002). *Moving past the politics: How alternative certification can promote comprehensive teacher development reforms.* Alexandria, VA: Author.

National Commission on Teaching and America's Future. (1996). *What matters most: Teaching for America's future.* New York: Author.

National Commission on Teaching and America's Future. (1997). *Doing what matters most: Investing in quality teaching.* New York: Author.

National Research Council. (2001). *Educating teachers of science, mathematics, and technology: New practices for the new millennium.* Washington, DC: National Academy Press.

National Staff Development Council. (2001). *Standards for staff development: Revised.* Oxford, OH: Author.

Odden, A. (2001). How teachers should be paid. *Education Matters 1*(1), 16–24.

Odden, A., Archibald, S., Fermanich, M., & Gallagher, H. A. (2002). A cost framework for professional development. *Journal of Education Finance 28*(1), 51–74.

Odden, A. R., & Kelley, C. (1997). *Paying teachers for what they know and do: New and smarter compensation strategies to improve schools.* Thousand Oaks, CA: Corwin Press.

Odden, A. R., Kelley, C., Heneman, H., & Milanowski, A. (2001). *Enhancing teacher quality through knowledge- and skills-based pay* (CPRE Policy Brief No. RB-34). Philadelphia: University of Pennsylvania, Consortium for Policy Research in Education.

Plecki, M. (2000). Economic perspectives on investments in teacher quality: Lessons learned from research on productivity and human resource development. *Education Policy Analysis Archives 8*(33).

Reichardt, R., & Van Buhler, R. (2003). *Recruiting and retaining teachers with alternative pay.* Aurora, CO: Mid-Continent Research for Education and Learning.

Rice, J. K. (2003). *Teacher quality: Understanding the effectiveness of teacher attributes.* Washington, DC: Economic Policy Institute.

Rivkin, S. G., Hanushek, E. A., & Kain, J. F. (2005). Teachers, schools, and academic achievement. *Econometrica 73*(2), 417–458.

Rowan, B., Correnti, R., & Miller, R. J. (2002). What large-scale, survey research tells us about teacher effects on student achievement: Insights from the Prospects study of elementary schools. *Teachers College Record 104*,(8), 1525–1567.

Sanders, W. L., & Horn, S. P. (1998). Research findings from the Tennessee value-added assessment system (TVAAS) database: Implications for educational evaluation and research. *Journal of Personnel Evaluation in Education 12*(3), 247–256.

Sanders, W. L., & Rivers, J. C. (1996). *Cumulative and residual effects of teachers on student achievement.* Knoxville: University of Tennessee Value-Added Research and Assessment Center.

Slavin, R. E. (1989). Students at risk of school failure: The problem and its dimensions. In R. E. Slavin, N. L. Karweit, and N. A. Madden (Eds.), *Effective programs for students at risk* (pp. 3–17). Needham Heights, MA: Allyn & Bacon.

Solmon, L. C., & Podgursky, M. (2000). *The pros and cons of performance-based compensation.* Santa Monica, CA: Milken Family Foundation.

Southeast Center for Teaching Quality. (2004). NCLB teaching quality mandates: Findings and themes from the field. *Teaching Quality in the Southeast: Best Practices and Policies 3*(7), 1–3.

SRI International. (2004). *Review of research on the impact of beginning teacher induction on teacher quality and retention.* Menlo Park, CA: Author.

Stein, M. K., & D'Amico, L. (1998). *Content-driven instructional reform in Community School District #2.* Pittsburgh, PA: University of Pittsburgh, Learning Research and Development Center.

Stout, R. T. (1996). Staff development policy: Fuzzy choices in an imperfect market. *Education Policy Analysis Archives 4*(2). Retrieved January 23, 2007, from http://olam.ed.asu.edu/epaa/v4n2.html.

Supovitz, J. A., Mayer, D., & Kahle, J. B. (2000). The longitudinal impact of inquiry-based professional development on teaching practice. *Educational Policy 14*(3), 331–356.

Supovitz, J. A., & Turner, H. M. (2000). The effects of professional development on science teaching practices and classroom culture. *Journal of Research in Science Teaching 37*(9), 963–980.

Teaching Commission. (2004). *Teaching at risk: A call to action.* New York: Author.

Teaching Commission. (2006). *Teaching at risk: Progress and potholes. Final report.* New York: Author.

Temin, P. (2003). Low pay, low quality. *Education Next 3*(3), 8–13.

Torres, J., Santos, J., Peck, N. L., & Cortes, L. (2004). *Minority teacher recruitment, development, and retention.* Providence, RI: Brown University, Education Alliance.

U.S. Department of Education. (2002). *Meeting the highly qualified teacher challenge.* Washington, DC: Author, Office of Postsecondary Education, Office of Policy Planning and Innovation. Retrieved January 23, 2007, from http://www. ed.gov/about/reports/annual/teachprep/2002 title-ii-report.pdf

U.S. Department of Education. (2005). *The secretary's fourth annual report on teacher quality: A highly qualified teacher in every classroom.* Washington, DC: Author, Office of Postsecondary Education. Retrieved January 23, 2007, from http://www.title2.org/TitleIIReport05.pdf

Vedder, R. (2003). Comparable worth. *Education Next 3*(3), 14–19.

Weiss, E. M., & Weiss, S. G. (1999). *Beginning teacher induction.* Washington, DC: ERIC Clearinghouse on Teaching and Teacher Education. Retrieved January 23, 2007, from http://eric.ed.gov/ERICDOCS/data/ericdocs2/content_storage_01/0000000b/80/2a/2f/a7.pdf

Weiss, I. R., Pasley, J. D., Smith, P. S., Banilower, E. R., & Heck, D. J. (2003). *Looking inside the classroom: A study of K–12 mathematics and science education in the United States.* Chapel Hill, NC: Horizon Research, Inc.

Wilson, S. (2003). *California dreaming.* New Haven, CT: Yale University Press.

Wilson, S. M., & Berne, J. (1999). Teacher learning and the acquisition of professional knowledge: An examination of research on contemporary professional development. In A. Iran-Nejad and P. D. Pearson (Eds.), *Review of Research in Education* (pp. 173–209). Washington, DC: American Educational Research Association.

Wilson, S., Floden, R., & Ferrini-Mundy, J. (2001). *Teacher preparation research: Current knowledge, gaps, and recommendations.* Seattle, WA: Center for the Study of Teaching and Policy.

Policy and Professionals: Commentary

Discussion of the Chapters

Allan Odden, Anthony Milanowski, and
Herbert G. Heneman, III

Tom Corcoran and Richard Ingersoll cover a broad swath of issues in their chapters on teacher policy, which together provide a succinct summary of what we know and don't know about multiple issues related to having a highly qualified teacher in every classroom in America. This commentary takes both a human resources management (HRM) and a labor market perspective in responding to the issues raised in these two excellent chapters. From an HRM and a labor market viewpoint, we want to know how to train, license, recruit, select, deploy, assign, develop, evaluate, retain, and compensate teachers to produce a qualified teacher in every classroom, focusing especially on classrooms in urban, high-poverty, high-minority-concentration and currently low-performing schools, the schools most in need of effective teachers (Lankford, Loeb, & Wyckoff, 2002). Our perspective is that both of these frames are important, the latter to provide the appropriate fiscal incentives and the former to help operate the systems so they work in getting good teachers into all classrooms.

In terms of initial training, Corcoran concludes that the case for current teacher education is weak and that other than requiring teachers to know the content they teach and to have good clinical training, the evidence is not strong enough to suggest specific policies on either the substance of teacher education or the accreditation of teacher training institutions. Corcoran also concludes that the evidence about the benefits of teacher licensing is not compelling, stating that the evidence suggests experimenting with new licensing policies, including alternative routes to licensure.

Neither author addresses the issues of teacher recruitment, selection, and deployment, although there is existing literature that finds teacher recruitment and selection policies in urban districts quite weak (e.g., Levin & Quinn, 2003).

Ingersoll's chapter largely focuses on teacher assignment, turnover, and retention. He first debunks the common allegations that there is an overall shortage of teachers, caused largely by retirements and insufficient supply. He argues that teaching is an "easy in and easy out" profession which, together with a large "reserve" pool of individuals trained to teach but not teaching, provides an ample supply of potential teachers. He also argues that a considerable portion of turnover is "natural" and caused by spousal moves, pregnancy, and decisions to leave the workforce altogether. His major indictment is that the bulk of teacher turnover that results in the absence of high-quality teachers in many classrooms is caused by schools themselves—requiring teachers qualified in their area of licensure to teach "out of field," which when combined with ineffective school leadership and poor working conditions, drives teachers to seek schools where they can be effective and experience the intrinsic rewards of being successful in their classrooms.

One way to help teachers become effective is, during the beginning years, a good induction program, and after that, effective ongoing professional development. This would help to reduce the turnover rate due to inept school leadership and management. Corcoran concludes, however, citing other Ingersoll research, that although we know the key features of effective induction programs, few states or districts operate such programs, thus missing one way to reduce unneeded teacher turnover. Similarly, Corcoran concludes that although we know the key features of effective professional development programs and many large urban districts invest heavily in professional development activities, most extant professional development programs are poorly designed and ineffective, thus missing another opportunity to enhance teacher quality and reduce unwarranted teacher turnover.

Neither author addresses the issue of teacher evaluation. If they had, they would have concluded, as have many other researchers have (e.g., Peterson, 2000), that typical teacher evaluation consumes time and energy of both teachers and administrators with few if any positive impacts and miniscule links of evaluation ratings to teacher effectiveness (Medley & Coker, 1987). Other Consortium for Policy Research in Education (CPRE) research, however, has found significant promise in new forms of standards-based teacher evaluation systems; this research shows that such teacher evaluation programs can apportion teachers into four groups, each with differential effectiveness in producing student learning gains, and are good enough to use in revised teacher salary structures (Heneman, Milanowski, Kimball, & Odden, 2006).

Corcoran's chapter does provide a quick review of alternative forms of teacher compensation, but concludes that not much is definitively known either about how to design such programs or what impacts they have. However, there is more known about these systems than Corcoran suggests, largely because there is a wide body of compensation theory outside of education that is having a hard time penetrating education policy design and research (Milkvich & Newmann, 2005; Odden & Wallace, 2006).

First, it is important to divide teacher compensation into at least two parts: base pay, or the monthly check, and variable pay, or a bonus for improved organizational performance such as gains in student learning. For the latter, there is considerable knowledge about the operation of effective school-based performance bonus programs (Heneman, 1998; Kelley, Heneman, & Milanowski, 2002; Milanowski, 2000). However, less is known about individual-teacher-oriented bonus programs, even though states and districts have designed several new such programs in the past year.

In terms of base pay, research is quite clear, as Corcoran concludes, that neither education units, degrees, nor years of experience (after the first 3 to 5 years), the elements of the single salary schedule, are linked to student learning gains. This conclusion begs for a salary structure with features that are linked to student learning gains. Milanowski, Kimball, and Odden (2005) conclude that the new forms of standards- or performance-based teacher evaluation systems are sufficiently reliable and valid to use in redesigned teacher salary structures that would link higher pay levels to greater levels of teacher effectiveness in producing student learning gains, although these authors agree that there is still need for research on the operation and overall impact of such new structures (see also Odden & Wallace, 2006).

Finally, in terms of base pay, both authors imply that salary incentives are probably needed to recruit and retain teachers in urban districts and in areas experiencing subject-area shortages, such as mathematics and science, conclusions reached by several labor market economists (e.g., Goldhaber, 2002; Loeb & Reininger, 2004). Unfortunately, there is scant research about how to design and operate such incentive programs; an exception is Milanowski (2003).

POLICY IMPLICATIONS

In sum, the two chapters and research on the other issues related to all the elements of the education system's human resources practices conclude that education's HRM system broadly conceived is weak, resulting in the inability of many districts to recruit, place, induct, and retain good teachers. This produces a highly unequal distribution of teacher quality across America's schools, with a concentration of the lowest-quality teachers in the highest-need urban, poor, low-performing, and predominantly minority schools, a situation further complicated by unnecessary teacher turnover in those schools. The policy implications are that labor market realities and more effective HRM systems should be the prime foci for enhancing teacher quality across America, particular in urban and high-minority, high-poverty, and low-performing schools. In short, on the assumption that teacher quality is a major contributor to student achievement, policymakers at all levels need to pay more attention to the systems that recruit, select, induct, train, evaluate, and compensate teachers. A similar argument can be made about school leaders.

Across the nation, we need to build the capacity of current teachers and to attract more and better teachers. We need a strategy for attracting more high-performing students into teaching, such as those who are now participating in Teach for America or other alternative routes into teaching, and then keeping the best ones, using a variety of strategies ranging from altering how people get trained to be teachers to new approaches to teacher compensation, including incentives for both geographic and subject-area shortages. The National Board for Professional Teaching Standards has been one organization to take a national view of the teacher labor market, and has promoted the idea of cross-state certification for accomplished teachers and support and incentives for receiving this certification. Some states are recognizing the need to change aspects of the system to support a quantum leap upward in teachers' instructional capacity. California has emphasized intensive teacher induction. Connecticut has developed a teacher licensing system that focuses on assessing content-based pedagogy, and Iowa has aligned teacher licensing closely with teaching standards and has closed marginal teacher and administrator preparation programs.

But there are few states or districts with *both* a coherent strategy for improving teacher quality, including appropriate labor market incentives, *and* comprehensive HRM policies that work together to help execute the strategy. Most states leave HRM issues beyond training and licensure to districts. At the district level, the components of HRM are often fragmented, with individual programs forming silos that stand unconnected to each other or to district strategies for improving student achievement. Moreover, much of district HRM practice and a considerable portion of local school management are driven by teacher contracts that are too inflexible and specify many processes in great detail. Most district HRM departments are aptly characterized as "bystanders" (Campbell, DeArmond, & Schumwinger, 2004) rather than strategic partners in supporting teacher quality and instructional improvement.

We also need to address some shorter-term, practical issues of teacher shortages, such as the level and type of incentives for teachers to work in urban and high-poverty schools as well as for subjects experiencing shortages, particularly mathematics, science, and technology.

MAJOR RELATED WORK IN THE FIELD OF HUMAN
RESOURCES MANAGEMENT

Current thinking in *strategic* HRM (Becker et al., 2001; Wright & McMahan, 1992) has emphasized the importance of human resources in carrying out organizational strategies to improve performance, and of organizational strategy as a basis for HRM program design. However, though researchers have shown empirical links between HRM practices and aspects of organizational performance in private sector organizations (e.g., Arthur, 1994; Huselid, 1995; McDuffie, 1995), the relationship between HRM practices and the performance of educational organizations has not been given much attention.

Although the potential importance of HRM has been recognized by some teacher quality reform advocates (e.g., the National Commission on Teaching and America's Future, the Education Trust), relatively little research or theorizing has been focused on the use of HRM to support district (or state) strategies to improve teacher quality and student achievement. In the 1980s, Darling-Hammond and her colleagues called attention to problematic district recruitment, selection, and evaluation practices that weakened district efforts to hire and develop quality teachers (Wise, Darling-Hammond, & Berry, 1987). More recently, the National Commission on Teaching and America's Future identified attention to several HRM functions, including improved staffing systems, induction and support programs, and incentives for improving practice as action steps in improving teacher quality (National Commission on Teaching and America's Future, 2003). Useem and her colleagues looked at how restrictive teacher selection and transfer policies of district HRM departments in Philadelphia hindered efforts to staff high-need schools with high-skill teachers (Neild et al., 2003; Useem & Neild, 2001). Levin and Quinn (2003) found that HRM practices that delayed hiring decisions caused large urban districts to lose substantial numbers of teacher candidates to suburban districts. Podgursky and Ballou (2001) studied the personnel policies of charter schools, finding that many employ more innovative practices than conventional public schools, and that these might make managing easier, but the authors did not assess the alignment of these practices with school goals nor assess the relationship of innovative practices to measures of school effectiveness.

There has also been little research on the alignment of HRM practices with each other and with strategies for meeting student achievement goals. Campbell, DeArmond, and Schumwinger (2004) examined HRM program reform in three large districts. But the progress made by these districts was mostly related to improving the efficiency of their extant HRM systems, especially with respect to teacher staffing, rather than aligning them with each other or with district strategies. CPRE research on teacher compensation innovations, such as school-based performance awards and knowledge- and skill-based pay, suggests that these interventions have potential, but their impact can be limited if other district human resource programs do not support them (Heneman & Milanowski, 2003; Kelley, Heneman, & Milanowski, 2002). This has also been recognized by others researching teacher compensation. For example, Ballou and Podgursky (1997) argued that if a district does not have effective procedures for selecting high-quality teachers, additional pay may not result in a more qualified workforce.

In response to these insights about the importance of mutual support among HRM programs, CPRE researchers Heneman and Milanowski (2004) developed an HRM program alignment model, and applied the model to an initial evaluation of HRM programs in two districts. They now are working in two additional districts to conduct an HRM alignment audit and help the district redesign the HRM system to enhance alignment, generally around a view of effective instructional practice.

Taken together, this work hints at the importance of HRM in achieving district strategies for improving instruction and student achievement, but it has not yet made HRM systems as a whole appear on the radar screens of many national, state, and district policymakers. Nor is there much research-based guidance of how a district might go about developing specific HRM programs to support their initiatives. As Campbell, DeArmond, and Schumwinger (2004) observed, although the need for HRM reform is apparent, "there are few signposts in education to guide an effort to transform HR" (p. 8), and "an investigation into the relationship between HR management practices and teacher quality could help identify those processes and structures that help districts attract and place quality teachers" (p. 40).

We believe that a connected program of research on how HRM programs and practices can support building capacity to respond to accountability would be one logical next step in CPRE's intellectual journey. Research from the private sector has shown that there are clear links between the nature and quality of HRM practices and various indicators of organizational performance. We believe that the expertise of CPRE researchers—Corcoran, Ingersoll, Odden, Milanowski, Heneman, and Kimball—could make a major contribution to finding these links in education, focusing attention on HRM issues at the national, state, and district levels, and disseminating promising ideas and practices.

TEACHER LABOR MARKET FOCUS

As both Corcoran and Ingersoll suggest, there also are significant areas for policy development and research directly related to the working of the current teacher labor market. Loeb and Reininger's review (2004) of how labor market economists view the teacher quality issues underscores many of the issues discussed above. Table 1 summarizes how the current labor market helps or hinders the goal of placing a quality teacher in every classroom.

As the authors of the chapters in this section and other researchers conclude, the structure of the current teacher labor market helps the nation's education system to place a quality teacher in the classroom in the following ways:

- Stable salary structures that retain those dedicated enough to make it through the first years and that are easy to plan and administer.
- Benefit systems and levels that contribute to teacher retention.
- Stable teaching forces in suburban and medium city schools.
- Localized teacher labor markets that tend to promote hiring teachers from the area served, with resulting understanding of and dedication to the community.

And as the authors of the two chapters and other researchers conclude, the current labor market hinders accomplishing this objective in the following ways:

- Uncompetitive salaries for people with math/science/technology skills.
- Teacher preparation and licensing institutions that make it hard to utilize nontraditional talent pools (e.g., high-ability college students, career changers, people wanting only a partial career in teaching, ethnic and language minorities).
- Salary and working conditions that make it difficulty to attract and retain high-quality teachers in high-need schools.

- Inflexible teacher compensation systems that do not support the development of teachers' instructional capacity or the importance of producing student learning gains.
- The undifferentiated design of teaching work that pulls teacher salaries toward the lowest common denominator.
- Inefficient benefit systems that cost money that might be better used for salaries.
- Localized markets that do not distribute teachers from overage to shortage areas.

On balance, the hindrances outweigh the helps, and as a result the teacher labor market does not work very well. Most of the labor market barriers have aspects at multiple policy levels. For example, the difficulty schools and districts have in utilizing nontraditional talent pools is influenced by federal No Child Left Behind (NCLB) Act "highly qualified teacher" provisions, state licensing requirements, undifferentiated job design and "egg crate" school structures at the school and district level, and limited HRM capacity at the district level. Similarly, the difficulty of

TABLE 1
Teacher Labor Market Problems by Policy Level

Labor Market Feature	Example Barriers by Policy Level		
	National	State	District
Attracting people with math/science/tech skills to teaching	Traditional occupational pay differentials	Lengthy certification programs that require extra forgone income	Working conditions that may turn off people with these skills
Difficulty utilizing alternative sources of supply	NCLB highly qualified teacher provisions	Rigid certification programs	Undifferentiated job design; limited district HRM capacity
Attracting and retaining teachers in high-need schools		School finance systems not adequacy based	Rigid pay schedules, poor working conditions
Redesigning teaching work and school structures to allow higher pay	Old-fashioned societal conception of one teacher for each class	Undifferentiated teacher licensing systems	Undifferentiated job design; rigid teacher contracts; limited district HRM capacity
Narrow geographical scope of labor market		Variation in state teacher preparation and certification systems	District inability or reluctance to recruit nationally or provide relocation incentives
Inability to adapt compensation systems to district and school needs		Inflexible school finance systems	Inflexible school finance systems; rigid teacher contracts
Inefficient allocation of compensation costs between pay and benefits		State-required benefit plans	Limited district HRM capacity

developing more flexible teacher compensation systems is influenced by state licensing systems and statewide teacher salary schedules (where present), state and local school finance systems that emphasize stability and equity over adequacy, state-level collective bargaining laws, bargaining at the district level, and limited district HRM capacity. Researchers need to consider the constraints and influences present at each level. CPRE is one of the few groups that have the depth of experience to conceptualize and research these issues at all the relevant levels.

Potential research projects and questions focusing specifically on these labor market issues include the following:

1. Attracting people with math/science/technology skills to teaching.

- Survey and focus group research at colleges nationwide on the pay-level and other working-condition changes that would make teaching more attractive to people with math, science, and technology skills.
- Study of content and effectiveness of state alternative and accelerated certification programs for math, science, and technology teachers.

2. Attracting and retaining teachers in high-need schools.

- Success of state and district programs providing incentives for teaching in high-need schools (in Fairfax County, New York City, Charlotte, Miami, Chicago).

3. Redesigning teaching work and school structures to allow higher pay.

- Research on differentiated staffing models from district experiments and whole school designs (Milken Teacher Advancement Program, for example).
- Research on district systems that define, recognize, and/or compensate teacher leaders and master teachers.

4. Redesigning school finance systems.
- How can state and district systems be redesigned to provide more flexibility for teacher compensation to be used for incentives for high-need schools, differentiated staffing, and building teacher instructional competency? Can moving to an adequacy framework help?

5. Developing and utilizing alternative sources of supply.

- How do state licensure systems facilitate or restrict alternative sources of supply (e.g., high-achieving college students, career changers)?
- How can staffing patterns and teaching work be redesigned to utilize nontraditional sources of supply?
- What changes in compensation and working conditions would be needed to attract and retain people from nontraditional sources?
- How can districts reinvent their HRM systems to recruit, retain, and develop people from alternative labor pools?

REFERENCES

Arthur, J. A. (1994). Effects of human resource systems on manufacturing performance. *Academy of Management Journal* 37 (3): 670–687.

Ballou, D., & Podgursky, M.. (1997). *Teacher pay and teacher quality.* Kalamazoo, MI: Upjohn Institute for Employment Research.

Becker, B., Huselid, M., Pickus, P. & Spratt, M. (1997). HR as a source of shareholder value: Research and recommendations. *Human Resources Management Journal 36*(1), 9–47.

Campbell, C., DeArmond, M., & Schumwinger, A. (2004). *From bystander to ally: Transforming the district human resources department.* Seattle: University of Washington, Center on Reinventing Public Education.

Goldhaber, D. (2002). Teacher quality and teacher pay structure: What do we know and what are the options? *Georgetown Public Policy Review 7*(2), 81–94.

Heneman, H. G., III. (1998). Assessment of the motivational reactions of teachers to a school-based performance award program. *Journal of Personnel Evaluation in Education 12*(1), 43–59.

Heneman, H. G., III, & Milanowski, A. T. (2003). Continuing assessment of teacher reactions to a standards-based teacher evaluation system. *Journal of Personnel Evaluation in Education 17*(2), 173–195.

Heneman, H. G., III, & Milanowski, A. T. (2004). Alignment of human resource practices and teacher performance competency. *Peabody Journal of Education 79*(4), 108–125.

Heneman, H. G., III, Milanowski, A., M. Kimball, S., & Odden, A. (2006). *Standards-based teacher evaluation as a foundation for knowledge- and skill-based pay* (CPRE Policy Brief No. RB-45). Philadelphia: University of Pennsylvania, Consortium for Policy Research in Education.

Huselid, M. A. (1995). The impact of human resource management practices on turnover, productivity, and corporate financial performance. *Academy of Management Journal 38*(3), 635–672.

Kelley, C., Heneman, III, H. G., & Milanowski, A. (2002). School-based performance rewards: Research findings and future directions. *Educational Administration Quarterly 38*(3), 372–401.

Lankford, H., Loeb, S., & Wyckoff, J. (2002). Teaching sorting and the plight of urban schools. *Educational Evaluation and Policy Analysis 24*(61), 37–62.

Levin, J. D., & Quinn, M. (2003). *Missed opportunities: How we keep high-quality teachers out of urban classrooms.* New York: The New Teacher Project. Retrieved January 23, 2007, from http://www.tntp.org/files/MissedOpportunities.pdf

Loeb, S., & Reininger, M. (2004). *Public policy and teacher labor markets: What we know and why it matters.* East Lansing: The Education Policy Center at Michigan State University.

McDuffie, J. P. (1995). Human resource bundles and manufacturing performance: Organizational logic and flexible production systems in the world auto industry. *Industrial and Labor Relations Review 48*(2), 197–221.

Medley, D. M., & Coker, H. (1987). The accuracy of principals' judgments of teacher performance. *Journal of Educational Research 80*(4), 242–247.

Milanowski, A. (2000). School-based performance award programs and teacher motivation. *Journal of Education Finance 25*(4), 517–544.

Milanowski, A. (2003). An exploration of the pay levels needed to attract mathematics, science and technology majors to a career in K–12 teaching. *Education Policy Analysis Archives 11*(50).

Milanowski, A. T., Kimball, S. M., & Odden, A. (2005). Teacher accountability measures and links to learning. In L. Stiefel, A. E. Schwartz, R. Rubenstein, & J. Zabel (Eds.), *Measuring school performance and efficiency: Implications for practice and research. Yearbook of the American Education Finance Association* (pp. 137–161). Larchmont, NY: Eye on Education.

Milkvich, G., & Newmann, J. (2005). *Compensation.* 8th ed. Homewood, IL: McGraw-Hill.

National Commission on Teaching and America's Future. (2003). *No dream denied: A pledge to America's children.* Washington, DC: Author.

Neild, R. C., Useem, E., Travers, E. F., & Lesnick, J. (2003). *Once and for all: Placing a highly qualified teacher in every Philadelphia classroom.* Philadelphia: Research for Action. Retrieved January 23, 2007, from http:www.philaedfund. org/pdfs/rfareport.pdf.

Odden, A., & Wallace, M. (2006). *New directions in teacher pay.* Book presented and distributed at the State Policy Forum on Teacher Compensation sponsored jointly by the Education Commission of the States and the Joyce Foundation. Madison, WI: University of Wisconsin-Madison, Wisconsin Center for Education Research, Consortium for Policy Research in Education.

Peterson, K. D. (2000). *Teacher evaluation: A comprehensive guide to new directions and practice.* 2nd ed. Thousand Oaks, CA: Corwin.

Podgursky, M., & Ballou, D. (2001). *Personnel policy in charter schools.* Washington, DC: Thomas B. Fordham Foundation.

Useem, E., & Neild, R. C. (2001). *Teacher staffing in the School District of Philadelphia: A report to the community.* Philadelphia: Philadelphia Education Fund.

Wise, A., Darling-Hammond, L., & Berry, B. (1987). *Effective teacher selection: From recruitment to retention.* Santa Monica, CA: RAND.

Wright, P. M., & McMahan, G. C. (1992). Theoretical perspectives for strategic human resource management. *Journal of Management 18*(2), 295–320.

VII

CONCLUSION

16

Conclusion: A Review of Policy and Research in Education

David K. Cohen, Susan H. Fuhrman, and
Fritz Mosher

Part I

Problems in Education Policy and Research

David K. Cohen

Education policy, research on policy, and the relations between research and policy, are the subjects of this book. Education policy refers to deliberate government efforts to shape everything from student attendance and school construction to race relations, resource allocation, and student learning (see Floden, this volume, for consideration of the nature of education policy). Research refers to systematic inquiry into policy and those aspects of schooling that bear on policy. Both research and policy are venerable enterprises in the United States. Governments have been making policy for schools since public education began in the 1840s, and systematic social inquiry into education began at the same time, arising then, as if often does now, in connection with controversies about schools. The chapters in this volume range over the period that began in the 1950s. In this part of the conclusion, I discuss several central problems in education policy and research on policy that figure in the chapters. My discussion is followed by a coda in which my coeditors, Susan Fuhrman and Fritz Mosher, consider ways in which the knowledge needed to reach the ambitious goals of current policies might be developed.

THE CHANGING SHAPE OF EDUCATION POLICY

Education and education policy changed dramatically in the decades that followed World War II, notably through the increased role of state and federal governance of education (see Fuhrman et al., this volume). For most of U.S. history, state and federal policies manipulated familiar resource inputs to schools: money, student attendance, curriculum, and teachers' qualifications chief among them. State school finance policies aimed to build a floor of minimum provision and to somewhat reduce revenue inequalities in order to improve school quality. State teacher certification and licensing policies sought to insure that teachers were at least modestly qualified. The reforms of the Sputnik era sought to create more engaging and intellectually serious curriculum materials. Federal desegregation policy, discussed in this volume by Henig, used judicial, legislative, and executive action to improve schooling for African American students, either by opening access to better schools or by improving neighborhood schools. Title I of the 1965 Elementary and Secondary Education Act directed federal financial aid to schools that enrolled children from poor families. State governments pressed schools to improve basic skills teaching in the 1970s.

These policies were quite consistent with the guiding ideas of U.S. education. As W. Norton Grubb suggests in his chapter in this volume, most educators, parents, and policymakers seem to have assumed that conventional educational resources, such as money, curriculum materials, facilities, and their regulation, influenced student outcomes. Many still seem to assume that, as they write about the "effects" that class size or expenditures have on learning, a phrase which implies that resources carry "capacity." If so, learning would be influenced directly by such things as schools' supply of books or teachers' degrees. Regulation had been thought to work by steering resources and thus capacity, within and among educational organizations, so that ability grouping or segregation would influence achievement by influencing access to resources. These assumptions made school improvement seem straightforward: allocate more resources, or regulate schools' allocation of them.

Yet as education policymaking and research intensified after World War II, policy began to shift, from the allocation and regulation of resources to the definition and regulation of results. Research played a significant part in the change, for in the late 1950s and the 1960s, researchers began to focus attention both on the outcomes of schooling and on the relationships among resources, regulation, and school outcomes. The *Equality Of Educational Opportunity Study* (EEOS), done by James Coleman and several colleagues and published in 1966, was not the first national survey of school resources and student achievement—Project Talent, a late 1950s study of high schools, had that honor—but EEOS was far better known (Coleman et al., 1966). The study was required by Title IV of the 1964 Civil Rights Act; Congress seems to have envisioned a descriptive study of race differences in educational resources, and even here, Coleman and his colleagues offered some surprises. They reported much less striking racial differences in access to educational resources than had been expected, but very large differences between the average test scores of advantaged and disadvantaged students, and between the average scores of African American and Caucasian students (see Henig, this volume, on racial implications of EEOS). These differences were familiar to educators and some researchers, but schools never made test results public. Coleman's report was big news in the midst of the civil rights campaigns of the 1960s, for combined with civil rights pressure for more equality, it helped to raise awareness of school outcomes and to move unequal outcomes onto the public agenda.

That was just the beginning. EEOS also probed the relations among school average student social background, school average resources, and school average student achievement. Contrary to what nearly everyone expected, schools with more resources did not have significantly better student scores, once students' social background was taken into account. School average differences in libraries, teacher experience and education, funds, science labs, and other resources had weak or no associations with differences in school average student achievement. Differences in the educational resources that most people thought significant were weakly related to differences in student performance. The most powerful predictors of school-to-school differences in student performance were school average parents' educational and social background, in contrast to which resources had modest or trivial effects. The seemingly weak effect of schools was especially troubling, given EEOS reports of achievement differences between schools that enrolled the children of affluent and poor parents. This was often taken to mean that schools did not "make a difference," a marvelously ambiguous idea that some conservatives embraced to attack liberal social policy, and that some liberals rejected to defend those policies.[1] But the research was much more limited: EEOS investigated whether schools were differentially effective, not whether schools "made a difference." To investigate the latter question, Coleman would have had to compare children with amounts of schooling that varied from little or nothing to a great deal. EEOS could not do that, because nearly all children in the U.S. completed elementary school at the time of the survey.

The late 1960s brought several other studies which found that conventional education policies, which added resources of various sorts, brought no significant change in student performance. These were taken to confirm the idea that schools made little difference to outcomes. The early 1970s brought another study—*Inequality* by Christopher Jencks et al. (1972)—that confirmed and amplified Coleman's results. The late 1970s and early 1980s brought the first cross-national research on student performance, which reported that U.S. students did less well than students in several developed nations on more or less common tests. These reports further added to the impression that public education was failing.[2]

These developments also focused attention on school outcomes, and began to discredit the idea that to allocate resources was to influence outcomes. Partly as a result, state and federal policy in the 1970s began to regulate instructional content, processes, and outcomes, as the Fuhrman et al. and Mosher chapters in this volume point out. Though this regulation began with minimum competency tests, the most prominent policies that aimed to regulate schools by way of their outcomes were standards-based reform policies, in the next decade. By the late 1990s most states had created policies that changed key technical and professional features of public education, adding more demanding academic goals, standards of student performance, assessment of students' academic performance against those standards, and schemes to hold schools or teachers accountable for students' performance.

These policies are conventional in the sense that they operate within the extant political economy of public education. Yet they are quite unconventional historically, for they seek to regulate instruction by its results, and aim to greatly reduce or eliminate class and racial inequalities in the outcomes of schooling. To do so they seek to turn fragmented U.S. educational systems, which had considerable autonomy for schools, teachers, and districts, and great inequality, into 50 state systems in which academic standards shape curriculum, tests, and teaching, and in which accountability creates strong incentives for educators to meet standards. They also focus unprecedented attention on the nation's weakest schools, in an effort to reduce class and racial differences

---

1. For a brief discussion of these developments, see Cohen, Raudenbush, and Ball 2003.

2. That "failure," widely accepted by the media, is contested by researchers. See, for example, Berliner and Biddle (1995) and Bracey (1997a, 1997b).

in student achievement. The No Child Left Behind (NCLB) Act, the Bush administration's signature education program, is the most recent expression of these ambitions.

Several other recent policies—choice, big-city school decentralization, and mayoral control—were unconventional in a very different sense. They linked school improvement to change in the political economy of schooling (see McDonnell in this volume on the role of political ideas and other political influences in education policy). The guiding ideas were that the school system's governance and fiscal structure were the central problem, rather than technical and professional matters like standards, resources, and assessments. Chicago radically decentralized authority in its schools in the late 1980s, and put community school boards, occupied by elected parents, in charge. Reformers believed that the former highly centralized and bureaucratic system frustrated improvement; if decisions about education were instead informed by the concerns of those closest to students, teaching and learning would improve. Structural change in school government was required. School decentralization in Chicago was the most radical and sustained effort of the sort ever tried in the U.S.: each school in the city has a governing board that can hire and fire principals, and has considerable authority to spend money as it sees fit. But in 1995 the state legislature and Chicago's mayor agreed on a rather different governance reform, which gave authority for city schools to the mayor. No other cities followed Chicago's example of decentralization, but New York soon moved control of the schools from elected local boards to the mayor. If one rationale for these changes was that elected boards had failed to hold schools accountable for their performance, one motive was the view of mayors and members of civic elites that unless schools were dramatically improved, cities could become economically and politically unviable.

Another set of policies sought to free schools with vouchers or charter schools (these initiatives are reviewed in Paul Hill's chapter). One idea behind both is that giving families choice among schools will compel schools to compete, and thereby change their incentives, for if public schools operated in markets, they would either improve instruction, as they respond to parents' and students' preferences, or go out of business. Most states now have charter school legislation, and the number of these schools has increased rapidly. Vouchers were less attractive and more controversial, though a few small or experimental programs do operate.

These governance initiatives are very different than standards-based reform in some respects, but they came to share a focus on outcomes. It is now accepted that even the mayors who take control of city schools and charter schools must be judged in terms of their effects on student performance. So deeply has this shift taken root that even nongovernment initiatives are judged in such terms. The National Board for Professional Teaching Standards (NBPTS) began, in the 1980s, with little direct reference to the effects that professionally more qualified teachers would have on learning, but in the past few years analyses of NBPTS and the program's own account of itself prominently focus on student outcomes. The turn toward outcomes, to which standards-based reform gave such impetus, permeates education policy.

NEW PROBLEMS AND OLD

That turn created several new problems for policy and practice. The most basic is the lack of adequate knowledge about how schooling processes work, and how to improve schools (in their chapters here, Cohen et al. and Mosher discuss aspects of this problem). These problems arise because the policies require states and localities to set academic standards, to create tests that fit the standards, and to hold schools and school systems accountable for students' test performance. If students fail, so do schools, and if schools don't improve, they can be put out of business. If many schools fail, so can school systems. For the first time in U.S. history, the fate of schools could depend on how well they help students to learn.

The catch is that these policies cannot work if educators don't know how to detect and explain differences in instructional effectiveness—i.e., why some classrooms and schools do well when others, similarly situated, do not. They also would need to know how to use that knowledge to improve practice. Such knowledge has grown recently, but it still is modest. Success of the new policies also depends on policymakers knowing how to embody knowledge of these relationships in policy instruments, and how to deploy them. That requires extensive knowledge of the relations between policy and practice, which is even more modest, as Cohen et al. stress in their chapter here. The success of outcome-oriented policy also depends on education professionals' knowledge of teaching and learning, and their knowledge of how to use the new instruments, which in turn requires extensive knowledge of the culture, organization, and management of state and local school systems and schools. These sorts of knowledge also are quite modest. The research that was sufficient to help undercut an old order is far from adequate to inform the new one.

That situation is due to a guiding idea of standards-based reform: if school outcomes were specified in standards and incarnate in tests, and if schools were accountable for students' performance on the tests, schools could solve the knowledge problems and produce the desired results. Though student performance in the era of standards-based reform has improved a bit in some states and cities, it has not improved in many others. Moreover, it has not improved very much anywhere (Perie, Grigg, & Donahue, 2005; Perie, Grigg, & Dion, 2005), and the large class and racial disparities in student achievement that these policies propose to eliminate have shrunk only a little. Recent (2004) National Assessment of Educational Progress (NAEP) reading and math reports show that the gap between Black and White performance has narrowed a bit at all three age levels for reading and math between 1971 and 2004. The narrowing was more significant for reading than math, and for nine-year-olds. However, Whites still outperform Blacks and Hispanics by more than 20 points (Perie, Moran, & Lutkus, 2005, Figs. 3–2 and 3–6). The same weak professional knowledge and skills, and modest knowledge of educational processes, that impeded the effective use of resources under the old regime, remain a key impediment to making outcome-oriented policies work in the new regime (the Slavin et al. and Neufeld chapters here examine ways to build professional knowledge). Weak knowledge about the relations between resources and results helped to discredit input-oriented policies, and that helped to inspire the new policies. Yet the new policies depend much more on scientific and professional knowledge, because they hold schools, states, and districts accountable for outcomes. If the knowledge problems are not solved, it is difficult to see how the new policies can remain viable.

In a world that behaved as reformers imagined, those knowledge problems would have been solved as standards-based reform was implemented. New knowledge would have been used to reorder, clarify, and winnow the accumulation of earlier policies and programs, many of which would have been informed by erroneous assumptions. That, in turn, would have led to much more rational decisions about policies and programs, based at least in part on their contribution to students' learning. But since most of the knowledge problems remain unsolved, outcome-oriented policies are in no position to rationally reorder the preexisting stock of education policies. They coexist with earlier policies and programs, rather than reordering or replacing them.

The hallmark of this era in education is that policy and practice subsist between two worlds, operating in both but belonging distinctively to neither. In one, schools are steered by the identification, allocation, and regulation of resource inputs, while in the other they are steered by the identification and regulation of learning outcomes. The inherited approach lost much of its authority without losing its utility, while the new approach gained authority without having the knowledge required to achieve much utility.

In what follows I explore the four most enduring policy problems in U.S. education—resource allocation, race, the quality of teaching, and access to schooling—in light of this curious situation.

Resource Allocation

Ever since school systems began, a central policy problem was to identify the important resources and allocate them to schools. Prior to standards-based reform, resources were identified by way of ordinary and professional knowledge. It was not difficult to name the key resources: books in the library, the quality of physical facilities, teachers' education, and the money that purchased them seemed self-evident signs of quality. District revenues were raised by a combination of local decisions about taxes and state government decisions about school aid, made in negotiation among the representatives of more and less well-to-do localities, other interest groups, and legislative and executive agencies.

When post-World War II social research undercut ideas about the efficacy of educational resources, it undercut the ordinary and professional knowledge that had informed resource identification and allocation. Doubts began to arise about whether schools could be regulated by allocating resources, and attention turned to regulating outcomes. The first sign of this shift was Representative Albert Quie's proposal, in the mid–1970s, to allocate Title I funds on the basis of students' test scores rather than family poverty. The proposal gained little support, but several others—including minimum competency testing and standards-based reform—were quickly adopted. Yet these policies are unlikely to work unless policymakers can solve the same old problems of resource identification and allocation: what are the professional knowledge, dispositions, and skills, the curricula, class size, and money that influence the quality of classroom work? What amounts of the identified resources are needed, in what combinations, in which classrooms and schools?

There are few answers to these and other questions. As a result, states and localities now deal with these problems at the site of a collision between radically different approaches to education policy, and the knowledge and political influence that are associated with each. In the past, state education policy consisted of relatively uncoordinated subdomains, each of which allocated resources that seemed self-evidently effective. Recent state and federal policies, however, embody a vision of decisions about curriculum, testing, teaching and teacher quality, and resource allocation which are made in a coordinated fashion, in light of statewide academic standards, tests, and accountability policies (Smith & O'Day, 1991). These policies assume that there is or soon will be knowledge to make effective resource identification and allocation decisions, a point that gains emphasis from the repeated requirement, in NCLB, that decisions be made on the basis of scientifically valid evidence. Despite this feature of standards-based reform, recent policies lack the intellectual leverage—research and professional knowledge—that could help to move states toward more effective resource identification and allocation. Despite the policies, state and local arrangements for identifying and allocating resources remain largely unchanged.

As a result, states and localities face several quandaries. One concerns the relationship between knowledge of schooling processes and resource allocation. Though researchers are far from being able to extensively specify the relationships among money, educational resources, and outcomes, enough evidence has accumulated to make it clear that, on average, other things being equal, some resources do matter to learning. Teachers' verbal ability, and their subject matter and pedagogical knowledge and skill, for instance, do influence students' learning, as does time on instructional tasks. These findings are a reason to urge resource allocation consistent with them. Work of this sort also offers social scientists a strong incentive to continue efforts to redefine resources in terms of their relationship to student performance.

Though such work is important, it comes with several problems. One is that the redefinition of resources will be a continuing, long-term effort, as researchers attempt to define the many influences in schooling processes and the many things that students learn, and to discern relationships between the two. As a result, there will be continuing ambiguity about the nature of educational resources, how they should be identified, and how they influence students' performance. Still another problem concerns the criteria for validating such knowledge, and the tensions between validity for science and validity for practice. Few of the current findings about resource effects have been validated in experiments, let alone in experiments in varied sorts of schools. They arise instead from large and varied populations; the findings reflect population averages from which possibly confounding influences are statistically removed. But no school head presides over the average school, and no teacher teaches in the average classroom. For practitioners, the confounding influences that researchers try to eliminate are essential elements of their situations. For instance, the schools with the weakest student achievement are also likely to have the least qualified teachers, the most mobile students, and the worst conditions of teaching and learning (Lankford, Loeb, & Wyckoff, 2002). Like any practitioner, therefore, teachers and school heads want to know what resources are the best for their use, in their situation, when particular confounding influences play an important part in defining both their situation and their practice. That question confounds the generalizing logic of social research, and there is no good answer. In theory, one could do experiments in many different circumstances, but that would make sense only if one already knew what the salient circumstances were, and if one had virtually unlimited money, time, and research capability (see Barrow and Rouse in this volume on key methodological problems facing research into educational resources).

An additional problem is that books, curricula, and money are not self-activating; their effects depend on their use by students and teachers, and there is convincing evidence that some teachers use resources much less effectively than others (Murnane, 1975). Even teachers are not a self-activating resource, for their effectiveness depends both on how students use them and on how schools and school systems use, which is to say, deploy and support them (for a discussion of these complications, see Cohen, Raudenbush, & Ball, 2003). These findings argue for research that investigates action in particular situations, and for policies and practices that support and reward effective resource use. Though there has been a craze for ethnographic studies in education in the past two decades, little of that work attends to practical action in ways that builds cumulative knowledge of practice that would be usable by practitioners. Rewarding effective resource use was part of the rationale for standards-based reform, but the policies have focused much more on penalizing schools that appear to use resources ineffectively than on rewarding effective use. Neither states nor the federal government have made much of an effort to identify effective resource use in particular situations, to analyze its causes, or to devise compelling rewards for it. States spend little or nothing on research, and NCLB sponsors summative national studies.

Federal policy tries to address the knowledge problem in two ways. One is NCLB's requirement to use only scientifically valid methods and materials. The other, also written into NCLB, is the Institute of Education Sciences (IES), established to sponsor scientifically rigorous research. The first is of real interest, because it is vivid evidence of the need for such knowledge in standards-based reform; yet the requirement is so broad and stated so often in NCLB that, covering nearly everything, it covers nothing. A study of NCLB's implementation found that the requirement has not been enforced (Center on Education Policy, 2004). That is no surprise; one reason is that the requirement is so broad as to be virtually unenforceable. Monitoring and enforcement would be gargantuan and impossibly intrusive. Another reason is the lack of scientifically valid knowledge that is usable in practice. Though outcome-oriented research is insufficient to permit enforcement of the requirement, the program operates partly in that frame.

IES has been more serious. It selects well-qualified panels, conducts serious reviews, has reasonable priorities, and has had well-conducted competitions. There are, of course, things that one can argue with, but IES is the best effort thus far in federal research and development. Its budget, however, is modest, and the list of questions about schooling processes and school improvement that need to be answered far outstrips the IES research program.

How do policymakers allocate resources when relatively convincing evidence about the effects of a few resources coexists with uncertainty about many others? The question is especially difficult, since the uncertainty has not relieved pressure for more money and more equal allocation, as recent litigation in New York and California demonstrates. One response is to use the uncertainty as a rationale for traditional resource allocation. Another is to use evidence on the importance of resource use to argue against more resources, and for policies like school choice or performance incentives, which are said to improve resource use. The answer to my question thus seems to be that states and localities allocate resources as before, save in those few cases—like the recent court decision concerning school finance in New York City—in which great pressure is brought to bear. Then resource allocation changes a bit, but only a bit.

These responses are especially troubling in light of a second quandary: though recent policies press states for both greater effectiveness and equal outcomes, the allocation of educational resources is grossly unequal, within and among states. How can states eliminate social class and race-based inequalities in the outcomes of schooling, when state and local policies and practices deliver very unequal educational resources to schools? Students in relatively poor states and districts continue to have access to substantially fewer educational resources than otherwise similar students in relatively affluent states and districts (see, e.g., Carey 2004; Stateline.org, 2004).

That problem is compounded by the enormous differences in income, wealth, and social advantages that divide Americans, for these influence both students' access to educational resources and their own capability to use those resources effectively. Poor and working-class Americans are unlikely to live in localities that offer them access to educationally effective schools, for local control of schools combines with residential segregation by income and race to limit that access. Less advantaged children also bring fewer educational resources to school, on average, so they are less able than their more advantaged peers to make effective use of whatever their schools offer.

Thus, state and federal outcome-oriented policies propose to equalize the results of schooling, at the same time that states allocate resources in ways that maintain inequality. That is certain to impede state efforts to improve outcomes. Perhaps for that reason among others, most states have used minimal standards for the "proficiency" that NCLB requires, since easier tests and criteria for proficiency can at least create the appearance of equal outcomes, despite very unequal educational resources.

The federal response to this quandary has been cautious. It deals with these issues from the relatively weak center of a large, fragmented, and very unequal system of domestic government. Short of a huge increase in federal funding, for instance, it has quite modest leverage on revenue inequality within and among states. NCLB allocates several billion dollars to the poorest schools, which could help, but Title I is only 8 or 9 percent of total local revenues, and the inequalities within most states are so large that Title I only makes a modest dent in them. Given these inequalities, how could one eliminate race and class differences in school outcomes? Even if we imagined that funding differences were eliminated within states, equalized funds alone would be very unlikely to equalize students' access to educational resources, for the monies would flow to schools and districts that vary greatly in the capability to use them effectively. Since disadvantaged schools typically lack those capabilities, equalizing funds does not equalize access to educational resources. Improved capability to effectively use resources would also be required for most weak schools and systems, a point that figures prominently in Norton Grubb's analysis in this volume.

More important, equal funds within states would not deal with fiscal inequality among them, and that inequality is even greater. Title I has only a modest effect on these inequalities, at best. In addition, it seeks to exert leverage mainly through accountability, not finance or human resource policies. Thus, for example, it tries to deal with possible differences in the stringency of state tests by using the state-by-state NAEP to check on state tests. The federal concern, that states like Alabama might ease their tests to reflect their fiscal and human resource problems, relative to others, is plausible. But quite aside from the effects that this may have for the NAEP, it is inconceivable that NAEP comparisons with state tests could generate incentives for test score increases that would make up for the differences in funding, human resources, and educational capability that separate New Jersey, Connecticut, or New York from Mississippi or Alabama.

Is there a way out of this quandary? The sharp contrast between state and federal pressure for equal outcomes, and huge inequalities in educational resources, will generate more awareness of the problems discussed here. That could stimulate efforts to reduce inequality; one bit of evidence for this is the recent proposal by a coalition of prominent conservatives and liberals to reduce funding disparities by tying equalized grants to students, and permitting the funds to be used when students choose schools (Thomas B. Fordham Institute, 2006). The proposal is fascinating evidence of the possibilities that the Improving America's Schools Act and NCLB have opened up, but enormous federal budget deficits make the central government an unlikely source of equalizing funds. It is more likely that resource inequality will continue, and that most states and cities will use tests with low ceilings to create the appearance of reduced outcome inequality. Lacking more leverage from politics or finance, the federal government will have few alternatives but to acquiesce.

*****

Policymakers and educators now operate in an unusual situation. Familiar battles over funds, and sporadic efforts to reduce resource inequality, are mixed with unfamiliar attempts to improve outcomes and enforce accountability. Education policy is caught between standards-based reform and the conventional policies that it was supposed to rationalize, but thus far has not. The logic of the two approaches could hardly be more different, yet they operate together.

Though the coexistence of the two worlds of conventional policy and standards-based reform creates many problems for practitioners, it offers unique research opportunities. One overarching issue is how states deal with the cross-pressures arising from the two policy frames. For example, have state standards-based reforms been accompanied by tighter coordination among the domains of education policy? So far, there are a few signs of that in the few states that have taken a more aggressive approach to standards-based reform and tried to bring state curriculum and testing practices into some rough alignment, but that may change. If it does, it would be important to investigate whether existing political arrangements will give way to the logic of standards-based reform, or the reverse. Another large issue concerns the extent to which state and localities pursue the logic of standards-based reform in domains that reach beyond fund allocation. For example, have states substantially revised policies to bring more rationality and coordination to state action in education? Have they tried to coordinate teacher education, certification, and licensing with state content standards? If so, how have they done this, and to what effect? If not, why has standards-based reform remained compartmentalized? (See the Fuhrman et al. chapter for discussion of attempts to coordinate policies.) To pursue these issues and others like them would enable researchers to investigate interactions between outcome-oriented policies and the politics of education, and the extent to which policy has reshaped politics.

Race and Education

Justice Thurgood Marshall said that when he argued *Brown* v. *Board of Education of Topeka* before the U.S. Supreme Court, he believed that if the court ruled for the plaintiffs, schools would desegregate, state-imposed inequalities would disappear, and educational equality would be achieved. Justice Marshall and many others saw a strong relationship among structural change in the laws governing education, the quality of schooling, and students' learning. Those relationships were central to the courts' reasoning in the line of cases that led up to *Brown*, and the plain implication of that decision was that racially equal access to schools would yield racially equal education. Like the educators and policymakers who used educational resources to regulate school quality, advocates of racial justice assumed that there was a strong connection between structural "inputs" to schooling and outcomes.

Brown and its progeny had enormous effects. Jim Crow schools were the most extraordinary system of educational inequality in U.S. history, and *Brown* began to break down the legally maintained, racially dual school systems of the old South. Many Southern schools were desegregated in the late 1960s and early 1970s, and, by 1980, African Americans were a large part of the teaching force in many places, in contrast to their containment, before the 1960s, chiefly in Black schools in the Jim Crow South. Access to schooling is much less unequal than it was in 1954, and racial differences in high school completion and college attendance have somewhat narrowed. The federal government and several states initiated programs to improve opportunity for Blacks in particular and poor people in general; the most prominent in education was Title I of the 1965 Elementary and Secondary Education Act.

Yet despite the dramatic effects of *Brown* and its progeny, racial equality in education remains elusive. Legal segregation ended, but segregated schools persist; in fact, schools are more segregated now than they were decades ago, and very large proportions of the Black and White school populations lead separate and unequal educational lives. Moreover, there still are large differences in the quality of schooling to which Black and White students have access, and differences in Black and White school performance are also large and seem to be little changed in decades.

If ending the legally sanctioned dual school system was a policy change of great consequence, it did not have many of the expected educational effects. The advocates of desegregation believed that breaking the stigma of enforced segregation and creating racially neutral schools would eliminate or vastly diminish racial inequality in public schools, but it did not. One reason is that desegregation was an unfinished revolution: fierce resistance blunted federal enforcement in the late 1960s and early 1970s, and political realignment eroded support for it. By the end of Ronald Reagan's presidency, court-ordered desegregation was all but dead. That left federal education policy with little leverage on racial inequalities that were pervasive in education.

Another reason was that the decision and its progeny seemed to suggest that the mere fact of majority-Black attendance meant that a school was not good, and that to correct segregation required school attendance with Whites. The inferiority of Black schools was a fact of the segregation system, but as a key to remedy, it carried an implication that was offensive to many African Americans. That made broad and lasting Black support for desegregation very unlikely.

Several other reasons for the persistence of racial inequality are rooted in the living legacy of racism. The residential segregation of Blacks in poor neighborhoods and jurisdictions, in large part the result of official discrimination (Singer, 1999), has meant that a larger fraction of African American than White children attend schools in which educational quality is weak. Black students are more likely to be exposed to poorly educated teachers, to attend schools in which teacher and student mobility is very high and working conditions are poor. In addition, centuries of slavery and discrimination left a disproportionately large fraction of the Black population economically and socially disadvantaged. Many children from these families enter school with knowledge and skills that are, on average, weaker than those of more fortunate peers. As they proceed through life they face economic and social deprivation, and as they proceed through school, their average performance relative to others further weakens (Burkham & Lee, 2002). Some of that loss seems to be due to differences in learning opportunities out of school, especially during the summer, but some of it is due to things that teachers do—or don't do.

Remedial programs, Title I chief among them, were to improve education in schools that enrolled disadvantaged students. Title I seemed a major initiative in Washington, nearly a billion dollars in 1965, but once the money was divided among thousands of schools, it added only a small fraction, perhaps 3.7 percent, to per-pupil expenditures in Title I schools (Snyder, Hoffman, & Geddes, 1997, Table 359). Moreover, that modest increment supplemented local outlays in a very unequal system. The Title I supplement was a very small contribution, and could not make much of a dent in the underlying inequalities. The poorest schools were at best only in a slightly better position relative to more advantaged schools. The best studies found that Title I had a modest positive effect on test scores, but that teachers' relentless focus on remedial basic skills, and the small size of the program in schools, limited that effect (Carter, 1980).

These reasons, as well as political and other factors discussed in Henig's chapter, help to explain why, decades after *Brown*, racial inequality is still so tightly woven into the fabric of U.S. schools. A complementary point is that desegregation turned out to be a relatively narrow intervention. Done well, it could fundamentally change race relations in schools, and in the South in the 1950s that was everything. Yet once the legal structure of Jim Crow began to erode, desegregation could not reach far enough into schools to influence many things that affect their quality. It might, for example, reduce inequalities in conventional indices of teacher quality, but it could not otherwise improve the quality of teaching, nor could it have much influence on teachers' working conditions, their salaries, or the patterns of teacher assignment that lodge the weakest teachers in schools with the most disadvantaged students.

Outcome-oriented policies express a curious stance toward racial inequality. Regulating school outcomes was proposed as a more effective way to improve schools, and NCLB announced that the achievement gap must close by 2014. Part of the rationale for this move was the presumed failure of both desegregation and Title I. Yet that leaves outcome regulation as the only substantial policy lever on racial inequality in education; state and local school systems must try to make NCLB work, despite large racial inequalities in nearly everything that is salient to education. Lacking much better knowledge about school improvement, and given deep racial inequality in educational resources of all sorts, policymakers are left with one policy instrument—accountability—that has proved much less powerful than its advocates fancied, and little other leverage on America's most pervasive inequality.

It should not be surprising, then, to find that standards-based reform has had little effect on racial differences in student achievement. There has been a slight gain in African American mathematics scores on NAEP, and several large cities report small gains on state or local tests. But there have been no changes in NAEP in reading, and the NAEP math and big city gains are very modest (Perie, Moran, & Lutkus, 2005). If the advocates of desegregation overestimated the potency of one sort of structural change, the advocates of standards-based reform made another version of that error, as they overestimated the power of accountability, and underestimated both the influence of Black-White inequalities and the role that knowledge would play in regulating schools by way of outcomes.

* * * * * * *

Much research has focused on the influence that school and environmental factors have on learning. My analysis suggests questions about the effects that learning may have on schools and their environments. For whatever the effects of standards-based reform, it seems likely to affect schools and their environments. For instance, depending on what these policies deliver for African American students' learning, one would expect effects on Black attitudes about public schools. If the policies deliver substantial gains in learning, will African American support for public schools grow, and will Black support for school choice, or privatization—discussed in more detail in Henig's chapter—weaken? Will any such learning gains have similar effects on the recruitment of African Americans, among others, to work in public education? Will small or nonexistent learning gains have the opposite effects? To investigate such questions is to probe the possible influence that schools have on their environments. Such influences have been relatively unfamiliar, but now are likely to become much more central, because outcome-oriented policies have made schools' performance the most significant feature of policy, politics, and public knowledge.

Teaching Quality

Teaching is the most important educational resource, a point on which nearly all commentators agree. They agree less on the attributes of teaching that matter most. Some have argued that caring for students is the key, while others contend that knowledge of the subject, or pedagogical knowledge, or knowledge of students matter most. For most of U.S. history such disagreements were muted, because the attributes of teachers—including gender, education, race, and experience—were treated as proxies for the attributes of teaching. The underlying idea was that teachers' formal qualifications were good indicators of the quality of teaching; hence regulating formal qualifications would yield good outcomes.

It was convenient to equate the two things. It made supervision and evaluation much easier, and it meant that there was no need to inquire into teachers' actual effectiveness with students. It also eased standard setting and personnel decisions in the processes of certification, licensure, and hiring. The equation worked for a long time, until researchers began to investigate the relationship among the attributes of teachers, teaching, and students' learning. There had been truckloads of earlier, small studies that cast doubt on the efficacy of teachers' attributes (see Duncan & Biddle, 1974), but James Coleman's EEOS was the first to bring the problem vividly to the attention of both policymakers and researchers outside of educational psychology. In Coleman's analyses, teachers' verbal ability was significantly related to school average student achievement, while the school averages of teachers' formal qualifications had little or no relation to average achievement. This meant that formal qualifications were not as salient as had been imagined, and that their equation with teaching quality rested on mistaken assumptions.

In response, educational researchers sought to learn more directly what attributes of teaching were effective for students' learning. In Jere Brophy and Tom Good's mid-1980s summary of the evidence (1986), the practice of unusually effective teachers, as judged by students' gains on standardized tests, seemed significantly different than that of their less effective peers. More effective teachers planned lessons carefully, selected appropriate materials, made their goals clear to students, maintained a brisk pace in lessons, checked student work regularly, and taught material again when students had trouble learning. They also made good use of the time they spent on instructional tasks (that was first reported by Cooley & Leinhardt, 1975, 1978). Such teachers had coherent strategies for instruction and deployed lessons, books, and other resources in ways that were consistent with the strategies. Finally, they believed that their students could learn and that they had a large responsibility to help. These attributes, which were consequential for student learning, would not be captured in conventional measures of teachers' formal qualifications.

The studies showed that what mattered to students' learning were specific attributes of teaching—what teachers did with students as they dealt with academic content—not their formal qualifications. The studies strongly implied, though they did not say, that formal qualifications would be a poor measure of teaching quality, and that more behavioral measures would be more valid indicators of the quality of teaching. Later studies showed that when formal qualifications were aligned with the elements of teachers' effectiveness, there was some connection to student performance. One example is academic degrees that reflect courses of study, which very roughly may proxy for teachers' knowledge of the subjects that they teach (Ferguson, 1991; Ferguson & Ladd, 1996). Subsequent research deepened these findings, but a great deal remains to be learned. One good example is the lack of knowledge about how to teach reading comprehension effectively (Hirsch, 2003).

Though these studies did not have any direct effect on policies, they did change the direction of research on teaching. In addition, the focus on teaching rather than teachers has recently been recognized in policy. (See Corcoran in this volume for a review of research on policy supports for effective teaching.) But, consistent with the divided character of the age, those policies offer a curious mix of old and new, as they define teaching quality in quite disparate terms. In some provisions they offer incentives for performance and leave it to schools and teachers to figure out how to make policy work. These provisions effectively ignore the attributes of both teachers and teaching, while attempting to offer strong incentives for effective practice. Here standards-based reform moves far beyond the evidence on teaching, because when these policies were enacted, there simply was no evidence that they would improve teaching or learning. Such policies never had been tried, in the United States or elsewhere. Nearly 20 years after standards-based reform began, there is only fragmentary evidence on this point, and it suggests that accountability has had either weak or no effect on student performance. There is some evidence from one state that accountability somewhat changed how local school leaders treat teaching: it encouraged schools to assign teachers who are believed to be more effective to classes of poorly performing students, in the subjects for which schools are held accountable (Coggeshall, 2006). It remains to be seen whether that improves student performance, or spreads beyond a few schools in one state.

At the same time, other provisions in the same policies take rather different approaches to the regulation of teaching quality. One provision of NCLB offers states incentives to hire only "highly qualified teachers," and defines those qualifications largely in formal and conventional terms. A second provision offers the states money to induce them to encourage localities to hire teachers with few or no conventional qualifications, apart from military service, an academic major in the subject that they would teach, or enrollment in an alternative certification program.

There is only modest evidence on these initiatives, but it offers no more than limited support for any of them. There is evidence that teachers who know an academic subject tend to have students who learn more of that subject, and a few studies report that academic majors seem to be a rough proxy for such knowledge (Ferguson, 1991; Ferguson & Ladd, 1996). Yet there also is evidence that knowledge of how to teach that subject is important, and it is likely that measures of academic knowledge to some extent pick up knowledge of how to teach it (Ball, Hill, & Bass, 2005). There is also growing evidence that various alternatives to conventional certification and licensing are no better and in some ways worse for students' learning. Two recent studies in New York City show that the students of alternatively certified new teachers do not score as well on tests as the students of teachers who had conventional teacher education and certification. It takes three years, during which the alternatively certified teachers had teacher education, for their students to catch up with the students of conventionally educated teachers (Kane, Rockoff, & Staiger, 2006; Boyd et al., 2006). Similarly, the students of Teach for America (TFA) teachers, who are academically the *crème de la crème* of U.S. college graduates, but have only a few weeks of teacher education, do no better on reading and only a little better on math tests than the students of conventionally educated teachers in the same schools, who are hardly the *crème de la crème* of conventionally educated teachers.[3]

These findings are far from conclusive, but they do little to support the claims either for alternative certification or for dropping conventional certification. At the same time, they offer little comfort for conventional teacher education and certification: given the weak average academic performance of U.S. students, and the much weaker average performance of disadvantaged students, conventionally educated and certified teachers are, on average, not an example of tip-top performance.

The findings do, however, offer solid evidence of the uncertainty that accompanies efforts to move policy concerning teaching from conventional to outcome-oriented terms. Richard Ingersoll's chapter in this volume offers an analysis of such uncertainty with respect to policies meant to improve teacher quality. Teaching and learning each are very complex practices, and their interactions are even more complex. It is very difficult to devise instruments that validly capture the attributes of effectiveness in either domain, and that problem is complicated by the large demographic and resource differences among both teachers and students, as well as organizational and cultural differences among the situations in which they work. Uncertainty about measures of quality in teaching is likely to continue, as more evidence is forthcoming. If experience in such matters is any guide, more research on the relations between teaching and learning will enrich our understanding without offering conclusive guidance for policy.

* * * * *

If teaching is the most important educational resource, it is not the easiest to understand or manage. Research made clear both the grave limitations of using formal qualifications as a guide to the quality of teaching, and the impressive differences in teachers' effectiveness in consistently

---

3. See Decker, Mayer, and Glazerman (2004). It is worth noting that this study's estimate of the TFA effect does not take account of the effects of the rather high dropout rate among first-year TFA teachers, so the finding may overestimate the effect that all TFA teachers have on student performance.

boosting students' test scores. But research has only begun to explore the attributes of teaching that are salient to student performance. There is a large gap between the knowledge that faulty assumptions underlie inherited teacher certification and licensure policies, and the knowledge that would be needed to support a defensible outcome-oriented approach to teacher certification and licensure. That gap notwithstanding, some recent policy concerning teaching has moved sharply toward outcomes, while some remains wedded to formal qualifications. That curious combination is typical of the age.

Though the combination of conventional and outcome-oriented approaches to improving teaching poses problems for policy and practice, it opens up unusual opportunities for research. As with research on race, much research on teaching in the last several decades has attempted to discern how the attributes of schools and school systems affect teaching and learning. In these studies, the causal arrows run from organizations to individuals who work within them. But recent outcome-oriented policies are likely to bring reversals in the direction of causality, because policies will generate evidence concerning teaching that may influence organizations. For example, do schools and school systems attempt to change teacher hiring and assignment, in response to pressure for learning outcomes, and evidence about outcomes, or in response to evidence concerning teachers' qualifications? Do colleges and universities change teacher education programs in an effort to respond to evidence on weakness in teacher education, and growing concerns with teachers' effectiveness? These and related questions concern the effects that policies may have on knowledge about teaching and learning, and how that knowledge may affect educational organizations.

Access to Schooling

Expanded access to schooling was the central element of education policy between the early 19th century and the late 20th century. Access is important, because whatever schools are thought to do, they cannot do it for students who are not there. But one reason that educators and reformers concentrated so much attention on building school systems and getting students to attend in those decades was their belief that if children attended, schools would do the rest. Schools were thought to be so potent that students from all sorts of backgrounds could get a good and common education. The policy problem was not whether schools worked, or how to make them work more effectively, but how to get students into them. These ideas made it possible for educators and reformers to energetically campaign for expanded access to schools, even though many schools had quite modest resources.

From one perspective, efforts to expand access met with appreciable success. Though in 1950, 76 percent of the age-eligible students attended high school, by 2000 the rate was 92 percent (Snyder, Tan, & Hoffman, 2006, Table 54). The same story can be told for access to higher education: in 1960, 45 percent of the age-eligible population went beyond grade 12, while in 2000 the comparable figure was 63.3 percent (Snyder, Tan, & Hoffman 2004, Table 185).

Inequality also decreased. In 1967, 90.3 percent of age-eligible Blacks attended U.S. high schools (U.S. Census Bureau 1969, Table 14), and 56 percent of those who had attended graduated (U.S. Census Bureau 2005a, Table A-5a); the comparable figures for Whites were 94 percent (U.S. Census Bureau 1969, Table 14) and 78 percent (U.S. Census Bureau 2005a, Table A-5a). In 2000, however, the comparable figures were 95.6 percent (U.S. Census Bureau 2000, Table 2) and 83.7 percent for Blacks (Kaufman, Alt, & Chapman, 2004, Table A-7), and 96.4 percent (U.S. Census Bureau 2000, Table 2) and 91.8 percent for Whites (Kaufman, Alt, & Chapman 2004, Table A-7). Similarly dramatic developments occurred in higher education: in 1967, 13 percent of the age-eligible Black population attended college, as compared to 27 percent of Whites (U.S.

Census Bureau 2005a, Table A-5a), and 5.4 percent of Blacks completed college, as compared to 15.5 percent of Whites.[4] In 2000, however, 55 percent of age-eligible Blacks attended college, as compared to 65.7 percent of Whites (Snyder, Tan, & Hoffman, 2004, Table 185) and 42 percent of Blacks who enrolled completed college, as compared to 62 percent of Whites (Journal of Blacks in Higher Education, 2006). The percentage of White students who complete a bachelor's degree within 6 years is 66.8 percent compared to the 45.7 percent of African Americans who complete their bachelor's degree within 6 years (Berkner, He, & Cataldi, 2002). There are still huge racial inequalities in access to higher education, but they are less than in 1950.

Yet the more access improved, the more its promise seemed to be compromised. One problem has been growing evidence that improved access does not, by itself, seem to reduce inequality in learning. On average, less advantaged students do less well on any measure of learning than their more advantaged peers, and Blacks and Hispanics do less well than Whites. NAEP is one sort of measure that has been even roughly stable over several decades, and it reveals large race and class disparities in learning. There was a significant narrowing of this gap between the mid 1970s and mid 1980s, but it widened in the 1990s (Perie, Moran, & Lutkus, 2005).

Another sort of measure that is germane to such inequality arises from longitudinal studies of students' achievement. Several studies of this sort suggest that schools do little to reduce inequality among groups. The correlations between students' test scores early in high school and their scores late in high school are strong and stable. This means that students' relative positions in the distribution of achievement vary only a little during high school. One group of scholars has produced evidence that some high schools have reduced the influence of social class and race on students' performance, and reduced the differences in achievement that divide students of different racial and social class groups in most schools. But the high schools that did this were quite unusual, and were a small minority of schools (Bryk, Lee, & Holland, 1993).

Both sorts of evidence suggest that, though many students learn in high school, the schools did little to reduce inequalities that divided students at the beginning of school. If so, schools were not the great "balance wheel of social machinery" that Horace Mann depicted and that virtually all advocates of expanded access promised. If school attendance was the ultimate educational input, because it summarized all the resources to which students had been exposed, these studies suggest that, on average, access improved academic learning over what would have occurred if students had not been in school, but it did little to reduce the race and class differences in knowledge and skill with which society endowed students. That was especially troubling, given the large role that improved access played in U.S. social and educational policy.

A second problem with expanded access arose from the differentiated offerings that schools devised to accommodate the growth in enrollments that expanded access brought. For differentiation meant that the education to which students had access often was distinctly unequal. As poor and immigrant children began to wash into city schools in the late 19th century, some localities differentiated elementary schools by students' academic progress or academic wishes. One aim was to enable students to progress at rates that suited them, and thus to hold them in school. Another was to avoid the one-size-fits-all approach to curriculum and instruction that was the initial reflex of mass public education in the United States. Still another aim was to make teaching more manageable, as more and more students, from more and more varied circumstances, surged into school. Such changes were introduced informally and often sporadically, in the 1880s and 1890s, but they took more stable form in the first few decades of the twentieth century, as ele-

---

4. This is as a percentage of people aged 24 to 29. The census does not rack college completers as a percentage of college attendees (U.S. Census Bureau, 2005b).

mentary schools introduced ability grouping based on students' scores on new standardized tests, and secondary schools introduced curricula that were differentiated by a combination of academic demands, students' presumed occupational destinations, students' elementary school performance, and test scores. These initiatives sought to change what schools did in order to accommodate what were seen as the much less academic tastes and abilities of a much larger and more varied set of students, and to help students to learn what they would need to know to succeed in the world. As the schools sought to expand access, they differentiated educational offerings and organization. The rationale was to adapt schoolwork to the interests, needs, and abilities of a rapidly changing student population, but the effect was to build equal access around unequal offerings.

Another step of the same sort was taken in the 1960s, as disadvantaged students' high school attendance grew, and social protest challenged the schools' legitimacy. Educators further differentiated the curriculum, not by adding more curriculum tracks, but by adding more varied, often less demanding and presumably more appealing courses, including such things as detective stories and science fiction in the English curriculum. The aim was to accommodate and engage disaffected students, whether from less or more privileged strata of society, but the effect was to accompany growing access with more unequal offerings.

These developments were slower in rural schools, until the post-World War II drive for consolidation. They also were less pronounced in nonpublic schools, which remain smaller, less impersonal, and in many cases academically more demanding than their public counterparts. Yet some nonpublic schools are quite unselective, and all charge tuition, which means that they are inaccessible to most disadvantaged families.

The growth in postsecondary education followed a similar pattern. There was a boom in institution and system building in the 1950s and 1960s, as high school attendance became nearly universal and postwar economic prosperity generated unprecedented state revenue. The result, by the beginning of the 1970s, was a highly differentiated system, in which most attendance was in public institutions, whether large public universities or community colleges. A minority of students attended private colleges and universities, some of which were very selective, while others took virtually all comers.

A third problem with expanding access lay in the organizational consequence of expanded access, namely, a mass system in which education increasingly became a matter of batch processing. Teaching and learning were organized in more impersonal terms, in schools whose size and operation tended to defeat deep connections between teachers and students. In high schools, most teachers had so many students, in so many different classes, that they did not have time to read students' work carefully, let alone become deeply acquainted with their thinking in class. Students were assigned to curricula by means of attributes such as test scores, and guidance counselors had so many hundreds of advisees that they could do only cursory work with them, at best. The size of many high schools and the variety of course offerings meant that scheduling classes and assigning students to them became very difficult and often quite irrational (DeLany, 1991). Most public postsecondary schooling is also organized around batch processing. At many state universities students can graduate with little or no contact with faculty, and with no need even to write essay exams. Course enrollments sometimes number in the thousands, many courses are offered on television, and students interact directly only with graduate teaching assistants. In contrast, the smaller, elite private schools offer more personalized education, as do the elite tracks in many large public universities.

These lines of policy and practice were challenged by evidence that policies and practices that aimed to make schools more accommodating had not made them more effective. Some evidence arose from studies of secondary schools in the 1980s, which portrayed high schools as places in which, for most students, academic work was almost beside the point: These students did little or nothing in class, owing to their resistance in some cases, and to teachers' impossible loads and inability to offer more ambitious and engaging fare, in other cases. Some other evidence arose in studies of the relationship between the quality of educational offerings and student performance. Researchers reported that students who were placed in academically more demanding high school curricula learned more than otherwise similar students who had been placed in less demanding curricula. Another research group reported that when advantaged and disadvantaged students attended high schools that had markedly less curriculum differentiation, and more equal offerings, the disadvantaged students learned more than otherwise similarly situated students who attended schools that had more differentiated and more unequal curricula.

The developments sketched here chipped away at the belief that schools could do the job, if students would attend. Two sorts of evidence from research emphasized that point. One was that poor and minority-group students continued to have weaker average achievement than their White and more advantaged peers, and that the weakness was especially pronounced in high-poverty schools. Another was that school completion was poor in urban secondary schools that enroll disadvantaged students. Valid data on dropouts is scarce, and there are disputes about the exact rates, but few contest that the incidence of dropouts is unacceptably high.

Those making efforts to respond to these problems agree that the quality of schooling should be improved, and that expanded access alone will not do the job. But there is no agreement about how to improve quality. One line of thought and practice centers on restructuring high-poverty elementary schools, so that they offer much more demanding instruction for students. The leading examples of such work include such reform designs as America's Choice, Core Knowledge, Accelerated Schools PLUS, and Success for All. These and other models devise changes in schools that support more ambitious instruction with more opportunities to learn for teachers, stronger and more effective leadership, change in professional norms and expectations, and much more. These designs are premised on the view that unless disadvantaged students have access to carefully designed, high-quality education, their average achievement will continue to lag. They redefine the meaning of access to include effectiveness.

Another line of thought and practice centers on restructuring secondary or tertiary schools so that they take students much more seriously as learners, in educational organizations that are smaller and more personalized, with academic work that is more demanding and engaging, and with much more attention to helping students to navigate the transition between secondary and tertiary schools. (The Kirst chapter in this volume considers the problems of this transition; similarly, the Barnett and Ackerman chapter examines transitional problems at the boundary between early and K–12 education.) Initiatives of this sort include the Big Picture Company, the Coalition of Essential Schools, some of the small schools in central cities that have been supported by the Gates Foundation, and efforts to improve teaching in some community colleges and in smaller colleges within public universities. Initiatives of this sort assume that if schools are to hold more students and offer more effective education, they should devise more intimate educational organizations, work more effectively with students' views and experience to offer more engaging and demanding work, and coordinate education across organizational boundaries. They depart from inherited ideas and practices, for they reflect organizational values that are typically found in small nonpublic settings, they imply costly investments in teaching, they depend on bridging very different organizations for students' benefit, and they reject efforts to accommodate students within batch-processed schooling.

A third line of thought and practice centers on the view that more stringent institutional accountability is the best way to improve quality in secondary and tertiary schools. The lever for change is externally imposed standards and tests of student learning, rather than more investment in teaching or changes in educational organization, content, and relations with students. The problem is thought to lie not in the organization of secondary and tertiary education or underfunding, but in the lack of disciplined resource allocation that would flow from clear accountability. If one judges by the experience with standards-based reform thus far, however, such initiatives would accentuate the batch-processing features of secondary and tertiary schooling.

A fourth line of thought and practice centers on the continued extension of access by conventional means. Public university systems and state legislatures are often at odds over appropriations and student tuition, and there are increasing legislative demands for accountability in higher education. Yet at the same time, legislators and educators can agree on proposals to open or expand branch campuses and community colleges.

*****

Extension of access is the most venerable U.S. educational policy, and schooling has improved in many ways since the 1950s. Research in the last several decades shows that there is less unequal access, there are more resources and better educated teachers. But research has also shown that these improvements were made to a system that embodied large structural inequalities in funding, educational resources, and race. As a result, large race and class inequalities in access to and the quality of schooling remain, despite the improvements. Research on the effects of schooling has gradually eroded the beliefs that underpinned policies that promoted access.

Access to education is a necessary condition of learning, but it no longer seems sufficient, especially if schools are to significantly reduce the educational effects of the inequalities that society imposes on students. The key problems here arise from improved access itself. One is that the success of these policies depended on the provision of quite unequal opportunities to learn, and less unequal learning will depend at least in part on redressing those inequalities. The other is that though effective teaching and learning depend on sustained personal relationships, the policies that improved access created mass systems of secondary and tertiary schooling, in which the modal educational transactions were quite impersonal.

In consequence there have been increasing efforts to redefine access to schooling not in the classical terms of common schools for all, but in terms of access to particular, carefully designed educational processes and opportunities. These ideas are manifest in such diverse endeavors as comprehensive school reform designs, secondary school reforms, the Abbott decisions in New Jersey, efforts to use conceptions of adequate rather than equal education as the basis for state school finance, and plans to devise opportunity-to-learn standards.

As the meaning of access changes, schools and school systems will find themselves operating in two rather different worlds. The differences are evident in contemporary ideas about how to make access more effective. Some initiatives seek to address the problems of impersonality and quality that have become general in secondary and tertiary schooling, while others seek to improve quality and manage resources with external accountability for student outcomes. Initiatives of the first sort promise to deal more directly with the educational and organization problems, but they are costly; would require quite extensive change in schools' size, organization, and content; and have been tried chiefly in rather protected, small, nonpublic schools and colleges. Initiatives of the second sort promise effectiveness in return for a relatively modest investment in institutional accountability, but they never have been tried, and there is no evidence that they would have the intended results. If these developments continue, schools will deal not only with very different conceptions of access, but also with competing conceptions of what it might mean for policies and school systems to succeed or fail.

RESEARCH AND POLICY

My discussion suggests that research was consequential in several ways during the post-World War II decades. For one thing, it helped to bring issues to public attention and to revise the ways in which things are understood. It played these parts quite effectively in drawing attention to school outcomes and to the effects that schools have on outcomes. Coleman and his colleagues' *Equality of Educational Opportunity Study* touched off significant attention to both of these matters in 1966–1967, and public attention has grown ever since. Coleman's work also helped to change how Americans understood schools and school quality. Quality previously had been seen largely in terms of the resources that were available, but Coleman's work began to move conceptions of quality toward schools' effectiveness in improving student performance. Research in this tradition has also contributed to a shift in the goals that Americans envision for schools, from relatively diffuse ideas about students' mastery of the "three R's" and social development to somewhat more focused ideas about performance on tests of achievement.

Research also helped to focus attention on unequal provision of educational resources, on unequal achievement, and on school failure. Coleman's study was a landmark there as well, and subsequent research on racial, economic, and fiscal inequalities helped to call attention to these problems. Research also played a modest role in provoking litigation concerning unequal resources and racial discrimination, and a key role in supporting such litigation.

Research was not the sole source of these effects. Rather, it helped to focus attention and change ideas in tandem with other developments. Coleman's survey was federally sponsored at a time of unprecedented interest in civil rights, and it was published during the nation's most intense engagement with that issue. That interest and engagement helped to provoke the survey and create an audience for Coleman's ideas; had the study been privately sponsored and done a decade earlier, it likely would have done little to focus attention or to prompt change in understanding. Similarly, Americans' attention to academic outcomes grew during decades in which federal and state policymakers, reformers, and business leaders kept up steady criticism of schools' weakness and devised highly visible policies that aimed to improve academic outcomes.

Research also contributed to Americans' evaluation of the schools' effectiveness and their satisfaction with the schools' performance. When the Gallup organization began asking Americans for their opinions about schools, in 1968, satisfaction was high, and most saw public education as an effective enterprise. At that time, however, there was little research on the schools' effects and effectiveness. By the late 1960s such research was enjoying a boom, and there were the first high-profile evaluations of the performance of schools and educational programs. Both sorts of research were taken to show that schools performed poorly, an impression that was reinforced by cross-national comparisons in which U.S. schools rarely did well. Several decades of such reports, and increasing criticism from civic leadership and policymakers, were accompanied by decreasing popular satisfaction and a decreasing belief in the schools' effectiveness. The most dramatic change occurred in the views of African Americans: at the beginning of this period they were very strongly committed to public schools and opposed to vouchers, but by the late 1990s their commitment to public education was very greatly reduced, and their acceptance of vouchers very greatly increased. Research alone would not have had these effects, but it did exert some influence as policymakers, civic leaders, and advocates used it to call attention to school problems.

In these cases and others, though research had important effects on ideas, it had no discernable independent effects on action. Those effects were indirect and typically modest for several reasons. One, already noted, was that research depended for its effects on the ideas and actions of other, more influential agents. Another was that the fractured political organization of U.S. schooling, and the weak capabilities of most state education agencies, meant that if knowledge were to be used, it would have to be noticed and understood in thousands of independent local jurisdictions and tens of thousands of schools. Still another reason was that the economic and racial segregation that was built into local jurisdictions created strong disincentives for well-to-do localities to address many of the problems of inequality on which research has focused.

Another still was that even if U.S. schools had been models of eager research use, there was rather little research to use. Few researchers attended to practice and practice improvement, and only a small number of studies reported on practices that would enable schools to improve instruction, organization, or management. Fewer still offered any discussion of what it would take for practitioners to learn to change practice. Finally, schools and school systems offered neither incentives for educators to use research, nor opportunities for them to do so.

In principle, that changed with standards-based reform. I state earlier in this chapter that outcome-oriented policies "require states and localities to set academic standards, to create tests that fit the standards, and to hold schools and school systems accountable for students' test performance. If students fail, so do schools, and if schools don't improve, they can be put out of business. If many schools fail, so can school systems. For the first time in U.S. history, the fate of schools could depend on how well they help students to learn. [Yet] . . . these policies cannot work if educators don't know how to detect and explain differences in instructional effectiveness."

In the world that federal policymakers imagined, NCLB and related policies would create a strong demand for improved knowledge, but that has not been the case. One reason has been the acute shortage of usable knowledge, and another has been federal nonenforcement of NCLB requirements for such knowledge use. Research on the implementation and effects of these policies does plays a significant role in informing policymakers and the public, but nearly all of it is sponsored and carried out by nongovernment organizations. There are no signs that this is likely to change.

One last role of research is its increasing importance as a language of discourse about policy. Americans now debate and understand schools in the input-output terms of the mathematical models of educational processes that sociologists and economists brought to research on schools in the 1960s. The effects of schooling are increasingly understood and discussed in terms of the tests that psychometricians devised. Even those who formerly argued for vouchers, charter schools, or intelligent design, on the basis of no evidence, now find it necessary to use research to make arguments and objections.

This development has been a mixed blessing. On the one hand, there is much more interest in research; journalists regularly consult researchers and offer interpretations of studies in the popular media. In addition, research on matters of concern to policy has improved, both in technical methods and in probing more deeply into matters that were formerly taken for granted. On the other hand, these technical improvements mean that research is less accessible to nonspecialists and that researchers know more and more about less and less. More important, these improvements have occurred at a time of intensely partisan policymaking. Though research is used much more than it was four or five decades ago, it is much more often used in the service of intensely partisan causes; that has hindered the development of common standards of inquiry, and enhanced the sense that research is made to say whatever its sponsors or authors wish. Though the Campbell Collaboration aims to deal with this problem in its careful research reviews, its work is limited to studies that meet pretty high standards of quality, on topics on which there is considerable work, and on issues of program impact. That leaves out most research on education.

CONCLUSION

Contemporary education policy is the site of a collision between novel policies that seek to govern and regulate school systems by learning outcomes, and a system of schooling that was long habituated to governance and regulation by resource inputs. That collision, and the consequent coexistence of two profoundly different approaches to education policy, defines the current era in education.

The collision had deep sources in post-World War II U.S. history. That entire period was marked by continuing criticism of public education, by increasing public dissatisfaction, by a succession of state and federal policies that were to correct the objects of criticism, and by one report after another that the policies had not succeeded. By the 1980s the criticism had grown more general and more fundamental, in part owing to the cumulative weight of three decades of discouraging reports. By then policymakers, politicians, and commentators had a strong scent of the schools' failure and a growing sense that criticizing failure and proposing improvement could yield political advantage. Many concluded that thousands of schools were simply failing, that the entire system was crippled at best, and that what was needed would have to be more fundamental than the reforms whose failures had been reported during the preceding decades.

Yet policymakers were far removed from knowledge of educational practice, and few troubled themselves to inquire into it. Practitioners did not help; they were not adept at representing themselves to politicians and policymakers, and had instead learned to duck their heads to let the latest policy enthusiasm pass. Though a few researchers did very useful work to understand schooling processes, to map the relations between teaching and learning, and to build knowledge of school improvement, they were the exceptions; neither many researchers nor education professionals devoted much attention to these matters. On all sides there was a dangerous combination of a strong sense that schools were failing and little understanding of what it might take to substantially improve them.

The U.S. school system had two characteristics that inhibited such understanding. It was very decentralized, and thus lacked the experience, dispositions, and capabilities suited to strong central direction and coherent policy. In addition, neither the public schools, nor the people who worked in them, nor those in related organizations like research institutes or teacher education colleges, knew how to devise and implement usable content standards and measures of educational outcomes, or how to manage schools, classrooms, and systems to achieve those outcomes. The very system that the new policies sought to overcome had created the incapacities that would cripple any effort to impose a novel, rational, outcome orientation. It seems an obvious point, but nearly everyone seemed to miss it.

The collision between the two approaches to managing and governing schools would have been painful even in the best of circumstances, because the two are so different. It was made more acute not only by extreme decentralization and incapacity to manage an outcome-oriented system but also by adding policies that demanded equal outcomes from a very unequal system of schooling. Recent policies ask the least advantaged schools and students to do things that the unequal allocation of social and educational resources weakly equips them to do. Though NCLB increased funding for the poorest schools, that does little to ameliorate enormous inequalities within and among states, and between students from very different racial and social class backgrounds.

These deficits of resources and knowledge help to explain the problems that recent policies have run into and their very modest effects on student performance. But students' achievement is not the only domain in which the effects of these policies should be observed. Since the policies insist that schools improve if they are found wanting, knowledge of schooling processes and school improvement is the key to the success of practice and policy. Will standards-based reform lead to improved knowledge of schooling processes, of the relations between teaching and learning, and of school improvement? Though there have been several efforts to improve knowledge, there is no evidence of work on anything like the required scale—although a few have called for such work (see Mosher, this volume).

In this matter as well as others, recent policies that required much better knowledge if they were to succeed outran the required knowledge. One question for the current period in education policy is how policy will deal with this situation. There seem to be two alternatives. One is to build the knowledge that might make the new policies viable, but at the moment there are no signs that federal and state policymakers or educators are about to embark on major knowledge building. The other is to weaken tests and reduce cut points for proficiency, to create the appearance of success.

What policymakers and other do with respect to these matters will have a large impact on the character of education policy in the coming decade or two. Much more serious and systematic knowledge development would improve the chances that outcome-oriented policies could have a significant effect on practice and that schools would improve. The lack of such knowledge development is likely to increase the chances that the markers of student success will be arranged to save face for the policies and for those who championed and made them.

Part II

Coda: The Research That Policy Needs

Fritz Mosher and Susan H. Fuhrman

We are grateful to our coeditor David Cohen for his willingness to take on the task of writing a reflective conclusion for this volume. We think he has gone well beyond summary to offer a deep and comprehensive perspective on the last half century or so of education policy and policy research.

We agree that this period has witnessed the beginning of an epochal transformation of the goals of education policy and the ideal criteria by which the success or failure of American public schools in their time-honored role of ensuring "equal opportunity" are judged. That transformation involves a shift from a focus on whether or not all students have a reasonably equal access to the educational inputs that have long been considered to characterize good schooling—qualified teachers, a solid curriculum, safe and well-equipped facilities, reasonable class sizes, equitable funding, and so on—to the question of whether or not substantially all the students as they proceed through school are on track at least to be proficient in core knowledge and skills when they leave the system, and whether they do in fact at least achieve proficiency.

We also agree with David that education research, in conjunction with the civil rights and other group rights movements and the pressures of international economic and political competition, provided the impetus for this shift in normative focus from inputs to outcomes by casting a continuing light on the unacceptable inequities in those outcomes and on the disappointing overall performance of American students on NAEP and/or relative to their counterparts in competing countries. In addition, it is clear he is correct that, while researchers have played a role in suggesting plausible bases for designing interventions and policies aimed at making schools more effective, the more consistent role of education policy research and evaluation has been to call into question the effectiveness of reform policies and to demonstrate their limitations. Research evidence on what doesn't work has been at least as influential as evidence about what works, and probably it has had a greater impact both by stirring a continuing sense of crisis and by motivating responses that promise to do better.

David leaves us with a picture of a system caught in transition, adopting standards- and outcomes-based accountability but stuck with patterns of regulation and pedagogical orientations deeply rooted in the earlier idea that equal access to conventional inputs and resources ought to provide sufficient opportunity. The system lacks the fundamental knowledge about, and tools for, approaches to teaching and learning and the social organization of schools and schools' contexts that would be necessary and sufficient to enable substantially all students to meet or exceed the desired standards. Such knowledge, if it existed, could reshape the system's conception of the relevant inputs and resources in ways that would tie them directly to outcomes and make possible a defensible definition of "opportunity to learn," which then could play a direct role in what David characterizes as the regulation of the system, and in what W. Norton Grubb, in this volume, calls "the new school finance." Absent such knowledge, as David says, policymakers will be sorely tempted to define standards and "proficiency" in terms of the lowest-common-denominator kinds of outcomes the system currently produces, even though these would leave the many students who would just meet such standards with precious little chance of being able to function in the real world in the way that the label "proficiency" should imply.

We share most of this vision of the current state of policy and practice and the knowledge that informs them, but we would like to extrapolate a bit further from the lessons learned in the work covered in the chapters of this book and from our own observations of the recent history of education research and development to consider what might increase the chances that research could help to produce the knowledge and tools needed to enable policy, and the schools, to succeed according to their new ambitions.

WHAT WOULD BE NECESSARY TO PRODUCE KNOWLEDGE SUFFICIENT TO ENSURE SUCCESS?

Our reading of the work reported here and of the current policy environment suggests some of the fundamental reasons why it is hard to develop the knowledge needed to inform policies that might enable standards-based reform to succeed:

First, there is no adequate conception of the goal of the system—i.e., "proficiency" in key subjects and skills—and how it should be measured. Use of the term proficiency carries a connotation that leans more toward conceptions of skill than it does toward amounts or breadth of knowledge, though they are not fully separable. It seems more relevant to areas like reading and mathematics that serve as foundational skills or literacies used widely in other aspects of school, work, and life. And those of course are the subjects where the term is being most widely applied in current policy. It will be interesting to see how it carries over to science, as that is added to the testing requirements under NCLB. It might be a closer parallel to require assessment of logical reasoning and the ability to apply it to practical and social problems as well as to scientific topics. In any case, proficiency implies a level of competence in the use of a skill that provides a substantial chance of success in the areas where it is applied—for instance in further study and study of other subjects, or in employment, or in carrying out the responsibilities of citizenship or parenthood, and so on. *None* of the measures used in state assessments or even in NAEP has any direct empirical validation for such an interpretation of the reported proficiency (or equivalent terms) levels. At best they are based on expert judges eyeballing the items in the assessments and trying to pick the ones that somehow fit what they would expect a proficient student would be able to do, and a less than proficient student would not. These judgments are never tested further against other observations and more complex assessments of students' effectiveness in real settings. *Neither*, for the most part, are any of these assessments referenced to any well-defined conception of how and in what particular order, steps, or stages knowledge and skill typically develop over time and with instruction in any of these subjects. Rather, the assessment scores take their meaning explicitly or implicitly from where they stand in the distribution of all students' scores. Given the time available for assessment, it would be hard to get reliable and valid information about specific academic progress even if the attempt were made to design assessments to provide it, but this all means that current assessments provide very limited information that could be used to guide instruction.

What this first problem means is that public discussion of standards and the outcomes of schooling is carried out in an empirical vacuum. There is no way to consider how close to, or how far from, a goal of proficiency for substantially all we are moving, nor is there a shared basis for considering what the trade-offs might be for setting the definition of the goal higher or lower in situations where people might legitimately differ on the relevant costs and benefits. We simply can't tell, for instance, whether it actually ought to be possible for schools to succeed with most children if they are doing the best that educators now know how to do, or whether more than normal effort or time might be sufficient, or whether it might require new fundamental knowledge to enable such success, or what we (and the least well-performing students) lose if we settle for a weaker proficiency standard. While we may be able to assume there is some correlation between a more empirically based standard of proficiency or of progress in knowledge and skill on the one hand and the scores provided by current assessments, on the other, so that *changes* in the latter provide at least some information useful for evaluating the effectiveness of education programs and policies, that relationship is nevertheless uncertain. It certainly is not adequate to provide information about the *sufficiency* of such programs and policies, since doing that would require an agreed and warranted measure of proficiency.

So, research and development that could better inform outcomes-based policy desperately requires the development of better measures of the outcomes themselves. Such work will take time and undoubtedly will require an iterative process working back and forth between basic work on the core subjects and skills, and the ways they are learned, and work in real settings on the role those subjects and skills play in effective performance in other areas. Still, it is time to get started.

Second, a number of the chapters in this book make the point that the teaching side of the teaching/learning interaction in instruction is clearly crucial, but that we know too little about what is crucial about it (besides David's discussion above, see Cohen, Moffitt, & Goldin; Barrow & Rouse; Corcoran). One implication of the shift to standards-based reform and accountability is that if substantially all children are to be enabled to succeed, instruction will have to be adapted to respond to the needs of children who are somehow not on the path to meeting standards or who are falling behind on it. Policy needs therefore to find ways to reach to what actually happens in specific classrooms between teachers and students. But as David's discussion of teacher quality and Tom Corcoran's review of the research in his chapter indicate, we really have very little direct evidence about what teachers do and how that affects students' learning. It seems, in the United States at least, that much of both policy and research stop at the classroom door, and we are left studying the relationships between proxy measures for teacher quality and behavior and overall student outcomes. There are exceptions, and there is now a beginning and growing literature based on direct classroom observation, analysis of video records of instruction, teacher self-reports, teacher logs, and the collection of the artifacts of instruction (for instance, the work of Rowan and his colleagues on the Study of Instructional Improvement at the University of Michigan; see Rowan, Camburn, & Correnti, 2004) that attempts to get at teachers' pedagogical behavior and decision making more directly. But as yet there is no clear agreement in the field about what categories of observation and behavior are crucial or fruitful to observe and/or how to sample them reliably and validly.

This work has to be pushed much further and more effectively if we are to have any chance of learning whether reform policies, or pre- and in-service teacher education, or any of the efforts to improve outcomes for students are having any effect on the teacher behaviors that might mediate such improvement, or, for that matter, what changes in pedagogy we should be hoping for. We badly need a common vocabulary and a common set of tools for the study of instruction, or most of the research we do will be little more than spinning our wheels. It also will be important to tie work on instruction much more closely to the specific content, subjects, and skills being taught, since it seems likely that "pedagogical content knowledge" (Shulman, 1987; Rowan, Schilling, Ball, & Miller, 2001) will prove to be a crucial element underlying effective instruction. One virtue of the new and growing enthusiasm for promoting the practice of "formative assessment" of various kinds, and for the use of evidence in instruction, is that it may help to call attention to what decisions teachers actually are making with respect to each of their students, and to whether and how those focus on students' progress in specific subjects and skills.

Third, we need to solve the problem of finding contexts in which multivariate research and, more particularly, development can be carried out in real school settings and at the scale and durations that are likely to be required to produce knowledge, tools, and policies warranted for and usable in practice. This is easier said than done.

As David summarizes, education research over the years has identified a number of factors at various levels of the system that are associated with increased student performance. Some of them are arguably necessary for improvement or success, but none of them, taken separately or together, has been demonstrated to be sufficient to assure success for all or most students, or even to be as strongly associated with success as students' family background or social class status. As we have argued above, part of the problem of this work has been that we lack agreement on and measures of what would be an adequate outcome, but even with current performance measures that clearly fall short of assuring that students who pass them will be able to function effectively in other real situations, research evidence fails to identify factors or combinations of factors that would enable most students to meet those standards. While we think that research that searches large data sets to identify correlations between variations in educational inputs and resources and variations in student outcomes, with appropriate statistical controls, is useful for suggesting hypotheses about which designs and interventions should be tried, we think it is unlikely that the current real world, and particularly variations in the real world available within the American system, will, on its own, turn up combinations with any real chance of sufficiency. This argues that what is needed is quite self-conscious development and design work that would seek to put together the best-bet lessons and hypotheses from both research and practice about promising resource combinations and "instructional regimes" (Cohen, Raudenbush, & Ball, 2003) and to make full-court-press efforts in real schools to test whether we can move closer to interventions that are sufficient to ensure success for most students.

A strong example of such a strategy is the Success for All work reported by Robert Slavin and his colleagues in this book. We need many more such examples, sustained over comparable periods of time and across a wide range of school settings. We also need for work of this sort to be monitored and formatively evaluated in ways that parallel the Boston work that Barbara Neufeld reports in her chapter, both to make running improvements in the designs as they are developed and also to identify problems that may require attention of funders and researchers at a much more fundamental level—work that then could inform and improve future designs.

Obviously this advice is difficult to act on, and we think that the reasons it is difficult are the reasons why education research has such a poor track record. In fields in which it is possible to take the results of basic laboratory work, translate them into designs, and test them relatively quickly in working settings and then modify them and test again if necessary, there is much greater historical evidence of progress due to such combinations of "science" and "engineering" (Nelson, 2001). The time required both to act and to see results is much greater in education (and other social institutions). The levels at which things have to be held equal or varied in measurable and replicable ways tend to be much greater—consider not just curriculum or pedagogy but also levels of funding available to schools; the background, experience, and training of teachers and the kinds of in-service training, time, and support available to them; the quality and behavior of school and district leadership; the coherence of curriculum and the degree of consistency between curricular and pedagogical expectations and the criteria for student, teacher, school, and system accountability; the degree of press and stress from the latter; the social backgrounds of students and parents and the levels of community resources and stress; positive and perverse incentives for performance or the lack of it, both in the system and in the local and student cultures; and much more. When we use the term full-court-press we mean to imply that interventions that are likely to have a chance of being sufficient probably have to push the variables at these other levels toward relatively benign ranges while at the same time solving detailed problems of instruction in specific subjects tied to the varying cognitive and social needs of specific groups of students and specific individuals.[5]

We don't pretend to know how to solve the problem of finding real settings in which something like these complex forms of design and intervention can be tried and tested. We just insist that it is a problem for which at least partial and progressive answers will have to be found before there is much chance of providing the knowledge we need in the form we need it. We also suggest, as the search for answers to these issues proceeds, that we will need to look beyond the current realities of American schools to identify hypotheses about what may happen if those realities change more radically. For instance, what if some state departments of education were to take on roles and responsibilities closer to those played by ministries of education in many countries, providing a more coherent setting in which to carry out more detailed experimentation with instructional regimes than is now possible in the fragmented American system described so well in many chapters of this book? Or are there ways to take advantage of the charter schools movement to encourage the development of somewhat insulated subsystems within which real experimentation might be carried out? This strikes us as an extremely high-priority set of issues that should be the focus of serious discussion among researchers, policymakers, and the funders of education research (a recent *Education Week* op ed essay by Paul Hill (2006) makes some parallel points directed specifically at the Bill and Melinda Gates Foundation and its newly augmented wealth).

And that brings us to a *fourth* point. None of our first three concerns has any chance of being addressed effectively unless those who fund and manage education research take a much more strategic view of what they are doing. By "strategic" we mean that funders and managers should focus on the key goals of practice or particular big problems that seem to impede attainment of those goals. They should try to determine whether our current levels of understanding of the factors affecting the focal areas seem to be sufficient to support the design of practical approaches and solutions that might have a chance of having big effects in moving practice toward the goals or toward solving the particular problems. If so, they should invest in developing, testing, and refining those designs. New design efforts should engage both researchers and practitioners in combining insights stemming from basic work with the wisdom of designers and practitioners to develop new approaches, materials, and policies that should support successful practice. If current understanding does not seem sufficient to support such work, funders and managers should consider providing programmatic support for basic disciplinary or multidisciplinary studies in areas that show promise of identifying understandings that could inform new designs which might produce big effects. Also, if design work of the former sort runs into new problems that stand in the way of success and seem to require new knowledge, that information also should lead funders and managers to devote resources to basic efforts to understand and remove those impediments.

---

5. It should be obvious, but it probably is worth saying, that even if we could identify forms of instruction that have really big effects with students who have difficulty in learning particular subjects or skills, there would remain the problems of putting that knowledge in the hands of teachers in ways that they can use, and of getting teachers who have that knowledge in front of the students who need them. Such teachers are likely to remain a scarce resource well beyond the happy time in which such knowledge is discovered, and designing and testing systems for increasing and spreading these resources and getting them to where they are required is a prime example of the fact that the solution of education problems demands work at many levels. In this case it should be clear that the solutions are likely to involve a deep engagement with politics, values, and pocketbooks, as the McDonnell and Hill chapters in this book should teach us.

Over time, strategic funding and management would generate interacting cycles of basic and design work in the focal areas, cycles in which the outcomes from each level would inform and set priorities for the other (RAND Mathematics Study Panel, 2003). This requires finding ways to monitor progress and problems at both levels and to shift, balance, and orchestrate resources among them depending on judgments based on that monitoring.

When we refer to "big effects," we mean effects at least as large as those that have been mediated by understanding that differences in an underlying ability called "phonological awareness" are key to understanding students' ability to develop fluent decoding in early reading, and understanding that interventions to improve and make such awareness explicit can shift low-performing students up into the normal range of functioning.

The problems of assessment that we identify in our first point provide clear examples whose solution will require both fundamental and practical design work, interacting in a reciprocal relationship playing out over time. The same is true of finding much better ways of tapping in to what actually is happening in instruction in ways that are derived from an understanding of what elements of instruction are key to making big differences in student outcomes. And there are many more specific problems of practice involved in addressing students' difficulties in learning particular subjects and skills that would repay strategic attention of this sort, though part of being strategic also involves making serious judgments about the trade-offs involved in focusing in depth on a few problems at a time as opposed to spreading resources more thinly across more areas.

The answer to striking that balance is not likely to be obvious; it does involve making serious estimates of the progress being made on each problem and the trade-off against the potential value of unexpected progress resulting from casting a wider net. The question of how and where these strategic judgments should be made is a major design problem in its own right. Clearly the major funders of research, both federal sources and private foundations—and states and commercial sources if they should decide to expand their roles—will have to take major responsibility, though they almost certainly cannot do this successfully without finding better ways than we now have in education (and related disciplines) of promoting a reciprocal interaction between the funders and the field in supporting judgments about strategic priority and payoff. Peer review is a crucial mechanism for ensuring basic quality and adherence to methodological standards and disciplinary relevance, but it is not a sufficient way of engaging the field in judgments about strategic priorities.

Part of the answer to this might come in the development of research management institutions in focused areas that would have a scale and level of resources, and degree of interaction between universities and other research organizations and schools or school systems, of a sort that for the most part do not now exist. Such institutions are not likely to appear spontaneously. They will have to be nurtured by the very funders who then will need them as partners in making strategic judgments. But certainly around the country there must be nodes of work, and talented research managers, that can provide the basis for growing such partners. As an example, more thought might be given to the roles that the federally funded National Research and Development Centers and Regional Education Laboratories might play along these lines. This problem requires much more attention than it has had so far, or than we can give it here (for a thoughtful consideration of related issues see Burkhardt & Shoenfeld, 2003).

Finally, we think that the public discourse on these issues has been clouded by a narrow or unbalanced understanding of what "science" entails. Federal legislation establishing NCLB and IES is full of language promoting "scientifically based" or "scientifically valid" research and evaluation and establishing the expectation that educators will adopt approaches to practice that are warranted by such research. We recognize that the language of the legislation and the way it has been implemented in the Department of Education imply some recognition that there are early stages of scientific work that involve such things as careful and replicable observations of phenomena and relationships and the use of an array of methods appropriate to the questions to be answered, rather than simply drawing the defining line at the use of rigorous experiments. Nevertheless, it seems to us that there is a clear bias toward work that can establish the effectiveness of identifiable and currently available pedagogical approaches, curricula, materials, tools, and education policies through the use of designs which rigorously support the inference that the education intervention causes outcomes which are demonstrably better than those produced by current practice or by interventions that might be seen as competing or alternative choices.

That bias is understandable. The Barrow and Rouse chapter in this book argues that one of the main reasons education research has been seen as being weak is that it fails to use methods that allow rigorous causal inferences about the relationships between education inputs and outcomes, and they provide a careful exposition about the kinds of methods that could and should be used to do better, with an assessment of what we know to date about the effectiveness of some key inputs when these standards are applied to existing knowledge. It is reasonable to expect that policymakers and educators would find information about what works in real settings, and what works when, more useful than journal articles reporting findings about the relationships among particular education variables when "other things are held equal," or the results of laboratory experiments. But there is a catch.

The catch is that the emphasis on summative evaluation of interventions using some form of randomized trials, or the closest possible equivalent controls, places a premium on working with interventions that already are identified and specified. But as Barrow and Rouse point out here, education interventions tend to be complex, so that even if a causal effectiveness relationship can be demonstrated, we are often left uncertain about just to what within the intervention the cause should be attributed. They argue that you cannot expect definitive results from a single big randomized trial and recommend that what really is needed are extended series of studies spread over time and settings that might eventually have a chance of clarifying what the effective elements are and how far they might generalize. In addition, as we have argued above, the effects, even when they can be conclusively established statistically, are often not particularly impressive when gauged against the standard of being sufficient to enable most students to reach proficiency. Randomized designs are expensive. They often require payment of incentives of various kinds to encourage schools to participate. And they tend to lock in a particular version of the intervention being tested over the period of the experiment. Further, because of the expense and the difficulty of maintaining control, the experimental periods tend to be relatively short—often one to three years. And yet the effects in education, if they are there, might reasonably be expected only to show up and play out in full over much longer time periods.

This all suggests that serious attention has to be given to when significant investments in carrying out these designs should be made, and to whether, when there are interventions of sufficient promise to justify an investment to confirm that promise, the resources and time made available for the study are sufficient to give them a real chance to show what they can do. It also suggests that more attention and investment should be aimed both at fundamental work designed to identify basic relationships that might, perhaps in new combinations, show promise of informing interventions that would have the kinds of big effects we really need. Attention and investment should also be aimed at iterative attempts to design, try, and modify interventions based on these new fundamental insights, and based on the necessary input of talented designers and accomplished practitioners, in order to build interventions whose promise would justify the bigger investments necessary to test their causal effectiveness more definitively (though we have to say, it may be true that if the effects are big enough, the demand for statistically and methodologically powerful designs may seem less pressing).

Once again, we really are appealing here to those who have responsibility for funding education research, or who could be encouraged to undertake it, to join in an effort to determine how we might develop a stronger capacity to provide strategic reflection on the progress of work designed to inform policy and practice and on the structures and institutions that might be able to monitor and carry out the resulting strategic judgments and choices more effectively over time.

As Donald Stokes (1997) pointed out, science and research are motivated both by the desire to understand and explain and by the need to inform action—what he called "use." The two are not exclusive. Individual researchers may hold both motives in varying degrees. When the balance is struck toward understanding, we characterize it as "basic"; when it emphasizes use, we call it "applied," or even "engineering." Frequently the balance may be struck somewhere in the middle, as famously with Stokes's point that Pasteur laid the foundations of bacteriology while figuring out how to keep wine from going bad longer. Stokes was making an argument for increasing the emphasis in federal research support for funding "use-oriented" or mission-related basic research, work to be given priority because it seemed to hold out promise of ultimately being useful in solving high priority problems, rather than simply devoting all or most of the support to basic work wherever it might lead and wherever scientists in the disciplines might feel like going.

As our discussion in the fourth point indicates, we would share his emphasis. Reinforcing that inclination, much of what we and our colleagues who do education policy research do could be characterized as searching for a use-oriented understanding of the way education systems work. Much of it is quite descriptive work looking for insights and hypotheses in the array of associations presented to us by the real world of schools, though the methods we use to identify and weigh those relationships are becoming more and more mathematical and sophisticated. A substantial part of the enterprise still involves refinement of definitions, identifying and finding ways to measure aspects of education reality that seem to be important because, when they are properly defined and observed, they yield strong associations with other things we care about. We also simply report the facts about these things—how they are distributed, or mal-distributed, among students and schools, and whether or not they change when policymakers and educators take steps intended to change them.

So we are happy to encourage an emphasis on use-oriented basic work. But we also join a growing group of observers (Burkhardt & Shoenfeld, 2003; Sabelli & Dede, 2001; Donovan, Wigdor, & Snow, 2003; National Academy of Education, 1999) in suggesting that education lacks a strong tradition of engineering and design, and the institutions and funding that would support it, an applied infrastructure that Stokes could take for granted as he focused on the support of basic work in the sciences, but one which we cannot. It is time for us all to pay much more serious attention to that problem if we hope to do as well for all our children as we claim to want to.

A CAUTIONARY NOTE

We end on a cautionary note. This coda has tried to identify some of what it might take to increase the chances of developing knowledge that could be sufficient to enable education policy and the schools to attain their goals. There is little in the history of the relationship between research and policy as it is described in the chapters of this book that suggests even if such knowledge existed it necessarily would be taken up and used by policymakers and the schools. We offer these reasons to hope for a better outcome: If our recommendations were followed, new knowledge would not be buried in journals but would instead be embodied in tools, materials, policies, and practical advice designed for and tested in use, taking into account the full complexity of the system, so that their relevance to practice would be obvious. Further, we are assuming that more effectively and strategically organized research and development will over time result in interventions that will demonstrate much bigger effects in outcomes with the full range of students. It ought to be harder to ignore such evidence of effectiveness than it is now to ignore, or to pick and choose among, the more anemic and ambiguous results of current studies. Finally, we hope that education researchers learn how to be more effective advocates for the value of their own work, based both on its integrity and its promise. None of that would be a guarantee that the work would be picked up in the reality of practice, but, again, it would be a start.

REFERENCES

Ball, D. L., Hill, H. C., & Bass, H. (2005). Knowing mathematics for teaching: Who knows mathematics well enough to teach third grade, and how can we decide? *American Educator*, Fall, 14–22, 43–46.

Berkner, L., He, S., & Cataldi, E. F. (2002). Descriptive summary of the 1995–96 beginning postsecondary students: six years later. *Education Statistics Quarterly 5*(1). Retrieved January 23, 2007, from http://nces.ed.gov/ programs/quarterly/ vol_5/5_1/q5_2.asp

Berliner, D. C., & Biddle, B. J. (1995). *The manufactured crisis: Myths, fraud, and the attack on America's public schools*. Reading, MA: Addison-Wesley.

Bracey, G. W. (1997a). *Setting the record straight: Responses to misconceptions about public education in the United States*. Alexandria, VA: Association for Supervision and Curriculum Development.

Bracey, G. W. (1997b). *The truth about America's schools: The Bracey reports, 1991–97*. Bloomington, IN: Phi Delta Kappa Educational Foundation.

Boyd, D., Grossman, P., Lankford, H., Loeb, S., & Wyckoff, J. (2006). How changes in entry requirements alter the teacher workforce and affect student achievement. *Education Finance and Policy 1*(2).

Brophy, J. E., & Good, T. L. (1986). Teacher behavior and student achievement. In M. C. Wittrock (Ed.), *Handbook of research on teaching*, 3rd edition (pp. 328–375). New York: Macmillan.

Bryk, A. S., Lee, V. E., & Holland, P. B. (1993). *Catholic schools and the common good*. Cambridge MA: Harvard University Press.

Burkham, D. T., & Lee, V. E. (2002). *Inequality at the starting gate*. Washington, DC: Economic Policy Institute.

Burkhardt, H., & Shoenfeld, A. (2003). Improving educational research: Toward a more useful, more influential, and better-funded enterprise. *Educational Researcher 32*(9), 3–14.

Carey, K. (2004). *The funding gap 2004*. Washington, DC: Education Trust.

Carter, L. F. (1980). *The sustaining effects study: An interim report*. Santa Monica, CA: System Development Corporation.

Center on Education Policy. (2004). *From the capital to the classroom: Year 2 of the No Child Left behind Act*. Washington, DC: Author.

Coggeshall, J. G. (2006). *High school teacher assignment and the new governance of teacher quality*. PhD dissertation, University of Michigan.

Cohen, D. K., Raudenbush, S., & Ball, D. L. (2003). Resources, instruction, and research. *Educational Evaluation and Policy Analysis 25*(2), 1–24.

Coleman, J. S., Campbell, E. Q., Hobson, C. F., McPartland, J., Mood, A. M., Weinfeld, F. D., & York, R. L. (1966). *Equality of educational opportunity*. Washington, DC: U.S. Department of Health, Education, and Welfare, Office of Education; U.S. Government Printing Office.

Cooley, W. W., & Leinhardt, G. (1975). *The application of a model for investigating classroom processes*. Pittsburgh, PA: University of Pittsburgh Learning Research and Development Center.

Cooley, W. W., & Leinhardt, G. (1978). *The instructional dimensions study: The search for effective classroom practices. Final report*. Pittsburgh, PA: University of Pittsburgh Learning Research and Development Center.

Decker, P. T., Mayer, D. P., & Glazerman, S. (2004). *The effects of Teach for America on students: Findings from a national evaluation.* Princeton, NJ: Mathematica Policy Research, Inc. Retrieved January 23, 2007, from http://www.mathematica-mpr.com/publications/PDFs/teach.pdf

DeLany, B. (1991). Allocation, choice, and stratification within high schools: How the sorting machine copes. *American Journal of Education 99*(2), 181–207.

Donovan, M. S., Wigdor, A. K., & Snow, C. E., eds. (2003). *Strategic Education Research Partnership* Washington, DC: National Academies Press.

Duncan, M. J., & Biddle, B. J. (1974). *The study of teaching.* New York: Holt, Rinehart, and Winston.

Ferguson, R. (1991). *Paying for public education: New evidence on how and why money matters.* Cambridge, MA: Harvard University, John F. Kennedy School of Government.

Ferguson, R., & Ladd, H. (1996). How and why money matters: An analysis of Alabama schools. In H. Ladd (Ed.), *Holding schools accountable* (pp. 265–298). Washington, DC: Brookings Institution.

Hill, P. (2006). Money, momentum, and the Gates Foundation: What will Warren Buffett's gift mean for U.S. schools? *Education Week*, August 9, 34, 44.

Hirsch, E. D., Jr. (2003). Reading comprehension requires knowledge—of words and the world. *American Educator 27*(1), 10–13, 16–22, 28–29, 48.

Jencks, C., Smith, M. S., Ackland, H., Bane, M. J., Cohen, D., Ginter, H., Heynes, B., & Michelson, S. (1972). *Inequality: A reassessment of the effect of family and schooling in America.* New York: Basic Books.

Journal of Blacks in Higher Education. (2006). *Black student college graduation rates remain low, but modest progress begins to show.* Retrieved January 23, 2007, from http://www.jbhe.com/features/50_blackstudent_ gradrates.html

Kane, T. J., Rockoff, J. E., & Staiger, D. O. (2006). *What does certification tell us about teacher effectiveness? Evidence from New York City.* Cambridge, MA: National Bureau of Economic Research.

Kaufman, P., Alt, M. N., & Chapman, C. D. (2004). *Dropout rates in the United States: 2001* (National Center for Education Statistics, Analysis Report 2005–046). Washington, DC: U.S. Government Printing Office.

Lankford, H., Loeb, S., & Wyckoff, J. (2002). Teacher sorting and the plight of urban schools: A descriptive analysis. *Educational Evaluation and Policy Analysis 24*(1), 37–62.

Murnane, R. J. (1975). *The impact of school resources on the learning of inner city children.* Cambridge, MA: Ballinger.

Nelson, R. (2001). *On the uneven evolution of human know-how* (Working paper 01-05). New York: Columbia University, Institute for Social and Economic Research and Policy.

National Academy of Education. (1999). *Recommendations regarding research priorities: An advisory report to the National Educational Research, Policy, and Priorities Board.* New York: Author.

Perie, M., Moran, R., & Lutkus, A. D. (2005). *NAEP 2004 trends in academic progress: Three decades of student performance in reading and mathematics* (National Center for Education Statistics, Analysis Report 2005-464). Washington, DC: Government Printing Office.

Perie, M., Grigg, W. S., & Dion, G. S. (2005). *The nation's report card: Mathematics 2005* (National Center for Education Statistics, Analysis Report 2006-453). Washington, DC: Government Printing Office.

Perie, M., Grigg, W. S., & Donahue, P. L. (2005). *The nation's report card: Reading 2005* (National Center for Education Statistics, Analysis Report 2006-451). Washington, DC: Government Printing Office.

RAND Mathematics Study Panel. (2003). *Mathematical proficiency for all students: Toward a strategic research and development program in mathematics education.* Santa Monica, CA: RAND.

Rowan, B., Camburn, E., & Correnti, R. (2004). Using teacher logs to measure the enacted curriculum: A study of literacy teaching in third grade classrooms. *Elementary School Journal 105*(1), 75–102.

Rowan, B., Schilling, S., Ball, D., & Miller, R. (2001). *Measuring teachers' pedagogical content knowledge in surveys: An exploratory study* (Consortium for Policy Research in Education, Study of Instructional Improvement, Research Note S–2). Ann Arbor, MI: University of Michigan.

Sabelli, N. & Dede, C. (2001). *Integrating educational research and practice. Reconceptualizing goals and policies: "How to make what works, work for us?"* Fairfax, VA: George Mason University, Project Science-Space. Retrieved January 23, 2007, from http://www.virtual.gmu.eduSS_research/cdpapers/policy.pdf

Shulman, L. S. (1987). Knowledge and teaching: Foundations of the new reform. *Harvard Education Review 57*(1), 1–22.

Singer, A. (1999). American apartheid: Race and the politics of school finance on Long Island, NY. *Equity & Excellence in Education 32*(3), 25–36.

Smith, M., & O'Day, J. (1991). Systemic school reform. In S. Fuhrman & B. Malen (Eds.), *The politics of curriculum and testing: The 1990 yearbook of the Politics of Education Association* (pp. 233–267). Bristol, PA: Falmer Press.

Snyder, T. D., Hoffman, C. M., & Geddes, C. M. (1997). *Digest of education statistics, 1997* (National Center for Education Statistics, Analysis Report 98–015). Washington, DC: Government Printing Office.

Snyder, T. D., Tan, A. G., & Hoffman, C. M.. (2006). *Digest of education statistics, 2005* (National Center for Education Statistics, Analysis Report 2006-030). Washington, DC: Government Printing Office.

Snyder, T. D., Tan, A. G., & Hoffman, C. M. (2004). *Digest of education statistics, 2003* (National Center for Education Statistics, Analysis Report 2005-025). Washington, DC: Government Printing Office.

Stateline.org. (2004). *Statistics fact: Gap in per-pupil spending between highest- and lowest-spending districts (adjusted for regional differences and student need), 2000 (dollars).* Retrieved January 23, 2007, from http://www.stateline.org/ stateline/?pa = fact&sa = showFact&id = 327881

Stokes, D. E. (1997). *Pasteur's quadrant: Basic science and technical innovation.* Washington, DC: Brookings Institution Press.

Thomas B. Fordham Institute. (2006). Fund the child: Tackling inequity and antiquity in school finance. Washington, DC: Author. http://www.100percentsolution.org/fundthechild/ FundtheChild062706.pdf

U.S. Census Bureau. (2005a). *School enrollment data: Historical tables.* http://www.census.gov/ population/www/socdemo/school.html

U.S. Census Bureau. (2005b). Percent of people 25 years and over who have completed high school or college, by race, Hispanic origin, and sex: Selected years 1940 to 2004. *Historical tables* (Table A-2). http://www.census.gov/population/socdemo/education/tabA-2.pdf

U.S. Census Bureau. (2000). *School enrollment—Social and economic characteristics of students: October 2000* (PPL-148). Retrieved January 23, 2007, from http://www.census.gov/population/www/socdemo/school/ppl-148.html

U.S. Census Bureau. (1969). School enrollment: October 1968 and 1967. *Current population reports* (Series P-20, No. 190). Washington DC: U.S. Government Printing Office.

AUTHOR INDEX

SUBJECT INDEX

R

Race and education, 358
  Black schools, 358
  dual school system, 358
Race and education, 358
  Brown and its progeny, 358
  inequality, 351, 356, 357, 358, 359, 360, 363, 364
    ethnic, 128
    legal, 358
    racial, 369
    residential, 359
  segregation, 350, 356, 358, 359
Race, 105–125, 159, 160, 234,354, 356, 360,
      see also Civic capacity and coalition building
  dominant driving force, 113
  nonracial solutions, 118
  polarizing race wars, 123
  race differences, 350
  race focus, 107
  race issues, 105, 108
  race relations, 123, 349
  race separation, 117
  race-based biases, 111
  race-based perceptions, 112
  race-based policy, 118
  race-based privileges, 112
  race-based programs, 118
    affirmative action, 118
    anti-redlining regulations, 118
    Black families, 118
    open housing, 118
    race-based inequalities, 356
  race-conscious policies, 120
  racial composition, 111
  racial data, 123
  racial inequalities, 359
  students' race, 112
Race-neutral policies, 106, 117
  putative beneficiaries, 117
Regression discontinuity, 143–145, 149, 151, 180
  regression discontinuity design, 143
  analytical design, 145, 151, 180, 144
  regression discontinuity estimator, 149
Remedial programs, 359
  title I, 350, 354, 357, 359
Resource allocation, 354, 356, 367
  key resources, 354
  redefinition of resources, 355
  uncertainty, 356, 362
  working-class Americans, 356
Resource allocation, 48, 164, 135, 165, 179,184, 349,
      354–356, 367
  economists' view of education resources, 138
  educational resource allocation, 184
  professional knowledge, 354

school-level resource allocation, 165
self-evident signs, 354
teachers' education, 354
traditional resource allocation, 356
well-to-do localities executive agencies, 354

S

School reform, 20, 23, 44, 115, 119, 120, 121, 182,
      246, 272, 281, 293
  exploiting the natural variation, 144
  flip flops in school reform, 119
  reformdu jour, 119
  school reform demonstration act, 166
  school reform designs, 367
  school reform development grant, 246
  school reform initiatives, 20
  school reform model, 144
  school reform models, 272
  school reform movement, 130
  school reform programs, 274
  school reform proposals, 121
  spinning wheels, 119
Second-generation discrimination, 106, 110, 113, 114, 122
  Black administrators, 114
  Black–White test gap, 112
  differential fallback, 112
  late bloomers, 111
  pockets of segregation, 117
  pygmalion effect, 112
  racial minorities, 112
  self-fulfilling prophecies, 112
  statistical desegregation, 111
  uppity nigger, 111
Segmented system, 129
Shifting terrain, 130
  colonial power, 130
  Napoleonic plan, 130
Shortages, 297
  reasons, 300
  revolving door, 298, 300
  turnover, 258, 298, 299, 337, 338, 339
Success for All, 166, 261, 262, 263, 268, 269, 270, 271,
      273, 281, 366, 375
  comprehensive reform models, 261
  cross-grade grouping strategies, 261
  elementary schools, 9, 70, 103, 111, 152, 159, 189,
      191, 351, 365
  facilitator, 262
    on-site coach, 262
  faddishness of education, 262
  quarterly assessments and regrouping, 262
  research-based instruction, 261
  roots and wings, 261
    randomized evaluation, 261